Photograph by Kathleen de Jonge

Alex de Jonge is a professor of New College, Oxford, England, and the author of five previous books. He and his wife divide their time between Oxford and Virginia.

Jacket painting Stalin in Front of Mirror
by Komar and Melamid
Collection of Frayda and Ronald
Feldman; photograph by D. James Dee

Jacket design by Barbara Singer

Printed in U.S.A.

STALIN

STALIN

And the Shaping of the Soviet Union

ALEX DE JONGE

WILLIAM MORROW AND COMPANY, INC. • NEW YORK

Library of Congress Cataloging-in-Publication Data

De Jonge, Alex, 1938–
  Stalin, and the shaping of the Soviet Union.

  Includes index.
  1. Stalin, Joseph.   2. Heads of state—Soviet
Union—Biography.   3. Soviet Union—History—1925–
1953.   I. Title.
DK268.S8D42   1986   947.084′2′0924 [B]   85-21554
ISBN 0-688-04730-0

Printed in the United States of America

First Edition

1 2 3 4 5 6 7 8 9 10

BOOK DESIGN BY ROBERT FREESE

For Kathy, a very wise woman
to whom I owe it all

Acknowledgments

Many people have helped with this book, starting with my wife, who put up with me when I was writing it, still worse, talking about it, and whose careful reading of the manuscript and pertinent, detailed comments are proof enough that editing can begin at home. I am very grateful to the BBC, which gave me the opportunity to talk to many of the leading figures of the present emigration and even conduct a brief but revealing telephone conversation with Mme. Solzhenitsyn. These meetings proved invaluable, but more valuable still were the long conversations I have held with Igor Golomstok, Lev Kopelev, Alexander Pyatigorsky and, above all, the perpetual conversation I seem to have been holding for some years now with my dear friend Zinovi Zinik. Without that particular conversation the book could not have been written, and any insight it displays into the Soviet cast of mind is largely thanks to him. I would also like to thank the incomparable Komar and Melamid for the generosity with which they made available another view of Stalin, which now graces the jacket of this book. I owe another great debt to the late Edward Crankshaw for the patience and enthusiasm with which he responded to my inquiries, for his immensely careful and helpful letters and for the kindness with which he received me.

John and Carol Garrard helped me formulate some of the ideas that are central to my account of the Soviet Union under Stalin, as did a generation of hard-driving British businessmen long since retired, under whom my understanding of Stalinism was born. I should like to thank the staff of the British Library, the Library of Congress, the London Library and the Public Records Office at Kew for their help and courtesy. However, my greatest debt of all is to my editor, Philip Ziegler, who labored so hard and so helpfully over my manuscript. I also owe a special thank-you to James Beam, who was always there when I needed him.

Contents

Introduction

Judged by the standards of worldly ambition, Stalin is one of the great success stories of modern history. Born and raised in poverty in a tiny land on the southern confines of a ramshackle empire, he died the most powerful man in the world, ruling over the first power to dominate Europe and threaten the Orient since the days of Tamurlaine and Genghis Khan. Not only did he win power, he kept it in a way that would have won the admiration of Machiavelli or Talleyrand. Stalin had a genius for politics and combined natural talent with another quality: the infinite patience of the poor. In the course of his steady climb Stalin never overplayed his hand, never moved on an enemy too soon or allowed vanity to cloud his judgment. Even today he still radiates a chilling and mythic presence, which is why he still remains the most powerful figure in Soviet culture. In comparison with Stalin, Adolf Hitler appears an inept blunderer.

Stalin was consistently underestimated by his colleagues and rivals, who seldom grasped the scale and temper of his character until it was too late. This same talent for disguise made Western politicians fail to understand whom they were dealing with, fail to recognize that there had never been anybody less avuncular than Uncle Joe. He was equally skilled at persuading the rest of the world that he was benign; for instance successfully disguising an anti-Semitism quite as rabid as Hitler's, which ran right through his life to become the ruling obsession of his closing years.

Yet Stalin could never have succeeded had he gone against the grain of his nation's culture. He exploited lines of force that had been present in it for centuries. More immediately he profited from the intellectual and moral climate of prerevolutionary radicalism with its emphasis on fashionable ruthlessness. It must be realized that even at their most extreme, at the height of the terror, Stalin's policies were popular; throughout his reign he enjoyed widespread and enthusiastic support, and hundreds of thousands of his subjects enjoyed marching in demonstrations, carrying red banners and baying for blood. Stalin was extraordinarily adept at tapping a capacity to assent to, even to enjoy, terror and dictatorial authority that is by no means unique to citizens of the Soviet Union in the 1930s.

I have drawn widely on memoirs, eyewitness accounts and the inexhaustible funds of Soviet humor to try to convey something of the atmosphere of the Stalin era. One of the richest sources of such material proved to be British Embassy dispatches. They have provided an invaluable and largely unfamiliar angle upon Soviet affairs. I have also drawn on them, along with more familiar material, to give some account of British and American attitudes to Stalin during and just after the Second World War. One of his most remarkable achievements was to have pushed the frontiers of the Russian Empire farther west than they had ever reached before, and an examination of his relations with the Allies helps us understand how this came about.

Stalin made a remarkable personal contribution to determining the political shape of the Soviet Union and the kind of society that it became. He also did much to determine its subsequent leadership. Many of those who came to prominence just before the Second World War were still in power forty years later. At first sight the country over which he and they ruled strikes Western observers as alien, as indeed it is when judged by the standards and the practices of Western political democracy. However, when considered from a different point of view, much that may seem strange at first sight will strike the reader as surprisingly familiar. My interest in Stalin began many years ago, when I was in a position to compare what I knew of him with the atmosphere in a large British corporation, ruled by a chief executive who believed in management by terror. Everyone, from the board of directors to the elevator man, existed under the continuing threat of dismissal without warning, while firings appeared to occur on a virtually random basis. The chairman set ambitious targets based on his intuitions, seldom listened to advice and never admitted he had made a mistake. He was surrounded by an entourage of sycophants who passed his management style down the line, subjecting their own subordinates to the same kind of bullying, with the result that the corporation operated in a terror-laden miasma of politicking, backstabbing, misrepresentation of personal achievement and the sophisticated "management" of company news. Nevertheless, the technique got results, and while the chairman's intuitive methods produced some spectacular failures, they could also be spectacularly successful. It was a world in which the dangers were colossal, but in which the rewards were commensurate with the risks.

For many years I had supposed this style of management to be unique and that those who had had the misfortune to know it were exceptionally unfortunate. However, I have come to understand that in the world of the nontenured, administration by fear, with the firing squad replaced by instant dismissal, is closer to the rule than the exception. Indeed, it appears to be the norm for any organization in which the administrators are not accountable to those under their authority and in which there is no job security. Academics tend to treat Stalin's Russia as a savage and alien society that requires sophisticated analytic techniques to understand it, because tenure protects them from that perpetual threat of job loss that, with all its attendant office politics, drawn daggers and smoking guns, is part of the fabric of most people's daily lives. They fail to appreciate that Soviet reality "begins at home."

Stalin built a hierarchical society based upon conditional tenure. Those at the bottom, peasants on collective farms, lived as badly as the Russian peasant has ever lived. Those at the top of the pyramid lacked for nothing. I remember meeting the son of a high-ranking official in Moscow in the late 1950s and discovering to my surprise that we shared the same London tailor. However, no one in the hierarchy enjoyed security of tenure, while all privilege was attached to office and inseparable from it. Thus life in the upper echelons of Stalin's society, though precarious indeed, was not so different in essence from life at the top of a large corporation, offering huge rewards to those prepared to operate without safety nets. The atmosphere of Stalin's Russia should be immediately recognizable to all whose jobs depend upon the whims of their superiors, although it must be conceded that not even the most ruthless style of corporate management has yet extended the principles of hire and fire to include the delivery of a bullet to the back of the neck.

STALIN

Men make their own history but they do not make it just as
they please . . . but in circumstances directly found, given
and transmitted by the past.

—KARL MARX

CHAPTER ONE

Georgia

Because of the absence of reliable sources it is extremely
difficult to be absolutely certain of things in Georgia.
—J. B. HUTTON

According to the as yet uninvented field of study known as geoalcoholics, the Western Hemisphere may be divided into a series of horizontal bands, determined by the dominant alcoholic staple for the zone in question and the way that it affects the drinker. The northernmost band is the grain-spirit zone. This covers Scotland, Scandinavia, Finland and the greater part of the Soviet Union. The drinker of grain spirits looks for oblivion. He tries to get drunk as quickly as possible, whereupon he tends to keel over. He can be violent and is capable of extravagant excesses that verge upon the poetic and is often to be seen in the streets on high days, holidays, and other times in a condition of considerable disorder. Although he will drink wine, indeed will drink anything, his favorite tipple is hard liquor; beer he regards as a chaser. The hard-liquor belt favors writers, journalists and those who lead active outdoor lives. It does not suit steady and regular indoor work at repetitive jobs and is the wrong place entirely to look for a willing and able industrial proletariat.

This is to be found in the second zone, which provided the work force for the first Industrial Revolution. Its staple is beer, and it includes England, northern France, the Low Countries and the Ruhr, while nowadays much beer is also drunk in Japan. Beer drinkers tend to get bloated rather than drunk, becoming owlish, morose or a little brutal. For those who work in overheated environments, such as steel mills, beer is positively beneficial since it replaces lost liquids. The beer belt has been the chief supplier of skilled and semiskilled industrial labor ever since the Industrial Revolution.

Below the beer belt comes the wine belt, the culture of southern Europe, from the Iberian Peninsula through southern France, Italy, Greece, southern Germany and Austria. The serious wine drinker seldom becomes drunk but is seldom sober; he remains perpetually pickled. While his liver holds out, he can be a charming companion, a raconteur at his best at a café table holding forth to friends. Peasants and small-business men, traders, civil servants and middlemen flourish in the wine belt. Unless one loves hard work or the poetry of absolute drunkenness, the wine belt is the pleasantest of the three. To its south alcohol ceases altogether and Islam takes over with mint tea, sweetmeats and hashish.

The Russian climate is such that the Soviet Union has no beer belt, and this is one reason for the shortcomings of its industries—vodka drinkers are notoriously unreliable on production lines. The vodka belt extends across the full stretch of Great Russia until it reaches the southern republics of Armenia and Georgia, where vodka gives way to wine.

Unlike the United States, the Soviet Union cannot be considered a culturally integrated whole. It is a political federation covering one-sixth of the earth's landmass, where approximately 200 different languages are spoken. Thus the differences between Leningrad and Tiflis, the capital of Georgia, are spectacular. Georgians tend to be extroverts with an overpowering capacity for hospitality. As you sit at a table in a Tiflis restaurant, you may be sent a bottle by a stranger simply because he wants you to think well of him and his country. Georgians like to be seen as big spenders, given to extravagant enthusiasms, characteristics for which the Great Russians mock them. One joke tells of a Georgian who has to have an artificial tooth. In turn the dentist offers him teeth of steel, silver, gold and platinum. He rejects them all, observing that he is not a poor or mean man and is anxious for all to see that he can afford an expensive tooth. It transpires that he wants one made from imported denim.

Georgians are the traders, wheeler-dealers and racketeers of the Soviet Union, although in this respect they are no match for the citizens of Odessa. They are familiar figures on internal Aeroflot flights wearing round black peaked caps of stupendous diameter, known as airfields, and bringing fruit, vegetables and wine up from the south to be sold at exorbitant prices. At one time wine used to arrive in a water tender attached to an engine that would stand at a siding in a Moscow station. Those in the know would come and collect their wine in kettles. In the Khrushchev era a combination of racketeering, bribery and government payoffs evolved to the point that Georgians would claim, with characteristic extravagance, that their republic had seceded, winning de facto independence. The announcer in the Tiflis station was known to refer to the "train now leaving Tiflis for the Soviet Union."

Georgians are a race apart, fitting into none of the main ethnic categories of Europe and Asia. A number of different languages and dialects are spoken, none of which is of Indo-European, Turkic or Semitic origin. The account of the national character provided by a Georgian prince of the eighteenth century has lost little of its relevance:

> In outward appearance, the men and women are comely and black of
> brow and hair; their complexion is white and rosy, less frequently
> swarthy or sallow. . . . They are brave and hard working with great
> powers of endurance, bold cavaliers and eager for a fray, nimble and
> quick off the mark. . . . They are doughty warriors, lovers of arms,
> haughty, audacious, and so avid of personal glory that they will
> sacrifice their fatherland or their sovereign for the sake of their own
> advancement; they are hospitable to guests and strangers, and cheerful
> of disposition; if two or three are assembled together they are generous
> and prodigal of their own goods and of other peoples' and never think
> of amassing possessions; they are intelligent, quick-witted, self-
> centered and lovers of learning. . . . They lend loyal support to one
> another and will remember and repay a good turn but will extract
> retribution for an insult. They change rapidly from a good mood to a
> bad one; are headstrong, ambitious, and apt both to flatter and to take
> offence.[1]

Georgian culture honors poets and warriors. As late as the 1930s one could still come across a mountain tribe, the Khevsurs, allegedly descendants of the Crusaders, who wore chain mail, carried long swords and a little round studded shield and had seven crosses embroidered on their tunics.[2] A British diplomat visiting Georgia during Stalin's purges, when Georgia suffered at least as much as the rest of the Soviet Union, found that recent events had done little to alter the national character:

> The Georgian is chivalrous, wine drinking (14–15 bottles of light wine
> per man at one night's sitting is not uncommon), pleasure loving,
> lazy, hospitable and quick tempered. He loves dancing and
> music. . . . Perhaps the most striking of all his characteristics
> considering the times is his almost aggressive independence. None of
> these characteristics seem to have changed much under Soviet power,
> least of all the love of independence. This often manifests itself in
> sheer indiscipline. . . . In Georgia the name of Stalin does not seem
> to evoke the awe and homage, much less "love" which . . . is so
> nauseatingly played up in Russia. It is true that in the few places he
> was mentioned one could detect a note of restrained pride and affected
> nonchalance about the fact Stalin was born in these parts.[3]

The Georgians consider themselves culturally superior to their Slavic
neighbors. Ancient Georgia was a part of the Greco-Roman world,
where it had been an independent and civilized kingdom when the an-
cestors of the Russians were still nomads, while Georgians adopted the
Christian faith six centuries before the conversion of the Eastern Slavs.[4]
The golden age of Georgian civilization occurred in the eleventh and
twelfth centuries, when it achieved a notable level of culture and maintained its political independence. Thereafter Georgian history grows
sad, becoming the story of continual subjugation, starting with the arrival of the Mongols in the thirteenth century and continuing to the
point when Georgia entered the Russian Empire, more or less voluntarily, early in the nineteenth. However, assent to Russification was by
no means universal, and it took the Imperial pacification programs
some sixty years to eliminate all resistance. Along with political subjugation, Petersburg sought to impose its culture upon Georgia, which it
considered a colony on the outer rim of the Empire. The leader of the
Georgian Church was replaced by a Russian Exarch, and the political
administration was conducted almost exclusively by Russians. In 1871
the study of Georgian language and literature was replaced by compulsory Greek and Latin, and a year later Georgian was banned as a
teaching language in the Tiflis seminary. That institution became a
center of opposition to Great Russian domination, and matters came to
a head in 1886, when the Russian rector Chudetsky, who had described
Georgian as a "language for dogs," was assassinated by an ex-student
whom he had expelled. The Exarch responded by placing the entire
nation under a collective curse.

The Georgian countryside has an exotic feel, a blend of harsh mountains, fertile valleys and lovely rivers, flowing fast over milk-white stones, in which water buffaloes can be seen cooling their heavy bodies, tended by peasants in their bright orange blouses.[5] The cities felt closer to Islam than to Christendom, a world of bazaars and caravanserais, where life was lived in the streets. Visiting Tiflis in the early 1930s, Arthur Koestler found in it a delightful combination of cultures:

> I loved Tiflis more than any other town in the Soviet Union. Perhaps because it was still so untouched by the drabness and monotony of Soviet life. The town has an irresistible charm of its own, neither European nor Asiatic, but a happy blend of the two. It has a carefree and leisurely rhythm of life which is bohemian rather than Oriental; but its fastidious architecture and the courteous poise of its citizens make one constantly aware that it is the product of the oldest Christian civilizations. In the distance the Caucasus provides the town with a background of austere grandeur; but its immediate surroundings are gently undulating hills with the amiable profile of the vineyards of Tuscany; and the Kura River, daughter of glaciers, displays a Danubian mellowness under the handsome old bridges.[6]

• • •

Iosif Vissarionovich Djugashvili, later to be known as Stalin, was born in the small town of Gori, set on a bend of the Kura, some forty-eight miles to the northwest of Tiflis. The little community was dominated by a fortress set high on a flat-topped hill and was situated on the railway line that linked Baku on the Caspian Sea to Batum on the Black Sea. Toward the end of the last century it had a population of 8,000 or 9,000. The writer Maxim Gorky, who visited the town in the 1890s, found it "different, savagely original," writing of its raging river and the multitude of caves set in the surrounding mountains that gave it a bleak and wild feel.[7] Stalin's daughter recalls it in a gentler light: a little town set in a fertile valley, surrounded by magnificent vineyards and orchards and lit by a golden sun.

The Djugashvili family was wretchedly poor, their house scarcely more than a hovel. It had wooden walls, an earth floor, a ceiling of planks and consisted of two rooms. The Djugashvilis lived in one; their landlord in the other. Outside was a cobbled street with a sewer running down the middle. Today things are different; in the mid-1930s Lavrenti Beria, Stalin's future chief of police, turned the cottage into a shrine to his master, encapsulating the construction within an elaborate marble casing that bore a marked resemblance to a small metro station.

The question of Stalin's family background is sensitive. From the moment that the Bolsheviks seized power in October 1917, the wrong set of "objective characteristics"—parentage, class, political affiliations—sufficed to get one shot, while it was desirable for a Bolshevik leader to possess proletarian origins. Stalin had every reason to render his background as humble as possible; that is why we should be wary of the official account of his childhood. He would often boast that his name, Djugashvili, indicated his proletarian origins. The wife of a Finnish Communist leader once went on a picnic with Stalin:

> As he became more relaxed he slapped his boot with the palm of his hand—I never saw him wear anything on his feet but riding boots—and cried: "I'm the only real proletariat here, for my name ends in "-shvili." All the other Georgian comrades, with names in "-idze" or "-adze," are either aristocrats or bourgeois." So saying he named three of his best friends, Yenukidze, Lominadze and Ordzhonikidze—who all had high positions in the government. A few years later, however, the first two were liquidated by their good friend Stalin, and Ordzhonikidze committed suicide. [8]

According to official history, Stalin's father Vissarion, or Beso, was a shoemaker who worked in a small shop in Gori, where he met and married Ekaterina ("Keke") Geladze. She was allegedly an Ossete. The Ossetes are an isolated mountain tribe that lacks the exuberance of other Georgians. Like many mountain people, they are inward-looking, suspicious of strangers and expert at the art of feuding. In Imperial Russia Ossetes were in great demand as policemen and prison warders. [9] Although official biography is at pains to present Beso as a workingman, "a cobbler by trade, later a worker in a shoe factory," the truth may be more complicated. Like any legendary hero, Stalin has been invested with the mythological apparatus of a mysterious birth. This is as much the creation of wishful thinking as any official account of his origins. Nevertheless, one version recurs with remarkable frequency and is even consistent with the facts.

Stalin's mother was allegedly working as a servant in a large house in Tiflis, where she was seduced and impregnated by a famous explorer, Nikolai Przhevalsky, en route for an expedition into Central Asia. A husband was found for her in the shape of Beso Djugashvili, who was set up in a shoemaker's business. According to Nestor Menabde, one of Stalin's few political enemies to have survived, Beso employed some forty workmen in the early days of his business, an economic position that gave him the status of petit bourgeois, before he drank his business away. The contention that Przhevalsky was really Stalin's father is based in part upon physical resemblance. As portrayed in Soviet encyclopedias, the explorer looks remarkably like Stalin, with the same unusual features of a shallow forehead and disturbingly low hairline, together with a mustache of identical cut. It must be said that Stalin's mustache attained its final, Przhevalskian form only in the 1920s. Before that it had jutted forth in a distinctly Levantine manner reminiscent of the more aggressive kind of Greek waiter. Perhaps Stalin began to model his appearance upon the man he believed to be his father as he went up in the world, in order to invest himself with a mysterious birth and noble origins. This would account for the strange prominence that Soviet historians accord to Przhevalsky. Schoolchildren had, and still have, his exploits positively crammed down their throats at the expense of other equally distinguished explorers of the age. It was this otherwise inexplicable prominence that kept the rumors alive.

Joseph Vissarionovich Djugashvili was born on December 21, 1879. The little we have been told of his early years has a mythological ring to it. His childhood was characterized by violent hatred of his father, who used to beat him when drunk, allegedly prompting the child to defend himself with a knife. His mother did what she could to protect her son, for whom she was very ambitious. She worked as a seamstress and took in washing to keep him in school, even after her husband was knifed to death in a drunken brawl in 1890. However, the picture of a young boy hating a crude and violent pseudofather and loving a weak but dutiful mother is almost certainly untrue. There is no evidence that Stalin ever loved anyone. In years to come he would refer to his mother in appalling terms—for example, as "that old whore." At the height of his purges Stalin decided that she needed a bodyguard and had Beria arrange one. It says much for her view of her son that when the guards arrived she fainted, assuming that they had come to arrest her. Stalin did not attend her funeral, and although she died a devout Christian, he did not permit a cross to be placed upon her grave.

The boy grew up in a violent and bitter household. He was beaten by both parents, for Ekaterina was also something of a thrashing mother. It is clear that he underwent an early and intense hardening, quite sufficient to inaugurate the hatred of any authority other than his own that would mark him to his death. Physical factors contributed to his sense of resentment and inferiority. The young Stalin was ugly: His eyes were set unpleasantly close together, his face was pitted by smallpox and, above all, he was short. He never grew beyond five feet four inches. Moreover, he was handicapped: A childhood accident had brought about a stiffening of the left elbow, the result of blood poisoning. He was also deformed: The second and third toes of the left foot were joined, a conspicuous handicap in a world in which children played barefoot. Stalin may not have been a hunchback, but he had enough physical shortcomings to give him the bitter drive of a Shakespearean bastard.

According to official biography, his mother, devout and ambitious, wanted her son to better himself by training for the priesthood, this being the only way in which a son of poor parents could hope to escape his father's condition. But unofficial versions show Stalin's mother in a different light, viewing her son as unfit for anything else. According to oral history in the form of concentration camp gossip, she used to speak of him dismissively to her neighbors: "He has been ill, you know, and he is rather ugly. I think it is a good thing if he becomes a priest. He will then have people's respect and will always be sure of a crust of bread." [10]

Whatever decided his mother, Stalin was enrolled in the church school of Gori in September 1888, and Ekaterina had to struggle to keep him there. It was not just a question of money. His father disapproved of the venture and wanted him to become a shoemaker, too. He even took him out of school and put him to work in a factory, the only known instance of Stalin's earning his living by the sweat of his brow. However, his mother persisted and sent him back to school. He seems to have had a successful school career, although little store should be set by the report cards on display in the Stalin Museum in Gori. These show him getting top marks in all subjects, but the museum's first curator would have been insane or bent on suicide had he mounted an exhibit suggesting that Stalin was less than perfect in any academic respect. However, we have a glimpse of Stalin the schoolboy left us by a contemporary, J. Iremashvili, who was by no means unprejudiced. His memoir, published in exile in Berlin in 1932, makes it clear that he had little reason to love his old school friend. Nevertheless, it remains one of the rare firsthand accounts of Stalin's early days.

The portrait Iremashvili paints of the young Stalin is a chilling one: "He had an unbalanced, unrestrained and passionate character when he decided to go for something or achieve something. He loved nature, but never ever loved a living being. He was incapable of feeling pity for man or beast. Even as a child he greeted the joys and tribulations of his fellow schoolboys with a sarcastic smile. I never knew him to cry."[11]

Iremashvili also recalled that academically Stalin was outstanding, the best pupil in the school. In the light of his subsequent successes this need not surprise us. Soviet versions of his schooldays portray him as hardworking, brilliant, defiant and the leader of the sons of the poor in their constant feuding with the sons of the rich. This may be; the accounts accord with what we know of Stalin's character, but his biographers would have described his schooldays like that anyway. School gave Stalin his first exposure to Russification. For his first two years Stalin had been taught by Georgians and in Georgian. Then, in 1890, most of the teaching staff was replaced by Russians, and Russian became the medium of instruction; henceforth Georgian would be taught as a foreign language. This produced a violent upsurge of patriotism, the boys resenting the implication that Georgians were culturally inferior to their Russian masters.

Stalin's response was more complex. Although it is true that he aligned himself with those who were rebelling against authority, he was also impressed by it. Feeling inferior himself, he would always aspire to the superior level of Russian culture. Over the years he would dissociate himself from Georgia to identify with the culture of Great Russia, precisely as the newly emerged intelligentsia of a colony tends to overadopt the values, attitudes and characteristics of the colonizing power. "Our father used to be a Georgian," Stalin's elder son once remarked to his sister. Stalin's complex attitude toward Russia as a hated but admired colonial power had its origins in Gori in 1890. However, admiration was counterbalanced by oddly theatrical expressions of hatred and rebellion. One of the characteristics of the mature Stalin is a capacity for role playing. What was the cult of personality with its iconic stylization of every aspect of his being if not the extreme rendering of a role? Stalin loved to project himself into a persona—modest, pipe-smoking ruler and father of his people balancing a small child on his knee or warlord supreme, the most powerful member of the Big Three.

In the meantime, we find the twelve-year-old Stalin playing a very curious role indeed. The first persona he adopted was that of a rebel outlaw. In the words of Iremashvili, "his dream figure and ideal was Koba, the hero of Kazbegi's novel. Koba was the leader of an oppressed mountain tribe, which was betrayed, in its struggle against the czar's administration, and lost its last chance of freedom." [12]

The novel in question, a dreadful extravaganza entitled *The Parricide*, tells the story of a daring Georgian outlaw and his struggle against the Russians. Its climax is a scene of vengeance, in which Koba disposes of a renegade Georgian. It is overdrawn, fourth-rate Walter Scott in a Georgian setting, but with a romantic appeal that we cannot easily associate with Stalin's otherwise chilling personality. Indeed, the French Trotskyite Victor Serge singled out Stalin's fascination with Koba as "Perhaps the only impulse he ever had towards a destiny colored by feeling *[une destinée pathétique]*." [13]

The young Stalin's identification with an outlaw figure from the local version of cowboys and Indians has a fascinating parallel in the childhood of another future leader of modest origins with a rather greater capacity for fantasy and extravagance. The young Adolf Hitler also had an ideal dream figure in the shape of Old Shatterhand, a Red Indian who fought a relentless war against white settlers in the novels of Karl May. However, where Hitler left Old Shatterhand behind him with relative ease, Koba would remain with Stalin for many years. He would provide his pseudonym in the revolutionary underground, and a handful of old comrades continued to address him by that name long after he had come to power.

Stalin left school with every prize conceivable, which might have made it possible for the fifteen-year-old son of a shoemaker to get into the Tiflis seminary with a full scholarship into the bargain. Alternatively we may choose to see his destiny being moved by a mysterious hand as his real father dropped a word in the appropriate quarter. At all events Stalin's mother had good reason to be pleased. Her son, no longer dependent on her washing and sewing, was on course for a lifetime's escape from the manual labor to which persons of his station were otherwise doomed.

Stalin, the fifteen-year-old seminarist, was a cold, self-reliant and spiteful boy who imposed his will upon his contemporaries by means of natural authority supported by an icily sarcastic tongue. Writing in *Life* magazine, October 2, 1939, Leon Trotsky provided a brief sketch of Stalin the seminarian:

> The young Djugashvili felt his poverty acutely. "He didn't have any money," related one of his fellow students, "whereas all the rest of us got packages and spending money from our parents." Already his

> comrades noted in Joseph a tendency to find only the bad qualities in
> other people, and to show an attitude of mistrust towards unselfish
> motives. He knew how to play upon the weakness of enemies, and
> how to turn them against one another. Anyone attempting to oppose
> him or trying to explain something he did not understand brought a
> pitiless hostility upon himself.

The young Stalin already knew how to hate; first his father, then by
extension anyone in a position of authority over him. It was hatred of
the upper classes that provided his first political impulses. Although we
cannot say when he first involved himself in politics, it is assumed that
he was drawn toward socialism in the course of the four years he spent
training for the priesthood.

The seminary was becoming a major center of political unrest, a center of Georgian nationalism and revolutionary ideas. There is a special
and important reason for this, one that applies throughout the Russian
Empire. Throughout Europe the root-and-branch extremism of the new
radicalism had a special appeal for the newly literate and the newly
educated. This was particularly true in Imperial Russia, where the development of radicalism in the early 1860s followed directly in the wake
of a massive expansion in the number of persons entitled to higher education. The illiterate or semiliterate parents of these students, lacking
that experience which teaches one that life seldom resembles the world
of textbooks, could offer nothing to counterbalance their offsprings'
newly acquired knowledge. Their children graduated possessed of an
excessive faith in the value of book learning, while their parents, instead
of counterbalancing that faith with common sense, could only point
proudly to the fact that their children were reading. The kind of student
to emerge from such conditions combined fierce idealism with a naïve
commitment to the utopias of political theory, which would be comic if
the ultimate consequences of that naivety were not so sad. Seminarians,
drilled to accept the sanctity of Holy Writ and to absorb doctrine by
rote, were especially susceptible to the tenets of the new radicalism. In
Dostoevsky's *The Brothers Karamazov* it is a lapsed seminarian, the infamous Rakitin, that the author chooses to expound the half-baked new
ideas.

Besides introducing Stalin to socialism, the seminary taught him
what it was like to be policed. Looking back on his schooldays, Stalin
once observed that the seminary had made a rebel out of him "out of
protest against the humiliating régime and its hypocritical methods. For

instance there was spying in the dormitories: at 9 a.m. the bell would ring for tea; we would go to the refectory and on returning to our rooms we would see that our closet drawers had been searched and ransacked." [14] The institution was a dark, oppressive and joyless place, designed, by dint of strict discipline and a rigid educational system, to turn unruly Georgians into loyal Russian subjects. In due course Stalin would make ample use of his experience, successfully converting the entire Soviet Union into something not unlike the seminary of Tiflis.

The portrait of a hard, cold fifteen-year-old, already father to the man, is not quite complete. Stalin, the first-year seminarian, still retained a touch of romantic fire. No one would credit the mature Stalin with a poetic nature. Yet now, for a brief period, we find him writing poetry, which was published in a Tiflis journal, *Iveria*. The first piece reads as follows:

> The rose bud opens
> Bluebells all around
> The iris too awakens
> Flowers wave in the wind.
>
> The lark flies higher
> It trills and warbles
> The nightingale sings softly
> And with great feeling
>
> Let my dear land prosper,
> My land of Iveriya,
> Iveriya the motherland.
> And you, men of Georgia,
> May your labors join you
> To your homeland.

The verses were published under a pseudonym, and Stalin may even have been credited with their authorship well after the event. As for the actual poetry, one can only hope that it has lost everything in translation.

In the seminary Stalin began as an exemplary pupil, but soon his natural defiance of authority and his interest in radical ideas made him turn away from schoolwork. According to an unofficial sketch, he was academically undistinguished but won the approval of the authorities through the zeal he displayed in prayer and fasting, greatly to the surprise of those who knew him.[15] However, in his second year Stalin turned, "And suddenly everything changed, the man of prayer began speaking against authority."[16] He began to direct his hatred against all those set over him, developing the angry politics of a hungry have-not.[17]

He read widely outside the school curriculum, with that lack of direction that characterizes the autodidact. His reading included Thackeray, Darwin, Hugo and, allegedly, a bootleg edition of *Das Kapital*. Some of the seminarists founded a study and discussion group, which Stalin joined, that solemnly compiled a six-year reading program of socialist studies. His behavior within the group is fascinating, setting a pattern that would hold throughout his political life. Intolerant of dissent, Stalin would insist that he alone was right and was never afraid of playing dirty to win, with the result that the group soon split into those who followed Stalin without question and the rest, who could not abide him.

In the meantime, his extracurricular reading was incurring the displeasure of the authorities. The seminary records for November 1896 show that an inspector confiscated his library card together with a copy of Victor Hugo's *The Toilers of the Sea* and had him put in a punishment cell. A year later another entry mentions that he had been caught reading prohibited books for the thirteenth time. Nevertheless, he did not neglect his studies entirely, continuing to apply himself in two areas, logic and history. The historian Abdurakhman Avtorkhanov knew someone who was at school with Stalin and who recalled one of his historical essays:

> One day the ancient history teacher set us an essay on "Why Caesar fell." Djugashvili wrote a highly original piece. He stated that in his opinion Caesar lacked the apparatus of personal power which might have controlled the machinery of state power, i.e. the Senate. He also submitted a plan of Caesar's power structure which included the Senate and the provincial governors. He noted certain blank spots, which he set in red brackets. These were the vulnerable areas of the regime, the brackets being defensive measures for their protection. In his commentary Stalin maintained that the provincial governors had too much power to feel the threat not so much of the Senate as of Caesar himself hanging over them like the sword of Damocles. The struggle with the Senate had ended in a pardon for the enemies of Caesar and the continuance of the Senate as the symbol of collective

power; this rendered the notion of enduring dictatorship valueless. Worst of all, Caesar looked to friends to share his power, as opposed to executives who would be bound to obey him. Consequently he died at the hands of his friends, Cassius and Brutus, having failed to enclose himself within an iron ring of devoted henchmen. The teacher asked him whether his plan smacked of absolute monarchy. "No, the power of an absolute monarch depends upon the machinery of state power; in my plan state power is sustained by the machinery of personal power." [18]

Stalin already had a firm grasp of the importance of a personal political machine, for the essay provides an outline of his future strategies as a seeker and holder of power. In due course he would secure a unique degree of control, over the people, the bureaucracy, the party, the army and even the police, all subordinated to his own personal apparatus, staffed not by friends but by loyal executives.

Stalin did not graduate from the seminary. His school record had gone from bad to worse, and it became obvious that there was no point in his trying to graduate since his reports were so bad that any reference the school might give would be useless. In later years Stalin would maintain that he was "expelled for disseminating Marxist propaganda," while maternal loyalty encouraged his mother to maintain that she took him out of school because of poor health. There is a more dramatic account of his expulsion, probably the creation of wishful thinkers, that would play its part in the mythology of the gulag in years to come. An inmate of a gulag psychiatric ward in the mid-fifties, a wonderful source of stories, rumors and fragments of oral tradition, had a tale to tell about an otherwise-unsung villain of Russian history, the head of the Tiflis gendarmerie at the turn of the century, Colonel Polozov:

> It is perfectly clear in retrospect that the corps of gendarmes was formed with the express purpose of bringing about the fall of Imperial Russia, but all its efforts would have been in vain had it not been for Colonel Polozov. On November 28, 1894, a group of bandits who had been arrested on the scene of their crime was brought before him. They had tried to rob a government treasury, and had used arms. Both sides had taken losses. Colonel Polozov was not a man who went by the book, and in order to avoid excessive red tape elected to "write off" the entire group—as the defenders of the toiling masses would subsequently be known to express themselves.

"Makharadze. 25 years old. Orthodox."

"Excellent. To be shot. Next."

"Kandaliya. 28. Muslim."

"Muslim, eh? Send him to Mahomet."

"Petrosian, Gregorian, 20."

"I know that face, let him follow the rest."

Then they brought in a fourth, an ugly red-haired adolescent, pockmarked and rickety, with frightened eyes and trembling hands. The colonel observed that he was wearing the uniform of a seminarian.

"What are you, a seminarian? Name?"

"Djugashvili."

"Djugashvili? Not Vissarion Ivanovich's son? A pretty picture I must say, the son of a church elder mixed up with bandits. Is that what they teach you in the seminary?"

"I won't do it anymore."

"Of course you won't, the most you'll try and do is rob Judas in hell of his thirty pieces of silver."

"Your Excellency, what shall we do with the seminarist?"

"Give the snotnose a smack in the head and kick him out."

Two days later he was expelled.[19]

I have come across no other version of this story, which is unflattering enough to have been repressed. But true or false there is no doubt that throughout the labor camps of Siberia, when the going grew exceptionally tough, emaciated gray-faced men and women would shake their shaved heads and sadly mutter, "Oh, Polozov, Polozov!"

The seminary did much for Stalin. Curiously he did not look back on his school days with that degree of unrelieved and vindictive hostility which one might have anticipated. At a time when he went to great lengths to dispose of anyone connected with his early years, Stalin displayed an uncharacteristic capacity for mercy. He ordered that the school inspector, Avarkidze, who had signed his expulsion order be permitted to die a natural death.[20] The seminary helped Stalin to learn Russian. It also developed his oratorical style: declamatory and repetitive, with liturgical overtones. The hypnotic repetitions of simple phrases; the catechistical structure of question, answer, explanation; the enumerations of "In the first place, in the second place"—all betray the ex-theological student. In the future his oratory would remind listeners of the intonation of a reader of the Scriptures; the theologian also emerged in his inquisitorial assaults upon heretics, recusants and sinners accompanied by the obligatory references to the works of the Holy Fathers to Marx, Engels and Lenin.[21]

Theological training exposed him to a doctrinaire literalism which taught him how to manage the Marxist insistence upon ideological orthodoxy. Provided the letter of the law be observed, Stalin discovered that its spirit could be left to take care of itself. It also taught him the virtues of hypocrisy and dissimulation, particularly important for a theological student who had lost his faith; Stalin would always maintain that it was Darwin who was responsible for that loss. But whatever else the seminary may have given Stalin, according to his daughter, a Christian education was not part of its legacy:

> I am convinced that [the seminary] was of the utmost significance for
> his character and his entire life, reinforcing certain innate traits of
> character. He had no religious sense. The endless praying, the
> tyrannical religious instruction could only have had a negative effect
> upon a young man who had never, for a moment, believed in God or
> the life of the spirit, creating an extreme scepticism with regard to all
> things "celestial" and "on high." In their stead appeared radical
> materialism, a cynical realism, somber pragmatism and a no-nonsense
> approach. Instead of developing his spirituality he grew to know
> hypocrisy, toadying and dissimulation. Since the young man had
> neither the purity of soul nor the sincere religious sense of his illiterate
> mother, he was, at the age of nineteen, well prepared for a form of
> "service" altogether different from the one which she had had in
> mind.[22]

Yet although Stalin was no Christian, he remained drawn toward the church. When speaking informally, he would frequently appeal to the will of God. A splendid example is his reaction to André Gide's funeral oration in honor of Maxim Gorky, whom Stalin had probably murdered in 1936. After listening to the translation of Gide's magnificent peroration, Stalin turned to the French writer Louis Aragon at his side and observed laconically: "God grant him long life—if he's not lying." In later years he used to seek out the company of senior churchmen. On one occasion he invited an old school friend, another rare survivor, now head of the Georgian Orthodox Church, to call on him in the Kremlin. He asked him whom he feared more, God or Stalin. An embarrassed silence ensued. It was interrupted by Stalin, who observed, laughing: "I know it is me that you fear more, or else you would not have appeared in secular dress."[23]

Stalin left the seminary with a touch of style all his own. In the words of R. Arsenidze, who got to know him about this time:

> When Soso [an abbreviation for Iosif] was threatened with expulsion he suggested that his comrades in the illegal study group all leave the seminary at the same time to undertake revolutionary propaganda work. They refused, observing that such a step would scarcely delight their parents. . . . Whereupon Soso . . . denounced all of them to the authorities as his partners in crime. When they were all expelled he calmly expounded his strategy to them. He had helped them escape the reproaches of their parents while opening the way to revolutionary activity for them. The end had been achieved, and so discussion of the means was pointless.[24]

Over the years Stalin would develop creative denunciation to the point that it became the national sport of an entire nation.

CHAPTER TWO

The Young Marxist

Ideology is fiction that doesn't realize it's fiction.
—MARIO VARGAS LLOSA

Shortly after leaving the seminary, Stalin took a job in the Tiflis observatory. He got it with the help of a close friend, Vano Ketskhoveli, who worked there and had a room in the building where Stalin would sometimes sleep. In December 1899 the observatory engaged him as a clerk and bookkeeper, and he continued to work there until March 1901. Stalin, at this time, looked not at all like his future icon—military tunic, trimmed mustache and boots. He was a slight young man with wavy reddish hair brushed back from its low peak. He sported a short, straggling mustache and a scrawny beard. He invariably wore a black blouse, a red scarf and an old brown overcoat, with dirty, unpolished shoes.[1] Curiously that is the last description we have of Stalin for nearly a decade. There will be occasional glimpses, but a coherent picture is lacking. Official histories, which are in anything but short supply, are imprecise, evasive and all too susceptible to change. As a Soviet historian once complained of his profession, "The trouble is you never know what's going to happen yesterday."[2]

The principal explanation for the lack of records derives from the milieu that Stalin now began to move in. As implied by the possibly apocryphal account of his brush with a firing squad, Stalin was never an armchair revolutionary. In the years to come, along with agitation and propaganda activity among the workers of Batum and Baku, Stalin was involved in the planning, if not the execution, of armed robberies. These were euphemistically known as expropriations and provided the funds that kept the Social Democratic, later the Bolshevik, party afloat. This introduces us to a vital aspect of Stalin's character. Along with the theological student turned revolutionary we find a figure of a different kind: the *kinto*, or street person. The *kinto* is a figure central to Georgian street life, a petty hustler with a quick wit and sharp tongue, "renowned as a cynic and a scoffer, a real cockney of the Caucasus, with a raucous voice and a grotesque earthy sense of humour."[3] A universal type, he would be at home in Villon's Paris, Dickensian London or a present-day New York, but he probably had his heyday in prerevolutionary Odessa. Stalin spent his early revolutionary years as a *kinto* living on the edge of ordinary society and very close to the criminal world.

In later years Stalin made an open declaration of his affection for criminals. He pronounced criminal prisoners "socially close," as opposed to the political inmates of his camps, who were "socially remote," and encouraged criminals to mistreat and exploit the politicals, as they did with gusto. There is more here than a desire to punish his enemies; Stalin liked and respected the criminal cast of mind, ruthless and realistic in its recognition of self-interest as the only motive and possessed of the skills and mental habits of the survivor. In due course Stalin would use terror to bring into being a society which, with its special version of the managerial principle of hire and fire, was the most elaborate development ever of Article I of the Russian criminal code: "You can die today, I'll wait till tomorrow."

Stalin was drawn to the *classes dangereuses* because they existed on the margin. He derived his very nature from the street culture of a semi-Oriental city, Tiflis itself being on the margin between Christendom and Islam. The street assembled criminals, petty traders and a kind of *Lumpenintelligentsia* of the bitter and the disinherited—a far remove from the cultural world of the Georgian intelligentsia proper, a gracious world a million miles from the young man in the brown overcoat with his unpolished shoes. The young Stalin was a clearly recognizable type; the product of the lowest grade of Russified Georgian intelligentsia, neither Georgian nor Russian, a southern wanderer on the fringes of two cultures with no roots in either. He moved in a shifting cosmopolitan world in which the values of the street provided a tenuous stability.

Along with an affection for the criminal milieu, existence on the fringe made him fiercely dismissive of the Georgian cultural tradition, which he would always despise as inferior. Yet Stalin's admiration for

Great Russian values never extended to the intelligentsia. He was too attached to the values of the street to be impressed by their endless talk, and this separated him from the mainstream of Russian Marxism at the turn of the century. When one considers Marxism as it appeared at that time, it is surprising that Stalin should have been drawn to that system of belief. It would be inappropriate to turn this book into a history of nineteenth-century ideas. What follows can be only the barest account, designed to isolate certain lines in Marxist thought, in an attempt to show how although it might have appealed to Stalin, it was really aimed at persons of a different kind, a difference that would be acted out with a vengeance in the 1930s, when Stalin dissociated himself from Marxists of the old style by sending them all to the gulag or the cellars of the Lubyanka.

The emotional coloring of Marxism is that of an elaborate closed system, developed by a combination of intellectual rigor and utopian wishful thinking. Its most important characteristic is its feel, all-embracing, all-explaining and complete. It is remote from the open-ended intellectual tradition of empiricism and the scientific method, based on verification by example and the concept of working solutions and provisional truths. It aims at nothing less than a total explanation of human history—the totality of human experience.

A philosophical aspiration of this kind is not unique to Marx. He belongs to a tradition that extends to Plato and that includes Rousseau and Hegel as his immediate precursors. However, one feature of his system distinguishes it from philosophy as such. Almost, it might seem, by chance, the thought of Marx slips from philosophy to action. For Marx, the capitalist world presents itself to the proletariat in an act of understanding which springs from the act of destroying it. The worker's movement came into being before the theory, and that theory is no more than the self-knowledge of the movement. It is not a set of values but a mode of being that can be achieved only through action, as awareness of an aim one was pursuing without theoretical understanding of the pursuit. Awareness is an act whereby participants in the historical process acquire theoretical insight into the course of action upon which they have already embarked. For Marx, action and thought become bound up with each other and exist independent of any separate system of values.[4]

Thus theoretical Marxism posits a system of truths of which we may or may not be aware. Any dissent from the system merely indicates lack of awareness. Ethics or an independent value system has no place in

Marx's thought. Moreover, truth must necessarily be one with action. The irrelevance of ethics to Marxism, though justified within the delicate skein of Marx's thought, would have consequences for practical politics of a kind that Marx could never have foreseen, to be endured by the hundreds of millions of victims of Lenin, Stalin, Mao and Pol Pot. At the same time the shift required by Marx's thought from understanding to action created a system that began by addressing itself to philosophers emotionally or intellectually drawn to all-embracing explanations. Somewhat to their bewilderment the philosophers then discovered that these explanations required them to supplement thought with action; proper commitment to Marxism required the thinker to become a revolutionary.

That element in Marx's thought which convinced him philosophically of the need to amalgamate theory with action created a whole generation of intellectual disciples committed to revolutionary action without any understanding of action's realities, of the way in which the exercise of power and the practice of terror override the finer shadings of theory to make them irrelevant. The history of Marxism before the Russian Revolution, and for some time after it, is the history of intellectual squabbles over abstruse theoretical issues which have no bearing on political reality. These bitterly contested arguments are the precise counterpart of the no less bitter quarrels among *fin de siècle* aestheticians and poets about the nature of the "symbol," whether it should be written with a capital S. The mood of the movement in these years is captured vividly in a photograph of Russian Marxists arguing on a Zürich street: Three old gentlemen with long beards, wearing broad-brimmed hats and flapping overcoats, are engaged in gesticulating argument like three theologians debating a particularly knotty problem. Viewed from today, the arguments of the early Marxists seem as remote and bewildering as the savage disputes of the Eastern Church.

The talmudic nature of Marx's account of history appealed to a particular kind of intellectual. It was a complete system, a doctrine which invited analysis and interpretation but which did not require empirical verification because it did not derive from experience. Marx's central tenet, his conviction that the proletariat would evolve a revolutionary consciousness, was an unfounded profession of faith, nothing more than ungrounded prophecy.[5] Moreover, the system was endowed with a satisfactory vagueness that made it imprecise enough to resist the challenge of hard fact. It was a self-confirming closed circle that resisted all attempts to refute it from the outside. Since it held a monopoly over truth, it could dismiss any challenge as a mistake. It thus combined the all-embracing quality of a religious faith with a component that might at first seem incompatible: a hard-headed, no-nonsense materialism that dismissed ethics, Christian values, aesthetics as so many forms of delusion, offering in their place a truly "scientific" explanation of history. This combination of faith and science proved irresistible to the kind of mind, encountered among first-generation students and academics of all description, that is excessively prone to believe what it reads in books. This kind of Marxist is both cerebral and ready to submit to higher intellectual authority, nursing the delusion that "in that submission the values of scientific thought can be preserved. No doctrine was so well suited as Marxism to gratify both these attitudes, or to provide a mystification combining extreme dogmatism with the cult of 'scientific' thinking, in which the disciple could find mental and spiritual peace. Marxism thus played the part of a religion for the intelligentsia."[6]

Marx's blend of faith and science was eagerly embraced by the newly educated students of late-nineteenth-century Russia whose idealistic aspirations and concerned decency were equaled only by their dogmatism and naivety. Anyone with experience of the European intellectual tradition, of Hobbes, Locke, Montesquieu, even Rousseau, who comes late to the sacred texts of Russian radicalism—Chernyshevsky, Plekhanov and Lenin—can only shake his head in bewilderment at their intellectual ham-fistedness and the way in which debate is replaced by bullying, making one realize that the Russian radicals were not so much thinkers as street fighters.

Yet the street fighters found a ready following. With its intoxicating combination of dogmatism, mystification, entirety and the promise of a "radiant future," when communism would be built and all contradictions resolved, it is no wonder that many young people found Marxism irresistible. They were attracted by its optimism and the belief that capitalism was creating forces that would sweep the autocracy away. "With the optimism of youth we had been searching for a formula that offered hope and we found it in Marxism."[7] Once society had passed through the proper stages along the high road to communism, Russia would finally cease to be a semi-Asian country and become truly a part of the West "with its culture, institutions and the attributes of a free political system."[8]

Marx was aware of the intellectual clumsiness of his Russian disciples. In a letter to Engels he declared himself amused and not a little bewildered by the popularity of his ideas in that barbaric land: "A funny position for me to be in, to be functioning as the representative of young Russia. A man never knows what he may come to, or what strange fellowship he may have to submit to."[9]

Georgian intellectuals began reading Marx in the early 1880s, developing their own brand of radicalism. They had repudiated the crudities of Great Russian socialism, which one of the Georgians, Noe Zhordania, perceived as "A thoroughly utopian and reactionary movement . . . if it should ever be put into operation anywhere, we should be plunged into barbarism."[10] Himself an ex-seminarian, Zhordania was a leading figure in the so-called Third Group, *Mesame Dasi*, which eventually became the Georgian Social Democratic party. An intelligent and relatively sophisticated thinker, he devoted himself to adapting Marxian socialism to the peculiar conditions and needs of Georgia. Well versed in the delicacies of Marxist theory, he had spent years in the capitals of Europe, and it was his familiarity with the European versions of socialism that had encouraged him to dissociate himself from the crudities of Great Russian radicalism.

Even at its Russian level, Marxism required mastery of a set of ideas intended for intellectuals and not the *Lumpenproletariat* of the streets or half-baked teenage revolutionaries. The young Stalin's first contact with a flesh-and-blood Marxist intellectual ended in humiliating rejection. When still a schoolboy Stalin had called on Zhordania and informed the older man that he intended to leave the seminary and devote himself to the cause of revolution. Zhordania responded like a pompous schoolmaster. Rather than encourage the young seminarist, he submitted him to an impromptu test on political economy, history and sociology. On concluding that his knowledge was "superficial, based on newspaper articles," he told him to stay in school.[11] Effectively he rejected Stalin because the young man could not pay his intellectual dues. Lack of the "necessary knowledge" rendered him worthless as a revolutionary since he lacked the theoretical framework necessary for effective agitation. No one swallows rejection easily; Stalin found it harder than most. His reaction now, as ever, was to wait. In due course he would embark on a program of revenge that would embrace the entire Marxist intelligentsia.

It is not easy to say why the young Stalin should have been drawn to Marxism. Certainly there were circumstantial reasons: The Caucasus already had a strong Marxist tradition. More important, Stalin was attracted by the aggressive tone of Marxist polemic and by its dogmatic qualities. The importance of dogma and "correct" interpretation appealed to the seminarian in him, as they had doubtless appealed to Zhordania. But to judge by the subsequent uses Stalin made of it, the appeal of dogma went further. It provided him with a framework of absolute truth, which would also accord him scope for maneuver. He would never be a slave to dogma, always able to reconcile it with his immediate interests, while using it to justify his every action.

Personal factors played a role, too. Stalin's roommate in the observatory, Vano Ketskhoveli, had an elder brother, Lado. He, too, had been a seminarian and was four years older than Stalin. He had done underground work in Kiev, had been arrested and was now under police surveillance in Tiflis. It seems likely that despite Zhordania's misgivings, Lado recruited Stalin into *Mesame Dasi* shortly before he left school. Stalin greatly admired the activist, who was at the head of the radical wing of the party. In later years Georgian Old Bolsheviks permitted to reminisce described Lado as a Bolshevik *avant la lettre*, whose attitude to all subsequent ideological issues would have been impeccable had he lived long enough to have one. However, he was to be shot by a prison guard in 1903 for shouting anti-tsarist slogans from a cell window. Had he survived the next thirty-five years of Russian history—no easy feat in itself—he would have been shot by Stalin instead.

CHAPTER THREE

In the Underground

Stalin started work as a revolutionary by leading discussion groups among the railway workers of Tiflis at a time of political and industrial unrest. The workers went on strike late in 1898, and this was followed early in the following year by a number of other strikes that culminated in a demonstration led by Lado Ketskhoveli on May 1. That day 70 workers and some socialist activists carrying red flags met outside Tiflis and swore to uphold the cause of revolution. A year later the 70 had increased to 200, and Stalin now played an active role. In the enthusiastic words of his future father-in-law, S. Alliluyev, a skilled mechanic in the Tiflis railway shops and a revolutionary, too:

> In the middle of April, we members of the underground groups were informed that a May Day meeting would take place on the following Sunday. . . . Soso Djugashvili who was in charge of the arrangements chose a group of workers whom he asked to find a suitable spot for the meeting. When this was selected he inspected it and approved the choice. . . .
>
> As the sun rose over the hill the crowd grew excited [and] . . . the red banner with portraits of Marx and Engels and its stirring slogans blazed in the sun. . . . The emotion was tremendous: men wiped away furtive tears of joy. One by one speakers clambered up on the rocky platforms. [They] spoke of the meaning of May Day . . . of bad working conditions in the factories, of workers' humiliation and the ill treatment meted out by their bosses. "We must fight for our rights," the speakers proclaimed, "we must protest, organise strikes, demand

better conditions." This was the first time that we had heard such courageous words expressed at a public meeting. Loud approval and cheers rose from all sides: "Long live the First of May, down with Autocracy!" Returning home we felt happy, filled with determination to fight and to conquer.[1]

The passage, published during Stalin's lifetime, is interesting not just for the picture it paints but also for its overlay of that official sentimentality which accompanies the description of any moment in the birth of the Soviet nation. Next year's demonstration was a still more ambitious affair which has been described as a turning point in the history of the Tiflis workers' movement.[2] Held in the town center, it was attended by a crowd of more than 2,000. Red flags were unfurled, and various revolutionary orations were greeted with cries of "Down with the autocracy," "Long live the republic." The demonstrators were attacked by mounted police and whip-wielding Cossacks, an onslaught that resulted in 14 deaths and some 30 arrests. Writing from the safety of Switzerland, Lenin hailed the event as one of great significance for the revolutionary movement of the Caucasus. Immediately after the bloodbath the police arrested many leading socialists, including Zhordania, who spent several months in jail.[3]

Stalin did not play a public part in the demonstration. Although there is no reason to doubt his courage, he disliked exposing himself unnecessarily and preferred to remain in the background on such occasions. Nevertheless, he thought it prudent to go into hiding and returned to Gori, where he held forth about the demonstration, dwelling upon its bloodier aspects, which he appeared to find exciting.[4]

There may be another reason why he did not participate. Stalin was not on the best of terms with Zhordania and the party leaders. Soviet historians suggest a falling-out over revolutionary tactics; Stalin advocated radical measures which were rejected by the moderate Zhordania. Émigré sources are less flattering and more plausible. Zhordania recalled that soon after Stalin joined the party, there were rumors that he was intriguing against the leadership. He was busy creating his own faction and calling for changes in the party committee. According to Zhordania, it was evident from the start that Stalin was interested only in leading. He would rather head a small splinter group than submit to authority of any kind. Moreover, again according to Zhordania, he had none of the qualities of leadership, being a "poor speaker who could only recite his speeches like lessons and had recourse to bad language for oratorical effect."[5]

Stalin's lack of polish made Zhordania underestimate him once more. Nevertheless, his account makes it clear that Stalin was already an excellent organizer. He bypassed the official leadership, undermining its authority by describing it as ineffective, and encouraged the workers to take to the streets—without doing so himself. He also succeeded in creating an organization within the organization, his own apparatus based upon workers, not intellectuals, and finally this got him into serious trouble. According to admittedly prejudiced émigrés, the party warned him several times about his divisive behavior. When the warnings took no effect, he was summoned before a peculiar institution known as a party court. The concept derives from military "courts of honor" held to try an officer accused of breaking the officers' code of conduct. A party court was a similar institution at which a member's behavior was judged by an assembly of his peers: "It was the first Party court held by the Georgian Social-Democratic organization to judge a Party comrade. It consisted of local representatives. On concluding its investigation the court voted unanimously to dismiss [Stalin] from the Tiflis organisation, as a slanderer and an incorrigible intriguer. After sentencing, he was stripped of his discussion groups."[6]

Undisturbed by the findings of the court, Stalin left Tiflis and removed himself to Batum. This was a nasty little boomtown, a railway terminus and the chief port of the Caucasus; a pipeline linking the Black Sea port to the oilfields of Baku on the Caspian had just been completed. There were also a number of factories, those owned by Rothschild and Nobel being the largest. A labor force of more than 10,000 worked up to sixteen hours a day for modest wages, providing plenty of scope for socialist agitation. The local branch of Zhordania's party was led by two of its founder-members, Chkheidze and Ramishvili, who, like Zhordania, were opposed to violence and direct action. Looking back on this time, Stalin's contemporaries already saw him as a loner. He had neither friends nor colleagues, only groups of followers. As a leader he had little charisma. Instead, he had patience, was a good listener and a better organizer, who found no detail beneath his notice.

On arrival Stalin plunged straight into party intrigue. He tried to take over the local organization and turn it against the Tiflis group. According to one memoirist, he insisted on absolute authority and, in a curious parody of his own rejection by Zhordania, had "opposed the co-option of industrial workers into the Social-Democratic Party committee in Tiflis, on the grounds that the workers had not yet attained the level of the intellectuals."[7] The issue is trivial enough, yet it is psychologically revealing. Lack of education had once caused Stalin's rejection; now he ascribed his own shortcomings to others. It would not be for the last time.

Stalin was not well received in Batum. The local leaders knew all about the Tiflis "sentence" and refused to become involved in his intrigues. Understanding that he could make no impression there and always quick to cut his losses, he left for Baku, at the other end of the railway line on the Caspian Sea. Although it still retained its mosques, its minarets, its Zoroastrian temple, its filthy narrow streets and its bazaar, the town had grown over the preceding quarter of a century and now had a population of about 115,000, which included a large work force of Persians, Armenians and Russians, employed in the oilfields and refineries. Although it offered excellent opportunities for agitation, Stalin did not stay for long. By a curious chance, shortly after he left Batum, most of the revolutionary leaders were arrested, leaving a vacuum which Stalin returned to fill.

There was a lot of unrest in Batum in the early months of 1902, and Stalin doubtless played his part in encouraging strikes in the Rothschild refinery and the Mantashev works. On March 8, 32 Rothschild workers were arrested. Their colleagues responded with a demonstration, and 600 more were arrested. It has been alleged by one of Stalin's more interesting biographers, Boris Souvarine, that he persuaded a large body of workers to march on police headquarters. They intended to demand the release of their associates, failing which, unarmed though they might be, they would secure that release by force.[8] They failed, and the army opened fire, killing 14 and wounding many others. Stalin seems not to have come under fire himself. The workers of Batum did not remember him kindly for his part in their activities. Neither did the authorities. Shortly after the demonstration they arrested Stalin at a meeting. After eighteen months in prison in Georgia he was sent to an eastern Siberian village, Novaya Uda, for a three-year term of exile. He arrived there in November 1903, and three months later he escaped.

Stalin would be arrested eight times and exiled seven, escaping with apparent ease from every term of exile except the last. Not only did he find escape easy, but he had no difficulty in living on the run. Certainly he learned from his experiences; escape from *his* Siberia would be virtually impossible, as would life on the run in *his* Russia. Tsarist exile was much laxer than the Soviet version; prisoners were merely required to reside in designated areas and report regularly to the police. Nevertheless, the ease with which Stalin took his leave of exile has led some biographers to suspect that he was in the pay of the tsarist police, the Okhrana.

The idea is plausible. The Okhrana was the most efficient organization in imperial Russia, and it infiltrated the leadership of all the major revolutionary movements. For example, Azev, the leading terrorist of the Socialist Revolutionary party and a member of its innermost circle, was an Okhrana agent for years. Lenin's party was easy to penetrate, much easier than the opposing, Menshevik, wing of the Social Democrats. This is because Lenin attracted hard men who enjoyed the underground life and were closer to the world of criminals and stool pigeons than respectable Menshevik intellectuals. Moreover, unlike the Mensheviks, the Bolsheviks needed money. Living in the underground, unable to earn respectable livings, they had to rely on party contributions and were susceptible to offers from the Okhrana's reptile fund. The best-known Bolshevik double agent, Roman Malinovsky, was a member of the party's Central Committee. He retained his position for many years, largely because Lenin refused to heed warnings about him. In fact, Lenin may have been well suited by an agent who served both masters effectively by ensuring that the Bolshevik and Menshevik factions remained divided. On the point of being shot by indignant revolutionaries in 1917, Malinovsky implored Lenin to reveal that he had acted to his orders. Lenin did not consider an intervention to be in the interests of the party and allowed the firing squad to proceed.

The Bolshevik leadership in 1917 believed that one or more of their number had compromising associations with the Okhrana. Shortly before he died in a Siberian camp, its last chief, General V. F. Djunkovsky, recalled the zeal with which the Bolsheviks destroyed police records, observing that the zeal was far from disinterested.[9] Granted that there is nothing implausible about a leading Bolshevik's working for the police, was Stalin a double agent? A clumsily forged document appearing to confirm the charge led one author, Isaac Don Levine, to explain Stalin's purges as an attempt to cover his tracks. Nevertheless, no evidence has survived to suggest that Stalin was a long-term police informer. Indeed, surviving records suggest the contrary. When he escaped from Novaya Uda, the police put out the local version of an all points bulletin:

> Circular of the Ministry of the Interior, Department of Police, Special Section, May 1, 1904, No 5500.
>
> To all city and provincial governors, chiefs of police, chiefs of provincial gendarmes, railroad police and all border posts:

The Department of Police has the honour of communicating to you
the following items to be dealt with as appropriate:
1. A list of persons wanted by the police. . . . List One. Persons
wanted in connection with political affairs. . . . Page 20, No 52:
Djugashvili, Iosif Vissarionovich; peasant from the village of Didi-
Lilo, Tiflis district, Tiflis province; born 1881, Orthodox; educated
Gori church school, Tiflis Theological Seminary; unmarried, father
Vissarion whereabouts unknown, mother Ekaterina resident Gori,
Tiflis province.

Banished for three years to Eastern Siberia under open police
surveillance for crimes against the state. . . . Residence assigned in
Balagan district, Irkutsk province, disappeared January 5th 1904.

Description. Height, 2 *arshins*, 4½ *vershki*, [c. five feet four inches];
average build, ordinary appearance; brown hair, reddish brown
moustache and beard; straight hair, no parting; dark brown eyes of
average size; ordinary head shape; small flat forehead; long straight
nose; long swarthy pock-marked face; missing front molar in right
lower jaw; shortish height; sharp chin; soft voice, average size ears;
ordinary gait; birthmark on left ear; second and third toes joined on
left foot. [10]

Besides mistaking the date and place of Stalin's birth, the document
gives a verbose, ill-organized and unsatisfactory description. However,
had Stalin been a police agent, it seems unlikely that a bulletin would
have been issued at all. Moreover, the document confirms that Stalin
had effected a successful escape from Siberia. If he could manage it
once, then why not five times more?

Yet there remain two reasons for suspecting some police involvement.
The first is circumstantial. Stalin liked to impute his shortcomings to
others. Over the years this tendency found increasing scope, as the
trumped-up charges which he used to destroy his enemies came to offer
a mirror image of his own criminal actions. It is curious that virtually
every protagonist of the major show trials would be charged, along with
sundry other crimes, with membership of the Okhrana. Beyond this
tenuous argument there were moments, over the next few years, when
comrades or rivals voiced the suspicion that Stalin had betrayed them to
the police; it also seems likely that he betrayed the party leaders in
Batum when they rejected him. Stalin, never one to put loyalty before
advantage, was quite capable of using the police to get his infighting
done. Indeed it is inconceivable that he should *not* have used them as a
means of self-advancement and revenge.

CHAPTER FOUR

Bolsheviks and Mensheviks

On his return from Siberia in 1904 Stalin went to Batum, hoping to find some kind of organization and support. A party member and subsequent émigré, V. Arsenidze, who saw Stalin at this time, has left one of the rare eyewitness accounts of the young man:

> I first met Stalin in Batum in 1904. He had just returned from exile, and had come straight to us. I saw a young man, dry, bony, with a pale-brown pockmarked face and lively, crafty eyes. His opening words dealt with what he perceived as certain shortcomings of our illegal publications; he disliked their lack of militancy. [When their tone was justified as tactically appropriate] this silenced him, though a crafty smile continued to play across his lips. After this he saw fit to ignore the committee . . . altogether. He devoted all his efforts to restoring direct contact with the workers, among whom, thanks to his earlier activities, he had a number of acquaintances. He spent the better part of a fortnight with them, having secret talks and discussions. . . . As far as I am aware the discussions did not reach a satisfactory conclusion and soon after Stalin left Batum. . . . I got the impression that Soso used them to try to gain support for his ambitious plans and approval for his earlier behavior in Batum, but he found neither, even though he had returned expecting them to welcome him with open arms. It is scarcely surprising that he was put out and disappointed by his reception.[1]

A hostile source adds that Stalin tried to provoke the workers into direct action, accusing the local committee of cowardice when it failed to support him.

That year the Social Democrats had elected to celebrate the first of May discreetly. They had planned to hold their annual demonstration by taking to the sea in rowing boats and proceeding some way out. En route to the meeting place an occupant of Stalin's boat began to tease him. Stalin expressed his displeasure by tipping him into the sea and rowing on. Fortunately another boat appeared to fish out the humorist, who was not a strong swimmer, but the incident took much of the fun out of May Day.[2]

After failing to find his footing in Batum, Stalin moved on to Tiflis. Once again we see him trying to hijack an organization, as an eyewitness recalls:

> [In Tiflis] he used the same tactics he had in Batum. . . . He did not appear before the committee but went straight to a meeting of radical workers where he offered them both his services and his proposals for revolutionary work. But the comrades of Tiflis greeted him coldly, suspiciously even, and their response to his plans was so ironic that he abandoned the struggle and left before the meeting was over. His motives were still to win over the militant workers, become their leader, and, if necessary, rely on their support to move in on the committee and take it over. This tendency was powerfully developed in him. He clearly loved to be number one, to manage, rule, issue authoritarian instructions. His entourage consisted exclusively of people who obeyed him and submitted, in all respects, to his authority; he could not stand anyone else, while no one else, not even among the Bolsheviks, could stand him. . . .
>
> Each time that I met him I came away with a painful impression: His words, deeds, behavior had a peculiar quality that did not feel quite right. I often asked myself what kind of man he really was: a revolutionary utterly dedicated to the cause or a dry, heartless, soulless machine cast in the image of a man. . . . He spoke without oratorical eloquence. He gave no sign of an inner flame, of spiritual warmth, sincerity or goodness. He spoke rudely, roughly, and you could sense an energy, strength, persistence in his crudity. He often employed irony and sarcasm, crushing his opponents with coarse humor, hammerblows which often went far too far.
>
> He lied, and brazenly accused his opponents of lying. No motion

could be passed . . . without an immediate challenge from Stalin, who would accuse its proposer of lying, or else would alter the sense of the motion to deceive honest listeners. . . . In order to refute him, you had to have copies of all the illegal literature to hand, and this was not always easy. At the next meeting he would simply resurrect all the objections [that] he had raised before and that had already been dismissed on prior occasions. He would persist until the audience would be convinced that he really was deliberately and brazenly lying. . . . Whereupon his face would show not the faintest trace of embarrassment or shame—merely irritation and anger since the "means had failed to reach their end" and his tactic had been exposed. He had recourse to bad language and was never above vulgar abuse. Only the protests of embarrassed audiences could restrain the foulmouthed torrent. When this occurred, he would apologize, observing that he had used the language of workingmen and that workers were not well versed in delicate manners and aristocratic modes of speech. They spoke straight and coarse truths, and he followed their example.[3]

It was during his stay in Tiflis that Stalin first met Sergei Alliluyev, a skilled worker from Russia. Alliluyev had two daughters. One, Nadezhda, was aged three when Stalin first met her. Sixteen years later he would marry her. Twelve years after that she would shoot herself. The other daughter, Anna, was aged eight. Forty-four years later Stalin would put her in jail.

Nineteen three had been an important year for the Russian revolutionary movement, marking the moment when the Social Democratic party split. The schism was the work of Lenin. Those who write admiringly of the future leaders of the Russian Revolution treat their every ideological squabble with a degree of detail that cannot be justified by the significance of the points at issue. The issues dividing the Social Democrats in 1903 do not merit detailed attention, except insofar as they help us understand Lenin and why it was that Stalin should have felt drawn to him. The Social Democrats had split over a motion defining what it meant to be a member of their party. Lenin wanted members to be activists, while his opponents were content for them to play a passive role. Since Lenin's faction emerged with a majority, they became Bolsheviks (Majoritarians), and the minority was known as Mensheviks (Minoritarians). However, their divisions went much deeper. The Mensheviks believed in a scientific evolutionary Marxism, accord-

ing to which society would evolve through certain stages, the penulti-
mate one being advanced capitalism, before the emergence first of
socialism, then of communism. In other words, they went by the book.
Lenin went by a different kind of book altogether. The most succinct
exposition of his attitude is found in a pamphlet written in 1903 entitled
What Is to Be Done?. The title has significant associations. It was originally the title of one of the worst novels ever written, which became the
bible of the Russian radical movement.

Chernyshevsky, a radical who endured years of prison and exile in the
cause of revolution, wrote the novel in a Petersburg prison, an extenuat-
ing circumstance which fails to redeem it. The book is a dreadful
wooden portrait of ideal revolutionary types, "New People," who devote
themselves to the cause, overcoming both sexual prejudice and weaknesses of the flesh in alternating bouts of resolute enthusiasm. The book
is as stupid, stylized and distortive as the crudest pornography. It is also
a work of considerable significance for the history of what, for lack of a
better word, must be referred to as ideas. For its success among Russian
radicals, and the real veneration which Lenin accorded to it, are revealing indices of the extent of their literacy and even their psychological
and intellectual development. It has recently been republished in England by a women's press. Chernyshevsky calls for a kernel of fearless
and superhuman revolutionaries, "the flower of the best people, the
movers of the movers, the salt of the salt of the earth." With their
ascetic devotion and their staggeringly humorless fanaticism, they would
lead the masses toward a new life.

Lenin rejected the evolutionary approach of scientific Marxism.
Whatever the shortcomings of his literary tastes, he never lost his grasp
on revolutionary priorities. He was in too great a hurry to wait for Russia to transform itself according to the rules. Rejecting the idea of a
Marxist party with a mass membership, he called for a small group of
hard men, dedicated revolutionaries, who would lead the masses. The
party would be the "avant-garde of the working class." It would be an
illegal conspiratorial organization, with emotional affiliations closer to
the ruthless traditions of Jacobinism than the moderate and Menshevik
interpretations of Marx. Lenin called for a tiny elite, who would permit
nothing, no scruple, no personal concern, to stand in its way. Where
conventional Marxism denied that great men could ever affect the
course of history, Lenin called for a party of heroes to lead the people
into a radiant future.

The Mensheviks found Lenin's views repugnant, comparing him to the coldest-blooded murderers of the French Revolution, Robespierre and Saint-Just. Lenin was more than happy to accept the comparison. He never forgot that the first priority was power and that anybody inhibiting this priority was at best an irrelevance, at worst an enemy. It is this clear vision of power and priority that earned Lenin the support of the young Stalin, who admired Lenin's ruthless maximalism and his dismissal of the wishy-washy and the sentimental. More important, Lenin rounded on the Mensheviks as feeble intellectuals whose moderation and gradualism disgusted him. One of his biographers has called his hatred of the intelligentsia the only passion in his life which could not be explained by politics:

> [His hatred] runs like a thread through his personal and public life,
> and provides much . . . of the emotional intensity behind the
> revolutionary strivings. Phrases such as "the revolutionary scum," the
> "scoundrel intellectuals" . . . run continually through his writings.
> Even the staunchest reactionary who blamed all of Russia's troubles
> on the Jews and intellectuals seldom approached Lenin's violence. His
> fury was aroused by any concept, any postulate, any phenomenon that
> in some circuitous way could reflect the mentality of the intelligentsia;
> liberalism, independence of the judiciary, parliamentarianism.[4]

Lenin gave his party a style of fashionable ruthlessness which came to a peak during the civil war, the golden age of leather-clad commissars who brandished revolvers at the slightest pretext and often used them. Already in 1904 Trotsky, who would pull a trigger or two himself over the years, foresaw the course of Lenin's revolution: "Lenin's methods lead to this; first the Party organization substitutes itself for the party as a whole; then the Central Committee substitutes itself for the organization; and finally a dictator substitutes himself for the Central Committee.[5]

Stalin would remain loyal to his leader for a remarkably long time and was never tempted by the Menshevik deviation. A number of factors influenced him. The Menshevik tendency was dominant in Georgia; Stalin despised Georgian values a priori. Besides, he associated Mensheviks not just with intellectuals but with Jews. Anti-intellectualism and anti-Semitism go hand in glove in Russian culture, and anti-Semitism is a theme that runs right through Stalin's life. We find the young Stalin repudiating the Menshevik leadership in language that is remarkably frank and forthright. "Lenin," Koba would say, "is un-

happy because God gave him the Mensheviks as comrades. Just look at
them, what a rotten crowd, Martov, Dan and Axelrod are circumcised
yids [sic], and V. Zasulich is an old bitch. Just try and work with them.
You can't fight at their side, you can't drink with them either; a bunch
of cowards and tradesmen."[6] The Mensheviks were led by Jews and old
women, while the Bolsheviks were the party of Great Russians and real
men. Stalin obviously did not know that Lenin had Jewish blood, and
on his mother's side to boot.[7]

•   •   •

Stalin did not stay in Tiflis for long. His squabbles and intrigues had
made too many enemies. Once he even came to blows with Filip
Makharadze, a Bolshevik moderate. There is hearsay evidence of a second party court that banished him from Tiflis again.[8] Stalin paid a brief
return visit to Batum, before moving on to the oilfields of Baku, where
he joined the local party committee. A young party member, F. Khu-
nyants, recalled her first meeting with Stalin:

> I found Koba in a small room. He was short, thin and somewhat
> dejected-looking, reminding me of a petty thief awaiting sentencing.
> He wore a dark blue peasant blouse, tight-fitting jacket and a black
> Turkish cap.
>
> He treated me suspiciously. After lengthy questioning he handed
> me a stack of illegal literature. I had my own copies of some of them,
> so I only took some of the ones he offered. He saw me to the door
> with that same guarded, mistrustful expression.
>
> [She confesses to Stepan Shaumyan, a leading Bolshevik, that
> Stalin made a bad impression on her as an] intimidating and
> depressing [person]. "Is he like that with everybody?"
>
> "What are you talking about? He's an old comrade, very
> committed, very experienced," Shaumyan assured me.
>
> [She goes on to describe Stalin's behavior at local committee
> meetings.] . . . It would be time to start, and Koba would not be
> there. He always arrived late. Not very, but it never failed. . . . When
> he got there, the atmosphere would change. It was not so much that it
> became businesslike as strained. Koba would arrive with a book under
> his shortened left arm and sit somewhere to the side or in a corner.
> He would listen in silence until everyone had spoken. He always
> spoke last. Taking his time, he would compare the different views,
> weigh all the arguments and, basing himself upon the most practical

and farsighted position, make his "own" motion with great finality, as though concluding the discussion. Thus there was a sense of special importance to everything he said.[9]

It is an interesting view of Stalin in action. We see him exploiting the format of a meeting in order to dominate it, virtually regardless of the opinions he happens to espouse. He shows an ability to summarize and exploit the views expressed quickly and succinctly, characteristics which would eventually turn him into a manager and committee chairman of the highest caliber. Always patient, he would never be so attached to his own ideas that he would impose them at all costs, proving surprisingly willing to listen to others before arriving at a decision which he stood behind as his own. Few chief executives have exploited the form of the committee as effectively as Stalin.

Shaumyan was Baku's leading Bolshevik. Although he stood up for Stalin, Stalin did not reciprocate. He viewed Shaumyan as a rival and intrigued against him accordingly. Matters would come to a head a few years later, in 1909, when Shaumyan was arrested. He realized he had been denounced by Stalin when the police began to question him about a safe house known only to the two of them. The police had arrested a number of other revolutionaries at the same time, on the strength of anonymous letters telling them where to find them. Curiously they all were enemies of Stalin.[10] It was widely believed that Stalin had been responsible for the arrests, and yet another party court was planned. Unfortunately all its members were arrested as it assembled, while Stalin was picked up on his way to attend it. An attempt was made to conclude matters in prison, but nothing came of this, and the scandal died away.[11]

For Arsenidze, Shaumyan was greatly superior to Stalin because he produced original theoretical ideas whereas Stalin remained content to be the disciple of Lenin. However, he concedes that Stalin had certain practical qualities:

> Among the Bolsheviks Koba distinguished himself by his energy, his tireless capacity for work, his tremendous thirst for power, but also by his great and peculiar talent as an organizer. He did not use this to create mass organizations, but rather developed his own groups of devoted and loyal supporters in the midst of such mass movements, then using them to try to take over the movement in question.
> As an organizer he was well served by his skill at summing people

up quickly. He seemed to sense instinctively how to pick the right
man for the right job.[12]

Stalin's reliance on insiders, a party within the party, sets the pattern
for his rise to power, while the careful exercise of his considerable managerial skills eventually mattered far more than any capacity for original
thought.

It may seem strange that critics of Stalin should bother to accuse him
of shortcomings in the field of political philosophy; outstanding leaders
are seldom great thinkers. But the Bolsheviks were different; any one
with political ambitions had to prove himself in the field of political
theory in order to win the respect of his comrades. This is because of
the paramount role of ideology for the Social Democrats. They believed
in the literal truth of the theories and prophecies of Karl Marx. "The
teachings of Marx shall triumph because they are true" was the foundation of this belief, one drummed into every Soviet child from kindergarten to graduation to this very day. In this light, it becomes vital that any
would-be leader interpret Marx "correctly" since "incorrect" interpretation would lead to critical deviation, delaying the advent of the millennium. Although ideology plays a different role in the Soviet Union
today, in the early years of this century it constituted a loose accumulation of doctrine which had to be interpreted correctly and which created
the basis for all decision making. Understanding of the doctrine was as
important to a Social Democrat as proper interpretation of Christian
dogma would have been to a medieval theologian, for whom heresy
meant the endangering of his immortal soul. Marxists, like Christians,
believed that they alone were possessed of the truth, a belief which, in
each case, had unfortunate consequences for others—infidels, heretics,
deviationists, *kulaks*—cast by dogma and doctrine into ideological outer
darkness.

The importance of ideology and the need to cope with situations
unforeseen by Marx helps explain the otherwise-puzzling amount that
Stalin would write and publish: thirteen volumes of collected works.
Admittedly their core consists of speeches, yet there is a large body of
political writing proper, some of which dates from the early years. In
1904 he published an essay in a Georgian newspaper, *Proletarian Struggle*, about nationalism and the Social Democratic movement. He defined his party as being above national divisions, in the sense that it
sought to unite the various races of the empire, aiming at the creation of
a pan-imperial proletariat. He also attacked the parochial nationalism of

Georgian and Armenian radicals, equating them with the Bund, the Jewish workers' revolutionary movement, a comparison which he felt was eloquent enough to condemn his opponents without further comment.

The article is of interest because it marks the moment when Stalin turned his back upon Georgian culture. He also adopted an attitude to the so-called national question, the relationship between Great Russians and the other 200 or so races of the empire, which would prove significant in a few years. Stalin suggested that all nationalities would have a part to play in the new society but that class, not race, was the chief consideration; national interests and demands were of no importance and required no attention. The inevitable consequence of such an attitude would be Great Russian dominance; Stalin dissociated himself from the little nations of the empire to identify with the Muscovite heartland.

CHAPTER FIVE

1905

Stalin devoted most of 1905 to fighting Mensheviks and promoting Lenin's cause in the Caucasus. He published a fiery article defending Lenin's views. Russia consisted of two armies at war, each led by a political party: the liberals and the Social Democrats—a group of militants who would lead the proletariat in the final struggle. It shows us Stalin's view of Lenin as the leading proponent of a militant line. It also anticipates the strain of military imagery, with all its talk of fronts and armies, that would play a vital part in Soviet rhetoric and political imagination. It also reveals something of Stalin's debating style. The opposition's ideas are never refuted; they are brushed aside by rhetorical invective. Stalin did not allow himself to get bogged down by debate; already he was the master, not the slave, of ideology.

That year Stalin traveled extensively through Georgia in support of Lenin. He spoke against Mensheviks and tried without much success to establish groups of Bolshevik supporters or "local committees." The disastrous war with Japan had combined with peasant unrest and the disaffection of the professional classes, which wanted representative government, to create an almost universal hostility toward the tsar, making for a growing wave of strikes, demonstrations and assassinations directed against the regime throughout the empire. Stalin seems to have taken little part in the assault upon the autocracy. He was more concerned with fighting Mensheviks; the revolution which broke out at the end of the year and which was particularly violent in Georgia passed him by.

By the middle of October 1905 the rule of law had largely collapsed throughout the empire. The tsar was persuaded that he had no choice but to offer his subjects a form of constitutional government in an attempt to win over moderate opinion. Reluctantly he issued a manifesto promising certain constitutional guarantees and summoning a new national assembly, or Duma. This was welcomed by the Georgian Mensheviks, who believed that it meant the end of autocracy, so that terrorists and workers could put away their arms. The Bolsheviks told the workers that they should content themselves with nothing short of overthrowing the monarchy and establishing a proletarian government. The monarchist right wing, which was no more delighted by the constitution than the Bolsheviks, signified its displeasure in the usual manner by beating up and killing Jews, liberals and anybody else it suspected to be short of patriotic fervor, all under the admiring eyes of the tsarist police.

The right-wingers were especially active in Tiflis, where, on October 22, they caused some forty deaths. Matters in the Georgian capital were further complicated by fighting between Turks and Armenians. Thereupon there ensued that particular pattern of chaos and farce, laced with bloodshed, that often characterizes a nation on the brink of revolution, as the fighting between Turks and Armenians was brought to an end by none other than the Social Democrats, whom the viceroy had armed with 500 rifles, allowing them to form a people's militia, on the understanding that they would give the guns back after order had been restored—a request with which the Mensheviks complied. Elsewhere states of emergency were declared as insurgents disarmed the police, took over the railways and assumed the maintenance of public order. One report concluded: "The Viceroy has had a nervous breakdown but his condition is not hopeless yet."[1]

Gradually the government regained the upper hand, first in St. Petersburg, then in Moscow, which held out far longer. However after a week of fighting, a combination of regular troops, Cossacks and Russian patriots brought the revolutionaries to a standstill, and by early January 1906 order had been restored. Open insurrection had failed, and once more the revolution had to go underground. One might have expected Stalin to have fished energetically in such troubled waters, but the profile he kept was so low that it has grown imperceptible. The only eyewitness account of his actions shows him fighting a battle of a different kind. Arsenidze describes the funeral of a Social Democrat martyr of the revolution which was attended by both Bolsheviks and Mensheviks. The funeral was followed by a debate between the two factions at which

Stalin spoke on behalf of the Bolsheviks. It soon became clear that he was getting little or no support from the floor and was obviously going to lose. Rather than allow this to happen, Stalin suddenly gave a signal to his supporters, who came onto the platform, lifted him onto their shoulders and bore him in apparent triumph from the stage, much to the amazement of the rest of the audience. They took him into the square, where Stalin hoped that the crowd would respond to this token of his debating success, only to find to his fury that no one paid any attention to the little group. As he observed to his supporters, "You've carried me out all right, but where *is* everybody?" However, in due course his official biography would note the occasion as a personal triumph, at which he was born out from a nest of hostile Mensheviks to acclamations of the crowd that was thronging the square and waiting to see him.[2]

Stalin's lack of conspicuous revolutionary activity in 1905 does not mean that he confined himself to fighting Mensheviks. With its lawlessness, chaos and turbulence, 1905 was indeed, as Lenin would put it, a dress rehearsal for the Revolution. The Empire was on the verge of new and violent times. This was as clear to the peasants, who had set fire to their landlords' houses, stables and livestock, not to mention the occasional landlord, as it was to sophisticated members of the intelligentsia, such as the poet Alexander Blok, who henceforward devoted his creative life to readying himself for the cataclysm that must inevitably come. Stalin was at home in the atmosphere of chaos, corruption and dissolution. It appealed to the street person in him, and he now began to put the skills of the street to good revolutionary use.

The Bolshevik party was always short of funds for its publications and for its full-time workers. Lenin got money from various sources, some more respectable than others. There were donations from millionaires with social consciences and at least one occasion when a party member married in order to gain control of a fortune, which duly found its way into Lenin's coffers. In 1917 Lenin also drew comfort from the enemy as the Germans provided him with substantial funds, casting their bread upon the waters with spectacular success. However, during and after the troubles of 1905 the Bolsheviks' principal resource was criminal action: robbery and protection rackets. It should be recalled that political robbery was fashionable throughout early twentieth-century Europe, where the incidence of terrorist action, political crime and assassination was higher by far than anything we know today. For example, there were 121 terrorist acts in Russia alone in October 1906, 362 expropriations and 47 shoot-outs with the police. The forces of law and order suffered about 500 casualties a *month*.[3] The Bolshevik readiness to resort to criminal action and, later, to high treason illustrates the significance the party attached to ideology. In order to accelerate the coming of the radiant future, any and all means are justified. To permit scruples to limit the scope of one's service to humanity would be an unforgivable weakness. Although belief in a radiant future no longer plays much part in Soviet ideology today, the relationship between ends and means remains unaltered. Today's leaders still behave as if their actions were justified by the promise of the millennium, enabling them to invade Afghanistan or shoot down Korean airliners for the good of the cause. Lenin's ruthless idealism created a legacy of ruthlessness which long outlived the ideals themselves.

Stalin's role in these criminal activities is not a matter of public record. He was moving in a zone beyond the reach both of record and respectable reminiscence. We have one scrap of evidence that suggests Stalin played a part in the organization, if not the actual execution, of political murders. One of his early biographers quotes from the unpublished memoirs of an ex-revolutionary, Alipi Tsintsadze: "After the defeat of the revolution a period of dark reaction set in. Early in 1906 comrade Arsene Djordjiachvili was ordered to kill General Gryaznov, a terrible reactionary ordered by the government to crush the revolutionary movement in Georgia. He kept postponing the execution. Koba-Stalin came to me and said: 'If Djordjiachvili does not murder Gryaznov within a week you are to take it on, and you'll need to pick some terrorists to help you.'"[4]

But Djordjiachvili did the job. While Stalin watched coolly from the sidelines, the young terrorist bombed the general to death, was arrested, tried on the spot and hanged in the main square at dawn on the following day.

The part played by Stalin in expropriations remains a matter for conjecture, but there is little doubt that play a part he did. It is scarcely conceivable that he should not have done so, in view of what we know of his character and his affection for the criminal world. There is another reason to suppose that he devoted a large part of his time to criminal activity—namely, the uncanny sketchiness of his official biographies, which bring him into occasional focus only to have him drift away almost immediately. Considered in the light of Soviet hagiographic practices, which seek to establish the whereabouts of the founding fathers at every moment of their sometimes uneventful lives, we can only conclude from this haziness that Stalin, even when judged by revolutionary standards of behavior, was up to no good.

Not all Social Democrats approved of expropriations. The party congress of 1907 voted to ban them, some of Lenin's supporters voting with the Mensheviks to carry the motion. Soon after there occurred the most spectacular expropriation of all. Stalin played no part in its hazardous and bloody execution, but there is reason to believe that he helped plan it. As the *Tiflis Times* for June 26, 1907, reports, "Today in the crowded Erevan Square in the center of town ten bombs were thrown. They exploded and did considerable damage. The square is covered with debris. There were many casualties. The authorities have cordoned off the square."

The follow-up story told of a robbery. Terrorists had attacked two carriages, escorted by Cossacks, taking 341,000 rubles to the state bank. Three people had been killed, and about fifty wounded. There were also a number of dead horses, which had had bombs thrown under their feet by an intrepid terrorist, Batchoua Kuriachvili, to prevent the carriages' escape. The terrorist group was led by a fearless Armenian, Ter-Petrosian, a killer that history has unforgivably glamorized.

Although the Bolsheviks got away with the money in the most spectacular of all their armed robberies, it consisted of large-denomination banknotes. The police had been warned of the raid and had responded by recording the numbers of 200 of the 500 notes, which somewhat reduced the value of the haul. At this point history and myth become confused. There are two versions of the fate of the recorded notes. Either these were burned, or their numbers were altered with the help of a skilled forger, so that they, too, could serve the cause.[5]

According at least to Arsenidze, Stalin's part in the robbery marked the end of his political activities in the Caucasus. The local party bureau set up a special commission to investigate the affair and recommended that all those involved, beginning with Stalin, be dismissed from the party. Nothing came of this recommendation, although Stalin did not show his face in tsarist Georgia again, except for a short visit he paid to Tiflis in 1909. Then he only saw close friends and kept bodyguards posted. It was not, says Arsenidze, "just the police that they were watching for."[6] Stalin, incidentally, would always deny that the party had expelled him. When the Menshevik Martov maintained as much in 1918, Stalin went as far as to take him before a party court to refute the charge.

In the aftermath of 1905 Stalin made a few appearances above ground. In 1906 he wrote some articles for a Bolshevik publication in Tiflis, defending Marxism against anarchism, which show that he had an excellent command of Marxist dogma. He quotes freely from both Marx and Engels and has a sound grounding in the doctrine. The writing makes it obvious that he was drawn to the all-embracing quality of their thought as well as to the militant rhetoric with which they described class conflict. It is usually assumed that Stalin wrote the articles himself, although if we take account of Arsenidze's assessment of his capacities at the time, he may well have had a little help. In Arsenidze's view Stalin's literary talent was conspicuous only by its absence, while he could not even pride himself on his spelling.[7]

Stalin's journalistic ambitions may explain the interest he now displayed in a clandestine printing press that the Social Democrats had established in Tiflis. Setting up a press was a major undertaking: For example, it was impossible to purchase a font of characters without a license; they had to be stolen piecemeal from a legitimate printshop. The press, which had been running successfully for some years, employed six typesetters and published papers and pamphlets in Georgian, Armenian and Russian. Its whereabouts were known only to members of the local committee. It was set under a house and reached by a tunnel at the bottom of a well shaft. The police had been looking for it for a long time when, in the words of the owner of the house beneath which it was located:

> On April 15, 1906 the gendarmes, the police, a squad of sappers and a company of mounted cossacks surrounded the Rostomashvili house. Two state attorneys and the chief of the Tiflis police were there also. As soon as the gendarmes arrived they went straight to a corner of the yard where they dug up two bombs. They were most certainly tipped off by an insider, since they went directly to the place where they found the bombs. They then dug the whole yard up but found nothing more. After a discussion the chief ordered them to abandon the search and leave. As they moved off, on their way past the great "hole," a sapper officer lit a newspaper and threw it down. The burning paper was sucked down quickly. One of the attorneys drew attention to it and ordered a man sent down to investigate. They let a cossack down on a rope. From the bottom he announced that he had found a door. More men were let down, who broke the door in and discovered the press.[8]

Unconfirmed rumors suggest that Stalin had tried to gain control of the press and, when he failed, took the appropriate measures to close it down. The officials certainly behaved as if they wished to protect an inside source, discovering the press "by chance" at the last moment. Stalin's role is a matter of conjecture. Despite efforts to track it down, the press had operated successfully for a long time; it was discovered shortly after Stalin's arrival. There is nothing farfetched about the notion that Stalin had reported its whereabouts to the authorities. The motive? A combination of pleasure and of profit. Trotsky later maintained that Stalin was actually arrested during the raid and then released; that would scarcely have been possible since he was out of the country at the time. Arsenidze suggests that Trotsky got his dates confused and that Stalin had already been arrested and released before the press was discovered, the presumption being that his information bought the police off.[9]

He was now moving toward the center of the Bolshevik party, although he still had a long way to go. He made his first appearance on the Russian stage late in 1905. Lenin had summoned a party conference in Finland, at the small town of Tammerfors. Stalin attended as a delegate from Tiflis, and it was then that he first set eyes on Lenin. His recollection of that moment is set in the tone of unctuous veneration which informs all Soviet accounts of meetings with that remarkable man. At first Stalin was disappointed; it was only upon reflection that he perceived the greatness of Lenin. He had expected to see a man of imposing physical presence since he was, in Stalin's words, "the mountain eagle of this great party of ours." Instead, he found a "man of the most ordinary appearance, below average height and in no way distinguishable from ordinary mortals." He did not even act like a great man, being content to conduct quiet conversations with individual delegates. However, the young Stalin gradually began to understand that this "simplicity and modesty, this striving to remain unnoticed, or at least to remain inconspicuous and not to stress his own importance was one of Ilich's strongest points as the new leader of the new masses."[10] It is unfortunately impossible to convey in translation the Uriah Heep-like tones in which Stalin describes this first encounter.

Stalin traveled abroad again in the spring of 1906, attending a party conference in Stockholm. It was a joint meeting of Bolsheviks and Mensheviks, with the latter in a majority. Indeed, all the official delegates from the Transcaucasus were Mensheviks. Although Stalin presented himself as a delegate from the Social Democrat organization of the district of Borchalo, this did not exist. He was refused accreditation and told to leave the conference. However, the Bolshevik faction secured permission from the credentials committee for him to stay as a nonvoting delegate. We can be sure that Stalin's touchy and vindictive character would have resented such treatment.

In 1907 Stalin attended another conference. It was originally to have been held in Copenhagen, but the Danish authorities withdrew permission, and its venue was moved to London. The delegates gathered in the Brotherhood Church, Southgate Road, Whitechapel, where they met for some three weeks. Stalin again had difficulties with his accreditation. He still claimed to represent the nonexistent Borchalo organization, and again he was challenged. This time the committee gave him an advisory vote, a concession which elicited energetic protests from Zhordania and another leading Menshevik, Martov, who pointed out that nothing was known about the young Djugashvili. Lenin agreed but suggested that they trust the findings of the committee, and the matter was allowed to rest there.

In London Stalin shared a room with a Pole named Wallach, once described by Lenin as having the "virtues of a clever and adroit Jew." [11] He was otherwise known as Maxim Litvinov and one day would be Stalin's foreign minister. He would also have the rare good fortune to survive both dismissal and a posting abroad, as ambassador to Washington during World War II, and succeeded in dying a natural death. The conference was attended by a number of other future leaders, including Kamenev and Zinoviev, who together with Stalin would form the triumvirate that succeeded Lenin; Tomsky, the first head of the trade unions; the writer Maxim Gorky; and Trotsky, a Menshevik at the time, whom Stalin dismissed as "pretty but useless," an assessment that came close to the mark in the long run. Stalin was much struck by the predominance of Jews among the Mensheviks. Reporting on the conference for the *Baku Proletariat*, he observed that there had been more genuine workers among the Bolshevik delegates. The Mensheviks had a preponderance of artisans, semiskilled men and intellectuals. He even pointed out that the majority of them were Jews, quoting the words of a colleague who said that the Mensheviks were the Jewish party while the Bolsheviks were "true Russians"—an expression used by extreme rightwing groups such as the League of Russian Patriots that believed Russia's salvation was to be sought through the pogrom. Stalin's friend capped his observation with the facetious suggestion that they should consider a pogrom of their own within the party. [12] In due course Stalin would take him at his word.

On Stalin's return he based himself in Baku, probably because he had outlived his welcome in Georgia (Baku was part of the province of Azerbaijan). Although the local party was dominated by Mensheviks, Stalin helped to set up a parallel Bolshevik committee led by Shaumyan. This included two of Stalin's comrades and future victims, Sergo Ordzhonikidze and Avel Yenukidze. Stalin devoted himself to propaganda and agitation among the workers in the oil industry. He also worked protection and extortion rackets and was involved in a counterfeiting operation. His long-standing rivalry with Shaumyan now came to a head in the incidents that culminated in Shaumyan's arrest. Whether or not Stalin betrayed him we cannot say, but if he did, the action failed to gain him immunity. In March 1908 the police arrested him, too, treating him as a political prisoner, not a criminal. He spent eight months in the local prison and was then sentenced to two years' banishment to Vologda in northern Russia.

Tsarist prisons were revolutionary talking shops, where Bolsheviks, Mensheviks, anarchists, Tolstoyans, Socialist Revolutionaries could argue freely with one another from dawn to dusk. Not only did they bring together people with similar interests and tantalizingly divergent beliefs, but they were one of the few places where it was safe to talk without running the risk of arrest. Yet in the midst of all this debating Stalin remained a loner. A fellow inmate, a Socialist Revolutionary named Simon Vereshchak, saw a lot of Stalin in prison, and his account of him brings out his character with uncomfortable clarity. At recreation time, when other prisoners gathered in eager little groups, he preferred to keep to himself, pacing up and down with short, mincing steps. Vereshchak found Stalin impressive, but unpleasant to argue with. He was rude and never too proud to hit below the belt. When he wasn't using bad language, his speech was dry and humorless. Yet he had clearly acquired an imposing command of the Marxist scriptures. He had remarkable powers of recall—a skill developed in the seminary, with its emphasis upon learning by rote. When it came to the recitation of dogma, Stalin was in his element:

> [When you looked] at his primitive brow and small head, it seemed
> that, were you to break it open, it would spew forth the entire works of
> Marx, like an exploding gasometer. Marxism was his element, and in
> it he was invincible. Once he had made up his mind on a subject,
> nothing could shake him, and he always had an appropriate quotation
> to hand. He made a tremendous impression upon young, politically
> inexperienced party members and in Transcaucasia had the reputation
> of being a second Lenin.[13]

This prophetic sketch gives a first hint of Stalin's undeniable mass appeal. His blend of impressive memory and exposition of a rigid ideology won over his unsophisticated and "politically inexperienced" audience, who were probably self-taught and combined dedication—why else would they be in jail—with the autodidact's uncritical veneration for the written word. It should be recalled that rigid doctrinal frameworks and their "correct" interpretation have always played a more important part in Russian intellectual life than flexible and critical forms of personal evaluation. It was Stalin's impressive, literalistic command of the Marxist canon, the steeliness of his expositions that won him the admiration and respect of his coreligionaries.

The most striking feature of Stalin's behavior in prison was his independence. Closed institutions such as prisons, hospital wards and boarding schools subject their inmates to a tremendous pressure to conform, if only to seek the comfort of the group in otherwise bleak surroundings. It was a pressure that Stalin resisted effortlessly. He never had close friends, never adapted to the group. For example, on the eve of an execution it was a prison tradition to stay awake, feel distressed and converse in shocked whispers. Stalin did none of this. He spent such evenings working on his Esperanto before sleeping the sleep of the just. When political prisoners engaged in demonstrations, he took no part, but neither did he discourage others from demonstrating; however preposterous the pretext, he always had a word or two to spur the hotheads on. He also revealed a talent for persuading others to take the law into their own hands while remaining on the sidelines. On one occasion a newcomer was knifed to death on his way to recreation. The killer was a Bolshevik who believed his victim to be an informer. Apparently it was Stalin who had said so, although there was no evidence to support his contention. He might just have been setting a personal score.

He stood apart from the other politicals in another respect. They considered themselves an elite of intellectuals and avoided the institution's other inmates, the common criminals. As persons of education who suddenly find themselves cheek by jowl with professional hard men, they were probably afraid of them. Not so Stalin; he sought their company out and respected them as the perpetrators of "real crimes." Once again he professed the values of the street. One final touch to this chilling portrait: The prisoners had a game in which by words alone and without the use of bad language, the player had to make his victim lose his self-control. Stalin could never be made to lose his, but he also proved incapable of provoking others. It seemed that he had no understanding of passion.

CHAPTER SIX

Exile

Yet the young Stalin was not entirely devoid of feeling, for he had a wife, of whom he was fond and about whom almost nothing is known. The absence of information about Ekaterina ("Keke") Svanidze is curious if only because one can see no reason why official biography should have consigned this aspect of the leader's life to history's dustbin. We can only conclude that the details of the marriage were insufficiently edifying. Excessive attention to Stalin's domestic life might also have raised the embarrassing question of how he supported his household. It would not have been appropriate to reveal that he lived from the proceeds of armed robbery and extortion, supplemented by occasional free-lance work as a stool pigeon. As it is, virtually all we know of his circumstances is that he once rented a modest house in Baku.

Stalin probably met Keke through her brother, with whom he was at school, and the marriage may have taken place in 1902. His wife was not a revolutionary. Reading the memoirs of the time, one would suppose the revolutionary movement to be bursting with stern, emancipated women who chain-smoked and practiced free love to demonstrate that they knew their Chernyshevsky and understood that morality had no part to play in the brave new world. They served as models to early Soviet womanhood, and their prestige and authority—which they never hesitated to exercise—were high indeed. Stalin chose a wife of a different kind. Ekaterina was a devout Christian, who believed in the traditional Georgian values. A woman's place was in the home; she should dress modestly, keep her eyes cast down in company and submit to her husband's authority in all things. Stalin's attitude to marriage was more

Asiatic than European, with a strong emphasis on male dominance, female modesty and decorum. Many years later the attitude reemerged in his treatment of his daughter. He had her raised according to these values and, insistent upon the need for modesty, would fly into a rage at the sight of a hemline that displayed too much leg.

Stalin's puritanical attitude toward women and his conservative view of their role would be curiously reflected in a major shift of Soviet culture in the mid-1930s, away from the sexual permissiveness of the early years, with its instant divorce and abortion on demand. The new direction emphasized a dreadful neopuritanism, which was accompanied by an emphasis on etiquette—when to crook the little finger while drinking tea—creating an atmosphere of refinement that emulated the worst kind of nineteenth-century stuffiness. The change of direction was certainly Stalin's doing, and a glimpse of his first marriage helps to explain it.

Ekaterina, it would seem, worshiped her husband, who responded by acting the bully.[1] All accounts we have of his treatment of women—wives, mother, daughter—suggest that he was foulmouthed, disrespectful and capable of physical violence. He despised gentleness, which he confused with weakness, and persecuted his gentle wife accordingly. While working in Baku in the thirties, a future inmate of the gulag, Pyotr Mozhnov, heard tell of an old man who had rented rooms to Comrade Koba in 1908. Mozhnov was secretary of the district committee of the League of Young Communists. A typical LYC leader, ardent and full of pep, he imagined himself gathering the activists to listen to an old man's recollections of the leader. Unfortunately the old man proved unhelpful. "We don't know anything; we remember nothing. Someone has led you astray," he told the group of eager young people. Suspecting that something was not quite right, Mozhnov returned a few days later with a bottle or two. The old man and his wife greeted him very differently. They found some snacks, took a drink or so and began to talk freely:

> "What did you bring that crowd of people here for? Do you think such shameful things can be revealed in front of just anyone? Yes, it is true that Koba and his wife Keto lived here in 1908. Listen, what kind of revolutionary is he? Scum, that's what he is. A swine. Keto was pregnant then, and he used to curse her in the most disgusting way. And kick her in the belly. We tried to look after her. She came down with TB afterwards. When Koba came home drunk he always cursed

> her till he fell asleep." The old man drained his glass in a gulp and
> said despondently: "Listen, don't you know what kind of leader you've
> got yourself? Ai yai yai."[2]

Although this is unsubstantiated gossip from a prejudiced source, it
does not portray Stalin out of character. Moreover, as wives throughout
the grain-spirit belt can testify, the fact that their husbands mistreat
them when drunk is not to say that they do not love them.

Stalin's wife gave birth to a son, Yakov, in 1908 and very shortly
afterward she died. Iremashvili gives a fascinating account of Stalin's
feelings at that time. Stalin had always prided himself upon his im-
passive nature. Never before had his school friend seen him show emotion. He was astonished to see Koba let his grief come out. Iremashvili
considered this a remarkable indication of his sense of loss; indeed, it is
one of the rare occasions that we see him give way to any kind of sentiment other than rage. According to his late wife's wishes, Stalin gave
her an Orthodox Christian burial, and at her graveside he indulged in
his only known piece of self-analysis. It is disturbingly accurate: "Koba
pressed my hand firmly, gestured toward the coffin and said: 'This crea-
ture used to soften my stony heart. When she died, all my warm feeling
for people died with her.' Placing his hand on his heart, he said: 'It is all
so desolate, so unbelievably empty.'"[3]

It is as if Stalin recognized his inability to love, saw it as a failing,
not, as one might have supposed, a source of strength. He understood
that he was a psychological cripple, excluded by his handicap from the
world of feeling, an exclusion that fired his capacity for envy and
hatred. Iremashvili, who placed his recollection of Stalin in the perspective of his old friend's devastation of Georgia, observes that the death of
Ekaterina removed the last trace of moral restraint; henceforward he
would be unbridled. Significantly Stalin recognized this hardening of
the heart. Although he would continue to use "Koba," "Ko," "K" as
noms de plume, it is after the death of his wife that he first uses a new
revolutionary pseudonym, "Stalin," in which we hear an echo of
"Lenin" and, no less important, the Russian for "steel" or "stal'."

·   ·   ·

Stalin left Bailov prison for the province of Vologda in November
1908. On arrival he was assigned to his place of banishment, the remote
township of Solvychegodsk. To judge by the way he later spoke of that
time, exile was no burden to him, as Khrushchev recalls:

I've never forgotten how he described his exile. The tale helped explain why he drank so much. He was sent somewhere in Vologda Province. Many political and criminal convicts were sent there. Stalin used to say: "There were some nice fellows among the criminals during my exile. I hung around mostly with the criminals. I remember we used to stop at the saloons in town. We'd see who among us had a rouble or two, then we'd hold our money up to the window, order something, and drink every kopeck we had. One day I would pay, the next someone else would pay and so on, in turn. These criminals were nice, salt of the earth fellows. But there were lots of rats among the political convicts. They once organized a comrades' court and put me on trial for drinking with the criminal convicts, which they charged was an offence."[4]

Stalin did not stay there for long; four months later he escaped and headed south by train, passing through St. Petersburg on his way. His old friend Alliluyev had moved from Tiflis to the capital where he lived in relative comfort in a four-room house. Stalin had written to him from Solvychegodsk, explaining his plans in guarded terms and ensuring that he would have a place to stay when he came through. When he arrived in the capital, Alliluyev arranged for him to stay for a fortnight with a fellow Bolshevik, a guardsman who had rooms in the Horse Guards' Barracks, next to the Tauride Palace. Stalin often went into the city to visit friends, strolling serenely past the guard at the barracks gate.[5]

From Petersburg Stalin traveled south, making a brief appearance in Tiflis before going on to Baku. The ease with which he moved about appears as surprising as his readiness to return to the place of his arrest. Yet freedom of movement is not prima facie evidence of his being a police spy. Had such behavior been suspect, Stalin would have proceeded otherwise. He never took unnecessary risks, and informers, once identified, enjoyed an uncertain future. Rather, it is an indication of the inefficiency of the tsarist police and the competence of the Bolshevik underground. We know little of Stalin's activities in Baku. One dubious source describes him as publishing a pamphlet attacking the local Mensheviks, among whom was Andrey Vishinsky, a lawyer of Polish extraction and Stalin's future chief prosecuting attorney.[6] The author, who is determined to establish that Stalin worked for the police, even suggests that the pamphlet had been printed on the police department press.

On March 23, 1910, Stalin was arrested again and sent back to Bailov prison. On this occasion the police recommended harsher treatment. Beria, Stalin's future chief of police, whose account of his master's activities in the Caucasus does not always correspond to the facts, cites a local police chief, Captain F. I. Galimbatovsky, who drew attention to Stalin's two previous escapes and recommended he be sent to Siberia for five years.[7] Galimbatovsky was overruled; Stalin was ordered back to Solvychegodsk to complete his sentence and forbidden to return to the Caucasus for five years. He did not try to escape again, serving out the rest of his exile and settling in the town of Vologda, where he lived under police surveillance.

He enjoyed the harsh northern climate and turned his back upon Georgia. Under no obligation to settle in the north he was clearly opting for European Russia. His political ambitions took a corresponding new turn, as he made a bid to remind Lenin of his existence. His timing was excellent. After the Revolution of 1905 Lenin's party had gone into decline and Bolshevik morale was low. Much to Lenin's scorn, many former revolutionaries had left the underground to work within the framework of the new parliamentary institutions; others were in prison. It was a time when Lenin needed all the loyalty he could find, and never, in any of his modest journalistic excursions, had Stalin departed from the Leninist line. Stalin's writing had also made the transition from Georgian to Russian. For the last three years he had taken to writing in that language, a medium which he would always use a little clumsily but in which he was capable of dealing crude hammerblows for the good of Lenin's cause. By now, 1910, he had an impressive body of work behind him with a total of 109 articles, leaflets and booklets published.[8]

Stalin did not suffer from that overwhelming faith in his own rightness that one encounters in founders of religions, writers such as Rousseau or Tolstoy and inmates of insane asylums; he lacked the maniacal unity of vision of the inveterate solipsist. Yet he believed in the efficacity of Lenin's plans for revolutionary upheaval, and it was as a believer, not just a pragmatic opportunist, that he wrote in Lenin's support. Now, in exile, he decided to capitalize on his loyalty, recalling his existence to Lenin by means of a particularly blatant piece of flattery.

In December 1910 he wrote to a colleague who was in Paris, helping Lenin organize a party conference. The letter is intended for Lenin to read and see what a loyal supporter Stalin was. It finds his line correct in all respects, notably with regard to a new bloc Lenin had founded with Plekhanov, and continues: "The plan for a bloc reveals the hand of

Lenin—he is a shrewd fellow and knows where crayfish hide in winter."
Stalin goes on to suggest that more important than realignments among
the Bolsheviks abroad was the work to be done at home:

> The most important thing is to organise the work in Russia. The
> history of our Party shows that disagreements are ironed out not in
> debates, but mainly in the course of work, in the course of putting
> principles into action. Hence the most important thing is to organise
> work in Russia according to a strictly defined principle. . . . I believe
> our immediate task, one to be carried out without delay, is to organise
> a central group in Russia, to co-ordinate the illegal semi-legal and
> legal work, at first in the main centres (St. Petersburg, Moscow, the
> Urals, the South). Call it what you like—the Russian section of the
> Central Committee, or auxiliary group of the Central Committee, it
> does not matter, but such a group is as necessary as air or bread. At
> the present moment lack of information and loneliness are prevalent
> among regional Party workers, and they are all growing discouraged.
> As for me I have another six months to go here, and then I shall be at
> your service entirely. If you really need Party workers urgently I could
> get away at once. . . .
>   With comradely greetings. K.S.[9]

The letter will sound familiar to anyone who has had dealings with
ambitious young executives. Stalin proposes a reorganization of the
home office, suggesting, as if by chance, that he would be the perfect
person to take charge of the process. He already had, as it were, one foot
on the corporate ladder since he had been appointed an agent of the
Central Committee, acting as liaison officer between the Bolshevik center and local organizations. He now attempted to establish an organizational need which would result in his own promotion. Like many a
corporate novice, he was naïve enough to suppose that an oblique approach would disguise his motives. Yet Stalin the ambitious young
thruster proved less than deft, actually incurring the displeasure of his
chief.

For some time Lenin had been engaged in a polemic with some
Marxist heretics, Mach and Bogdanov, who had developed Marxism
along idealist as opposed to materialist lines, thereby opening some interesting philosophical avenues. Lenin's response, the book *Materialism
and Empirio-criticism*, was a torrent of insult and rage rather than a
philosophic rejoinder. As a reviewer, N. N. Valentinov, put it: "[The

book's] lack of literary restraint and propriety reach truly Herculean proportions and make a mockery of the most elementary demands of decency." [10] As a piece of philosophy Lenin's book is worthless; indeed, it attacks all philosophers who are, in Lenin's words, "the learned salesmen of theologians." [11] It is an intellectually embarrassing exercise in dogmatism and mediocrity masquerading as thought, low-grade street fighter's polemic. As Valentinov wrote many years later, "If someone had told me that these ideas . . . would one day be dinned like divine revelation into the heads of tens of millions of people in Russia, Eastern Europe, France, Italy, China, Korea—I would have laughed at him, or rather I should have told him that his joke was so stupid that it was not even worth a laugh. But what should have been a stupid joke has turned into a fact of world history!" [12]

It is important to establish the feel of the work that has been termed Lenin's only incursion into pure philosophy because it marks a further milestone in the development of intellectual terrorism. So convinced is the author that he is correct that abuse is substituted for argument; waverers might as well be browbeaten into assent. It is vital to an understanding of the age of revolution and the early years of the Soviet regime to realize that this form of debate was not thrust down the throats of a reluctant following. It was hailed with enthusiasm as a serious piece of thinking because its tone of militant abuse and absolute certainty had vast appeal.

Although Stalin would recognize the epoch-making nature of Lenin's treatise in due course, its appeal was lost on him at the time, which is why he incurred Lenin's displeasure. He had written to a colleague in Switzerland dismissing Lenin's differences with the empirio-critics and even suggesting that Mach had his points. The letter is the work of a man of action "at the sharp end" of revolutionary politics, dismissing the idle chatter of émigré café society squabbling in the safety of Switzerland. He wrote again in similar terms from Solvychegodsk in January 1911. The letter breathes self-importance and is dismissive of the leaders, who are getting out of touch "with the rank and file":

> I finish here in July. Ilich and Co. are calling me to one or two
> centers, without waiting for the end of the term. . . . If there should
> be a great need, of course, I'll fly the coop. . . .
>   We have heard, of course, about the storm in the teacup abroad,
> the blocs of Lenin and Plekhanov on one hand and Trotsky, Martov
> and Bogdanov on the other. As far as I know the workers look

favorably on the first bloc, but in general they are beginning to be contemptuous of those abroad, saying: Let them crawl up the wall as much as they want, but we feel that anyone with the interests of the movement at heart should get on with things. The rest will take care of itself. This, I think, is for the best. [13]

Stalin, the plain blunt man more interested in results than polemic, aligns himself with the practical workers, as opposed to theorists and intellectuals with their heads in the clouds. It was a persona that would serve him in good stead for many years, as he discovered his constituency, not among intellectuals, but among the party's lower echelons, newly literates who did not always find reading easy.

Stalin's letters made Lenin very angry. Incapable of laughing at anything, least of all himself, he took unkindly to the disparaging dismissal of his current concerns. In a conversation with Sergo Ordzhonikidze Lenin observed that although there was much to like about Koba's earlier words and actions, he was guilty of "inconsistency." He continued: "Nihilistic jokes about a storm in a teacup reveal Koba's immaturity as a Marxist." [14] Lenin countered Stalin's mockery with that puritanical censoriousness with which the Marxist Pecksniff disguises an attack *ad hominem* while going for the throat. Whether or not Ordzhonikidze passed Lenin's comments on, Stalin learned his lesson. He would not be disrespectful to Lenin again for many years, not until Ilich, incapacitated and deprived of the power of speech, would no longer be in a position to answer back.

In his second letter Stalin had described himself as "stifling, literally choking here with nothing to do," sensing that exile was denying him valuable opportunities for advancement. However, despite his high hopes, no summons came from Lenin, who doubtless saw fit to have him learn the significance of Marxist polemics the hard way. Soon the inactivity became intolerable. After three months in Vologda Stalin decided to escape again. He obtained a false passport in the name of P. A. Chizhikov and took the afternoon train to the capital on September 6, 1911. Together with a friend, Sila Todria, he presented himself at the Alliluyevs. Anna, his future sister-in-law, answered the door: "I loudly expressed my pleasure at seeing our grown-up friend Sila Todria, but suddenly stopped in my tracks when I saw a stranger standing behind the shortish Todria. The stranger was very thin in a black overcoat and a soft felt hat. When he stepped into the corridor, I looked more closely at his pale face and attentive hazel grey eyes under the thick, sharply curved eyebrows." [15]

While Sila chatted with the girls, Stalin kept to himself and read the papers, talking to Sila from time to time in "an abrupt but unhurried tone of voice." [16]

Stalin did not stay at large for long. Police activity had been stepped up as the result of the assassination of the Prime Minister, Peter Stolypin, in the Kiev Opera House. He had been shot before the Emperor and Empress in circumstances that have never been cleared up, but which suggest police complicity. Alliluyev had warned Stalin to be careful since the police had grown very active; indeed they netted him within days, and after a short spell in a Petersburg jail, he was returned to Vologda with a further sentence of three years' exile. The continuing mildness of his treatment suggests that the authorities did not have much against him—while their infiltration of the party sufficed to convince them that it posed no threat to the regime.

CHAPTER SEVEN

Promotion

Out of filth you can make a prince.
— STALIN

Nineteen twelve was a good year for Stalin. It marked his move to the center of the Bolshevik movement. Looking back, we can see a clear pattern to the last few years. First came the shift from Georgia to Vologda, a jump-off point for the capital; next Stalin brought himself to Lenin's attention, not as a Georgian bank robber but as a coordinator and potential executive in charge of the Russian end of the organization. His earlier moves now paid off. The year 1912 marked the moment when the two wings of the Social Democrats split into separate sections, and at a conference held in Prague in January the Bolshevik Party as such was born. Of the twenty-eight delegates at the conference, four were subsequently identified as police spies.

A Central Committee was set up; it consisted of seven members, including Ordzhonikidze, Zinoviev and the informer Malinovsky. It was a time when Lenin was well aware of the poor quality of the leading Bolsheviks. It was now that he dismissed Litvinov as an adroit and clever Jew and described Anatoli Lunacharsky, his future minister of education and toast of educational progressives, as a "moral gigolo." Lenin was happy to agree to Malinovsky's proposal that Stalin be co-opted onto the committee and made one of the four members of the new Russian Bureau, which would direct party activities at home. After all, he had proved himself a tough activist with a practical turn of mind, and although Stalin may have seemed many things to many people, no one ever thought of him as a gigolo. Stalin was nominated, not elected; as a political introvert he always operated from within a close-knit organization, rather than courting votes. Evidently he resented the fact since in 1938 he corrected his party's official history accordingly: "The Prague Conference, (January 1912) elected the Bolshevik Central Committee. It consisted of Lenin, Stalin and others. Comrades Stalin and Sverdlov were elected on a show of hands. A practical centre was created to direct revolutionary work in Russia, (the Russian Bureau of the Central Committee, headed by comrade Stalin).[1]

Not only was Stalin not elected, but he did not even head the bureau; that post was filled by Ordzhonikidze, who was conveniently dead by the time the new history came out.

Stalin celebrated his promotion with another escape. Five days after Ordzhonikidze had brought him the good news, he reappeared at the Alliluyev house in evident high spirits, behaving in a manner that was uncharacteristically human and even charming, as he took the Alliluyev family on a treat:

> "Who'd like a sledge ride? Well, get dressed and hurry—we're leaving right away!"
>
> We all jumped up, shouting with excitement. We had just been sitting glued to the window, admiring the sledges as they raced by, and suddenly we were invited by none other than Koba—Soso himself! During this visit to Petersburg he often came to see us. We now know Soso more intimately. We know he can be simple and gay, and that although he is usually uncommunicative and reserved, he can also laugh and joke boyishly and tell amusing stories. He sees the funny side of people and imitates them to such perfection that everyone roars with laughter. "Come on, all of you, get dressed! We're all going!" Fedya, Nadya, Fenya our domestic and I grab our fur coats and run downstairs. Soso calls out to a sledge-driver: 'What about giving us a ride?' We take our places in the sledge. Every word which is uttered makes us laugh. Soso laughs with us at everything. . . . The sledge glides down the Sampsonievskii Prospekt, past the station. . . . "Stop! I'll get off here, and you ride on back home." Jumping off the sledge, Stalin walks hurriedly to the station.[2]

We have another still more curious glimpse of Stalin at this time, in triumphant mood yet again:

The son of a famous Bolshevik tells this revealing episode. In 1912, when he was only nine, a Caucasian came to his parents' apartment. After a little talk his father went out, leaving the Caucasian, who was pleased with the boy's conversation. Four hours later the doorbell rang. The boy jumped up but the man stopped him. "Wait, wait," he said, taking the boy by the shoulder and hitting him on the cheek as hard as he could. "Don't cry," the Caucasian said, "don't cry, little boy. Remember to-day Stalin talked to you." When the boy told his parents about their guest's strange behaviour they were outraged and baffled, until, later on, they heard of a custom in many mountain villages of Georgia: if a prince comes to peasant's hut, the peasant would call in his son and hit him hard on the cheek, saying "remember that to-day Prince So and So visited our house." [3]

Stalin was quite ready to do his own hitting, as if understanding he had a destiny, the first indication that he thought of himself as more than a junior member of the leadership, that, in fact, he was a Bolshevik prince in the making.

Along with his work in the Russian Bureau Stalin wrote pieces for the underground press and played a minor part in the establishment of a legal Bolshevik newspaper named *Pravda* which enjoyed a measure of success. Much would later be made of his participation, yet none of the early histories of the party mention it, and a series of forty articles commemorating the paper's tenth anniversary name him only two or three times.

In April 1912 Stalin was arrested again and finally treated with some severity. He was exiled to the Narym region of Siberia, in the province of Tomsk, about 1,600 miles from the capital. He shared his exile with a number of acquaintances such as Jakob Sverdlov, a fellow Central Committee member, and Simon Vereshchak, whom he had first met in Bailov prison in 1908. There was also a Socialist Revolutionary, Surin, who turned out to be a police spy. Stalin's behavior was not exemplary. Once again he aligned himself with criminals against the politicals.[4] He also made no secret of his anti-Semitism. More serious, he seemed to be on suspiciously friendly terms with the local chief of police. There was further talk of a party court, a proposal which proved as futile as ever.

Late in the summer of 1912 Stalin escaped. He departed by steamer, picked up the Trans-Siberian Express at Tomsk and proceeded to the capital. He and Sverdlov paid regular calls on the Alliluyevs, where they spoke of their life in exile. Although the tone of their recollections is benign enough, they paint a picture of two men forced together and getting on one another's nerves:

> Stalin used to describe life with Sverdlov in exile. The day the mail arrived was like a long-awaited holiday, but they had to walk several kilometers to fetch it. They agreed between themselves that the person who went to fetch these letters should be relieved of all domestic chores for the rest of the day. "I liked slipping out for the mail an extra time or two," said Stalin, chuckling. So willy-nilly, Sverdlov had to do the housework, lighting the stove and cleaning up and suchlike.
>
> Much later, shortly before Sverdlov's death [in 1919], he and Stalin recalled those distant days.
>
> "There were numerous occasions when I tried to fool you and escape from domestic chores. I'd wake upon my duty day and pretend I was still fast asleep," said Stalin.
>
> "Did you think I didn't know about it?" Sverdlov answered good-naturedly, bursting out laughing.[5]

Stalin saw much of the Alliluyevs at this time. One senses the kind of attachment that bachelors form for a household that welcomes them, feeds them, does their laundry and sewing and gives them glimpses of family life. Stalin would drop in at all hours of the day or night, and the womenfolk would make a fuss of him, tell him he looked exhausted and make him up a bed in the back room.

Late in 1912 Stalin completed this phase of his climb up the hierarchy by traveling to Cracow, in Poland, to visit Lenin. In later years he enjoyed describing his journey, which was not a simple one, since he lacked satisfactory papers. On his way to the frontier he shared a compartment with two passengers who read aloud to each other from publications of the League of Russian Patriots. Stalin grew increasingly irritated by his fellow passengers and claims he began to berate them for reading such rubbish, suggesting they try more enlightened publications. The story sounds like something Stalin wished he had done in retrospect.

When he reached the frontier, he discovered he had mislaid the address of the contact who was to have taken him across. Fortunately he met a Pole who offered to help him and who turned out to be a cobbler. After a little verbal fencing Stalin told him he wanted to cross the frontier, and the obliging Pole took him part of the way and showed him how to complete the crossing. When he told the story in latter years, Stalin would wistfully observe that "he would very much like to know where that man is now and what happened to him. What a pity I forgot his name and cannot trace him."[6] Lucky Pole; all we know of Stalin suggests that if he had found him, he would have had him shot. The man might have had some inappropriate recollections, and besides, as Stalin was wont to observe, "Gratitude is a dog's disease." Once over the frontier Stalin had some trouble getting served in a Polish station restaurant. The waiter was slow in bringing him soup, waiting until his train was about to leave, and Stalin, in a hungry man's tantrum, threw it to the floor. He arrived at Lenin's lodgings full of bitter complaint, while Lenin, laughing for once, told him his mistake. Never speak Russian in a Polish restaurant if you want to be served; better by far to point. In that respect, at least, Polish restaurants have not changed over the last seventy years.

Stalin arrived in Cracow at a time when Lenin was preoccupied by the "question of nationalities," the situation of the minority races of the empire. Nationalism was a major issue of the age in Russia, Austria-Hungary and the British Empire, offering a valuable basis for agitation. The Bolshevik position required particularly careful formulation since all the other Russian political parties had expressed views on the subject. The Mensheviks had called for "the creation of institutions necessary for the free development of every nationality," which was tantamount to home rule on demand.[7] Lenin's attitude was based on the wish to have one's cake and eat it. On the one hand, he wanted to win national minorities over by promising as much as possible; on the other, he envisaged a highly centralized state which would govern in the interests of a class, the proletariat, as opposed to any ethnic group.[8]

Lenin chose Stalin to describe the Bolshevik position very largely because he was there, while it helped that he was a Georgian and thus free of "Great Russian chauvinism." True, there were other non-Russians quite as qualified as Stalin—the names of Shaumyan and Ordzhonikidze spring to mind (although admittedly there were doubts about the latter's literacy)—but they were not in Cracow. Had Lenin truly wanted an author sympathetic to the fate of small nations, he could have made a better choice than Stalin, who suffered from the ethnic equivalent of a short man's inferiority complex. However, he was both crude and deferential enough to please Lenin, who wrote in a letter to Maxim Gorky of "a splendid Georgian here, who has settled down to write a major piece for *Enlightenment* [a Bolshevik underground publication], bringing together all the Austrian and other material. We will really get down to this."[9] The "Austrian material" refers to the considerable amount of thought that Austrian socialists had devoted to the issue. Stalin was expected to work through an impressive reading list of Austrian and other socialist writers in order to refute incorrect views and present the Leninist line. Lenin also suggested that Stalin do a little fieldwork in Vienna, where he could review the Austrian situation for himself.

Stalin was not well equipped to carry out his assignment since much of the reading was in German, and his command of languages did not extend beyond Georgian and Russian. Fortunately he was able to call upon help, from Aleksandr Troyanovsky, a future Soviet ambassador to the United States, and, more important, from Nikolai Bukharin. Bukharin was a brilliant young Marxist intellectual and future Soviet leader, who would eventually have cause to regret helping his uncultured colleague stumble through the essays of German socialists, for Stalin never forgave anyone who had once proved his superior. It was also in Vienna that Stalin renewed his acquaintance with Trotsky, whom he disliked already; only a fortnight before their second encounter he had described him in print as "a noisy champion with fake muscles." Curiously Trotsky wrote about this meeting only in the last year of his life. One day he was visiting the Menshevik Skobelev, his former assistant, when Stalin dropped in: "Without knocking . . . there entered . . . a man of medium height, haggard, with a swarthy greyish face, showing signs of smallpox. The stranger, as if surprised at Trotsky's presence stopped a moment at the door and gave a guttural growl, which might have been taken for a greeting. Then, with an empty glass in his hand, he went to the samovar, filled his glass with tea and went out without saying a word."[10]

Trotsky retained a vivid memory of his future adversary and of the perturbing impression Stalin then made on him. He noticed the Caucasian's "dim but not commonplace" appearance, a "morose concentration" in the face and an expression of set hostility in "the yellow eyes."

Much ink has been devoted to the analysis of Stalin's essay in an attempt to determine how much of it was "his own work." Stalin may have been helped, by Lenin, Troyanovsky and Bukharin, but since the essay is an unremarkable rendering of the "correct" interpretation of the question, it is hard to be excited by the question. The piece attempts to define the nature of a nation, incidentally denying the principle of extraterritoriality. The Jews were not a nation, and the sooner the Jewish population of the Russian Empire assimilated, the better for all concerned. Stalin proclaims the right of all nations to self-determination on the one hand, condemning decentralization and federalism on the other. However, to aspire to national independence in a socialist state would constitute the betrayal of what you ought to want.

Stalin's article is of interest only because it is his first major publication and gained him the reputation of being the Central Committee's nationalities specialist. The importance with which it has subsequently been invested has nothing to do with the intrinsic merits of a clumsy little essay. It took time for it to acquire its reputation. Not even mentioned in a retrospective study, published in 1923, of the publication in which it appeared, when reprinted shortly after the end of World War II, it sold millions of copies. In 1948, during the Allied occupation of Vienna, a marble plaque was set on the house in the Schönbrunner Schloss Strasse where Stalin stayed, announcing that "J. V. Stalin resided in this house during January 1913. He wrote his important work *Marxism and the National Question* here." Although the plaque is sometimes daubed with paint at times when feelings run high, the paint is always removed and the plaque endures.

CHAPTER EIGHT

Siberia

Stalin returned to Russia in February 1913 after the last trip he would ever take abroad, apart from a brief visit to Persia in 1944. Henceforward his experience of foreign cultures would be derived from secondhand sources and increasingly, in latter years, from the cinema. Soon after he got back, he was arrested again and for the last time. Local Bolsheviks had secured police permission to hold a fund-raising concert to commemorate *Pravda*'s first anniversary. Stalin was eager to attend but not convinced that it would be safe. He consulted Malinovsky, who told him to go ahead but be careful. On arrival at the concert hall he was taken to a dressing room to put on a disguise, but as he was changing, the police, tipped off by Malinovsky, burst in and arrested him. It was a little more than a year since the police spy had got Stalin onto the Central Committee, and one wonders why he should now betray him. Those who believe Stalin to have been an agent of the Okhrana suggest either that Malinovsky disposed of him as a rival, or that he feared that Stalin might betray him. If Stalin was a loyal Bolshevik, and Malinovsky primarily an agent, he might have decided that Stalin was abler and more dangerous than hitherto supposed. Alternatively he may have needed to throw someone to the wolves that month, and Stalin happened to be available.

Stalin did not escape again. He was given four years of exile in the territory of Turukhansk, in far northern Siberia. In July 1913 Stalin was sent by train 2,500 miles to Krasnoyarsk and then went 1,300 miles down one of the great rivers of the world, the Yenisei, to the village of Monastyrskoye, the administrative center of Turukhansk. Rather than disperse members of the same revolutionary party, the authorities preferred to concentrate them in designated areas. Turukhansk was for Bolsheviks. By the time the Great War broke out and resulted in the arrest of all Bolshevik members of the Duma, Turukhansk counted four ex-deputies; Kamenev, a future member of the Politburo; and Sverdlov, first president of the Soviet Republic.

Stalin was given a warm reception by the Bolshevik colony. Prison protocol required newcomers to report on what was happening in the world; their report would then be carefully analyzed and discussed. But Stalin refused to play; picking up the presents his fellow exiles had prepared for him, he made off to his room, observing that he had nothing to say. Whereas the Bolshevik party in these early years was notable for an unremitting babble of ideological debate, Stalin was distinguished by his silence. We have a second account of Stalin's arrival, which makes him appear even more disagreeable. Vera Shveitser, an old Bolshevik who served a term in the region, recalled that many exiles did not trust "Comrade" Koba, whom they regarded as an intriguer and *provocateur*:

> When Koba arrived in the Turukhansk region . . . we all decided to
> boycott him. He had a reputation as a confirmed careerist and
> intriguer, capable of any kind of anarchistic action. There was definite
> talk in Party circles in Petrograd and Moscow about links between
> Stalin and the gendarmerie. Subsequently he was able to win the
> confidence of some of the exiles. The explanation for this is probably
> that such Old Bolsheviks as Petrovsky and Lev Kamenev were so pure
> of heart themselves that they could not suspect other comrades of
> treachery.[1]

Stalin's reception had been organized by his onetime companion in exile Jakob Sverdlov, who had also been arrested recently. Lenin felt the loss of both Stalin and Sverdlov to be serious and set a rescue plan in motion. Unfortunately he picked Malinovsky as his co-planner, and he informed the police. They immediately moved Sverdlov and Stalin from Monastyrskoe to Kureika, a tiny settlement north of the Arctic Circle. Stalin left Monastyrskoe under a cloud and in danger of yet another party court. After he had left, it was discovered that he had removed the books of a recently deceased comrade, although it had been agreed that these should be used to start a lending library. Another Bolshevik, Philip Zakharov, was sent to Kureika to demand an explanation: "Stalin 'received' him more or less as a tsarist general would receive a common private who dared to enter his presence with a demand. Philip was outraged (as was everyone!) and retained the impression of that conversation for the rest of his life. His unflattering opinion of Stalin never altered."[2]

Sverdlov was not overjoyed to start a second period of exile with Stalin, for he knew what to expect; life would not be led according to the principle of share and share alike, and relations soon grew strained in the little house they shared. The strain comes through in Sverdlov's letters. In March 1914 he wrote: "I am much worse off in the new place. Sharing a room is what does it. There are two of us. With me is an old acquaintance, the Georgian Djhugashvili, whom I know from an earlier exile. He's a good fellow, but wants his own way too much in day-to-day life. I happen to like a certain amount of tidiness, and there are times when I get nervy, but never mind.[3]

Two months later the break came: "I have a comrade with me here, but we know one another too well. The saddest thing about exile or prison is the way that a man's character comes out and reveals all its petty side. Worst of all, the petty side of a person is all you see. There is no scope to display the big features. My comrade and I live in separate quarters now, and we seldom meet."[4]

Sverdlov paints a sad picture. He and Stalin were the only exiles in a tiny settlement of fishermen, yet fired by that nerve-jangling irritation peculiar to closed circles, they upset each other so much that they preferred not to meet. However, they may have been driven by more than mere irritation. According to the late Boris Bazhanov, who was one of Stalin's private secretaries before leaving the Soviet Union, the two men were also rivals. Vera Aleksandrova Delenskaya was an actress in the Moscow Arts Theater, who had become involved with some politically suspect associates of Maxim Gorky and had agreed to conceal some illegal literature for them. The police were tipped off, and the young woman was arrested and sent into exile. Since it was Bolshevik literature she had been caught with, she went to the Bolshevik center at Monastyrskoe. There she was courted both by Stalin and by Sverdlov. Whatever their relative merits in other respects, Sverdlov, with his kind, warm manner, dark hair and gentle eyes, was by far the more attractive of the two, and Vera Aleksandrova did not hesitate.[5]

Stalin consoled himself with a local woman by whom it seems that he had a child. Her aunts told Stalin's daughter that during his exile her father had lived with a peasant woman and that she had borne him a son, who received a modest education and had no social or political ambitions. There are other traces of the rumor; for example, Anton Ciliga, a foreign Communist who spent some time in a Siberian labor camp, used his stay to do some research:

> Learning that Old Bolsheviks had lived in Krasnoyarsk and Yeniseisk I did my best to find out about their lives there. In Yeniseisk they had continued their activities, agitated among the population, issued illegal leaflets, possessed their own office for false passports and the preservation of their illegal archives. There were two factions among the Turukhansk Bolsheviks. One set around Sverdlov and later Kamenev, which studied a good deal, read and discussed, actively prepared for the future; the other, around Stalin, which chose the simpler, more pleasant life, and drank a good deal waiting for better times. The whole Yeniseisk region remembers Stalin's drinking bouts. Stalin left another souvenir of his stay in Turukhansk, a son by the wife of a peasant away at the front. In 1935 this young man was about twenty years old, and still lived in the Yeniseisk region. He had not desired to join his father in Moscow, preferring to work as a fisherman. And—a curious thing, the woman with whom Stalin had lived had nothing good to say of him. She had brought up her son to dislike his father intensely.[6]

The account is inaccurate since it ignores Stalin's move to Kureika. Clearly the "two groups" relate to his last days in Monastyrskoe, while his son was born after the move north. Another version has the peasant girl unmarried and Stalin giving a written promise to marry her. A first child was stillborn; the second survived:

> On May 9, 1951 among the photographs that appeared in a local paper showing heroes of the Great Patriotic War was one of a major, with slightly slanted Tungus eyes. But this detail hardly altered the resemblance between the major and the Generalissimo. Many residents of the Turukhansk region knew of Stalin's behaviour in exile. Later on this story became well known in the Yeniseisk region, to which many Turukhansk residents moved in the post-war years. Stalin's illegitimate son said that his mother sometimes received money from Moscow. Soon after the war the Master sought to persuade the mother and her son to come to Moscow. But they wouldn't go. What they feared was not the long trip but some short, swift blow in Moscow.[7]

In Kureika Stalin recognized that he would not be escaping again. Although life north of the Arctic Circle would have seemed a living death to any other Georgian, Stalin tolerated its isolation and bleakness. In later years he told his daughter that it was only then that he acquired a feel for Russia. Unlike his fellow exiles, he did not devote himself to self-improvement. He spent as much time as he could out of doors, and for the first time ever, we find him simply enjoying himself. He loved to fish in the Yenisei and, an interest he shared with Trotsky, to hunt, although, as Trotsky was at pains to point out, he used a gun, while Stalin preferred traps.[8] Stalin even had a dog, called Tikhon Stepanych, or Tishka, and he used to enjoy taking him hunting or simply talking to him:[9] "He used to keep me company . . . during the long winter evenings. . . . I would sit reading or writing, and Tishka would run in from the cold and lie down, pressed against my legs, growling as if trying to say something. I'd bend down, ruffle his ears and say something like this: 'Well, Tishka, are you frozen? Warm yourself, now, warm yourself.'"[10]

Stalin never kept another dog. One may suppose that he despised them for the ease with which their affection and loyalty could be won. It will be recalled that he had diagnosed gratitude as "a dog's disease."

Kureika was a commercial fishing settlement, and Stalin loved to fish in both summer and winter, when he set lines in the ice holes. In later years he enjoyed telling stories of his heroic fishing exploits and would boast that he was so good at discovering the feeding grounds that the locals credited him with supernatural powers. Stalin looked back on his stay in Kureika with ever-increasing warmth. It was his only period of ordinary, settled existence and the only time that he lived an outdoor life. It is to this that he would revert in the senile and drunken ramblings of his table talk in the latter years, alleging exploits with rod and gun so exaggerated that they embarrassed his most sycophantic listeners. Once he claimed to have traveled over thirty miles on skis and killed twelve brace of partridge with twenty-four shots.[11] But less important than the lie is the fact that he bothered to tell it. Success as a hunter was important to him, perhaps to show how well he had adapted to the culture and climate of the north.

However, that was not entirely the case. Stalin kept in touch with the Alliluyevs, and once he let his hair down to them:

> We had an address to which to send parcels . . . and letters. Stalin
> recalled how happy he was when, in his lonely exile, he unexpectedly

found a note bearing greetings from us in the pocket of his jacket. We had placed this note in the jacket when we sent him a winter suit.

He often corresponded with Father. From his letters which we all read we received an impression of that distant place with its cruel winters. He lived in the hut of an Ostyak fisherman in a tiny hamlet lost in the gloomy tundra. Here is a letter he once wrote to Mother:

25 xi, For Olga Evgenievna:

I am more than grateful to you, dear Olga Evgenievna, for your kind and good sentiments toward me. I shall never forget the concern which you have shown me. I await the time when my period of banishment is over and I can come to Petersburg to thank you and Sergei personally, for everything. I still have two years to complete in all.

I received the parcel. Thank you. I ask only one thing: Do not spend money on me; you need money yourselves. I should be happy if you would send me from time to time postcards with views of nature and so forth. In this forsaken spot nature is reduced to stark ugliness, in summer the river and in winter the snow, that is all there is of nature here, and I am driven by a stupid longing for the sight of some view, even if it is only on paper.

My greetings to the boys and girls. Wish them all the very best from me. I live much as before. I feel all right. My health is good as I have grown accustomed to conditions here. But nature is pretty fierce: three weeks ago we had 45 degrees of frost.

Until I write again.

Respectfully yours,
Joseph.[12]

When Stalin's sister-in-law published her memoirs in 1948, and was jailed by Stalin for doing so, it was this letter that did the damage. It portrays him in an inappropriate light, deferential, obsequious even, and a little sorry for himself. For all his protestations of love for the frozen north, the white expanses are clearly not enough; perhaps he even missed the mountains and green valleys of Georgia. The letter also shows him to be dependent on others and reveals a private side that he would have preferred to keep hidden.

The Alliluyevs maintained a tenuous liaison between Stalin and Lenin. Stalin finished his essay on the national question in Siberia and sent the manuscript to Alliluyev for transmission to Lenin. It was probably in response that Lenin wrote one of those letters that official biography prefers to forget. In later years it was important to Stalin that he should feature as Lenin's closest associate, prior to becoming "the Lenin of today." It was embarrassing to have to admit that as late as 1915 Lenin had forgotten what his "wonderful Georgian" was called. Twice he wrote asking associates for help, inquiring of Zinoviev, "Do you remember Koba's last name?" and of another comrade: "Big request; find out . . . the last name of Koba (Iosif DJ . . . have forgotten). It's very important."[13]

A cynic might argue that the tsarist government did the Bolshevik leaders such as Stalin and Sverdlov an unwitting service by banishing them to the farthest confines of Siberia when they did, thereby preserving them from the killing fields of World War I. Russia entered the fight very early, much too early for its own good, advancing rapidly into East Prussia in August 1914 before its armies were properly mobilized, gallantly coming to the assistance of its French ally, sore pressed by a German attack that had taken the enemy virtually to the gates of Paris. After advancing farther into enemy territory than any Russian unit would penetrate until 1945, Russian forces under General Samsonov met with terrible defeat in the Battle of Tannenberg.

Even so, they succeeded in saving Paris and producing the so-called miracle of the Marne. Although the Russians continued to take terrible losses over the war years and had to retreat before the Germans, losing much of Poland in the process, the war record of the imperial army was not the unmitigated disaster it has sometimes been made out to be. In three years of fighting they never broke before the Germans—unlike the Red Army in 1941—and they always outfought the Austrians on their southwestern front. It was a Russian general, Brusilov, who evolved tactics that restored the advantage to the attacker in trench warfare, while ironically enough, the Russian armies may well have been poised for a series of major victories at the moment the Revolution broke out. The war was surprisingly popular to begin with. Tsar Nicholas was hailed by crowds, who cheered him as he had never been cheered before, and for a moment the country, for all its acrimonious political divisions and its hostility to the autocracy, seemed to stand curiously united as it waved its young men off to the slaughter. In the summer of 1914 the only political party opposed to the war was Lenin's.

The Bolshevik deputies in the Duma had been arrested and sent to Siberia for voting against the granting of war credits, and representing Lenin's view that a German victory was desirable. At the trial their leader, Kamenev, had attempted to extricate himself and his colleagues by denying that they had directly supported Lenin's calls for defeat. Lenin was not pleased to learn of his behavior and conveyed that displeasure to the Bolsheviks of Turukhansk, thereby giving us a final glimpse of Stalin in exile as a political figure. In 1915 a special meeting was convened to tell Kamenev how wrong he had been; Stalin came in from Kureika to attend it. According to his official biography, he followed the Leninist line and stigmatized the behavior of Kamenev and his colleagues.[14] The truth is more complicated. The chief topic of the meeting was Kamenev's behavior, which Stalin proved unwilling to condemn. He preferred to remain silent, an attitude which took most of the edge off the issue. Although Stalin was instructed to join Sverdlov in drawing up a resolution condemning Kamenev, he went straight back to Kureika as soon as the meeting ended and took no further part.[15] This introduces an important characteristic, Stalin's capacity for creative fence sitting. Why antagonize a senior Bolshevik such as Kamenev to no purpose? This sense of restraint would prove very helpful to Stalin. Like his silence, it distinguished him in a party of doctrinaire intellectuals each one ready to press his case with an urgency that stemmed from the conviction that he was right. Stalin never insisted that his opinions must be heard and believed in a waiting game. He may have refrained from criticizing Kamenev in 1915, but he shot him in 1936 just the same.

Although by 1916 the imperial armies had succeeded in stabilizing their northwestern front and were enjoying considerable success against the Austrian armies in the southwest, Russia had paid a terrible price for their relative success. By the end of the year the fifteenth million was being called to the colors and the government could no longer afford to maintain able-bodied political prisoners. The exiles of Turukhansk were ordered to muster in Monastyrskoe, where they would make up a draft that was to report to the depot in Krasnoyarsk 1,000 miles away. The Bolsheviks had been looking askance at Stalin for some time, above all because he lacked party spirit and had withdrawn from the fold to keep exclusive company with a Bolshevik named Maslennikov. The comrades hoped that the prospect of military service would bring the two renegades back to the group. However, it did nothing of the sort. When Stalin arrived in Monastyrskoe, he stayed with Maslennikov and avoided the other exiles, including Sverdlov and Goloshchekin, his colleagues on the Russian Bureau. He remained as aloof and hostile as ever and displayed implacable hostility toward Sverdlov.[16] The latter was the first

Bolshevik to appreciate the stony temper of Stalin's character, and it was a pity that he died young, in 1919, since he was the only member of the leadership capable of seeing through and curbing Stalin before it was too late.

Stalin's account of the journey to the Krasnoyarsk recruiting center suggests it was spent in carefully camouflaged political discussion: "During the breaks in the journey they made arrangements to meet their friends, but in order not to rouse the suspicions of the authorities, they organized drinking parties; it was assumed the army recruits were having a final fling with their companions before induction."[17]

Stalin has left us a gorgeous piece of grain-spirit rationalization. Of course, the Bolsheviks en route to be turned into cannon fodder did not want to take a drink. They needed a cover for their discussions, and the authorities would have grown suspicious had they not used real vodka for their "drinking bouts." In December 1916 the Bolshevik contingent arrived in Krasnoyarsk, where Stalin was rejected for military service because of the weakness of his left arm. There is no record of his reaction, which must have been one of relief. Yet Stalin never took kindly to rejection. The thirst for military recognition that culminated in his promoting himself to the newly invented rank of generalissimo may have had its origins in the declaration of the imperial recruiting officer that Stalin was unfit to serve.

Stalin's official biography makes no mention of his failing a medical; the authorities rejected him because "he was too dangerous." The Alliluyev memoirs are less tactful. They suggest that "traces of his [old] injury remained, and it was this which gave the officials at Krasnoyarsk the excuse to reject him."[18] Since his term of exile was nearly up, the authorities decided that it was pointless to send him back to Kureika. He was ordered to reside in Achinsk, a small railway town 100 miles to the west of Krasnoyarsk. There he was joined by Kamenev and his wife, who was Trotsky's sister. Another exile, A. Baikalov, remembered him there. His recollections fail to confirm Stalin's subsequent contention that he devoted himself to the dissemination of revolutionary propaganda among troops on their way to the front. In fact, he had some difficulty in recalling Stalin at all:

> There was nothing striking or noteworthy about Stalin's appearance or his conversation. Thick set, of medium height, with a swarthy face pitted with smallpox, a drooping moustache, thick hair, narrow forehead and rather short legs . . . he produced the impression of a

man of poor intellectual abilities. His small eyes, hidden under bushy eyebrows, were dull and deprived of the friendly, humorous expression which forms such a prominent feature of his flattering post-revolutionary portraits. His Russian was very poor. He spoke haltingly, with a strong Georgian accent: his speech was dull and dry, and entirely devoid of any colour or witticism.

In this respect the contrast with Kamenev, a brilliant speaker and accomplished conversationalist, was striking. To chat with Kamenev was a real intellectual delight, and we spent hours at the customary Russian tea table . . . discussing international and Russian problems . . . or exchanging revolutionary reminiscences. Stalin used to remain taciturn and morose, placidly smoking his pipe. . . . I remember how the poisonous smoke irritated Olga Davidovna [Kamenev's wife]. She sneezed, coughed, groaned, implored Stalin to stop smoking, but he never paid any attention to her.

Stalin's rare contributions to the conversation were usually dismissed by Kamenev with a brief almost contemptuous remark. It was evident that he thought his reasonings unworthy of serious consideration.[19]

The date of these conversations was February 1917, and their subject the prospects for imminent revolution. Stalin nodded in silent agreement when Kamenev predicted that the Germans would win the war and that defeat would bring about a bourgeois revolution in Russia. This, according to Marx, was the necessary preliminary to an eventual socialist revolution which might be expected in the neighborhood of 1937. About this time Lenin in Zürich told his wife to explore the possibility of establishing a small printing business to support them since it was not likely that they would live to see a revolution in Russia.

CHAPTER NINE

Revolution

The Bolsheviks did not seize power, they picked it up.
—ADAM ULAM

In the middle of February the old regime disintegrated. The tsar and his ministers had lost all authority, and military discipline in the Petrograd garrison was very weak. What began in the capital as a series of strikes, bread riots and demonstrations slid into revolution as the rule of law melted away. On February the 26 the Duma was prorogued, as troops in the capital started to mutiny and shoot their officers, while unit after unit sent to control them joined forces with the mutineers. Faced with the disappearance of his authority, the Emperor was persuaded to abdicate, and a provisional government was established, headed by the liberal Prince Lvov.

When Stalin and his fellow Bolsheviks in Achinsk heard the news, they took the first available train to the capital and were the first senior Bolsheviks to reach the Revolution. Stalin went straight to the Alliluyev apartment, where the family welcomed him like a prodigal. Four years of exile had changed him. His face had grown thinner, and his cheeks had hollowed. Although he had aged, his eyes remained unaltered, and "that mocking smile never leaves his lips, it is still there."[1]

Stalin began to speak laconically about the Revolution; there was little talk of the bliss of being alive on that dawn. On the contrary, he entertained the family with his account of the enthusiasts he had observed at provincial railway stations, indulging in heady flights of that

94

sentimental and bombastic oratory to which the Russian language lends itself so admirably: "He imitated them to perfection. You can see them choking with pompous phrases, as they beat their chests and exclaim: 'The holy Revolution, the long awaited dear Revolution has come at last. . . .' We all collapse with laughter."[2]

Stalin was pleased to discover that the family was looking for somewhere to live near to the city center and urged them to keep him a place to stay. He spent the night with them and went to work the next morning. The new government had declared all political parties legal—contrary to the expectations of Lenin, whose immediate response to recent events was understandably confused. His chief fear was that Russia would disintegrate in a welter of disorder. "The socialists," he wrote, "need the state and authority."[3] The Bolsheviks had a reasonable organization in Petrograd. This included a local committee and three members of the Russian Bureau, Molotov, Shlyapnikov and Zalutsky. On the day of Stalin's return, they held a meeting which criticized the latter's behavior in exile. They accepted that he was entitled to a place on the Russian Bureau, but "in view of certain personal characteristics the Bureau decided to give him only a consulting vote."[4] Stalin had the authority and strength of character to brush these reservations aside; the next day he became a full member of the bureau and also a member of the editorial board of *Pravda*. By March 15, the paper was referring to Stalin, Kamenev and Muranov as its editors with no mention of the other members of its board.

The Bolshevik party needed to resolve a series of vital questions, the most important of which concerned the war. Not even Lenin had a ready answer. Although he formulated a slogan with which it was impossible to argue, calling for "Peace, bread and freedom," he declared himself opposed to making peace with German imperialism and called for a revolutionary war against the German bourgeoisie.[5] The second question was more complex still for a Marxist. The party had to define the Revolution in terms of Marx's predictions. If it had been a bourgeois-democratic revolution, this would turn the Provisional Government into a necessary stage in the ascent toward socialism. In that case the Bolsheviks should collaborate with it while awaiting the advent of the next stage in twenty or thirty years. However, fearing that it would continue to fight the Germans, Lenin decided that the Provisional Government was an enemy. Only the collapse of the war effort could bring down the government and create a power vacuum for the Bolsheviks to fill. It was therefore vital that they oppose the government and resist power sharing or collaboration of any kind.

The Petrograd Bolsheviks, led by Shlyapnikov, had followed Lenin in calling for an end to the fighting; Russian peasants and workers should join their German brothers and turn their bayonets against imperialism. However, Stalin and Kamenev changed all that. They opted for an orthodox Marxist analysis of the Revolution and called for collaboration with the Provisional Government and reconciliation with the Mensheviks. In an article in *Pravda* Stalin dismissed denunciations of the war as pointless; the Provisional Government should be encouraged to secure a negotiated peace. Stalin was approached by a delegation of puzzled Bolsheviks who asked him why the party did not attempt to seize power by siding with the Petrograd Soviet, the revolutionary council of soldiers and workers which had established itself as an independent body and challenged the authority of the Provisional Government. Stalin's reply was cautious. The government was not that weak, it enjoyed as much support as the soviet and prudence suggested that the party wait and see.[6] Stalin advanced similar views at a party conference in early April. Three factions were represented: a radical Leninist line, a right wing that inclined toward reconciliation with the Mensheviks and collaboration with the government, and a moderate center. Stalin, as usual, kept to the middle ground. He proposed moderate support for the Provisional Government, but also encouragement for the Petrograd Soviet, which was perceived as the embryo of revolutionary power.

Stalin was no revolutionary demagogue. He made no impact beyond the confines of the party's "smoke-filled rooms." Indeed, the most famous of all descriptions of him portrays him as an invisible man. Nikolai Sukhanov was a Menshevik, who left an invaluable though interminable day-by-day account of the Revolution. His depiction of the Bolsheviks is usually impartial, and he admitted that many of their leaders were impressive public figures, but Stalin was not among them. Sukhanov had seen him at the Petrograd Soviet, where he made absolutely no impression: "Stalin however, with his modest activity, . . . produced, and not on me alone, the impression of a grey blur, dimly looming up now and then, and leaving no trace behind him. And that, really, is all that can be said of him."[7]

Sukhanov was one of the first victims of Stalin's terror. He was arrested in 1931 and presumably died in prison.

Stalin's de facto leadership of the party was short-lived. News of his conciliatory policies had brought Lenin to the boiling point. On April

7, the irate leader finally arrived at the Finland Station in Petrograd, where he was given a triumphant reception with countless banners, red flags, delegations and troops presenting arms in his honor, while the railway station was decorated with triumphant red and gold arches, in a scene strangely forecasting the Ayatollah Khomeini's return to Teheran.[8] Lenin made a triumphant entry onto the revolutionary scene and clarified his position immediately. After listening to a speech from a Menshevik, who expressed the hope that Lenin would not compromise the unity of the Revolution, he started to speak. He ignored appeals for unity and denounced the imperialist war, soon to become a civil war that would rage through Europe. The collapse of imperialism was imminent: "The Russian Revolution, which you have accomplished, is its beginning, the start of a new era. Long live worldwide socialist revolution!"

To the sound of the "Marseillaise" and the shouts of thousands, surrounded by red and gold banners and in the light of a searchlight, he came out of the station and tried to get into his waiting Rolls-Royce. But the crowd would have none of it. He had to climb onto the car roof and make another speech. "Participation in a disgraceful imperialist slaughter . . . lies, deception, capitalist robber barons. . . ." He was then taken to the mansion of the ballerina Kseshinskaya, a former mistress of the tsar, which had been commandeered by the Bolsheviks, a wise choice since it was one of the few establishments in the capital which still had a supply of heating fuel.

Lenin's dogmatism, narrow-mindedness and truculence are unattractive qualities, more appropriate to a prophet than a great political thinker, which Lenin was not. His genius—and the word is not too strong—lay elsewhere. Despite the ideological apparatus which put blinkers upon most of the lesser political figures, Lenin always managed a clarity of analysis which was never clouded by doctrine or by sentiment and which enabled him to pinpoint tactical priorities. At a time when Russia was full of confused, bemused, floundering persons of goodwill and varied political persuasion, who suddenly found themselves in command, if not control, of a vast empire, Lenin towered above the rest. He never forgot that the important thing was to win, which is why his chief contribution to political science is to be found not in any of his ideological elucubrations, but in a simple and virtually untranslatable Russian phrase: *kto kovo*, literally "who whom." "Nice guys finish last" is the phrase that comes closest in tone. His most important characteristic was a pragmatism, which never obscured his sense that the final end was to serve humanity. The incarnation of fixity of purpose and narrowness of mind, he viewed everyone and everything in terms of their relation to the coming revolution. One may surmise that it was this ruthless sense of *kto kovo*, together with the refusal to be sidetracked by sentiment or moral scruple, that Stalin recognized in Lenin and which won his admiration.

Boris Bazhanov was well placed to develop a worm's-eye view of Lenin which brings out his resemblance to Stalin and takes us a long way from the stylized icon of genial, smiling "Ilich" created by official biography:

> I was amazed at how much [Lenin] had in common with Stalin: They both had a maniacal thirst for power. Everything Lenin did was shot through with the *leitmotif*, "to seize power, whatever, and stay in power whatever." Admittedly Stalin may have aspired to power to exploit it like a Genghis Khan, without burdening himself with suppositions such as "And what might this power be for?" while Lenin hungered after power in order to possess himself of a mighty and unique instrument for the construction of socialism. I think there is something in that. Personal considerations played a lesser, different role in Lenin's aspirations.[9]

Bazhanov comments unfavorably on Lenin's moral sense, which "was not high," since he considered "no method unworthy of himself. . . . Alas, the morals that Lenin introduced to the Party became common currency among its leadership both during and after the Revolution. I found them in both Zinoviev and Stalin."

Lenin took possession of his party the moment he arrived. He dismissed gradualist views and went straight for the throat. His *April Theses* declared that there could be no compromise with the Provisional Government, no alliance with the Mensheviks, which would constitute a betrayal of socialism. Far from being twenty years away, a socialist revolution was imminent. Instead of collaborating with bourgeois parliamentarianism, the party should strive for "a republic of soviets of workers, soldiers and peasant delegates; the confiscation of all landlords' estates, nationalization of land and the banks, the elimination of the army and the police." Lenin also called for a cessation of hostilities through fraternization.[10] He wanted immediate socialist revolution, disregarding the orthodox Marxist model that called for a bourgeois interregnum.

Moderate Bolsheviks were not easily persuaded. Lenin's views were rejected by *Pravda* as "unacceptable because they assume that the bourgeois democratic revolution is ended."[11] Lenin was not going by the book, and Kamenev was particularly vocal in his opposition, while Stalin, too, was unconvinced. As he put it unctuously many years later, as a "practical worker" he had suffered "inadequate theoretical preparation," failing to understand that the present revolution would "grow into" a socialist one.[12] However, he soon began to fence-sit, and while Kamenev and others were still advocating unification with the Mensheviks, Stalin fell silent.[13] No one managed to hold out against Lenin for long; his personal authority was too great. As more orthodox socialists watched in astonishment, he obliged his party to accept his ideas *en bloc*, with the result that everything that had hitherto seemed an arrant deviation from Marxist orthodoxy became Holy Writ overnight.[14] It was Lenin's personality and authority alone that caused this ideological about-turn. The Bolshevik party was his and was inconceivable without him, while the Bolshevik rank and file were content to follow him and were unconcerned by the finer points of Marxian prediction.[15]

Stalin quickly trimmed his sails. His incorrect behavior was forgiven, and now, for the first time, he was actually elected to the Central Committee, receiving the greatest number of votes after Lenin and Zinoviev. This was an important moment. Stalin had been considered a useful nonentity by the older Bolsheviks, the intellectuals in exile. Those who voted for him now saw him differently, as a practical revolutionary who lived at the business end of party affairs. As the party expanded, increasing its constituency among the less educated, support for the down-to-earth man of the people increased proportionately.

With his slogan "All power to the soviets" Lenin excluded the Provisional Government from his projected new order. However, the soviets were unfit to govern; the Petrograd Soviet consisted of a loosely constituted body of some 2,000 to 3,000, with an executive committee of 90. Lenin understood that once all political authority had been eliminated in the soviets' name, the Bolsheviks could take over. The Russian Revolution would then sweep across Europe and bring down the old order. In the meantime, Lenin encouraged peasants to seize the estates of their landlords and workers to take control of factories, proposals which increased his popularity among workers and peasants.

It would be a grave mistake, though, to suppose that Lenin called for the instant capitulation of the Russian armies or that the policy of peace at any price was popular in the spring of 1917. Lenin called for peace with German workers and soldiers and the overthrow of imperial Germany, not for a shameful capitulation. He placed his hopes upon the international solidarity of the proletariat, fired by agitation and fraternization between the opposing armies. Peace at any price was not an acceptable option at that time. Indeed, there were frequent demonstrations in support of the war, and Lenin lost much of his popularity when he was accused of being a German agent, which he was, in the sense that he had accepted German funds. He felt so threatened by the charges that he even appealed to the Mensheviks and other non-Bolshevik socialists to defend him. Their belief in socialist solidarity was such that they obliged, confident in the supposition that Lenin and his party would do as much for them.

Stalin did not play a prominent part in the early months of the Revolution. He continued to edit *Pravda* and also worked as Lenin's assistant. Early in July the Bolsheviks attempted to seize power. Following Lenin's orders, Stalin, as he later claimed, called on the sailors of the Kronstadt naval base—a Bolshevik stronghold—to gather in the capital for a peaceful demonstration. They wondered whether they should bring their rifles. Stalin allegedly replied: "Rifles? Comrades, it is up to you. We journalists always carry our weapons, our pencils, with us. As for your weapons, you had better judge for yourselves." [16]

Although one can imagine Stalin giving an evasive answer, his oily reply is almost certainly the creation of wishful thinking on the part of Stalin or his biographers. The sailors assembled outside Bolshevik headquarters, to be addressed by Lenin, who called for firmness, courage and revolutionary initiative. The Bolsheviks then laid siege to the Tauride Palace, but revolutionary activity rapidly shaded into the looting of a trigger-happy mob. In the meantime, Lenin learned that frontline troops were moving on the capital in support of the Provisional Government, and it was obvious that the sailors would be no match for them. To make matters worse, some army units stationed in town that had hitherto remained neutral came out in defense of the Provisional Government. This was enough to persuade the sailors to abandon their demonstration and retire to their base, complete with pencils.

The Bolsheviks were now in trouble. No one believed in the peaceful nature of their demonstration, and they understood that in such stirring times they ran a risk of being shot. After pleas to the Petrograd Soviet to defend Lenin and, more important, Zinoviev had fallen on distressingly deaf ears, Zinoviev ran from the building and went into hiding for several months. Stalin asked the Menshevik leader of the Soviet, Tseretelli, to protect the Bolsheviks from the mob. Tseretelli was pleased to inform him that there was no danger of a lynching but that Bolshevik HQ would be occupied by government troops. The Bolshevik press was shut down, its machinery destroyed, and the sailors meekly handed their ringleaders over to the government. The day after the sailors' demonstration Lenin, too, went underground. After twenty-four hours on the run he reached the Alliluyev apartment. He found Zinoviev there already, speechless with fright. The next day the Provisional Government, acting with uncharacteristic and short-lived decisiveness, issued a warrant for the arrest of Lenin, Zinoviev and Kamenev; Stalin was not considered worth bothering with.

Senior Bolsheviks debated the question of whether Lenin should submit to arrest and stand trial. Kamenev favored surrender, and suggested Lenin follow suit. Stalin's position was equivocal. Subsequent accounts have him urging Lenin not to submit at any price; however, an Old Bolshevik named Romanovsky contests this view, saying that Stalin was in favor of Lenin's appearing in court, provided that the soviet guaranteed his safety. When it refused, Lenin decided that it was time to leave. He felt himself to be in real danger, writing to Kamenev asking him to publish "my sketch on Marxism and the State" in the event of an untimely death. He even had Stalin shave off his mustache and beard, making him unrecognizable, and giving him the broad, open face of a Russian peasant. Dressed in a cap and coat supplied by the Alliluyevs, he fled to a Finnish town, Sestroretsk, twenty miles north of Petrograd.

The decisiveness which had made the government nearly arrest Lenin soon faded. He could easily have been picked up at the Alliluyevs and could certainly have been taken from Sestroretsk, where he continued to work peacefully on his essay and received numerous callers. He remained untouched because many members of the government considered that his arrest would be too embarrassing. Public acknowledgment of his treasonable acceptance of German funds would have besmirched the cause of socialism and, more serious, might have turned the army against the government. For the first but not the last time, a moderate socialist leadership declined to move against Communists because although they "went too far," they were still comrades—only to find greatly to their surprise that a little later those very comrades had put them in jail.

Lenin was further embarrassed by his own rank and file. At a party congress held in July and August junior Bolsheviks, who regarded accusations of treason as an unforgivable slur upon their leader, urged

Lenin to turn himself in. They envisaged a spectacular show trial which would provide Lenin with a platform upon which he would appear as "a second Dreyfus." They were finally dissuaded by their more sanguine seniors, and Lenin remained in Sestroretsk. In Lenin's absence Stalin played an important part at the congress. He made two major speeches and was considered Lenin's representative. No longer the moderate fence sitter of the spring, he stood foursquare behind Lenin's radicalism. The government, he claimed, had sold out to liberals, militarists and capitalists, but soon workers, soldiers and peasants would rise and sweep it away. There would be a world revolution, and society would be reconstructed along socialist lines. But, Stalin went on, in anticipation of his own contribution to Marxist doctrine some years later, Russia did not necessarily require revolution in the West: "The possibility is not excluded that Russia will become the country that blazes the trail to socialism. . . . It is necessary to give up the erroneous idea that Europe alone can show us the way. There is a dogmatic Marxism and a creative Marxism. I stand by the latter."[17]

These are fascinating words. A few months had brought Stalin a long way from the orthodox Marxist who nodded his agreement at Kamenev's view of the timing of the socialist revolution. Recent events, and the single-minded energy of Lenin, had shown him that the predictions of Marx could be adopted "creatively" to meet particular needs. We also seek a second important orientation in his thought. The majority of Bolsheviks, especially the Jews among them—Kamenev, Zinoviev and Trotsky, who had recently aligned himself with the party—were internationalists who considered that socialism could only be built in Russia if the Revolution should spread to the West. Already Stalin was dissociating himself from extraterritorial internationalism and appealing to that Great Russian chauvinism that can never, at any stage in Russian history, be described as anything less than blatant. He now dropped the hint that Mother Russia could go it alone.

During the congress Stalin reappeared at the Alliluyevs to claim the room they had promised him. He moved in with a small basket of belongings and stayed there for the better part of three months. Often he would be away for days at a time, reappearing so tired that he would fall asleep with a pipe still alight in his hand, burning a hole in the blanket. Although his sister-in-law's recollections are somewhat summary, she recalls that Stalin often spoke of Siberia. She also describes his sense of humor, which, as usual, expressed itself in mockery as he imitated the booming northern accent of a country girl staying with the family. He also enjoyed playing with language, inventing nicknames for his friends or addressing the girls by invented names which have a strange ecclelsiastical ring to them. The girls in question were becoming increasingly interested in politics. The elder, Anna, was working at party headquarters while the younger, Nadezhda, though still at school, announced that she had become a Bolshevik.

CHAPTER TEN

October

What happened in Russia coincides in many ways with what
the Marxists were talking about. But what *didn't* they talk
about?

—ALEXANDER ZINOVIEV

After the failure of his *Putsch* Lenin changed his tune. Instead of relying on "peaceful demonstrations," he decided on direct action, a shift of
emphasis reflected in his slogan "All Power to the Revolutionary Proletariat." He renewed the call for an armed take-over, claiming that
history would never forgive the party if it missed this opportunity. The
party disagreed. Lenin's proposal was turned down, notably by Kamenev
and by Zinoviev, who was afraid of being shot. Stalin, for all his fiery
rhetoric, remained noncommittal.

Early in October Lenin returned to Petrograd, recognizing that power
was there for the taking, that after the disastrous military campaigns of
the early autumn peace at any price was daily becoming a more attractive option. Where a less decisive leader would have been happy to
remain in Sestroretsk and work on his book Lenin saw that he must act.
If any single event justifies his reputation as a revolutionary, it must be
this decision to seize the time.

He held a meeting of his Central Committee at Sukhanov's apartment at which he urged action. The decision to "shake the world" was
carried by ten votes to two. Stalin voted, silently, with the majority
while Kamenev and Zinoviev continued their opposition to armed

struggle, publishing an open letter criticizing the decision. Lenin was furious and demanded their expulsion from the party. Stalin, the moderate, opposed the motion. When he was defeated, he offered to resign from the board of *Pravda*, but the offer was declined. Once again he was hedging his bets: agreeing with Lenin's policies but keeping in with the other side. The two rebels were reinstated eventually, but their mistake was never quite forgiven them. Lenin's faith in coincidence was slight, and he would refer to any form of dissent as "no accident"—the expression with which Lenin subsequently described Zinoviev and Kamenev's failure to agree with him.[1]

Stalin's role in the Bolshevik seizure of power grew steadily with time, until he eclipsed everyone, including Lenin. Stalin's favorite general, Voroshilov, wrote in the 1930s: "As for Stalin, the founder of the Red Army, its inspirer and the organizer of its victories, the author of the strategic and tactical laws of proletarian revolution, many volumes will be written about him. . . . He alone was the immediate organizer and leader of the proletarian revolution and its armed forces."[2]

In order to preserve the record as Stalin would have it, the first three editions of Lenin's works were withdrawn as "harmful" because they contained documents revealing Stalin's situation at the time. Volume 21 of the third edition of Lenin's collected works contains records of the Central Committee's meetings for October 10 through 16, 1917. These describe the preparations for the coup, establish its command centers and record a decision to establish a Politburo consisting, in order of importance, of Lenin, Zinoviev, Kamenev, Trotsky, Sokolnikov and Bubnov.[3] The minutes for a meeting on October 16 read: "The Central Committee is organising a military-revolutionary centre consisting of Sverdlov, Stalin, Bubnov, Uritsky and Dzerzhinsky."[4]

Whatever part Stalin may have played in events, he cannot be considered the Revolution's only begetter. It also proved necessary to alter the record in another respect. During the period when Lenin was in hiding, and most of the Bolshevik leaders were wondering whether he was right to call for an insurrection, the man of the hour was Trotsky.[5] He had a unique ability to bring a crowd to the highest pitch of tension and to use the power of oratory to win converts to his cause, rather as Hitler would subsequently do. Originally hostile listeners would leave his speeches bemused at their speedy and unanticipated conversions.[6] He displayed tremendous energy and dazzling oratorical skills during the days that led up to the coup. His speeches canvassed support for the cause, taunting the Mensheviks with threats of an armed uprising, only to reassure them that being orthodox Marxists, the Bolsheviks were, of course, incapable of anything of the sort. He also turned words into deeds, using pure oratory to persuade the supposedly hostile garrison of the Petropaviovsk Fortress to hand 100,000 rifles over to the Military Revolutionary Committee and come over to the Bolsheviks.[7]

On October 22 the government ordered the closure of the Bolshevik press. It could as easily have ordered the arrest of the party's leaders and had them shot on the spot. Instead, Trotsky's Red Guards were allowed to occupy bridges, post offices and railway stations, and by the next day they had complete control of the city. Prime Minister Kerensky escaped in a car flying the Stars and Stripes belonging to a prominent liberal politician, the father of Vladimir Nabokov. Total casualties in the capital on the first day of Revolution numbered six dead and about twenty wounded.

We cannot say what role was played by Stalin. He seems to have kept to the background, failing, on the morning of the twenty-fourth, to attend a Central Committee meeting which assigned specific tasks to the leaders of the Revolution.[8] Trotsky later maintained that Stalin kept his head down and his options open, which sounds consonant with his preference for caution.

Moscow was not taken easily. Lenin's supporters established themselves only after a week of street fighting in which artillery was used to bombard the central districts of the city. The Red Guards were reinforced by demoralized deserters from the front to whom the Bolsheviks had promised much in return for their support. They were also helped by apathy and lack of support for the Provisional Government among the middle classes and the intelligentsia. As a British observer put it, "Cruel as it may sound there were many observers of the revolution who contended that the middle classes of Russia did not deserve a better fate than that which was ultimately theirs."[9] The fighting also saw the emergence of a new quality that would characterize Bolshevik behavior over the coming years. Ruthlessness became a vital part of the party style.

> It was my lot to be in Moscow throughout these times, and what
> impressed me most was the callousness of the almost fanatical leaders
> in the fighting. I saw brutal executions carried out without a sign of
> pity or humane feeling on the part of those who committed these acts.
> On the other hand, the people of the town were themselves
> surprisingly calm. Even during the bombardment, railways, postal

services, and many other public services functioned as usual, and it was not uncommon to see bread queues standing on one side of a square whilst the other side . . . was subjected to rifle fire. The theatres functioned as usual, and I first saw Chekhov's *Cherry Orchard* at the Moscow Arts Theatre during the days of the bombardment. Incidentally I had to take cover from machine gun fire on my way home from the performance. [10]

In October 1917 there was only 1 Bolshevik for every 600 inhabitants of Russia. Yet the party enjoyed widespread support. Lenin had promised peace and land to a largely peasant army, and his party was also popular among workers in the big cities. Moreover, his Revolution was both the climax of that steady encroachment upon the powers of central government that had been developing over the past century and the high point in a tide of anarchy that had been rising steadily since the murder of Rasputin in December 1916, an event which marked the beginning of a breakdown in the rule of law at every level. The prospect of social anarchy was the more acceptable to many because much of the population, like that of a third world country, was self-sufficient. It had no stake in a social system which provided it with very little: no education; little protection of property; no public health service or social security. The average peasant, worker or solider had little to lose, much to gain from Lenin's take-over and promise of peace, freedom and bread. Only those with a personal stake in public order or an understanding of the technical problems of government were outspoken in their condemnation.

CHAPTER ELEVEN

Communism

> When people are taught this kind of nonsense, the devil
> knows where it will all end.
>
> —PEASANT, 1918

The body that would govern Russia under the new order was known as
the Council of People's Commissars, abbreviated to Sovnarkom. It consisted of fifteen commissars under the chairmanship of Lenin, with Stalin's name last on the list as people's commissar of nationalities, or
Narkomnats. Trotsky and Stalin arrived together for the first meeting.
The committee room was divided by a thin partition from the outer
office in which there was a telephone. This was being used by P. Du-
benko, a large, bearded sailor who was having a torrid affair with a
leading Bolshevik woman and advocate of free love, Alexandra Kollontai. According to Trotsky, Stalin gave an ugly display of locker-room
behavior, making lewd observations about the admittedly incongruous
couple. Trotsky responded like a self-righteous and genteel prig, revealing all that stiff-necked high-mindedness that sometimes characterizes
the Russian intelligentsia:

> His gestures and laughter seemed to me out of place and unendurably
> vulgar, especially on that occasion and in that place. I dont remember
> whether I simply said nothing, turning my eyes away, or answered
> drily, "That's their affair." But Stalin sensed he had made a mistake.
> His face changed and in his yellow eyes appeared the same glint of

animosity that I had noticed in Vienna. From that time on he never attempted to engage me in conversation on personal themes.[1]

Trotsky confirms that Stalin worked with Lenin at this time but suggests that he functioned as a kind of clerk.[2] Certainly he was a personal assistant of some kind, since some of the decrees signed by Lenin and sent to the printers are in Stalin's hand—an interesting reflection on the state of a government which lacked both secretarial staff and typewriters. Walter Duranty, an American journalist who came to Russia in 1921, became one of the first of the old Soviet hands whose sympathy for the country sometimes encouraged them to flatter the new order. He learned that in these early weeks "Stalin sat outside the door of Lenin's office like a sentry, watching everyone who went in and came out, no less faithful than a sentry and, as far as we know, not much more important."[3]

S. Pestkovsky was a graduate of the London School of Economics, and he wanted a job. First he tried the People's Commissariat of Finance. This consisted of a commissar, V. Menzhinsky, and a sofa upon which he sat. Pestkovsky was first offered the directorship of the State Bank, but its officials declined to serve under him. He then tried Foreign Affairs, but Trotsky observed that once the commissariat had published Russia's secret treaties, it would be closing down. Finally he turned to Stalin and helped him establish his ministry. He found him an office and a table upon which he placed a sign indicating the table's significance, looking to Stalin for approval. The Narkomnats emitted a noncommittal grunt and sent him to borrow 3,000 rubles from Trotsky. Although Pestkovsky worked hard to get the new department going, he was not happy in his work, finding his boss silent, gloomy and not disposed to gossip.[4]

Stalin's department had little to do at first, as secession and civil war reduced Bolshevik territory to the heartland of old Muscovy. It dealt with minority populations within those bounds, calling on non-Russians to support the new government, making propaganda among POWs, and closing down organizations of Jewish veterans and the Central Bureau of Jewish Communities, which had been established during the war. A little later, and in anticipation of Soviet policies in World War II, it tried vainly to assume control of revolutionary underground movements in neighboring countries. Stalin already made it clear that his minorities policy was based on Great Russian dominance. His colonial inferiority complex, strong as ever, encouraged him to call for "A strong Russia-wide state authority capable of decisive suppression of the enemies of socialism and the organisation of a new communist economy."[5] In other words, the national question was reduced to *kto kovo*. First the minorities must be brought under control; time enough to discuss the niceties of their situation later.

Although Stalin's ministry was staffed haphazardly, it became his first power base. Within a year or so the staff of Narkomnats included a number of people who would remain close to Stalin for many years and formed the nucleus of his personal machine. The first of these, a Ukrainian named I. P. Tovstukha, joined Narkomnats early in 1918. As the first head of Stalin's personal secretariat, later the curator of the Lenin Archive and eventually Stalin's first biographer, he would play a vital and covert role in his master's rise to personal power.

In March 1918 Lenin moved his capital to Moscow; the civil war had made it too dangerous to stay in Petrograd, which had become a frontier city. Stalin, as a commissar, was given quarters in the Kremlin but needed a building to house his commissariat. He made a move on the Great Siberian Hotel, ordering his secretary, who was none other than Nadezhda Alliluyeva, more of a Bolshevik than ever, to prepare notices announcing that his ministry had taken over the building. But when Stalin and Pestkovsky arrived, they discovered that they had been forestalled by the Supreme Council of National Economy. Although they tore its notices down and substituted their own, they had to yield. "One of the rare occasions," Pestkovsky observed, "when Stalin emerged a loser."[6] Yet despite the humble status of his commissariat, it became clear that Stalin had penetrated to the inner circle when the Central Committee established an executive subcommittee of four, consisting of Lenin, Stalin, Trotsky and Sverdlov, with power to decide all emergency questions without referral. Stalin also continued to operate as Lenin's executive assistant, and he and Lenin were continually in and out of each other's offices.

The Provisional Government had promised the nation a freely elected Constituent Assembly, and Lenin had claimed that only the Bolsheviks could guarantee such an election. Although it was certain that a free election would return a Socialist Revolutionary majority, Lenin did not dare cancel it. The only free election based on universal suffrage in Russian history gave the Bolsheviks under a quarter of all votes cast— they did well in industrial centers and in the army—while the SRs won an overall majority. When the Assembly rejected a Bolshevik motion on the first day that it met, January 5, 1918, Lenin ensured that it would not meet again by posting Red Guards at the entrance of its place of assembly. Nobody said much, and an unarmed demonstration by non-Bolshevik socialists was broken up by armed Red Guards. Although Lenin's treatment of an elected majority may dismay readers accustomed to democratic traditions of a different kind, his action was ideologically justified. By voting as it did, the majority of the nation had demonstrated its political immaturity. It had failed to see that the Bolsheviks were the standard-bearers of Marxian truth and that they alone were correct. Therefore, the majority must be disregarded in its own interests.

Lenin was faced with the uncomfortable fact that his country was still at war with Germany, even though the Russian Army as an organized body of men had ceased to exist. Trotsky had opened peace negotiations with the German High Command, but convinced that a German revolution would break out at any moment, he had come ready to deal from strength. Unprepared to agree to German demands, unwilling, indeed unable, to continue fighting, he had come with a policy, "Neither peace nor war," which enjoyed no currency beyond its status as a form of words. Intended to suggest a holding operation pending the spread of revolution, it was without relation to the facts; on one side a well-trained and well-equipped army, on the other a mutinous rabble. Like some twentieth-century shaman, Trotsky coined an ingenious turn of phrase and credited it with the power to shape reality; time and again he would repeat that mistake, supposing the magic of rhetoric an adequate substitute for action, only to find himself damaged by sticks and stones. Stalin saw through his verbiage at once. "Neither peace, nor war, nor a policy," he commented.

The Germans responded to Trotsky's hot air by stepping up their demands and continuing their unopposed advance on Petrograd, while the Allies, anxious to keep Russia in the war, offered military aid and unlimited advice. Many leading Bolsheviks permitted their knowledge of Marx to obscure their grasp on reality. Bukharin called for the rejection of imperialist aid and the prosecution of a people's war, with propaganda as the people's main weapon. Lenin was more realistic, resuming the Soviet attitude to aid and trade for all time: "Please add my vote to those in favour of accepting food and weapons from the Anglo-French Imperialist robbers."[7]

The Allies' offers came to nothing. The Germans announced that unless their demands were agreed to at once, they would march on Petrograd within forty-eight hours. Even now Lenin had the utmost difficulty in convincing his comrades that since the German revolution was not running on time, they had no choice. The Central Committee remained divided. Far from being Lenin's unswerving supporter, Stalin tried to sit on the fence, suggesting that peace negotiations could be conducted without actually signing a treaty. Lenin replied sharply: "If you don't sign, you'll sign the Soviet death warrant instead within three weeks."[8]

This was enough to persuade Stalin to vote with Lenin, who carried the motion with seven votes against four with four abstentions. But his problems were not over. Trotsky was unwilling to return to Brest-Litovsk to sign the treaty and threatened to resign. Feeling that Trotsky was protesting too much, Stalin dryly observed that some comrades kept offering to resign to make their colleagues implore them to stay. Although Trotsky had moments of glory to come, it was now that his support within the party began its steady decline.[9]

Once again Lenin distinguished himself by his grasp on realities, accepting that the Germans had left him without a choice. He also managed to persuade his colleagues to accept a truth both unpalatable and obscured by ideological wishful thinking, dismissing their verbiage with the observation that "the policy of the revolutionary phase has ended."[10] The reality facing his party was indeed harsh. According to the Treaty of Brest-Litovsk, which was signed on March 3, 1918, Lenin had lost Poland, Finland, the Baltic territories, the Ukraine and parts of the Transcaucasus—three centuries of territorial gains. Much has been made of Lenin's "trading space for time," as great a nonsense as the notion that the Red Army in 1941 deliberately withdrew to a line of defense somewhere between Moscow's international airport and the city suburbs. Lenin traded space for survival; time had nothing to do with it.

He had had difficulty enough in persuading his Central Committee to sign the treaty, more still in persuading the Seventh Party Congress to ratify it. The congress, held in March 1918, was a sorry affair. Its predecessor, in August 1917, had been attended by 270 delegates; this time only 69 managed to come. However, following in the wake of Russia's free election, it, too, was an occasion: the last time that a party congress decided anything, in this case the ratification of the treaty, by a majority vote—even though the majority was probably rigged.[11] It would be wrong to suppose that opposition to ratification stemmed from patriotism; it stemmed from a commitment to revolution by the book, which blinded its adherents to reality, in the shape of a German army moving, quite fast, upon Petrograd. The opponents of peace believed that cessation of hostilities would impede the otherwise imminent world revolution without which the Bolsheviks were doomed.[12] A revolutionary war in Europe was indispensable, and a regime which preserved itself by avoiding it would be obliged to assume a nonsocialist form.[13] Revolution must proceed to plan or not proceed at all.

At the congress Lenin outlined the nature of his regime. There would be no question of parliamentarianism or the separation of powers; who needs checks and balances if their policies are correct? He made it clear that the state would be governed via the party, the vanguard of the industrial proletariat, and on the latter's behalf alone. For the first time we find that virulent and doctrinaire hostility which the Bolshevik party leaders felt toward the vast majority of their subjects, the peasants. Workers were the standard-bearers of virtue; peasants were dark, unenlightened, embryo capitalists, corrupted by the ineradicable and sinful urge to own land and animals and exploit the labor of others. This aspect of Marxist mythology was deeply rooted indeed and must be recognized if the course of Soviet history is to be understood. True, Lenin hoped to win the support of poor, landless peasants, who would side with their proletarian counterparts against their exploiters, but essentially he proposed the dictatorship of city over country.

• • •

Lenin was now confronted by civil war. This had started in the south, where a tsarist general, Kornilov, allegedly possessed of the heart of a lion and the brains of an ass, led a so-called Volunteer Army against the Soviets. Largely consisting of officers of the Imperial Armed Services, it also contained anti-Russian factions: Ukrainians, Georgians, Armenians and assorted bands of Cossacks. Lenin was also faced with opposition of a different kind. For many voters his party stood for soviet rule, government by locally elected councils. But already in 1918 his supporters discovered for themselves an enduring feature of Russian politics— namely, that the requirements of a central government, determined to survive in reasonable style, are inconsistent with the population's having a say in the conduct of its own affairs. It would be foolish to maintain that Lenin's administration by coercion was inevitable; inevitability is the stuff of Marxist myth. But there were a number of factors which made it likely, factors almost as important in the present day.

The first of these was the peasants' self-sufficiency. The Russian peasant was never just a food grower; the long winters saw to that. During the many months when agricultural labor was not possible, peasants practiced cottage industries such as shoemaking or weaving. This vital fact, the significance of which the Soviet leadership never understood, made them largely self-sufficient and reduced the need to produce a cash crop; subsistence farming was always a viable option. Secondly, Russia lacked an advanced industrial economy based on interdependence and voluntary cooperation. There was no equivalent of the Protestant work ethic or a readiness to submit to political and industrial discipline. With all the ebullient maximalism of a grain-spirit culture, the liberated workers of 1917–18 interpreted their new-won freedom as a cue for anarchy and the greatest drinking bout since the emancipation of the serfs. As a result, experiments in worker control of factories did not succeed, and a system of production and distribution, which had been ramshackle enough in the first place, started to fall apart.

Lenin countered with a policy that came to be known as war communism, although it did more to start the civil war than it did to win it. He felt he could only ensure the survival of the new state through an assault upon anarchy and spontaneity and the use of compulsion to take the place of a nonexistent work ethic, an attitude that has been the keystone of Soviet administrative practice ever since. The Soviet style of government is to be explained by the ambitions of a superpower obliged to rely upon a people without a work ethic.[14]

War communism lasted some three years. Really the term is a misnomer since it refers to Lenin's attempt to implement socialism. Of course, the state of emergency accentuated the harshness of his methods, but civil war or not, there would have been some kind of great experiment very much along the lines of war communism, for Lenin considered it an important staging post along the high road to utopia: "Now that organisation of the proletariat's communist activities and the entire policy of the Communists has fully acquired a final stable form . . . I am fully convinced that we stand on the right road,"[15] he wrote at the height of war communism in 1919, while Bukharin considered that the civil war "lays bare the true physiognomy of society."[16]

War communism attempted to abolish the market economy. Instead, there would be three ways in which the peasants would part with their produce: by bartering grain for industrial goods, a plan which failed owing to the peasants' self-sufficiency and the collapse of the manufacturing industries; by setting up committees of poor peasants (Kombedy), which would expropriate their richer neighbors, with whom they in fact had much more in common than they did with any enthusiastic ideologue from the city; by means of armed food-gathering detachments "crusading," as Lenin put it, for bread. This succeeded up to a point. Food collection at pistol point produced something like half the average cash crop yield for the war period, a time when the fields had been worked by women, old men and children. Yet despite its economic shortcomings, politically speaking the experiment was a success in that the town gained control over the country.

The attempt to establish workers' control over industry was not a success. All the innate virtues of the proletariat did not suffice to turn it into management material overnight, and workers' control was rapidly replaced by state control, in the form of widespread nationalization. The immediate consequence was overnight chaos and something more than a doubling in the number of bureaucrats needed to supervise the same number of production workers. The only thing that prevented total industrial paralysis was the existence of an unofficial, semilegal system of private enterprise and interorganizational fixing that bypassed normal channels. Thus war communism saw the emergence of four of the chief attributes of the Soviet economy: state control of agriculture and a flourishing agricultural private sector to make up for its shortfalls, and state control of industry, plus that semilegal system of unofficial dealing between the middle managements of various enterprises that, even today, acts as a lubricant so vital that without it the system would seize up. War communism meant highly centralized control, the rejection of an official market economy, the distribution of basic goods and services at very low prices and an egalitarian wage structure. It also brought about an *Alice*-like world of bureaucratic absurdity as officialdom flourished to a grotesque extent. Thus in the Forestry Department, where a subdistrict had formerly required one civil servant and a couple of clerks, the new regime employed literally hundreds of persons, while a moneyless accounting system demanded paper work on an unprecedented scale.[17]

The peasants were bemused by the new bureaucracy that robbed them of their crops and devastated by the war that raged through their villages.

> What was happening in Russia was incomprehensible to them. They knew that the tsar was no more and that freedom had been given to the peasant. But they felt that some huge deceit had been played on the "dark people" by those in high places. They were constantly harassed by the military: soldiers of every kind and armed men without uniforms kept swooping down upon the village, taxing, confiscating

and pillaging. One by one their male folk had been drafted, often not knowing into what army, and then the boys began to be taken, as young as sixteen. Generals and commissars kept coming and carrying everyone away and now all the cattle are gone and the fields cannot be worked except by hand in small patches, and even the smallest children must help. Frequently the older girls are dragged away by the officers and soldiers, returning later damaged and sick. In a nearby village eighteen peasants hanged themselves after the commissars had left.[18]

The situation in the cities was less desperate, though no less absurd. At the height of war communism in Odessa everything was nationalized. Written permission was required to ride for more than one stop on a tram or to transport a mattress from one apartment to another. An American visitor who was puzzled to find that the cabdrivers were not nationalized asked a commissar why. The reply: "We found that if we don't feed human beings they continue to live somehow. But if you don't feed horses the stupid beasts die. That's why we don't nationalise them."[19]

A further and more Odessite anomaly: The police were paid in Imperial rubles, worth many times their equivalent in Soviet money, but to possess them was a capital offense.[20]

Although there was no shortage of organizers, organization was conspicuous only by its absence. An analyst of the city archives of Smolensk for this time writes: "The impression derived from the archive is one of almost chaotic disorganization, with the Party itself more a helpless victim than the master of the whirlwinds it had helped unleash. Indeed as one studies the record, the wonder is, not merely that the Party was victorious, but that it managed to survive at all.[21]

Considering that the Bolsheviks had attempted to install a new system of government along with a radical reform of methods of production and distribution while fighting a vicious war, it is scarcely surprising that their experiment failed. One understands why the experimenters found excuses for the failure and would be prepared to try again at a later date. In the meantime, the people suffered, from hunger and from cold. As the composer Shostakovich recalls, those were days when a log made a welcome birthday present: "for all you do, this log's for you."[22] Yet the "evident failure of war communism did not shake the faith of the majority of the communist leaders that all problems could be solved by more centralization, more control and more decrees."[23]

Many leading Bolsheviks looked back on war communism as a golden age, when the country was well on the way to socialism until incidental pressures put an end to the experiment. It was Stalin whom Lenin associated in retrospect with war communism and its techniques of administration by decree and firing squad. In conversation not long before he died, Lenin observed that Stalin was "rude and disloyal" and stated *in the same breath* that war communism had been a mistake. He thereby linked Stalin's abruptness and lack of scruple with a time when the end—the construction of socialism—was considered to justify the means, which took the form of the infliction of great misery.[24]

CHAPTER TWELVE

Civil War

Once the countryside understood what Bolshevik rule entailed—centralization, confiscation and coercion—opposition grew throughout the empire. By the summer of 1918 there were eighteen separate governments in competition with the Bolsheviks, five others in territories under German control; not to mention countries such as Finland and Georgia that had proclaimed their independence. As one historian has put it, by 1918 "Russia had ceased to exist."[1] There was also an increasing threat of foreign intervention. In the course of the war the Bolsheviks would be variously confronted by Czech ex-POWs, Germans, Poles and Allied forces: British, French, American and Japanese. Initially intended to restore the eastern front, which had collapsed owing to Bolshevik policy, Allied intervention turned into an attempt to overthrow the regime itself, but one that was never more than halfhearted. There were also internal enemies: various armies led by ex-tsarist generals, revolutionary adventurers, peasant partisans and Ukrainian separatists. Yet in retrospect it is clear that the most determined and efficient opposition would have found the Bolsheviks hard to beat. Their overthrow would have required Allied intervention on a scale that was not acceptable after four years of total war, together with a Russian Joan of Arc with the charisma to unite the various factions under one command. It would also have presupposed among White Russian civil and military authorities a capacity for humane common sense and rational cooperation, qualities which would have prevented a revolution from breaking out in the first place. As it was, all sides behaved abominably. No one emerging from a European conflict that had seen 7 million Russian casualties was much impressed by arguments about the sanctity of human life.

• • •

In May 1918 Stalin took charge of grain collection in Russia's fertile southlands. Together with his secretary, Nadezhda Alliluyeva, a detachment of infantry and two armored cars, he proceeded to Tsaritsyn, now Volgograd, previously Stalingrad, situated on a bend of the lower Volga. Strategically important and also a key supply point, the town was defended by the Tenth Army commanded by Voroshilov, an ex-tsarist NCO who would become Stalin's closest military associate. Stalin's assignment was to maintain the supply of grain to the capital. His ambition was twofold: to obtain a military command and to undermine the authority of Trotsky, people's commissar for war, then active on the southern front. It was also here, in Tsaritsyn, that he began to build a core of supporters in the military, starting with Voroshilov, who would play an important part in his rise to power.

Stalin arrived in Tsaritsyn like an executive on a "new broom" assignment, shooting from the hip. Having promised Lenin that "his hand would not tremble, we shall treat our enemies as enemies," he reorganized the police and, according to a White refugee, showed great efficiency.[2] This was reflected by an increase in the prison population and the discovery of a growing number of counterrevolutionary plots. Stalin had the plotters and *all known associates* executed and kept Lenin informed by telegrams combining self-congratulation with expressions of urgency. When Tsaritsyn came under pressure, Stalin used this as an excuse to take a hand in its defense:

> I am rushing to the front. I write on business only. The line south of
> Tsaritsyn has not yet been restored. I am chasing and yelling at
> everyone who deserves it, and hope to restore it quickly. Be sure we
> will spare no one, neither ourselves nor others, and we'll produce the
> grain come what may. If only our military "specialists," the fatheads,
> had not been idle and asleep, the line would have held; if it is restored
> it will be despite and not because of them. . . . Communications with
> the centre are so bad that we must have a man on the spot with the
> full authority to take urgent decisions without delay.[3]

Anyone familiar with the modalities of executive ambition will recognize Stalin's empire-building aspirations. The telegram is a flank attack on Trotsky, who had introduced military "specialists," ex-tsarist officers, into the Red Army. The move was opposed by those who believed that a revolutionary army should consist of a people's militia fighting as partisans. It was a view shared by Voroshilov, who felt happier handling small units, and by Stalin because he hated Trotsky. Stalin now made a bid for military authority. Three days later he sent Lenin a second telegram: "For the good of the cause I must have military powers. I've already written of this but received no reply. Very well. That being so I shall myself, without ado, get rid of the bungling military commanders and commissars. The good of the cause obliges me to do so, and of course the absence of a written order from Trotsky is not going to stop me."[4]

A. A. Avtorkhanov has suggested that Stalin blackmailed Lenin into giving him his appointment by threatening to withhold grain supplies but produces no evidence to confirm this contention.[5] (It is not hard to imagine Stalin stooping to blackmail but difficult to believe that such behavior left no detectable trace, in the shape, say, of an indignant response from Lenin.) He used his new command to undermine the authority of Trotsky, heading a "military opposition" led by Voroshilov, Egorov, and a flamboyant cavalry commander, Semyon Budenny, another ex-NCO, whose ample mustaches extended farther than his strategic skills. Stalin first noticed him in July 1918, when he won a tactical argument with Trotsky's appointee Snesarev. He then led a successful cavalry raid with Voroshilov. When the ex-NCO asked Trotsky to develop a Bolshevik cavalry, Trotsky made a silly objection: The Red Army could not develop cavalry since this "is a very aristocratic family of troops, commanded by princes, barons and counts."[6] Budenny got his cavalry anyway, and some of the Red Army's greatest future leaders, Timoshenko, Rokossovsky and Zhukov—served among its commanders. Like Voroshilov, Budenny remained close to Stalin, displaying a loyalty which Stalin rewarded by permitting him to outlive him.

Stalin proceeded against Trotsky's commanders in a spirit of willful insubordination. He imprisoned the senior "specialist" and most of his staff on a barge anchored in the middle of the Volga. Trotsky sent an angry telegram, which Stalin dismissed with the instruction "Disregard."[7] The specialist was eventually released, but his staff was less fortunate: The barge went down with all hands in circumstances that remain unexplained.[8] Stalin continued to bombard Lenin with telegrams demanding increasing quantities of matériel—including a submarine and a number of minesweepers of modest size. In return he promised dramatic breakthroughs. Yet as a military commander Stalin was undistinguished and profligate in his use of men. Once he committed an entire division of green troops which was captured to a man. When some were subsequently rescued, Stalin, and not for the last time, wanted the "traitors" executed.[9] Assessing Stalin's performance, Lenin observed: "It is permissible to sacrifice 60,000 men *[sic]*, but . . . can we just throw 60,000 away! I am perfectly aware that you killed many of the enemy. But had there been specialists, had it been a regular [not a guerrilla] army we would not have had to throw away 60,000 men."[10]

A wasteful way with men was not Stalin's only failing. He was insubordinate and logistically incompetent. His forces were poorly handled and inadequately supplied. He also exaggerated the importance of the Tsaritsyn sector.[11]

His behavior at the front was uncharacteristic. Stalin was not prone to making promises which he could not deliver, nor did he move against rivals before he could be sure of crushing them. Perhaps executive authority went to his head. There is also the question of his attitude toward Trotsky. An intellectual, a brilliant orator, a charismatic public figure and a Jew, Trotsky inspired a loathing tinged with envy unusual even by Stalin's standards, until he became the focus of everything that Stalin hated most. If anyone or anything could make him abandon calculation and fence-sitting to act irrationally, it was Trotsky, and this probably explains Stalin's behavior as he mounted his first direct challenge to his rival. Certainly that is how Trotsky explained the episode, observing that Stalin joined forces with Voroshilov, whom Trotsky considered crude and incompetent, "but did so in such a way that he could beat a retreat at any moment."[12]

Looking back on the conflict between the Tsaritsyn group and Trotsky, Bazhanov gives it an interesting and plausible coloring. Discussing the makeup of Stalin's private secretariat, he observed: "At the time of the Civil War, Stalin, at the front, was the leader of a military splinter group that hated Trotsky, his associate Sklyansy and their Jewish colleagues in the Peoples' Commissariat for War."[13] In October Trotsky's patience ran out and he sent a telegram to Lenin:

> I absolutely insist that Stalin be recalled. Things on the Tsaritsyn
> sector are going badly despite superior forces. Voroshilov is capable of
> handling a regiment but not an army of 50,000 men. However, I will
> leave him in command of the Tenth Army if he reports to . . . the

front commander. Until now there has not been one communiqué
from Tsaritsyn. I ordered reports on reconnaissance and operations to
be sent twice daily. If this is not done by tomorrow, I shall have
Voroshilov court-martialed and publish it in army orders.[14]

Stalin had tried to short-circuit Trotsky; had their military operations
succeeded, Stalin and Voroshilov could have claimed exclusive credit.
Although Stalin was behaving monstrously, Lenin did not come down
too hard, although he did recall him. Late in October 1918 he sent
Sverdlov to fetch him with a special train. He did not want Stalin to
consider his recall a disgrace though, and gave him a series of appointments, including membership in the Revolutionary War Council. He
also put him on a new committee to coordinate the war effort and use
of resources, the Council of Workers' and Peasants' Defense, on which
he sat as Lenin's executive assistant. Trotsky, writing years later as a
loser, explained Stalin's new posts as sops to his ego and added that it
gave him a chance to express his views on military matters without
getting in Trotsky's way. Stalin, the beneficiary of Trotsky's defeat, let
the appointments pass without comment.

Late in 1918 Stalin, together with Feliks Dzerzhinsky, the head of the
Cheka (secret police), went to the Siberian front on a fact-finding mission. Soviet forces had not been doing well there, and the Third Army
had just lost the city of Perm through incompetence. Stalin always had
a good eye for organizational problems. Never allowing sentiment to
stand in his way, he had proved himself a talented troubleshooter. Now
he quickly recognized that the problems were partly related to personnel, partly to lack of proper channels of communication between the
local organization and "head office." He responded by making some
organizational changes and instituted a recruitment and training scheme
to deal with staff deficiencies. Stalin also took the opportunity to renew
his attack upon Trotsky, while producing, in the words of an unbiased
military historian of great distinction, a report that was "a model of
incisiveness in its display of the present weaknesses, and action taken in
the light of these recommendations produced a noticeable strengthening
of the Soviet left wing to the north."[15]

The report was critical of Trotsky and his military council, whose "so-
called instructions and orders disorganized the control of the front and
the armies,"[16] a criticism confirmed by another Bolshevik, secretary to
the Central Committee and no party to the rivalry between Stalin and
Trotsky. He, too, disliked Trotsky's administrative style: "Trotsky sets the

tone for the whole of this system. Frequent changes of political workers and commanders, crowding the . . . front with a great number of Party workers and Trotsky's princely journeys along the front. All these are symptoms of the system of organized panic."[17]

Stalin also criticized the use of ex-officers and traditional as opposed to partisan tactics, suggesting that Trotsky was an inexperienced and foolhardy commander.[18]

* * *

The Eighth Party Congress, held in the spring of 1919 with the war in full swing, discussed the use of ex-officers at length. Although Trotsky's policy had the support of Lenin, it came in for harsh criticism. Stalin maneuvered with exemplary delicacy, never going out on a limb in public, professing support for Lenin, while siding with Voroshilov in his criticism of Trotsky. The latter rightly singled Stalin out as the leader of the "Tsaritsyn Group," which was bent on destroying his authority and attacking his supporters. Already the lines of the Stalin-Trotsky antagonism were drawn. Trotsky, the thinking man's revolutionary, a brilliant, charismatic figure, was backed by a number of loyal supporters, many of them Jewish, but remained a political lightweight within the party. Stalin's supporters were less educated and harder men, with experience of life in the underground, men who were not ashamed of a slight movement of the lips as they read. They supported "proletarian" strategies and tactics, favoring loosely organized informal units—effective enough against poorly led opposition in open country.

Tsaritsyn gave Stalin a taste for command and provided him with his first military supporters. When Voroshilov was transferred to the southern front, Stalin suggested to Lenin that he proceed there, too. Trotsky opposed his request, anticipating that Stalin would make trouble. Declining to take sides, Lenin temporarily assigned Stalin to the defense of Petrograd, which needed defending. It was threatened by a White army led by General Yudenich, and the discipline of the Bolshevik troops was not good. When a local garrison mutinied, Stalin used the opportunity to take a personal hand. He recaptured a fort, Krasnaya Gorka, occupied by the mutineers, and sent Lenin a telegram:

> Naval experts maintain that it is contrary to naval science to capture
> Krasnaya Gorka from the sea. I can only deplore such so-called
> science. The swift capture of Gorka was due to the grossest
> interference in operations by me and and civilians generally, even to

the point of counter-manding orders on land and sea and imposing
our own. I consider it my duty to declare that I shall continue to act
in this way despite all my veneration for science.[19]

Again we hear that boastful tone. The strident clamor of "me, me,
me" is a new sound for a man with a reputation for silence and fence-
sitting, one that he now began to favor whenever he was away from
headquarters. Distance emboldened him to take a harsh, independent
line to a degree that would surprise even Lenin.

Stalin returned to Moscow early in July, satisfied with the state of
Petrograd. However, the city came under threat again in the autumn,
when Yudenich nearly took it. It was Trotsky who rushed north, turned
defeat into a brilliant victory and was given a triumphant welcome on
his return to Moscow. Hitherto the new regime had not decorated its
heroes; successful field commanders were given wristwatches. The Politburo now voted to invest Trotsky with the newly invented Order of the
Red Banner. Toward the end of the meeting, or so Trotsky alleged,
Kamenev proposed that Stalin be given a decoration too and, when
asked why, replied: "Can't you understand, this is Lenin's idea. Stalin
cannot live unless he has what someone else has. He will never forgive
it."[20]

It is not easy to work back from a piece of bitchy gossip to the original
event. Lenin's assessment of Stalin's character was accurate enough, yet
it is unlikely that he decorated him to placate his ego, more probable
that he wished to keep a balance between Trotsky and Stalin. Historic
precedent had great prestige for Marxists, and the danger of Trotsky, the
military hero, following in the footsteps of the young Napoleon did not
escape Lenin. There is something hair-raising about the notion of
anyone's using Stalin as a counterweight, but that seems to be what
Lenin did.

The counterweight was now sent south at last. The White Army under Denikin had had a good autumn campaign, capturing Kursk,
Voronezh and Orel, thereby offering a modest threat to Moscow. On
this occasion Stalin did not intrigue against Trotsky, although his historians have exaggerated his contributions. There were two schools of
thought about the way to counterattack. One wanted a flanking movement from the southeast; the second favored a push down from the
north. Stalin had originally favored the former plan, but once he understood the logistic problems it entailed—attacking across the axis of numerous rivers and railway lines rather than moving down them—he

began to favor the alternative, which proved successful. In time Stalin became the architect of the plan, and the part played by Trotsky found its way into history's dustbin. According to Voroshilov, Stalin's court historian for military matters, Stalin went to the front with an order signed by Lenin ordering Trotsky to take no part in the fighting. Trotsky's account of the campaign lists at least eighty documents, signed by him, relating to it.[21]

The southern campaign concluded the civil war as Wrangel's front collapsed in the autumn of 1920. The remnants of his army and a considerable civilian population found themselves at the mercy of the Bolsheviks. An Allied fleet, in the process of making a hasty departure, took off some but by no means all of those anxious to leave before the Reds arrived, sometimes using machine guns to discourage the remainder from attempting to join their more fortunate friends and relations.

Stalin's last experience of active service took place in 1920, when he acted as political commissar for the southwestern front during a brief Russo-Polish conflict. Poland, a state reconstituted by the Treaty of Versailles, sought to establish its eastern frontier by force of arms as a Polish army, led by Marshal Pilsudski, successfully invaded the Ukraine and captured Kiev. Budenny's First Cavalry Army threw it out and pushed it back to Polish soil, while the main body of the Red Army advanced on Warsaw. It was led by Mikhail Tukhachevsky, a former tsarist officer of aristocratic origins and the outstanding Bolshevik commander of the civil war. An ambitious career soldier, he was perceived by the Tsaritsyn Group as Trotsky's man; indeed, they had criticized Trotsky for giving a "former aristocrat" responsible military command.

The Red Army mounted a two-pronged attack. Tukhachevsky led a drive that took him to the gates of Warsaw while the First Cavalry Army and other units on the southwestern front pushed down and away from Warsaw toward Lwow. They expected to be welcomed with open arms by Polish peasants and workers, in which expectation they were disappointed. As their advance petered out, they were ordered north to cover Tukhachevsky's left flank, which was extended and dangerously exposed. The orders were disobeyed at the instigation of Stalin, who was, in Trotsky's expression, "waging his own war."[22] Unconcerned by the state of Tukhachevsky's flank, he continued his advance on Lwow. The Polish Army counterattacked in front of Warsaw, broke Tukhachevsky and threw him back, while Budenny had to cut his way home with heavy losses. Early Soviet historians took the view that Stalin's disobedience was one of the principal causes of the defeat. Although Stalin attempted to shift responsibility onto Ivan Smilga, political commissar of the western front and an appointee of Trotsky's, he convinced nobody. Lenin's only recorded comment was: "Ech, who on earth would want to get to Warsaw by way of Lwow!"[23]

CHAPTER THIRTEEN

The Bolshevik Character

Anyone trying to understand the Soviet Union at the time of Stalin's rise to power, or even today, can find answers to much that might otherwise remain a mystery in the period of revolution, war communism and civil war, a period that defined the nature and style of the new regime.

Marxism gave Lenin a monopoly upon the truth, and possession of the truth meant that for Bolsheviks "everything was permitted"; to suppose otherwise was both sentimental and wrong. It was this that had legitimized the Bolshevik seizure of power, an event of mythic significance. The party would never forget that it had taken power as an enlightened minority acting on behalf of a majority ignorant of its best interests. It was a tiny handful of men and women dedicated to improving the human condition regardless of the cost to others or, to be fair, to themselves. They had won power because they were organized, dedicated and correct. It behoved them, in the interests of humanity, never to relinquish their grasp. There could never be any question of inefficient "consensus politics." As Bukharin once observed, he had no objection to a multiplicity of political parties, always provided the Bolsheviks were in power and the rest in jail.[1] There could and can be no question of permitting a diversity of political opinion or seeking a popular mandate. It was ideology, not a mandate, that legitimized the party. Even today, without ideology the rulers of the Soviet Union would be no more than a group of third-generation gangsters, while the countless millions of Soviet citizens who had died unnatural deaths, instead of having contributed to the eventual building of a radiant future, would turn out to have died for nothing. In the meantime, for the party to relax its powers would be to betray a trust. However, the party could never expect popular support, and it recognized that given the chance, an unenlightened populace would tear its leaders limb from limb; hence the need for the tightest of controls. Anyone outside the party was a potential enemy, while party members must stick together even though they might not always agree.

Three years of war and the miraculous survival of the regime obviously play another vital part in Bolshevik mythology. Victory created the image of the Bolshevik as military superman. "There are no fortresses that a Bolshevik cannot storm" was a favorite saying of the age. The party was an elite able to shake, if not move, the world. The storming of fortresses introduces a further aspect of the myth, the image of war. Lenin had always envisaged a party organized along military lines; the notions of discipline, hierarchy and centralized command were vital to his conception. The party thought of itself as an army, and victory in the civil war acted as a powerful validation of that view. As late as 1951 no fewer than thirteen full members of the Politburo had exercised military authority during the civil war.[2] Such was the impact of that war that it tended to militarize everything the Bolshevik turned his hand to. The young Bolsheviks of that age formulated their beliefs in terms of armed struggle, as Petr Grigorenko, future Red Army general and subsequent dissident, wrote:

> Together with our great dream of the future happiness of all humanity we were convinced that in order to achieve this dream the whole of society had to be reorganized, through the dictatorship of the proletariat. The sonorous term . . . resounded with strength, inflexibility and the romanticism of struggle. We . . . did not reflect on the fact that it involved the subjugation and repression of millions. We only remembered the alluring slogan "We shall convince the majority and reeducate it, crushing the minority with the dictator's iron fist." And our spirit responded rapturously, "Yes, yes, we shall overcome. We will tell the people the truth. . . . They will understand us, trust us and join us, marching into the future, shoulder to shoulder and keeping rank."[3]

Military imagery permeated Bolshevik prose to an intolerable degree, producing a language that militarized everything from chess to gymnastics. In the words of his admiring biographer, "It was Trotsky who

first systematically applied military terms, and symbols and thus introduced a fresh, vivid *[sic]* style into the Russian language, a style which
later became ossified into a bureaucratic mannerism and spread to other
languages."[4] For all the damage that this kind of portentous vulgarity
did to the Russian language, it also did damage of another kind. The
seizure of power combined with the war to make a virtue out of terror;
the practical reflection of that intellectual brutality favored by Plekhanov
and Lenin. A new figure emerges from the civil war, ruthless and idealistic Bolshevik Action Man; clad in leather from head to toe, he sports
a revolver, which he loves to brandish and does not hesitate to use.
Readiness to kill for the cause was a sign that one was a good Bolshevik,
free from bourgeois morality and ready to sacrifice the means to the
end. The police magazine *Red Sword* made the point: "Ours is a new
morality. Our humanism is absolute, for it has as its basis the desire for
the abolition of all oppression and tyranny. For us everything is permitted, for we are the first in the world to raise the sword, not for the
purpose of enslavement and oppression, but in the name of liberty and
emancipation from servitude."[5]

And in 1918 the appropriately named journal *Red Terror* declared:
"Do not seek incriminating evidence as to whether a person has opposed
the soviet with arms or with words. Your first duty is to ask what class he
or she belongs to, what were his or her origins, education and occupation. It is these questions which should decide the fate of the accused.
This is the true meaning and essence of Red Terror."[6]

The Soviet police established a policy of executing persons on the
basis not of their actions but of their "objective characteristics." The
wrong characteristics were enough to make anyone a potential enemy,
to be eliminated without ado. Yet according to Bolshevik mythology,
the police of that age were not thugs or sadists, but idealists prepared to
wash the dirty laundry of revolution. One ex-Red Guard wrote:

> I can only say that we young people believed, believed to the point of
> exaltation, in the work and cause of revolution, and adored our
> leaders of those days, Lenin, Trotsky and the others as saints, with
> haloes, looking on them as sincere and disinterested leaders of the
> people. And so we marched, marched gladly into the fire storm,
> without hesitating, and died with the faith and sublime knowledge
> that we had done our duty as citizens. And we did not notice, or
> scarcely noticed, the groans and cries of those who fell in those
> battles.[7]

The epitome of this heady blend of idealism and murder was the first leader of the Cheka, the Pole Feliks Dzerzhinsky. An emaciated figure with burning eyes who looked more like Don Quixote than a mass murderer, he was also a person of shining moral purpose. As a young man he had been imprisoned in Warsaw's Paviak prison, where he had insisted on cleaning the latrines. Holding that the most developed member of any community must take on the lowliest tasks, he observed: "Some day there will be a really dirty job to be done, someone will have to do it, and it will be me."[8] At meetings of the Politburo he used to express revolutionary enthusiasm so vociferously that he obliged embarrassed colleagues to remind him he was addressing a meeting, not a crowd.[9]

From the outset both Lenin and Trotsky held terror to be a crucial instrument of government. "How can a revolution be made without executions and purges; the courts must not abolish the practice" was Lenin's guideline to the Soviet judiciary.[10] "Terror is a mighty political instrument, only a clod could fail to see that," Trotsky observed.[11] Lenin also stated that people might be shot for expressing views that could "objectively serve the interests of the bourgeoisie" or for belonging to the wrong social category.[12] He thereby laid down the groundlines for Stalin's purges when hundreds of thousands were arrested and shot because of who they were, not for what they had done.[13] Those believers in socialism Soviet-style while abhorring the excesses of Stalin, who call for a return to "Leninist norms," either do not or will not understand to what they would be returning.

Lenin's use of the word *objective* introduces another concept vital to the understanding of the Bolshevik mind. Lev Kopelev, an ex-believer and the model for one of Solzhenitsyn's characters in *The First Circle*, told me that he believed the greatest curse of Marxism to be the "dialectic" notion of objective and subjective. This is a key instrument of control and persuasion. It maintains that in the quest for truth "why" is more important than "what." The party has a monopoly over truth since it always acts in the best interests of humanity. However, if one is ignorant enough to consider an issue from an incorrect viewpoint, this objective truth may elude one, leaving one blinded by one's own subjectivity. In other words, the party is able to make its adherents believe that should the party require it, black is truly white. This ability to persuade one to fly in the face of facts accounts in great measure for the appeal of communism, both to the naïve enthusiasts of the early twentieth century and to intellectuals such as Sartre and Aragon, who should have known better.

By imposing its discipline, the party created the sense that one belonged to an elite shock force, shaped by an intellectual training which reshaped truth itself to suit party interests, in a manner that recalled the methods of the Jesuits. It permitted one to ignore empirical evidence, rendered objectively irrelevant by the justice of the cause. In place of evidence, as Kopelev put it, the young idealists of his generation felt that "if the party decrees it, it must be necessary, if it is necessary, it is correct and, since it is correct, it must be true." In later years this would bring about the most remarkable paradoxes. For example, even believers recognized that Trotsky could not at one time be both an agent of the Gestapo and not an agent of the Gestapo. It was widely understood that subjectively speaking, he was innocent of that charge but that the party required him to be an agent for reasons of historical necessity; thus he could at one time be both subjectively innocent and objectively guilty.

This intellectual casuistry gave party members an extraordinary sense of belonging to an elite, a team with a command over special procedures that made it invincible. A Bolshevik and future victim of the purges tried to explain that feeling:

> According to Lenin the Communist Party is based on the principle of a coercion that recognises no limitations or inhibitions. And the central idea of this principle of boundless coercion is not coercion by itself, but the absence of any limits whatsoever, moral, political or even physical, as far as that goes. Such a Party is capable of achieving miracles, and doing things which no other collective of men could achieve.
>
> A real Communist, that is a man raised in the Party who has absorbed its spirit deeply enough, becomes himself a sort of miracle man. An ordinary man cannot honestly change his views quickly, but a Communist, by an effort of his own free will, can honestly and earnestly call white to-day what was black for him yesterday and *vice versa*.[14]

This brings us to the core of the Communist mentality. The objective-subjective alternation enables believers and leaders to decline to be influenced by experience. Once one is committed to the view of a radiant future, current reality loses its import, carries less weight when it comes to governing or making decisions than it does in a nonideological culture in which people have a vote. This is because facts are not really facts at all; they simply appear as such when considered subjectively. Hence one cannot view the horrors of civil war, terror, and war communism or the still greater horrors yet to come as manifestations of evil and cynical indifference on the part of Russia's rulers. To most of them these seemed regrettable necessities, and to have yielded to their sense of pity would have been tantamount to the weakness of a frontline commander afraid of casualties. As Kopelev observed to me, faith in the radiant future was terribly destructive. There was a belief, widespread among ordinary Bolsheviks, that they were truly leaving a gloomy past and were on their way to the light, working if not for themselves, then for future generations. Present miseries were unimportant; only the future mattered, and that was on its way.

Bolshevik mythology created a generation of stern-faced young men and women bent on sparing neither themselves nor others in their pursuit of the millennium, an attitude which did little for the quality or indeed the quantity of life. It was a generation unsophisticated enough to believe that the end justified the means (a notion Trotsky described as an ethical universal [15]). One does not have to be an admirer of Dostoevsky, who foresaw what would happen if half-baked radical idealism were allowed its head, or even a believer in the Christian ethic to appreciate the dangers inherent in such attitudes. Indeed, sympathetic observers soon noticed that the Bolsheviks were becoming corrupt. Shortly before his death in 1920 the American journalist John Reed confessed to his disillusion with the Bolshevik leadership, incidentally singling Stalin out as the man to watch: "He's not an intellectual like the other people you will meet. He's not even particularly well informed, but he knows what he wants. He's got will power, and he's going to be on top of the pile some day." [16]

Another foreign revolutionary, Angelica Balabanoff, concluded that the revolution went wrong when terror "became a habit," while the leadership resorted to coercion as the easiest way to govern. This led her to conclude that Stalin's later crimes were merely "links in a chain that had already been forged by 1920." [17] For by 1920, as Nadezhda Mandelstam put it, the ordinary virtues were out of style: "For goodness is not just an innate quality; you have to cultivate it, and this only happens when it is in demand. For us goodness was old-fashioned, an extinct category, and the good man something like a prehistoric beast. Everything that the age taught us encouraged the development of everything except for goodness." [18]

The effect of these attitudes is illustrated by a dreadful vignette. A friend of Alexander Pyatigorsky was traveling down the Volga by steamer and happened to meet Zinoviev on the boat. The Soviet leader informed him that he was going south to put down a peasant insurrection. He was taking with him his two sons, aged eleven and thirteen, and had equipped each with a revolver. He had authorized them to fire without hesitating at anyone who appeared potentially hostile, and they were greatly looking forward to landing. Not only does the story capture the spirit of those times, but it helps explain the spirit of unhappier ones to come.

CHAPTER FOURTEEN

Promotion and a Marriage

John Reed was exceptional in his ability to foresee Stalin's rise; others who met him at this time were much less impressed. The Scotsman Robert Bruce Lockhart, who had met many of the Bolshevik leaders, did not think a lot of Stalin: "a strongly built man with a sallow face, black moustache, heavy eyebrows and black hair worn *en brosse*. I paid little attention to him. He himself said nothing. He did not seem of sufficient importance to include in my gallery of Bolshevik portraits."[1]

The French socialist Victor Serge did not consider him officer material; the overall impression was of a vaguely unnerving NCO in some Oriental cavalry regiment. A friend filled him in on Stalin's personality: "Very forceful, crafty, confused ideas, too much blood" (apparently a view that was widely held in the party at that time).[2] Yet for all his unimpressive appearance and despite his relentless intriguing, Stalin was now part of the inner circle. Early in 1919 Lenin created a seven-man Politburo, consisting of Lenin, Zinoviev, Kamenev, Trotsky, Sokolnikov, Bubnov and Stalin. It was probably the latter's eye for organizational shortcomings that earned him his next appointment. Lenin, whose answer to every administrative problem was to create new administrative bodies, wanted a department to oversee and control other departments while acting as a training ground for future administrators. Stalin was a founder member of the People's Commissariat for Worker Peasant Inspection, better known as Rabkrin. Lenin considered this a key appointment, for Rabkrin was to take the place of those checks and balances which he would always consider redundant. He envisaged it as a staff agency designed to inspect and control the work of the line administration. "A gigantic job. But in order to cope with the inspection work, you have to have a man with authority at the head of it. Otherwise, we'll bog down and drown in petty intrigue."[3]

Another important committee was set up that year. The Orgburo would consist of five Central Committee members and was to concern itself with senior party appointments and the design of the administrative structure. It was subordinate to the Politburo, its function being to allocate forces while the Politburo determined policy. Both subcommittees were supposed to report to the Central Committee, but, since they were empowered to make decisions without referring to it, they soon became autonomous. Stalin thus found himself on the two administrative bodies that mattered. A third was now founded, which might be termed an ex-officio subcommittee, the party Secretariat. Initially a modest affair, it grew steadily over the years. The first secretary of the Central Committee was Sverdlov, but he died of Spanish flu in 1919. Soon afterward the body expanded to consist of three secretaries, each a member of the Central Committee. It was to be responsible for organizational and executive issues too trivial to be referred to either of the subcommittees. It grew from 30 members in 1919 to 600 by 1921. It concerned itself with matters of day-to-day routine, but it also had the authority to make decisions.[4]

Thus, besides the Central Committee, there were three administrative bodies of descending prestige and importance. The Orgburo and the Secretariat dealt with matters of recruitment, training and appointment beneath the notice of planners of world revolution, such as Trotsky and Zinoviev. Yet they were important, nevertheless, and wonderful places from which to build a power base, especially since the party was expanding and, more important, changing.

The Old Bolsheviks had joined the party because they believed in the good of the cause. They were selfless men and women, who had never expected their devotion to be rewarded by political power. Relatively educated, they read "difficult" books, not always without difficulty. The new Bolsheviks were different. For a start they were younger. By 1920 half the party's members were under thirty and no more than ten percent over forty. Many "closet revolutionaries" had flocked to join for a multitude of reasons, among which ambition ranked high. For years coal miners, like Nikita Khrushchev, and others of humble origin, like Lev Kopelev, had seemed condemned to lifetimes of manual labor. At a stroke the Bolsheviks had given them a future, not just the radiant future of Marxist promise but a personal future in the shape of a career in their party. If they were successful, they could expect to be given a vocational training which could take them right up the administrative or industrial ladder—prospects inconceivable two or three years before. Consequently the party was flooded by ambitious and often semiliterate young people, politically and intellectually naïve, their characters shaped by war, war communism and civil war and out of touch with their parents, whose experience had nothing to offer them. They had little more in common with the Old Bolsheviks and were closer in temperament to men like Stalin. By judicious control of the party's personnel department, Stalin would ensure that the newcomers provided him with the support he needed to win personal power; later still, and at some cost to their persons, they would also help him keep it.

Nineteen nineteen was an important year for Stalin in another respect; he married his secretary. Passion, as far as we can see, never played a determining role in Stalin's life, so that even though he was some twenty years older than Nadezhda Alliluyeva, we may suppose that he married her for companionship and perhaps out of respect for her practical qualities. Certainly he did not marry her for her intellect; he hated intellectual women, referring to them disparagingly as "herrings with ideas." One might also adduce the "Asiatic" pleasure he derived from asserting his authority over a meek and demure woman, together with the view that it would do no harm to have his wife for a secretary. There was another, less tangible motive. In his underground years we saw him returning to the Alliluyev household with its happy marriage and its two lively young daughters. He found there a kind of domestic happiness that he had never known or seen before, a home life very different from his own poverty-stricken and brutalized childhood. A belated discovery that family life can be happy may leave a profound impression and make one long for that kind of happiness, too. It is possible that Stalin married Nadezhda out of a wish for the kind of domestic warmth that he had known only as a visitor to the Alliluyev household.

Nadezhda Alliluyeva was not a secretary of the mouselike variety. She belonged to a prerevolutionary generation of women who were uncompromising in their idealism, severe in their manner and wore their hair in braids. Over the years she made many friends and no enemies. "Nadezhda Alliluyeva was an outstanding personality. Among the Kremlin womenfolk there are many who put on airs, but she was always simple; her every gesture was unassuming, there was never anything strained or forced about her; she was always the soul of frankness and honesty." [5]

A young Russian woman of such character, raised in a revolutionary household in those years, could never have given herself to a man whom she did not admire and, above all, respect. The concept of respect is vital to an understanding of Russian personal relationships. The ultimate reproach addressed by a woman to her seducer or by one drunk to another is "You don't respect me." The fact that Nadezhda Alliluyeva married Stalin proves that he had won her respect, a curious token of the Bolshevik spirit, with its blend of idealism and ruthlessness, since the respecting Alliluyeva was no political innocent. All the kind things said about her notwithstanding, there is reason to believe that she, too, had blood on her hands, or at least on her typewriter. She had accompanied Stalin on his Tsaritsyn expedition, and we may presume that she saw him in action and handled the paper work pertaining to the arrests and executions that he ordered. Whatever her subsequent opinions of Stalin, this glimpse of him in action had done nothing to diminish her respect.

Stalin created family life of a sort. Nadezhda bore him two children, Vasily, in 1921, and Svetlana, in 1926. The couple lived comfortably. They had a town apartment in the Kremlin and a fine home in the country, Zubalovo, which Stalin completely rebuilt, transforming it from a gloomy country house into an airy mansion, displaying for the first time a passion for architecture which would never leave him. A little later Stalin obtained the use of a summer estate also called Zubalovo, on the Black Sea. The name reveals something of Stalin's sense of humor. Both residences had belonged to Zubalov, an oil magnate who had owned refineries in Batum and Baku that had been targets for strikes organized by Stalin. At a time when it was fashionable to cancel names associated with the bad old days, Stalin preferred to keep his Zubalovos unaltered as an ironic reminder that he was their master now.

Stalin ran the Moscow Zubalovo as a thriving country estate, with livestock, beehives, gardens, orchards and beautifully tended birch woods. He loved to spend time in his gardens, working or pottering about, with some garden shears doing a little pruning, a form of "gardening" which brought him great contentment. Judged by prerevolutionary standards, the couple lived the life of a comfortable upper-middle-class family. In a land devastated by civil war and experimental socialism, in which people gave one another logs for presents and there was cannibalism in the countryside, it was a life of luxury. When it is said that the Bolshevik leaders lived modestly, were driven about in used American cars and only occasionally dined off the

Imperial gold plate, we should recall that this was a time when the majority of the population could scarcely be thought of as living at all.

Nadezhda had too much character to be a housewife. No longer working for her husband, she found a job in Lenin's secretariat, where she nearly suffered a curious fate. Shortly after she had joined, she, of all people, was "purged"—that is to say, expelled from the party—because she did not do enough party work. When Lenin heard the news, he wrote to the purge committee reminding it that her family had helped him at a difficult time and was politically reliable: "It is possible that in view of the youth of Nadezhda Sergeeva Alliluyeva the commission has remained in ignorance of this circumstance."[6]

Stalin's household included a number of bodyguards, one of whom would serve as his chief security officer until a month or so before his master died, making him the longest-serving member of the entourage. Nikolai Sergeevich Vlasik was a Red Army man detailed to head Stalin's guard. As such he was, in one sense, closer to him than anyone else, and over the years he acquired tremendous power, combining the roles of bodyguard and majordomo and rising to the rank of major general. Nadezhda seems to have kept Vlasik in his place; it was only after her death that he took over the household—and more besides. As Stalin's bodyguard he would accompany him to the theater, opera, ballet and concerts and interpret "his" responses to the performers. He also gave advice to Kremlin cooks, to filmmakers and even to architects, exploiting his power with that particular arrogant insolence encountered in the chauffeurs and personal servants of the rich and the powerful. For Vlasik was a crude, insufferable oaf, the sort that gives "rough diamonds" a bad name and also the sort that appealed to Stalin, who enjoyed the company of those who seemed to incarnate humanity's lowest common denominator; he knew where he was with them.

CHAPTER FIFTEEN

Cannibalism and Reform

By 1921 the fighting may have been virtually over, but the country was in poor shape. Production had come to a standstill, and the transport system no longer transported anything. Confiscation by the state had replaced legal commerce, and illegal commerce, otherwise known as speculation, was punished by death. Peasants had been ordered to hand specified amounts of their crop over to the government in return for the promise of manufactured goods. Since they were called on to deliver more than they produced and could keep no seed corn, they were not cooperative. As for the cities, any visitor who had last seen Moscow before the war would have found it unrecognizable. The only familiar sight would have been the graffiti, which, as ever, read "Save Russia and kill the Jews." Russia's cities were falling to pieces. In summer grass grew between the flagstones, and nothing worked in the overcrowded tenements. There was little electricity, and the water supply was intermittent. Apartment blocks used to be heated centrally, by single furnaces, and since these no longer functioned, the apartments would have stayed cold were it not for their homemade stoves, ironically called *bourzhoiki*. Their iron pipes protruded through the windows of every apartment of an eight-or ten-story building. The inhabitants of those apartments went about in rags. To the journalist Walter Duranty, freshly arrived in Moscow, it all seemed familiar:

> The city was incredibly broken and dilapidated. Physically and
> morally it reminded me of Lille when the French troops entered it in
> October 1918 after four years of German occupation. . . . The street

was full of holes where the water mains had burst and there had been digging in an attempt to clear choked drains. . . . There was also a break down in running water and sanitation. Those who lived in old wooden houses did all right, but the inhabitants of buildings once fitted with modern plumbing had a terrible time.[1]

Petrograd was no better. The winter of 1921 was exceptionally hard: "The cold is extreme and there is intense suffering in the city. Snow-storms have cut us off from the provinces; the supply of provisions has almost ceased. Only half a pound of bread is being issued now. Most of the houses are unheated. At dusk old women prowl along the big wood pile near the Hotel Astoria but the sentry is vigilant."[2]

In the countryside there was often nothing at all to eat. In *Doctor Zhivago* Pasternak describes a character walking through a devastated cornfield which appeared alive, teeming with rats and mice desperately on the move in search of food. It was this passage that convinced my grandmother of the book's authenticity. She recalled those moving fields all too clearly, for they had focused her memory of country life at the time, the kind of detail that imagination does not invent. For country life was grim indeed. Agriculture had come to a standstill, which resulted in famine. In 1921 and 1922 the Volga area knew hunger so dreadful that there were frequent, well-documented incidents of cannibalism. One Volga peasant, when asked what human flesh tasted like, answered calmly that it was "quite good and does not need much salt."[3] Farther east in Bashkiria authorities reported more than 2,000 cases of cannibalism: "We hear . . . that women cut the arms and legs off a human corpse and eat them. Children who die are not taken to the cemetery but kept for food."[4]

The Volga famine would have been more serious still had it not been for the American Relief Administration, which did a magnificent job and saved some 2 or 3 million lives by its work. The Soviet of People's Commissars wrote, "The people of the Soviet Union will never forget the generous help of the American people"—and arrested all Soviet citizens who had worked for the organization as potential spies. The victims of the famine were lucky that the government admitted the ARA at all. A domestic committee for aid to the starving formed by non-Bolsheviks was arrested to a man. Its president, the populist writer Korolenko, who was dying at the time, described the Bolsheviks' action as politicking of the worst kind and voiced the suspicion that "history will show one day that the Bolshevik revolution dealt as severely with genuine revolutionaries and socialists as the tsarist régime."[5]

The widespread cannibalism was shocking—more shocking still the fact that it would occur twice more within twenty-five years, a record unsurpassed in Europe since the Thirty Years War (1618–48). The famine posed a threat to the regime, and not just because its citizens were dying. The behavior of the survivors made for the breakdown of good government.

> No one who was ever in that famine area, no one who saw those starving and brutalized people, will ever forget the spectacle. Cannibalism was common. The despairing people crept about emaciated like brown mummies. And in the course of their own destruction they dragged thousands of people to death with them. For in the great famine areas the starving people went in crowds in search of regions in which food was still to be had; and when these hordes fell upon an unprepared village, they were apt to massacre every living person. The inhabitants of the regions not yet starving therefore organised guards, and drove away the starving people with rifle and machine gun fire as they appeared. When the international relief organisation started work their missions had to be given military protection. The distributors of relief were placed in the middle of a square of troops who saved them from being overwhelmed by the starving recipients.
>
> The famine-stricken victims came as far as Moscow. They encamped in the gigantic square in which are most of Moscow's railway stations, the living lying among the dead.[6]

It is clear that the Bolsheviks had had no inkling of the likely outcome of their policies. They were an urban party, their ignorance of peasant conditions matched only by the optimism of their expectations. Just a year before Russia underwent the worst famine in recent history, Bukharin told the English writer Arthur Ransome that he was looking forward to a revolution in Europe, remarking: "Once civil war ends in Europe, Europe can feed herself. With English and German engineering assistance, we shall soon turn Russia into an effective grain supply for all the working men's republics of the continent."[7]

Not all the peasantry was content to fight for scraps of food or passively accept its role as a guinea pig in a great experiment. There was widespread, if disorganized, resistance, notably in the Tambov district, where resistance developed into something close to war. The Red Army used tanks and even aircraft to suppress the rising and also employed a new technique to subdue the insurgents. It set up barbed-wire perimeters around open spaces in the countryside, and within these spaces, known as camps, it located the families of any peasant suspected of participating in armed rebellion. If the man did not give himself up within three weeks, the family went to Siberia. The young military commander Tukhachevsky was so proud of this new technique that he wrote it up in the journal *War and Revolution*.[8]

These rebellions were spontaneous and inarticulate, but the same period saw protest of a different kind. One of the more tiresome aspects of Soviet histories is the way they always describe sailors of the Kronstadt naval base as the "pride, glamour and glory of the Revolution." Such was the prestige of the revolutionary sailors that it came as a severe shock to the regime when Kronstadt mutinied in 1921. There had been much unrest in Petrograd; strikes had broken out and strikers had been arrested, while groups of workers being escorted to prison were a regular feature of city life at the time.[9] The strikers made an appeal to the pride, glamour and glory of the Revolution, where libertarian traditions were still alive. The sailors responded, issuing a proclamation calling for a new government with democratic institutions, free, unrigged elections to the soviets and an end to the tutelary dictatorship of the party. When the authorities ordered the sailors to submit to revolutionary discipline, they mutinied and appealed to the country at large to overthrow the dictatorship of the party. The mutiny was suppressed, bloodily, by the Red Army, which went in, shooting, on March 18. Coincidentally it was the anniversary of the Paris Commune, a date hailed by the press as a landmark in revolutionary history.

The party leadership, which was genuinely disturbed by the mutiny, did all it could to present it in the light most favorable to itself. Trotsky suggested that the sailors had been misled by a White general and that the mutiny was inspired by counterrevolutionaries and foreign agents. So successfully were foreign Communists taken in that those who later came to Moscow were shocked to discover that the episode was rather more than a minor postscript to the civil war.[10] Nevertheless, the mutiny obliged the leadership to recognize that all was not well with the country, and various forms of response were proposed, some more in tune with the state of the nation than others.

Trotsky had discovered in the conditions of civil war and war communism a magnificent basis on which to build the future. Since the Red Army had less to do now that hostilities were ended, it should be converted into an army of labor. As his admiring biographer puts it, "Nothing could be simpler than that the army, before releasing its men, should take a census of their productive skills, mark every soldier's trade in his service book, then direct him straight from the demobilization point to the working place where he was wanted."[11] While describing the idea as "imaginative," the biographer concedes that it had drawbacks: "Its flaw was that the released soldier, anxious to re-unite with his family or look for a better living, was likely to abandon the working place to which he had been directed."[12] Trotsky tried to deal with this problem by planning communal feeding centers to be located at the workplace, but these could never be more than plans in a country starving to death. He began his militarization of labor by placing railway workers under martial law, a move that met with considerable resistance from their union; unions were not yet as they would become, in party jargon, "transmission belts" that conveyed the directives of the party to the shop floor.

Looking back on Trotsky's ideas, one is struck less by their coercive nature, than by their naivety. It was preposterous to assume, now that peace had come after seven years of war, that there could be assent of any kind to the principle of further conscription and military direction on the part of a peasant population that had seen its land ruined and its families starved to death. However productive the ideas themselves might have been, and we shall see Stalin implement something very similar within a decade, the party lacked the muscle to impose them in 1921.

Lenin was the first to grasp that fundamental truth. His realization that *kto kovo* was more important than ideology made him recognize that for the time being at least, the great experiment had failed and that if the party were to remain in power, ideology must yield to hard fact. Privately he conceded the failure of communism as such and the need to revert to an exchange economy. It was not possible to change people's mentality and age-long habits overnight.[13]

At the Tenth Party Congress Lenin announced the change of direction, known as the New Economic Policy (NEP). At its heart was a concession to the peasants. In place of barter and forced grain deliveries, the peasants would meet their obligations by paying a tax in kind and were permitted to sell the rest of their crops. In order to create the other end of a market economy, Lenin also authorized private trade, or speculation, and private industry in the shape of manufacturing enterprises employing up to forty persons. Although NEP smacked of ideological heresy, an attempt was made to justify it. Lenin wrote a series of articles that set about the ludicrous task of determining the nature of the revolution of 1917 according to categories such as bourgeois-democratic and socialist. Once again we encounter the *Alice*-like notion that events could be defined according to preexisting categories, coupled with the awesome knowledge that it was possible to make mistaken classifications. History was again required to proceed according to plan. Were it not for the fact that Lenin was using analytic intelligence, not intuition, to consider recent events, he might be compared to an Old Testament leader trying to reconcile current reality to a corpus of revealed prophecy.

To a non-Marxist NEP appears a triumph of common sense over book learning. It encouraged the production of food and the rebirth of industry. Yet for all his flexibility even Lenin found that aspects of it stuck in his ideological craw. According to the scriptures, the peasant was the greatest obstacle to the building of socialism; he had the mentality of a petty-bourgeois hoarder; he was and would remain the enemy; the measures designed to save him from starvation could be no more than generous concessions. Even though Lenin recognized the new policy was essential to the survival of his party, he felt he had yielded to the forces of evil, to peasants, speculators and hawkers, the Odessite elements of Soviet society. NEP was seen as a partial abdication of his party's power in the face of superior forces. Shortly after its introduction a secret Politburo report recorded that peasant influence was growing apace and that:

> a conflict with one hundred million reactionary peasants awaits the party, a victory over whom would scarcely be possible. The peasants are still, as they were a hundred years ago, behind a stone wall which the Communist party is powerless to surmount or destroy. The conservative masses in the villages, with their fixed conviction of oppression, their elementary distrust of town populations and their narrow-minded local patriotism, have a strong influence on the more advanced villagers, by whose aid the party had hoped to build a bridge of mutual understanding and confidence between workmen and field laborers, between town and village.[14]

In other words, the party had hoped that poor and landless peasants would persuade their more prosperous neighbors to give up their small holdings and voluntarily enter state farms, thereby increasing productivity and giving the government control of agriculture. It was well known that large units were more efficient than small ones; only ignorant peasants would suppose otherwise.

The party faithful were appalled by NEP. Reversion to a market economy favoring the peasants flew in the face of socialism. They viewed the policy as "a slow-burning mine placed under the as yet insecure structure of the new regime."[15] For there were powerful objections to Lenin's bid to retain power. Marx had maintained that society's superstructure is determined by its economic base so that a free-market economy must needs alter the political superstructure and cause a reversion to capitalism. Less sophisticated analysts simply regarded NEP as a betrayal of the workers in favor of their peasant inferiors.[16]

In the meantime Russia became something approaching a land of plenty. Streets filled with petty traders, and there were even strange assortments of goods to display in shopwindows; it was common enough to find loaves of bread, pastries and boots laid out side by side.[17] To anyone growing up under Soviet rule with no memory of tsarist times, NEP was a miraculous time of plenty when one could eat one's fill and buy things in shops. General Grigorenko recalls: "Never again did I live as well as I did as a simple working man in the NEP years, not even when I became a general."[18] That standard of living would not be matched until long after Stalin's death.

The new policy did much for Lenin's popularity in nonparty circles. As late as the 1940s ordinary people recalled him gratefully as the architect of NEP, the leader who had given them a shorter working week and a higher standard of living. They also remembered him as a Russian, as opposed to Trotsky, who was the Jew.[19]

CHAPTER SIXTEEN

The Stalin Machine

NEP had meant a defeat for Trotsky, the advocate of labor conscription and infinite compulsion. At the Tenth Party Congress, which met in 1921, his trade union policy had been heavily defeated. He had suggested the unions be incorporated into the state economic administration. Lenin's policy, supported by Stalin, was to allow them an independent existence as "schools of communism," supposedly preparing the working class to conduct its own affairs but without granting it the authority to do so. Trotsky's defeat made for significant adjustments in Stalin's favor. A number of Trotsky's supporters lost their places on the Central Committee and were replaced by Stalin's men, Voroshilov, Ordzhonikidze and two other key Stalinists of the future, Kuibyshev and Kirov, while Molotov was made a candidate member of the Politburo itself. The realignments also prepared Stalin's entry into the Secretariat. The basis for his stunning rise to power was now complete, and the time has come to consider the nature of his political machine.

He devoted a lot of time in the early twenties to putting his team together. He was in his element at last, and what followed was the culmination of his habit of creating parties within the party, splinter groups owing their loyalty to him first, with the cause coming a remote but not disgraceful second. In 1922 Lenin appointed him General Secretary of the Central Committee. His situation was now unique, since he alone was on the Politburo, the Orgburo and the Secretariat. Since he presided over the latter two bodies, all matters involving personnel were under his control together with most routine administrative decisions. This put him in an unassailable position, dominating the machinery of the party.[1] Kronstadt and NEP had been primarily responsible for his advancement at a time of serious division. One faction favored labor conscription and the ideological purity of war communism; another, the Workers' Opposition, sympathized with the rebel sailors and called for genuinely independent unions and workers' control of industry. Lenin turned to Stalin because he trusted him, because politically he was a moderate and because he was a practical man, not an ideologue. He had spoken in favor of inner party discipline, recalling Lenin's insistence on organizational toughness.[2] He later supplied his own explanation for Lenin's choice: "Lenin from the outset favoured a hard-boiled policy and picked men who could stick it out and endure."[3]

Moreover, Lenin recognized Stalin's exceptional gifts as an administrator and patient executive officer who had the support of the rank and file of the party. The historian Adam Ulam writes:

> Stalin's simple manner must have contrasted favourably with the airs
> the other leaders of the proletariat had begun to give themselves. Up
> to now he had spoken infrequently at Party gatherings and
> congresses—he enjoyed a reputation for taciturnity, again an
> exception among the rather gossipy Communist types of that era. His
> personal following lay mostly with the intermediate level of Soviet
> officialdom. Many of these people resented the airs and intellectual
> pretensions of Zinoviev, Trotsky and Bukharin, and felt closer to this
> simple, uncomplicated Georgian.[4]

Stalin enjoyed the support of Zinoviev and Kamenev, who saw him as a check to Trotsky. He also appealed to the new generation of hungry young Bolsheviks, who combined ambition with ruthlessness and read neither Marx nor anybody else for pleasure. This was the raw material from which he built the machine that revealed his political genius; success, for Stalin, meant having the right supporters. "Cadres determine everything" was a later catchword of his, one as valid now as it would ever be. Policies alone were never enough. "After the correct line has been described, success depends on organizational work . . . and the correct choice of people."[5]

While building his machine, Stalin displayed qualities that appear at odds with the picture we have of the foulmouthed, coarse intriguer or the compulsive loner. At a time when other leaders had a growing sense of their own importance, Stalin differed from them in his willingness to devote time to little people. Alexander Barmine was a successful Soviet diplomat until he defected in 1937. He first saw Stalin at a party gathering in 1922, and his portrait reveals Stalin the politician at work:

> He was about to leave the imposing Hall of St George . . . when I first saw him. . . . As he approached the stairway, wearing a military greatcoat over his semi-military tunic and boots, an obscure young clerk employed at the Comintern Office stopped him and asked him a question. . . . The Comintern clerk was undersized, and, as is frequently true of people of very short stature, he was inordinately active. Although Stalin himself is not above five feet six, the little clerk hardly came up to his shoulders. Stalin towered above him, nodding, occasionally dropping a word, listening impassively. The little fellow hopped about, tugging at Stalin's sleeve, lapel or button, talking incessantly and with what would be to me an irritating ardour, as though burning up with more enthusiasm than he had room to contain. What held my attention and made me remember the scene was Stalin's amazing patience. He struck me as an ideal listener. He was on the verge of departing, had one foot on the edge of the stairs, yet he stood there for almost an hour, calm, unhurried, attentive, as though he had all the time in the world to give to this agitated little clerk. There was something monumental in his manner.[6]

Almost as important when it came to winning support was Stalin's ability to seem the kind of man who would not make a worker feel inferior. The writer Alexander Zinoviev suggests that Stalin understood that "The people like a leader to be distinguished not by his intelligence, or his beauty, but by some clearly perceptible blemish."[7] This, suggests Zinoviev, is why Stalin did not alter the Georgian accent which always marked his speech, its chief characteristic a deliberate, un-Russian intonation and the inability to render the Russian speech sound *ye*. It was an accent that made no interlocutor feel inferior and encouraged people to underestimate him. In like manner Hitler never lost his strong southern Bavarian accent.

The machine that Stalin built had three interlocking components with overlapping functions; the Orgburo, the Secretariat of the Central Committee and his personal secretariat. The Orgburo played an important part in making senior appointments in the capital and filled all key posts in provincial party organizations. As Bazhanov put it, "The Orgburo became [Stalin's] chief instrument for the selection of his own people, enabling him to take control of local party organizations."[8]

Patience was a factor here. The Bolsheviks felt that all the glamour and seemingly the power were to be found in Moscow. No one bothered with the political life of the provinces, no one except for Stalin, who found it easy to get a grip on the provincial party organizations and thence, in time, on the entire party. The Orgburo also kept a close track of every prominent party member since, as Stalin observed, "It is necessary to study every worker through and through."[9] So notorious was he for his seemingly inexplicable obsession with keeping careful records about personnel, that he was known to his comrades as "Comrade Kartotekov" (*kartoteka* means "card index"). He was thus in a position to block any potential enemy.

Until Stalin took it over, the Secretariat had been headed by Molotov, the first and for long the closest of his associates, one who played a vital role in the building of Stalin's machine. Molotov would always have the reputation of an imperturbable and immovable bureaucrat, quite without personal initiative. He was known to his colleagues as *kamenny zad*, or "stone-arse," while a British ambassador subsequently referred to him, in a dispatch to his foreign secretary as "Old Boot Face." He took his staff from the Central Committee staff proper, displaying that very attention to detail which Stalin appreciated.[10]

One of the most important sections of the Secretariat was the Orgotdel, which dealt with local organizations and also the inspection and control of administration. Soon after Stalin took over the Secretariat, he appointed L. M. Kaganovich as its section head. He was another figure who would stay close to Stalin. Like Molotov, he even managed to survive him, almost a miracle when it is recalled that Kaganovich was a Jew. The price of his survival was high, though, requiring the renunciation of both culture and family. When Stalin inquired at a later date whether his brother, a minister of aircraft production, should be shot, Kaganovich replied that it was for the police to decide; in any event, his brother shot himself.[11] Kaganovich was a man without pity, but intelligent, and a first-class administrator, who remained a workaholic to his dying day. Stalin used him as a troubleshooter, a role in which he excelled. Paul Scheffer, a German journalist and probably the finest foreign correspondent ever to work in the Soviet Union, described him in 1931, before the rise of Beria, as the only person of real quality in Stalin's entourage.[12]

The Secretariat of the Central Committee also had a secret department, which was almost indistinguishable from an element in Stalin's *personal* secretariat, the unofficial "engine room" of his political machine. Over the years the secret department became a parallel system of government, operating at every level of the administration, as both a control and an information-gathering device. Arguably Stalin's greatest creation, it provides the key to his political triumph. Remarkably, we know virtually nothing about it. Its existence is reflected in hints and pieces of secondhand speculation. For much of the time we do not even know its name, yet it was undoubtedly the most important element in the administration almost from the moment that Stalin became general secretary.

We know something of his personal secretariat thanks to the memoirs of Boris Bazhanov. It dealt with Stalin's routine paper work and helped prepare the agenda for meetings of the Central Committee, the Orgburo and the Politburo, while junior secretaries such as Bazhanov often found themselves making decisions in Stalin's name and on his behalf. In later years the body also functioned as an HQ staff, a planning department and a department for special assignments. It was manned by ambitious young men who owed their positions and hence their loyalty to Stalin personally and who carried out their assignments in his name.

The other part of the cabinet was the so-called special sector. It is hard, if not impossible, to separate this from the secret section of the official Secretariat, for the two departments shared the same staff. It seems to have begun as a department of private intelligence and dirty tricks, which was also responsible for Stalin's personal security. As far as we can tell, he began by using it for protection and information gathering. Later it developed into an extraordinary instrument for control, the perfect realization of the group within a group that Stalin always looked for. It served him well, better by far than any more conspicuous Praetorian Guard, for it derived its strength not from force but from superb organization, which gave it an access to intelligence that was second to none. By the thirties the special sector had representatives at every level of the administration, including the army and the security services. It dealt with matters ranging from internal security to relations with foreign Communist parties, espionage, executions and assassinations—in short all matters that might be thought of as sensitive.

Stalin's secretariat was first headed by Tovstukha, whom he had taken from Narkomnats. He also had other assistants. The most important of these, and the least conspicuous, was G. M. Malenkov, who seems to have headed the special sector from the beginning, while maintaining the lowest of profiles for many years.[13] His role was as inconspicuous as the section he headed, but he was party to everything falling within the scope of the department and hence to every secret of Stalin's regime. Unaccountably he, too, survived.

Working under Tovstukha were Stalin's young aides, Mekhlis and Kanner. According to Boris Bazhanov, Kanner was Stalin's secretary for so-called black affairs while Tovstukha dealt with the gray ones.[14] By *black affairs* Bazhanov meant "dirty tricks," and he provides an example. As they are to this day, senior members of the inner circle were linked by a special telephone system, the *vertushka*, then consisting of some eighty terminals. Kanner had arranged for its installation in the Kremlin by a Czech engineer. Its most interesting feature was a special facility which enabled Stalin to monitor all other conversations. Once the engineer had installed the system, Kanner had him shot. Stalin used to spend a lot of time listening quietly to the telephone.[15]

Mekhlis, Stalin's personal secretary, had a distinguished career, succeeding Tovstukha as head of the secretariat in 1924 and eventually, during World War II, becoming head of the political wing of the Red Army, a post in which he failed to win the respect of the fighting commanders. Himself a Jew, he would never turn a hair when Stalin held forth about "filthy yids,"[16] which did not save him from Stalin's last bout of anti-Semitism in February 1953.

Early in the days of the Secretariat its members were embarrassed to discover that there were no workers in their party collective, which needed a new secretary. Bazhanov observed that there was a suitable young man in the packing department, short, bald and by no means unintelligent. Largely out of a spirit of fun he got him the job, thereby launching the spectacular career of Alexander Poskrebyshev, the man whom Khrushchev would one day describe as Stalin's squire, and who was also known as his Grey Eminence and even his Rasputin—which does a grave injustice to both those remarkable but dissimilar men. Poskrebyshev was in his early thirties. During the civil war he had been active as a director of executions and had been one of the signatories to the death sentence of the Emperor and his family. He evidently impressed Stalin and soon became his personal assistant. By 1928 he had taken charge of the entire Secretariat, thereby acquiring enormous power, since he controlled access to his chief. As a novelist close to the Kremlin put it, "Every one had long been accustomed to the fact that Stalin could only be reached through Poskrebyshev's office, that, as a rule it was the voice of Poskrebyshev that spoke over the telephone before Stalin came on the line . . . that all papers Stalin had to read passed through his hands and that Stalin gave Poskrebyshev all the most important documents to finish off." [17]

In other words, Poskrebyshev won that special control over the outer office that can make a secretary more powerful than any department head, although the fact that he reached the rank of major general during the war suggests that Poskrebyshev was more a *chef de cabinet* than a secretary.

When considering the machine that Stalin was now building, certain factors stand out. First, over a protracted period during which heads rolled easily, most of the men he now picked either outlived him or went close; he would work with Malenkov, Mekhlis, Molotov, Kaganovich and Poskrebyshev for more than thirty years. Secondly, there was nothing flamboyant about his empire building, no obvious vanity engaged, as there had been in his moves on Trotsky and his military ambitions. He created an instrument designed to win power, disguising it as a technical apparatus. By a process of osmosis and dual responsibility, to himself and to the Central Committee, he brought about such an interpenetration of functions that it was no longer possible to distinguish his own staff from the administrative machinery of the party. Finally, he camouflaged his organization so successfully that its most important elements have remained virtually invisible to this day.

CHAPTER SEVENTEEN

Immeasurable Power

Soviet foreign policy in the early 1920s was both curious and familiar. The Soviets had no reason to love the West, which had made a half-hearted attempt to bring them down, and the notion of "capitalist encirclement" played an important part in Bolshevik mythology. Capitalist nations were the enemy, and it behooved the regime to endeavor to bring them to their knees. Yet this did not prevent it from seeking to trade with them or from accepting their disinterested assistance in time of famine. George Kennan has summarized the two aspects of the Soviet attitude to the capitalist powers:

> We despise you. We consider you should be swept from the
> earth. . . . We reserve the right to do what we can to bring this about
> . . . to do everything in our power to detach your own people from
> their loyalty to you . . . and to work for your downfall in favour of a
> Communist dictatorship. But since we are not strong enough to
> destroy you to-day . . . we want you during this interval to trade with
> us; we want you to finance us. We want you to give us the advantages
> of full fledged diplomatic recognition. [1]

Lenin was confident that the West would oblige since its own greed and the contradictions inherent in capitalism were such that given the chance of turning a profit on the deal, it would trade with the devil himself. Capitalism would continue to trade with Russia and bring it material assistance with sublime disregard for the fact that, as Kamenev put it on the day an Anglo-Soviet trade agreement was signed, capitalism was thereby digging its own grave.

Although the Soviet Union was obliged to take a long-term view of the decline of the West, it was able to act more promptly close to home. Georgia had not followed the Bolsheviks in 1917. Still a Menshevik stronghold, it had declared its independence and established itself as a socialist republic governed by consensus, not coercion. For more than three years it symbolized the struggle between Bolshevism and more benign versions of socialism. The Social Democrats of Europe held "gallant little Georgia" up as proof that the relationship between peasants and workers could be solved by democratic means; Tiflis was to avenge the defeat of social democracy in Petrograd and Moscow.[2] Socialist delegations visited Georgia and returned with shining eyes; the Belgian leader Vandervelde brought home accounts of enthusiastic groups of peasant converts to socialism waving red flags and singing the "Internationale" as they came to greet him. By a curious chance the scene of this rapturous reception was Stalin's native village of Gori.[3] Trotsky, the theoretician, trying to analyze a political situation developing contrary to predictions, found himself in a position resembling that of Molière's doctor who maintained that a sick man could not get better contrary to medical rules. He tried to account for "the relative (and incorrect) stability of the régime" by the "political powerlessness of widely scattered peasant masses,"[4] forgetting that peasants in the land of the Bolsheviks were no less powerless.

Georgia did not endear itself to the Bolshevik leadership, least of all to Stalin, whose dislike of Tiflis was almost as great as Hitler's loathing of Vienna. Putting into practice for the first time a basic tenet of Soviet foreign policy—namely, that any adjacent nation too weak to defend itself should be assimilated—the Red Army acted as the agent for an *Anschluss*. The invasion of Georgia for its own good was very similar to Hitler's asssimilations of Austria and Czechoslovakia—not to mention subsequent Soviet excursions into Hungary and Czechoslovakia. On the basis that Georgia was trading with capitalist Europe, Stalin declared it a jump-off point for imperialist aggression. Besides, the Georgian government was "oppressing" workers and good Georgian Bolsheviks, who, like the Sudeten Germans or Hungarian and Czechoslovakian Communists, were in urgent need of help. Georgia was accused of violating its treaty with the Soviets, while it was maintained that the country was upon the brink of revolution. In January 1921 Stalin called for an armed uprising to be led by Sergo Ordzhonikidze with the assistance of the Red Army.

The Russians went in on February 15 and, to their surprise were not made welcome. It took ten days' hard fighting to reach Tiflis, which then received the kind of treatment for which Soviet troops later became famous, as the city was given over to murder, pillage and rape.[5] It took the army three more weeks to complete its conquest. Many Georgian units fought to the end, at which point their officers committed suicide. Before they died, many of them spoke bitterly of Great Britain's failure to offer any assistance, having recognized Georgia as a sovereign state some two months before. They had the "contradictions of capitalism" to thank for that, together with a traditional reluctance to indulge in fruitless acts of altruism. According to the terms of a recent trade agreement, His Majesty's government had given the Soviets carte blanche in all territories previously part of the Russian Empire. There was little to be done about the rape of Georgia beyond the expression of righteous indignation and the washing of hands.

An enthusiastic English biography of Stalin, published at the height of Uncle Joe's popularity during World War II, describes the invasion as a rescue mission, saving Georgia from an imminent coup led by nationalists and Socialist Revolutionaries. Stalin did the right thing, for "No further outbreak of Georgian nationalism has occurred since those steps were taken, which, bearing in mind the country's turbulent past, speaks highly of its reorganised administration."[6] In fact, a tragic and bloody anti-Bolshevik uprising would take place three years after the invasion. In the process of crushing it, the Bolsheviks killed more than 10,000 prisoners and hostages, men, women and children.

Lenin was a little worried by the invasion of Georgia. Like Napoleon considering the failure of his Spanish policy, he feared that the "immorality of the proceedings might have been too great" and presented the action as a war between Georgia and Armenia in which Russian troops became spontaneously involved. As a result, the designs of the Armenian bourgeoisie backfired and a Soviet government was established in Tiflis.[7]

Lenin still proceeded with caution. He told Ordzhonikidze to try to form a coalition with the Mensheviks, who sensibly declined his offer and emigrated en masse. However, despite Lenin's calls for kid gloves, Georgia was promptly sovietized. The administration was taken over by Russian officials nominated by the Orgburo, while the Cheka established its own organization, which also favored Russians at the expense of Georgians. Despite Lenin's protestations, Ordzhonikidze was far from mild. He was a tough man, very much Stalin's protégé and, like him, a Russified Georgian. He put his own people in key positions, one of the appointees' being another associate of Stalin's, S. M. Kirov, who took over the party organization in Azerbaijan. Lack of regard for local feelings provoked resistance from Georgian patriots and from good Communists, too.

One senses the hand of Stalin behind this brutal administrative style. His treatment of his native land cries out for psychoanalytic consideration, in terms of revenge upon his parents and all those—feudal aristocracy, churchmen and Menshevik intellectuals alike—responsible for his growing up an underdog. It is therefore curious that he should have been surprised by his reception when he appeared before a mass meeting in a working-class district of Tiflis, scene of his heroic youth, in the summer of 1921. He was given something less than a hero's welcome. As soon as he appeared on the platform surrounded by Chekist:

> guards and agents the crowd began to hiss. Old women in the audience, some of whom had fed and sheltered Stalin when he was in hiding from the Tsarist secret police, shouted: "Accursed one, renegade, traitor!" The crowd reserved its ovation for the veteran revolutionary leader Isidor Ramishvili and another of their leaders Alexander Dgebuadze, who asked Stalin straight out: "Why have you destroyed Georgia? What have you to offer by way of atonement?" Surrounded by the angry faces of his old comrades Stalin turned pale and could only stutter a few words of self-justification, after which he left cowering behind his Russian bodyguard. [8]

Such abuse did more harm than good to the Georgian cause. Stalin made a scene at local party headquarters and promised its leaders, whom he accused of organizing the demonstration "on purpose," that he would abolish Georgia, merging it into a Transcaucasian federation together with Armenia and Azerbaijan. Meanwhile, the party must "smash the hydra of [Georgian] nationalism." [9]

As People's Commissar for Nationalities Stalin was pursuing an independent line. There was nothing wrong with this; Bolshevik leaders treated their areas of command as satrapies in which they could do as they pleased. However, there was more at stake here. Stalin was beginning to detach himself from Lenin's policies and pursue lines of his own, his Georgian policies being in direct conflict with the conciliatory attitudes advocated by Lenin. It would seem that his loyalty was at an end. Lenin, in turn, was beginning to have misgivings about Stalin. In 1922, when Zinoviev, moving against Trotsky, pressed to have Stalin appointed general secretary, Lenin observed: "This cook will prepare nothing but peppery dishes." [10] Stalin clashed with Lenin directly over another issue: whether the state should retain its foreign trade monopoly or establish trade concessions. Lenin favored the monopoly, but Stalin opposed him directly, maintaining a relaxation of the monopoly to be inevitable. Stalin subsequently confessed himself to have been mistaken, but by then Lenin was safe in his mausoleum and could be invested with retrospective infallibility.

• • •

While Stalin was busy accumulating political power, Lenin's physical strength was fading, doubtless one reason why Stalin dared turn against him. Lenin had fallen seriously ill toward the end of 1921, being obliged to rest for several weeks, and then, on May 25, 1922, he had a stroke, which paralyzed his right arm and leg and impaired his speech. As he subsequently put it, he could neither speak nor write and had to relearn both processes. He did not start work again until early October and never really recovered. Fearing he had tertiary syphilis, Lenin ordered elaborate examinations of his own and his wife's family health records. [11] But whatever the causes of his condition, it became clear in the course of 1922 that his days as leader were numbered and that the issue of succession would soon be posed.

Stalin continued to clash with Lenin. Drafting the constitution which would define Russia's relations with other republics, Stalin took a strong centralist line which emphasized Russian dominance over its smaller associates and dismissed the Jewish principle of extraterritoriality. He also showed himself to be opposed to any form of Ukrainian autonomy, displaying a hostility toward that country which he retained to his dying day. Lenin objected to policies in which he perceived that Great Russian chauvinism which he had always abhorred. For him, as for many of his contemporaries, the term had connotations of an administration, staffed by thickheaded Russian policemen, that practiced cultural, religious and political bullying. Lenin's opposition to Stalin on the nationalities issue stems from a genuine difference of feeling, an innate emotional repugnance and the inability to admit that his centralized dictatorship must necessarily lead to Russian domination over the other republics. This truth was not lost upon Stalin as a realist and an admirer of the Great Russian way. He showed little respect for Lenin's objections, accusing him of "liberalism" and brushing aside a number of his criticisms as stylistic. [12] He reacted to Lenin's charge that he was being "overhasty" with a scornful dismissal, while the tone of his letters veered from rude to disrespectful, as if he already understood that Lenin's strength was gone.

Stalin had proposed that the Ukraine, Byelorussia, Azerbaijan, Georgia and Armenia should enter a Russian federation as republics to be governed by the supreme bodies of the Russian Socialist Federative Republic. The plan was not well received by the territories in question and, despite the urgings of Kirov and Ordzhonikidze, was rejected by the Central Committee of the Georgian party. A running battle between local Communists and Stalin's centralizers resulted in a complaint to Moscow about Ordzhonikidze's high-handed and boorish behavior. (He had described his opponents as "chauvinist rot that has to be thrown out."[13]) Lenin gave the "rot" short shrift. He sent their complaint to be dealt with by none other than Stalin, accusing local Communists of infringing party discipline by airing their differences in public. He also charged them with impertinence and "lack of upbringing." The Georgian Central Committee responded by resigning en masse. This made Lenin suspicious enough to appoint a commission of inquiry, which, at the suggestion of Stalin, was headed by Feliks Dzerzhinsky, another Russified foreigner opposed to the principle of self-determination.

The commission seemed designed to whitewash Ordzhonikidze, but something happened that made Lenin recognize the true nature of the latter's administrative style. Lenin had asked his deputy Rykov to go to Tiflis to see for himself. During Rykov's visit to Ordzhonikidze, someone mentioned a white stallion which a mountain tribe had presented to Ordzhonikidze and on which he liked to parade through the city streets. Ordzhonikidze took this as a slight upon his honor and gave the man a smack in the face. The incident appalled Lenin. For all his polemics and his capacity for spiteful rage Lenin had never lost a small-town puritan's belief in the need to keep up appearances.

There is something genuinely tragic about the last phase of Lenin's life, in which understanding and weakening grew together, as they do in Lear. A political opportunist of genius he had not had enough experience of political power to lose his naivety. He expected his fellow revolutionaries to share his own moral standards, being possessed of "a natural asceticism of character which power did not corrupt."[14] He had never understood that thuggery is only a short remove from revolutionary ruthlessness. Now, for the first time, he came to realize that he had brought forth a regime of thugs.

The slap in the face and Dzerzhinsky's subsequent cover-up were the catalysts that made Lenin face the truth, distressing him to the point that they probably caused his second stroke. Dzerzhinsky reported to him on December 12 and was told to return to Georgia and renew his investigations. On the following day Lenin had two minor strokes, and three days later a major stroke brought back the paralysis. However, he was determined not to allow his body to let him down and attempted to work again within the week. He shocked his colleagues by informing them that unless they allowed him to give dictation, he would refuse all medical treatment. A subcommittee of the Politburo consisting of Stalin, Bukharin and Kamenev met to discuss the matter and proposed that: "Vladimir Ilich has the right to dictate every day for five to ten minutes, but this cannnot have the character of correspondence and Vladimir Ilich may not expect to receive any answers. It is forbidden for him to have any [political] visitors. Neither friends nor those around him are allowed to convey to him any political news."[15]

The hectoring tone of this communication is something of a puzzle. It is the kind of language that many doctors long to use, yet it is curious to find it here. What right had anyone to tell Lenin what to do? The usual answer to that question—that Lenin was obliged to submit to party discipline—might have satisfied at the time, but it is scarcely convincing. Although there is no evidence to confirm the supposition, one cannot help feeling that the decision was designed, at the instigation of Stalin, to take Lenin out of the game just when he was about to turn on his ex-disciple. Indeed the stroke could not have come more apropos. In the words of Karl Radek, self-appointed jester to the leadership and the author of many excellent jokes before Stalin had the last laugh: "On this occasion God voted for Stalin."[16]

Although the timing of Lenin's decline was opportune, the deterioration came as no surprise and the political realignments which it entailed were already under way. A key factor here was hostility to Trotsky. Despite his popularity with the rank and file, leading Old Bolsheviks loathed him, considering him an "arrogant unbearable intruder."[17] Lenin, in the meantime, had begun to look to Trotsky for support. Early in December he had asked him to call and proposed that they form an alliance "against bureaucracy" and, more important, that Trotsky become his deputy. Trotsky subsequently maintained that Lenin suggested he succeed him, and that they should make common cause against Stalin, but this seems improbable. Whatever the truth of the matter and whatever his motives, Trotsky failed to seize the time. With Lenin's open support and a minimum of political acumen he would have been unstoppable. He was popular with the party's left wing and, more important, with the army. Moreover, he was politically glamorous, unlike other members of the Politburo, including the "gray blur" Stalin. With the succession his for the asking, incredibly Trotsky refused. There can be few sadder cases of political ineptitude than Trotsky's behavior during his last years in Russia. He constantly misread the mood of the country—his advocacy of labor conscription was a case in point—and lacked all sense of political timing. Moreover, he kept resorting to words when only deeds would do and underestimated Stalin because he was a purely practical man with no command of theory. Alas for him, Trotsky had too much. He could not cope with the infighting of machine politics and remained an intellectual blinded by his awareness of the larger issues.

Lenin, though a sick man, was not yet a beaten one. Nine days after his stroke he dictated his so-called testament. It consists of two parts; an overview of the party and an assessment of the Politburo. Although these are incisive enough, the document as a whole is not. It begins by stating that the stability of the Central Committee was threatened by the antagonism between Stalin and Trotsky. To deal with this, Lenin proposed doubling the size of the committee. This, the only tangible proposal he made, was unlikely to have had the desired effect. The piece continues with criticism of the two rivals, beginning with Stalin: "Comrade Stalin having become General Secretary has immeasurable power concentrated in his hands, and I am not sure that he always knows how to use that power with sufficient caution." This is muted criticism, implying that Stalin might be rash, but no worse.

Lenin now turns to Trotsky: "Distinguished by his exceptional abilities, he is personally, to be sure, the ablest man in the Central Committee but distinguished also by his too far-reaching self-confidence and a disposition to be too much attracted by the purely administrative side of affairs."

Lenin then acknowledges that Stalin and Trotsky are the two ablest men in the Politburo. He moves on to Zinoviev and Kamenev, recalling that their behavior in October was "no accident" but that consideration should matter no more than the "non-Bolshevism" of Trotsky. Bukharin "is not only the most valuable and biggest theoretician of the party, but also should legitimately be considered the favorite of the whole party; but his theoretical views can only with the gravest doubts be regarded as wholly Marxist, for there is something scholastic in him. He has never learned and I think never fully understood the dialectic."

These are strong words for the party's "biggest theoretician." Yet Lenin's judgment is extraordinarily perspicacious. If by "the dialectic" he means the pragmatic manipulation of the categories of "objective" and "subjective," then Bukharin would indeed never understand it and would go by the book until the bitter end. Pyatakov, the other young leader, was possessed, according to Lenin, of both will and ability but was too much the administrator to be relied on in a crisis.

The testament is a strange document that has been interpreted in a number of ways. Although it soon became known to the party elite, it would not be published in the Soviet Union until 1956, in the aftermath of Khrushchev's denunciation of Stalin. It is hard to say what Lenin wanted. He was not paving the way for Trotsky to succeed him, nor was he hard on Stalin, who emerges rather well, though with a touch of menace. No one comes out looking good, and no serious recommendations are made for the future. The document fails to nominate an heir; instead, it suggests that no member of the Politburo deserves to succeed him, while making collective leadership difficult, since everyone is provided with mud to sling at his colleagues. Lenin did not even cover the entire Politburo, omitting Rykov and Tomsky as beneath his notice. Assuming that he was not expecting to return to active politics, and few men are realistic enough to know when comebacks are no longer possible, he seems to have wanted to cut the entire Politburo down to size, perhaps in the hope that it would subordinate itself to a newly constituted Central Committee manned by good men and true.

He was only just beginning to understand the kind of men who controlled the country. The testament had been critical of their abilities but had not touched on their political morality. Now, thinking anew about Stalin and Ordzhonikidze, Lenin produced criticism of a different kind. He dictated three notes on the nationalities issue and the Georgian affair which show that he finally had Stalin's measure. Sadly he recognized that the brutal administrative traditions of tsarism had been translated wholesale into the new Russia. His notes single out the two Georgians for special mention; Russified non-Russians were the worst of all. Ordzhonikidze's "laying on of hands" (the word *rukoprikladstvo* is much used in Russian and has nothing to do with confirmation) was inexcusable, and both he and Stalin had conducted themselves with all the sensitivity of a Great Russian *derzhimorda*, literally "shut your face." The name refers to an unpleasant provincial policeman in Gogol's

Government Inspector. The character is a corrupt and disagreeable bully who became something of a national type.

Lenin's meditations upon Great Russian chauvinism led him to reconsider Stalin's personality, recognizing him for what he was, a thug, who should not be permitted to keep a job for which he was unsuited. On January 4, 1923, he dictated a postscript, or codicil, to his "will": "Stalin is too rude, and this fault, entirely acceptable in relations between us communists, becomes completely unacceptable in the office of General Secretary. Therefore I propose to the comrades that a way be found to remove Stalin from that post and replace him with someone else who differs from Stalin in all respects, someone more patient, more loyal, more polite, more considerate to comrades, less headstrong."[18] Lenin then stressed that this was a matter of some importance, especially if the Stalin-Trotsky conflict was not to split the party.

For the time being Lenin kept these documents to himself. Only his wife and his secretary knew of their existence. Either he was waiting for the right moment to publish them, or else he did not know what to do with them. Yet whatever his intentions, Lenin had clearly come to see Stalin for what he was. One may wonder what took him so long. The explanation lies partly in Lenin's respect for practical men, partly in Stalin's own behavior. Although it had been clear for years that he was intriguing against Trotsky, this had seemed to be the healthy rivalry of an ambitious man. On major issues such as the ratification of the peace treaty or the announcement of the NEP, Stalin had either supported Lenin or radiated moderation. It was in Georgia that he and his supporters had shown their hand for the first time, helping Lenin realize the nature of the general secretary's political style. The Russian word for "rude," *grub*, is stronger and richer than its English counterpart. It embraces notions of rudeness, coarseness, a primitive, unpleasantly rough-hewn, barbaric quality. In the recognition that such a person was unfit to hold high office Lenin was admitting that he had backed the wrong horse. He had found ruthless fanatics to help him bring his party to power, and only now did he begin to understand that they were unfit to govern.

CHAPTER EIGHTEEN

God Votes Again

By the end of 1922 it had become obvious to the Politburo that Lenin's day was done. Already the chief concern of its members was power and how to keep it. Already the Soviet Union distributed power and privilege according to a pattern it would follow to this day, that of the pyramid. The apex was formed by the Politburo, beneath which came the Central Committee, then local party administrations; lower still were the party rank and file, and below them the rest of the country entirely without rights or privileges, existing in outer darkness. The Politburo was now anxious to prevent erosion of its power by the Central Committee, which adopted a similar attitude toward the rank and file, which in turn adopted the same attitude to nonparty members. Such attitudes derived from the seizure of a power which the Bolsheviks retained by compulsion. This made for a readiness to close ranks, especially in the Politburo, anxious to defend its authority and the situation of its members, most of whom were also anxious to oust Trotsky. These factors combined to create a majority in favor of a collective leadership, which emerged, early in 1923, as a triumvirate.

It was headed by Zinoviev, whose original name was Radomylsky, a man of great vanity, capable of remarkable meanness of spirit.[1] He had a magnificent head on a less than magnificent body, with a shrill, scratchy voice that made his listeners think of eunuchs. Not afraid of enjoying the benefits of power, he had kept on the late tsar's chef, and at a time when much of the population was starving, this helped confirm him in his belief that he was irresistible to women. He was, however, an outstanding orator, though his speeches had more power than content.

Some day he may look back on his whole life as one continuous
sacrifice to his eloquence and his own belief in its powers. It is, in
truth, a kind of narcotic that induces pleasant dreams. His speeches
begin with dry not very elegant introductions, then they are under
way! His audiences are weaned from their thoughts, their memories,
the world they see about them, the wisdom of their experience, to
follow the flood of his eloquence, which is not, curiously enough,
sustained by a very pleasing voice. Otherwise sane and sound people
have confessed to me that they are completely at the mercy of
Zinoviev's temperament, and recover their wits only when he has
vanished from the platform. . . . In Zinoviev everything turns to
excitement and passion. . . . He is just temperament, with strong
instincts of hate. He seems to be nothing apart from this temperament
and the motives that determine it. There is something sinister and
something peevish about him. His face, keen and intelligent in
profile, looks like a sponge from in front.[2]

His colleagues felt that he talked too much and nicknamed him
vodoley ("the spouter").[3] A Bolshevik of the older generation, he had
little grasp of the realities of politics and allowed himself to be dazzled
by words. He is said to have "moved in a world of verbal constructions
[leading] a bloodless paper existence."[4] A contemporary characterized
him more succinctly with the well-known Russian tag "Lustful as a
tomcat and timid as a hare."[5]

L. B. Kamenev, born Rosenfeld, was less flamboyant. His name is
usually linked with that of Zinoviev, who overshadowed him. He was
born in 1883 and after a taste of higher education became a full-time
revolutionary. He, too, had been a close associate of Lenin. Over the
years he adopted a conciliatory approach to major issues, and this did
not always meet with the master's approval. If Zinoviev declined to support the Bolshevik seizure of power because he was afraid, Kamenev's
refusal stemmed from a dislike of radical measures. Nevertheless, Lenin
never lost respect for his abilities. He was known to be an intelligent,
sensible and relatively decent man, possessed of the rare ability to chair
a meeting. Business was dispatched quickly and without anyone's feeling he had been bullied or cut off in midstream.[6] He owed his position
in the triumvirate to his past and to the fact that he had charge of the
Moscow party machine. He would have made an excellent socialist politician in a Western democracy; by no stretch of the imagination was he
a match for Stalin.

Stalin was the team's junior member; his name was always mentioned last. Although Kamenev, in particular, was not overfond of him, he was considered a useful organization man and party workhorse. Moreover, a coalition that excluded the effective head of the departments of party organization and personnel would have been unworkable. At the end of 1922 Stalin was seen as a little-known figure but an able one, a plausible outsider in the succession race. The correspondent of the *New York Times* ended his review of the contenders as follows: "There is also the Georgian Stalin, one of the most remarkable men in Russia and perhaps the most influential here today. During the last year he has shown judgment and analytic power not unworthy of Lenin."[7]

Stalin provided further evidence of his "rudeness" in a brush with Lenin's wife, Nadezhda Krupskaya, late in December 1922. The Central Committee had appointed Stalin to "supervise" Lenin and ensure that he was following doctors' orders, keeping political activity to the minimum. On December 22 Stalin learned that Lenin had given Krupskaya a short piece of dictation. He telephoned her in a fury and, as she put it in a letter of indignant and bewildered complaint to Kamenev, subjected her to "unseemly abuse and menaces," threatening to have her prosecuted for insubordination. He allegedly went as far as to call her a "syphilitic old whore." A simple telephone call could have told him that Krupskaya had the doctor's permission to take Lenin's dictation, but Stalin had apparently lost his temper, while fairness was never his strong suit.

It was the letter itself that had enraged Stalin. Discovering that the Central Committee had altered its position on the foreign trade monopoly in his favor and that Stalin had withdrawn all objections, Lenin dictated a note to Trotsky congratulating him on getting "their" policy through: "It seems that we have captured the position by manoeuvring, without firing a shot, I propose that far from stopping now we press home the attack."[8] This suggestion of an effective alliance between Lenin and Trotsky would have sufficed to make Stalin overexcited, since it would put them in an unassailable position and leave him dangerously exposed with respect to the Georgian affair. We do not know when Krupskaya told Lenin of her conversation with Stalin, although tell him she did in due course. It may or may not have been this incident which prompted Lenin to add the codicil concerning Stalin's rudeness, but his only direct response to it comes later.

The three months or so that separate Lenin's second stroke from his third were an unreal time. The restrictions imposed upon him, allegedly for his own good, made him a virtual prisoner, and there is every reason to suppose that the person responsible for those restrictions was Stalin. Lenin seemed to grasp their extent only gradually and did his best to resist them; he did not give up easily. A party congress was to be held in April, and it seems that it was there that he planned to make his next move. This would probably have taken the form of a reading of his will and codicil culminating in the proposal that Stalin be dismissed from his posts. In the meantime, he prepared more material for the congress at which he hoped to steer the party onto a new course. He wanted to know the results of a recent census of government officials in large cities. Reluctantly his secretary told him that Stalin had forbidden him to see the papers. Moreover, his own doctor accused him of requesting political information.

Lenin now voiced the suspicion that he was under political, as opposed to medical, control. He was also concerned by problems of party organization, trying to alter its nature by tinkering with its structure. His essays on the subject constituted a veiled attack upon Stalin, since they came to focus on the shortcomings of Rabkrin, which Stalin had administered. He expressed the hope that the right kind of inspectorate, staffed with "good people," trained in Germany and England, might cure bureaucratic abuse. Moreover, and here he aimed directly at Stalin, he hoped that a new inspectorate would "abandon the qualities of ludicrous affectation and self-importance" which had hitherto signed the style of both party and state organizations.

Stalin was not pleased by Lenin's essays and tried to oppose their publication in *Pravda*. He even suggested the printing of a single dummy copy to satisfy Lenin. However, Trotsky and Kamenev, no doubt with some degree of malicious satisfaction, insisted upon publication, and the pieces appeared in early March. In the meantime, Lenin returned to the Georgian question. The complaints of the Georgian Central Committee had been discussed again in the Politburo, which again exonerated Stalin and Ordzhonikidze. Lenin asked to be shown the papers, and his secretary passed the request to Stalin. At first Stalin stalled, replying that the matter was trivial and would anyway require the authorization of the Politburo. Eventually there was a discussion between Stalin and Kamenev, who observed that Lenin was entitled to see the papers. Stalin, recognizing that he had lost a round, answered that Lenin could do as he pleased.[9]

When Lenin read them, his understanding of the bullying style of Stalin's methods developed a stage further. One of his notes relating to "the affair of bio-mechanics," or Ordzhonikidze's blow to the face, reads: "Did Stalin know? Why did he not do something about it?" [10] Once again Lenin turned to Trotsky, writing a letter to be read to him over the telephone in which he asked Trotsky to defend the Georgians against Stalin and Ordzhonikidze, signing himself with the warmest of formulas: "With very best comradely greetings." [11] If Trotsky were not prepared to defend the Georgians, would he please return the material that Lenin was sending him (his December note on the national question)? He also wrote to the Georgians, with copies to Kamenev and Trotsky, informing them that he now supported their cause and was appalled at the behavior of Stalin and Ordzhonikidze.

Not only was Trotsky of no help to Lenin, but he managed to shoot himself in the foot. First he asked Lenin's permission to show the material to Kamenev. Lenin replied that this was out of the question since Kamenev would immediately tell Stalin, who would "do a rotten deal and deceive us." Lenin's secretary then told Trotsky that in her master's view Stalin was no longer to be trusted and that he, Lenin, was preparing a "bomb" against him. Trotsky returned Lenin's letter but kept a copy for himself. In other words, he refused to help the Georgians but mentioned the letter to nobody. He later made some feeble criticisms of Ordzhonikidze but said nothing about Stalin—or about Lenin's letter. Matters could have ended there had Lenin's secretary not written to Kamenev exposing the whole affair. Manifestly Trotsky had ignored Lenin's wishes on the one hand, and failed to inform his colleagues of a crucial letter on the other, letting both sides down by trying to sit on the fence. Once more the architect of the formula "Neither peace nor war" was out of touch with political reality.

On the same day, March 5th, that Lenin wrote to Trotsky asking him for his support, he also wrote to Stalin:

> Dear Comrade Stalin,
>
> You had the rudeness to call my wife on the telephone and insult her. While being prepared to forget what you said, she repeated your words to Zinoviev and Kamenev. I do not intend to forget what you do against me so easily, and of course anything done to my wife is done against me too. I must therefore ask you if you are prepared to withdraw your words and apologize or whether you would prefer that all relations between us should cease henceforth.
>
> Yours, Lenin [12]

Lenin did not send the letter at once. Indeed, since he may have known of the incident for more than two months, he could have been acting in cold blood, hoping to elicit an apology to be used against Stalin at the next month's congress. That is how Krupskaya interpreted the letter when Lenin showed it to her, making her observe to Ka- menev: "He would never have decided to break off personal relations if he had not thought it necessary to crush Stalin politically."[13] She rec- ognized that Lenin would always put politics before his wife's honor. Despite Krupskaya's objections, the letter was delivered upon March 7, and Stalin dictated an answer on the spot. We have no record of his reply but can only assume it to have been an apology. Lenin's letter made a surprisingly profound impression upon Stalin, whom one might have expected to have shrugged it off with a sneer about an old whore and an invalid. Its existence remained a secret for more than thirty years until Khrushchev and Stalin's successors stumbled upon it in a secret compartment in Stalin's desk.[14] Khrushchev first made its contents known to the party in his secret speech of 1956. It is pointless to wonder why Stalin kept it. Although it may have been out of veneration for Lenin, it might equally well have been a source of amusement; it is not hard to imagine Stalin rereading it occasionally and smiling to himself as the man who had the last laugh. He did, it is true, permit Krupskaya to live out her natural life in a Kremlin apartment, but that is all he allowed her. On the one occasion, at the height of the terror, when she attempted to criticize Stalin's actions, he brought her to heel with the magnificent threat that "If you don't shut up, we'll make somebody else Lenin's widow."

Together with his expression of support for the Georgians, the letter to Stalin was the last thing Lenin wrote. On March 9 a third stroke paralyzed his right side, deprived him of the power of speech, and re- moved him from the political scene. A few days later a bulletin sug- gested that he had been politically inactive for some time and stated that he was accepting doctors' orders "unconditionally." To anyone reading between the lines this meant that he was under the authority of the Politburo, in the first instance of Stalin. The latter, who knew when to keep to the background, did not sign the bulletin.

If God voted for Stalin by incapacitating Lenin in December, He seems to have done so again in March. Had Lenin been able to appear at the April congress, he would surely have dropped his bomb on Stalin, who had not yet gained control of the Central Committee. Lenin's hos- tility, if not his testament, was no secret to Stalin. In the circumstances one cannot help wondering if he may not have given God a little help. Trotsky, who would subsequently recall many otherwise unconfirmed details, sometimes contradicting himself in successive accounts, wrote that according to Stalin, Lenin had once requested poison. Trotsky implies that Stalin probably obliged. Certainly he was in a position to effect a medical murder since he was in control of Lenin's doctors, while the technique itself appealed to him. He made ample use of it in later years, and it also featured in the scenario of his final purge, the "doctors' plot." Besides, we shall see him accuse others of murdering Lenin during the Moscow trials of the late 1930s, and Stalin liked to tax his enemies with his own misdeeds.

We shall never know whether Stalin was responsible for the timing of Lenin's strokes; the evidence is purely circumstantial. Certainly he had method, opportunity and motive. In future years it becomes safe to presume that anyone who crossed Stalin and died quite suddenly did not die a natural death. Most certainly it would appeal to Stalin's sense of humor to inaugurate a monumental cult to celebrate a man whom he had murdered. The writer Jean Cocteau once defined coincidence as "the alibi of the gods." The coincidence that removed Lenin from active politics when he was about to drop his bomb might well have been "Stalin's alibi."

CHAPTER NINETEEN

The Triumvirate

The congress that opened in April would be the first to be held without Lenin, and the confusion created by his absence is reflected in the greetings that factories and youth organizations transmitted to their leaders on such occasions, since it was by no means clear who their leaders were. "Some of them hailed Lenin and Zinoviev, some coupled Trotsky with the sick man in their greetings. The more prudent saluted 'Lenin, Zinoviev, Kamenev and Trotsky,' or still more wisely omitted any name but Lenin's. But no one thought of paying a special tribute to the modest self-effacing man who was the General Secretary of the Party."[1]

Stalin displayed remarkable political sense at the congress, exercising finesse and exceptional adroitness in what remained a tight spot; Lenin or no Lenin, he was still at risk. Many delegates had a clear idea of the thrust of Lenin's memorandum on the Georgian issue, and there were also those who knew about the testament, its codicil and the letter to Stalin.[2] Stalin countered with a whispering campaign. He began to undermine the authority of the document as his agents spread the word that the postscript to Lenin's testament was written immediately after the incident involving Krupskaya, implying that Lenin had been driven by rage.[3]

Trotsky remained a threat. He was still very popular and a plausible successor to Lenin. Moscow was full of rumors suggesting that the old man had named him his heir, understandably enough at a time when many considered him the second great leader of the Revolution and the architect of victory. His reputation had just been given a boost by Radek, who published a major piece in *Pravda* on March 14 entitled "Lev Trotsky Organizer of Victory," which made the point that the Red

Army, Trotsky's creation, was the only institution in Soviet Russia that worked. Radek's piece, which had irritated Voroshilov and the Tsaritsyn group, was dismissed by Stalin as "idiotic babbling," but nevertheless, Trotsky came to the congress as a charismatic figure, and Stalin had too much sense to mount a frontal assault upon him. Instead, he had his secretariat run a second whispering campaign, suggesting that Trotsky was a potential Napoleon and "gravedigger of the Revolution."

Yet Trotsky's was a popularity based on past, not present, performance, and although it was not apparent at the time, it was crumbling. Trotsky did not understand how to increase his support; he was incapable of "pressing the flesh." In the words of an old friend, "He behaved like a man who knew his own worth and was sure of his place in the party. Unlike the role-playing Stalin, prepared to consort with anyone, his enemies even, for the sake of his ultimate aim, Trotsky was felt to create an invisible barrier in his relations with others, and though the degree of distance could vary, still it was almost always there."[4]

Yet it was not just that Trotsky was aloof and arrogant. He was temperamentally unsuited to the climate of Russian politics. Writing in *Pravda* just after the April congress, he mounted an attack on Russian thuggery, in this case as it was reflected in the language, writing with remarkable perspicacity about the existence of "Two streams of Russian abuse—the swearing of masters, officials and police, full and fat, and the hungry desperate and tormented swearing of the masses, that have colored the whole of Russian life with their despicable patterns."[5] Trotsky looked to the Revolution as a means of raising the human spirit above these levels. He never understood that a successful political leader must needs have command of both streams of abuse, both components of Great Russian thuggery. It was a lesson that Stalin had learned by consorting with both criminals and policemen, one that he would never forget.

In his public attitude toward Trotsky Stalin displayed a new maturity. He no longer allowed his loathing of the man to dictate his behavior. He had more self-control now and could proceed with greater delicacy. He started by setting a trap for his rival's vanity. At past congresses the Central Committee's general report had always been presented by Lenin. Stalin suggested that Trotsky take his place, thereby revealing that he aspired to the succession. Trotsky had the sense to refuse, while Zinoviev was vain and foolish enough to propose himself, an offer which was accepted.

Stalin still had his problems. The delegates knew of Lenin's criticism of his nationalities policy and had read the articles criticizing Rabkrin.

Stalin dealt with both issues magnificently; his speech on the Georgian issue is something of a masterpiece. His chief technique consisted in appropriating the arguments of his opponent or misrepresenting his words to show either that there were no disagreements or that he, Stalin, was in the right. The whole thrust is one of willful but subtle manipulation of differences between letter and spirit, which leave an opponent angered and frustrated by the monstrous unfairness of the proceedings but unable to deliver a satisfactory counterblow.

Stalin did not know if the delegates had read the text of Lenin's strictures but assumed they knew its tenor and were familiar with key phrases such as the one accusing him of "undue haste." His speech adopted all Lenin's criticism of Great Russian chauvinism and made it his own. He suggested that such chauvinism probably came about because Lenin had established relations between the republics with "undue haste," but now there was plenty of time to modify those relations. He then pronounced his own indictment of chauvinism, which he associated with the NEP, suggesting that it was Lenin, the architect of those reforms, who had brought about its recrudescence. Then, with a stroke of genius, he faced the issue of Lenin's memoranda. He quoted passages from two of Lenin's early articles and continued:

> Many have referred to notes and articles by Vladimir Ilich. I should have preferred not to have quoted my teacher and comrade Lenin, since he is not here, and I am afraid I might refer to him incorrectly or out of context, nevertheless I am obliged to quote a certain key passage. . . . Allow me to refer once again to comrade Lenin. I ought not to, but since many comrades attending the congress quote comrade Lenin at random and distort him, permit me to read a few words from one well known article. . . .[6]

He gave the impression that he had no time for distorted rumors, gossip and below-the-belt polemic, while making it clear that there were no differences between himself and Lenin, reducing the Georgian affair to a storm in a teacup. The only man who could have answered Stalin and demolished his speech was Trotsky. He had the intelligence, the information and the political authority to do so, yet once again, for reasons best known to himself, he preferred to keep silent. He continually underestimated Stalin the crude empiricist and even persisted for years in believing him to be the instrument of an abler and more intelligent enemy such as Bukharin.

In reply to Lenin's strictures about the tyranny and inefficiency of its bureaucrats, Stalin spoke about the organization of the party. Pronouncing himself in complete agreement with his absent colleague, he made some tangible suggestions. The time had come to prepare a "generation of future leaders" and bring fresh blood into the Central Committee. He therefore proposed to enlarge it by introducing local party workers. The Politburo should also be enlarged to include four candidate members. On the surface Stalin was following Lenin's desire to remove some of the power from the apex of the pyramid and allow lower-ranking elements a part in the decision-making process. In fact, he was developing the scope of the Stalin machine. It was his Secretariat and his Orgburo that would select the new members of the Central Committee, while of the four new candidate members of the Politburo, three—Kalinin, Molotov and Rudzutak—were his men. Since the new system ostensibly diminished the powers of the Politburo vis-à-vis the Central Committee, it reduced the authority of his senior rivals. Finally, the emphasis on youth is important. Stalin would rely increasingly upon the support of young newcomers to the party, selected by his own machine. He would employ them first against Trotsky and then against the Old Bolsheviks themselves.

Stalin's speech was remarkable for one further reason. In his unctuous references to his mentor Stalin first used the term *Leninism* in a positive sense. It had been coined and used pejoratively in 1904 by the Menshevik Martov. Now, in Stalin's mouth, it anticipated Lenin's death and future apotheosis. He then summed up the mood of the congress with sublime hypocrisy and total disregard for the divisions and antagonisms which his oratory had papered over, observing "That I have not for a long time seen a congress so united, so imbued with one idea. I am sorry that comrade Lenin is not here. If he were he would be able to say 'For twenty-five years I have been forging a Party, and now here it is, complete, great and strong.'"[7]

• • •

The dictatorship of the proletariat is being replaced by that of the Secretariat.

—RADEK

Not counting Lenin, the Politburo now numbered six full members: Zinoviev, Kamenev, Stalin, Trotsky, Bukharin and Tomsky. The latter was a trade unionist and bitterly opposed to Trotsky's plans for the work force. The triumvirate had announced their intent of voting together at the April congress, and henceforward the only vote Trotsky might hope to collect was that of Bukharin, who was closer by temperament and interests to Trotsky than any other member of the Politburo without always agreeing with him. Trotsky maintained that Bukharin used to cry on his shoulder and complain that his colleagues were "turning the party into a sewer."[8] Certainly Bukharin had stood up for the Georgian Communists, but whether he behaved as Trotsky described remains an open question. At all events it is clear that the triumvirate had an effective majority in the committee and that with or without the support of a tearful Bukharin, Trotsky was isolated.

Although Stalin still needed allies within the Politburo, the balance of power was to shift appreciably over the following two years as a result of Stalin's suggestion that the Central Committee be reorganized along "Leninist" lines. In 1922 it had numbered twenty-seven full members, at least nineteen of whom supported Zinoviev, and nineteen candidates. Two years later it had been expanded to sixty-three full members and forty-five candidates. All the new appointments had been made via the Stalin machine. Years of patient work by the Secretariat and the Orgburo, which kept a careful record of every party member—"It is necessary to study every member through and through"[9]—were paying off. For it was the Central Committee which determined membership of the Politburo, and thanks to the committee's new Stalinist bias, the most recent members of the Politburo—Molotov, Voroshilov and Kalinin—all were Stalin's men.

He did not get his nominations through without a struggle. It was obvious that he was packing the Central Committee, and there was considerable resistance to his practice of making appointments which were automatically ratified by his stooges. In August a number of party leaders were on vacation in the southern resort town of Kislovodsk. Among those present were Zinoviev, Bukharin, possibly Ordzhonikidze and some senior army men, Voroshilov, Frunze and Lashevich. They met quietly in a cave on the city outskirts to discuss the increasing influence of the Stalin machine. They were aware that the Orgburo was making appointments and transfers without referring to the Politburo, and it did not require an acute political sense for leaders suspicious of Stalin to feel the ground shifting a little where they stood. They all had heard something of Lenin's testament, and his comments on Stalin's power were beginning to ring true. Zinoviev suggested that the Politburo be dissolved and replaced by a formally recognized triumvirate consisting of Stalin, Trotsky and either himself, Kamenev or Bukharin. He also called for a change in the nature of the Secretariat which would be subordinate to the triumvirate and cease to be Stalin's exclusive domain. Loyal Stalinist that he was, Voroshilov objected, and it would seem that Bukharin did so too.

Stalin quickly got to hear of the plans and reacted with characteristic subtlety. Without commenting on a proposal that was obviously a threat to his power base, he said "that if the comrades were to persist in their plan, I was prepared to clear out without a fuss and without any discussion, be it open or secret."[10] He implied that the meeting of those whom he referred to disparagingly as "troglodytes" was a furtive little affair. He was above such hole-and-corner behavior and quite ready to resign. It was not the last time he would make such an offer, which became a favorite tactic. It acted as a trap; anyone appearing to favor the proposal became suspect. It also served a further purpose: Stalin realized that his resignation would make things easy for Trotsky and that this would not delight the other members of the leadership. By giving them the choice between maintaining the status quo and a resignation which he knew to be unacceptable, Stalin outmaneuvered his weak and divided opponents.

He did not treat all enemies so delicately. Sultan-Galiev was a Tartar Bolshevik who had hitherto favored centralization and opposed Muslim separatism. However on observing the effect of the new chauvinism in the eastern territories, he changed his mind. The police intercepted a letter to party colleagues in which he complained that the Soviets were no better than their tsarist predecessors and suggested that non-Russian Communists form a bloc to represent their regional and racial interests. Stalin had Sultan-Galiev arrested, an action requiring the approval of Zinoviev and Kamenev. It was the first time that a prominent party man had been subjected to such a fate. According to the historian E. H. Carr, the occasion provided a precedent that was both "significant and fruitful."[11] The fruit it was to bear, consisting of thousands of arrests, imprisonments and executions, was strange indeed.

Stalin observed that in the past he had protected Sultan-Galiev in the hope that he might become a true Marxist, but he had disappointed him, as had those who failed to condemn his behavior with the necessary vigor. Like so many after him, Sultan-Galiev was accused of heading an illegal organization within the party, offering the mirror image of Stalin's own procedures. He was also accused of conspiring with foreign powers and counterrevolutionary forces. In further anticipation of things to come Sultan-Galiev confessed to all charges. Stalin wanted him shot, but his colleagues disagreed, and he had to settle for expulsion from the party. However, within a few years Stalin proved able to dispose of Sultan-Galiev definitively in the cellars of the Lubyanka.

Despite growing misgivings about Stalin, hostility to Trotsky kept the triumvirate together. In September 1923 they moved against his personal power base, the Red Army (Trotsky was still Commissar for War and President of the Revolutionary War Council). The Politburo proposed to increase the size of the council by adding a number of Trotsky's enemies, including Stalin, thereby depriving him of his majority. Trotsky countered the power play with oratory. He made a fiery speech to the Central Committee, denouncing the machinations of his intriguing enemies, saying that he had no intention of dirtying his hands, which were solely at the service of the Revolution. He asked to be relieved of all offices and to be allowed to serve as a simple soldier in the revolution that was about to break out in Germany. The speech rang splendidly and did not please the triumvirate. But Zinoviev, to use a metaphor that would have pleased Trotsky, shot his fox.

He turned Trotsky's oratory into a joke, requesting the Central Committee to release him, too, from all duties, so that he might stand shoulder to shoulder with his old friend in that coming revolution. The speech had a particular appeal for those aware of the limitations of Zinoviev's personal courage. Stalin then entered into the spirit of the affair by declaring that the Central Committee would never permit such "beloved leaders" to risk their necks and moving that they be forbidden to do so. His motion was seconded, and the Central Committee solemnly proceeded to vote. At this stage the proceedings were interrupted by a voice from the floor, speaking with an exaggeratedly coarse accent and wanting to know why "Comrade Trotsky is pussyfooting about?" The word *pussyfooting (kochevryazhetsya)* was too much for Trotsky. He asked to be "relieved of his role in this unseemly farce" and made off dramatically, all eyes upon him. He decided to complete his exit by slamming the door behind him. Unfortunately the meeting was being held in the old imperial throne room, which had a massive iron door with pneumatic hinges that, alas for Trotsky, closed as slowly as they opened. As he departed, he gave the door a mighty heave, to no effect whatsoever; it continued to shut with a majestic slowness. Rather than leave with a bang, Trotsky flounced away with an impotent gesture. From now on the triumvirate and Trotsky fought with the gloves off. Although he continued to attend meetings of the Politburo, he spent his time ostentatiously reading novels in French—a skill that has since been lost to Soviet leaders.[12]

Boris Bazhanov has given a fascinating account of the confused political situation at the end of 1923. First it must be understood that active politics, argument, dissent were reserved for a tiny proportion of the population, a few hundred thousand party members. Beyond the party, politics was no longer possible; the rest of the population lived entirely under the arbitrary rule of the GPU (successor to the Cheka), which had the power to arrest, torture and imprison as it pleased. Sentimental historians who look back on the twenties as a golden age appear to forget that the gold was not equitably distributed. The British consul in Leningrad, an intelligent and perceptive observer, provided a salutary reminder of what ordinary life could be like:

> Terror is kept up at red heat. It is perfectly obvious that the reins of
> government could not be held by the present rulers by any other
> means. Arrests and domiciliary searches continue. The policy of
> combing out from the population all persons, particularly of the
> intelligentsia, known or suspected to be of anti-Bolshevik views, is
> being pursued with what is, even for the Bolsheviks, unusual vigour.
> In many instances the authorities do not bother to find a pretext for
> arresting their victims.[13]

Although NEP had made living conditions tolerable, it had not produced universal economic satisfaction at a stroke. The chief problem of the twenties was the inability of the regime to achieve an acceptable balance between agricultural and manufacturing prices—the so-called scissors problem. Although the advantage fluctuated between town and country over the period, neither side considered the state of affairs satisfactory. Peasants complained that produce prices were too low; workers, of poor conditions and oppression at the hands of a bureaucracy that governed in their name and on their behalf, while retaining all the benefits. Peasant discontent was not reflected in the party since peasants were considered a potentially hostile class (their first supporter in high circles would be Khrushchev in the 1950s). Workers, on the other hand, could make their grievances felt, there being a Workers' Opposition within the party, which was opposed to bureaucratic centralism and wanted more power for the unions. Despite the seemingly united front of the April congress, discontent with the leadership was widespread among ordinary party members, who considered its policies economically unsatisfactory and were opposed to the high-handed way with which those at the apex of the pyramid conducted their affairs.

Trotsky attacked the triumvirate in early October. In an open letter he accused it of making excessive use of nomination instead of election; all power was now vested in a secretarial apparatus created from above. He called for the dictatorship of the Secretariat to be replaced by party democracy. His letter circulated widely until it was banned by the Central Committee on October 15. Ironically it was on that same day that the so-called Platform of the Forty-six was published. The Forty-six were a group on the left wing of the party which had sympathized with Trotsky's radical attitude to labor conscription but from which he had kept aloof to avoid exposing himself to charges of factionalism. They declared the party leadership inadequate, too much under the domination of the "secretarial hierarchy," while ordinary party members, the "quiet people," were afraid to speak their minds in public or even in private unless they were certain that those present were "discreet." The present regime had outlived its usefulnesss, and a conference of senior party members should be called to discuss what should be done.

The triumvirate did not ignore the charges. It began a sharp polemic with Trotsky and called a meeting of the Central Committee and other prominent Bolsheviks to discuss the Platform of the Forty-six, some of whom were even allowed to attend. The meeting concluded with a resolution condemning both them and Trotsky for factionalism, while agreeing to the principle of inner-party democracy. At the same time the triumvirate made private overtures to Trotsky. Throughout the autumn Trotsky argued with them about the form of party resolutions when he should have been out canvassing votes.[14]

The triumvirate still had good reason to fear him. He could easily have headed an opposition that was uncomfortably numerous, extended into the Central Committee itself, and which would have become infinitely more threatening under his leadership. That he did not do so is in keeping with his character; why he should not have done so, be it for reasons of cowardice, stupidity or out of a genuine wish to preserve party unity at all costs, is a question that cannot be answered. He rationalized the failure in retrospect, by suggesting that such a bid would have looked like "casting lots for Lenin's mantle."[15] His motives, however laudable, were of no help to Trotsky. Stalin's world was not one in which nice guys finished last; they did not finish at all.

Boris Bazhanov offered a further reason for Trotsky's refusal. He believed that the opposition consisted largely of intellectuals and educated believers who had expected Communist society to deliver its promises. When they saw that everyone except the party privileged was worse off under Soviet rule and that peasants and workers alike were impoverished slaves, they began to wonder whether it had all been worthwhile. It was an attitude that found no expression among the leaders, the Forty-six, the Workers' Opposition or, least of all, Trotsky because in essence it proposed the winding up of the regime. In those circumstances the opposition could express its disagreement only by voting for Trotsky, rather as voters in Western democracies signify discontent by voting for no-hopers. Late in 1923 the GPU reported to the Politburo that there was widespread disagreement with its policies, even within the Central Committee, and that this was the case throughout the country.[16] Another source records that in Tashkent, and despite intense pressure from the GPU leadership, forty-five percent of the GPU rank and file voted for Trotsky, and the only reason the vote was that low was "because our lot were counting."[17] The triumvirate then discovered that it had actually lost its majority in the party cells of Moscow. Zinoviev and Kamenev both greeted the news with dismayed speeches, holding forth at length while Stalin drew quietly on his pipe. When they were finished, they asked him for his opinion, whereupon he observed that in such affairs it mattered not at all who voted for whom; what mattered was who counted the votes. He then arranged for his secretariat to rig the election.[18] Once the local organizations saw Moscow support the official line, they grew more circumspect in their expressions of dissent, and the affair began to die down.

Trotsky's situation became weaker accordingly. He had been openly criticized for the first time, was no longer the inviolate companion of Lenin, and it was now that the word *Trotskyism* began to be used in unflattering contrast with *Leninism*. Considering those months of struggle, Trotsky later imparted a pathetic character to them, quoting his wife's unpublished memoir to focus the atmosphere, as he described himself battling with his enemies in the throes of a fever which he had caught shooting duck: "He was alone and ill and had to fight them all. Owing to his illness the meetings were held in our apartment. . . . He spoke with his whole being; it seemed as if with every speech he lost some of his strength, he spoke with so much 'blood.' And in reply I heard only cold, indifferent answers. . . . After each of these meetings [his] temperature rose; he came out of the study soaked through, undressed and went to bed."[19]

The use of oratory to win over a subcommittee that has been meeting regularly for years is inappropriate at the best of times, futile when it is dominated by Stalin.

CHAPTER TWENTY

We Vow to Thee, Comrade Lenin

After his stroke in March 1923 Lenin had been moved to the village of Gorki. Cut off from active politics, he had no further contact with any political leader; according to Krupskaya, any such meeting would have been unbearably painful. He still made appearances before delegations of workers, young Communists and other organizations of enthusiasts, and it was still hoped that he would get well again. Indeed, Lenin did recover in some degree from the paralysis of his right side, although he never regained his powers of speech, and he also made progress in the process of learning to write with his left hand. He continued to take an interest in politics and was able to indicate which newspaper articles he wanted read to him. By October he could even walk a little and climb stairs.

It is clear that Lenin felt great distress; he could be seen sitting alone for hours at a time, crying, as an observer put it, not just from impotence but from outrage.[1] The newspapers gave him some idea of the disturbances within the party that autumn, and these drove him to a final effort, which health and circumstances prevented him from making good. On October 18 he asked to be wheeled to the garage and placed in his Rolls-Royce. A caravan of three cars, including Krupskaya, a team of doctors and his bodyguard, set off for Moscow, where they arrived long after dark. Lenin went directly to his apartment in the Kremlin, where he looked in vain for a certain file of papers. On discovering the loss, he signified great distress by means of excited and inarticulate cries. We do not know what he was looking for, but it was probably a dossier he had compiled against Stalin.

Lenin spent that night in the Kremlin, a fact that was not admitted by Soviet historians until 1964. Although several officials saw him there, orders were given to clear the corridors, "in case he be upset by the sight of familiar faces." The next morning he was driven around the city and taken to an agricultural exhibition, at which he was observed smiling fixedly and doffing his hat in mute greeting to the crowds. The macabre performance was presumably intended to establish that he was still alive and kicking, as the preliminary to a final move against Stalin. One does not have to be a disciple to be moved by the notion of the old leader and onetime spectacular orator reduced to addressing the crowds with a single mechanical and futile gesture. When Lenin returned to his apartment, he found an order signed by Stalin. Lenin was in breach of party discipline, having "willfully gone to the garage," and must return home at once. For some time after his trip Lenin seemed even more depressed than usual. No mention of the visit appeared in the newspapers.

In the meantime, Stalin was changing Lenin from a human being into an institution. He had produced vast quantities of polemic writing, including some savage attacks upon Trotsky, excellent ammunition for the triumvirate. They proposed the establishment of a Lenin institute, to be the sole depository of all manuscript materials pertaining to Lenin. Any person in possession of such material must hand it over at once. The institute was to be headed by a scholar of Marxism, Ryazanov, but his assistant was to be Stalin's secretary, Tovstukha. This gave Stalin control over the Lenin Archive, providing him with an ideological and polemic tool of the first importance. Tovstukha learned to know his way about the archive better than anyone. He was able to supply Stalin with material against Trotsky, or any other enemy, and provide appropriate quotations in support of any policy he might adopt.

Early in 1924 Lenin's health began to improve. He attended a joint Christmas and New Year's party on January 7 to which all the children in his sanatorium were invited. There was a sixteen-foot Christmas tree, decorated by Lenin's GPU guards. (One would like to know more about that tree. What decorations did the policemen use, and did they put a red star on the top? It was curious that there should have been a tree at all; in later years Christmas trees were declared illegal, relics of a Christian past, and were only restored to favor, as symbols of the New Year in 1937.) Lenin was in excellent form at the gathering, signifying approval of various party pieces and staying to the end. The news disturbed Stalin, ever aware that Lenin posed a continuing threat.

Stalin attacked the master at a conference which opened on January 16. His speech criticized attempts to divide the party, while defending its leaders against charges of bullying, and disclosed a secret memorandum of Lenin's that insisted on party unity at all costs. His speech then took an unexpected turn. There had been attempts to hold up the values and attitudes of the old generation as superior to those of younger comrades. But this was not necessarily true. Moreover, one could not possibly respect *every old man*. This was an explicit attack upon Lenin, who was regularly known as the old man. Stalin also dropped dark hints about parallels to be drawn between the Old Bolsheviks and German socialists who had collaborated with the kaiser during the Great War— possibly a threat to bring Lenin's reliance on German funding into the open. He then spoke of the corrupting effects of the NEP. The next day he attacked Lenin again. Conceding that Lenin was a genius, Stalin observed that Lenin's pupils were excellent learners and that not even Lenin was infallible, at which point he mentioned Brest-Litovsk, the civil war and Kronstadt.

Trotsky, a beaten man now, was still unwell; he took two months' leave from all political work and left for the south on January 18. Curiously his departure endangered Stalin. The threat of Trotsky was all that kept the triumvirate together. Now he was gone, and with Lenin threatening a counterattack, Stalin felt vulnerable. Indeed, Zinoviev, Kamenev and Bukharin apparently tried to see Lenin at some time in January, although Stalin's men were able to prevent the meeting, obliging the three Politburo members to content themselves with watching Lenin being trundled through the park. In any event, Stalin had no reason to be afraid. At six o'clock on the evening of January 21, Lenin had another stroke, and fifty minutes later he died. Solemnly the Bolshevik leaders Zinoviev, Kamenev, Bukharin, Kalinin rode out in sleighs to view the body, accompanied by Stalin, who would in time have every member of that group, except Kalinin, shot.

As soon as the news of Lenin's death was made known, the rumors started. It was claimed that he had been poisoned by Stalin, perhaps at his own request, perhaps not. There was also much discussion of Lenin's visit to the capital. People reacted to his death in differing ways. Many who considered him the architect of communism were far from displeased. Others, with shorter memories, saw in him the architect of

NEP and remembered him gratefully as such; as late as the 1940s ordinary people still looked back to him warmly for that reason.[2] Others remembered him in a different, characteristically Russian manner as someone who "loved Russia in his own way," despite the fact that "he had a good many Trotskyite hangers-on, Jews mostly" whom the patriotic Stalin disposed of in due course.[3] Party members felt the loss more keenly, while throughout the capital there was an extraordinary sense of the passing of a great leader, as Nadezhda Mandelstam, wife of the poet, recalls: "It was like long long ago, like the funeral of a tsar of Muscovy. Lenin's funeral was the last spark of the people's Revolution, and I could see that his popularity was created not by fear, as would be the case with the adoration and apotheosis of Stalin, but by the hopes which the entire nation had of him. For the only time in my life Moscow willingly took to the streets and stood in line. They stood patiently, quietly, somberly."[4]

Stalin was far from somber. For fourteen months he had been under threat, and now the threat was gone. In private he was radiant, while offering the public a sober and grieving appearance.[5] At the same time, acting like the villain of a soap opera, he played a dirty trick on Trotsky. The latter was on his way to the Black Sea when he was overtaken by a telegram from Stalin, which reached him on the twenty-first. It informed him that Lenin had died and that the funeral would be held on the twenty-sixth; since he would be unable to return in time, he should continue traveling south. The telegram lied: The funeral was to be held a day later, on the twenty-seventh, giving Trotsky ample time to attend it as one of the pallbearers. But only the triumvirate featured in the ceremony; Trotsky, it was widely felt, had not bothered to turn up. As the *New York Times* man put it, "Trotsky's failure to pay his last tribute to the dead leader horrified the people of Moscow as a want of respect and good taste. It was, moreover, a political error of the first magnitude and dealt a fatal blow to Trotsky's prestige."[6]

•   •   •

On the eve of the funeral there was a session of the All-Union Congress of Soviets at which the Bolshevik leaders honored Lenin. Stalin spoke fourth, after Kalinin, Krupskaya and Zinoviev, yet his speech is the most remarkable he ever made. It revealed a totally unfamiliar side. No longer the *kinto*, intriguer or machine politician, he appeared the master of a monumental and ritualistic oratory that, stylistically speaking, inaugurated the Stalin era and marked the beginning of the Soviet cult of the dead. The party was depicted as a band of humble disciples honoring and obeying their former lawgiver and leader. On their behalf Stalin pledged that they would not betray the sacred trust. The style of the speech was not just monumental but liturgical, too, shot through with Stalin's recollections of the seminary and ringing with ecclesiastical rhetoric. Its appeal was overwhelmingly emotional, inviting its listeners to assent to a ritual that both celebrated the dead and united the living. With its repetitions and oppositions its style was remarkably close to that of the American gospel preacher. Like him, Stalin looked for the "hook," the emotional catchword, which, as it returned time and again, would capture the attention of the audience.

> Comrades! We Communists are people of a special cast. We are fashioned of special stuff. We are the ones who form the army of the great proletarian general, the army of Comrade Lenin. There is no higher honor than that of belonging to this army. There is nothing higher than the calling of a member of the party whose founder and leader is Comrade Lenin. Not to every man is it given to be the member of such a party. Not to every man is it given to endure the tribulations and tempests that go with membership in such a party. Sons of the working class, sons of poverty and strife, sons of unparalleled privations and heroic struggles, these are the men who, first and foremost, are worthy to be members of such a party. . . .
>
> Leaving us, Comrade Lenin ordered us to hold high and keep pure the great calling of member of the party. We vow to thee, Comrade Lenin, that we will honor this, thy commandment.
>
> Leaving us, Comrade Lenin enjoined us to keep the unity of the party like the apple of our eye. We vow to thee, Comrade Lenin, that we will with honor fulfill this, thy commandment.
>
> Leaving us, Comrade Lenin enjoined us to keep and strengthen the dictatorship of the proletariat. We vow to thee, Comrade Lenin, that we will not spare our strength to fulfill with honor this, thy commandment.
>
> Leaving us, Comrade Lenin enjoined us to strengthen with all our might the union of workers and peasants. We vow to thee, Comrade Lenin, that we will with honor fulfill this, thy commandment.
>
> Leaving us, Comrade Lenin enjoined us to strengthen and extend the union of republics. We vow to thee, Comrade Lenin, that we will fulfill with honor this, thy commandment. . . .

The speech has the full ring of mature Stalinism: massive, ritualistic, yet a parody, reeking with vulgarity, a gimcrack imitation of its ecclesiastical models. Stalin introduces to Soviet public life a solemn and shoddy unctuousness, inaugurating a house style that might have been designed by Uriah Heep and which endures to this day.

The speech established a celebration of Lenin that has properly been termed a cult. There is no need to explain this by the survival of some ineradicable trace of the Slav's religious feeling. It is simply an example of the kind of mass propaganda made possible by rapid developments in the media and an increase in literacy. The cult began with a series of decrees. The anniversary of Lenin's death was to be a day of mourning. Petrograd was rechristened Leningrad. Editions of Lenin's work would be published in a multitude of languages. Finally, in keeping with the increasingly pharaonic style of public life, rather than have Lenin cremated, as earlier leaders had been, his body was to be embalmed and placed on public display, to be visited by millions of pilgrims in lines stretching far into the radiant future. Initially the glass coffin was housed in a wooden mausoleum, which was replaced in 1929 by the familiar structure of red granite. Lenin became, at one and the same time, both a mummy and an icon. His portrait acquired that remarkable stylization and ubiquity which it still enjoys today, while his every word was accorded the state of Holy Writ.

Obviously the cult was not the work of one man; it appealed to the mass of the party and to its leaders. The notion of the sanctity and infallibility of the founder derived naturally from Bolshevik conceptions of ideological correctness. Nevertheless, Stalin played a major role in both its inauguration and its design, and the treatment it accorded Lenin must have appealed to his sense of humor. Despite his early loyalty to Lenin, for the last two or three years of his life Ilich had been an enemy, and Stalin loved to exploit his enemies, as he liked to ascribe his own crimes to his victims. As the only man with the power to destroy him, Lenin had become the greatest threat of all, and now Stalin took exceptional delight in putting his satisfactorily dead opponent to good use. Henceforth Stalin had him under his control and could distort his image to suit his own ends. Thus official history exaggerated his closeness to the dead leader with a breathtaking cynicism well illustrated by the photograph which shows Lenin and Stalin apparently sitting side by side in a garden. So ineptly has the picture been cobbled together out of separate originals that Stalin is obviously seated on a garden bench while Lenin is seated both on the bench and in a wicker chair! That the photographers could do no better reflects the lack of closeness between the two men. Bazhanov recalls Stalin's actual view of Lenin:

> I could easily see through the false and hypocritical celebration of Lenin "the genius" which the ruling group indulged in to turn Lenin into an icon and govern in his name as his loyal disciples and heirs. . . . I saw straight through Stalin swearing public oaths of loyalty to his genius mentor and actually sincerely hating Lenin because Lenin had become the major obstacle on his road to power. Stalin did not bother to pretend in front of his secretaries, and I could clearly tell from individual remarks, phrases, tone of voice what he really thought of Lenin.[7]

As for his reaction to Lenin's death, "Stalin was jubilant! I never saw him in a happier mood than during the days following Lenin's death. He was pacing up and down the [office] with satisfaction written all over his face."[8]

•   •   •

His self-appointed role as Lenin's disciple and eventual successor required Stalin to be the interpreter of his master's work. If he was to lead the Bolshevik party, he had to demonstrate that he, too, was a master of ideology. So important was the role of ideology that Stalin even engaged a private tutor. Jan Sten, a leading Marxist philosopher, gave him bi-weekly tutorials in which the unlikely couple devoted themselves to the study of Marx's *Das Kapital* and, stranger still, Hegel's *Phenomenology of Mind*. The notion of Stalin laboring over one of the densest works of Western philosophy has its preposterous side. Stalin's tutor spoke to a friend of "the difficulties he . . . was having due to his pupil's inability to master the material of Hegelian dialectics. Jan often dropped in to see me after a lesson with Stalin in a depressed and gloomy condition. The meetings with Stalin, the conversations with him on matters philosophical . . . opened his eyes more and more to Stalin's true nature, his striving for one-man rule, his crafty schemes and methods for putting them into effect."[9]

Interestingly, Sten focused on his pupil's anti-Semitism, fully expecting him in due course to mount trials of Jews that "will put the trials of Dreyfus and Beylis in the shade."[10] Stalin did not forget his old tutor in later years and had him shot on June 19, 1937.

Significantly Stalin's first major excursion into ideology, *Foundations of Leninism*, is dedicated to "his people," the young generation his machine had just brought into the party. It consisted of some lectures he gave at Sverdlov University, a college for Central Committee officials. They provided an overview of Lenin's ideas, characterizing Leninism as Marxism of the phase of imperialism and proletarian revolution. His account emphasized political strategy and tactics and the contrast between "objective" and "subjective." Although both this and a military strain are present in Lenin's thought, Stalin's account brought them to the foreground. He also asserted that the fundamental concern of Leninism was not the need to win peasants to the proletarian cause, but rather the creation and consolidation of the dictatorship of the proletariat. Any need to preserve peasant allegiance was a secondary consideration and one which Stalin would solve in a different way.

It might seem curious that it should have been Stalin, by no means the party's most distinguished thinker, who produced the first, indeed the definitive, study of "Leninism." In fact, it was a masterly piece of opportunism which exploited the vanity of finer minds. The other leaders would have considered it beneath them to study Lenin. They were "original thinkers" and did not need Lenin's help to study Marx. "I am not prepared to call myself a Leninist, I am a Marxist," observed Professor Ryazanov, Russia's leading authority on Marxism, whom Stalin subsequently shot. [11]

Bazhanov has maintained that Stalin, who was incapable of expressing any thought requiring more than five minutes' attention, made extensive use of ghostwriters and, indeed, ghost thinkers and that hardly anything he published was his own work. [12] Research assistants were certainly responsible for his familiarity with Lenin's every word and the elegance with which the material is deployed. However, the writing has a consistency that runs through every word he ever published. Judged by literary standards, Stalin was an awful writer. He has the clumsy style of an autodidact, full of repetitions; he once repeats the words *constitution* and *constitutional* fourteen times in 135 words. [13] He has difficulty in developing a chain of thought and is incapable of easy and elegant expression, finding writing about abstractions painfully difficult. He employs a thick, crude style, dotting every *i*, conducting his argument on a level so basic that its oversimplifications reduce fine gradations to a set of primary colors. The crudity and clumsiness are typical of someone writing in a foreign language, which is what Stalin was doing. He clearly had difficulties with written Russian and could not cope with two of its characteristics. Russian, unlike Georgian, has no present tense of the verb *to be*. "I am here" becomes "I here." The result, for someone not entirely at home in Russian, is an uneasy sense that there are gaps in one's prose that ought to be filled. Stalin fills them with a series of near synonyms for *is*, the one used most often being *yavlyaetsya* ("appears"), which make his writing feel overpadded. The second characteristic is the inability to control subordinate clauses, which creates prose of great clumsiness that has a pseudo-Germanic quality, shot through with cliché and ringing with the flat and refined tones of the bureaucrat. Beside the bloodier consequences of Stalinism one must count the severe damage which it has done to the Russian language. The authority of Stalin's example sufficed to impose the tones of low-grade officialese upon the Soviet stylistic register, contaminating the middle ground of day-to-day prose, which continues to make excessive use of circumlocutions and *yavlyaetsya* to this day.

Yet Stalin the writer was not unsuccessful. He found it hard to work with words but recognized his shortcomings. The one quality he sustains is a simplicity which makes the writing well suited to the intellectual and educational level of his readership. Russia, in those days, was not remarkable for the high degree of literacy among its population. In 1917 thirty percent of the people were fully literate, about the same level as France in 1789. The Bolsheviks had mounted a vigorous campaign against total illiteracy, with the result that Stalin's audience, the young men and women now joining the party, had acquired some ability to read and even to write, but not to think. The outcome of the increase in literacy was the creation of a half-educated generation with uncritical faith in the written word. Stalin's prose was well suited to such readers who were literalistic, dogmatic, inflexible, with high regard for "book learning," trained to accept the official word without question—in short, perfect targets for propaganda. Virtually the only words they would ever see would be those they read in government-produced newspapers. Stalin's prose reached and found these new readers with remarkable ease. As Milovan Djilas has put it:

> Stalin understood his Russians extremely well and made full use of their need to be given a simple, easily digestible fare. . . . He reduced Marxism and Leninism to the mental level of worthy but somewhat slow-witted bureaucrats who didn't have the time or curiosity to be bothered with the obscure dialectics of the founding fathers. . . . But false or not, Stalin satisfied a need, not only in the Soviet Party, but

throughout international Communism as well, where his dull, scholastic but easily assimilated compendium became very influential. Stalin's role as a theorist has been much underrated. The skill with which he linked Marxist-Leninist theory to power and turned it into a guide for action had great appeal and gave him enormous strength.[14]

The Triumvirate Destroyed

Stalin had reason to feel a growing confidence; it must have been clear that he was on his way to power. He had no illusions about the caliber of his rivals. Trotsky was a windbag, Zinoviev a weakling and Kamenev a moderate to be outmaneuvered at will. No member of the Politburo had the qualities necessary to squash him, and he could always win a voting majority by balancing his alliances. True, the Central Committee was not quite under his control, but it already contained his closest associates: Molotov, Voroshilov, Kirov, Mikoyan, Ordzhonikidze. As for the rank and file, this now underwent a transformation which put it firmly behind Stalin. To commemorate Lenin's death, the party admitted 200,000 new members. They joined at a time when party membership did rather more than satisfy a sense of political idealism. Not only did it protect one from the more extravagant attentions of the GPU, but it also put one on the first rung of that ladder of ever-increasing privilege that characterizes the Soviet system. As a party member you had *bron'*, or protection and priority, which made it incomparably harder for you to be kicked around. In times of unemployment party members were the last to be laid off, the first to be rehired. Once in the party you need not limit your ambitions.

Of course, the newcomers were carefully sifted by Stalin's machine since, as Molotov put it at the time, "The development of the Party in the future will undoubtedly be based on this Lenin enrollment."[1] He probably did not understand the full import of what he was saying, for the "Lenin enrollment" might better be termed the "Stalin generation," the rock upon which he would found his personal rule. The chief victims of the purges would be Old Bolsheviks and those joining the party before 1924. They would be replaced by these latecomers, ignorant, unsophisticated and avid readers of Stalin, who had never seen Lenin or, more important, Trotsky, in full cry. Their enrollment altered the nature of the party. By the end of 1925 it numbered slightly over 1 million members and candidates, only 8,500 of whom had joined before 1917. Now, more than ever, it was a party of the young, the naïve—and the ambitious. The expansion was accompanied by a modest purge. The machine got rid of anyone suspected of Trotskyite or Opposition sympathies, a process which had the effect of discouraging dissent.

However, Stalin was yet not in power, and for a moment it must have seemed that he never would be. Krupskaya had diligently followed Lenin's injunction not to open the envelope containing his will and codicil until after his death. She opened the envelope a day or so before the closed session of the Central Committee that always preceded a party congress and immediately sent the contents to Stalin. When he read the letter, he exploded. "Krupskaya is an old whore," he screamed,[2] and was scarcely more complimentary about Lenin, choosing to regard the posthumous bombshell as the work of a weakling, afraid to attack him in his own lifetime. "Couldn't even die like a *real* leader," he was heard to mutter.[3] In the climate of those or indeed later times, that remark was tantamount to an act of blasphemy.

Stalin was at risk once again. Zinoviev and Kamenev could easily have turned on him, and pursuant to the wishes of the recently canonized leader, the Central Committee could have voted him out of office. However, the other triumvirs decided to stand by their comrade. It is tempting to call them fools for doing so, but they still went in fear of Trotsky, while there was a second fear that had always haunted Soviet leaders: the fear of splitting the party and bringing it down, at which point no one's head would be safe, for it was recognized that given the chance, the rest of the population would tear them limb from limb.

The will still had to be presented to the Central Committee. As it was being read, Stalin stared out the window with the ostentatious composure of a man inwardly in torment—one of the rare occasions on which his feelings were too agitated to be disguised.[4] Zinoviev made a speech in support of Stalin which, as Bazhanov put it, "was difficult to match for sheer hypocrisy." While conceding the principle of Lenin's infallibility along with the sacred nature of his every word, he continued: "We are happy to say that on one point Lenin's apprehensions have not proved to be well founded. I refer to the point concerning the General Secretary."[5] He then spoke of Stalin's unblemished record, lack of rudeness and sterling qualities as a colleague, although as Radek observed to Bazhanov, "The proof Zinoviev offered of Stalin's unblemished record reminded one of . . . the case of the virgin who protested that yes, yes she did have an illegitimate baby, but it was exceedingly small."[6]

The Central Committee voted by thirty to ten to read the will to heads of delegations only and to withhold it from the congress at large. Trotsky remained silent throughout the discussion, although together with Radek, he did at least vote against the motion. There can be no doubt that he had missed yet another opportunity, allowing Stalin to escape again. As it happened, party delegates to the congress discovered the contents of the will soon enough; numerous copies were circulated and read before the document was banned, a curious fate for the last words of Lenin. Nevertheless, the congress was a triumph for Stalin. It was agreed to expand the Central Committee by adding thirteen full members and seventeen candidates, all Stalin's men, while Radek lost his place. In contrast, Stalin's associate Kaganovich joined the Central Committee, the Secretariat and the Orgburo, increasing Stalin's hold over the apparatus still further. The congress radiated docile unanimity, as if the various oppositions of recent months had never been. Once again unity was considered more important than the expression of dissent and the attendant danger of splitting the party.

Stalin was now in a stronger position than ever, and he knew it. For the first time he made a modest move against Zinoviev and Kamenev, criticizing both men for ideological error. In each case he took casual remarks from their original context to suggest that the views they had apparently professed were in some respects incorrect; once again Stalin's method of arguing was exasperatingly unfair. He also replaced the secretary of Kamenev's Moscow organization by one of his own men. In the meantime, the triumvirate was still fighting Trotsky, and it now attacked his position as commissar for war by appointing M. V. Frunze, one of his chief opponents, as his deputy. Frunze effectively took over the office, while Voroshilov replaced one of Trotsky's closest supporters as commander of the Moscow Military District, and a series of other promotions favored the old First Cavalry Army at the expense of Trotsky's adherents. By the summer of 1924 he had lost his hold over both the military and political sections of the army.[7]

Trotsky counterattacked by taking to the pen. In the autumn he published his *The Lessons of October*, which analyzed the nature of the Revolution, castigating Zinoviev, Kamenev and Stalin, suggesting that Lenin and Trotsky together were the architects of victory. There ensued a polemic conducted in the language of outrage, each triumvir in turn refuting and criticizing Trotsky and steadily reducing the part he had allegedly played in the Revolution. It was now that Stalin began revising history. He invented a "practical center for organizational direction of the insurrection" in which he had played a leading role and in which there was no room for Trotsky. He also unearthed some letters Trotsky had written in 1917 containing fierce denunciations of Lenin. The triumvirate laid on a well-orchestrated concert of protest at Trotsky's charges, which included howls of indignation from party cells at home and abroad. In Moscow there were even electric light displays advertising various "replies to Trotsky."[8]

Trotsky made no effective counter. As Paul Scheffer put it, "In publishing his *[Lessons of October]* he made the disastrous mistake of misjudging the effectiveness of a verbal attack upon an enemy equipped with all the elements of real power. Were he not a sick man he would know that after such an error he could win out only by fighting on in spite of his defeat, by coming out into the open with his own proposals. The only alternative would be a long long silence."[9]

Choosing neither combat nor silence, Trotsky wrote a letter to the Central Committee which reiterated his submission to party discipline—the reason for his refusal to defend himself against the monstrous charges laid against him—and offered to resign from his last effective post, the presidency of the Revolutionary War Council. Zinoviev wanted him expelled from the Politburo and even the party. But Stalin opposed any further sanction, and the Central Committee contented itself with his resignation. Stalin was *not* playing cat and mouse with Trotsky. About to engage in a delicate change of horses in midstream, he was content to let Zinoviev occupy a position of extreme hostility, while he could appear a moderating influence. Stalin always looked long and hard before committing himself to any extreme course of action. Now, in marked contrast with Kamenev and Zinoviev, he continued to refer punctiliously to "Comrade" Trotsky, radiating correctness and moderation and making his two colleagues seem "rude" in contrast.

It may have been because he was still uncertain of the army that Stalin continued to proceed with caution. Trotsky had, it is true, been replaced by Frunze, but it soon became clear that Frunze was his own man and therefore left much to be desired as head of the armed forces. An Old Bolshevik of Rumanian origins, he quickly showed too much independence both of Stalin and of the GPU. He could not have picked deadlier enemies. Discussing the promotions made by Frunze with his secretaries, Stalin declared himself unhappy with many of them and suggested that Frunze might be planning a coup.[10]

For some years Frunze had suffered from ulcers, but was making a steady recovery when, in October 1925, Stalin decided that the Politburo was neglecting his health and arranged for that body to order Frunze to have an operation. The order did not delight the commander, and the day before he went into hospital he wrote to his wife telling her that he felt perfectly well, that the operation seemed pointless and that he was puzzled by the doctors' recommendations.[11] He might have found the decision more sinister than puzzling had he known that the operation had been organized by Kanner, Stalin's secretary for dirty tricks, together with the Central Committee's surgeon, Pogosyants. Curiously Frunze proved allergic to the anesthetic, and thirty hours after the operation his heart failed. We do not know if he ever saw the note that Stalin and Mikoyan left for him at the hospital: "We wanted to visit you, but the doctor would not let us. . . . Don't worry old friend, we'll come again, we'll come again. . . . Koba."[12]

Frunze was given a splendid funeral, at which Stalin grieved conspicuously. Viewed in the light of subsequent events, his funeral oration appeared a blend of wishful thinking and black humor when he observed: "Perhaps this is exactly the way, so easy and so simple, that all old comrades should go to their graves."[13] Frunze's widow, for one, did not believe that her husband had died by accident and made her suspicions evident by committing suicide. A little later a Soviet writer of distinction, Boris Pilnyak, made Frunze's death the subject of a story, *The Tale of the Extinguished Moon*. It tells of a senior military commander made to submit to an unnecessary operation which proved fatal. Pilnyak seems to have got his information from Yakov Agranov, a senior member of the GPU—Stalin had both men shot in 1938—and further details from the irrepressible Radek, who observed that "all's fair when you're at war."[14] Frunze was succeeded by Voroshilov, Stalin's most loyal military supporter. If Stalin did indeed have Frunze killed, his plan would have required the approval of the Politburo, and doubtless he frightened his colleagues with warnings of a possible coup. At any rate, by the autumn of 1925 Stalin seems to have been powerful enough to have made those colleagues assent to the cold-blooded murder of a distinguished comrade.

With Trotsky no longer any kind of threat, the triumvirate came apart, as Stalin made an elegant move against both Zinoviev and Kamenev. It will be recalled that they controlled the party organizations of Leningrad and Moscow respectively. In the summer of 1924 the secretary of the Moscow committee, Zelensky, had been replaced by Uglanov. Zinoviev had pushed his candidacy against Stalin's man, Kaganovich. Stalin agreed, grudgingly, to Uglanov's appointment. He and Molotov then proceeded to win Uglanov over. Bazhanov recalls coming upon the three of them in private sessions, at which point he understood that Stalin was quietly taking over Moscow, working, to use a favorite expression of his for covert operations, *tikhoi sapoi*, ("by a silent sap"). Uglanov did a deal with Stalin, while ostensibly continuing to support Kamenev and Zinoviev. However, at the end of 1925 he transferred his allegiance and his whole delegation to Stalin, thereby destroying Kamenev's power base and openly opposing Zinoviev.

The fight was now on between Stalin and Zinoviev, and between Moscow and Leningrad, too. As yet Stalin had not been able to penetrate the Leningrad machine, and it is perhaps from now that we should date his hostility toward that city and its inhabitants. The northern capital represented openness, sophistication, contact with Western culture, while Moscow stood for those values of conservative and introverted old Muscovy with which Stalin aligned himself. As he moved against Zinoviev and Kamenev, Stalin, who had not yet packed the Politburo and still had to work for a majority, started a tentative new alliance with Nikolai Bukharin. Bukharin, the thinking man's Bolshevik, had the support of the party's younger intellectuals, notably those in the Institute of Red Professors, a Bolshevik establishment for the training of university teachers. He also had strong ties with the Moscow organization, and this was an additional reason for Stalin to move closer to him in the summer of 1925. Having previously believed that socialism must be brought about by radical and coercive methods, Bukharin had moved to the right on the issues of industry, agriculture and the role of state control. He believed in the NEP and felt that the way to socialism lay through a prosperous peasantry. Many of his colleagues found his view's ideologically unsound, conducive to the reemergence of capitalism and all the moral corruption which that involved. Even his new ally Stalin felt Bukharin had gone too far when, in 1925, he echoed Guizot's famous injunction to the French voters who had just brought him to power, by telling the Soviet peasantry to "Get rich."

Stalin was not the only one to regroup. The year 1925 saw a futile attempt to form an anti-Stalin opposition, consisting of Zinoviev, Ka-

menev, Krupskaya and Sokolnikov, commissar for finance and a firm
believer in the NEP, a mixed economy and a prosperous peasantry.
They held widely differing views on matters of policy; Krupskaya, for
example, took strong exception to recent manifestations of the propeas-
ant policy, maintaining the orthodox Leninist view of peasants as class
enemies.[15] Kamenev and Zinoviev, who for years had been closer to
Sokolnikov than to Krupskaya in this respect, were beginning to incline
in her direction—in other words, to the "left," the faction favoring
rapid industrialization at the peasants' expense and the elimination of a
market economy. Krupskaya also tried to recruit G. P. Petrovsky, president of the Ukrainian Central Committee, but he refused to move
against Stalin. By some curious chance he survived him. Although Petrovsky would later regret his failure to oppose the dictator: "In view of
what we knew at that time, in 1925, I cannot condemn myself."[16]

There is evidence of a plan to replace Stalin with Dzerzhinsky as
general secretary, but it petered out, one reason for the failure of the
opposition being that nothing united it except dislike, and perhaps by
now fear, of Stalin.[17] According to Trotsky at least, the fear was there all
right. Kamenev allegedly warned him that Stalin was not at all concerned with countering his opponents' arguments, preferring to "liquidate you without being punished for it." Both Zinoviev and Kamenev
had prepared documents stating that should they die unexpectedly, it
would be Stalin's work.[18] In any event, neither man died unexpectedly,
and their documents were no help at all.

•   •   •

The opposition was to make its stand at the Fourteenth Party Congress, which had already been postponed several times. The delay was
Stalin's doing, and he had used it to win over waverers.[19] The congress
was finally scheduled to assemble in December, and Zinoviev lost the
first battle when the Politburo decided that Stalin would make the initial
major speech. Zinoviev insisted on referring the issue to the Central
Committee, and there he lost the second battle. Stalin's groundwork
had paid off, and the committee endorsed the decision. At the congress
Zinoviev and Kamenev expected to have the support of Leningrad,
Moscow and possibly the Ukraine, all other organizations being in the
hands of Stalin. The Ukraine failed them, and Moscow deserted Kamenev, leaving the Leningrad organization as the sole remaining, and
inadequate, bastion of opposition. Political rivalries had hitherto been
expressed obliquely, in squabbles about the proper interpretation of the

recent past or as doctrinal differences on issues such as the desirability of supporting the peasant. Although this congress had its share of ideological squabble, it differed from past assemblies in two respects. For the first time both Zinoviev and Kamenev made personal attacks upon Stalin, while Kamenev maintained that the country was on the brink of a dictatorship. "We are against creating the theory of a leader; we are against making a leader. We are against having the Secretariat combine both politics and organization. . . . We cannot regard as normal . . . a situation in which the Secretariat . . . decides policy in advance. . . . I have become convinced that Comrade Stalin cannot perform the function of uniting the Bolshevik general staff." [20]

The word Kamenev used for leader, *vozhd'*, has all the charismatic connotations of *Duce* or Führer, and was an epithet soon to be reserved for Stalin alone.

The Fourteenth Congress also differed from earlier ones by virtue of its brutality. The reasoned arguments of the opposition were countered with jeers, catcalls and insults. Stalin's delegates simply shouted the speakers down. For the first time the techniques the young Stalin had developed in Georgia, seeking victory through packed audiences, claques and rigged votes, had become the political house style of the nation. That the style should have been imposed so successfully was a measure of Stalin's control over his party and of his understanding of its nature. The new Bolshevik was neither a talmudic intellectual of the old type or a Petersburg worker with decades of political experience. The newcomers had more ambition than political sophistication—or idealism for that matter (the idealists had supplied the cannon fodder of the civil war and paid a commensurate price). The new men would rather shout an opponent down than argue with him, just as Lenin had once shouted down the Marxist "deviationists" Avenarius and Mach.

Stalin did not win over his new supporters simply by appealing to the thug in them. He revealed a curious kind of charisma—not that of the leader-prophet with fiery eyes and an inspirational appeal but that of the holder of high office who did not allow his importance to go to his head and who still had time for little people. By presenting himself as a simple man, Stalin won considerable popularity among newcomers made insecure by the spectacle of intellectual, and frequently Jewish, fireworks. For example, it was at this congress that Nikita Khrushchev first saw Stalin, who had agreed to pose in a group photograph. The Kremlin photographer, Petrov, was making a fuss about arranging the group when Stalin was heard to observe, "Comrade Petrov loves to order

people around. But that's forbidden here now. No one can order anyone else around again."[21] News of such behavior travels fast and does
wonders for the reputation of a bigwig. Stalin knew how to present himself as a humble man, a pipe-smoking embodiment of common sense.
He had the self-control never to allow his craving for power and the arid
hatred of potential rivals to be glimpsed in public.

In the meantime, Stalin answered Kamenev's charge of "leaderism"
in a speech of considerable interest to students of the role of hypocrisy
in public life. He maintained that it was Zinoviev who was the guilty
party since he sought to undermine the principle of collective leadership. How could a party be led without such stalwarts as Rykov,
Tomsky and Bukharin? It was not possible to lead it other than collectively.

The opposition was outvoted at the congress, and Stalin tightened his
grip. Kamenev was reduced to a candidate member of the Politburo,
which was increased to nine full members with the addition of Molotov,
Kalinin and Voroshilov, giving Stalin a guaranteed majority, while Uglanov got his reward for delivering Moscow by becoming a candidate
member. The Central Committee was further expanded and packed
with more of Stalin's men, and a final mopping-up operation was completed when Stalin sent a team to Leningrad to purge the local organization of Zinoviev's supporters; a task they accomplished with remarkable
ease. Henceforward the organization was to be headed by Stalin's loyal
and long-standing associate S. M. Kirov.

The Fourteenth Congress marks the moment when Stalin gained
complete control over the party's upper echelons, the Central Committee and the Politburo. It also marks the effective end of politics within
the party. Henceforth all appointments and promotions would be controlled by Stalin's machine, and no one was permitted to dissent from
his policies; all that was required of party members was an unquestioning support of the "General Line."

CHAPTER TWENTY-TWO

The Beginnings of Stalinism

Q. Is socialism in one country possible?
A. Yes.
Q. Is life in such a country possible?
A. No.
      —SOVIET ANECDOTE

The mid-1920s were a time of disagreement within the party, focused largely upon economic issues and conducted according to principles derived from ideology and myth. Positions ranged from unqualified support for the NEP to belief in superindustrialization, a process which, it was felt, for reasons which have more to do with mythology than economics, could be achieved only "at the expense" of the peasants. Essentially the issue lay between favoring agriculture and developing a consumer economy which would produce goods that the peasants might actually want to buy and a coercive policy toward the peasants, which would take no account of the marketplace and favor the development of heavy industry. The arguments of the superindustrializers are derived from a concept of Marx's that has borne strange fruit. The term *primitive accumulation* had been coined by Marx to describe the first phase in the growth of capitalism, a time when industry was not yet sufficiently developed to expand from its own resources. At this stage capitalism relied upon the ruthless exploitation of the yeoman peasantry, piracy and the rape of its colonies to develop its industries to the point at which they became self-financing. According to Marx's predictions, a socialist revolution could occur only after the stage of mature capitalism, the fruits and profits of which would be employed to build communism. But the fruits had been rare enough in prerevolutionary Russia, when industry was poised on the brink of rapid state-directed expansion. After six years of war and revolution the fruits were non-existent. Hence, Trotsky suggested, the new industrial society would require, for its development, a phase of "primitive socialist accumulation." The socialist state must regard its peasant population as a kind of colony within, which would have to be exploited to bring industrialization about. The concept was rejected by Bukharin and, for the time being, by Stalin. It was much favored by the left wing of the party, which considered an independent peasantry an alien element because unlike industrial workers, peasants were able to own their own means of production and also because both Marx and, more important, Lenin had described them as the enemy.

Primitive socialist accumulation boils down to the principle that the well-being of classes and individuals is subordinate to the economic interests of the state; development of those interests is to be funded by deprivation to be endured by the masses. It can be seen that the Soviet economy has been run according to the principle of primitive socialist accumulation for more than half a century; there is no need to defer to the economic interests of dispersed individuals in societies in which such individuals do not have an effective vote.

In the earlier phases of the debate Stalin appeared to be a moderate trimming cautiously between right and left. As Zinoviev and Kamenev inclined toward coercive methods of industrialization in 1924 and 1925, Stalin moved closer to Bukharin. It has been argued that Stalin's shifts in attitude over these years were dictated not by political opportunism alone but by a changing view of Soviet agricultural resources.[1] However, at the risk of oversimplifying, everything we know of Stalin suggests that he was more interested in power than in policies and would never hesitate to adopt a line that might "subjectively" be incorrect if its "objective" consequence were to strengthen his own position.

Yet it would be wrong to say that Stalin had no long-term political strategy, no conception of the direction that the Soviet Union ought to take. Anything but a mere opportunist, he had a vision of the Soviet state, not only one which he would succeed in realizing but also one which endured long after his own death, serving to determine the shape of the country as we know it. That in itself is a remarkable achievement, albeit a costly one. Although it would take years to bring it about, its first and in some ways most important element was formulated by Stalin in the mid-1920s and constituted his sole original contribution to the canon of Bolshevik ideology.

Marx had expected socialism, the first phase of communism, to arrive hard on the heels of revolution. It was a view modified by Lenin, who stated that socialism, by which he meant an economically and culturally advanced society with machine technology and an educated populace participating actively in the process of government, would have to be "built" and that its construction would be a lengthy process.[2] According to Lenin, the transformation could never occur in Russia alone; it would require the "most active cooperation of at least several advanced countries among which we certainly cannot classify Russia."[3] Thus, for the orthodox Marxist-Leninist, the Russian Revolution was part of a wider movement; it could not stand alone. However, by the end of 1925 the prospects for further revolution were poor. Internationalists such as Trotsky, Radek and Zinoviev had worked for a revolution in Germany, in the wake of the French occupation of the Ruhr and the ensuing inflation, but this had come to nothing. It was clear, at least to Stalin and the less doctrinaire leaders, that whatever Marx might have prophesied, Russia would have to pursue its revolution alone. In the latter months of 1924, as part of his campaign against Trotsky, Stalin and his research assistants made an exquisitely ingenious use of Lenin's writings to turn ideology on its head. They came up with some lines Lenin had written in 1915 which maintained that in view of the unequal development of capitalism in various lands, revolution, too, might develop unequally and break out in a single country. Stalin used this passage to justify his own spectacular theory "Socialism in one country," which maintained that although the cooperation of the pro-letariat of several countries was necessary to guard against the restoration of a bourgeois order, it was possible to build *socialism in one country alone*. The qualification is important, for it develops the Bolshevik myth of capitalist encirclement. Russia, *if left in peace*, could complete its revolution and build socialism in isolation. But it depended for its security upon world revolution, for this alone could guarantee her the peace it needed to complete the process.

To trained Marxists, Stalin's "theory" appeared hilarious. Radek collapsed with laughter when he heard the formulation, in which he saw further evidence of the general secretary's stupidity. Why, he wondered, did Stalin restrict himself to socialism in one country? What was wrong with socialism in one district or even in one street?[4] In the meantime, Stalin used his formula to attack both Trotsky and Zinoviev, who were Jews, rootless cosmopolitans and internationalists. He skillfully misrepresented their view that the Russian Revolution must necessarily be succeeded by others to suggest that they lacked patriotism. For all his lack of Marxist orthodoxy, Stalin knew just what he was doing. The notion of socialism in one country appealed to those millions who were unfamiliar with the philosophy of Karl Marx, mistrustful of Jews and foreigners and deeply imbued with that Great Russian chauvinism which Lenin used to castigate. To many ignorant enthusiasts of the age Trotsky's internationalism was dismaying, while Stalin brought reassurance.

The new doctrine also suggested that Lenin's cautious deference to market forces and the peasantry was unnecessary, and it came to be regarded as the negation of the NEP. Stalin thereby appealed to Bolshevik idealists who considered that policy to have been an unholy compromise with the spirit of capitalism and who still looked back nostalgically to the days of war communism. There was still, in the mid-twenties, a considerable fund of enthusiasm and revolutionary idealism both in the party and among the young. Stalin's doctrine appealed to these idealists, who wanted to industrialize rapidly and at all costs and who wanted to build their socialism now. Critics of the policy, who preached caution and gradualism, were considered negative skeptics, if not worse. At a stroke and perhaps to his surprise, Stalin had created a rallying point for idealists. As the future General Grigorenko wrote:

> I read *Lessons of October* . . . and felt lost. I despaired. Was Trotsky really correct? Were we really unable to create a socialist society? Would we really perish without world revolution? I did not want to live, did not want to think, I was not the kind of person to wait for others to help me. I had to act. [He then read Stalin's refutation of Trotsky.] With his characteristic simplicity . . . he refuted Trotsky's arguments point by point. It appeared that socialism in one country could not only be built but be completed. The delay in world revolution would not hold us back. . . . From then on I carried Stalin's article wherever I went, and kept explaining its significance to my friends. It was my weapon in my struggle against Trotsky.[5]

Stalin recognized that the notion of Russian socialism was a heady one and a perfect stick with which to belabor Trotsky. More important, it was a notion that he believed in. It appealed to his chauvinism and his isolationist conception of the state, echoing his mistrust of the west-ward-looking Leningrad. According to his conception, Russia would go it alone, while doing everything in its power to secure its frontiers by revolution or conquest, in order to preserve itself from capitalist inter-ference. It is no coincidence that, at the time that Stalin was developing his theory, he should have defined his country's role in the next Euro-pean war, which he already considered inevitable. Russia could not stand idly by; it would be obliged to involve itself, but it would ensure that it was the last nation to do so.[6] In other words, as it would attempt to do in the Second World War, it should wait for the opposing sides to fight each other to a standstill before taking a hand. The diplomats and politicians who were horrified and surprised by the Hitler-Stalin pact of 1939, as they had earlier been by the discovery of Hitler's aggressive intentions as outlined in *Mein Kampf*, had once again failed to do their homework.

• • •

Kamenev did not have to be clairvoyant to warn his party of the dangers of "leaderism" in December 1925. It soon grew clear that a leader was precisely what Stalin was. By the spring of 1926 we find diplomatic dispatches describing him as the most powerful man in the land, effectively in charge of the government, although it was conceded that he still had rivals. He had himself informally recognized the princi-ple of dictatorship, thereby revealing a remarkable lucidity of vision. At a dinner to celebrate Kirov's take-over of Leningrad there was a discus-sion about collective leadership, which was felt to be a good thing. Stalin did not agree. According to one of those present he observed: "Do not forget we are living in Russia, the land of the tsars. The Russians like to have one man standing at the head of the state. Of course . . . this man should carry out the will of the collective."[7] In so many words Stalin had recognized that the emotional needs of the Russian people could be met only by one-man rule.

We have seen that Russia's "tsar in waiting" was a master of the com-mon touch. Indeed, he radiated it: short, a little thickset, his face heavily pitted with smallpox, many of his teeth already reduced to rotten stumps. (We cannot say whether it was from ordinary phobia or a fear of medical murder, but Stalin would never consent to be treated by a den-tist.) Along with his unprepossessing appearance went behavior which suggested that Stalin could take his common touch a little far. The wife of the Finnish Communist leader Otto Kuusinen recalled an encounter with Stalin on a holiday by the Black Sea. She had met him before and found him impressive, admiring the terse and businesslike way in which he handled meetings. Her view of him changed considerably after the day she and her husband spent aboard his small and very ordinary motorboat:

> He received us cordially in a cabin and said to a sailor: "I shall serve these guests myself." There was fruit on the table and a lot of wine and champagne bottles. Stalin filled our glasses and put a record on the gramophone: it was the delightful Georgian folk-song *Suliko*. [The corniest and most hackneyed of all Georgian songs, it can be heard to this day being chanted by drunken Georgians and their friends in every restaurant and café in Tiflis.] I am afraid it rather lost its charm as he played it over and over again. He also drank glass after glass of wine, and after a while he began to dance. It was a gruesome sight and the more he drank the more fearful he looked. The whole performance seemed like a bad dream. He bellowed with laughter, staggering and stamping around the cabin completely out of time with the music. The general impression was not only coarse and vulgar but so bizarre that it seemed a kind of sinister threat. The most frightening thing of all was that despite his drunkenness *he still seemed sober enough to observe my reactions to his conduct*[8] [author's italics].

Stalin was probably trying to humiliate her. He disliked women, especially the priggish "herrings with ideas" to be found among the Bolshevik leadership, and enjoyed treating them with less respect than they felt they deserved. On the same trip he misbehaved at a dinner in Ordzhonikidze's apartment, singing obscene Georgian songs in the presence of Bolshevik ladies known to be "highly moral women." He also visited his mother and abused her in public, referring to her as "you old whore."[9]

Stalin's rude and bullying personality matched the mood of the land. As a Swedish diplomat reported from Leningrad, the entire country seemed haunted by fear, notably fear of the GPU, which kept bringing to light "real or imaginary" conspiracies.[10] Those historians who would maintain that terror only began in the 1930s and seek to present the twenties in a rosier light are victims of their own wishful thinking. Hand in glove with fear went lawlessness. The sad, run-down cities were terrorized by crime and street violence, perhaps the greatest menace being the *besprizornye* ("unsupervised")—gangs of homeless children who depended upon their wits for survival and who displayed all the pitiless capacity for violence of the young. They were regularly rounded up by the GPU, who would shoot some out of hand and send others to institutions. These contained a high percentage of alcoholics and cocaine users among their inmates, some of whom were doing up to five grams a day, supporting their habits by begging, stealing and murdering.[11]

Glimpses of street life in the mid-twenties, later considered a period of relative prosperity, give some indication of the atmosphere of the age:

> A vagrant boy snatched a loaf of bread from a woman's hands, and took to his heels. The woman raised a hue and cry; the boy was tripped, fell bruised and bleeding to the cobbles, and was kicked in the spine and ribs by the woman who had joined the chase. Some student in the crowd ultimately felled the woman with a heavy blow to her face. But this is not all. Prone on the ground, bleeding and beaten, smarting under his injuries, and protecting himself as best he could, the boy continued to tear the loaf with hungry teeth, and simply bolted the dirty and blood-stained chunks of bread. He finished the loaf on the way to the police-station.[12]

> The calm of the workers' city of Leningrad was suddenly broken. . . . About fifteen young workers had raped an unfortunate girl . . . on a piece of waste ground. . . . The Party had an epidemic of collective rapes to investigate. . . . Books like those of Alexandra Kollontai propagated an over-simplified theory of free love; an infantile variety of materialism reduced "sexual need" to its strictly animal connotations. "You make love as you drink a glass of water, to relieve yourself."
>
> The accused fifteen had the faces of gutter-kids . . . with primitive brutality as their salient feature. They offered confessions and denounced one another with no inhibitions about going into details. . . . What was more natural than sex on waste sites? And what if she disliked mating with four, five or six, she would have got just as pregnant and diseased if it had been only one. And if she did mind, probably it was because she had "prejudices."[13]

After talking of the "new culture" and "our wonderful Soviet morals," the magistrate condemned five of the rapists to death. Since rape was not a capital offense, he convicted them of banditry instead.

A confidential report by an American on the state of the cities in 1926 suggested that the Soviet government was practically on its knees, with rising unemployment and factories closing down or laying men off daily. The British consul observed that although the report was exaggerated, a radical change of some kind was certainly necessary.[14]

It is not easy to get a clear picture of the Soviet economy at any time, partly because the statistics are unreliable, partly because those who have written on the subject in the greatest detail often have axes to grind. It is, above all, agriculture that presents a confusing series of problems, some real, others false. Essentially crops were produced by peasant smallholders using old-fashioned methods. However, this was not to say that they were incapable of producing enough to feed the nation. Agriculture did not have to undergo massive modernization to achieve that goal. However, it was certainly difficult to persuade smallholders to grow nonedible cash crops such as flax and hemp or even, for that matter, sugar-beet. Before the Revolution these had been produced by the large agricultural estates. The real problem facing Soviet planners was how to induce peasants to market their surplus, while maintaining control over agricultural prices and in the absence of anything that the peasants might wish to purchase. The planners seem to have found the problem insoluble.

The genuine problems posed by agriculture were overlaid by demonology. This put peasants into three categories, good, neutral and bad: the *bednyak*, or poor peasant; the *serednyak*, or middle peasant; and the *kulak*, or rich peasant, literally "fist," respectively. According to this ideologue's view of rural life, the landowning *kulak* exploited the labor of the landless *bednyak* while the *serednyak* had just enough land to work himself and thus exploited no one. It was ideologically unacceptable to encourage the successful farmer because he was evil, yet the need to grow as much food as efficiently as possible did not appear to leave an alternative. It was no doubt the party's hostility to peasants in general, and successful ones in particular, that had brought forth the theory of primitive socialist accumulation, with its assumption that industrialization could take place only at the peasants' expense. The supposition that industrialization required an assault upon successful farmers was an important part of that policy's emotional appeal. Encouragement of the *kulak*, which category eventually came to include any peasant with two or more animals, came to be thought of as rejection of industrialization and of yet another ideological sacred cow, the industrial plan.

For believers, the words *plan* and *planned economy* had a significance bordering upon the magical. One of the chief arguments against capitalism was that since it was founded upon a market economy and the principles of laissez-faire, it made for a wasteful and uncoordinated use of economic resources. Socialism would create a rational economy that would inevitably be more efficient. Encouraging the smallholder, that most inefficient of all forms of private enterprise, was the antithesis of socialist economic ambition. Consequently the combination of a peasant-based agriculture and industrial planning came to be considered incompatible. As was the case with socialism in one country, the primitive patterns of Bolshevik demonology oversimplified and distorted complex economic issues, reducing them to the stark alternatives of "either/or."

Stalin was in no hurry to commit himself on the issue since Zinoviev and Kamenev were growing increasingly hostile toward the smallholder. Admittedly there is an *Alice*-like quality about many aspects of Soviet history, but it is still surprising to find Zinoviev, in 1925, wondering out loud whether a marked economic revival in the agricultural sector should be viewed "positively or negatively."[15] Stalin, without sympathizing with Zinoviev, had wisely refrained from joining Bukharin in his injunction to the smallholders to enrich themselves. However, at the congress of 1925 he had, in a curious form of words, charged the opposition with demanding "the blood of Bukharin"—it had done nothing of the sort—and observed that "we shall not give you that blood."[16] His own view of agriculture was naive enough to have him talk of "isolating the *kulaks* and speculators and separating the toiling peasants from them,"[17] thereby supposing divisions in village life that did not exist and presuming that prosperous peasants sat back and watched the hired hands work their fields for them. It was also in 1925 that he began to imply that peasants were politically unreliable. While conceding that they were allies, he continued: "This ally, as you know, is not very firm; the peasantry is not such a dependable ally as the proletariat of capitalistically developed countries."[18]

Unlike Bukharin, Stalin was not immediately concerned by issues of economic prosperity. Economic hardship might be the price that others would have to pay if the Bolsheviks were to consolidate their power. Since they stood to gain so little from the regime, Stalin rightly perceived the peasants as *politically* unreliable and hence as a potential threat. This would remain the principal issue for Stalin; he was not fond of placing his trust in dubious allies. However, he could always separate strategy from tactics. For the time being he needed Bukharin to undercut Zinoviev, Kamenev and the archsuperindustrializer Trotsky. For the time being the peasants could wait.

Trotsky Leaves the Stage

Trotsky failed to understand that the issue of the struggle was
determined not by the availability of arguments, but by the
control and manipulation of the levers of power.

—E. H. Carr

In 1926 Stalin consolidated his victories over Zinoviev, Kamenev and,
later in the year, Trotsky—the Jewish members of the Politburo. Bazhanov subsequently expressed the view that this marked a major shift
in the leadership. The prerevolutionary party had had a strong Jewish
element at every level. By the mid-1920s this was no longer the case; by
the end of 1926 the number of Jews on the Central Committee could be
counted on one's fingers. Although the shift derived in part from Stalin's own anti-Semitism, the new orientation was by no means unwelcome. Curiously, the popular interpretation of the Kremlin power
struggle was close to the truth. The Smolensk Archives give the following peasant's-eye view of the Politburo in 1926: "Our good master
Vladimir Ilich had only just passed away when our Commissars began
to fight among themselves, and all this is due to the fact that the Jews
became very numerous, and our Russians do not let them have their
way, but there is nobody to suppress them and each one considers himself more intelligent than the others."[1] Another peasant commented
bitterly: "Formerly there was one tsar, now there are many, every Communist is a tsar."[2]

After Zinoviev and Kamenev had lost Leningrad and Moscow, they at last turned to Trotsky to form a "united opposition," the only source of unity being their common enemy, Stalin. An attempt was made to involve the army. Voroshilov's deputy, Lashevich, was a Zinoviev man who tried to win support for the new bloc among the armed forces, and Stalin took this as a pretext for his dismissal. Thus the most important "achievement" of the new opposition was to consolidate Stalin's hold over the Red Army since Lashevich's departure left Voroshilov firmly in the saddle.

In October members of the opposition signed a document of unconditional surrender, agreeing to submit to party discipline on every issue and repudiating their supporters. They could scarcely have done otherwise since they had no effective following at the higher levels of the party pyramid and were unable or unwilling to take the fight elsewhere, a course that might split the party—or earn them GPU bullets to the backs of their necks. Bukharin had played an important part in the opposition's defeat, supplying Stalin with appropriate ideological ammunition and making a speech at the Fifteenth Congress which attacked them with a cynical and mocking coarseness that Stalin himself would have been proud of. The opposition was permitted to speak at the Congress and once more attempted to fight naked power with hot air. Zinoviev devoted ninety minutes to an oratorical assault upon the notion of socialism in one country. Trotsky asked for two hours' speaking time and, on being accorded one hour, expressed indignant surprise when he was silenced after it had expired. However, oratory availed nothing. By the end of October 1926, accused of having sought to disrupt the unity of the party, they all had lost their places on both the Politburo and the Central Committee. Zinoviev was replaced by another of Stalin's men, Jan Rudzutak, while Ordzhonikidze, Andreev, Kirov and Mikoyan, all important cogs in the Stalin machine, became candidate members. Stalin now had a working majority within the Politburo and no longer required the support of Bukharin, who had just maneuvered himself out of power.

Stalin immediately started to distance himself from Bukharin's position on economic issues and the construction of socialism. He made a speech condemning the notion of primitive accumulation, as Bukharin did, but whereas the latter had maintained that it would take generations to build socialism, Stalin suggested that the process could be accelerated; in other words "he was envisaging . . . a revolutionary rather than an evolutionary approach to the problem."[3] It was a vital shift of emphasis and one with great political appeal.

Stalin recognized that he could consolidate his position by tapping the revolutionary idealism and energy that were still to be found within the party. He also understood how suspect the NEP appeared to the idealists, whose simplistic sense of political good and evil considered the policy a compromise with the devil. It was here that Stalin's rank-and-file support would lie. Many young party members looked on Stalin as a new man, as their representative. Recalling his own attitude at the time, Khrushchev wrote: "It should not be overlooked that Stalin's name had not been widely known among the masses in the first years of the Revolution. He had come a long way in a short time, and he had brought our Party and our people with him."[4] A British diplomat went further, expressing the view that Stalin had become the prisoner of those young adherents he had recently brought into the party.[5] It is certainly an exaggeration to describe Stalin as the prisoner of the Lenin enrollment, but there can be no doubt that he was aware that his supporters disliked the moderation of Bukharin and favored radical rather than gradualist solutions.

Stalin considered 1927 the year in which he became leader of the party. Henceforward, as he remarked to an intimate, who subsequently repeated his words to a cellmate in the Lubyanka, the leadership could be changed only by force of arms.[6] The Politburo had become Stalin's rubber stamp, a situation which had an interesting reflection in his personal secretariat. It underwent a major expansion, its form being altered to correspond to the structure of the people's commissariats, while a new apparatus which processed all the administrative work of the Central Committee was created. This reflected a shift in real power away from the party's political appointees in the Central Committee and the Politburo toward Stalin's personal administration, which had become something rather more than a kitchen cabinet of the kind associated with Prime Minister Wilson or President Nixon:

> What makes the Stalin variant something special is . . . the
> consideration that his staff . . . enjoyed a quite extraordinary
> superiority in the acquisition of information, compared to other Soviet
> authorities, by means of water-tight control of all lines of
> communication. Stalin's "cabinet" was part of the Party's secret
> department, but from 1927 or earlier it also contained a so-called
> "special sector" that . . . took care of personnel and . . . security
> questions. [It] could . . . accumulate information which . . . not even
> other leading Bolsheviks were entitled to see. It could . . . make direct

contact with the Secret Police, and . . . ensure that Stalin did not become dependent on [them]. In other words, it had all the prerequisites to function as the innermost core of Stalin's own chancellery.[7]

This was the engine of Stalin's personal machine. It was manned by young administrators such as Tovstukha, Mekhlis, Kanner and Poskrebyshev. Without personal ambition, security of tenure or power, they wielded great authority in Stalin's name and possessed considerable influence through their control of access to their master, functioning, in this respect, very like White House aides. They staffed the perfect apparatus for the exercise of a highly centralized, indeed personal form of power. Not only did Stalin's machine control all appointments of significance throughout the land, but it also acted, albeit in a staff rather than a line capacity, as a government within government, able to short-circuit the official chain of command at any level, rendering impossible the formation of those independent fiefs and satrapies that had characterized the regime in its earlier years.

Throughout 1927 Stalin maintained pressure upon the united opposition. Pressure alternated between carrot and stick, advancement or loss of party card. In the meantime, he also played on the political helplessness of the opposition leaders. He tantalized them with promises that the party would forgive and forget if only they would repudiate past objections and submit to party discipline; when they complied, he would complain that they had not gone far enough. Zinoviev in particular allowed himself to be carried away by wishful thinking and agreed to all of Stalin's suggestions, only to be accused of "grave disloyalty" when conceding that he had opposed Stalin's policies in the past. In August 1927, together with Trotsky, he produced a document which admitted that they had violated party discipline and attempted to divide the party. Stalin resisted the Central Committee's calls to have them deprived of their party cards. Exercising his celebrated moderation, he insisted that the committee content itself with the delivery of a severe reprimand. Trotsky, in the meantime, continued to speak against Stalin, while supporters of the opposition, which had been thoroughly infiltrated by the *agents provocateurs* of the GPU, now became liable to arrest for printing or circulating political material. Yet weak though their position may have been at the higher levels of the party, they enjoyed support elsewhere, notably in Zinoviev's old stronghold, Leningrad.

At that city's October celebration of the anniversary of the Revolution, Trotsky, Radek and other members of the opposition occupied a viewing stand next to Stalin's. As the parade filed past, they were greeted with shouts of "Long live the opposition," "Down with Stalin," "Long live Trotsky." According to one GPU man, mounted police with sabers drawn rode in to keep the procession moving. The demonstrators, mostly factory workers, yelled, "Red police out," and pulled the riders down. They were eventually dispersed by a company of GPU infantry. The author comments naïvely: "And that is free proletarian Russia for you."[8]

Yet whatever support it may have enjoyed on the streets, within the party the opposition was powerless. At a meeting to determine the agenda for the next congress, Trotsky made another speech, attacking official history's distortions of his role in the Revolution. He backed his words up with documents showing that he had enjoyed the support of Lenin, and then he mentioned the unmentionable. Trotsky actually described Lenin's break with Stalin and the contents of his will. But by now it was much too late. Trotsky's appeal was directed at an unreconstructed audience of Stalin's appointees. Nevertheless, it must be conceded that Stalin's riposte was magnificent. Of course, he had had a long time to prepare himself for a revelation that he must have known to be inevitable, yet one may still admire the broadside which blew Trotsky out of the water.

Instead of speaking in the first-person singular, he referred to himself throughout as "Stalin." He began by disparaging Trotsky's attack as a "personal factor," phrasing his speech in a way that made it clear that he was above such spiteful infighting. He went on to observe, quoting him chapter and verse, that Trotsky had been more abusive still of Lenin. Stalin then had the supreme self-confidence, or gall, to read out Lenin's criticisms verbatim, conceding that it was perfectly true that he was rude "Toward those who rudely and treacherously seek to wreck and divide the Party. Stalin has never made a secret of this. It may be that such persons should be treated gently, but not by Stalin." He then told his audience that he had offered his resignation in response to the will, but that Trotsky, Kamenev and Zinoviev had "*obliged* Stalin to remain at his post" and that Stalin was not the sort to run away. Once again he had proved himself the master of the "unfair" argument. Besides, the atmosphere of the meeting did not favor rational debate, for along with verbal abuse and catcalls, objects, ranging from a glass of water to a heavy volume of statistics, were hurled at Trotsky's head, providing a clear indication that he would get little support from the floor of the house. The meeting had a curious aftermath. The 1,669 delegates present were each given a copy of Lenin's will, and all those who failed to destroy theirs in time were eventually arrested, and for the most part shot, for being in possession of a "counter-revolutionary document, the so-called Testament of Lenin."[9]

Overencouraged by his October reception in Leningrad, Trotsky attempted a similar appeal in Moscow the following month, on the tenth anniversary of the Revolution. But this proved too late by years. The police were ready and waiting for those isolated supporters of the opposition who appeared on the streets with their curiously wordy banners: "Against opportunism, against a split, for the unity of Lenin's party"; "Fulfill the Testament of Lenin. Let's turn our fire to the right, against *kulaks*, nepmen and bureaucrats." (The slogans sound just as pompous and labored in the original.) The police quickly bustled the demonstrators away. Trotsky and some friends then drove around Moscow, looking for supporters, in an overcrowded open car on an exceptionally cold day, while the police loosed off live rounds behind them. A foreign correspondent observed that he would never "forget the bitterness written on Trotsky's face after hours of such futile effort."[10] Some of his supporters tried to make rousing speeches from suitable balconies, only to be assaulted by the police, who dragged them, and their banners, out of view. Trotsky had looked for a spontaneous mass demonstration that would topple Stalin like a tidal wave, hoping that as workers and soldiers filed past the reviewing stand on Red Square (from which he had been excluded), they would rally to his cause. Reality fell short of his expectations; the only persons to rally were:

> A group of Chinese Communist students of the Moscow Sun Yat Sen University [who] lifted the long sinuous *papier-mâché* dragon off their heads, threw Trotskyist proclamations into the air and shouted "Death to Stalin." GPU men quickly arrested them. Nobody else demonstrated.
>
> Near Red Square . . . is a government building with a second-storey grill-work balcony. Many of the civilian marchers passed this spot on their way into and out of the square. At about 2 P.M. Trotsky appeared on the balcony with several associates. A picture of Trotsky was hung from the grill-work and he commenced to harangue the citizens who immediately congregated below. But a young man climbed up to the balcony and pulled down the picture. In a few minutes Trotsky was silenced with boos.[11]

Soviet Russia in 1927 was no place in which to lead from political weakness. Within a week of their feeble efforts Kamenev was expelled from the Central Committee, while Zinoviev and Trotsky ceased to be members of the Communist party. Trotsky announced that he would be leaving his official Kremlin residence as soon as possible, while Zinoviev departed from his ostentatiously bearing a death mask of Lenin with him.

Adolf Joffé, a distinguished Old Bolshevik diplomat and a close friend of Trotsky's, reacted to news of the latter's expulsion by blowing out his brains, thereby sparing Stalin the trouble of doing it for him. Joffé left Trotsky a letter, echoing the charge that Stalin was the "gravedigger of the Revolution." He declared his death to be "the protest of a combatant reduced to such a state that he cannot respond in any other way. . . . The fact that, after twenty-seven years of revolutionary activity my plight is such that nothing [else] remains for me simply goes to show the kind of régime we now have." [12] The letter continues with an uncomfortably telling analysis of Trotsky's lack of political backbone.

Joffé's funeral, attended, at least according to Trotsky, by some 10,000 sympathizers, was the last time that Stalin's archrival made a public appearance in the Soviet Union. Within a month he was banished to Alma Ata in the remotest eastern corner of Kazakhstan. When they came for him, the GPU had to carry him from his apartment kicking and screaming; he should have begun his forcible resistance many, many years before.

Stalin made sure that Trotsky did not use his departure to make a final appeal to his supporters. Instead of letting him board the Trans-Siberian Express in Moscow, he had him join the train at a small station down the line. In the meantime, in Moscow the departing demagogue, crushed and uncharacteristically silent, was played by the actor who had specialized in doing Trotsky in films about the Revolution and who would have to start looking for another role since Trotsky would not be appearing upon the Soviet screen again.

After spending a year in Alma Ata, Trotsky was expelled from the Soviet Union. Initially he moved to the Turkish island of Principo, near Constantinople, before beginning an unhappy final phase of his life, which took him first to France and then to Norway (whence Stalin had him driven in 1936 by threatening the Norwegians with a trade embargo), before settling in Mexico. Throughout his years of wandering, years during which all his children died in suspicious circumstances, he sustained his paper polemic against Stalin and his brand of socialism.

Although one might have supposed that Stalin would have been more afraid of sticks and stones than Trotsky's paper bullets, the fact remains that Trotsky continued to feature as the archfiend in Stalin's demonology, almost as if Stalin's remarkable political acumen obliged him to recognize that Trotsky's policies, which he would adopt himself in considerable measure, had an innate appeal which rendered their author a continuing threat to his own authority. The threat was laid finally to rest on August 20, 1940, when one of Stalin's assassins finally caught up with Trotsky to sink an ice pick into his skull.

The Fifteenth Congress was a triumph for Stalin. The opposition had been dispersed; henceforward opposing his policies would entail expulsion from the party, with all the consequences of such a fate. The triumph of the "general line" was celebrated by Rykov, who solemnly presented Stalin with a steel broom, to "sweep away our enemies."[13] The young Khrushchev attended the congress, which was dominated by the mood of "us" and "them": "We realised that a merciless struggle against the opposition was inevitable. We justified what was happening in the terms of a lumberjack; when you chop a forest down, chips fly."[14] The lines render clearly the mentality of Stalin's supporters. The opposition of "us" and "them" leads logically to the notion of "merciless struggle." Since there could be only one correct course of action, there could be no possibility of compromise; compromise was a sign of weakness, of the readiness to waver under pressure. More important still is the lumberjack metaphor. Far from being Khrushchev's invention, it is a familiar Russian proverb which should be translated: "You can't make an omelet without breaking eggs." Time and again one finds Stalin's supporters using it to justify the events of the following decade, a period during which eggs were broken in all disproportion to the omelets produced.

Stalin's new Politburo consisted of Bukharin, Voroshilov, Kalinin, Kuibyshev, Molotov, Rykov, Rudzutak, Stalin and Tomsky. Only Bukharin, Rykov and Tomsky were not out-and-out Stalinists, so that there was no way in which he could be outvoted. At last he was in a position to impose his will. At some time before, or during, the congress Stalin had decided upon a change of policy so radical that it has properly been termed a "revolution from above." Having disposed of the party's left wing, he appropriated its policy of superindustrialization and prepared to declare war upon the luckless smallholders, the *kulaks*. We do not know when he decided on this course of action, or, for that matter, why. Eulogists have seen his plans as the farsighted provision for war with Germany. This is nonsense. There was no such prospect in 1927, the heyday of the Weimar Republic, when Hitler was only just recovering from the failure of the Beer Hall *Putsch* of 1923 and his subsequent prison sentence. Besides, Stalin displayed no capacity for farsightedness in matters of foreign policy until he hoodwinked his allies, who made it easy for him, in the 1940s. Up to then everything he did, including assisting Hitler in his rise to power, would prove to be a mistake.

It did not require a threat of war to make good Bolsheviks want dramatic industrial development without foreign investment. Moreover, Stalin recognized the need to win over erstwhile followers of Trotsky, who had been implacable in their opposition to the NEP. A radical policy of industrialization at the peasants' expense, a call for monumental sacrifice and effort in the interests of a great leap forward, had great appeal to the party militants. More important, the revolution from above promised a final solution to a peasant problem that was becoming increasingly acute. Not only were peasants failing to market their produce, but it was obvious that they lay beyond effective party control. They were as independent and mistrustful of party officials and city bureaucrats as they had once been of the well-meaning intellectuals who had "gone" to them in a proselytizing campaign of enlightenment half a century before.

Collectivization has sometimes been presented as Stalin's struggle against hostile *kulaks* who sought to blackmail his regime by withholding their produce from the marketplace. His response was admittedly a little extreme, but if a forest is to be cut down, then chips must fly. Apart from the notion that any farmer would ever conclude that, for political reasons, he would sell no crops that year, the so-called *kulaks* did not produce much more than three percent of all grain marketed—at least according to Molotov at the Fifteenth Congress. The real objection to them was that they enjoyed a degree of authority and prestige in village life that posed a real challenge to Soviet authority. The party had failed in its preposterous attempts to turn the poor peasants against their "exploiters," seeking antagonism where none existed. The increasing independence of village life was significantly characterized by a marked religious revival. In 1927 there were twice as many religious communities as there had been in 1923.[15]

To be fair, the decision to move against the peasants was possibly triggered by an economic crisis. The grain harvest of 1927 was approximately the size of the harvest of 1913, but a far smaller proportion was marketed partly because the poorer peasants were living better and producing more meat for their own consumption, partly because the official price of grain was set too low. Since meat and dairy products were sold on an open market, it paid farmers to use grain as feed rather than market it directly. This is a problem that has continued to beset Soviet agriculture ever since, as one may judge from the innumerable decrees forbidding peasants to buy bread to fatten their livestock. As matters stood, the only way that a significant number of peasants could be persuaded to market more grain was by increasing the official price.

CHAPTER TWENTY-FOUR

A Visit to Siberia

First Soviet Citizen: How are things today?
Second Soviet Citizen: Better than tomorrow.
　　　　　　　　—SOVIET ANECDOTE

Nothing that happens in Russia surprises me.
　　　　　　　　—STALIN

Having disposed of Trotsky and the left, Stalin elegantly assumed their policies as he moved against Bukharin and the right. In January 1928 he took a trip to Siberia, where he spent three weeks in Novosibirsk, Barnaul and Omsk, studying questions of grain procurement with local party officials. He considered the problem an administrative one, which did not oblige him to visit a single village or speak to a single peasant. Reliving the heady days when he used firing squads to organize food supplies around Tsaritsyn, he reintroduced the language and practices of war communism. Party officials should resort to all possible means to extract grain from farmers, who were actually "speculators," in other words, who were waiting for a rise in price before bringing their crops to market. At the same time future yields must be assured by setting up state and collective farms, which should, within three or four years, meet a third of the country's food requirements. Stalin understood that in the long run he could not hope to control recalcitrant farmers by threats. He subsequently observed to the German journalist Emil Ludwig that it was not possible to govern peasants by fear.[1] Although Ludwig, an admirer, took this to mean that Stalin governed by assent, the remark really signified that peasants required measures more drastic than fear alone.

Stalin's trip to Siberia was one of the unhappier turning points in Russian history, marking the moment when a market economy was replaced by administrative violence. It was also the first time that Stalin took a major step on his own initiative. In no way was this a joint Politburo decision; in fact, it was directed against Bukharin, Tomsky and Rykov, all of whom were opposed to such coercive practices. Stalin's call for radical measures, and hands that would not tremble, appealed especially to the younger members of the party, whose recollections of war communism had been shaped by official mythology and who were eager to sacrifice themselves, and others too, for the sake of a great leap forward. General Grigorenko recalls the mood of 1928, when he was a young believer:

> [It was] a time of great deeds. It must be admitted that Stalin was able to keep discovering new challenges, and we looked to the beckoning horizons as if under a spell. I remember—I know it was a little later, but during the same period, the enthusiasm aroused by Stalin's article "The Year of the Great Change." Bread was in dreadfully short supply, there were queues, rationing and famine were just round the corner, and yet we were carried away by Stalin's piece and rejoiced. "Yes, a great change indeed, the liquidation of peasant small holdings, the destruction of the very soil from which capitalism might reemerge. Let the sharks of imperialism just try to attack us now. Now we are on the high road to the triumph of socialism."[2]

The grain collections that replaced the marketplace were conducted by enthusiasts from the towns, who went to the countryside "explaining" the need for grain and subsequent collectivization. Sometimes they were rational and civilized in their conduct. Lev Kopelev, a longtime believer in communism, now a dissident, is a man who radiates gentleness and decency, and there is no doubt that his grain expeditions were based on rational explanation—for example, of the threat of capitalist encirclement.[3] Another refugee described his part in the "horror campaign" of 1928: "In spite of my sympathy for the feelings of the peasants, I did not question the need for the executions; I regarded my functions as an unpleasant but necessary duty. I was young and, as a Party member, my first loyalty was to the Soviet Government, which

alone could rescue and develop our country along wholly new and revolutionary lines."[4]

The young party men went to the country shooting, not always meta-
phorically, from the hip, with results that were predictable. In the first
half of 1928 the GPU put down more than 150 peasant rebellions in the
Ukraine alone, the first time in history that fighter planes and tanks
played an active part in agricultural life. For the peasants did not receive
the party emissaries gently, and many of them were found lying by
roadsides with their skulls split open. Sometimes the party men resorted
to subterfuge, taking grain as representatives of "grain centers," and paying for it by vouchers to be placed toward the purchase of the tractors
that were going to be available any day now.[5] The party also made use
of scapegoats, occasionally shooting overzealous grain collectors in order
to persuade the peasants that they were victims of local and uncharacteristic excess. Such was the efficiency of Soviet news management that
the peasants had no way of knowing that their fellows were being treated
just as badly throughout the length and breadth of the land.[6]

There is no evidence to suggest that Stalin intended to make war
upon his people. He genuinely appears to have expected both poor and
relatively well-off peasants to turn upon their more prosperous neighbors
and to do his work for him. Moreover, it must be recognized that he
lacked the machinery to fine-tune the collecting process. Relying as he
did upon revolver-toting young Bolsheviks vicariously reliving the heroic
days of the civil war, he could not have hoped to control their excesses
and still expect them to deliver the grain. Stalin may have put the col-
lectivizing process in motion, but he cannot be held solely responsible
for the way in which it was carried out.

The peasants' response combined predictable hostility with the super-
stitions of a primitive Christian culture. Collectivization was the work of
Antichrist. In one area there is a record of peasant sectarians (i.e., non-
conformists) reading the Bible collectively and predicting that "there is
not much longer to live, so do not succumb to the temptation of collective farms."[7] There were numerous instances of mass suicides, especially along railway lines, where whole families threw themselves under
trains.[8] As yet there was no awareness of what collectivization really
entailed, but there was a conviction that it would mean free love and
the pooling of all the wives in the village, just as the land was to be
pooled. All the men and women would have to sleep under a single
blanket in a single hut; the size of the blanket varied from 10 to 200
square meters. There would be special machines to burn up the old and

the infirm, children would be sent to China and collective farms would bear the seal of the devil.[9]

Foreign observers responded to the campaign in surprising ways. Anna Louise Strong, a famous believer in socialism, had prophesied that collectivization would improve the peasant's lot, bringing enlightenment and, eventually, tractors. On learning what was really happening, she sought reassurance from a Soviet official, who told her: "I think that what worries you most is not so much the cruelty as the anarchy."[10] A moment's reflection convinced her that he was right. For there was anarchy aplenty. As a British diplomat observed, "The essential element of successful collectivization is sound organization, and this, in the nature of things, cannot be extemporized overnight, especially in Russia."[11] The last word on the unhappy subject is attributed to Radek. Stalin allegedly came to him with a problem: The entire Politburo was infested with lice that could not be got rid of. "Simple," replied Radek. "Collectivize; most of them will die and the rest will run away."[12]

Shortly after Stalin's return from Siberia, where he had established the process he described as the "Sibero-Ugaric form of grain collection," he clashed with the right wing of the Politburo. Once again he avoided a confrontation and instructed his operators to exercise moderation on what the awful jargon of the day now described as "the grain front." In the meantime, he began to probe Bukharin's defenses. He sent Mekhlis to address the Institute of Red Professors, a Bukharinist stronghold, where he made a remarkable speech full of appropriate quotations, explaining the incorrect nature of Bukharin's views on agriculture. Similar moves were made in all other institutes in the capital. As usual Stalin distinguished himself by thoroughness and attention to detail, seeking to win students and faculty over to his point of view. Using "unfair" arguments, he accused Bukharin of being opposed to the building of socialism, magnificently ignoring the fact that he and Bukharin had identical aims and differed only in respect of method.

He also began to look beyond debate to other ways of dealing with opponents. One of his original contributions to Soviet ideology was his contention that the closer the country came to socialism, the more resistance to the process would develop, creating an increasing need for vigilance and coercion. By the middle of 1928 virtually all of Trotsky's supporters were either exiled or behind bars. In parallel with the attack upon the peasants, the same year saw a renewed assault upon a different anti-Soviet element, organized religion. By the end of the year all surviving monasteries had been closed, and their monks sent to Siberia. Thousands of churches, mosques and synagogues were torn down. St. Basil's Cathedral in Red Square was itself nearly removed to assist the traffic flow on May Day parades.

Terror had long been a part of everyday life for prominent nonparty men and women, and it was common practice for such persons to keep small suitcases permanently packed.[13] A comedian of the time began his patter as follows: "I heard a ring at the doorbell at midnight last night, so I picked up my case. . . ."[14] Another joke tells of Stalin's attempt to test the loyalty of a worker, a peasant and a Jewish engineer. The three men are taken to the top of the Central Committee building and one by one are invited to demonstrate their loyalty by jumping to their deaths. The worker and the peasant both refuse, but the Jewish engineer, no sooner asked, makes a headlong dive for the edge and is only just caught in time by Kaganovich. "Wait," says Stalin. "Stalin is more than happy to see that you are ready to die for the party, but Stalin says that for the moment that is unnecessary. But please tell him why you, of all people, a Jew, were so willing to jump." "Simple," replies the engineer. "Better a horrible end than endless horror."

Endless horror started in March 1928, when the GPU announced that it had discovered a plot involving engineers and foreign spies bent on sabotaging the Shakhty mines in the industrial complex of the Donets Basin. There were fifty-five arrests and almost as many confessions when the accused were put on public trial in the old Nobles' Club in Moscow, now the House of Trade Unions. It was Stalin's first show trial, the first time that those facing death sentences eagerly outlined their prosecuting attorneys in the description of their crimes. Eugene Lyons covered the trial for an American wire service:

> For over two months the Soviet press, radio, official speeches had built up towards the climax of this show. Dark hints of enemies within conniving with enemies abroad, villainy that cut production and took food out of the mouths of hungering masses, treachery that threatened the socialist fatherland—all brought to a sharp focus at last in this case. In recent months there had been many laconic announcements of executions for economic counter-revolution—here at last was a public demonstration of the reasons for such extreme measures.
>
> The tightening pinch of goods and food shortages was making people grumble with pain. The ruthless extermination of Trotskyism and other communist deviations was eating into the faith of more

conscious workers. The Shakhty trial offered a tangible object for hatreds smoldering in the heart of Russia. That morning's newspapers in every city and town shrieked curses upon the bourgeois plotters and their bloodthirsty foreign confederates. Week after week the press, radio, schools, newsreels, billboards had waved the promise of traitors' deaths aloft like crimson flags. They had treated every accusation and every far-fetched implication as established fact. [15]

Lyons was right to emphasize the theme of the scapegoat. Nonparty specialists were to carry the blame for failures of the economy, failures which were in anything but short supply. Thus around the time of the trial a report written by the Latvian consul mentions the rapid increase in railway disasters, due to lack of discipline and drunkenness among the staff. [16] In view of the important part played by conspiracy in Bolshevik mythology, such failures were never considered "accidental." Besides, people positively wanted to blame the shortcomings of everyday life on hostile intervention, as opposed to incompetence. Throughout the time of terror and the show trials there persisted a widespread belief in the guilt of those accused, because the population actively wanted them to be guilty. Lev Kopelev was friendly with the daughter of one of the engineers involved, and while he believed in the innocence of that particular man, he presumed that he had been the innocent victim of wicked associates.

When considering the show trial phenomenon, we must appreciate that these spectacles gave people what they wanted. Not only did they provide acceptable explanations and scapegoats for shortcomings that would otherwise have to be laid at the door of the leadership, but people also took great delight in the spectacle of the public downfall of *Prominenz*, who only a moment ago "had had everything"—the soft life, enough to eat, a home and perhaps even a car—and now were destitute and worse.

However, there was more to the trial than the judicious use of scapegoats. It initiated a pattern that would be completed only with the purge of the Red Army some ten years hence. Stalin had begun a methodical attack upon his *potential* enemies in every sphere of public life. He started with the nonparty technicians and specialists who had worked for Russia, as opposed to for Soviet power, and who were therefore suspect. The Shakhty trial was directed not just at the fifty-odd accused, but at the *kind* of people they were, as thousands like them were to be arrested, and often shot, in their wake. To take two examples, it was now that Stalin ordered the execution of Kondratiev, the most distinguished economist in the land, and of von Meck, an ex-millionaire and railway engineer of the old school, who had refrained from emigrating and devoted the last years of his life to an attempt to keep the Soviet railway system running.

Stalin also used terror to make room for his friends. Soviet educational institutions were turning out a new generation of working-class engineers and technicians, loyal supporters of the regime. In the wake of the trial Stalin began to stress the need to train specialists ready to step into dead men's shoes, shoes which would not be in short supply. He thereby harnessed the ambitions of young careerists, who would be rushed through higher education and pushed hard as long as they continued to succeed, tossed onto the scrap heap when they broke. The rush to appoint persons of the right political background to senior positions without regard for their intellectual qualities had its comic side. Professor Pavlov, the psychologist, remarked of some elections to the Academy of Sciences that their only precedent was the occasion when Caligula made his horse a senator.[17]

The Shakhty affair was also a blow against Bukharin, who had favored the use of nonparty experts. In April 1928 Stalin made a speech in which he declared, in the classic language of conspiracy, that the Shakhty affair was "no accident" and that to cope with enemies without and within, the class struggle in the countryside would have to be intensified, elegantly, if illogically, grouping engineers and smallholders under the common rubric "internal enemy." Bukharin, who had kept his political innocence after more than ten years of Soviet rule, at last began to understand the kind of man Stalin was and the policies he was advancing. He also recognized Stalin's readiness to misrepresent any argument in order to win a debate. Together with Rykov and Tomsky he was genuinely horrified by Stalin's new policies and his intention of abandoning the NEP. Stalin, still biding his time, tried to placate him, even observing that he and Bukharin were "the Himalayas"; their colleagues mere pygmies. He then grew very upset when Bukharin quoted him and tried to deny that he had said anything of the sort.

Believing they had a chance of winning a majority in the Politburo and the Central Committee, Bukharin and the right now began a belated propaganda campaign. They had considerable support outside the party, including a strong right-wing element in the GPU. They also controlled *Pravda* and *Bolshevik*, the official newspapers of the Central Committee. Trotsky displayed his characteristic political acumen by predicting that Bukharin would soon be hunting Stalin down like a mad dog. But the right had underestimated the power of Stalin's machine. Support for the general secretary in the Central Committee and the lower echelons of the party was solid, and he also carried the Politburo. The only vote Bukharin might have counted on was that of Kalinin, but he too was won over by Stalin. Of his colleagues' defections Bukharin could only remark sadly that "Stalin has some special hold over them." [18]

It says a lot for the stealth with which Stalin had built his machine that Bukharin seriously believed that he could carry the Politburo and the Central Committee. Admittedly Bukharin was a poor judge of politicians; still, his failure to grasp the extent of Stalin's power says much for the general secretary's powers of camouflage. Yet Stalin did not owe his victory to machine politics alone. The change of direction he favored was popular with the activists, while the Bukharinist alternative, based on the NEP and a class of prosperous peasant farmers, was perceived as a threat to the regime. Many of those who supported Stalin did so from the belief that were Bukharin to prevail, the party might succumb to the forces of capitalism, at which point it would be their heads that would roll. In the meantime, they could only continue to ride the tiger and try to sit tight.

Stalin also enjoyed the support of the party's practical politicians such as Ordzhonikidze, Kuibyshev and Kirov, men committed to the development of the Soviet Union as a modern industrial power. Stalin for them was an able, realistic leader who possessed all the organizational and administrative abilities that Bukharin lacked. They saw the latter's gradualism as a form of cowardice, at a time when Stalin was calling on them to gird up their loins and, in a famous phrase, "catch up and overtake the West." They did not yet appreciate that Stalin would take their country to the brink of civil war in his efforts at agricultural reform. They probably failed to understand the irony behind Stalin's choice of pictures in the Kremlin; only one portrait of a tsar still hung there, a gigantic canvas of Alexander III distributing land to a gathering of peasants. [19]

Forgetting political differences, Bukharin now turned to associates whom he had recently castigated on Stalin's behalf. At the time Kamenev was in comfortable exile in Kaluga, a medium-size town southwest of Moscow. The day after his defeat in the Central Committee Bukharin arranged to meet him in secret, in an attempt to form an alliance. In the political climate of 1928 Bukharin was risking his politi-

cal reputation, at the very least, by paying a clandestine visit to the
enemy. He warned Kamenev against a reconciliation with Stalin, for he
had finally understood what kind of man he was. Obviously distressed,
he described him as an unprincipled intriguer and a "debased Genghis
Khan," thereby recalling the prophecy uttered by the nineteenth-century liberal Alexander Herzen, who foresaw the day when Russia would
be governed by "Genghis Khan with a telegraph." If Stalin were to see
his policies through, they would lead to a civil war that would drown
the country in its own blood. However, nothing came of his *démarche*
since both Zinoviev and Kamenev decided that they had no alternative
but to continue to support Stalin. Since he had control over the party,
they felt obliged to follow him; in view of their acceptance of one-party
rule, there was no alternative.[20]

Collectivization

The social order that was established in Russia after the
revolution took shape is in many ways a reconstruction of the
Russian serfdom that had existed for centuries.

—ALEXANDER ZINOVIEV

Q. Why is the USSR like Liberia?
A. In neither country do white men have the vote.

—SOVIET JOKE, 1929

Accounts of Bukharin's talk with Kamenev soon found their way into
circulation. We get a worm's-eye view of the power struggle from Lev
Kopelev, who outlines his attitude of February 1929, just after Stalin
expelled Trotsky from the USSR, an action that Kopelev thought excessive:

> Pamphlets and brochures signed "Bolshevik-Leninists" demonstrated
> that Trotsky was leading the party along the correct road. Stalin and
> Rykov were indulging *kulaks*, nepmen and bureaucrats. I knew
> Bukharin to be the nicest and least aloof of all the leaders. But first
> and foremost he was a theoretician, a gentle dreamer. . . . Once upon
> a time he had been farther to the left than Trotsky, but apparently he
> had been corrupted by the NEP. He had started to call on the peasants
> to "get rich" and believed that the *kulaks* would "grow into socialism."
> . . . The opposition pamphlets told me that Bukharin, Rykov and
> Tomsky had quarreled seriously with Stalin and even wanted to make

227

> peace with the opposition. Bukharin had come to Kamenev to talk it
> over. Perhaps there would be another discussion like the one in 1927,
> but more extensive and more honest. Then it would become clear
> who was correct. [1]

Kopelev is fascinating. He had had no experience of shifting political
allegiances and so considered the issue in terms of "correct" and "incorrect," viewing political alignments in terms of absolute right and wrong
and hoping that in the course of discussion the proper course of action
would emerge. His was the generation that was easily convinced that
when all was said and done, Stalin must be right.

Bukharin continued an unequal struggle against Stalin, who had, of
course, learned of his meeting with Kamenev. The Central Committee
rebuked him for this and other failings. However, together with Tomsky
and Rykov, the "right deviationists" as they were now known, he kept
his seat on the Politburo. He was still popular, while his policies had
little support within the party, so that nothing would be gained by moving against him. Trotsky had been a different case altogether. His policies had been attractive, while his charisma made him a perpetual
threat. Stalin's spies kept him under continuous surveillance, referring
to him by a code name that he would retain until his assassination in
Mexico some fifteen years hence—"Judas Iscariot."

In April Bukharin lost the editorship of *Pravda* and the chairmanship
of the Comintern, while Tomsky lost his post as leader of the trade
unions. Kaganovich conceded that his dismissal was a violation of proletarian democracy, but, "Comrades, it has long been known that for us
Bolsheviks democracy is no fetish." [2] In the summer a new campaign
was mounted against Bukharin and his "rotten liberalism." It ended
with his expulsion from the Politburo on November 17; a week later the
right deviationists signed a document stating that they had been mistaken in their views and would join the party's struggle on behalf of the
"general line," particularly against the right deviation. Stalin's victory
over both right and left was now complete. That victory inspired the
celebration of his fiftieth birthday in December 1929 and marked the
moment when the personality cult began. From now on it was customary to refer to Stalin as *vozhd'*, or leader, a term soon reserved for him
alone. According to a joke of the time, Stalin ordered Radek to stop
telling jokes against the government. "All right," Radek answered, "but
the latest, that you are our *vozhd'*, is not one of mine." [3] The birthday
also marked the introduction of the term *Stalinism*. As late as 1927 its

use would have seemed embarrassingly inappropriate, but now Mekhlis set the new tone by writing articles with titles like "Under the Wise Direction of Our Great Genius Leader and Teacher Stalin." Other journalists soon took the hint, and it rapidly became impossible to refer to Stalin as anything but "wise" and a "genius." One unfortunate typesetter who allowed the word for his "countenance," *vzor*, to be altered to his "nonsense," *vzdor*, did not live long enough to repeat a mistake that was doubtless no accident.

To date the only birthday that the party celebrated had been Lenin's, so that the chorus of acclaim that now greeted Stalin from every newspaper and broadcast in the land marked a definite new departure. This was also reflected in other practices. Hitherto, members of the Politburo had always been cited in alphabetical order; now Stalin's name headed the list. The language used by the press to celebrate his elevation is consistent enough to suggest that it had been carefully orchestrated, and its tone is revealing. Stalin is referred to as a leader of colossal stature and monumental hardness. He is a man of iron, a warrior of steel, a Leninist of bronze and a Bolshevik of granite. The expressions all suggest a colossus towering over his people.

Stalin was about to embark upon the creation of a pharaonic state, in which millions of slaves and functionaries would toil away to celebrate its glory, a state which would be the fullest realization of the hierarchical pyramid structure that already determined the organization of the party. The monumental mode would affect everything, from architecture to the style of Stalin's speeches; henceforward he would only refer to himself in the third person as "Stalin." Of course, the notion of such a society is not peculiar to ancient Egypt. Indeed, the society that Stalin brought forth was the realization of social and political lines of force that had been present in Russia for centuries. However, we possess hitherto-unnoticed evidence that Stalin had a particular interest in ancient Egypt. He was a great admirer of the novels of a Polish writer, A. Glovatski, who wrote under the pseudonym of B. Prus.[4] Prus's most popular work was *The Pharaoh and the Priest*, which is enthralling to read in the light of Stalin's known interest. Some of its themes have an immediate and obvious relevance. The book abounds in the description of massive public buildings that sound remarkably like Stalin's postwar skyscrapers, and there are descriptions of armies of slaves digging canals; canal construction would become another of Stalin's obsessions. There are descriptions of public ceremonies with plenty of stiff and spectacular pageants that resemble Soviet ceremonial, notably at funerals, and much is made of the cult of dead pharaohs.

The novel's plot is also strangely relevant. The young pharaoh Rameses is engaged in a running battle with enemies within, a caste of priests who are full of deceit, though appearing to be his allies. Rameses is eager to regain the lost prosperity of his country by a combination of war and the practice of austerity that would get rid of both expensive imports and Phoenician moneylenders. In other words, he wishes to create a version of socialism in one country. He fails because he is undone by treachery and deception from within. The novel describes the development in the young prince of an idea of the state as "something grander than the pyramid of Cheops, something more enduring than granite" and also contains something close to a conception of the party:

> Draw on the earth, O lord, a square and put on it six million unhewn
> stones; they will represent the people. On that foundation place sixty
> thousand hewn stones; they will be the lower officials. On them place
> six thousand polished stones; they will be the higher officials. On
> these place sixty covered with carvings; they will be thy most intimate
> councillors and chief leaders, and on the summit place one monolith
> with its pedestal and the golden image of the sun. That will be
> thyself. [5]

In a major speech Stalin would make in 1937 he seemed to echo the passage we have just quoted. Reviewing the structure of the party he described it as consisting of 3,000 to 4,000 "generals," 30,000 to 40,000 "officers" and 150,000 "NCOs." It would be foolish to suggest that Stalin drew his political designs from novels, yet the revolution from above he was about to embark on had much that might explain his interest in the book.

The country over which Stalin now ruled was not a happy place. Food was no longer very easy to come by, and one consequence of the shortages was a reluctance to leave Moscow for the summer and move to the country, since food could still be found in the capital, while in the country it was almost impossible for outsiders to feed themselves. [6] Even in Moscow sausage was scarce, and its new nickname, Budenny's First Cavalry, indicates its presumed origins. The impact of the shortages was aggravated by Soviet propaganda, which broadcast the impression that all was wonderful in the workers' paradise. There was a series of bitter jokes about the Filipovs, a "typical Soviet family that was featured regularly in foreign language propaganda magazines, beautifully dressed, enjoying a large meal at a table complete with samovar in a room with a piano and side tables covered with splendid embroidered cloths."[7] Already passersby displayed that gray deadpan expression, the Soviet street face. Not a projection of the sadness of the Slav soul, it was a look that people donned for safety—only a fool would display his feelings in public—and it made for a thoroughly miserable atmosphere in the streets, which were depressing enough as it was.

> Shops are dingy in appearance, both the outsides, which are in need of repainting, and also the goods displayed in the windows. These are few, poor and heterogeneous. There are price tickets on some of the articles of clothing, and the prices are high for goods which look like the stock-in-trade of a second-hand dealer in London. Outside the big provision stores stand a line of private traders, offering a chicken or some carrots or eggs or baskets or brooms to people on their way to the stores.[8]

> The appearance of people in the streets is very bad, and I cannot remember once having seen either a middle-aged or an elderly person smile, except when drunk or at the ballet.[9]

It was prudent to put one's street face on before one left a cinema and avoid all eye contact, let alone discuss the film, for fear of disclosing attitudes that would require one or other party to play the informer.[10]

Visitors to the Soviet Union at this time were, for the most part, enthusiasts anxious to admire the great experiment for themselves. Their enthusiasm was not always welcome. A group of American tourists spoke to women waiting in line outside a bakery, and one of the women asked the visitors what they thought of Soviet life. "Difficult but interesting" came the reply. "Interesting! Obviously it is interesting to watch a burning house, but the trouble is that we are in it,"[11] was her astoundingly honest rejoinder. The suffering and misery to be noticed in the cities were yet another manifestation of the principles of primitive accumulation. Paul Scheffer wrote in the middle of 1929:

> Here great ambitions are confronted with the inertia of tradition, but at the same time with the very consequences of a head-strong and one

sided policy. . . . In many departments of life the worker . . . is
paying for the system for which he fought, which has been erected in
his interest, but the results of which, also, are determining his
lot. . . . The present generation is defraying many costs by which only
the generations to come will profit. This is becoming apparent, and
increasingly so, as regards food, housing, and general comfort, in
respect of which the present calamities are all consequences of
socialisation. [12]

In the meantime, the heads of scapegoats and class enemies continued to roll. An American correspondent observed that 1929 was the year
when executions ceased to be news. The mood of that time was well
captured by one of its jokes. On his birthday Stalin had a dream in
which he saw Lenin to whom he described his revolution from above
and his plans for the future. "And look, Comrade," he observed, "the
masses are with me." "No, Comrade," replied Lenin, who suddenly
started reeking of the grave, "I think you'll find they are with me." [13]

•   •   •

Stalin understood creative democracy, and formalism of every
kind was alien to him. At every stage in the building of
socialism he committed the people on a mass scale.

—N. GOLD

Just after his fiftieth birthday, and two months after the Wall Street
crash, Stalin declared war on his peasants, calling for the "liquidation of
the *kulaks* as a class." The party went into immediate action, rounding
up those peasants and their families, right down to breast-fed infants,
that local activists had decided were *kulaks*. They were shipped to Siberia, unloaded in areas designated as future concentration camps and
ordered to set about their construction. The GPU slang for peasants in
transit was "white coal." [14] At first the peasants fought back, with agricultural implements largely, which proved ineffective against the new
Soviet tanks which enjoyed their baptism of fire on the grain front. [15]
We do not know the extent of the war, but it seems to have been comparable to the peasant risings of the 1905 Revolution. The liquidation of
the smallholders was not just a piece of ideological slum clearance,
ending in the relocation of several hundreds of thousands of peasants.
Frequently it entailed the physical annihilation of the peasants in question, as it became clear that it was impossible to control the "field-

workers." The Smolensk Archive gives the following, almost certainly typical account:

> Despite apparently precise directions and instructions, many authorities went their own way, interpreting the *kulak* category broadly to embrace middle, and even poor peasants who were opposed to collectivization [and] evicting *kulak* families who had Red Army connections [Stalin prudently exempted the latter to reduce unrest in an essentially peasant army] . . . certain members of the working brigades and officials of lower echelons of the party-soviet apparatus deprived members of *kulak* and middle peasant households of their clothes and warm underwear, directly from their body, confiscated headwear from children's heads and removed shoes from people's feet. The perpetrators divided the confiscated goods among themselves. The food they found was eaten on the spot; the alcohol they uncovered was consumed directly, resulting in drunken orgies.[16]

It is fashionable in some circles to hold Stalin alone responsible for the horror of collectivization. Certainly it was he who gave the signal to start liquidating, but liquidation could never have taken place without the willing participation of many thousands of activists who set about their task with that blend of idealism and power-crazed, often self-interested brutality familiar to students of movements as remote from one another as witch-hunting, National-Socialism and the Ku Klux Klan. The consequences were dreadful. Rather than surrender their livestock, the peasants slaughtered their beasts en masse, or had their women make ramparts of their bodies around cattle about to be confiscated, daring the activists to shoot. Women undressed in their houses, mistakenly supposing that no one would deport them in that condition. Peasants left for Siberia by the trainload. "Old folks starved to death in mid-journey, new born babies were buried by the roadside, and each wilderness had its crop of little crosses of boughs of white wood."[17]

It is not surprising that the peasants should have been treated as enemies after years of propaganda describing them as the embodiment of social evil. Young idealists went to the countryside as crusaders. Sometimes they justified their behavior in military terms; in the words of one young activist, "We cannot help it, there is such a thing as revolutionary discipline, and we have no right to question the administration of the Party. This is just like war-time: ours is not to reason why."[18] A little later a British diplomat, J. D. Greenway, produced a fascinating analysis of such activists, writing of:

a relatively small body of genuinely honest, but lamentably ignorant
enthusiasts, drawn almost exclusively from the ranks of the younger
generation, who, with all the generosity of youth, have listened to the
endless propaganda of their masters, and accepted the implacable
credo of the danger to Russia from the outside world, and the
potential greatness which they believe themselves to be bringing forth.
So much zeal and self-sacrifice are worthy of a nobler cause. . . .
[Instead of finding] the high ideals and elements of humanity, which
the prophets of communism claim lie at the root of this vast and
unwieldy fabric, I found generally speaking only misery, exploitation,
terror, and perhaps the most tragic of all the blind helpless confidence
of the young in a future that is not to be made manifest.[19]

It was also the case that government news management was so efficient that many young men and women in the party did not appreciate
what was going on. They heard vague rumors of resistance, which took
the form of so-called women's rebellions, ignorant opposition to the
notion of sleeping under the collective blanket. However, many young
people were deceived because they wanted to be. Their belief in the
need to build instant communism was such that they were prepared to
justify any crimes as long as these could be presented in Communist
phraseology. No one wanted to consider his actions in a broader perspective. "We preferred to concentrate on concrete events and convince
ourselves that they were isolated phenomena, and that by and large all
was as the Party said it was. One had more peace of mind that way,
and, let us be honest, it was *SAFER.*"[20]

The use of Communist phraseology as a form of self-deception was
widespread. Viktor Khravchenko, another who "chose freedom," remembers how he took refuge in "the high flown euphemisms of Party
lingo. . . . In order to live with ourselves we had to smear the reality
out of recognition with verbal camouflage."[21] When he was sent into
battle, his group was addressed by a member of the Central Committee
who urged them to do their duty without flinching or yielding to rotten
liberalism: "Throw your bourgeois humanitarianism out of the window
and behave like Bolsheviks worthy of Comrade Stalin. Beat down the
kulak agent wherever he raises his head. It's war, it's them or us! The
last decayed remnant of capitalist farming must be wiped out at any
cost. . . . The class struggle in the village has assumed the acutest
forms. This is no time for squeamishness or rotten sentimentality."[22]

•   •   •

It must also be recognized that refusal to take part in this holy war meant dismissal from the party, and "Without his revolver and the one for all, all for one protection of the governing clique [an ex-Communist] has little chance of staying alive. This is the reason why many of those purged prefer to blow their brains out before their revolver is taken from them together with their Party card."[23]

When considering the failure of the West to understand Stalin in the 1940s, we will have occasion to accuse the British Foreign Service of serious shortcomings in its perception of Soviet realities. The same cannot be said of British Embassy staff in the 1930s, when they displayed a remarkable grasp of political and social conditions, never permitting prejudice to affect their judgment. From the outset, they recognized the horror of collectivization. Dispatches abound in accounts of peasants' being herded, sometimes naked, into cattle trucks. They had no illusions about the meaning of the term *liquidation*. They also understood that despite the risks and human cost involved, Stalin would see his policy through. One dispatch quotes the situation perfectly. Remarking that Western analysts had failed to understand the Soviet leadership, notably Stalin, it continues:

> The Russian government were perfectly prepared to ruin themelves, their country and the world rather than yield an inch to the idol of compromise, or retract one syllable of their doctrine. He went on to prophesy that they would be prepared to bring the country to the brink of famine, but that both famine and resistance would only occur in isolated areas and that the spirit of sacrifice and endurance was such that the policy would eventually triumph.[24]

The role played by Stalin in this great experiment was variously interpreted by foreign observers. Eugene Lyons saw it "As if in the midst of a terrible volcanic eruption, one were to catch sight of someone turning a crank that kept the hot lava pouring over men and towns."[25]

Foreign believers admired the courage of the Soviet leadership: "Strong must have been the faith and resolute the will of men who, in the interest of what seemed to them the public good, could take such a momentous decision."[26] They regarded the liquidation of the small-holders as an issue that separated soft "idealists" from the "realists" who would let nothing stand in the way of their pursuit of the "general line." Reinforcing the view that the campaign against the smallholder was political rather than economic, its intensification was accompanied by a stepping up in the campaign against all forms of religion. Decisions to deport well-to-do peasants and a new category invented in the course of the year, *podkulachniki* ("subkulaks"), were accompanied by orders to close and destroy village churches, while ecclesiastical buildings were no longer protected monuments, so that numerous churches, cemeteries and monasteries were vandalized for building materials and firewood. Moscow, at the end of that year, was full of red-letter instructions reading, "Do not celebrate Christmas," and the cutting and sale of Christmas trees were forbidden by law, although an exception was made for the diplomatic corps.[27]

The new collective farms were not models of efficiency. Most of them were managed by party members from the towns, more than 2 million of them by the end of 1930, at which time forty-three percent of the managers were under twenty-three years old.[28] The peasants who had escaped deportation were, by definition, the least successful. In the words of the correspondent of the *New York Times*, who did not live long enough to eat them, "With the removal of the *kulaks* the rest of the village was little more fitted to handle the complicated management of a collective farm than the coloured population of the Southern states was capable of self-government."[29]

In its original conception, aspects of the collective system guaranteed failure. In the early stages a hardworking peasant received no more than his lazy counterpart, and the efficient collective retained no more of its crop than an inefficient one. The result was that both peasant and collective lost all sense of a relationship between reward and performance. By about mid-1930 the peasant had grown convinced that there was no sense in working; however hard he labored, the government would take all he produced.

It was not so much the wholesale destruction of livestock in collectivization's early phases that brought about the famine that was shortly to ravage southern Russia, but rather the systematic and cumulative damage wrought by so-called grain deliveries—in other words, the confiscation of the annual crop. Arbitrary demands for predetermined amounts were made of each collective farm, regardless of whether it was able to meet them out of cash crop, seed corn or not at all. Peasants stopped working, and grain ceased to grow in the fields.[30] It is no wonder that the Moscow cabbies of the time would refer to an especially lazy horse as a "kolkhoznik," or collective farm worker.[31]

When considering the violence, chaos, disruption and tragedy of collectivization, one cannot help wondering why Stalin did it. A moment's thought will make it clear that *whatever the circumstances*, whatever the shortages or shortcomings, it makes no kind of economic sense to declare war upon the 5 million or so ablest food producers in the land and ship them to a place in which they can grow nothing. One cannot even consider the cost of the operation a necessary preliminary to massive investment in industry. Despite all the statistics and the rhetoric, it is obvious that economically speaking, collectivization was a nonsense.

To Stalin, however, it made perfect political sense. He believed that the peasantry had the ability to hold the party to ransom by withholding food from the marketplace. Whether or not that vastly dispersed body was capable of any such coordinated response is another matter, but Stalin certainly believed that to be the case. In the second place, the peasantry fell largely outside Soviet rule and might be thought of as offering an eventual threat to the regime via the Red Army. Stalin must have been aware of the danger of serious unrest in the countryside; Russian history had always made much of its peasant rebellions and of leaders such as Pugachev and Stenka Razin leading their "dark people" in assaults upon Moscow. The peasant had no reason to love the Bolsheviks. Besides, Stalin's supporters wanted mighty deeds and heady action.

It may be true that the violence with which collectivization was conducted had not been ordered from the top and was beyond the power of the central authorities to control. It may even be that Stalin had seriously expected that poor and middling peasants would welcome collectivization and the discomfiture of the prosperous smallholder. But these are secondary factors. Stalin envisaged collectivization as a means of consolidating and extending the authority of the party by purging an opposition. It was, as he liked to term such actions, a prophylactic measure. Moreover, by committing the party to such a course, he committed it to him. With so much blood and so much hostility in the country, this would be no time to break ranks. Finally, and this perhaps is the point at which his own personality plays its part, he had never attached excessive value to the lives of others. It was not as if, he might have observed, peasants were potentially immortal. Sooner or later they would all have died anyway.

Before they did so, they killed their livestock; if they could not have their beasts, then no one would. In February and March 1930 some 14 million head of cattle were destroyed, along with a third of all the pigs in the nation and a quarter of its sheep and goats. In the meantime, the number of collectivized households increased dramatically, 10 million joining in the first two months of 1930. The Soviet historian Roy Medvedev adds the comment "In many [areas] enemies of collective farms succeeded in provoking anti-Soviet outbursts from the peasantry."[32] One seemingly cannot escape the language of warfare and the sense of "for us or against us." In fact, far from conducting anti-Soviet propaganda, the peasants were simply reacting to the disruption of a way of life that had not, in many respects, changed for more than 1,000 years and had scarcely been affected by the Revolution.

By March 1930 Stalin recognized that he had underestimated the ferocity of peasant resistance and that he would have to rein his enthusiasts in. Various sources, including a British diplomat, suggest that it was alarm and discontent in the army that obliged him to take one step back, with Voroshilov and Budenny representing that they could no longer guarantee the loyalty of their troops if the terrorization of the countryside were to continue.[33] It is even possible that the excesses of his agricultural policy had caused the raising of an eyebrow or two in his Central Committee. World opinion may have played a further part. Pope Pius XI had called for a worldwide day of prayer on behalf of the persecuted faithful of the Soviet Union, and the antireligious campaign had also succeeded in antagonizing the worldwide Jewish community.[34]

Stalin's response was both sensitive and brazen. On March 2 *Pravda* published his famous article "Dizzy from Success," which stated that some comrades had been overzealous in their invitation to peasants to join the collective farms. These were to be established not by force, but by seeking the "active support of the main mass of the peasantry."[35] The article also criticized antireligious elements by suggesting that some would-be revolutionaries thought the proper way to collectivize a village was to begin by removing its church bells. Stalin went on to warn those executing his policies against becoming dizzy from success and "losing their grip on reality." Yet significantly the article continued to present the agricultural policy in terms of war, dizziness from success bringing "a tendency to overestimate one's strength and underestimate the strength of the enemy." The piece also warned against attempts to build socialism too fast. The fight itself was still on; this was simply a time for consolidation.

The peasants greeted the article with jubilation. They celebrated it with torchlight processions, and copies of the actual piece were so sought after that they commanded a high price on the black market:

> They paid four or five roubles for a copy of such a paper, that was how eager they were to see the letter with their own eyes. In the market

places peasants gathered in groups and read it aloud and discussed it
long and violently, and some of them were so overjoyed that they
bought all the vodka they could pay for and got drunk. Others stuck
the paper inside their bosom and rushed home to show it to the
neighbours and went to the Soviet offices and flashing it before the
officials and the organizers, gave them a piece of their mind.[36]

As Paul Scheffer shrewdly observed, it seemed unlikely that the celebrations would continue for long.[37] In the meantime, Stalin, who
clearly felt the need to distance himself from his zealots, had managed
to find scapegoats for his own policies. Reducing his personal responsibility still further, he followed his piece up with a second, in which he
made it clear that he had not acted alone when calling for a halt to the
excesses; that was not the way of the Soviet government. Playing down
his own role, Stalin reminded his colleagues that they were all in the
boat together, introducing the doctrine of collective responsibility.

> There are those who think that the article *Dizzy from Success* is the
> result of the direct intervention of Stalin. That of course is nonsense.
> The Central Committee does not exist to permit the individual
> initiative of just anyone on such issues. It was a piece of deep
> reconaissance [sic] on the part of the Central Committee, and when
> the depth and extent of the errors emerged the Central Committee did
> not hesitate to attack the errors with the full strength of its authority.[38]

To enthusiastic ignoramuses in the cities, happily unaware of the horrors and violence of country life, Stalin's article came as a bolt from the
blue and was seen as proof of his extraordinary farsightedness, the
wisdom of a true leader, counseling restraint at the appropriate moment
and displaying a clarity of political vision tantamount to genius.[39] This
was the easiest and also the safest response, although there were others,
such as the letter printed in *Pravda* on June 25, 1930, cautiously pointing out that if Stalin's piece had appeared sooner, a lot of misery and
wasted effort might have been spared. This was the last occasion that
the paper published any criticism of Stalin or the "general line."

His retreat is only conceivable against a ground swell of protest from
within the party as well as from outside it, for it took colossal pressure
for Stalin to concede that he might have made a mistake. In retrospect
this appears a perfect moment for the right opposition to have moved
against him. But once again they had no stomach for the fight. Party

discipline proved too strong, as Rykov, Tomsky and Bukharin all expressed the view that opposition to the "general line" would entail supporting successful smallholders, petty bourgeois and other counter-revolutionary elements and would probably result in a peasant uprising.[40] Once again the impossibility of opposing Stalin without causing a potentially fatal breach proved too much for them.

The peasants responded to Stalin by a mass withdrawal from the new collectives, on a scale that surprised even the Politburo, suggesting that the government had seriously underestimated the extent of their hostility—further evidence of their misunderstanding of the rural mind. Nevertheless, and despite the number of deserters from the new farms, the old ways were gone forever. By the summer of 1930 twenty-four percent of the peasants were collectivized, as opposed to forty percent the year before, but traditional patterns of land tenure had been disrupted, so that private farmers now held the poorest land in the community and the plots farthest away from their villages. More than 2.5 million of the most efficient farmers and their families had been deported, and the really able ones, the professional survivors, understanding that they no longer had a future on the land, had contrived to move to the cities.[41] There had been appalling losses in livestock and hence, eventually, in fertilizers; the stock levels of 1928 were not to be recovered until the late 1950s.[42]

While Soviet propaganda would celebrate the tractor as a symbol of the radiant future and the answer to all agricultural problems, the truth is that tractors were hard to come by and proved harder still to maintain. However, the tractor became a political issue, "an end in itself, a fetish, a symbol of the new age,"[43] and those who suggested that there were circumstances in which it might be useless were denounced as enemies of progress. Lack of mechanical skills apart, peasants tended to treat government tractors less lovingly than they had treated their own beasts, while others, still awaiting mechanization after all their draft animals were long gone, shared the lot of some inmates of the gulag who regularly found themselves on an assignment known as TFFOH, or temporarily fulfilling the functions of a horse.[44]

The Plan

The only country to cope with its workers' movement.
—NADEZHDA MANDELSTAM ON SOVIET RUSSIA

Various reasons have been advanced to explain the decision to industrialize at breakneck speed. The most popular, for Soviet historians at least, suggests the move was both correct and necessary to prepare the country for a war which the farsighted leadership already recognized as inevitable. One may wonder whether collectivization and industrialization were the best way to prepare the country for war, in view of the waste of manpower and resources that they entailed. Most probably they were not, but that is not to say that the threat of war argument should be dismissed. Stalin stated that war was imminent since capitalism had entered its so-called third phase, a time which would bring economic and political cataclysm, by no means an idiotic prophecy on the eve of the Wall Street crash and the Great Depression. Certainly threat of war was a potent element in Soviet domestic propaganda, helping build that atmosphere of feverish urgency which helped make Stalin's revolution acceptable.

Threat of war may have been less a cause than an excuse. Considering Stalin's change of direction, it appears that once he had eliminated his political rivals, he took the party in a direction that would appeal to its radicals, while committing the waverers to a course from which there could be no turning back. The party radicals were a more reliable source of support than a right wing that favored compromise with the peasants, believed in the NEP and would rather be governed than led. Moreover, the men Stalin had picked as his immediate supporters, the Ordzhonikidzes, Kirovs and Kaganoviches, administrators with plenty of ambition and a taste for power, would not welcome a policy that appeared to mark time and falter.

Alongside the impersonal factors there were also the personality and ambitions of Stalin to be considered. It is not fashionable to account for historical developments by the actions and attitudes of great men. But even if, say, collectivization had been inevitable, it would never have taken such a bloody and rapid course had it not been for Stalin. Over the period from 1929 until his death we shall see Stalin gradually formulate and bring about a certain conception of the Soviet state and of the proper extent of Soviet power. This is surely one of the greatest achievements in modern times. Not only did Stalin successfully impose his political vision upon one-sixth of the world's landmass, but his creation, far from dying with him, has survived virtually intact to this day, imparting to the Soviet Union a degree of political stability and continuity that is unique in modern times.

Stalin had an acute sense of Russian history, and his actions can be understood only when considered in a historical perspective. Many of his policies bear a curious relation to the sixteenth-century Muscovy under Ivan the Terrible; above all, he sought to restore its introverted insularity. Equally he was conscious of a need to restore to his country the territories it had held at its apogee, before the Japanese War of 1905. Finally he was also conscious of the achievements and style of the creator of the Russian Empire, Peter the Great. Peter comes down in history as a dedicated, violent ruler, with a colossal vision, the man who would drag Muscovy willy-nilly into Europe, at considerable cost to the Muscovites but to the ultimate benefit of their descendants. A one-man revolution from above imposed upon them a modern capital, a standing army, a navy and modern industry.

Stalin was very aware of Peter's example. Peter's love of grandiose projects, notably the construction of mighty and ultimately useless canals, is echoed by some of Stalin's more ambitious and futile undertakings, though where Peter simply attempted to reverse the flow of rivers, Stalin had more ambitious plans, such as a project to heat Siberia by diverting the Gulf Stream.[1] However the scale of his industrial enterprises—great dams across the Dnieper, new towns mushrooming overnight in Siberia—and the use of coercion to drive his land forward to greatness, all have an unmistakably Petrine ring about them. Stalin actually confirmed this. When explaining to the Fifteenth Congress why he had opted for massive investment in heavy industry, he reminded delegates of Peter the Great, who "feverishly built mills and factories to supply the army and strengthen the country's defences."[2] This is not to say that Peter "caused" the First Five-Year Plan. Rather, Stalin had a sense of Russian history which helped shape his political vision, and this in turn determined the kind of collectivization and industrialization that the Soviet Union was to enjoy.

In the mid-1920s Soviet economists had done serious work on the mathematical analysis of large-scale state-run economic development, their leader being Kondratiev, now regarded as a pioneer in the field of mathematical economics. Initially the State Planning Commission, Gosplan, produced a carefully worked-out scheme which related to Soviet needs and realities. However, it, or rather the planners, encountered one of Stalin's less explicable hostilities: his hatred of mathematical abstraction. He dismissed the whole field of mathematical economics on the ground that it was "idealist," not Marxist. The action is that of a powerful man made angry by concepts that he cannot see, touch or understand, and it might also be thought of as an administrator's mistrust of theoreticians. At all events his rejection of mathematical and technical planning aids would have repercussions in years to come. Stalin would refuse to invest in the development of computers in the 1940s, and would not even allow the production of desk calculators or cash registers. Soviet accountants were obliged to rely upon the abacus. He also mistrusted statistics, which, he alleged, again with some reason, could never be politically neutral, and called for "class statistics," which would presumably serve the cause objectively at the cost of "subjective" accuracy.

Stalin's mistrust of Kondratiev's economics extended to having Kondratiev shot. However, his treatment of Gosplan's proposals is fascinating. It recalls the kind of manager who doubles the targets that his planning staff have proposed on the basis that back room boys are cautious to a fault and that there is nothing wrong with making sales and production sweat blood to meet their quotas. Stalin set aside a plan which had tried to create a certain growth rate by the rational allocation of resources. He required Gosplan to set targets based on the crudest assumptions, which he then increased on his own initiative. There was much emphasis upon the immense and the grandiose, athough there was also an attempt to establish a plan for a socialist form of chess.[3] At the same time collectivization had succeeded in eliminating the peasant artisan long before the new industries were capable of replacing him. This made for shortages of certain goods such as domestic utensils, shoes, baskets and the simpler agricultural implements.

The plan itself soon lost all significance as an attempt to coordinate the nation's economy. Rationality gave way to immensity as its guiding principle, and overfulfillment of targets was considered essential, as party activists and Komsomol auxiliaries goaded the populace forward in a frenzy.[4] Soviet industry developed in an atmosphere of chaotic and urgent campaigning that was the antithesis of planning, as each enterprise sought to overfulfill its target at all costs and, if needs be, at the expense of others. The result was a kind of disorder that has been the bane of the Soviet economy ever since.

> One Soviet enterprise purchased its nail supply from a nail factory fifteen hundred miles away, while a nail factory across the street from it was shipping goods a similar distance. . . . A truckful of bath tubs was dumped on an empty lot in Moscow; three years later the apartments they were intended for began to be constructed on the lot. Valuable . . . imported turret lathes were plunked down on the wet, uneven ground that served as the floor of a Siberian factory, where they could not be used because they were not level, and where they rusted irretrievably in three weeks. A factory on a tributary of the Volga was completed just in time to be flooded by a lake that piled up behind a dam that had been built a mile down stream.[5]

Russian has a word, *pokazukha*, which means "the need to show off even though one may have nothing to display." It played a major part in the way that the plan was presented to the world, as heroic plants were celebrated for having fulfilled and overfulfilled their targets, while the actual achievements existed only upon paper.[6] As the British journalist Kingsley Martin observed in 1930, America's early development of the techniques of mass production provided the dominant model for *pokazukha* on "the industrial front": "Russia is in fact going through a stage of machine madness. There is a good deal of Americanism about the whole thing and the Communists have acquired the habit of boasting that their factory or dam or whatever is 'the largest in the world' and when I remarked that a new building was 'very American' my guide nearly fell on my neck and kissed me."[7]

It is now largely forgotten that foreign engineers and experts, Americans especially, did much to help establish Soviet industry. They came partly out of excitement, partly out of belief, partly because of the depression. An American journalist who visited Russia in 1930 estimated that there were about 1,000 of his fellow countrymen there. They did not find Soviet life easy, although it was a great deal easier for them than it was for the natives.

> Americans, who had come to set up the Stalingrad tractor plant, had the style of men in a hurry, and were infuriated by the frequent necessity to stand patiently in what used to pass in the USSR for a line, especially after a glass or two; they were notorious for their habit of smashing in the windows of street cars, to climb aboard as a crowd of pushing, struggling and vociferous Russians jammed the exits as they variously endeavoured to get on or off.[8]

In fact, their life was not bad at all; they had their own canteen in the tractor plant, in which a visiting American journalist observed the following curious notice: "The scoundrels who spread the rumour that the body of the dead American was taken from its grave and robbed of its clothing are nothing other than counter-revolutionaries."[9] The tale has a ring of truth to it, for these were times when it would have been a sensible thing to have done. The early years of the plan were not easy despite undoubted achievements in the industrial sector. Once more the mood of the moment is caught by its jokes:

> "Where are you going so fast?"
> "I'm off to jump in the river, there's no bread, no meat, nothing to wear, nothing to heat the apartment with."
> "But wait till the Plan's completed, there'll be plenty of everything."
> "If I wait that long there'll be no water."[10]

One of the more unsettling aspects of the plan was the temporary abolition of Sundays, in the sense that days off were staggered so that six-sevenths of the labor force were always working. People began to lose track of what day of the week it was. Leningrad Orientalists were lucky to find a fixed point provided by the local hammam, or ritual Muslim bath, which always took place on what used to be a Saturday.

It would be foolish to ignore the enthusiasm with which the plan was prosecuted if only because failure to display enthusiasm could have disastrous consequences. The point, once again, is driven home by a joke:

> The Politburo finding its work increasingly difficult and uncongenial

decides to provoke a revolution which will allow it to resign with
dignity. They hoped to provoke it by ordering every Soviet worker to
whip himself, and so it was decreed. Days passed and nothing
happened till at last they beheld a mighty crowd approach the
Kremlin, and assumed that the people had come to relieve them of
their office, in which assumption they proved mistaken. As the crowd
drew nearer they could see it carried banners, "Through whipping to
Socialism," "Whip harder for our Revolution" and then a small group
broke away and came forward with another banner. "We of the
engineering corps, because of our strategic importance to industry,
demand to be whipped out of turn." [11]

The workers were whipped indeed. They were underpaid and under-
nourished. By 1932 a skilled man's standard of living had fallen to a
quarter of the 1928 level and was considerably lower than that of his
unemployed counterpart in France, Britain or the United States.[12] Idealists such as Willie Campbell, the son of the Scots Communist leader,
who came to the workers' paradise to earn a living wage, were brought
abruptly to their senses. Campbell survived only because of his skills as
a jazz musician. We get an oblique view of the workingman's life from
this glimpse of a Soviet hospital:

> It was filled with cases of sickness or accident casualties whose true
> sickness or accident lay in chronic under-nourishment aggravated by
> alcoholism. The workers who lived on sour-cabbage soup, without a
> fat content, would acquire an abscess as a result of a simple
> bruise. . . . Children were covered in cold sores; whole wards were
> full of peasants with frozen limbs . . . they offered little resistance to
> the cold. . . . Bandages came in inadequate quantities so that
> dressings which should have been changed daily were only attended to
> every three days. . . . I heard arguments and bargaining going on
> among the nurses. "Give me back the three yards of gauze I lent you
> the day before yesterday, I've a patient here who can't wait any
> longer." [13]

The Russian worker's traditional response to poor conditions was
drunkenness and moving on. Many workers retained links with the land
and would go home to help at harvesttime. Now the work force had been
increased by dispossessed or prescient peasants who had moved to the
towns. Thus for a number of reasons the Russian worker was unusually

prone to wander—at least until now. In October 1930 the free movement of labor was forbidden, and factories were not allowed to employ anyone who had moved without permission, while unemployment relief was abolished—since there was no unemployment. Absenteeism was severely penalized; anyone arriving more than twenty minutes late for work automatically went to prison. The year 1932 saw the culmination of labor restrictions with the reintroduction of the internal passport, a hated symbol of workers' oppression in tsarist times, which made freedom of movement or unauthorized change of residence impossible. The measure was partly intended to keep starving peasants out of the towns; peasants were not given passports at all, a state of affairs that did not change until the 1970s. They thus reverted to the condition of their grandfathers, the serfs who had been emancipated seventy years before.

The plan also had indisputable positive aspects, one of which was the emergence of a new managerial caste. Often the sons of workers or poor peasants, young and hungry, they owed their rapid promotion to the party, and ultimately to Stalin, and were the material beneficiaries of a regime which obliged them to develop unusual managerial skills with remarkable speed. The confusion brought about by the plan and the breakneck pace of its obligations and objectives made a manager's task impossible if he stuck to orthodox channels. Yet if he failed and fell short of his norm, he would at best be dismissed and might well face a charge of sabotage. Soviet managers rapidly developed certain skills not unknown elsewhere, but essential in the USSR during the 1930s, which would serve the nation in good stead during the Second World War. The successful Soviet manager had to be a master of unofficial wheeling and dealing. He had to know how to lure skilled workers away from other enterprises or kidnap them even—by using contacts in the GPU to order their transfer or to borrow prisoners for the same purpose. He had to be able to manipulate an elaborate system of unofficial bribes, backhanders and quid pro quos to obtain the favor essential to fulfillment of the norm. The system, known as *blat*, the equivalent of the French *système D*, was a kind of semicriminal black market. It was a vital lubricant, a "nether world of unplanned, harshly competitive private enterprise under the surface of the Five Year Plan."[14] In that world the hustlers from Odessa were as important as they had ever been in the heady days of the NEP. Just as Soviet agriculture came to depend on the peasants' private plots for its fruit and vegetables, so industry depended in considerable measure on the sector of *blat*, making for an economy rather more mixed than might meet the eye. As a saying of the times went, parodying an official slogan, "In the age of socialist construction *blat* determines everything."

Along with *blat* was another practice essential to the survival of both management and labor, *tufta*, or the creative misrepresentation of socialist achievement. It was thanks to *tufta* that the impossible targets of the plan could appear to be met. The process was made easier by complex bureaucratic evaluative procedures such as time-and-motion techniques for job rating so complex that they could have been designed only by white-collar party men who had never done a day's work in their lives.[15]

Excellent examples of *tufta* were to be seen in work reports of snow clearance:

> Snow shovelling was priced by the cubic metre, having regard to how far the snow had to be thrown off the road—in other words, if it went sufficiently far, and the type of snow. In the norm sheets snow was of many different classes; there was loose, light snow, solid, crushed snow, snow that had thawed and frozen again. . . . When two or three hundred prisoners with shovels were . . . clearing a stretch of road onto which the blizzard kept piling up fresh snow a man had to be very clever to determine the cubic measurement of snow removed in a day or week.[16]

To add to the problems created by unrealistic targets and bureaucratic idiocy, the government had disposed of its old industrial experts. They were replaced by newly trained, loyal, but not necessarily skilled managers of its own creation. After the Shakhty trial a British engineer wrote: "I was to see many chief engineers—men of long experience and men who I believed were working loyally for the Soviet Régime— ruthlessly removed from their posts and replaced by young Party men whose theoretical and political training were without doubt excellent but who possessed exceedingly flimsy practical qualifications for the high positions in which they were now placed."[17]

The phenomenon, all too familiar to anyone with experience of newly independent African states, made for serious managerial mistakes as a generation learned on the job. Their task was not helped by a rapidly expanded work force that was mechanically unsophisticated. Russian peasants could do remarkable things with wood—one even invented and built a wooden bicycle in the early 1920s, only to discover that someone had anticipated him—but they had little experience of working metal. People at every level had to "pay to learn" with predictable results: "Tens thousands of freight cars left the rails . . . (according to the records of Kaganovich, People's Commissar for Transport there were 62,000 accidents to rolling stock in 1935.) . . . Hundreds of thousands of tractors rusted in their iron sepulchres. Millions of men worked themselves to death in stupidly arranged jobs quite beyond their capacity."[18]

The inability to treat machinery, especially agricultural machinery, properly was widespread. According to one American expert, a combine, good for ten years, or twenty weeks of harvesting in the States, lasted two years in the Soviet Union.[19]

A certain touchiness when it comes to admitting mistakes is not peculiar to the Soviet leadership of the early thirties. However, such feelings were compounded by a kind of paranoia born of a naïve sense of determinism, whereby every misfortune was considered the result of a coherent and concealed set of causes, and nothing could be ascribed to sheer bad luck. Besides, it takes experience of industrial management to understand how industrial disasters occur, as a series of minor errors combine imperceptibly to create a major one without there being one obvious and isolatable cause. In such circumstances it is not surprising that all the shortcomings that accompanied the attempt to change a rural society into an industrial one should have been blamed on sabotage. Not only was the Soviet Union surrounded by enemies, but it had been infiltrated by hundreds of thousands of saboteurs conspiring to bring about the failure of the plan. Throughout the thirties the press and radio called for perpetual vigilance in the face of the saboteur since it was axiomatic that things did not go wrong by themselves: "Not one mistake, not one accident should pass unnoticed. We know that assembly-lines do not stop by themselves, machines do not break down by themselves, boilers do not burst by themselves. Somebody's hand is behind every such action. Is it the hand of an enemy? This is the first question we should ask."[20]

•　　•　　•

> Splendid illustrated magazines . . . crowds of brightly dressed
> well-fed happy looking workers are shown with their palatial
> dwellings . . . nobody who ever sees these publications will
> ever believe tales of a half-starved population dwelling in
> camps under the lash of a ruthless tyrant.
> —GEORGE BERNARD SHAW IN A LETTER TO THE TIMES

The steady proliferation of arrests helped swell the population of the gulag, that third component of Stalin's revolution from above. Its history is too well known to require retelling here, except to touch on the role of forced labor in Stalin's Russia. The Soviet state made use of forced labor from its inception. In 1921 the economics department was already one of the three largest in the GPU. Later it became the largest, while its head, Feliks Dzerzhinsky, became head of the Supreme Economic Council. From the beginning the secret police attracted young people with technical backgrounds and managerial skills, just as it does today, and used forced labor on various enterprises throughout the twenties. However, it was not until collectivization that it began to employ forced labor upon a colossal scale.

It was a Turk, N. A. Frenkel, an ex-millionaire and himself a prisoner at the time, who in 1929 proposed to Stalin a novel strategy for the exploitation of labor, based on a sliding scale of rations which were determined by the laborer's work rate and took no account of their physical capacity to carry out the tasks assigned.[21] In other words, they were to be worked until they dropped and then permitted to starve to death. The suggestion played an important part in the formation of the Chief Administration of Camps, the gulag. Frenkel was released and soon became head of a major construction undertaking; he was later awarded the Order of Lenin.

Like so much of Stalin's revolution, the gulag might be thought of as the extension of Trotsky's ideas, here for the creation of a "labor army." Stalin simply developed it and, instead of conscripting labor, created an entire subcontinent of slaves. No one can say what the gulag population was at its peak; estimates range from 5 to 25 million with considered opinion favoring a figure between 6 and 10 million. Interestingly enough, the dramatic expansion of the camps came at a time when there was serious overpopulation in the countryside—25 million peasant farmers in 1928 as opposed to 18 million in 1913. It was also a time when the plan created a huge demand for industrial labor. This soon absorbed the pool of urban unemployed, while it was not at all easy to draw in peasants who were afraid that if they moved to the cities, they might forfeit their share in the land. Forced labor together with collectivization and the plan provided an elegant solution to these problems; especially since, as one historian has put it, "A particular advantage of NKVD [successor to GPU] enterprises was that they did not need to attract labour by the promise of better conditions of living."[22]

The camps served a further purpose. The mid-twenties had been a time of serious unemployment, a problem which Stalin solved at a stroke. Millions of deported peasants were put to work on labor-intensive enterprises, such as the White Sea Canal. Moreover, the work force was treated in such a way—i.e., badly—that there was a perpetual demand for fresh labor and thus no unemployment. The enterprise undertaken by the gulag might thus be thought of as Stalin's equivalent of Hitler's autobahns or Roosevelt's WPA projects; it was just that Stalin's version of the New Deal was a little different. By relying upon a huge and expendable population of slaves, he was able to deploy his manpower as he pleased.

Although Isaac Deutscher, the biographer of Stalin and Trotsky, has made the wondrous observation that forced labor was "a factor marginal to the system," on the basis that slaves constituted only ten percent of the work force,[23] it played a vital part in the calculations of the First Five-Year Plan, and from 1931 the gulag was expected to be self-financing. From a Marxist point of view this was unorthodox; Marx had stated that slavery was uneconomic since slaves had to be fed whether they worked or not and had no incentive to work harder. However, it was not the case that inmates of the gulag had to be fed. The difference in rations was colossal, varying from ten to forty ounces of bread a day.[24] Since the cost of acquiring slaves was comparatively low, and the supply limitless, why spend money on keeping them alive? It has been calculated that the cost of keeping a prisoner in the thirties was about a third of the average workingman's wage. Curiously, the notion that the purpose of the gulag was to provide cheap labor came as a comfort to loyal Communists, especially those in prison. It helped them accept an institution that was obviously necessary.

Slave labor was much used in industry since it replaced expensive machinery that had to be bought with hard currency, although some of the enterprises seem pointless. The White Sea Canal, for example, proved useless, and within a year or so of its completion its only traffic consisted of launches moving from one camp to another, while the canal was already silting up.[25] Slave labor was used successfully in the mining industry and other uncongenial or hazardous areas. The gulag also rented labor to civilian employers:

> The NKVD agreed to supply two thousand prisoners to begin with, the number to be enlarged in the spring. . . . There was a lot of cold-blooded bargaining on the qualifications of the slaves to be supplied and the price to be paid. An outsider intruding midway . . . would have assumed that horses or mules, rather than living men and women, were concerned. . . . The NKVD spokesman explained that

there was no dearth of prisoners, including the necessary percentage of
skilled workers and foremen. He could provide five thousand, ten
thousand, any quantity we wished. The only difficulty was where to
put them.[26]

Pace. Isaac Deutscher, an ex-member of the State Planning Commission, has maintained that by the end of the decade the gulag was the
main construction agency in the land. It supplied ten percent of the
timber, furniture and kitchenware, twenty-five percent of Arctic freight
towage, forty percent of the chrome and seventy-five percent of the nation's gold. There were also significant numbers of prisoners working
under police guard in normal places of employment.[27] Solzhenitsyn has
observed that rather than enumerate the ways in which forced labor was
employed, it is easier to name the one field in which it was not—the
food-processing industry.

Thanks to numerous memoirs by fugitives and defectors, a full picture of the gulag and all its horrors was available to the West decades
before the publication of Solzhenitsyn's books. The bizarre reluctance
of men of goodwill to accept or even to discuss these early accounts of
life in the workers' paradise is the subject for another book altogether. It
is an attitude summarized by Jean Paul Sartre's magnificent observation
that even if Stalin's camps did exist, their existence should be ignored;
"otherwise the French proletariat might be thrown into despair."[28]

Gori, Georgia. From *Le
Monde Illustré*, 1867.

Iosif Djugashvili in 1894.

Ekaterina Djugashvili, Stalin's mother.

Stalin in 1900. These photographs were found in the files of the tsarist police in Tiflis.

A card from the register of the tsarist secret
police of St. Petersburg with photos of
Stalin, 1912 or 1913.

Stalin, 1917.

Feliks Dzerzhinsky, 1917.

Stalin, Lenin and Kalinin at the Congress
of the Russian Communist Party in March
1919.

Stalin in 1920.

Trotsky at Petrograd railway station, 1920.

Soviet souvenir, April 1920. *Top, left to right*: Rykov, Radek, Pokrevsky, Kamenev. *Middle, left to right*: Trotsky, Lenin, Sverdlov. *Bottom, left to right*: Bukharin, Zinoviev, Krylenko, Kollontai, Lunacharsky.

Lenin and Stalin, 1922.

Kamenev, January 1924.

Bukharin and Marie Illyievna Oulianova
of Pravda.

Stalin, Rykov, Kamenev and Zinoviev.

Radek.

G. K. Ordzhonikidze.

The coffin bearing Dzerzhinsky, July
1926. Stalin is on the right in the white
shirt.

Stalin, December 21,
1929.

Nadezhda Alliluyev,
Stalin's second wife,
mother of Vassily and
Svetlana. She died
November 8, 1932.

Serge Kirov. He was assassinated in Leningrad, December 1, 1934.

Andrei Vyshinsky, the Pole who spoke for the Soviet Union.

Stalin, Roosevelt, Churchill and Molotov
at Yalta.

Stalin, Truman and Churchill at Potsdam.

Beria.

Stalin.

A State of Terror

By 1930 the better diplomats were getting Stalin into focus. The Polish minister characterized him as "A man of great courage, determination and even brutality. At the same time of singular astuteness. To any attempt to entangle him in abstract discussion he invariably replied that the question had already been disposed of in the writings of Marx or Lenin. . . . On the other hand he was a master of tactics. Before clashing with an opponent he was careful to steal that opponent's best weapons."[1]

A British report goes further, isolating an important aspect of his style:

> Stalin is said to be a man of extraordinary force of character and ability. . . . Lenin it is generally believed disliked and distrusted the young Georgian and in his will, which has never been published, is said to have bidden the Party beware of Stalin as disloyal, coarse and untrustworthy.
>
> Stalin deliberately makes himself a figure of mystery, rarely issuing from the Kremlin. (It is generally believed that he is suffering from persecution mania and fears assassination.) His public utterances are very few. . . . By surrounding himself with mediocrities and by the employment of an iron discipline, aided partly by luck and the natural apathy of the Russian people, he has reached a position of absolute despotism, such as no Mussolini ever attained. . . . His chief asset seems to be a faculty of divining the policy of possible opponents, condemning it as "deviation from the Party line" and then adopting the policy.[2]

It is a shrewd assessment, which emphasizes the role played in his style of leadership by mystery; one might cite the three principles by which Dostoevsky's Grand Inquisitor governed: miracle, mystery and authority. Stalin was unlike Hitler, who projected his power by the instruments of mass publicity—loudspeakers, photographs, public appearances and newsreels—seeking to impose his living presence upon the people, in an anticipation of a modern U.S. presidential campaign. Stalin preferred to remain mysterious. Where Hitler would receive quantities of well-screened outsiders and was always ready to talk to the press, Stalin scarcely ever gave interviews. He never addressed open meetings and made only two public appearances a year, on May 1 and November 7, behind ranks of police and soldiers and in front of hand-picked demonstrators, to whom he appeared remote and removed upon a distant reviewing stand. He even exercised control over his appearance, rarely posing for photographs, preferring stylized pictorial representations to candid camera shots and thereby turning his face into a formalized icon. People literally did not know what he looked like, and when an updated photograph was published in 1945, it came as a shock to the nation to see how he had aged. Outsiders, diplomats included, did not even know where he lived. They supposed, right up to his death, that he resided in the Kremlin, as opposed to his villas, Zubalovo and later Kuntsevo, failing to understand why the only decent road in the country was a short stretch connecting Zubalovo to the Kremlin.

· · ·

Stalin had made some changes in his secretariat early in 1930. Tovstukha was replaced by Poskrebyshev at its head, while its scope and functions were increased. The changes were consequent upon Stalin's coming to personal power. They also prepared for the purge of government and party that the Secretariat was to set in motion in the run up to the Sixteenth Party Congress scheduled for July of that year.[3] It sifted government and party staff, seeking potential opponents of Stalin's policies, and eventually thirty percent of the administration and ten percent of the party were purged, though not, at this stage, arrested. The purge functioned at every level and was no respecter of seniority. Its victims included Uglanov, who was replaced as head of the Moscow organization by Kaganovich, and Tomsky's supporters in the unions, who were dismissed for displaying "Trades-unionist tendencies."[4] Senior local vacancies were seldom filled by local men and women; almost all the replacements came from the Central Committee apparatus, the

Secretariat or one of the top party schools. It was now that members of the Stalin generation began to surface, as names like Malenkov, Khrushchev, Suslov, Ponomarenko, Beria, Serov, Gromyko started to figure prominently.

In the circumstances it is scarcely surprising that the Sixteenth Congress appeared an assembly of yes-men. On the day it opened the front page of *Pravda* was almost entirely taken up by a picture of Stalin, with a tiny insert of Lenin in one corner. Bukharin had avoided the congress, pleading that he was sick, but Rykov and Tomsky were obliged to make public confession of their errors. However, confession no longer brought absolution. A sinister note was struck with the observation that those who confessed did not always mean it, that they merely moved from open to covert opposition.[5] Stalin's increasingly demonological view of opposition had developed a stage further. It is a short step from the concept of covert opposition to the view that no one can ever have a clean bill of health. As Stalin later observed, the greatest saboteurs are those who never sabotage.[6]

Stalin gave a composed and studied seven-hour report on the state of the nation. According to an American journalist, he presented himself as a "calm engineer building a new world, diverting great rivers of national history, blasting out millionfold classes, bridging centuries of backwardness, levelling mountains of opposition."[7] In other words, he was a twentieth-century Peter the Great. He also gave a truly staggering reply to those who questioned the human cost of his undertakings, inquiring of them whether they were "afraid of cockroaches" (creatures, incidentally, toward which Peter the Great had entertained an implacable hostility).[8]

Beneath the official unanimity of the congress there were faint stirrings of opposition. Hitherto-loyal Stalinists were beginning to feel that the human misery was too great, the achievements not significant enough to justify it. Understandably many who were out of sympathy with Stalin preferred to remain silent, so that it becomes increasingly difficult to gauge resistance to his policies. However, in 1930 two young men of the Stalin generation, both members of the Central Committee, Lominadze and Syrtsov, circulated a memoir criticizing the "general line" for its authoritarianism, its mistreatment of peasants and workers and its economic shortcomings. They were both expelled from the Central Committee, and Lominadze committed suicide a few years later.

Suicide showed no sign of going out of style. In 1930 the poet Mayakovsky, once an ardent celebrant of the Revolution, took his own life—shortly after Stalin had put an end to what literature there was left by declaring that henceforward nothing should be printed that did not promote the "general line." In the meantime, the use of terror and arbitrary arrest was stepped up, aimed for the moment at ex-NEP traders, the old intelligentsia, engineers and, as ever, the peasantry. For G. Agabekov, a GPU man who defected in 1930, this was the year in which the moral deterioration of the police became total; no longer a "defender of proletarian interests," it had become the instrument of Stalin and his clique: "In the struggle for power within the GPU the notion of socialist competition between departments became the order of the day. Competition resulted in the number of persons in prisons and camps increasing in geometric proportion to the size of the population."[9]

The year 1930 inaugurated the golden age of the *donos* ("act of informing"). Its advent was heralded by the opening of a new section in *Pravda* for letters of "self-confession and denunciation" and was soon reflected in the jokes and anecdotes of the time:

> A couple asked the GPU for permission to invite a dozen guests to a party. The police replied that they could invite ten guests and that they would supply the other two. The couple agreed, saying that they were inviting only their closest friends and submitted the list, which the police returned saying that they would not need the extra couple since more than two of their people were on the list as it stood.

> A man looks at himself in a looking-glass and observes "One of us must be an informer."[10]

One rough estimate was that every fifth person in an average office was a stool pigeon.[11] The office would contain various kinds of informer. The special department had agents, as did the local party committee, the GPU, and the city committee, while the regional committee received reports from its people on the city committee. This made for an interlocking pyramid of surveillance which extended to the very top.[12] Anyone could expect to be invited to become an informer or "secret collaborator" *(seksot)*. It was dangerous to refuse and necessary to produce results, failure to do so being an offense in itself. Informing became the national pastime; as the writer Isaac Babel observed, it was a time when one could talk only at night, to one's wife, with a blanket pulled over the head—precautions which did not save him from a firing squad. Everyone possessed the power of life and death over his neighbor—and people used it: to dispose of jealous husbands and wives, to gain possession of more living space, out of spite or for fear that if they did not talk, somebody else would and they would be arrested for "failing to inform."[13]

Informing was a Russian tradition of long standing. In the age of Peter the Great it was customary to report friends and neighbors for "word and deed"—treasonable talk or behavior. If the charges were found proven, the successful informer would be rewarded with half the victim's worldly goods. However, in those days the law discouraged mischievous informing. Both informer and accused would be subjected to judicial torture, and the one to hold out the longest would be deemed to have truth on his side. In Stalin's day informing was easier, but the reward only amounted to twenty-five percent of a victim's wealth, the only form of private enterprise encouraged at the time. "Informing became a way of life, and not out of police pressure and fear alone. Two authors in an article on Soviet ethics claim that anything furthering the cause is 'moral and ethical.' Soviet patriotism is the most profound manifestation of a new ethic . . . a new psychology of man. . . . Soviet patriotism is the highest stage of moral behavior and ethics in man and society."[14]

Soviet citizens happily informed on one another out of honest conviction, as the *donos* became a form of state-directed gossip. Evgeniya Ginzburg, a good party member at the time, found herself in a group of newly arrested women waiting to be searched. She was approached by one of them with a moral problem. She had seen another woman conceal jewelry in her hair. As a good Communist would Comrade Ginzburg tell her whether she was morally obliged to inform on her fellow prisoner? After due thought Ginzburg solemnly replied that in view of the unusual circumstances it was not necessary. The martyr-hero of collectivization, the Communist Horst Wessel, was the young Pavlik Morozov, a good Komsomol member murdered by his relatives for denouncing his parents as covert *kulaks*.

One of the strangest stories from a strange time is the account of how the GPU classified its arrestees: according to the number of people who had informed on them. It established four categories that rely on the Russian language's capacity to generate increasing orders of diminutive: enemy *(vrag)*, lesser enemy *(vrazhok)*, small enemy *(vrazhonok)*, tiny enemy *(vrazhonochek)*. Arrestees were charged with crimes corresponding to their positions on the scale.[15] That great analyst of Soviet reality

Alexander Zinoviev has suggested that informing is an essential feature of Soviet life. Far from being an aberration, the "organs," or secret police, express the very essence of Soviet reality. Even if it were not "necessary" to track down spies and enemies of the people, Soviet society would evolve a secret police anyway.[16] The contention is vital to an understanding of the Soviet people's assent to Stalin's terror. The denunciation of enemies was a national sport of long standing, a simple variant upon that passion for telling others how to live which runs through Russian culture from *The Instruction of Vladimir Monomakh* of the late eleventh century via *The Housebuilder* of the sixteenth, through Gogol, Belinsky, Dostoevsky, Tolstoy, to the redoubtable voice of Solzhenitsyn ringing out from his New England fastness. It is a compulsion found not just in literature but in life, as a responsible Soviet citizen wags the finger and instructs one to desist from photographing a perfectly harmless building or leans over one's shoulder to correct an indifferent move in a game of chess. Dostoevsky himself is all too aware of the Russian eagerness to tell others how they should live. "Show a Russian . . . a map of the night sky that he has never seen before, and he'll immediately start correcting it," he once observed.

Of course, a readiness to tell others how to live does not *necessarily* lead to Stalin's terror, or Peter the Great's Secret Chancellery, or Nicholas I's Third Department or the Okhrana of Nicholas II, or the continuing hordes of *stukachi* ("knockers," or informers) in the Soviet Union of today. The proliferation of informing in Stalin's Russia was due to many factors besides nebulous notions of national character, the shadow of the gulag being but one. Yet it is important to realize that in a civilization which has no verbal equivalent for the expression *Live and let live*, there was more than a faint undertone of real approval in the officially orchestrated jeers, catcalls and howls of opprobrium which the public was ordered to bring down upon the heads of Stalin's "enemies of the people." Significantly the Russian language is unusual in that it has a word, *zloradstvo*, that is the direct equivalent of the German *Schadenfreude*, the taking of delight in the misfortunes of others.

CHAPTER TWENTY-EIGHT

New Society

Moscow, in 1930, was taking on an increasingly run-down appearance, yet it appeared to be a city dedicated to leisure pursuits:

> Musical instruments, French horns predominating, fish hooks, hockey sticks and skis are the chief commodities on display . . . there is absolutely nothing else to buy.
>
> No other feature of Moscow's streets is so impressive as the endless rows of empty dusty windows. . . . They are the shop windows of a deserted city. The milling crowds that surge along their sides make their vacancy bizarre. . . . It has been calculated that the average time taken up by standing in line to obtain sufficient food and supplies for each family is at least two hours a day [three hours in 1983]. In order to buy a [railroad] ticket it was necessary to stand in line from midnight until ten o'clock the next morning a full week in advance of the departure of the train.
>
> There go two youths wearing chopped off ancient rubber boots. An ill-clad bearded man has his feet wrapped in rags . . . wait for a good pair of boots to go by. . . . Nine cases out of ten it will be a soldier or one of the uniformed troops of the GPU. [1]

Our most vivid sense of the shortage of virtually everything is conveyed by the memoirs of a fugitive. As he crossed the frontier from Russia into Finland, he realized that he had escaped when "I saw a piece of yellow paper in the grass. It turned out to be a grocery bag composed of two layers of strong well-glued paper, such as could not be found in Russia. . . . Crumbs of white bread were scattered inside, clearly indicating its bourgeois character. We also found a piece of string; this also is a rarity in Soviet Russia. Yura solemnly rose and embraced me ceremoniously."[2]

Stalin dealt with the shortages by discovering more scapegoats. The year 1930 saw the second show trial, of the "Industrial Party." A group of economists and engineers was accused of participating in a gigantic conspiracy directed by capitalist governments and Russian émigrés. The accused, headed by a Professor Ramzin, all made public confessions of their sins. In the meantime, the Soviet Union stepped up its anti-French and anti-British propaganda, accusing the Western powers of sabotaging the Soviet economy as a preliminary to declaring the war that was to take them out of the slump. British workers were called upon to "stand by your class."[3] The British ambassador, Sir Esmond Ovey, saw through the "trial" at once, and his dispatch provides an impeccable analysis:

> First it is not a trial at all in the Anglo-Saxon sense of the word. It is definitely a demonstration. The accused, who have theoretically nothing to look forward to but the certainty of being executed, appear on terms of pleasant and entirely courteous intimacy with their judges, and even with the Public Prosecutor. They evidently take the greatest pains to omit no detail in their self-accusatory statements, and in rare cases of forgetfulness their attention is drawn to their lapse by the prosecuting counsel in the manner of a schoolmaster showing off the skill of a favourite pupil.[4]

The trial was accompanied by hundreds of meetings at which those attending howled for the blood of the accused. "The proletariat thanks the glorious GPU, the unsheathed sword of the revolution, for its splendid work in liquidating the dastardly plot." In due course the ringleaders were sentenced to death, although the sentences were commuted to terms of imprisonment, enabling Ramzin to win a Stalin Prize in 1943 for the invention of a new type of boiler. No foreign observer seems to have been taken in by the trial, with the exception of Duranty of the *New York Times*, whose dispatches follow the official Soviet line. Of the trial he writes: "To your correspondent the most surprising thing is that the punishment was so long delayed. . . . It is hard to believe that there was no sinister attempt behind such appalling waste."[5] When he described the trial again in a book he published in 1942, Duranty concentrated on the way Ramzin tied the prosecution in knots and offered no comment on the delay in punishment.

• • •

The Soviet Union was short of hard currency with which to continue financing its industrial development. Its chief exports were commodities, such as timber and, though it could ill afford it, grain, which fetched declining prices on the depressed world markets. The gold mines of Kolyma had not yet reached their subsequent remarkable production levels, but the authorities discovered a simpler method of extracting gold—directly from their citizens. Of all the violence, terror and pain that Stalin inflicted upon his people, the gold extraction campaign was probably the worst. The GPU gathered up anyone who might "objectively" possess gold, ex-traders, priests, jewelers, dentists, clockmakers, and invited them to exchange it for tokens that could be used in hard-currency stores. Those who would not, or could not, deliver were put in overheated cells, fed salt fish and denied water. They were also beaten. Those who had nothing to offer were often beaten until they died, for there was no way out for them. Others could postpone their beatings by handing over their hoards, but there was always the risk that the police would think there was more and start to beat them again. Not everyone arrested was beaten to death. Some died of other causes; others survived. Yet the believers accepted even this treatment as "necessary" since the nation must have its gold. In a society in which there is no public opinion and no means of redress against illegal procedures, why *not* beat citizens to death in the hope that the process might yield a little gold?

Not all of Stalin's campaigns were brutal. This was also the time of the celebrated "Stalin cow," also known as the rabbit, which was to end shortages of meat and poultry at a stroke. Rabbits were imported and distributed by the million: to hospitals and party organizations, to housewives and even to the clergy. Refusal to accept rabbits was deemed a form of sabotage.[6] The rabbit became a celebrity; its pictures were featured in papers and on billboards throughout the length and breadth of the land, while the academic community published learned papers extolling its virtues.[7] Unfortunately the rabbits proved disloyal and sterile. "They forgot how to breed and began to die off as fast as class enemies in concentration camps. . . . A few forlorn bunnies now still lingered on billboards, and a few arrests for disrupting the rabbit breeding programme were still being made—great campaigns die slowly. But the rabbit was through."[8]

Meanwhile, Soviet agronomists evolved a substitute for the hay, oats and barley that were no longer being produced in sufficient quantity to maintain the nation's livestock. They discovered a new form of silage:

> It was proven officially that the small branches of pine and fir trees were remarkably rich in calories and vitamins, and the "authorities" began to inculcate the idea of "twig fodder." The question as to whether the horses and cattle would eat it never occurred to them. However as in the case of the famous rabbits, whoever protested was sent to a concentration camp. The *kolkhoz* [collective farm] peasants wandered sadly through the forests, cutting off twigs, which were subsequently crammed into the silo. . . . As long as there was a little hay left, the poor horses managed to survive somehow, but when they were restricted to one hundred per cent tree fodder they died off. The chiefs of the camp unit were in no hurry to send in reports concerning the pine-tree ensilage. While not responsible for the experiment, they would, nonetheless very likely be answerable for its failure.[9]

> The condition of the surviving collective farm horses was so pitiful that they were unable to draw an empty cart . . . and I myself visited hundreds in which the horses were supported by ropes under their bellies because they were too weak to stand.[10]

•   •   •

In the summer of 1931 Stalin instituted a change which did more than any other action of his to determine the kind of society Soviet Russia became under his rule. Hitherto, at least officially, equality of income *(uravnilovka)*, had been an important feature of the regime. Even the income of party members had to observe a maximum. Of course, this egalitarianism was relative and did not extend to party members' going hungry or unshod, like the rest of the population, nor did it prevent Communists of rank from riding in Fords, Packards and Cadillacs, while their wives never had to stand in line.[11] However, in June 1931 Stalin abolished the party maximum, calling for a wide-ranging differentiation in incomes, amplifying that principle of privilege which had already played its part in earlier years. At a time of increasing shortages the practice of distributing benefits in greatly varying proportions had exceptional impact. The degree of differentiation was truly remarkable. Alexander Pyatigorsky came from a professional family that was relatively well-off; that is to say, they had all the bread, flour and sugar that they wanted, but no candy and very little meat. At the level above, though, people lived like royalty. Pyatigorsky recalled a reception given by his father's superior at which evening dress was worn and white-gloved servants distributed imported wines and all the meat, smoked fish and caviar one could wish for. This was also a time when he recalled seeing peasants dying of hunger on city streets.

The father of a subsequent refugee, A. Granovsky, ran a chemical plant. He had a large official residence, decorated, furnished, stocked with china, silver and linen, all free. There was a villa near Moscow and a five-room apartment in the capital—at a time when an ordinary family was lucky to have a room to itself and use of a communal kitchen—three cars, a stable of horses and a motorboat. Food and clothing were also provided, while his workers lay in crude wooden barracks and could scarcely afford a change of clothes.[12] Differences in pay and purchasing power were not always so blatant; then, as now, the elite favored surreptitious as opposed to conspicuous consumption. For example, GPU men received special ration cards which could be used to buy food and consumer goods at special prices in shops open only to them, increasing the real value of their salaries by a factor of ten. There were, in fact, hundreds of different sorts of ration card, for various categories of goods and shops.[13] The result was an ever-increasing differentiation, as Arthur Koestler discovered when he was in Kharkov in 1932: "The rights and privileges of the individual were entirely dependent on the rank his organisation, administrative department, factory, occupied in the social pyramid, and on the rank he occupied in that organisation. There has never perhaps been a society in which a rigid hierarchical order so completely determined every citizen's station in life and governed all his activities."[14]

My favorite illustration of Koestler's point is a sign posted upon the door of a Moscow canteen: "The open canteen is closing, a closed canteen will be opening in its place."[15]

The uneven distribution of benefits proved a great success. It provided, and provides, a powerful incentive—much stronger than the key to the executive washroom. It focused the ambitions wonderfully, developing vigilance and loyalty to the regime. The joy of the system, for Stalin, was that no one owned the benefits he enjoyed. They could be taken away as easily as a company car, leaving the fallen official with nothing, not even a roof over his head. If the Western democratic tradition derives from the development of freehold, then Stalin's service state was its antipode; no one owned anything that was not recoverable at a moment's notice. Such a system discouraged its beneficiaries from reflecting too much upon the fate of fallen colleagues, while there were, of course, no alternative employers. Sinking or not, the rats had to stay on board the ship; they were, effectively speaking, nailed to its mast. It was a system that brought forth a new type of manager, the type Stalin wanted: brutal, hungry and pitiless.[16] The higher the new men rose, the greater their privileges, and they could rise only on the backs of others. The system created a form of natural selection, the survival of the most ruthless. "A man with a heart would have been a poor factory director at the time."[17]

●   ●   ●

It is by no means true in the Soviet Union that dog does not eat dog.

—SIR ESMOND OVEY

No bread in the villages: left deviation.
No bread in the towns: right deviation.
No bread anywhere: "general line."

—SOVIET JOKE

Students of the most somber chapters of Russian history can usually find a flash of farce to lighten them. December 1931 provided such an occasion in the shape of a visit to the Soviet Union by George Bernard Shaw and the intrepid Lady Astor. Shaw conducted himself like a buffoon, who knew all about the country before he arrived. He informed a meeting that his friends had loaded him with canned food to prepare for his visit, but as he crossed the frontier into the Soviet Union, he had thrown it out of the train window. His underfed audience gasped; the idea of the wasted food seeming a bitter mockery. Shaw went on to assure them that he knew that the tales of shortages were "poppycock." Had he not himself just eaten a magnificent meal? "He spoke at length that night. But his cynical talk of throwing food away was the one memory that remained deeply chiseled in a thousand minds when the celebration dispersed."[18]

Lady Astor was different. As far as we know, that redoubtable lady is the only person in history not to have been egregiously deferential to

Stalin when meeting him for the first time. She inquired of him point-blank when he was going to stop killing people. Although her inter-preter nearly died of stress, Stalin, to his credit, remained unperturbed, replying that the process would continue for as long as it would take to build communism. Lady Astor emerged very well compared to Chur-chill, on his first meeting with Stalin. To make conversation, Churchill observed that Stalin must have had a grievous time of it during collec-tivization, and Stalin, who liked the feel of his tongue in his cheek, answered earnestly that yes, it had been a difficult time indeed—surely the only occasion in history when two political leaders have made small talk about genocide.

Shaw excelled himself on his return from Soviet Russia, writing and speaking extensively, revealing his ignorance of its realities with every word and helping convince persons of goodwill that socialist Russia was a happy, prosperous and enthusiastic country, with youth at the helm and an enlightened attitude to the arts and physical culture (he was especially impressed by displays of mass gymnastics and by the heroic girl parachutists). Addressing the Soviet people themselves as he was about to leave for home, he stirred them with a promise: "When you carry your experiment to its final triumph, and I know that you will, we in the West, we who are still playing at socialism, will have to follow in your footsteps whether we like it or no."[19] The same idea was later expressed by a Red Army commander with a sense of humor, looking forward to liberating Europe in the aftermath of the Second World War: "We shall stretch out a fraternal helping hand to you, the feet you will stretch out yourselves [stretch out your feet, i.e., drop dead]" *My pro-tyanem vam bratskuyu ruku pomoshchi, a nogi vy sami protyanite.*"[20]

• • •

It is curious that the two areas in which the Soviet Union has been most successful should be the development of the world's finest secret police and the presentation to the world of a face which many people, often people of power, influence and undoubted intelligence, should find not simply acceptable but downright respectable. The Soviet gov-ernment was as good at public relations in the early 1930s as it is today, and it is scarcely surprising that the blackest chapter in its history, and in Stalin's biography, too, should be so little known. To most non-specialists collectivization means deporting millions of peasants and forcing the rest into collective farms, the tearing asunder of families and appalling hardship. Yet one could say to a Russian peasant in 1932, after four years of collectivized life, that true horror was still to come. The Sixteenth Congress gave Stalin authority to pursue his policy of collectivization and grain collection. The 1932 harvest was a poor one, about twelve percent below average, but grain was needed to finance the plan even though this entailed selling into a falling market. Grain exports had risen from under 200,000 tons in 1928 to nearly 5 million in 1931. Undeterred by the poor harvest, Stalin set out to recollectivize those peasants who had responded to his "Dizzy from Success" speech by leaving the new farms. He also stepped up grain procurement targets by forty percent. Those about to go into action upon the grain front received a new kind of briefing. Stanislas Kossior, secretary of the Ukrainian party, observed to his activists:

> The peasant has adopted a new tactic. He refuses to get the harvest in. He wants the crops to perish in order to throttle Soviet power with the bony hand of famine. But the enemy has miscalculated. We'll teach him what famine is. Your assignment is to stop him from sabotaging the harvest. To collect it all down to the last grain and take it at once to the delivery point. The peasants are not working, relying on the grain they hoarded and hid in pits in past years. We must make them open those pits. [21]

The January edition of a Ukrainian publication entitled *Collective Farm Activist* mounted an assault upon peasants who, although "they have grain, deliberately starve themselves and their families to death in order to sow discontent among other collective farm workers." [22] In Gogol's play *The Government Inspector* a flustered police chief, who has irresponsibly had a woman flogged, suggests that "she flogged herself." On the threshold of probably the greatest man-made famine in history peasants seemingly were starving themselves to death. For starve they did, in their millions, as the grain collectors took everything, down to the seed corn. Men, women, children were arrested for stealing their own crops, sometimes using scissors to trim ears of wheat off the stalks at night. Thanks to the passport system, peasants were supposedly tied to the soil, forbidden to move to the towns where food might still be found, but some got through nonetheless and could be seen dying on their feet in the streets:

> It was horrible to see the starved people dragged along the road, their bare, swollen feet scraping against sharp stones. . . . Scurvy and boils

covered their bodies. Their legs were bloated. Some were insane and
spat at the Guards and Young Communists who teased them.

The children of well-fed Communist officials, Pioneers, stood by
and parroted phrases of hate learned in school. . . . I was witnessing
myself how human beings were being tossed into the high lorries like
sacks of wheat. . . . There were cries of pain rending the air as the
swollen and blistered captives were tossed into the trucks.[23]

The trucks took the peasants out of town and dumped them at the
roadside, while "Every night trucks with canvas tops collected corpses
from train stations, from under bridges, from doorways. They drove
about the town [Kharkov] at night."[24] Not all the corpses were collected
at once. There was a fashion among the dying which will appeal to
those for whom only the blackest humor will do. It was customary at the
time to take the bodies of dead friends—or strangers—and pose them at
the feet of the statues of Lenin that were to be found in many city
squares.[25]
The villages were worse:

We came across a dead horse and a dead man at the side of the road.
The horse still lay harnessed to the wagon. The man was still holding
the reins in his lifeless hands. Both had died from starvation it
seemed. The village we reached was the worst of all possible. . . . The
village was dead. Going up to one of the shacks we looked into a
window. We saw a dead man propped up on a built-in Russian stove.
His back was against the wall. He was rigid and staring at us with his
faraway dead eyes. . . . We found more dead people in what had been
their homes. Some bodies were decomposed. Others were fresher.
When we opened the doors huge rats would scamper to their holes
and then come out and stare at us. At one house there was a sign
printed on the door . . . "God bless those who enter here, may they
never have to suffer as we have." Inside two men and a child lay dead
with an icon alongside of them. . . . Many of the houses were empty.
But to the rear the graves told a story of desolation and ghastly death.
More signs were stuck up by these graves by those who buried them.
"I love Stalin, bury him here as soon as possible." "The collective
died on us." "We tried a collective this is the result." On our way back
people told us that the village was to be burnt. Three or four others in
the vicinity had been burned already.[26]

Horror became an everyday spectacle. "On no occasion that I can remember did I fail to see a death from starvation during my travels to the city."[27]

It was not always the case that villages were razed, not at least in the north. There dwellings were often left standing and being sturdily built log cabins, they stood for a long time. Igor Golomstok, once one of the Soviet Union's leading historians of art, told me that in the late 1950s it was the fashion among Moscow intelligentsia to make trips to the north and explore it by boat, visiting deserted villages, where one could find pieces of peasant craft—utensils, spindles, carvings—that had been lying there for a quarter of a century.

In their search for food the starving ate everything, from the horse manure which still had a few grains of wheat in it to the bark of trees. In the Urals and western Siberia there were outbreaks of pulmonary plague spread by the fleas of marmots. The peasants caught the disease by digging out their burrows in search of the grain stored there.[28] There were also numerous reports of cannibalism—for the second time in just over a decade. A Ukrainian language paper, *Dilo*, published in Poland, printed an interview with a refugee collective farm manager who alleged: "The Soviet Government does not allow corpses to be buried until they are decomposed because if fresh corpses were buried the population would open their graves and eat them. Cannibalism is spreading wholesale. Peasants often eat their dead children. The Soviet government punishes cannibalism by shooting without trial, but that does not help much because death has lost its terror."[29]

A U.S. journalist, Harry Lang, had a bizarre encounter with a Soviet official who had an anticannibalism poster in his office. Embarrassed by his foreign visitor, he tried to explain it away with the remarkable excuse that *some of the local people were still pretty primitive*, trying "to suggest that cannibalism was the result of the cultural backwardness of the Russian people."[30] The situation was aggravated by the official view that the famine did not exist, so there could be no famine relief. The most that was conceded was the existence of "temporary local supply difficulties" which in fact were not difficult at all. Khravchenko recalls seeing stores of grain, guarded by Red Army men, hard by villages in which the native population was starving to death,[31] administered by officials who had more than enough to eat:

> I thought of the new privileged class in the village, the Party and Soviet functionaries who were receiving milk and butter and supplies from the cooperative shop, while everyone around them starved.

> Slavishly they obeyed orders from the centre, indifferent to the
> suffering of the common people. The corruption of character by
> privilege was fearsome to behold; these men who only a few years ago
> were themselves poor peasants had already lost the last trace of
> identification with their neighbours. They were a caste apart, living in
> an intimate clique, supporting each other, banded together against the
> community.[32]

The government was remarkably successful at concealing the famine
from the world. Anyone talking or writing about it abroad tended to be
branded as a tsarist reactionary, for as an embassy dispatch put it, "Soviet organisations can now do anything they like in or outside of the
Soviet Union, as the majority of educated and responsible opinion in
Europe and America is simply incredulous of any criticism of the Soviet
Union, Soviet decency or good faith."[33]

The view that reports of the famine had been exaggerated was reinforced by Intourist, which took selected visitors on tours of the alleged
famine areas, where peasants were on view smiling happily, if a little
wanly, on station platforms. However, this did not always work. A German journalist tried throwing bread at a group of allegedly well-fed
peasants, with results indistinguishable from a stampede. On the whole,
foreign correspondents did not know much about the famine and were
urged by the press office to remain in Moscow. However, some discovered it for themselves, notably Malcolm Muggeridge, who reported
from the Kuban that it had become a desert inhabited by starving peasants and occupied by well-fed troops.[34] Walter Duranty, whose dispatches had done much to play down the famine, finally made a trip to
see for himself. He returned from the stricken areas and told his colleagues that the horrors were real enough but concluded his account
with the curious observation "But after all they're only Russians."[35] Yet
even famine could be justified by the appropriate objective/subjective
juggle. An American believer, whose faith had been shaken by tales of
cannibalism and megadeaths, was told: "Don't worry, Comrade Smith,
because you do not find conditions as good as you expected to find them
here. Don't worry that you saw people dying of hunger. If twenty million die of hunger, we will still have plenty of people to continue our
work. And what does it matter if millions of people die, as long as we
are building socialism."[36]

In his own attitude toward the temporary supply difficulties Stalin
surpassed himself. At the height of the famine he addressed a congress

of collective farm stock workers and spoke to them on the subject of an altogether different hunger, that of the year 1918, "when the workers of Leningrad and Moscow were issued two ounces of bread a day, and that continued for the whole year. But the workers put up with it and stayed cheerful because they knew that better times were coming. Just compare your hardships and deprivations with the hardships and deprivations endured by those workers and you will find that they are not even worth discussing." [37]

In old Muscovy, where channels for the expression of discontent were scarcely better than they were in Soviet Russia, the established form of protest was to leave an anonymous letter *(podmyetnoye pis'mo)* lying in a public place to be picked up and circulated. Few people in Soviet Russia cared to live that dangerously, but some letters found their way to foreign embassies in the hope that someone, somewhere, might gain an inkling of what was going on. The number of letters increased appreciably in the second half of 1932. The following is typical, written by a factory worker from Saratov:

> Listen, comrades, and hear how they live in the land of intensive collectivization. You are told of the achievements of the USSR but you must see the realities in order to value at their true worth the achievements of Comrade Stalin. You cannot buy bread at the market; it is forbidden and other foodstuffs are so dear that a worker's wage for a month is only enough for five days. The other twenty-five days the worker goes hungry or sells his chattels, for the communal eating houses feed you only filth. People are dying of starvation at the rate of 150–200 a day. There is no room left in the cemeteries. We Russians have never been in such a position, not even in the famine year of 1921. [38]

Other letters complain of purges, and arrests, giving a vivid picture of concentration camp life. While most complain of the socialist experiment, they also contain a pronounced anti-Semitic strain, blaming Jewish-socialist machinations for their misfortunes. This casts an interesting light upon Stalin's subsequent purge of the predominantly Jewish Old Bolsheviks. Ordinary people would have viewed his action as punishing Jewish socialists for the misery they had inflicted upon the masses; those who survived collectivization did not suffer nearly as much as party members in the actual purges. Once again Stalin made scapegoats of his Jewish victims.

In his little talk with Churchill Stalin mentioned that 10 million peasants had had to be dealt with, which is not to say that they all were liquidated. Analysis of population figures shows that it ceased to grow in 1928 and resumed only in 1936, and suggests that his victims probably numbered a little more than 5 million, a body count which makes some of Hitler's achievements seem modest.

CHAPTER TWENTY-NINE

Terror Begins at Home

By no means all the victims were nameless peasants. For Stalin terror may be said to have begun at home. His eldest son, Yasha, had long been at odds with his father. He had been raised by his aunt and uncle in Tiflis and then insisted on completing his studies in Moscow. Very much against his father's wishes he joined the Stalin family; he was only seven years younger than his stepmother, and they were apparently close. Stalin disliked his son, who failed to give him that unquestioning obedience which was the only kind of loyalty that he recognized. Yasha objected to the set of his father's mind and the dogmatic way in which he expressed himself. The boy did not find life in Moscow easy, had difficulty in learning Russian and was distressed by his father's lack of support.

Yasha angered Stalin still further by announcing his intention to make what Stalin considered an inappropriate marriage, and the ensuing strain drove him to a suicide attempt. He shot himself in the kitchen of their Kremlin apartment. The bullet missed his heart, and although he was very ill, he eventually recovered. Stalin reacted to the news with a derisive snort, mocking his son for failing to do the job properly. The episode is a curious echo of another shooting by the eldest son of a Russian ruler. Peter the Great's son once tried unsuccessfully to shoot himself in the hand to avoid having to demonstrate nonexistent skills in technical drawing, thereby incurring his father's scorn for yet another failure.

Nadezhda Stalin was very upset by her stepson's attempt to die. She had grown increasingly unhappy in her marriage, as she discovered that

Stalin, far from the hero she had supposed him, was a coarse, brutal bully who cared for her not at all. By all accounts she was a woman of resolute character, not given to accommodation or compromise. She had enrolled as a student in the Industrial Academy, where she had gradually learned the truth about Soviet reality, notably from fellow students recently returned from the Ukraine.

According to an acquaintance of Stalin's bodyguard Pauker, there was a series of angry arguments between husband and wife in which Nadezhda gave as good as she got.[1] Stalin ordered a purge of all her fellow students who had been to the countryside to help with collectivization and told his wife to stay away from the institute for two months.[2] She became increasingly depressed in the course of 1932, telling her friends that she had lost all love of life. An acquaintance of hers, the diplomat Alexander Barmine, saw her that year with her brother, Paul Alliluyev, at the anniversary celebration of the Revolution. She looked pale, worn and listless; it was obvious that her brother was deeply concerned.[3]

That was her last public appearance. On November 8 Voroshilov gave a party in his Kremlin apartment which the Stalins attended. There are a number of versions of what happened, but they all agree that Stalin offended his wife in public and that the humiliation was too much for her. The "weak" version provided by their daughter is that Stalin said something like "Oy, you, have a drink" to which she answered, "Don't oy me," and ran from the apartment. Another version has him arriving after her, drunk. A remark of hers enraged him, and he threw a burning cigarette at her, which fell down her dress. She left at once, and Stalin followed her.[4] Another source, E. Lermolo's *Face of a Victim*, which cannot be cross-checked and is suspiciously full of fascinating encounters, suggests that there was a further reason for the quarrel. Throughout the 1930s there were rumors that Stalin was having a liaison with a sister of Kaganovich's named Rosa. The rumors are even found in diplomatic dispatches. Some claim that he eventually married her. His daughter dismisses the story, denying that Kaganovich even had a sister, while it is hard to believe that her father would have slept with, let alone married, a Jewess. However, Lermolo alleges that Rosa was already Stalin's mistress and that this was a further humiliation for his wife.[5]

We do not know what happened next. It appears that Nadezhda returned to her apartment. It is certain that the next morning she was dead and that a pistol, a lady's Walther, which her brother had bought her in Berlin, was at her side. According to her daughter, Molotov's wife, Zhemchuzhina, had seen her back to her apartment and left her in a reasonable mood. The next morning it was found that she had shot herself. The Lermolo version has her accompanied by Voroshilov. She was hysterical and declared herself to be at the end of her tether. When she calmed down, her maid began to undress her, whereupon she fainted. The maid telephoned the Voroshilovs and told Stalin what had happened. He returned to find that she had come to. A violent quarrel then took place. There was a blow and the sound of a body falling, whereupon the maid came in to find her mistress lying dead on the floor. Yet another version suggests that Stalin strangled her.

Besides the two hypotheses of suicide and murder there is a third which is perhaps the most interesting. This has it that Stalin found Nadezhda waving her pistol about and that a struggle took place in the course of which she was shot by accident. This version is supported by one piece of reported evidence that rings with authenticity as the kind of item no one could invent. In later years Stalin took to thinking a lot about the death of his wife. Characteristically he considered it to have been a breach of loyalty, and his mind would reach out to try to find the guilty party. Sometimes this was the author Michael Arlen, whose novel *The Green Hat* Nadezhda had just been reading. He also blamed her brother for providing the gun, and here his daughter cites a phrase that rings so true that it could not have been invented. It was, he said, "such a piddling little pistol" *(takoi plyugaven'kii pistoletik)*.[6] While the phrase would fit the suicide scenario, it seems more appropriate in the context of an accidental death. At all events it is not the observation of a murderer. On this occasion one cannot easily accuse Stalin of anything graver than manslaughter.

Stalin was deeply affected by his wife's death; he did not dismiss that event with a derisive snort. Although it was usual for distinguished Bolsheviks to be cremated, he ordered that his wife be buried in the Novodevichii monastery, on the western side of the city, which also held the grave of his first wife, the sister of Peter the Great and many members of the nobility. In Soviet Russia it has become the last resting place for distinguished figures who fail to make it to that holy of holies, the Kremlin Wall. Although one might have expected a quiet funeral, it was nothing of the sort. Despite his fear of assassination, Stalin announced to Yagoda, his chief of personal security, that he was going to walk behind the coffin through the streets of Moscow to the cemetery, a distance of more than four miles. Yagoda could not believe his ears;

Stalin never made public appearances. When inspecting a newly opened factory, he would have it cleared of workers and occupied by GPU men and would fall into a rage if he even glimpsed an employee while passing from his Kremlin apartment to his office.[7]

The funeral began at 3:00 P.M. on November 10. The cortege was headed by a squadron of GPU cavalry and a GPU band. Then came a wagon full of wreaths drawn by red-caparisoned and black-plumed horses; Stalin followed on foot.[8] In the event, he did not walk long. After ten minutes he transferred to a car and drove ahead. Nevertheless, his readiness to expose himself, for ten whole minutes, to the genuine danger of an assassin's bullet is extraordinary. He thought a lot about his wife in latter years, and as late as 1950 he used to pay regular visits to her tomb.[9]

It was officially given out that Nadezhda had died of appendicitis. Foreign correspondents' telegrams were censored if they dwelt upon the suddenness of her death, for, as a dispatch put it, "It is possible that the broadcasting of the cause of death might be considered a reflection upon the efficiency of Soviet medicine." The report continues with the speculation that she might have committed suicide. It also bears a comment in its margin which provides the saddest of epitaphs: "Interesting but unimportant—Poor Madame Stalin mattered not at all to anybody, and least of all to her husband."[10] In the aftermath of her death Stalin left Zubalovo, which one presumes held too many memories for him. He moved into a new villa at Kuntsevo, which began as a single-story building and was regularly rebuilt over the years until it became unrecognizable. Stalin lived on the ground floor, which consisted of a series of identically furnished rooms, each one being a bedroom and living room combined.

●　　●　　●

One would have to assume that all members of the party were idiots or sadists for there to have been no opposition to Stalin's methods of collectivization. There was opposition, although "opposition" in the political sense was no longer possible. There is a further factor of some significance: By now many of Stalin's potential opponents were exhausted, had lived through too much history. Arthur Koestler describes the Old Bolsheviks as they appeared in 1932 and 1933:

> They were all tired men. The higher you got in the hierarchy, the more tired they were. I have nowhere seen such exhausted men as

> among the higher strata of Soviet politicians, among the Old
> Bolshevik guard. It was not only the effect of overwork, nervous strain
> and apprehension. It was the past that was telling on them . . . and
> sticking to the rules of a game that demanded that at every moment a
> man's whole life should be at stake. . . . Nothing could frighten them
> any more. Nothing surprised them. They had given all they had.[11]

He then contrasts them with the ruthless and ambitious managers of
the up-and-coming generation.

Yet even if Stalin's potential opponents were largely exhausted, there
seems to have been a quietly growing opposition toward his treatment of
the peasants, in the light of industrial output figures that showed that
the plan was falling short of its targets, that the end was failing to justify the means. It is impossible to gauge its extent. Officially the party
presented an unqualified unanimity, and any expressions of dissent fall
beyond the reach of written records. However, we know that Stalin was
not entirely unopposed in 1932 and 1933, that there were documents in
circulation calling for his replacement as general secretary. It also appears that certain Red Army commanders—the name of Blyukher is the
one that occurs most often—called on him to relax his war upon the
peasantry. More important, Stalin was no longer able to carry his Politburo on certain issues.

In the summer of 1932 Mikhail Ryutin, once an ally of Uglanov's in
the Moscow organization, together with some younger members of the
right opposition, had composed and circulated an attack upon Stalin.
Describing him as the evil genius of the Revolution motivated by lust
for power and revenge, who had brought his country to the brink of an
abyss, it called for the reinstatement of all expelled party members, including Trotsky, and painted such a vivid picture of the shortcomings of
the regime that many Trotskyites who read the document supposed it to
be a GPU provocation.[12] There was also a second piece in circulation
which called for a change in leadership and dissolution of the collective
farms.

Stalin chose to regard Ryutin's attack as a threat of assassination and
called on the Politburo for his head: execution to be followed by the
physical extermination of his supporters within the party. However, the
Politburo turned him down. Molotov and Kaganovich would certainly
have voted with Stalin, but he was apparently opposed by Ordzhonikidze, Kossior, Rudzutak, Kirov and perhaps even Kalinin. Instead of
going before a firing squad, Ryutin was expelled from the party and

banished from Moscow, treatment mild enough to be construed as a major snub to Stalin and a triumph for the forces of moderation. Certainly, as we shall see in exactly four years' time, Stalin considered his defeat an act of betrayal. However, as usual he was slow to move against his enemies. For the time being he was content to defer to the spirit of moderation that had overtaken the Politburo.

Early in 1933 the British ambassador, Sir Esmond Ovey, sent a ciphered report expressing the view that Stalin had lost support within his party: "While the government is still reported strong, acute observers feel the present dictatorship has outrun the general views of the Party and that the country under Stalin is now almost exclusively [governed] by the army and the secret police regardless of any councils of moderation."[13] This was not quite the case; both police and army counseled moderation at one time or another, while the country was governed through the machinery of the party. However, the report properly emphasizes a sense that Stalin had gone too far for many of his supporters. Speeches he made to the Central Committee reflected this mood. They made it clear that there would be no going back from collectivization; at the same time, by announcing that the battle to collectivize had been won, he recognized that the time for punitive proceedings was over. However, he warned his audience not to overestimate the new farms, saying that their socialist "forms of organization" were less important than their content; in other words, they could still conceal enemies. He also admitted that there had been difficulties with grain deliveries, explaining these as the work of saboteurs and wreckers.

The result was a pronounced increase in arrests among nonparty intelligentsia, such as the entire school staff of Tsarskoye Selo—all accused of sabotage. Many of them were simply exiled for the time being, to be rearrested in due course. The arrests continued until the summer holidays, a period which regularly saw a seasonal slackening.[14] It was this wave of terror that brought the poet Osip Mandelstam to full understanding of the regime. He declared to his wife that the point of the terror had become perfectly clear: nothing less than the annihilation of everyone left in the land who retained a scrap of sanity.[15] Collective insanity was increased by rumors such as the one that the GPU "Big House" in Leningrad had "an elaborate mincing machine in which . . . the GPU destroyed their victims before washing the remains out into the Neva."[16]

•   •   •

The campaign against wreckers and saboteurs made renewed use of the notion of foreign devils and the capitalist threat, culminating in another show trial which would explain the failure of the plan. The British firm of Metropolitan Vickers Electrical had employees working in every branch of Soviet industry that used electrical power. The company's leading engineers were now arrested, to star in a superplot that would account for failures in every aspect of the economy.

In an attempt to impart an air of juridical solemnity to the proceedings which might convince foreign observers of its bona fides, on this occasion the courtroom did not have the appearance of a stage set, with swatches of red bunting, revolutionary slogans and portraits of the nation's leaders. The chief defendants were six British engineers who were accused of sabotage and who had previously signed confessions to that effect. Unfortunately they withdrew them the moment they appeared in open court. Their prosecutor was an ex-Menshevik of Polish extraction, Andrey Vishinsky, whose star was very much in the ascendant. In due course he secured a conviction from his court, and two of the engineers were given token prison sentences, two and three years, while the rest were to be deported. However, after the British imposed an immediate trade embargo, the sentences were commuted and the guilty men sent home. As a show trial the affair was a mixed success. It convinced few foreigners but gave a lot of Soviet citizens the kind of explanation for failures and shortcomings that they wanted to hear. The trial also elicited an observation from Vishinsky that should become a classic comment on Soviet life. Foreign observers were informed that in the Soviet Union, "We have our own reality." [17] The notion used to be conveyed more idiomatically to the newly arrested who tried to complain of the illegality of the proceedings. "This isn't England, you know," they would be told. [18]

While stepping up terror in appropriate quarters, Stalin relaxed his assault upon the peasants. He announced the abolition of forced grain deliveries and their replacement by a tax in kind. This was set at two hundredweight an acre, regardless of the yield, providing an incentive to produce as much grain as possible. At the same time grain was actually purchased on the Baltimore Exchange and Red Army reserve granaries were opened. The party mobilized once more, this time to convince the peasants that Stalin could be trusted. A new party organ was created, the political section of the MTS, or machine tractor station—that vaunted replacement for private beasts of burden. The party worked hard to restore confidence among surviving peasants, and it succeeded.

They went back to work, and the harvest of 1934 was excellent. They were also given a further reward, permission to cultivate private plots of vegetables, the *priusad'byennye uchastki*, which were to become the mainstay of Soviet agriculture, restoring the principle of a mixed agricultural economy. Thus in 1937 the private sector produced fifty-two percent of the nation's potatoes and vegetables, seventy-one percent of its meat, fifty-seven percent of its fruit and seventy-one percent of its milk.[19]

As he made his concessions, Stalin insisted that Bukharin and the right should confess that they had been wrong to condemn the breakneck pace of collectivization, ensuring that no one could suggest that Stalin and the "general line" had been incorrect. This tactic prompted the British ambassador to observe: "Were it not for the utter unreality of all published Soviet political opinion it might seem bewildering that the very moment when an argument is proven correct should be utilized by its exponents to renounce that argument."[20]

One of the explanations proposed for this retreat upon the agricultural and to some extent the industrial "fronts"—the Second Five Year Plan set much more realistic targets than the First—is the influence of a man who may still have had Stalin's ear, the writer Maxim Gorky. Gorky is an artist of uneven quality, whose reputation has been exaggerated in some circles because of his support of the Bolshevik and subsequently the Soviet cause. This earned him the place of "Russia's greatest living writer" throughout the regime's early years. He was not universally loved among the intelligentsia, some of whom were not impressed by articles he wrote in support of the trials and his celebrations of Soviet achievements such as the White Sea Canal. On a cell door in the far northern prison of Solovki a famous occasion was commemorated by a graffito reading: "Today Maxim Gorky honoured us with a visit. He seemed pleased with his handiwork."[21]

Nevertheless, it has been maintained that Gorky, in the early to mid-1930s, tried to persuade Stalin to slow things down. As we shall see, Stalin had a surprising degree of respect for the arts, and it may be that Gorky really had some influence, especially when reminding him of the judgments of posterity. For by now Stalin had a sense of his own stature, and considerations such as the findings of the court of history were becoming important. It may be that Gorky managed to persuade him that the time had come for moderation.[22]

CHAPTER THIRTY

The Cult

In the early thirties Stalin began to grant interviews to carefully chosen journalists and persons of distinction, in which he presented himself as a plain, superficially simple and overwhelmingly modest man, who never forgot that he was just a disciple of the great Lenin. These interviews have produced comments of a quite magnificent fatuity such as that of the journalist Emil Ludwig, who saw him as a "dictator to whom I would readily confide the education of my children."[1] H. G. Wells opined that Stalin owed his position to the fact that "no one is afraid of him and everyone trusts him."

There was indeed an air of austere simplicity about him, because his sole passion was power and he had no time for the trappings of small-scale amour-propre. His sense of self operated on such a colossal scale that at the heart of it he could present himself as a genuinely humble and simple man. Yet we should recall that the mid-1930s also saw the development of the cult of personality, the greatest celebration of a single man in modern times. "If there was a cult of the individual in the Soviet Union who was responsible for it? It is an absurdity to charge Stalin with responsibility for it. It is not possible for a man to create a cult of himself."[2] So wrote an unrepentant Stalinist in 1956, at the time of Khrushchev's Secret Speech and in one sense he was right; the pyramid shape of the party hierarchy tends toward the celebration of whoever happens to be at its apex. Khrushchev and Brezhnev may not have been dictators in the sense that Stalin was, but in their day, they came in for their share of adulation, which even contrived to turn them into distinguished military figures. Nevertheless, the scale of the Stalin cult was not just the consequence of a system; it could have come about only with his assent and active encouragement. His own explanation—"If this is what the people want I see no harm in it"[3]—will not do at all. No one, certainly not the once-talented writer Count Aleksey Tolstoy, could "want" to write: "I want to howl, roar, shriek, bawl with rapture at the thought that we are living in the days of the most glorious, one and only, incomparable Stalin! Our breath, our blood, our life—here, take it, O great Stalin."[4]

Equally it would be hard to understand how philosophers could suggest that "certain prognostications of Aristotle have been incarnated and explained in all their amplitude only by Stalin," who, "together with Socrates," represents the "peak of human intelligence."[5] It is perfectly clear that the "cult" was Stalin's doing. Ultimately it was he who was responsible for, say, the 151 statues and portraits of him to be counted in Moscow's Kazan Station.[6] As the writer Ilya Ehrenburg put it, "The deification of Stalin did not come about suddenly, nor did it stem from an explosion of popular feeling. Stalin organised it himself."[7] It was organized to the point that kindergarten children were trained to thank Stalin for their happy childhoods as they rose from the table,[8] to the point that typesetters had to follow an elaborate protocol that required, for example, the full word *Comrade* never the abbreviated form *c*, to appear before Stalin's name; it could appear on only one line and had to be accompanied by certain epithets. It was incorrect for those reporting to Stalin to remain seated when speaking with him on the telephone.[9]

The cult had its comic sides, not the least of which was provided by the strange case of the Kazakh folk poet. A Russian journalist working on a Kazakhstan newspaper printed some "translations" of local folk poems composed in praise of Stalin. They were well enough received in Moscow for him to be invited to bring forth their author, thereby obliging the journalist to confess that he had invented him. However, it was decreed that an author be found regardless. An old folk poet, Dzhambul, was discovered who performed his poetry to the accompaniment of a primitive musical instrument, and for whom a rich new life was about to begin. An entire factory of writers was assembled to create "translations" of his work, among which an ode to Stalin featured prominently, making a national hero of the bewildered old nomad who knew no Russian. Shostakovich, who tells the story, observes, "As usual people will say that none of this is typical, and I'll reply why not, it's very typical."[10]

There is no reason to suppose that the cult did not please Stalin enormously. A political leader who refers to himself in the third person is likely to have vanity to spare. This is not to say that he supposed all that was said of him to be true, although one may presume that his skepticism waned over the years. But since the cult was practiced by millions with every reason to hate him, their worship provided him with gratifying evidence of a personal power so absolute that it obliged millions of his victims to profess love for him whether they felt it or not. Orchestrated adulation also had practical uses. It worked upon the naïve and the young, who seem actually to have felt what the cult taught them to feel. Those Red Army soldiers who ran to their deaths in battle in 1941 shouting, "For Stalin," were all young; their elder comrades-in-arms may also have died with words on their lips, but those words were certainly not "For Stalin."

Before pouring scorn upon unfortunates such as the philosophers who were obliged to mention Stalin in the same breath as Socrates, we should understand that they had no choice. This was truly a time when no one could afford not to love Stalin. Equally, no one could afford to fall behind in the race to find new superlatives for the expression of his love, for any hesitation was suspect, and suspicion led directly to arrest. The result was a dreadful inflation of rhetoric, as the value of expressions of love, adulation and worship of the "great man" plummeted daily. There is no better illustration than a case recalled by Solzhenitsyn. At the end of a local party meeting there was a standing ovation in honor of Comrade Stalin. Everyone stood and applauded, for minute after minute, until the meeting gradually realized that no one dared be the first to stop. At the end of eleven minutes a factory director took it upon himself to desist and sit down. He was followed at once by the rest of the meeting, who gratefully fell back into their seats. That night the director was arrested, charged with sabotage, and told never again to be the first to stop clapping.[11]

•   •   •

Stalin used the period of relative moderation to make some important changes and promotions. For some years, due to the prolonged illness of Dzerzhinsky's successor, Menzhinsky, the actual head of the GPU had been his assistant Genrikh Yagoda, a former pharmacist and, as Dzerzhinsky had been, a supporter of the policies of Bukharin. In 1931 Stalin had demoted him to second assistant under Ivan Akulov (*akula* happens to be the Russian for "shark"). The move was not a success, for Yagoda had too many supporters in the police and Stalin needed their full cooperation during his war with the peasants. Within four months Akulov was removed, and Yagoda restored. But in June 1933 Stalin brought Akulov back to a new position which made him supervise and control the actions of the police. In early 1934 the police itself was renamed the People's Commissariat of Internal Affairs, the NKVD, and deprived of several of its judicial functions. For six months it remained a commissariat without a commissar, until Yagoda, who seems to have triumphed again, was awarded the post. Despite the loss of its judicial branch, the police grew stronger in other respects. Besides controlling political police, frontier guards and internal security troops, it took over the militia, to become an immensely powerful force, a blend of army, police and secret police, that answered directly to Stalin.

This period witnessed the rise of another policeman, Lavrenti Beria, whose reputation as an exterminator has successfully concealed the man himself. Any description of him should begin with his exceptional intelligence. When Stalin put him in charge of Russia's atomic energy program, he gained a grasp of the principles of nuclear physics which amazed one scientist, who, trembling, had expounded them to Beria in, as he put it, "the lecture of a lifetime," only to hear his pupil deliver his own version of that lecture soon after to members of the Central Committee, displaying greater clarity and precision than the professor could ever have mustered. As he spoke, Beria occasionally caught the eye of his "tutor" and smiled. The tutor did not smile back.

Beria, a Georgian, was born in 1899, and he already had a reputation for police work by the time he left school in 1915, displaying a talent for tracking down school thieves, which earned him the nickname of the Detective. He joined the party in 1920 after living a dubious existence in the criminal underground of Azerbaijan and had links with the separatist Mussavat party, a serious blot on his Bolshevik copybook about which Stalin knew but cared nothing. For Beria possessed the kind of criminal temperament that Stalin appreciated and trusted because he could understand it. He was ambitious, opportunistic and free of all idealism. A very hard worker—the only Bolshevik who worked in his car—he was also a good man to work for, one who stood up for his staff. Sources hostile to him have alleged that he was a compulsive womanizer who enjoyed seducing or, failing that, raping young girls and who did not hesitate to make use of his powers in order to secure his pleasures. As a policeman he was reputed to be an accomplished interrogator thanks to his skillful use of the blackjack.[12] From the early twenties he had displayed a remarkable ability to get rid of any colleague who stood in his way, and by 1928 he was already a legendary figure in the GPU. Within the agency this was attributed to his closeness to Ordzhonikidze. A fellow policeman described him as a political illiterate, with no concern for the "general line" and more interest in the politics of the Tiflis street. [13]

Beria, who had risen to be head of the Georgian GPU, took over as secretary of the party there in 1931. He grew close to Stalin in the following years, asserting an influence to which Nadezhda Stalin objected strongly. Stalin answered her protests by asking her for proof that Beria was evil. According to their daughter, Beria's personal hold upon Stalin increased after his wife's suicide. He appeared to fill a void and provide Stalin with the companionship of a kindred spirit in his loneliness and, again according to Svetlana, to act as an evil counselor and encourage him to develop the dark side of his personality. While there is a tendency here to "blame it all on Beria," it is plausible that Stalin should have enjoyed the intelligence and cast of mind of his fellow Georgian and felt drawn to his unsentimental and practical temperament.

In 1933 Stalin introduced another character who played an important part in the next few years. Nikolai Ezhov had worked for some time in Stalin's personal secretariat. Unlike Beria no one anticipated that he would make a suitable head of the secret police. Those who knew him in the twenties found him a pleasant young man, devoid of arrogance or any distinctive feature except for his diminutive stature—five feet. He seems to have fallen under the spell of Stalin, who recognized his capacity for blind obedience and pushed him up the ladder as a result. In 1933 Stalin put him at the head of a committee that was to purge the party in the aftermath of the Ryutin affair. Later he was placed in charge of the newly created Special Secret Political Division of State Security, itself part of the Secretariat. Shortly afterward Poskrebyshev was officially declared to be Stalin's secretary and head of what was henceforward known as the special sector, *(osobyi otdel)*.

The development of Stalin's machinery of government was now complete. It represented the fusion of his personal secretariat with the party's special sector, which had acted as an instrument of staff control in every branch of the administration, including the police. By 1934, on the eve of the great purges, Stalin ruled the country with a personal apparatus which controlled all levels of administration and which was responsible for security and communication with the secret police; certain departments of the police were part of the special sector. The special sector's network extended to all local party organizations, giving Stalin control of a highly centralized kind.

The extent of the system's centralization was astonishing. A few years later, at the height of the terror, a Pole, Alex Weissberg, shared a cell in Kharkov with a local ex-lieutenant of state security, who revealed that there were only *two administrative levels* between himself and the top. He would see the head of the Kharkov NKVD at least once a week, and once every two months his chief would see the head of the secret police.[14] This enabled Stalin to transmit not just direct orders but nods, hints and winks as to how he wished his police to proceed.

Stalin made another important appointment in 1933. He created the office of prosecutor general of the USSR and made Andrei Vishinsky of Shakhty and Metrovickers fame its first deputy. A professor of law, Vishinsky had even been appointed rector of the Law Faculty of Moscow University. As an academic he specialized in aspects of the law of evidence and the nature of judicial proof. He published books on those subjects which cast an interesting light on the Soviet theory of show trials: "The court has an educational function which consists of using the public dissection of the case to reveal and present to general opprobrium the disgraceful deeds of enemies of the Soviet State."[15] "In conspiracies the question of how one treats the evidence of the accused must be posed with quite particular care."[16] As a prosecutor he was renowned for the relish with which he abused his victims, making use of expressions such as "human garbage," "beast in human form," "mad dogs," "hideous scoundrels," "scum" and, a favorite throughout police and judicial agencies, "reptile."

Reconciliation

We shall offer decisive and united resistance to all who
endeavor to disunite our ranks.

—S. M. KIROV

The Seventeenth Congress of February 1934 was termed the Congress
of Victors. Stalin's speech announced the triumph of Leninism, the
elimination of a Trotskyite opposition and of all other deviations. In a
spirit of conciliation Kamenev was restored to favor, and made a speech
extolling the virtues of personal dictatorship. Another victory speech was
made by the head of the Leningrad organization, S. M. Kirov, who had
been associated with Stalin since his days as commissar for nationalities.
Very much a Bolshevik of the new type, he was five years younger than
Stalin. Kirov was popular within his fief, where he was perceived as one
of the few leaders who were not afraid of the people they led; unlike
Stalin or Molotov, he was always prepared to talk with ordinary workers
on the shop floor. He was also an excellent orator who could reach an
audience with simple language, and he was particularly popular with
the young.[1] His speech to the congress was in the plain style fashionable
at the time. It ended as follows: "Our successes are really huge, colossal,
the devil knows; to put it frankly, you just want to live and live. Just take
a look at what's actually happening. It's true all right."[2]

The congress was not quite as united as it appeared. Indeed, expressions of dissent were actually permitted, and erstwhile members of the
opposition allowed to speak without being interrupted by those jeers and

catcalls with which the faithful usually signified their disapproval of dissent. Thus Bukharin, who had also been restored to partial favor, made a speech that was implicitly critical of a vital aspect of Stalin's unfortunate foreign policy.

Stalin had displayed consistently poor judgment in foreign affairs. His greatest mistake had been his failure to bring about a joint Social Democratic/Communist opposition to the rise of Hitler. Instead, he decided that social democracy was the true enemy, only a step away from "social fascism," and that the German Communist party should cooperate with the Nazis to bring down the Weimar Republic. At this point Germany would fall like a ripe fruit into the waiting basket of communism. (In a sense Stalin was right, except that he got only half the country and it took eleven years and more than 30 million deaths to get it.) However, now in 1934, a year after the German president, Paul von Hindenburg, had invited Hitler to become chancellor, his policy appeared a total disaster. Not even Stalin's wondrous scheme to undermine Hitler's government by persuading the kaiser's son to head an aristocratic opposition had succeeded in creating a counterweight to National Socialism.[3] Bukharin spoke at length about the Nazi menace, making it clear that he believed Stalin's foreign policy to have been mistaken. Nevertheless, the left wing of the party continued to maintain a pro-Nazi stance; early in 1934 Radek observed to a Nazi professor visiting the country on official business: "In the faces of the brown-shirted German students we see the same dedication and inspiration that once brightened the faces of Red Army officer candidates. There are magnificent men in the SA and the SS."[4]

Foreign policy was not the only point of dissent. According to L. Shaumyan, one of the few delegates to survive the next thirty years of Russian history, there was even opposition to Stalin himself: "Some of the delegates had come to the conclusion that it was time to remove Stalin from the post of general secretary and find other work for him."[5]

The statement is somewhat suspect; it was published at a time when it was fashionable to blame Stalin alone for the misfortunes of the thirties. Nevertheless, there is reason to believe that it was suggested to Kirov that he assume the post of general secretary, a suggestion he rejected out of hand.[6] This was not all. According to the same source, when the votes for the Central Committee election were counted, it transpired that 292 out of 1,225 delegates had voted against Stalin. Face was saved by the annihilation of 289 of those ballot papers, but news of the voting leaked. A British Embassy report on the congress cited a rumor that

Kalinin had polled the most votes and that Stalin had come in only third. It was not clear who had come second.[7]

Yet although Kirov was much applauded at the congress, his reception was no warmer than that accorded Stalin's henchmen Molotov and Kaganovich, nor can he be thought of as standing for anything other than the "general line." He may, though, have been considered the right man to lead the party away from the horrors of collectivization and the higher lunacies of the plan. Certainly he exercised moderation in his fief and was well known for his readiness to employ repentant members of the opposition. Finally there is one curious feature of the congress. It elected a new Secretariat consisting of Stalin, Kaganovich, Kirov and Zhdanov, an up-and-coming protégé of Stalin's. In *Pravda's* account of the election Stalin was referred to as "secretary" as opposed to "general secretary," the title that he had used since 1922. This, it should be recalled, was a land in which misprints were a shooting matter, and such changes were never accidental. It would suggest either that there was a genuine reduction in Stalin's authority or, more plausibly, that he felt it prudent to respond to the opposition he could clearly sense by taking a less prominent role and allowing the spirit of moderation to persist for the time being. A reliable source has suggested that there was a struggle for "influence over Stalin's soul" between moderates and extremists such as Kaganovich and Molotov, who knew that they would go under should the moderates win.[8] For the moment, though, Stalin displayed a remarkable capacity for trimming and even for mercy.

In 1934 Osip Mandelstam wrote the only direct attack on Stalin known to have been produced and circulated by a nonparty man. It is a poem, not a very good one, that describes the state of numbed silence in which the country had its being. The piece also contains a caricature of Stalin the lover of executions and, in one variant, the murderer of peasants. Foolishly Mandelstam read his piece to a tiny circle of his closest friends, and one of them reported him. In the perspective of the age his crime should have brought him before a firing squad without delay. It is not easy to piece together what happened, but it appears that Bukharin interceded with Stalin, who indulged in a curious Harun al-Rashid-like move. In order to find out more about Mandelstam, he telephoned the writer Pasternak, who was called to the communal instrument outside his apartment to find himself speaking with Stalin. Stalin told him that Mandelstam's case was under consideration and asked him what he thought he should do. Pasternak replied noncommittally that Stalin should proceed as he thought fit, but Stalin continued to press him: "But he's a great writer (*master*), is he not, a great writer?"

Pasternak again was noncommittal, and Stalin then observed with a sneer if *he* were a poet and a fellow poet were in trouble, he would behave differently. Pasternak retorted that that was not the issue.

"What is?"

"Life and death."

Stalin hung up.[9]

One of the most hair-raising telephone conversations in history resulted in Mandelstam's life being spared, for the time being. He was exiled first to Siberia and then to Voronezh in southern Russia and was eventually rearrested to die in a camp. It is extraordinary that the only man of the age to voice such public criticism should not have been shot at once. This may not just be due to Stalin's temporary spirit of reconciliation, but may also reflect a strange respect he displayed for the arts. At a time when persons of prominence in every walk of life seemed doomed, most of the leading artists, writers, musicians and theater people of the age survived; an anomaly that can only have been Stalin's doing.

In 1934 Stalin sought a new kind of popularity, as he began to encourage an upsurge in patriotism and Russian nationalism. The word *rodina*, "motherland," as in "betrayal of the motherland," was introduced for the first time: Soviet Russia was a mother, whereas prerevolutionary Russia had been *otechestvo*—a fatherland. Hitherto it had been easy for foreign believers to obtain Soviet citizenship. Now citizenship became hard to acquire, and foreign Communists were placed at a disadvantage, no longer being admitted to party meetings. This was put down partly to a fear of spies and sabotage, partly to Stalin's understanding of the popularity of appeals to Great Russian chauvinism. He wanted the support of the masses now because he was about to embark upon the next phase of his revolution, one to be directed at members of his own party. Over the next four years more than sixty percent of the delegates attending the Congress of Victors would be arrested and seventy percent of the Central Committee would be shot.

THIRTY-TWO

The Kirov Affair

To those who have served Russia faithfully Stalin has always
been a loyal friend and generous colleague. He does not
remove a man as Hitler does, nor does he kill by stealth as
Mussolini.

—COLE

On December 1, 1934, at 4:30 P.M. S. M. Kirov was shot dead outside
his office in the Smolny Institute. The shot, which signaled the start of
four years of terror, was an act of such significance for the history of
Europe that it has been compared to the assassination of the archduke
Franz Ferdinand in Sarajevo in 1914. George Katkov, the distinguished
historian of twentieth-century Russia, has suggested that had the murder
not spurred Stalin into destroying the Bolshevik Old Guard and notably
Bukharin, he could never have made the pact with Hitler which
brought about World War II.

Kirov was killed by a young man named Nikolaev, a party member of
thwarted ambition, unstable, and possibly an epileptic, who believed he
was ridding his party of an evil leader. That is all we know about the
killing; everything else is speculation founded on hearsay and circumstantial evidence. We cannot say whether it was planned by Stalin, although everything suggests this to have been the case. In his secret
report to the Twentieth Congress Khrushchev implied the assassination
was the work of Stalin and his secretariat. But Khrushchev had good
reason to suggest as much. His chief rival at the time was Malenkov, a

306

long-standing member of the secretariat who could be thought of as having been implicated in the murder.

There are various ways in which the assassination may have taken place; Nikolaev could have acted alone; the killing could have been planned and run by the local NKVD without Stalin's knowledge but to his benefit; it might have been a plan that went wrong, the intention being to bring about a "near miss"; Stalin could have been behind it all. The probabilities favor that last and most obvious explanation. Kirov had emerged as a possible rival to Stalin, the only beneficiary of his death. Besides, an assassination that unleashed terror after a breathing space was a favorite technique of Stalin's. It seems unlikely that the local NKVD acted on its own initiative, for it could not expect Stalin to thank it; he would have welcomed the chance to pillory ready-made scapegoats. Finally, too much was known of Nikolaev's intentions before the killing to make it plausible to suppose he had acted alone. We are left with a strong presumption that the killing was Stalin's work.

Shortly after the Seventeenth Congress Stalin had tried to lure Kirov away from Leningrad by putting him on the Secretariat of the Central Committee. However, Kirov had refused to move to Moscow, and his office there remained empty. It has been alleged that he recognized he was finished when Stalin insisted upon his appointment.[1] He had no need of precognitive powers to reach such a conclusion; it sufficed to know that Stalin was aware of the proposal that Kirov should replace him as party secretary. The inevitability of his doom was much discussed in NKVD circles. Kirov spent part of his holiday that year with Stalin's family on the Black Sea, and an assassination seems to have been attempted while he was in the south. According to a source close to the security services, his car went over an embankment in suspicious circumstances, but he was unhurt. The same source mentions a second attempt to have him killed through the agency of two brothers, criminals released from a Leningrad jail by some NKVD men. However, they too failed and were shot soon afterward.[2]

Stalin's next move had been a bid to get rid of Filipp Medved', head of the Leningrad NKVD and a loyal friend of Kirov's, replacing him with Evdokimov, the most decorated officer in the service, who had been close to Stalin for many years. Kirov objected so strongly that the order was rescinded and Medved' allowed to remain. Instead, someone, presumably Stalin, had Medved's second-in-command reassigned and replaced by a certain Zaporozhets, also a policeman of long standing. When Kirov complained, Stalin told him to submit to party discipline.

We presume that Stalin had picked Zaporozhets to plan Kirov's assassination, although it is hard to imagine anyone as careful as Stalin ordering a relatively junior policeman to arrange the assassination of a member of the Politburo. He would have been more likely to have used an intermediary and a series of hints. What follows is pure speculation based on an observation of Stalin's daughter.[3] She recalls that during the civil war Beria was arrested by the Bolsheviks as a double agent. Kirov ordered Beria's execution, which for some reason never took place. However, Beria knew of the order and might suppose that one day Kirov could recall his inconvenient past. In the circumstances it is easy to imagine Beria being the intermediary.

Among the local NKVD reports, Zaporozhets would have found a file on Nikolaev, whose ex-wife was Kirov's secretary. He had been expelled from the party for incompetence and was so embittered by his treatment that, he observed to a friend, he wanted revenge upon the party leaders, notably Kirov, who readily found work for Trotskyites, Zinovievites and other scum but not for a loyal Bolshevik like himself. Zaporozhets followed the lead and even arranged to have Nikolaev's diary stolen and copied. The diary was full of professions of hate and the desire to emulate famous political assassins of yore. According to an ex-NKVD man, Zaporozhets then made the mistake of interviewing Nikolaev in person to get a closer feel for his character.[4] We do not know how the police talked Nikolaev into trying to assassinate Kirov. We do know that they provided him with a pistol, which he could not possibly have come by on his own. It was later stated that he got it from an Old Bolshevik named Avdeyev, a loyal supporter of Kirov. However, Avdeyev claimed that his gun had vanished in mysterious circumstances. When the police later tried to make him acknowledge the murder weapon as his own, he refused when he saw that its serial number had been filed off.[5]

Nikolaev now started to follow Kirov through the streets of Leningrad. Twice he was picked up by Kirov's loyal bodyguard, Borisov, and twice Zaporozhets ordered his release, saying that he was not to be touched.[6] Borisov, who had allegedly warned Kirov that he was in danger, was not with his charge on the afternoon of December 1; curiously he had been detained on NKVD business. This enabled Nikolaev to follow his target into the Smolny Institute and wait for him outside his office. When Kirov emerged, he shot him dead and then shot himself incompetently, following with an equally unsuccessful attempt to cut his own throat.

When news of the killing reached Stalin, he immediately issued what was in effect a charter for terror. It urged all investigators to speed up their preparation of cases against suspected terrorists. All pending death sentences should be carried out forthwith since no appeals would be considered. Future executions should take place immediately after sentencing.[7] The decree bears no direct relation to Kirov's murder but uses it as a catalyst to accelerate the tempo of terror. It was as if Stalin understood that the killing could be used to create a sense of emergency in which the thrust of the decree would seem appropriate.

Stalin's next action makes it almost certain that he knew of the murder. Together with Molotov, Voroshilov, Ezhov, Zhdanov and Yagoda he took the night train to Leningrad; perhaps the only occasion that he unwittingly laid every card he held faceup on the table. Had Stalin known nothing of the plan to murder Kirov, he would have concluded on learning of his death that the assassination could be part of a larger conspiracy. In those circumstances he would have remained in the Kremlin, surrounded by battalions of security forces. It is inconceivable that he would have exposed himself by traveling to Leningrad, which he always regarded as bandit country. It was not in his nature to take unnecessary risks. He would have proceeded to that city only had he been certain that he was not running into danger, and there was only one way in which certainty was possible.

When Stalin arrived in Leningrad, he was met by Medved'. Without removing his glove Stalin hit him in the face and announced that he would take over the interrogation.[8] However, his questioning of Nikolaev was not a great success. When Stalin asked him why he had killed Kirov, Nikolaev pointed to the NKVD men and screamed that they had made him do it. He was promptly beaten into silence. According to one version, he had previously been interrogated by Zaporozhets, who had hoped to present Stalin with a cut-and-dried "case" complete with conspirators and scapegoats. He particularly hoped to include Zinoviev and Kamenev in the plot. However, Nikolaev, who proved tougher and more alert than had been expected, recognized Zaporozhets immediately from their earlier meeting and understood that the NKVD had exploited him.

Stalin realized that his police had bungled, necessitating urgent damage control. Not only would Nikolaev be impossible in open court, but Stalin would have to move fast to mop up traces of the crime. The immediate danger was Kirov's bodyguard Borisov who had long suspected that something bad was going to happen. He was called for questioning, but the truck in which he was traveling had an unaccountable accident en route. It glanced into a wall, denting a fender; luckily no one was hurt except for Borisov, who was dispatched by two blows of an iron bar to the skull.[9] Miraculously the driver survived the next twenty years to give Khrushchev a full account of what had taken place.[10] Further loose ends were cleared up with the dismissal for "negligence" of both Medved' and Zaporozhets, who received a singularly light punishment. Instead of being executed, they were sent to work for the NKVD in the Far East. Medved' was allegedly returned to Moscow and shot in 1937, but Zaporozhets was last seen running a road-building operation in western Kolyma in 1938.[11]

The British Embassy first assumed that Nikolaev had killed Kirov because he thought that he was sleeping with his ex-wife. The British consul in Leningrad agreed but added the qualification that "an alternative and perhaps rather wild explanation has been current from the first, according to which Kirov, a Russian, and a proletar[sic] was becoming too powerful and too popular," while in factories in both Leningrad and Moscow discipline was disrupted and some workers even observed that Nikolaev would have done better to have disposed of Stalin.[12] The official reaction took Stalin's decree as its point of departure, as party members were informed that the leadership was in danger, and renewed vigilance called for, since other Nikolaevs could be lurking, even in the bosom of the party. The news also brought a sense of doom: "People suddenly started to act as if they had been told by their doctor that they suffered from a malignant growth which might or might not be cancer. There was a general suspension of opinion and speculation. Men just waited."[13]

The believers continued to believe; Lev Kopelev was convinced that Trotsky was behind it all.[14] Others were under no illusions. From the moment Mandelstam heard the news, "Everything became clear."[15] It was no longer possible to give the regime the benefit of any kind of doubt, while the burying of one's head in sand no longer brought comfort.

Kirov was given a magnificent send-off. At the funeral Stalin blamed himself vociferously for his trustfulness and lack of vigilance. When he beheld the corpse, he was so overcome by some emotion that he leaned forward to kiss it on the cheek.[16] It is tempting to see his action as evidence of the general secretary's sense of humor. In the aftermath a total of one ballet company and no fewer than eighty towns and villages would be named after Kirov, only one fewer than Stalin named after himself.[17]

The only aspect of the case that suggests that Stalin may not have known about it is the hesitancy with which he lashed out in search of a scapegoat. Initially the assassination was ascribed to a conspiracy of "White Guards," who had infiltrated the country from Poland and Rumania. Within twenty-four hours 103 suitable candidates had been rounded up and shot, while thousands of Leningrad party members, notably those associated with Kirov, were arrested and shipped east—a curious way of avenging his death.[18] Almost immediately afterward, doubtless on the pretext that Kirov's wife was Latvian, it was stated that Nikolaev had been bribed by the Latvian consul, Bissenieks, who was ordered to leave the country forthwith. (Somewhat to its shame the diplomatic corps did not accompany him to the station en masse to see him off, although the proposal had been widely canvassed. However, four months later he was recalled, and bygones were allowed to be by-gones.) It was not until the end of the month that appropriate culprits were found, in the shape of Kamenev and Zinoviev; they and their sympathizers were arrested and indicted on charges of forming a "Moscow Center" that had directed the conspiracy against Kirov. While pleading not guilty of plotting to kill him, Zinoviev and Kamenev admitted their "political and moral responsibility." Zinoviev was sentenced to ten years, Kamenev to five, although six months later he was retried and given ten more.

An important aspect of the Kirov affair was Stalin's hostility toward Leningrad. He had first revealed this when he attacked Zinoviev and would show it again on more than one occasion, culminating in the disgrace, in 1948, of Kirov's successor, Zhdanov, and the so-called Leningrad affair. Certainly he now moved on the city with unusual savagery. One explanation for his actions is provided by the British ambassador, Lord Chilston:

> Leningrad is perhaps the only town in the Soviet Union where there remains any trace of "public opinion." This is due to the presence there, in considerable numbers, of survivors of the governing classes of the old regime. The removal of the Academy of Sciences to Moscow in the spring of 1934 was a step towards destroying this survival of bourgeois opinion, and the present purge, instituted as a result of the Kirov murder, is intended to settle it for good and all.[19]

Stalin hit the city hard. Virtually all its "former people," members of the prerevolutionary educated classes, were either arrested and deported or simply ordered to leave. Those sent to Siberia were deposited in various towns and villages with no provision for their support since they were exiles, not prisoners. Solzhenitsyn has estimated, and waits to be proved wrong, that up to a quarter of the city's population was arrested or banished.[20] Certainly its housing problem was solved at a stroke. Since the exiles had to move at short notice and could not always arrange for the storage or transportation of their possessions, others, notably the good citizens of Moscow, reacted to their plight according to that excellent criminal precept "You go today, I'll wait till tomorrow." Hundreds traveled to Leningrad to buy up the furniture, paintings and carpets that were being disposed of at rock-bottom prices.[21] The opportunistic speed with which they exploited the misfortunes of others bears witness to the atomization of a society in which all sense of mutual dependency and decency had given way to a desperate readiness to grab with both hands. It also helps explain why it became so easy to assent to the purges, which were no cause for dismay as long as they were happening to someone else. There are various Russian sayings which indicate that the misfortunes of others are no concern of yours: "Your own shirt's nearer to your body," and, when the center of a village is on fire, "My hut's on the outskirts," the Russian equivalent of "I'm all right, Jack."

Bukharin had once described Stalin as a genius at applying and decreasing pressure. He was careful never to make war on all the people for all the time. Now, as he concentrated on the urban intelligentsia, he left the peasants well alone. He also began a campaign to convince ordinary people that their life was improving, as in a number of ways it was. Shortly after announcing the first wave of executions, Stalin informed a delighted nation that progress on the food front was such that basic foodstuffs need no longer be rationed—a matter of far greater import than a small pile of corpses, that had probably, in their lifetime, "had everything." As the Trotskyite Victor Serge put it, "Executions, jailings and deportations had long since ceased to interest the masses. By contrast the abolition of bread-rationing made everybody happy. This country, for the sake of a little progress in the direction of prosperity, would walk over any number of corpses without noticing."[22]

Terror by Day, and by Night

The tree of liberty must be refreshed from time to time with
. . . blood. It is its natural manure.

—THOMAS JEFFERSON

"Chip" Bohlen, an American diplomat who had first seen Stalin two years earlier, found him changed in early 1935, reflecting the pressure of recent events: "Stalin had visibly aged. His face was more deeply lined and his hair had turned grey. He gave the impression of general weariness and strain."[1] At the same time his true stature was becoming apparent to Western observers. Lord Chilston provides a remarkable assessment of Stalin immediately after the death of Kirov. His report is full of respect and suggests that Stalin owed his position to his remarkable personality alone and that he was, in historiographic terms, "a great man."

> Seen at a public function he appears to be more human, sociable, friendly with people than would be expected. One is impressed by an air of calm assurance and strength in the Georgian and somewhat Oriental face. . . . He certainly loves power and he is certainly a capable intriguer, but it must now be admitted that he is more than that. The mere intriguer generally doesnt know what to do with power when he achieves it; but M. Stalin has always known that, though he

has sometimes changed his mind and is prepared to change his policy
at any time even in disregard of cherished Communist principles. . . .
[He then considers H. G. Wells' belief that Stalin was a kindly man
who owed his position to the universal love he inspired.] Kindliness is
not a quality easy to reconcile either with M. Stalin's actions or with
his public statements . . . it is equally absurd to say that no one in the
Soviet Union is afraid of him . . . millions both fear and loathe
him. . . . But if by trusting is meant that everyone knows he will carry
out a policy once undertaken then perhaps there is some truth in the
second half of Mr. Wells' dictum.[2]

Lord Chilston was even more impressed after his first audience with
Stalin in 1936. Sir William Hayter, himself a future ambassador to the
Soviet Union, then *en poste* in Moscow, recalls the entire embassy staff
gathered in the hall, eagerly awaiting the ambassador's return from the
Kremlin. On Chilston's return, he stroked his mustache reflectively and
then, with his tongue only slightly in his cheek, observed: "Do you
know, I think the chap's a gentleman." Once more Stalin showed he
could be all things to all men. Anthony Eden, who also met him at this
time, was even more impressed. His passionate support for the Soviet
Union, which did so much to affect British policy in World War II,
dates from this encounter.

Stalin followed the Kirov killing with his first assault upon the party,
making further use of murder to eliminate potential enemies. In January 1935 V. V. Kuibyshev, a strong supporter of Kirov's policies of reconciliation, who had insisted upon heading a special Central
Committee investigation of the NKVD's handling of the Kirov affair,
died suddenly of a stroke. We are now entering a period when sudden
death is unlikely to be from natural causes and in which coincidence
plays as great a part as it did in Jack Ruby's murder of Lee Harvey
Oswald. As the NKVD used to say, "Any fool can commit a murder,
but it takes an artist to commit a good natural death." It is possible that
Kuibyshev died naturally, but the death was too convenient to make this
likely.

Stalin now proceeded to dispose of anyone suspected of entertaining
sympathies for Kamenev, Zinoviev or, ultimately, Trotsky. That Trotsky
was always the greatest enemy is confirmed by the remarkable fact that
no Soviet Trotskyite is known to have survived the purges. Suspect party
members were rounded up in every major city, while others with no
obvious links to the fallen leaders were gathered in their wake. Once

again the embassy analysis is illuminating and accurate. It views the purge as a power struggle, combined with a means of providing career opportunities for a hungry generation waiting in the wings. It points out that Trotsky served both as a bogeyman and an opposition in exile and continues with the view that Stalin no longer wished to export revolution but was content with his own brand of "low-brow national and industrial socialism." The purge also represented the attempt to prevent the formation of settled classes or power centers:

> The periodical hacking off of limbs growing diagonally from the main trunk has been the work of the highest oligarchs themselves. . . . It is therefore conceivable that the various excrescences or deviations have been removed not because they threatened the growth of the socialist state but because their continual growth would threaten the position of M. Stalin and his coterie of the faithful. . . . Essentially therefore political power in this country remains in the hands of very few men, if not ultimately in the hands of one.[3]

The prime targets of the purge were party members of long enough standing to have been supporters of Zinoviev and Kamenev, at the time when they were the senior members of the triumvirate. Now it was their turn to sleep with bags ready packed and to shudder every time they heard the lift door slam shut outside their apartments. To such persons arrest could actually come as a relief since the fact was that "for years past we Old Bolsheviks who lived in this new society, this new State we had created with our own hand, had been living with fear and horror in our hearts . . . worse than anything we had known under tsarism."[4]

In terms of personal strategy Stalin was right to mount an attack upon the older generation of party members. It was there that a potential opposition might yet be found, and their removal would create vacancies for the Stalin generation to fill. Accordingly he now dissolved a prestigious party organization and possible opposition center, the Society of Old Bolsheviks. This had acted as a club, in the Soviet sense: an organization for the distribution of special privileges—extra rations and access to special health centers—as well as provided a sociopolitical base.[5] Stalin wisely decided that it had outlived its usefulness. Next he introduced a measure calculated greatly to increase compliance. In April 1935 he made children aged twelve and over subject to criminal charges up to and including capital offenses. Many fascinating explanations have been advanced for the public confessions of the Moscow trials, notably in Koestler's brilliant *Darkness at Noon*. But in the majority of cases one need not look beyond the desire to save one's wife and children to understand why so many brave men confessed to crimes they could never have committed.

The purge of the party was administered by Yezhov, who had succeeded Kirov as joint secretary to the Central Committee, while Malenkov became his deputy in charge of personnel. Stalin had thus filled two more key positions with the handpicked products of his secretariat. It is now, too, that a protégé of Kaganovich's, Nikita Khrushchev, became first secretary of the Moscow party organization. Reviewing the purge at the end of the year, Yezhov reported that he had cleansed party ranks of an impressive list of enemies, rogues, *kulaks*, White Guards, Trotskyites, Zinovievites, traitors and other hostile elements. Eighty percent of the party had been meticulously screened, and about twelve percent, or 315,000 had failed the test.[6]

Although the politically aware may have awaited arrest with their bags packed, political "outsiders" had little idea of what was happening. Soviet citizens depended on word of mouth for their knowledge of current events at a time when careless talk cost lives. There was no "news" in the sense that we know it. Thus a young Leningrader on the eve of his own arrest in 1935 could be in a state of almost blissful ignorance.

> Just nineteen at the time of my arrest, I was a student in one of the technical institutes in Leningrad. I was diligent and quite proficient in my studies, and as for politics, my interest was strictly confined within the limits graciously set down from on high for us Soviet citizens. I did not regard the Soviet régime as the best in the world, but neither did I think of it as exceptionally bad.
>
> All I knew of political terror in the country was based on vague rumours, and it never seemed as widespread and terrible as it was. What appeared at that time to be the errors of the Soviet government such as forcible collectivization of peasant holdings and the famine of the early thirties, I blamed partly upon the wrecking activities of counter-revolutionary elements in the ruling circles and partly on forgivable slips in Soviet domestic policies. As a matter of fact I viewed the Soviet government in an optimistic light and felt sure that in due time everything would be straightened out. There was no justifiable reason for my arrest that February night.[7]

Once again Stalin revealed his skill in the manipulation of the carrot as well as the stick. On May 4, 1935, he made a speech of considerable importance to the up-and-coming generation. It was built around the statement that "Cadres are all-decisive," a shift of emphasis from tractors to personnel. The speech acknowledged the significance of the generation born around 1910, which was too young to have heard Lenin or Trotsky and would owe its successes to Stalin alone. It also emphasized the need to "treasure and not waste the human element."

> To me it seems that the attitude of some of our leaders towards their people and towards the cadres, and their inability to appreciate the human element are relics of that terrible attitude of men towards other men. If we are to live through the period of famine in human material, if we are to win through to a state of affairs when our country shall dispose of an adequate system of cadres capable of manning and developing our technical resources, then above all we must learn to appreciate men, realise the worth of every labourer who is able to do his bit for the common cause. In a word we must understand that of all the capital values which the world possesses the most precious and the most decisive in its influence is man himself, and the cadre.[8]

Stalin dissociated himself from the traditions of Bolshevik ruthlessness. He appealed to the young managers and administrators, promising them that their efforts would be appreciated, developing the policy initiated by the introduction of large-scale privilege. In any event, the younger generation would not find the going as simple as the speech implied, yet the thrust of Stalin's strategy favored the young and the hungry at the expense of settled middle age.

Stalin also eased the pressure in other areas. Shortly after the Kirov killing, there was much acclaim for the People's Republic of the Ukraine, which had suffered so dreadfully during the famine. This saw three Ukrainians, Chubar, Kossior and Petrovsky, admitted to the Politburo and Khrushchev's promotion in Moscow. There were also significant changes in the army. Although there are unsubstantiated rumors of arrests after the Kirov affair, Stalin had left it largely untouched and had not moved against commanders who had complained to him about collectivization. Now, in 1935, as he turned against the rest of the party, Stalin greatly increased the army's status and independence. Hitherto it had eschewed traditional military titles and ranks but these were now reintroduced, together with a series of decrees de-

signed to make the officer corps a privileged body set apart from the
rest of society. They included immunity from arrest by civil authorities and an increase in material benefits and special privileges. Officers were now required to conduct themselves in a proper manner: Like
their Western equivalents, they were not permitted to carry packages
in uniform and even required their COs' permission to marry. At the
same time the corps was greatly expanded, and this created a significant "generation gap." The senior officers were veterans of the civil war
and had often seen service in the imperial army. They formed a sharp
contrast with their juniors. The senior officers resented Stalin's political
control over the army; by contrast the younger generation did not object
to this to the same degree.[9] Significantly Stalin addressed himself in
particular to young officers, especially to those graduating from military
academies in 1935, a generation so successful that it was known in
military circles as the "lucky graduating class" *(schastlivyi vypusk)*.[10]
The support Stalin enjoyed in military circles and the power of his charisma are illustrated by the peculiarly Russian story of how Commander
Zabrodny lost his leg:

> [Zabrodny, a party member and an outstanding young officer, was]
> not a raw young man from the back of beyond, but an intelligent, well
> educated, polished Soviet gentleman, a model, on all normal
> occasions of polite, civilized and responsible behaviour.
>
> He was invited to attend the First of May reception that Stalin gave
> for senior officers in May 1935, an occasion on which he had
> occasion to speak to Stalin himself, and from which he emerged
> "psychologically drunk."
>
> In the morning Zabrodny started for home at the hour when
> ordinary folk are packed tight into trams on their way to work. The
> tram Zabrodny wanted to board was full and obviously going to run
> past his stop. His head turned by the magic of the scene he had just
> left, Zabrodny leapt off the pavement onto the track, barred the way,
> drew his pistol and commanded the driver to halt.
>
> The driver braked hard and halted.
>
> "What's the matter, commander?"
>
> "Nothing is the matter . . . I only wanted to tell you that Stalin has
> just said to me, 'Zabrodny you are a fine fellow,' and I want all
> Moscow to know it, I want to tell you. Stalin took me by the hand and
> said, 'Zabrodny you are a fine fellow.'"
>
> The driver . . . thought Zabrodny was merely drunk with alcohol,

and as he had a tram full of passengers and a time table he pushed the obstructing commander aside and tried to drive on. Zabrodny then fired a quick shot at the driver, fortunately missing, followed this by trying to board the tram, but fell, and lost one leg under the wheels. [He went on to become a one-legged lecturer at the Zhukovsky Military Academy].[11]

Stalin did not favor the army alone; he made a more general concession. Declaring the era of class antagonism to be ended, he announced the drafting of a Soviet constitution that would guarantee the rights and freedoms of every citizen, and as a further conciliatory gesture he placed both Radek and Bukharin upon its drafting commission. This seems to have been devised to divert his opponents' energies and tantalize them with the prospect of a legal order that would enable them to pursue their policies protected by constitutional guarantees.[12]

A new direction was also taken in Soviet cultural life. Intellectuals in the West had admired Soviet society for its daring: Free abortion, easy divorce, progressive education, leaderless orchestras and experimental theater all caught the eye. Stalin now turned his back on radicalism and introduced a new kind of culture. Modernism was abandoned. Soviet music now required tunes that could be whistled. Divorce and abortion became harder to come by, and the virtues of fecund family life were extolled, while progressive education was replaced by a return to traditional discipline. Along with other frivolities such as cosmetics, ballroom dancing was restored to favor and Soviet diplomats were required to take courses in etiquette. A British Embassy report informs us that stiff white collars began to be worn again, together with felt hats and a new style of Soviet suit with ridiculously overpadded shoulders and those enormously wide trousers with sagging crotches that continued to symbolize the values of the Stalin era into the 1960s. The necktie made a return to favor and quite junior officials were expected to shave every day. Jazz was declared acceptable, and foreign musicians with the appropriate skills could earn good money, as theatrical journals carried articles with titles such as "On the Way to Jazz Culture."[13]

Finally, at the end of 1935, the Christmas tree was declared legal once again. A whole series of elements, hitherto condemned as trappings of bourgeois decadence, had been relegitimized, establishing a kind of Central European revival of antimacassar Victorianism, a petty and prudish respectability, the style to which the new generation was invited to aspire. The last vestiges of egalitarianism and proletarian values were dispensed with, and *kul'turnyi* behavior was the new norm for a people who thanked Stalin for a life that was growing "better and more cheerful" by the day.

CHAPTER THIRTY-FOUR

Four Years Late

Stalin always plays for keeps.
—ALGER HISS

With Zinoviev and Kamenev safely behind bars, the only political leader left at large was Bukharin. Throughout 1936 Stalin played cat and mouse with him, although his final pounce was delayed by circumstances beyond his control. It is fashionable to admire Bukharin these days partly because he was an intellectual, partly because the policies he favored made sense; they did not sacrifice reason to ideology. Moreover, he was a kind and civilized man who, for example, had helped save Mandelstam from a firing squad, an intervention that took courage. He seems to have been a delightful companion and a great animal lover; he had a menagerie of hawks, hedgehogs and even a tame fox that resided in the Kremlin and outlived him by many years.[1] He was probably the nicest of Bolshevik leaders, although one should never forget that he, too, had his share of blood upon the hands. However, for all his personal qualities, as a political tactician Bukharin was hopeless, and as an intellectual he could be naïve enough to make a professor blush.

Kirov's killing may have made things clear to intelligent outsiders such as the Mandelstams, but it had done nothing for Bukharin. Far from understanding that if he did not oppose the arrest of Kamenev and Zinoviev, it would be his turn next, he not only condoned Stalin's action but commented on it with the Soviet equivalent of "There's no smoke without fire." This was a classic response to the arrest of others and an important feature of the age. People had grown so isolated from one another, there were so few social bonds remaining that not only was it easier to assume that newly arrested colleagues or neighbors were guilty, people even seemed to welcome the news—which made police work that much easier.

Stalin continued his game with Bukharin by sending him abroad in the spring of 1936 to negotiate the purchase of Karl Marx's archive, which German socialists had brought out of Hitler's Germany. Stalin may have been providing him with the rope to hang himself, the opportunity to make contact with Trotskyites, saboteurs and agents of foreign intelligence, but at all events Stalin knew Bukharin well enough to be certain that he would return. In Paris Bukharin had a conversation with two leading Mensheviks, the Dans, in which he painted a deadly portrait of Stalin. So little was known of Stalin's character at the time that Bukharin's chilling account amazed his listeners. He depicted him as a man with a huge inferiority complex and overpowering vanity. Stalin would like to erect a statue of Marx dwarfed by a huge statue of Stalin correcting his works. He suffered from his inability to convince others and even himself of his stature and would always seek to destroy anyone who was his superior in any way. He was "a small, spiteful man, no, not a man, a devil."[2] When the Dans wondered why the leadership still obeyed him, Bukharin revealed the casuistic skills of a sublime idiot:

> You do not understand; that is something completely different. You give your trust not to him, but to the man the party trusts, so that it has come about that he is as it were the symbol of the party; the masses, the workers, the people trust him—our fault perhaps, but that is how it turned out, and that is why we are all putting our heads in his mouth, knowing that he will probably eat us up. He knows this quite well and is just biding his time.[3]

In response to this blend of clarity and self-deception the Dans asked Bukharin why he was returning, to which he replied that life outside the party would not be worth living. He then spoke about the terrible course that Soviet history had taken, how it all had seemingly gone wrong, and then made possibly the stupidest observation in Russian political history: He was going to read through the unpublished manuscripts in the Marx archive in the hope that he might come upon some hitherto-unknown body of Marx's writing that might explain what was amiss in Russia today.

There can be no better illustration of the idiot grip of ideology. Bukharin had been involved in the government of a great nation for nearly twenty years, quite long enough to learn something of practical politics, how decisions are made and mistakes occur, enough to know that day-to-day administration has nothing to do with political theory. Yet here we find him, suspecting that he is near the end of his life, still expecting the unpublished musings of a mid-nineteenth-century philosopher to explain what was wrong with his country nearly a century later. After twenty years of practical politics Bukharin still believed what he read in books.

· · ·

In August 1936 there occurred the first of the three great Moscow trials, with their press campaigns and public calls for execution, their set piece confessions and their deadly aftermath. Yagoda had been working on the case of Zinoviev and Kamenev for months, trying to extract confessions from their supporters that would show them conspiring with Trotsky to assassinate the political leaders of the Soviet Union. Both Kamenev and Zinoviev had been put under severe pressure to oblige; for example, the heating in their cells was kept at boiling point throughout a hot summer. Eventually, in return for the promise of their lives, they apparently agreed to perform in a public trial at which they would admit to being part of a Trotskyite Zinovievite center. The trial was held in a former ballroom of the old Nobles' Club, now known as the October Hall, before an audience of NKVD men and foreign observers. A policeman later alleged that it had been preceded by a series of rehearsals each of which was presented to the participants as the genuine article. Anyone failing to play his part correctly was severely dealt with.[4] Certainly the use of rehearsals became common practice in the preparation of show trials at a later date.[5]

Judicial spectacles designed to demonstrate, not ascertain, the guilt of the accused were no stranger to the Russian tradition. Both Peter the Great and his father, tsar Aleksey Mikhailovich had made use of that ritual in the seventeenth and early eighteenth centuries. In his novel *The History of a Certain Town*, the nineteenth-century satirist Saltykov-Shchedrin describes the "case" of a liberal arrested on a charge of atheism because he owns a book entitled *How to Destroy Fleas, Bugs and Other Insects*, which he is accused of having written, regardless of the fact that it had been passed by the censor and published by the University of Moscow. After two witnesses have testified against him, he asks for his defense counsel to be heard. Counsel gets so carried away that he speaks for the prosecution; at which point the luckless liberal gives up. "So powerfully did it affect him that not only did he admit everything at once, but even confessed to many things which had never happened . . . such as having discovered in the course of his experiments that frogs possess souls which are very small and not immortal."[6]

Something similar occurred at this trial. One of the accused stated that he had had a conspiratorial meeting with Trotsky's son in the autumn of 1932 at the Bristol Hotel, Copenhagen. There had indeed once been a Bristol Hotel there, but it had been pulled down in 1913. The NKVD men composing the scenario had asked the minister of foreign affairs for lists of grand hotels in Copenhagen and Oslo respectively, and someone had confused them. Stalin was furious. "What the devil did you need a hotel for?" he allegedly said. "You should have said they met at the railway station, a railway station is always there."[7] The trial was otherwise a tame affair. "The demeanour of the accused varied. M. Zinoviev appeared cowed and scarcely able to speak. (He was once the Party's greatest orator.) M. Kamenev made a feeble attempt to maintain his dignity, but soon collapsed; the rest were either frightened and demoralised or superior and even jaunty. . . . The Soviet press as usual prejudiced the whole issue by calling for the execution of the accused even before the trial opened."[8]

The actors confessed to murdering Kirov and happily incriminated a number of old comrades, such as Tomsky, Rykov, Radek, Pyatakov and Bukharin. Almost immediately afterwards Stalin called on Tomsky, described by Lord Chilston as one of the "least unattractive" of the Soviet leaders, with a bottle of wine. At first they "talked quietly," and then Tomsky's son Yuri heard his father shouting and swearing, accusing Stalin of murder.[9] Shortly afterwards he blew out his brains. Tomsky was lucky; when Rykov tried to commit suicide his family tore the gun from his hands, and all concerned survived for a year or so, time enough to regret their intervention.[10]

Despite Stalin's promises, the "mad dogs" were condemned to death, and it was announced that the sentences had been carried out—at which point Zinoviev and Kamenev, still alive, were displayed to some of those, such as Radek and Pyatakov, destined to perform in the next trial, as proof that Stalin kept his promises. Then they were shot.

Although Soviet history has its share of brutality, it largely lacks the refined sadism that we associate with Nazi Germany; Soviet cruelty was cruder. There is an exception, though. A Hungarian NKVD man, a

close friend of Stalin's bodyguard, Pauker, has provided an account of
Zinoviev's death. At a banquet to commemorate the founding of the
Soviet secret police when everyone was fairly drunk:

> Pauker gave an impromptu performance in Stalin's honour. Supported
> by two comrades who acted as prison warders, Pauker played the part
> of Zinoviev, who was being led to the cellar for execution. Zinoviev
> hung helplessly on the arms of the "warders" and, dragging his feet,
> moaned, looking around with eyes wild with fear. When he was in the
> middle of the room he fell on his knees, embraced the boot of one of
> the "warders" and cried out in anguish: "Please for God's sake
> comrade, call up Iosif Vissarionovich. . . . ." Stalin watched every
> move of "Zinoviev" and roared with laughter. When they saw how
> Stalin enjoyed that scene, the guests demanded that Pauker repeat the
> performance. Pauker obliged. This time Stalin laughed so boisterously
> that he bent down and held his belly with both hands. And when
> Pauker introduced a new improvisation and, instead of kneeling,
> raised his hands to heaven and screamed "Hear Israel, our God is the
> only God!" Stalin could no longer bear it and, choking with laughter,
> began to make signs to Pauker to stop the performance.[11]

• • •

No Soviet I have spoken to admits to having believed the charges
against Zinoviev and Kamenev, although some conceded that they were
doubtless objectively necessary. The West was different. The defector
Igor Khravchenko never met anyone who believed in the guilt of those
accused at the Moscow trials until he reached the United States, a
country where, as I discovered, pockets of belief in their guilt survive to
this day. But even in the West by no means everyone was taken in.
Once again one can only admire the analysis of the British Embassy
staff. The ambassador dismissed the possibility of actual guilt; Zinoviev
and Kamenev were either scapegoats or victims of a power play, while
the purpose of the trials was the elimination of all those who had ever
opposed Stalin, at which point "His isolation from all forms of criticism
will be complete."[12]

Not all observers were so shrewd. Stalin's comment on foreign reaction to the trial marks the beginning of his understanding of foreign
affairs. "They'll swallow it all right," he promised, and swallow it they
largely did.[13] The U.S. ambassador, Joseph E. Davies, who still holds
the all-time record for gullibility in Soviet affairs, was convinced of the

guilt of the accused and said as much to Alfred Chollerton, a canny British journalist, who replied, "Mr. Ambassador, I believe everything but the facts."[14] Edward C. Carter, secretary-general of the Institute of Pacific Relations, found the Kremlin's case "terribly genuine, it makes sense, is convincing."[15] The greatest swallower of all was D. N. Pritt, a British Member of Parliament and King's Counsel who attended the trial. Even granted a pro-Soviet bias, his judgments are extraordinary, sufficient to reduce any Soviet who heard them to that state of hysterical despair in the face of Western stupidity that has unhinged so many émigrés. Writing in a British daily paper, the *News Chronicle*, he described Vishinsky, a man known to foam at the mouth as he clamored for sentences of death, as "looking like a very intelligent and mild mannered English business man." As for the trial itself, "The executive authorities of the USSR may have taken, by the successful prosecution of this case, a very big step towards eradicating counter-revolutionary activities. But it is equally clear that the judicature and the prosecuting attorney have taken at least as great a step towards establishing their reputation among the legal systems of the modern world."[16]

It may be that Pritt was willfully distorting the truth for the good of the cause. However, he might well have accepted what he saw at face value because to an English lawyer the alternative was inconceivable:

> . . . the critics who refuse to believe that Zinoviev or Kamenev could possibly have conspired to murder Kirov, Stalin, Voroshilov and others, even when they say themselves that they did, are in a grave logical difficulty. For if they thus dismiss the whole case for the prosecution as a "frame-up" it follows inescapably that Stalin and a substantial number of other high officials, including presumably the judges and the prosecutor, were themselves guilty of a foul conspiracy to procure the judicial murder of Zinoviev, Kamenev and a fair number of other persons.[17]

Stalin was not entirely pleased with his trial. Too many sophisticated Soviets had been able to read between its lines; according to a Soviet journalist, Zinoviev and Kamenev had outwitted Stalin in one respect. They had maintained that (a) they had no political program of their own that differed from Stalin's line, and (b) they had been driven by naked lust for power. It took time for it to dawn on Stalin that "If they had no political differences with Stalin . . . that meant that Stalin himself had no political differences with them, and was fighting solely for his personal power . . . and that Stalin was ready to send . . . friends of Lenin to death simply to defend his own position."[18]

That autumn, accompanied by Zhdanov, Stalin traveled south to vacation by the Black Sea. On September 26 he sent a telegram to Moscow that inaugurated a period when terror reached a new peak. It called for the dismissal of Yagoda on grounds of incompetence in the unmasking of the Trotsky-Zinoviev bloc and for bungling the trial. Ezhov was to replace him as head of the NKVD, thereby becoming the first Great Russian to head that body. The telegram stated that the NKVD was four years late in its unmasking of enemies of the state; it was four years to the day since the Central Committee had rejected Stalin's call for the execution of Ryutin, opposing a plan to unleash terror upon the party. Stalin's timing shows what careful note he took of such slights. Patience was now rewarded, and he proposed to make up for four years of lost time.

The news that an unknown bureaucrat of diminutive stature had replaced Yagoda was greeted with widespread relief since things could obviously not get worse—or so it appeared on the threshold of the longest Night of the Long Knives in history. For Ezhov came to glory in cruelty; as one NKVD man put it, "In all my life I have never known a villain like Ezhov, he does it for pleasure."[19] The chief target of the new terror was Bukharin. Zinoviev and Kamenev's indictment of him was the culmination of a public campaign that had been running since his return from Europe; at one point the columns of *Izvestiya* were calling for his arrest while the paper still bore his name as its editor. However, the campaign did not run to plan. Stalin went to his Central Committee with an order for Bukharin's head; Ezhov had come up with an impressive scenario that made Bukharin part of a conspiracy of long standing, which had plotted to assassinate Lenin, Stalin and even Sverdlov. His group had collaborated with Trotsky and, at one and the same time, with the Gestapo. Ezhov concluded with the demand that Bukharin and Rykov be expelled from the party and charged with treason. Instead of the usual storm of statutory applause, the committee greeted the speech with silence. Bukharin then replied. He said that there was indeed a conspiracy, but that it was Stalin's. Together with Ezhov he wished to take over the party, was determined to dispose of anyone in his way and would resort to any means to bring this about. It was Stalin and the NKVD, not Bukharin, that planned a seizure of power. He then called for a return to the "traditions of Lenin," forgetting that Lenin was the greatest power seizer of modern times. Much to

Stalin's dismay Bukharin carried the Central Committee. Fewer than a third of its members voted for Stalin; the rest returned blank papers or voted no. All military members except for Voroshilov voted with the opposition.[20]

Stalin yielded immediately, thanking the committee for its healthy self-criticism and adding that nobody wanted the blood of Bukharin and Rykov. His lack of support indicated that changes would have to be made. Within twelve months only 15 of the committee's 140 members and deputy members would still be at liberty, and eight of those were members of the Politburo. Stalin also made a second retreat; he had probably planned to move against the Red Army, the last independent institution in the USSR, in the autumn of 1936, but now felt it prudent to delay this until Ezhov had conducted a covert purge of the NKVD. In the meantime Bukharin, deprived of all party duties, remained in his Kremlin apartment, writing conciliatory letters to Stalin that began: "My dear Koba," while Stalin continued to play with him. Thus at the November 7 parade Bukharin found a position on a minor viewing stand only to be greeted by a respectful army officer who relayed Stalin's order to take his proper place on top of Lenin's tomb.

A further bouquet was tossed him when his constitution was published and made law. It was the subject of great public celebration and described by Stalin as the Magna Carta of proletarian democracy. Others compared it to Beethoven's Ninth Symphony.[21] It was an attempt to court those outside the party, increase the popularity of the regime with ordinary people and gain a degree of assent to the war that was about to be launched on the party itself. The electoral system was changed from indirect to direct voting, while citizens were accorded rights, such as freedom of speech, freedom of the press, freedom of assembly—provided these were exercised to strengthen the socialist system. Although the constitution has never been invoked successfully, it made an impression at the time. Osip Mandelstam, for example, found real cause for hope in it. "First people vote like this and gradually get to learn and eventually we'll have proper elections," he said.[22] Not everyone was so sanguine. Gorky, who read the draft as a dying man, observed that "in this country even the stones sing."[23] The popular reaction was also mixed. When the Obelisk to Freedom, which used to stand in Soviet Square in Moscow, was transformed into a monument to the constitution, it was observed: "They've liquidated freedom to make room for the constitution."[24] Once again the British Embassy was accurate and not without humor:

One is irresistibly reminded of the similarity between the scientific theory of conditioned reflexes and the political theories of to-day, of which Soviet leaders have been notable exponents. The mass human vivisections of the last twenty years have enriched human knowledge by the valuable discovery that, given a sufficiently prolonged course of repression and suffering, the human mass can be brought to such a point of docility that it will at last respond automatically in the direction of continued obedience to its own accumulated suggestions of pain, and the tedious business of inflicting actual torture can be suspended. Thus despotism is relieved of its last burdens of ferocity and fatigue and the revolver or bludgeon in a tyrant's hand can be replaced by a bunch of innocent spring flowers. [25]

Up to Our Elbows in Blood

One death is a tragedy, a million just statistics.

—STALIN

The second of the three Moscow trials featured Radek, Pyatakov and Sokolnikov as its main protagonists. Pyatakov was the most important; as deputy commissar for heavy industry he served as a scapegoat for the continuing shortages on that front. He had been unwilling to confess until his wife persuaded him to do so to save their child, and his chief, Ordzhonikidze, brought him Stalin's promise that his life would be spared. He testified that he had conspired with Trotsky, and with Germany, to overthrow the régime, maintaining that he had contacted Trotsky in Oslo, having flown there in December 1935. Unfortunately the script writer had bungled again; it did not take Norwegian journalists long to discover that no civil aircraft had used the city's airfield that month. Nevertheless the trial went smoothly enough; responding to Vishinsky's invective, Pyatakov described himself as "standing before the court in filth, crushed by my own crimes, bereft of everything; a man who has lost his Party, his friends, his family, lost his very self."[1]

Radek played the fool. On arrest he had inveighed against Stalin's "ingratitude" but after a talk with his master had devoted much time and effort to perfecting the script of the trial, adding body to Trotsky's past and establishing the role of the German government in the conspiracy. He assumed responsibility for this during the trial but insisted on threatening to reveal all by referring to the crimes as "man-made." He based his final plea upon his contribution to the scenario, reminding the court that it was he who had disclosed the Trotskyite conspiracy. It was a characteristically brilliant and useless display of acrobatics on thin ice.

Radek's efforts appeared to be rewarded; when the rest of the accused were condemned to death, Radek and Sokolnikov were given the remarkably light sentence of ten years' imprisonment. After listening gravely to a series of death sentences, Radek, an actor to the last, reacted to his own sentence of "ten years" with a splendid simulation of surprise; his face lit up, and he shrugged his shoulders as if bewildered by his unexpected luck. For some time he must have thought he had escaped. A subsequent fugitive from the gulag saw him in 1938, living in relative freedom in Magadan.[2] (The same source reveals that Stalin was known to criminal inmates as the Black Thief or the Gypsy.) However, soon afterward a murder was arranged. A fellow convict, a criminal, picked a fight with the diminutive Radek whom he lifted and dashed headfirst upon a cement floor, death resulting soon after.

Western observers responded variously to the trial. Walter Duranty maintained that the accused were guilty, a view shared by the U.S. ambassador, who wrongly presumed that it would have required the genius of a Shakespeare to falsify the affair. Sir Bernard Pares, for years considered the leading British authority on Russia past and present and an ardent supporter of the regime, published a piece on the trial in the *Observer* on March 10, 1937. He stated that he had returned from the Soviet Union with a most favorable impression and that he found "the wrecking activities proven to the hilt"; behind them he had detected the vindictive hand of Trotsky, its presence "confirmed by careful expert evidence." Once again it was the British ambassador who came closest to the truth:

> The opportunity is taken to saddle the latest Trotskyite group with the
> blame for all those accidents and disasters which innate Russian
> inefficiency coupled with over hasty industrialization and record fever
> have brought in their train. Rightly or wrongly the great majority of
> my colleagues are convinced that the facts cannot be adequately
> explained without assuming that unavowable methods were employed
> on the prisoners.[3]

The immediate consequence of the trial was the untimely death of

Pyatakov's boss, in the words of the Soviet encyclopedia, "the favorite comrade-in-arms of the great Stalin," Sergo Ordzhonikidze, who, as commissar for heavy industry, had won the respect and affection of his subordinates. Allegedly he had told Stalin it was time to stop the arrests. Stalin responded by sending him three NKVD men, a doctor and a revolver, offering him the choice of suicide or execution. Ordzhonikidze said good-bye to his wife and duly shot himself, whereupon the doctor diagnosed failure of the heart.[4] There are a number of versions of his death, which range from shooting through "voluntary suicide" to poisoning; one has Poskrebyshev delivering Stalin's ultimatum.[5] It appears that it came two hours after the Politburo had discussed Georgian affairs and followed the arrest of two Georgian communists and old friends of Stalin, "Budu" Mdivani and Torozhelidze, chief of planning for the Georgian Republic.[6] When Mdivani's interrogator suggested he save his skin by testifying against himself and others, he replied: "You tell that to me, who has known Stalin for thirty years. Stalin won't rest until he has butchered all of us, beginning with the unweaned baby and ending with the blind grandmother."[7]

Ordzhonikidze was given an impressive funeral at which Stalin, giving eloquent public expression to his grief, honored his ashes by having them buried next to Kirov's in the Kremlin Wall—another of his jokes. Shortly afterward Stalin attended a session of the Central Committee to discuss the cases of Bukharin and Rykov. Bukharin had tried to express his discontent by going on hunger strike, which prompted Stalin to tell him he looked terrible and wonder why he was not eating. Stalin assured him that no one wanted to expel him from the party, whereupon Molotov attacked with a magnificent piece of dialectic. He invited Bukharin to confess his crimes. When Bukharin refused to "tell lies against himself," Molotov retorted that such failure to oblige the party proved he was guilty and a fascist hireling. Bukharin then suggested that in view of the quantities of false confessions they were extracting from his sympathizers, something must be wrong with the NKVD. This time it was Stalin who had the answer. "Why, then, we'll send you there to have a look for yourself," he replied.

There were some last attempts to persuade Stalin to restrain himself, notably from Postyshev, party secretary in the Ukraine, who was making a speech about the improbability of the charges against Bukharin when Stalin interrupted him: "And just what are you in fact?" Postyshev paled and replied: "A Bolshevik, Comrade Stalin, a Bolshevik." Postyshev's speech doubtless explains why he was arrested and shot within the year and may also account for the savage purge of the Ukraine that autumn.

The committee set up a commission, headed by Mikoyan, to determine the fate of Bukharin and Rykov. All except for Stalin came to one conclusion. "Arrest, try, shoot," they wrote; only Stalin, moderate as always, disagreed. "Let the NKVD handle the case," he suggested.[8] Bukharin and Rykov were duly arrested although they only came to trial a little more than twelve months later.

It was at this session of the Central Committee that Stalin made the famous pronouncement that the most dangerous saboteurs were those who never sabotaged: "A genuine saboteur has to be successful in his work because that is the only way he can maintain his position as a saboteur, work his way into people's confidence and continue his sabotage." He then made it clear that he was declaring open season on everyone. To date, he observed, the spies and wreckers who had so successfully infiltrated the party had gone untouched because it had proved necessary to train tens of thousands of replacements. But now this had been accomplished. One might have expected Stalin to distinguish between the older and younger generations, but he did nothing as obvious. Although he concentrated on those who had joined the party before the Lenin recruitment of 1924, he did not make the mistake of letting later comers get overconfident.

Stalin made it chillingly clear that nobody was immune by an astounding call for the training of a series of backup replacements for key party and industrial posts, whereby second and even third understudies should be trained to take the place of their superiors.[9] In any event, it often transpired that not even two levels of backup would be enough; sometimes five or six replacements would be used before the "front" was stabilized. The speed with which promotion could take place was remarkable. For example, two Central Committee representatives visited the School for Foreign Trade, in Moscow, a kind of staff college, and asked for the names of two politically reliable students. The next day one had been appointed people's commissar for trade, and the other was also made a member of the government.[10]

Stalin also addressed the Central Committee on the subject of the shortcomings of Yagoda, and as his audience applauded, Yagoda snarled at them that six months before he could have arrested them all. Stalin and Ezhov now turned their attention to the police. In March Ezhov ordered all NKVD department chiefs except for Pauker and the head of the foreign department to proceed by train to various destinations on a collective inspection tour and had each of them picked up at the first stop after Moscow. He then used the same technique to gather their deputies. Next, he summoned a meeting of senior NKVD men at which he denounced Yagoda as a tsarist spy, a thief and an embezzler and arrested all his appointees. There were numerous suicides among the police, many of them in the NKVD apartment building. Sometimes they proved to be a mistake; a midnight knock at one apartment setting off a suicide shot next door.[11] The families of the arrested policemen suffered dreadfully; often they were turned out into the street. There is at least one report of a mass suicide bid by teenage children of arrested NKVD men.[12] Children were often arrested with their parents, one ten-year-old confessing to membership in a fascist group which he had joined when he was seven.[13] All in all some 3,000 NKVD men, including the infamous Pauker, were shot that year. Yagoda himself was arrested in April, and Molotov moved into his dacha. When Ezhov took over the NKVD, he had brought with him 200 men from the security branch of Stalin's special sector, and these now assumed key posts vacated by the old guard, securing Stalin's personal control of the security forces and perpetuating his policy of creating an organization within an organization. With the police in hand the tempo of the purge could now be accelerated.

Henceforth no one could consider himself safe. By the nature of things everyone was bound to be the friend of a friend who had been taken, and that was enough. The only way to avoid arrest was to keep moving from city to city; it proved surprisingly easy to stay ahead of police paper work. Alternatively one dropped out of ordinary life. I know of several party members who survived by fleeing to the woods and living like peasants until it was all over, recalling the fugitives who escaped Peter the Great's revolution from above by fleeing to the forests of Siberia.

•   •   •

Stalin was now ready to move against the last potential source of opposition, the armed services. Hitherto he had been meticulous in his protection of them; from collectivization onward they had been virtually immune from arrest. The army had developed into a highly privileged body, as Stalin increased its size and reduced political control over it. In earlier times the use of the commissar system had made for a pattern of dual command. However, the importance of commissars had been much diminished in recent years. A British staff officer acting as an observer at the Red Army maneuvers in 1936 noted that commissars were treated with scant respect by their commanders.

Granted that Stalin was a leader of frustrated military ambition, who had failed in the wars in which Tukhachevsky had made his name, the patience with which he handled the army is remarkable. Stalin had every reason to dislike Tukhachevsky, beginning with his dismissive treatment of the general secretary during the Polish campaign. Tukhachevsky was an intelligent man of independent spirit, who enjoyed the authority and glamour of his position. Besides, he was associated with Leningrad, having commanded the Leningrad Military District, and had been a close friend of Kirov. He was also well known for his hostility toward Germany. In all respects he was the antipode of the mediocre and subservient toady Voroshilov, down to his view of military strategy. He offended the cavalrymen Voroshilov and Budenny by maintaining that it would be tanks and aircraft, not horses, that would win the next war. He enjoyed teasing them by speaking over their heads about the application of Einstein's new theories to military strategy; no one was capable of understanding that he, too, was talking rubbish.

Although this may have made Tukhachevsky an obvious target, it does not explain why Stalin chose to move against the armed services themselves. Once again he seems to have decided that it would be prudent to eliminate a generation—any officer old enough to have known a world beyond Stalin's Russia. The purge would also bring on the new officers, the "lucky class" of 1935. Stalin was the kind of chief executive who delighted in "imaginative appointments," singling out a man or group and dramatically thrusting responsibilities upon them. He liked to pull a face that caught his eye out of a passing parade and push the young officer into the limelight. During the purges he did as much with whole generations, particularly with respect to the army.

The timing of the purge may not have been determined by Stalin; there were other factors in play. He was already extending feelers toward Nazi Germany. At the same time elements in the German security forces were anxious to compromise some of their own military commanders, seen as potentially anti-Nazi, and also Tukhachevsky, who was recognized as no friend to Germany. They forged a dossier suggesting that he had been in treasonable contact with certain Wehrmacht commanders. The papers were conveyed to Stalin, possibly via the German Communist underground and Czech intelligence. We cannot say whether Stalin believed in the material or was simply happy to have it as a pretext. However, if German intelligence intended the move as an attack upon the Red Army, it succeeded beyond its wildest dreams.

Although the first moves on Red Army officers had occurred as early as April, the main blow fell on June 9, when Tukhachevsky, Yakir and Uborevich were relieved of their commands. Two days later *Pravda* announced the conclusion of the case against them, together with Eidemann, Kork, Primakov and Putna. On the dawn of June 12 they were all shot.

Stalin did not risk putting them on trial probably because he doubted their willingness to give a satisfactory performance. He need not have worried about Yakir. After his arrest he wrote Stalin a letter professing honesty and decency, observing that he would die with words of love for him, the party, the country and with a boundless faith in the eventual triumph of communism. "Scoundrel and prostitute," Stalin wrote in the margin, and on hearing that Yakir's last words really were "Long live the Party and Stalin," he cursed him roundly.[14] Among the peripheral victims of the arrests were Tukhachevsky's wife, who went insane, and his twelve-year-old daughter, who hanged herself.

The purge fanned out down the chain of command, as officers presiding over a court-martial one day found themselves facing a firing squad the next. The charges were "subjectively" preposterous, although considered objectively, they appeared in a different light. Once again we find that blend of irony and deadly farce that marks so much of Russian history. For example, a certain General Lukirsky was shot for the role he played in Tukhachevsky's last war game. The marshal, in command of Blueforce, attacked the USSR from the west. Lukirsky, who ran the game, concluded that Redforce would be obliged to retreat to the east, but that they would stabilize their line just outside Moscow. He was arrested and shot for "letting the enemy get to the gates of Moscow"—more precisely to the very point that the Germans would reach in 1941.[15]

The Red Army's death roll in 1937 and 1938 includes 3 out of 5 marshals, 13 out of 15 army commanders, 57 out of 85 corps commanders, 110 out of 195 divisional commanders, 220 out of 406 brigade commanders. Estimates of the total loss vary from twenty to fifty percent of the officer corps with best opinion favoring the high range. The purge affected the top of the pyramid most severely, while Stalin seems to have spared commanders, such as Voroshilov, Timoshenko, Budenny and Zhukov, associated with the old First Cavalry Army. A significant proportion of the victims were Jews.

•   •   •

By the end of the summer diplomats had come to accept arrests and executions as a feature of daily life, giving rise to dispatches observing that "the number of executions which have come to our notice during the last fortnight is a good deal smaller than usual, another fifty Party people have been shot at Irkutsk on the usual charges. . . ."[16] One of the more interesting sets of victims was the Central Statistical Organization of the All-Union State Planning Commission. It had been responsible for a census taken earlier in the year, which was officially annulled, almost certainly because it would have enabled analysts to calculate too precisely the number of premature deaths over the past seven years. It was accused of "grave violation of the elementary rules of statistical science and instruction approved by the government."[17]

One of the more puzzling features of the purges remains the fact that all those arrested, regardless of whether or not they were destined for public trial, were put under tremendous pressure to confess to preposterous crimes, the interrogators devoting much time and trouble to each victim. Since there was no relationship between crime and punishment, it is curious that the security organs should have bothered. A great deal of rubbish has been written about the Slav soul, not the least of which relates to its need to confess, though admittedly public confession features generously in the works of Dostoevsky. Confession also used to play an important part in the judicial process. In the days of Peter the Great Russian jurisprudence had it that no one could be convicted solely upon circumstantial evidence or the testimony of others. Conviction was not possible without confession. However, it was perfectly acceptable to extract this by torture, and indeed, it was widely held that confession without torture was no confession at all.

Thus the confessions produced at the show trials fitted into a historical perspective. Yet this alone cannot explain the effort and expense of extracting individual confessions from every victim of Yagoda, Ezhov and Beria. There were various reasons why the effort was deemed worthwhile. In the first instance, no one was prepared to risk *not* interrogating a prisoner till he had broken. It might transpire that he really had been guilty of something, in which case the lax interrogator would risk being shot for negligence. Secondly, the security services needed confessions as insurance against the charge of illegal procedures. Everyone from Stalin down seems to have been careful to maintain the appearance of legality, permitting H. G. Wells, the Webbs and numerous

French intellectuals, such as Aragon, Sartre, Malraux, Barbusse, to express public admiration for Soviet justice, contrasting it with Hitler's brutal elimination of Röhm's SA on his Night of the Long Knives.

There was also the fact that those still at large believed in the guilt of those inside. Certainly no sophisticated Communist believed in the crimes to which Zinoviev, Radek or Pyatakov had confessed; however, it was widely assumed that viewed "objectively," there was a deeper level at which they were indeed guilty. More important, countless less sophisticated persons continued to believe in the guilt of those arrested, greeting the disappearance of friends and neighbors with the recollection that they had always thought there was something odd about them. The idiot fanatics took the process further still. In 1937 Evgeniya Ginzburg used to know a fanatical Communist lady who was never known otherwise than by her family name, Pitkovskaya:

> [She] was one of those who had carried over into the thirties all the habits and attitudes of the Civil War. . . . You could load her with enough work for four people, you could take her money and not return it, you could laugh at her—she never took offence at those whom she called her family.
>
> [The one cloud in her life was the fact that her husband, in 1927, had joined the Opposition.] Even to her five year old son she tried to explain in simple terms how gravely his father had sinned. She insisted that he should steep himself in the proletariat spirit. [In due course the NKVD came to arrest him, and] she carried on in a manner worthy of a Greek tragedy. . . .
>
> "So he lied to me!" she exclaimed dramatically, "so he really was against the Party all the time."
>
> With an amused grin the agent said: "Better get his things together."
>
> But she refused to do this for an enemy of the Party, and when her husband went to his sleeping child's cot to kiss him good-bye she barred his way.
>
> "My child has no father."
>
> Then shaking the policemen fervently by the hand she swore to them that her son would be brought up a faithful servant of the Party.
>
> All this she told me herself, and I do not for a moment believe that there was the least calculation or hypocrisy in her actions. Absurd as they were, they were prompted by the naïve sincerity of her soul, rigidly devoted to the ideals of her militant youth. The idea of possible

degeneration of scoundrels lusting for power, of treachery . . . had no
place in her honest single track mind.[18]

The most famous song to emerge from the Stalin era was written by
the author Yuz Aleshkovsky. It has entered the folk art of the Soviet
Union—so much so that when he once told a stranger somewhat in his
cups that he wrote it, the stranger assumed that Aleshkovsky took him
for a fool, fell upon him and tried to beat him up. The song features an
inmate of the gulag addressing Comrade Stalin the great scholar; it contains a couplet of remarkable insight into persons such as Pitkovskaya,
describing Stalin's cynical exploitation of their idiot idealism:

> We believed in you, Comrade Stalin,
> More perhaps than you believed in yourself.
> *My verili v tebya tovarisch' Stalin*
> *Kak mozhet byt' ne verili i vy.*

Thus the militants remained convinced of the justice of Soviet justice, as the charges of terror, sabotage and espionage sowed panic and
paranoia, keeping the nation subdued, obedient, divided and, above all,
ignorant. Despite the 10,000 daily papers, with their 38 million copies,
that appeared in 1937, the people had no news of what was going on.
For most important of all, perhaps, the charges served as a force of
disinformation. The fact that students of the purges still wonder why
Stalin unleashed them, when it is obvious that he wished to eliminate
the social groups and categories most likely to contain enemies, proves
that his method worked, that he was extraordinarily successful in disguising the basically simple idea behind the terror.

The first reaction of an arrestee was to keep asking "why" until his
fellow inmates told him to "change the record."[19] Record number two
would be "The horror of it," while the most interesting would be the
next piece, a variant upon the theme "If only Stalin knew." That record
played a vital part in believers' attempts to explain their fate. Obviously
it could not have been Stalin's doing; it was either a mistake or the work
of wicked minions. This explanation perpetuates a Russian tradition according to which the tsar is the embodiment of justice, goodness and all
the virtues but is cut off from his people by a dividing wall (*sredostenie*)
of wicked counsellors. If only the dividing wall could be broken, and
the tsar really know his people, justice and virtue would prevail.

Although all kinds of reason have been put forward to explain the confessions, it is obvious that there can be no single explanation. Pain, fear, loyalty to the party—all played their part. But there is one common factor—namely, the newly arrested person's sense of isolation and helplessness. No one, not even lawyers, visited them, there was no scope for heroics, no "bearing witness," no opportunity for scaffold speeches, and to all complaints there was one answer only: "You'll get used to it and if you don't you'll die."[20] As for those carefully staged public confessions, a security man, now himself an inmate of a Moscow prison, gave the following account of the ways of making them talk:

> Some idealists can be persuaded that they are no longer needed and will best serve the interests of their country by disappearing in such a manner. But most are more difficult and must be coerced, usually by destroying any hope they may have of ever obtaining justice and by threats to the lives of their wives and children. Sometimes drugs are used. . . . There was a case once when a man was required to make a public . . . confession of treason and was told that if he did not do it exactly as arranged his small son would have his head crushed in. The man apparently did not believe this. . . . His son was picked up by the feet and his head shattered against the wall.[21]

One Old Bolshevik's explanation was even simpler: "We were all up to our elbows in blood."[22] The investigators themselves were without illusions about the legends they concocted, although it was considered "good party manners' to pretend to believe in one's own conspiracies when discussing these with outsiders.[23] Both arrests and charges operated according to a quota system, so many arrests, so many charges per city, as a cellmate of Evgeniya Ginzburg made clear: "as a Tartar it was simpler to put down 'bourgeois nationalist.' Actually they had me down as a Trotskyite first, but they sent the file back saying they had exceeded the quota for Trotskyites but were short on nationalists."[24] Many of the legends were surreal: "A workman from Kiev . . . gave a detailed account of attempts to blow up a bridge a kilometre long with several kilos of arsenic. Another explained his activities in an organisation aiming at the construction of a number of artificial volcanoes in order to explode the entire Soviet Union . . . another prisoner admitted that he had informed the Polish consul of the weather as shown in a forecast put up regularly in a public park."[25]

Sometimes one had to prove the impossible; one army officer was required to prove that he was not Polish. Moreover, the interweaving of fact and fiction called for ingenuity; a willingness to confess was not always enough. In 1934 the writer Ivanov-Razumnik shared a cell with a cabdriver whose interrogator wanted him to confess to his crimes without being told what they were. Eventually, after a long night of interrogation, the prisoner returned to the cell looking even sadder than usual.

"I finally confessed," he said miserably.

"Well and what happened?"

"He hit me in the face."

"When?"

"When I confessed."

"Why?"

"I'm still not sure."

For some time he had been listening to his cellmates, all members of the intelligentsia, discussing Hitler's outlawing of the German Communist party on the pretext that they had burned down the Reichstag on February 25, 1933 (in fact it was Hitler who had engineered it). At a loss for anything to confess to, he thought he would choose a crime substantial enough to get the interrogator off his back and informed him that it was he who had burned the Reichstag down, at which point the interrogator started to beat him hysterically.[26]

No one pretended that the fictions were true. Rather, it was necessary to acknowledge the supremacy of party-directed fiction over fact. The point is illustrated by an anecdote. Stalin loses his pipe and orders the NKVD to find it. Two hours later he discovers it in his boot. He calls again to ask what progress has been made and is informed that ten men have been arrested and the investigation is continuing.

"I've found my pipe, so release them at once."

"But seven have confessed already."[27]

Evgeniya Ginzburg has the last word. When she heard that she had been given ten years' hard labor, she protested she was innocent: "Shut up! Of course you're not guilty! Would they have only given you ten years if you had been?"[28]

The Final Phases of the Terror

When trying to determine to what extent the purges were Stalin's doing, we should recognize that they were merely the accentuation of a trend. From its beginnings the regime had been happy to liquidate anyone whose face did not fit, and there had been no shortage of willing hands to execute its directives. Moreover, terror had its beneficiaries. The British consul in Leningrad, a highly intelligent observer, saw it as a third revolution, collectivization having been the second:

> Stalin's object in launching the third revolution is to get rid of all the eye-witnesses of the first revolution, whom the communist youth of to-day accuse of having become too bourgeois, by acquiring certain property etc. and whose jobs they covet. . . . It is merely what the Russians call a *shkurnyi vopros*, skin question, or, if you like, a matter of getting jobs. What we may have in the near future is Stalin at the head of a new régime of young communists.[1]

The wish to remove or isolate the older generation explains attempts to cut children off from their parents, encouraging them to inform on them or reject them, with the doctrine that "The child is not responsible for its parents"—which was not to say that the child could not be used against them if needs be. The ambitious young benefited from the terror and were ready to live by the criminal code of "Your turn today." As much was true of anyone enjoying the privileges of office. Such persons found themselves riding tigers and could only hope to remain on top for as long as possible, while no one who had assented to collectivization could object to the methods of the purges—only to being purged themselves.

In that sense the purges were not an "abnormal phenomenon"; they were in harmony with Soviet administrative methods, and there was no shortage of administrators, judges, executioners to see them through. Moreover, the arrests had a momentum of their own: No NKVD man could afford not to arrest a suspect, for this would immediately result in his own incarceration. In that sense the purges lay beyond the control of one man and, especially at regional levels, had a life of their own. Their casualties cannot be laid at Stalin's door alone; any Soviet leader who survived the thirties emerged with blood on his hands.

Writing in a British Communist party publication, *The Reasoner*, R. W. Davies, subsequently director of the center for Russian and East European Studies, made it clear that Stalin did not act alone in the purges and that he was actively supported by many of the USSR's subsequent leaders as well as by a large section of the industrial working class. As he put it with some elegance, "The Soviet proletariat was insufficiently mature to be able to make a distinction between treachery and political error."[2] He also referred to the "contradictions in Soviet life that were overcome by the purges," by which he meant that "a high proportion of the leading positions in the Party were still held by intellectuals not workers." However, he conceded that "injustices were not prevented by the Soviet State machinery, because the Soviet Union had not proved able to develop a proper system of checks and balances."[3]

Yet clearly Stalin was responsible for beginning the purges, and he proved able to maintain a fair degree of control over their nature. For example, up to the middle of August 1937 interrogators did not use torture as such. Their chief resource was the "conveyor," interrogation by relays, which gave the prisoner no chance to sleep for days on end. Although it broke most people eventually, it took time and was almost as exhausting for the interrogators as it was for their victims. It appears from the memoirs of ex-prisoners that on August 17, interrogators everywhere went over to "simplified interrogation," in other words to physical torture, a change apparently ordered by Stalin. We also know that he read and revised the execution lists Ezhov submitted to him. (Ezhov used the name and patronymic of Ivan the Terrible, Ivan Vasilievich, when referring to Stalin to his colleagues.[4]) It has been claimed that Stalin received 380 such lists, containing some 40,000 names.[5] He sometimes added comments: "Arrest everyone"; "No need to check, shoot them."[6] According to Khrushchev, he encouraged Ezhov to "Beat, beat and beat again." It would be fair to say that the purges were initiated by Stalin, that they could never have taken place without him and that he played an active part in their prosecution.

We gain a unique insight into the climate of that time from the diary of the Arctic explorer Papanin. He was put down on an ice floe near the Arctic Circle together with three other associates, one of them a NKVD man, and a dog named Loyal. He was supposed to winter there and be picked up later, but the floe broke away and began to drift south. Papanin's group maintained radio contact with "mission control," but as they drifted farther and farther, it became increasingly unlikely that they could be picked up before their floe melted away, and they began to reconcile themselves to death. When they were eventually rescued, the event was properly hailed as a great Soviet achievement, and the diary Papanin kept on the ice was pushed rapidly into print. Too rapidly. The book now available is an amended second edition. The first was withdrawn and destroyed. Only a few copies have survived. That is regrettable since the diary is an extraordinary record of Stalinist madness in its most acute form as the explorers became increasingly unbalanced. One was determined to use socialist educational methods to teach the dog not to steal food and developed fundamental doubts about the system when these failed. The explorers and the dog celebrated Stalin's birthday and other Communist festivals by holding demonstrations on the ice, marching up and down with banners, since none of the quartet would dare suggest that the activity was preposterous. In the meantime, they got news of the purges on the radio and learned that all those who had sent them on their mission, their replacements and the replacements of those replacements were foreign spies. The inference was obvious: One of them must be spying, too. The policeman began indulging in ostentatious target practice, after which he would clean his revolver meticulously. Every night he stripped down the piece, a cherished trophy presented to him by Yagoda, and reassembled it in the morning. One day he came close to breakdown. After reassembling the revolver, he found himself left with an extra part and no place to put it. He never realized that one of the others had added the piece in the night and continued to agonize over it for days. By the time the team was rescued they all were half-mad, trusting no one, not even themselves and giving rise to a joke popular at the time: "I'm alone on an ice floe, and there must be an enemy somewhere." It would be no exaggeration to say that the first edition of the Papanin diary spoke with the voice of a nation.

The view that the purges were Stalin's doing is reinforced by the fact that he was their only certain beneficiary. Of course, others benefited too from the Khrushchevs, the Suslovs, the Malenkovs down to junior army officers, who found their superiors taking casualties at a rate unknown in any war. But no group emerged as having done so well out of the purges that it could be thought of as their instigator. No one could be sure he would benefit, no one be certain that he was immune. True, a Jewish Old Bolshevik with Trotskyite sympathies could not hope to escape arrest, while a young nonparty factory hand stupefied by work, malnutrition and vodka would probably fall outside the danger zone. That the party itself was the principal target is reflected in anecdotes:

> "Knock knock."
> "Who's there?"
> "NKVD."
> "You've got the wrong floor; the Communists live upstairs."

A sense of the transitory quality of life within the danger zone was to be found everywhere. Soviet banknotes ceased to bear the signature of bank officials since their signatories disappeared too quickly. Offices in the *Izvestiya* building no longer had the names of senior staff members painted on their doors. Streets were constantly having their names changed since streets had to be called something—unlike the public parks, which tended to remain nameless after the disgrace of the leader they were originally named after. In the meantime, the government attempted to check a serious threat to the nation's plumbing by making it illegal to put books and newspapers down the lavatory.

Terror at this level suited Stalin, because it brought about the atomization of society. Social ties vanished; people, as Nadezhda Mandelstam put it, "ceased to meet one another."[7] Stalin had succeeded in doing something the tsars had never managed: His terror had loosened the very bonds of humanity and made those exposed to it live in a void.[8] An American journalist describes the destruction of all ties and obligations, as if the very stuff of civilization had perished:

> Women I knew, fine intellectual women, with government jobs,
> would meet after hours and just drink themselves into a stupor.
> Citizens who had always followed politics at home and abroad with

keen interest escaped into apathy. Suicides multiplied. Youth took refuge in cynicism. Everybody played Safety First. Lying, hypocrisy, humiliatory obeisances, violence towards one's deepest conviction, and disloyalty to friends were a small price to pay for keeping out of prison. To divert suspicion from yourself you accused the other fellow. You yelled loudest at meetings when resolutions were voted calling on the government to execute Pyatakov, Radek and their accomplices. When Stalin's name was mentioned you applauded and you did not stop even though it might go on for ten minutes.[9]

Disintegration was not confined to educated circles. The British Embassy received an anonymous letter that described a comparable process in the villages. It complained of poor food since many mills had been burned down and flour was ground by hand. People reacted to arrests by taking their bitterness out on one another. Hooliganism was on the increase, and all moral principles appeared to have collapsed. Families broke up as the terror loosened all binding ties, while no one dared raise a voice in protest for fear of being accused of being anti-Soviet.[10]

These were times when everyone felt guilty. By the exacting standards of that age innocence was impossible. The Soviet Union had become the land of universal guilt. As one scientist put it, although he was a loyal Soviet scholar, he was ready for arrest because like any citizen, he carried with him a nagging sense of guilt, combined with the certain hope of inevitable punishment. After every lecture he would wonder whether he had veered from the "general line" and whether he had done so "intentionally" or by mistake, so vague yet strong was his sense of guilt that he could not decide for himself.[11]

This atmosphere created a readiness to assent to terror, as an informer or even an executioner, because as Mme. Mandelstam put it, "But does it matter who actually signed the death warrants? In those years everyone was prepared to sign everything and not just because to refuse would have meant an instant firing squad. The power of our sense of being organised was such that people like us . . . destroyed, tortured, killed, annihilated our fellows, justifying our actions with 'historical necessity.'"[12]

There is more to such behavior than simply obeying orders. The atomization of Soviet society was the outcome of that ruthlessness and lack of respect for human life that were in style from the moment the Bolsheviks seized power, making it easy for people to assent to or par-

ticipate in the annihilation of others. With every man become an island, no man's death diminished anyone anymore.

• • •

> Very treacherous weather. In such times a man must be
> careful to protect the back of his neck.
> —BARON STEIGER ON THE EVE OF HIS
>   DISAPPEARANCE

Every student of this period has their favorite story of absurd arrests.
One of the strangest is the case of an illiterate seventy-three-year-old
woman in hospital with a broken hip. A doctor asked her whom she was
going to vote for in the forthcoming elections. She replied that the candidate for her district was Bukharin—who had been in prison for the
last six months. She had confused his name with that of Bulganin,
Khrushchev's future associate and was taken to the Lubyanka by am-
bulance at once.[13]

The country's mood was reflected in the November 7 celebrations for
the year 1937. Security was tighter than ever, and diplomatic invitations
were restricted to first secretaries and above. The only "crowd" consisted
of a handful of schoolchildren placed on the far side of Red Square,
behind five rows of troops and a good quarter of a mile away from
Stalin. He emerged from a private door and slipped onto Lenin's tomb
when all eyes were on the parade, for the greater part of which, an
embassy report continues, "he stood quietly smoking and spitting." In
the absence of a real crowd cheering was provided by loudspeakers.

> The volume of sound was carefully amplified or dimmed in order to
> denote the exact degree of popularity suitable to the object of the
> cheering. The GPU troops were given a particularly enthusiastic
> reception. . . . All officers' holsters were empty. The space around the
> tomb which on previous parades had been occupied by generals of the
> Red Army, Old Bolsheviks and other persons of distinction was this
> year left empty except for a handful of GPU men . . . the dominant
> impression . . . was one of nervousness and suspicion amounting to
> mania.[14]

Another report develops the theme of mania. Commenting on a
batch of executions, Stalin's friend, and his late wife's godfather,
Yenukidze, being one of the victims, it talks of the standardized quality
of the confessions:

All political suspects must be found to be Trotskyites, all Trotskyites must seal their own death warrants with full confessions . . . there must be no ragged ends. This is state planning carried to a pitch of madness and unquestionably the note of insanity sounds very loud in the Soviet Union to-day. M. Ezhov himself is stated to be in an acutely neurotic condition and unable to sleep for more than a few minutes at a time. The machine seems to be running away with him.[15]

As the terror approached its climax, Stalin began to appeal to its beneficiaries. In January 1938 the press was full of the need to promote workers to responsible positions, and there were sinister references to the survival of Communist arrogance among the party's old guard. A piece in *Pravda* on January 27 called for bold and rapid promotions; only a bureaucrat could object to making dramatic advancements from the rank and file, omitting intermediate grades. "It is necessary to help people along and break the opposition to new cadres that have already been advanced to responsible work." Opposition came from Trotskyite-Bukharinist wreckers, who "dread above all the arrival of new people devoted to the Stalinist Central Committee and to the Soviet government."[16]

Stalin was setting the new generation against the old, which was to have its final pillorying in the third of the Moscow trials the stars of which would be Bukharin, Rykov, Krestinsky and Yagoda. Ezhov seems to have found it difficult to create the appropriate legends for his performers; it had been the better part of a year since Bukharin's arrest. Part of the softening-up process consisted of drawing the attention of the accused to a change in Stalin's attitude toward children. In the autumn of 1937 an NKVD man working abroad heard a rumor that children were to be charged with the crimes of their parents: "No wonder the accused of the third trial who had children of their own, *e.g.* Bukharin and Krestinsky, were ready to pay Stalin any price."[17]

Yagoda had been arrested in 1937, necessitating the dynamiting of a gigantic statue of him, carved from solid rock, at the entrance to the White Sea Canal.[18] He had flourished in prison, putting on weight; every week Ezhov reported on his health to Stalin.[19] The trial was held in the Trade Union Hall of Columns, in an upstairs chamber seating about 200 people. The cast included familiar figures, such as the presiding judge, Ulrikh, and Vishinsky playing his usual role as prosecutor. The charges against Bukharin included plotting to assassinate Lenin and trying to undermine Lenin's work in collaboration with Trotsky and British intelligence. Yagoda was charged with conspiring with Bukharin to murder Kirov, Gorky and his son. There was also an attempt to poison Ezhov.

The charges against Bukharin were intended to discredit his brand of communism once and for all. Those against Yagoda are more revealing. By making him responsible for Kirov's death, Stalin was mending his fences. It was common gossip in NKVD circles that Nikolaev had not acted alone. It was logical to assume that the death had been Stalin's doing. As usual his response was to find a scapegoat, and he now made Yagoda responsible for the killing, while the charge that Yagoda had arranged for the medical murder of Gorky suggests that this was probably how he died, for "this was a time when people did not believe in natural death."[20]

The third trial had an unusual start as Krestinsky played a variation on the standard theme, startling his audience by entering a plea of not guilty. Many thought that at last someone would expose a trial for the farce it was. However, the next day he stated that he had pleaded not guilty by mistake. It was assumed that he had passed a lively and uncomfortable night, although the explanation may be simpler. The initial plea and the retraction were probably part of the script. Stalin had recognized that the mechanical admissions of guilt appeared unconvincing to foreign observers and used Krestinsky for a change in the plot.[21]

At first Yagoda's performance was impressive and appears to have included a measure of improvisation. Among other crimes he was accused of arranging the medical murder of his predecessor, Menzhinsky. He replied that his accusers were lying. When Vishinsky asked Yagoda whether he too had lied, he replied: "Don't dare ask me that question! That question I shall not answer" and observed to Ulrikh: "You can drive me but not too far, I'll say what I want to say but do not drive me too far."[22] It was as if he were reminding the court that he might still expose the whole charade, hoping that his life might be spared as a reward for his discretion. But the next day things were different: "All the spirit had been knocked out of Yagoda. He looked ten years older than the Yagoda who had given evidence the night before and thirty years older than the Yagoda who had formerly held sway at the Lubyanka. In the course of his statement which he read out as though he were seeing it for the first time . . . he confessed to all the crimes with which he had been charged."[23]

He concluded with a plea for mercy: "Even from behind bars I would like to see the further flourishing of the country I betrayed."[24]

The trial, with its charges of conspiracy with British intelligence was discussed in Parliament. *Hansard* for March 9, 1938, records the following exchange:

> Mr. Leach. Can the Prime Minister take any steps to protect the innocent victims of these fantastic stories?
> Mr. Gallagher. They are true stories.
> Mr. Leach. Will he do so?
> Mr. Gallagher. Are we to understand that the British Intelligence Service has no interest in Russia, or that there is no British Intelligence Service; and does the Prime Minister mean to tell us that men who are facing trial voluntarily make statements of this kind without there being any base for them?

Bukharin made a courageous attempt at a "scaffold speech," which vainly relied on the ability of foreign observers to read between the lines. He stated that he had decided to give evidence—in other words, to collaborate—because if he were to die unrepentant, he would die in vain. Then he alluded to the coming struggle against fascism which made all other considerations appear trivial. It was a view he had held ever since Hitler took power, and it may have been the decisive motive for his collaboration. Better that socialists of all complexions rally to Stalin's cause than allow Hitler to destroy the Soviet state. He then confessed to "crimes" that constituted an alternative to the path his country had taken. He conceded that he had aimed at state capitalism, the abolition of the collective farms, the establishment of a prosperous peasantry, the introduction of foreign trade concessions and the end of the foreign trade monopoly. Although he refused to accept the charge of murdering Lenin, he conceded that "my counter-revolutionary confederates and I endeavoured to murder Lenin's cause, which is being carried on with such tremendous success by Stalin."[25]

This is the point at which Bukharin wanted to be understood. It was clear that Stalin's perpetuation of Lenin's line had been a disaster. Therefore, either Bukharin was repudiating Stalin's interpretation of Lenin's cause or he was suggesting that Lenin himself had been wrong. However, Bukharin was too subtle for the majority of an audience which, though small, was not undistinguished, since it included none other than Stalin himself! For as Sir Fitzroy Maclean, then on the embassy staff, reported, "At one moment during the trial a clumsily directed arc lamp clearly revealed to attentive members of the audience a drooping moustache and yellowish face peering out from behind the black glass of one of the private boxes that commanded a view of the court-room."[26]

In a final speech, which secured the death penalty for all the accused, Vishinsky concluded:

> Our whole country is awaiting and demanding one thing. The traitors and spies who were selling our country must be shot like dirty dogs. Our people are demanding one thing. Crush the accursed reptile. Time will pass. The graves of the hateful traitors will grow over with weeds and thistles. But over us, over our happy country our sun will shine . . . as bright and luminous as before. Over the road cleared of the last scum and filth of the past, we, with our beloved leader and teacher the great Stalin at our head, will march as before onward and onward toward communism.

This was the last of the great trials. The tempo of the terror began to abate now, although some of the country's most distinguished heads rolled as Stalin rounded it off. Moving up from commissars and members of the Central Committee, he liquidated loyal Stalinists such as Rudzutak, together with five members of his own Politburo. He also shot A. V. Kosarev, a member of the Orgburo and secretary of the Komsomol, after a hair-raising encounter. At a reception to celebrate the return of the intrepid Papanin Stalin approached Kosarev, clinked glasses with him, embraced him and whispered in his ear, "If you're a traitor, I'll kill you."[27]

Stalin suffered a different kind of loss that year when his mother died. He neither attended the funeral in Tiflis nor put a cross upon her grave, despite the fact that she was a devout Christian. She had lived out her last years in great loneliness, neglected by her son, and was heard on more than one occasion to regret that he had never become a priest. Stalin further reduced his immediate circle. He shot J. Redens, the husband of his sister-in-law; Alexander Svanidze, the brother of his first wife; and Pavel Alliluyev, the brother of his second. The thinning out was a source of sad bewilderment to his young daughter, Svetlana, who wondered why the family dacha had grown so empty. While Stalin went to some lengths to exterminate anyone who had known him in early life, he permitted himself the occasional caprice. Although he had his old friend and onetime rival Budu Mdivani shot, he kept an associate of Mdivani's, S. I. Kavtaradze, in a death cell for some time but then released him. Stalin seems to have "taken him up"; he reunited him with his wife in Beria's office and arranged for him to have an apartment in Moscow. On one astounding occasion, in the company of Beria, he played Harun al-Rashid and appeared at Kavtaradze's front door with a bottle of wine. At dinner Stalin would act the Georgian host, pour the soup and propose toasts, which did not prevent him from reproaching Kavtaradze: "And still you wanted to kill me."[28]

Yet Stalin, at this time, remained a surprisingly loving father. He was hard on his son Vasily but obviously fond of his daughter, to the point of spoiling her. When they were apart, he wrote tender little notes to his "Little Mistress" (*khozyaika*), which he would sign, in comic self-deprecation, "Your wretched secretary the poor peasant J. Stalin," a form which echoes the way Peter the Great was wont to sign himself in letters to his wife. From his daughter's account it is obvious that what he required of his children was blind obedience and unquestioning adoration. Anything less would have been a form of disloyalty—a view of father-daughter relations that boded ill for the future.

Stalin was beginning to show signs that his healthy sense of suspicion was getting out of hand. After all the blood he had spilt, he found it inconceivable that no one should be seeking to assassinate him. He even suspected his own police. When Khrushchev complained to him that the NKVD had arrested an innocent man, he replied: "I know what you mean, they're gathering evidence against me too."[29] He took elaborate precautions against being poisoned and even had a servant whose sole function was to make his tea from sealed packages kept in a locked cabinet. They were opened in the presence of a security man who checked the seal; the appropriate amount would be taken and the rest of the packet disposed of. One day a packet was found with its seal broken, and the teamaker duly made her way to the Lubyanka. Stalin's security mania could be counterproductive. A German diplomat returned from a Black Sea vacation with a story of Stalin's coming under fire. He was due to go for a spin in his launch, and the NKVD coast guards had been ordered to fire on any boat other than Stalin's. "Apparently as an additional measure of caution, M. Stalin at the last moment had the number of his launch changed, but failed to notify the local coastguard. . . . As a result of this he was greeted with a broadside as soon as he was sighted by them. . . . Even if all this did not actually happen it is quite the sort of thing which might happen here."[30]

The incident may have been "arranged" by Beria, for there are rumors of his having rigged an assassination bid at sea in order to demonstrate his loyalty to Stalin by coping with it.

• • •

The triumph of mature Stalinism was marked by a publication which was a cynical demonstration of his victory, making it clear that henceforward the truth was whatever he might want it to be. *The History of the Communist Party* rewrote fifty years of Russian history, and its study was immediately made obligatory for all party members. Stalin was so pleased with the work that he presented a copy to his daughter and was furious when he discovered that she had not read it.

> It was bold, specious, conscienceless fiction. There was a certain magnificence in its unabridged cynicism, its defiance of the common sense of the Russian people. The roles of leading historical figures were perverted or altogether erased. New roles were invented for others. Leon Trotsky . . . was presented as a fiendish agent of foreign capitalists who had sought to sell out his country in collusion with Rykov, Bukharin, Zinoviev, Kamenev, Krestinsky and Pyatakov. . . . Iosef Stalin . . . emerged as the sole leader inside Russia before the revolution and as Lenin's one intimate and trusted associate thereafter. All books, articles, documents, museum materials which contradicted this . . . fantasy . . . disappeared throughout the country. More than that living witnesses, as far as possible, were removed.[31]

In the autumn of 1938 Stalin began to wind the purges down. It has been worked out that at the rate at which the arrests were proceeding, with each arrestee required to name at least five accomplices, it would not have taken long to put the entire nation in prison. The first sign of a change of policy came at the January plenum of the Central Committee, which criticized careerists who had made their way up the ladder by informing on their superiors—precisely what they had been encouraged to do. Stalin was repeating the technique of "Dizzy from Success," blaming others for his own excesses. The chief scapegoat would be Ezhov. Stalin moved on him with some delicacy. In April he gave him the additional appointment of commissar for water transport, logical enough since canals were built and maintained by forced labor. The chief accountant of the gulag, Inzhin, who went to work for him, found him under great stress, drinking heavily and treating visitors with extraordinary cynicism and rudeness.[32] Stalin next appointed a commission, headed by Beria and Malenkov to examine alleged NKVD excesses under Ezhov. Beria was then made Ezhov's deputy and, by the autumn of 1938, had replaced him as head of the NKVD, although

Ezhov remained in charge of water transport. By now he was totally demoralised; he attended departmental meetings in silence, sometimes making paper darts, which he threw and retrieved, always in silence.[33]

The news of Ezhov's dismissal caused widespread rejoicing in the camps, especially among devout Communists. They hailed it as proof that Stalin had finally understood what had been going on. Others, remembering how they had celebrated the fall of Yagoda, were more cautious. Ezhov's last recorded appearance was at the Eighteenth Congress, held five years late in early 1939. When his name came up for reelection to the Central Committee, Stalin ordered him to assess his own fitness to belong to that body. Ezhov answered, stammering, that he did not understand the question, that he had devoted his entire life to serving Stalin and the party. Stalin puffed his pipe and asked him what had become of the senior NKVD men, including Ezhov's deputy and his secretary, who all had been arrested. Ezhov tried to remind Stalin that it was he who had "discovered" that they were plotting against him, but Stalin promptly trumped his ace by observing that it was inconceivable that Ezhov himself was not part of such a plot. He then accused him of running the security forces at too high a pitch and also, crime of crimes, of arresting innocent people. Of course, it was up to the floor to decide Ezhov's candidacy, but he, Stalin, had his doubts. When Ezhov was arrested a few days later, his expression was almost cheerful. "How long have I been waiting for this," he observed.[34] Stalin sustained the pretense that the purges were Ezhov's doing, later observing to the aircraft designer A. S. Yakovlyev: "Ezhov was a rat; he killed many innocent people. We shot him for that."[35]

In his report to the congress Stalin announced the end of the purges. He conceded: "It cannot be said that the purges were conducted without serious mistakes. Unfortunately there were more mistakes than might have been expected."[36] However, both the party and the country had been strengthened by the process, for whole classes whose existence elsewhere weakened the capitalist countries had been eliminated. The Soviet Union now consisted, as it were, of three estates—workers, peasants and intelligentsia—firmly united. Stalin offered a wonderfully simple view of Soviet society. He considered class anomalies, conflicts, antagonisms to be destabilizing and had dealt with the problem by eliminating the antagonists. He went on to emphasize that the purges had also narrowed the gap between the leaders and the rank and file, creating a party with a more developed sense of practical reality. (In other words, he had got rid of ideologues, intellectuals and Jews.) He then

addressed himself to the beneficiaries of the purges, the young generation. He emphasized the importance of the young cadres and reminded
them that he believed in rapid promotion before youth grew stale.[37] He
conceded that the older generation also had a contribution to make and,
with the greatest of all his examples of black humor, went on: "But . . .
there are always fewer old cadres than are needed, and their ranks are
already beginning to thin out by dint of nature's laws."[38] In other words
he accounted for the elimination of an entire generation in four years by
natural wastage! He stressed the achievements of the eager, ambitious,
practical younger generation, pointing out that more than 500,000
young members, including 100,000 women, had recently been promoted to managerial posts. This and not the Seventeenth Congress was
the true Feast of the Victors, for Stalin made it clear that the spoils were
theirs, that the future lay with them, not with their seniors.

There were not many seniors left. The purge had accounted for four
full members of the Politburo, two candidate members and eighty percent of the Council of People's Commissars. In 1934 the average regional party secretary had been in the party for twenty-one years; the
average commissar, for twenty-three. In 1939 the corresponding figures
were fifteen and eighteen years respectively. It was a time when future
leaders started spectacular careers; Kosygin and Brezhnev both graduated in 1935, and now the former was people's commissar for textiles,
the latter a regional secretary. Ustinov graduated in 1934 and was commissar for armaments by 1941. Kirilenko graduated in 1936 and was a
second secretary of a regional committee by 1940. Among Stalin's many
achievements, by no means the least remarkable is his bringing on a
generation of party men able enough still to be governing the Soviet
Union nearly half a century later.

CHAPTER THIRTY-SEVEN

Foreign Policy

Since our concern has been with Stalin's rise to power and its effect upon his country, we have ignored the subject of his foreign policy. However, it would be true to say that up to, if not beyond, 1941 this consisted of a series of misjudgments. Neither Stalin, nor the majority of those close to him had any grasp of foreign affairs. Stalin's personal experience of the world beyond the Soviet Union was minimal, and he spoke only one foreign language, Russian. Moreover, he was not the kind of man to seek advice from those more knowledgeable than himself. The Bolsheviks who knew Europe and were fluent in foreign languages, such as Radek, Bukharin, Zinoviev were never welcome precisely because they outshone Stalin.

His first major misjudgment is the most easily forgiven, for it concerned China, a land about which nobody knew anything. The mistake was Stalin's insistence that the Chinese Communist party accept the leadership of the Kuomintang and his encouragement of that body to establish an armed force regardless of the social origin of its officers. A promising young commander, Chiang Kai-shek, was trained in Moscow and sent to Canton to establish a military school, the famous Whampoa Military Academy. As he increased his dominance over the Kuomintang, Chinese Communists made anxious representations to Stalin, who refused to admit that he had backed the wrong man and insisted that the party continue to collaborate with him.

In 1926 Chiang advanced upon Shanghai and the treaty ports. As he drew near, the Shanghai Communists rose in his support, whereupon Chiang delayed his advance until the rebels had brought their fight to a successful conclusion. It was a move after Stalin's own heart: cynical and effective. Stalin would play a variant of it in 1944, halting the Red Army at the gates of Warsaw while the Wehrmacht eliminated the Polish Home Army. The triumphant Communists invited Chiang into the city, where he fell upon them, eliminating their leaders by feeding them fully conscious into locomotive furnaces. Undismayed, Stalin ordered the remnants of the party to place themselves under the liberal wing of the Kuomintang, with consequences no less disastrous. As usual a scapegoat was found, in the form of the party leader, Chen Tu-hsiu, who was expelled and denounced as a Trotskyite. From that moment the Chinese Communists, led by Mao, were left to go it alone, opening a rift between the two parties that may yet prove the most disastrous of Stalin's legacies.

In the late twenties Stalin developed certain tenets of foreign policy. These were based on an erroneous assessment of the encircling capitalist powers which were seen as perpetually threatening the USSR with war. One of the justifications for superindustrialization and the mass murder of the peasantry was the need to "catch up and overtake" the threatening countries. At this time Stalin made another mistake, one which would cost a total of some 30 million lives. Stalin judged that advanced capitalist societies from Germany to the United States were on the verge of collapse and ordered foreign Communist parties not to collaborate with other socialists and to establish rival trade unions. They were to fight any gradualist or reformist policies, purge themselves of "right deviationists" and recognize that Social Democrats were the real enemy. "Social Democracy is objectively the moderate wing of fascism. . . . They are not antipodes they are twins."[1] It is a view that Stalin seems to have arrived at from obstinate reliance upon his own intuition.

At the Sixth Congress of the International held in Moscow in 1928 it was established that the chief target of the German Communist party, the KPD, should be the Social Democratic party, or SDP, thereby creating a hopeless division in the German left. Stalin was afraid of SDP moderates, who worked within the framework of the Weimar Constitution, afraid of their potential influence over his own Bukharinist right wing on the eve of collectivization. He believed that the Weimar Republic must be destroyed, that this alone could pave the way for an eventual Communist take-over. Here his interests coincided with those of the Nazi party and their desire to smash what they referred to as the Weimar *System*. They spoke scornfully of the period they lived in with its punctilious insistence on legality as the *Systemzeit*, while, like the

Green party today, they made heady appeals to principles beyond the law.

Up to the moment that Hindenburg invited Hitler to form a government in January 1933 the KPD supported the Nazis against the socialist and Catholic parties that were trying to keep parliamentary democracy alive. The collaboration had bizarre results, captured by photographs of working-class districts in which Nazi and Communist flags hang side by side from the same windows. The strangest episode of all was the Berlin transport strike in 1932, when Nazis and Communists jointly manned picket lines, each dressed in the uniform of his private army, decorously taking it in turns to chant his party slogans. The strike is no longer acknowledged to have taken place by East German historians.

Hitler did not seize power; he won it constitutionally. Had the KPD, the world's largest Communist party outside the USSR, voted with the Center party and the SDP against Hitler, it would have beaten the Nazis comfortably. Three months before Hitler came to power, the SDP leaders implored Stalin to support them to that effect. No one can say whether the KPD could have prevented Hitler from seizing power in the end, but certainly Stalin did nothing to stop him.

Hitler was not the only politician Stalin supported in 1932, election year in the United States. The American Communist party had tried to run its own candidate, a union man named William Z. Foster, with a black running mate, James Ford, a student at the Lenin School in Moscow. Their campaign was financed by the Comintern, which expected to win by concentrating on the black vote. When they failed to collect enough signatures to enable Foster and Ford to run, the American party was ordered to switch its vote to Roosevelt. The notion that Stalin played a part in the election of one of America's greatest presidents has its comic aspects; Stalin may not actually have brought Roosevelt to power, but it cannot be denied that he helped.[2]

As Hitler consolidated his power, Stalin's attitude to Social Democrats altered to one of collaboration—the policy of united fronts. Through coalition with other socialist parties, Communists in national governments were to use their position to pack key departments and then eliminate their allies to govern alone. Such was the long-term aim; the immediate one was to seek allies against Hitler. In 1934 the Communists signed a limited agreement with the French Socialist party, and a year later France and the USSR signed a pact of mutual aid and assistance aimed at Germany. The following year the *Front Populaire* coalition led by Léon Blum won the election, but Blum declined to admit Communists to key positions in the government or the trade unions.

In the summer of 1936 Stalin was presented with a new problem in the shape of the civil war that had broken out in Spain, when Franco and his fascists moved on the forces of the republic. This put Stalin in a cleft stick. France, an ally of sorts, had opted for nonintervention, but Stalin was already extending delicate feelers toward Germany, while a Communist victory in Spain might unite France, Germany and Britain against the Red Peril. Yet to allow the republic and its left-wing Popular Front to go under would bring a grave loss of international prestige. Stalin maneuvered with some elegance. He accepted the principle of nonintervention while intervening—with large numbers of Soviet volunteers and matériel, tanks and planes—in return for the republic's gold deposits, to be lodged in Moscow for safekeeping. Moreover, Stalin was accorded tight control over republican forces, taking over many areas of government, including internal security. Soviet military units operated independently of other forces and were themselves controlled by the NKVD.

Stalin's portrait began to appear in the streets of Madrid "with something of the aura associated then with the images of the saints."[3] But increasingly the attention of the NKVD was turned against anarchists and other splinter groups deemed to be infiltrated by Trotskyites. Early in 1937 Soviet aid began to be run down as Stalin made his contribution to Franco's victory. His treatment of the advisers and experts he had sent to Spain is typical. He arrested virtually all of them, on the ground that they could have been contaminated abroad, and disposed of them together with the Spanish refugees who fled to the USSR to escape Franco. At least the war produced its share of anti-Soviet jokes:

> "Have you heard they've taken Teruel?"
> "Family too?"
> "Dont you understand Teruel's a town."
> "Aha, they've started arresting whole towns, have they?"[4]

*   *   *

Stalin had declared a European war to be inevitable, expecting his country to enter it late—and on the winning side. A keen student of history, he must have been aware of the foolish generosity of Nicholas II, who entered World War I too early, to save France at the expense of

Russia. He also understood that war had toppled a regime which had done much less harm to its subjects than they had suffered in twenty years of Soviet rule. Stalin may even have recognized that from the point of view of Russia and the autocracy, Nicholas had been fighting on the wrong side. Imperial Russia stood to gain very little, apart from eventual further foreign loans, from siding with France and Great Britain, whereas an alliance with Germany and Austria-Hungary would have preserved its frontiers and saved the autocracy. Nicholas had even attempted to form an alliance with the kaiser some years before, only to have his prime minister chivy him out of it. For once Nicholas had been right; a friendly neutrality in the Great War would have preserved the empire.

Stalin had further reason to seek a German alliance. Unlike his anointed predecessor, he was free from messy involvements in the Balkans and no longer had a threatening Austro-Hungarian presence on his southwestern flank. Moreover, he must have recognized that his regime had more in common with Nazi Germany than it did with the Western democracies, right down to a certain attitude toward Jews. There was nothing preposterous about a deal with Hitler; it was the sensible thing to do. Stalin secretly sought such an accommodation, while publicly negotiating with France and promoting the principle of collective security. His policy in the late thirties remained one of fence-sitting; he was determined that his country would never have to fight Hitler alone. Early in 1937, just as he was reducing the Soviet involvement in Spain, Stalin tried to reach an agreement with Hitler, only to be rebuffed.[5]

The unimpressive and duplicitous Soviet performance in Spain did not recommend Stalin to France and Britain as a potential ally. In the circumstances one can understand why the two countries did not seek an alliance with Soviet Russia or even consult it before signing the Munich agreement with Hitler in September 1938, which countenanced a German annexation of part of Czechoslovakia. Nevertheless, their action came as a shock to the Soviet Union. A member of a Soviet anti-Stalinist group writes of the Western democracies: "Tragically they offered us no hope. Both in the eyes of the thinking opposition and the man in the street the Munich agreement had destroyed their moral authority. By that agreement Britain and France committed moral suicide."[6]

The Allies helped bring about the conjuncture that Stalin had been seeking for the last four years. Assuming the political leaders of France and Great Britain to be as clear-sighted and ruthless as himself in their pursuit of advantage, Stalin concluded that they wished to provoke a war between the USSR and Germany in which they would ally themselves with Hitler. Stalin's view of the Allies has sometimes been said to have been colored by unreasonable suspicion, but all he did was to put himself in their place. Having no experience of other leaders, it was reasonable to assume that their sense of *Realpolitik* was not unlike his own.

In the spring of 1939 Stalin addressed the Eighteenth Congress on foreign policy. He said that a second imperialist war was already raging from Shanghai to Gibraltar and that democratic states were giving way to the Axis all along the line. By their policy of nonintervention they sought to involve the Soviet Union, Germany and Japan in an internecine war from which they alone would benefit. The Soviet Union wished for peace, would defend the integrity of its frontiers and would not be inveigled into fighting on behalf of others.[7] Shortly afterward Stalin dismissed Litvinov, his minister of foreign affairs, a Jew and an advocate of collective security, replacing him with Molotov.

During the spring and summer of 1939 Stalin negotiated openly with the British. They did nothing to help what was probably a lost cause anyway by failing to send a top-level negotiator. William Strang was a career diplomat who had served in the embassy as counselor and had accompanied Anthony Eden on a visit to Stalin in 1935. He was now an assistant under-secretary and was sent to Moscow at Eden's suggestion. There was also a military mission which was unable to agree to Stalin's condition for joint military action: namely, right of passage through Poland and naval bases in the Baltic states.

Stalin probably went through the motion of negotiating with the Allies to strengthen his hand in the secret negotiations he was conducting with Germany. Nevertheless, the British government made a grave diplomatic error when it guaranteed Poland, without extracting a quid pro quo from Stalin, for Prime Minister Chamberlain was thereby offering him free protection against a German invasion.

On August 21 Stalin was able to announce the imminent arrival of the German foreign minister with whom Molotov would sign a nonaggression pact. Von Ribbentrop's visit posed problems, not the least of which was a shortage of Nazi flags with which to celebrate his arrival. Eventually a supply was tracked down in a film studio where they had been used in anti-Nazi films.[8] At his meeting with the foreign minister Stalin opened with the observation that although both sides had "poured buckets of filth" over each other for years, there was no reason not to make their quarrels up.[9] Later at dinner Stalin professed a long-standing admiration for Hitler.[10] As the assembled guests drank his health, the anti-Semite von Ribbentrop clinked glasses with the Jew Kaganovich.

The agreement reached with Hitler was twofold. Germany and the Soviet Union agreed that in the event of either nation's being attacked, neither would lend support to the aggressor. They also established spheres of interest, partitioning Central Europe. Russia's sphere included Finland, Estonia, Latvia, Bessarabia (then part of Rumania), and the eastern half of Poland. Everything to the west of that line would be Germany's. There was also an economic agreement, whereby Russia would supply Germany with specified quantities of raw material in return for military hardware and technology.

Much ink has been devoted to justifying or explaining the pact, and wondering who was deceiving whom. According to von Ribbentrop's interpreter, Gustav Hilger, an able diplomat, Hitler believed that the political side of the agreement would hold in the medium term, while understanding that Stalin could never be bound by a scrap of paper.[11] In the short term he had secured significant quantities of raw materials, including oil. According to the trade agreement, which was only completed in February 1940, Russia agreed to ship 1 million tonnes of grain, 900,000 tonnes of oil, 100,000 tonnes of chrome, two and a half tons of platinum in return for machinery and military matériel.[12] More important, once Poland had been taken care of, Hitler would be free of the threat of war on two fronts. Stalin, too, had made important gains. He had recovered a significant portion of the territories lost at Brest-Litovsk. Moreover, Germany was at war with France and England as of September 1939. If the Great War was anything to go by, this would prove a protracted affair from which all parties would emerge exhausted, leaving the Soviet Union untouched.

Stalin seems to have believed that the treaty would hold; certainly he saw it to be in the interest of both parties; as he observed some years later to his daughter, allied with Germany, the Soviet Union would have been invincible.[13] The Soviet government went far beyond paying lip service to the pact. Anti-Nazi films and propaganda vanished overnight, while France and Britain were denounced as plutocracies that had launched an imperialist war against Germany; Hitler, it was explained, was only trying to right the injustices of the Treaty of Versailles.[14] All things German became fashionable, and Stalin even ordered a production of Die Walküre to be mounted at the Bolshoi Theater.[15]

The pact was well received in the Soviet Union; a two-line couplet popular at the time went as follows:

> *Spasibo Yashe Ribentropu*
> *Chto on otkryl okno v Evropu.*
> Thanks to Yasha Ribbentrop
> For opening a window on Europe.

Abroad devout Communists welcomed the pact, considering that it provided an excellent opportunity to further the cause at the expense of warring capitalist powers.[16]

It has been suggested that like Chamberlain at Munich, Stalin was playing for time and never believed in the agreement. If so, he had a funny way of showing it: Not only did the raw materials he shipped make a substantial contribution to the German war effort, but he made no attempt to use the time bought at such cost to prepare for war with Germany. It seems more likely that he settled down to watch the Second World War from the sidelines, until the appropriate moment should come to take part—on whose side it would remain to be seen. Looking back on the situation as it appeared in the autumn of 1939 this would have been the most sensible course—with the proviso that it was essential to have a fallback plan. Stalin's mistake was his failure to provide one. One of the greatest puzzles of modern history is why Stalin, who had never trusted anyone in his life before, apparently trusted Hitler. Part of the explanation derives from the fact that what, at the outset of World War II, had seemed an excellent deal quickly turned into a bad bargain. But by then Stalin, bereft of a contingency plan, was left without a choice; he had to continue to cooperate with Hitler because there was no alternative.

Hitler invaded Poland on September 1 1939, without declaring war. The speed with which he disposed of the Polish Army came as a great surprise to Stalin, not to mention the Poles, who as late as August 1939 were confident of their ability to hold off the Wehrmacht. Toward the end of the first two weeks of September the German commanders began to wonder politely when the Red Army was going to invade its half of Poland. The Soviet government was unprepared for the speed of the German advance and had not expected to move for several weeks. In the meantime, it had been engaged in local but intensive military action against the Japanese in the Far East, where it had defeated a Japanese army at the battle of Khalkin Gol. The Red Army, led by Zhukov, had performed impressively, learning from its mistakes and fighting hard. Zhukov had proved himself a capable commander, at least in the judgment of some military historians. However, General Grigorenko's memoirs paint a different picture. He mentions a study of the campaign compiled by a group of staff officers which underlined serious shortcomings at the highest level of command without actually naming Zhukov. Grigorenko comments as follows: "We took enormous losses, largely because of inexperienced commanders. Moreover we had sight of Georgii Konstantinovich's [i.e., Zhukov's] character—he was not afraid of losing men. . . . He was a cruel and vindictive man."[17]

Now that the Japanese affair was over, Stalin was ready to occupy his share of Poland, and Soviet cavalry and tanks crossed the frontier on September 17, ten days before Warsaw fell. The Red Army quickly moved up to its demarcation line, and despite a few scattered incidents, the two forces met peaceably enough. Although Maisky, the Soviet ambassador in London, described the invasion as carried out "in order to save the working people of the Western Ukraine and Western Belorussia from the threat of German occupation,"[18] it has always seemed to most observers that the Soviet occupation was no less a violation of Poland's territorial integrity than Hitler's invasion earlier in the month. Consequently it has never been easy to understand why Great Britain did not fulfill her treaty obligations by declaring war on the Soviet Union. There were practical reasons why this might have been deemed unwise, but the question of whether or not Britain was obliged to do so by virtue of her guarantees is seldom raised.

The Soviet invaders enjoyed Poland, notably the shops full of goods and provisions that no one in Russia had seen for years. Combat officers could be seen emerging from them to rejoin their units, pushing their acquisitions under their tunics as they ran.[19] The troops themselves looked sloppy, their uniforms carelessly worn, while some soldiers even had towels around their necks. They were jumpy, too, and there were frequent instances of Soviet units firing on one another.[20]

Stalin prosecuted his attack on Poland with exceptional energy for a number of reasons. First, he considered that country a serious threat; he once observed that countries such as Poland and Hungary, with strong aristocracies, were the most dangerous opponents and the hardest to break.[21] Moreover, Poland was the old enemy. A Soviet defector has characterized the Russian attitude to Poland in a manner that is timeless:

Informant states that the general opinion is that the Soviet government considers Poland a political and strategic keystone. The Soviet statesmen consider the Poles as a most difficult nation for Communist policy, and owing to the Polish national and cultural traditions as well as a very strong Catholic spirit, special attention must be paid to the development of Polish affairs. Moreover Poland is the enemy number one of the Soviet Union and in fact Poles are looking to the west and wait only for the collapse of the Soviet régime to take revenge on the Russians. [22]

At no stage did the Soviets act as liberators; they did not even take the Polish Army's guns and horses and tell the soldiers to go home. In the words of a Soviet participant, "The territory occupied by the Red Army was immediately submitted to complete Sovietisation. In this respect the Soviet authorities and the NKVD had great experience."[23] Sovietization entailed the neutralization of all Poles possessed of the wrong objective characteristics, a majority of whom were conveniently to be found in the officer classes of the active and reserve armies. They sent all Polish servicemen to Soviet camps, separating the officers from other ranks. Admittedly their criteria for determining who was an officer were shaky. One young Pole, G. A. Herling, was picked up on suspicion of being an officer because he wore good leather boots. Since the Russified version of his name, "Gerling," sounded like Göring, he was charged with being a German spy. [24] When a defiant Pole observed to an NKVD man that there were 30 million Poles, "and you won't find it as easy as you think to dispose of us," the Russian replied: "What's thirty million? We've more than that in our prisons as it is."[25]

Although some officers with an instinct for survival disposed of their badges of ranks to join the enlisted men, the vast majority, the best of the Polish upper classes and intelligentsia, did not. They believed Marshal Timoshenko's assistant, Nikita Khrushchev, when he told them that they would be freed to return home or to join a new Polish army being raised in France. They gladly entered the trains that were supposed to take them to the border. The trains were guarded by NKVD men and took them, some 15,000 in all, to camps prepared for them by Beria. Eventually some would be released, 4,000 would be found in the mass graves of the Katyn Forest and 6,000 have never been found at all. The name of the policeman in charge of the Katyn operation was a Colonel Pogrebny, a name coming from the same root, *grob*, from which words such as *coffin* and *burial* derive. [26]

Stalin's intended sphere of influence had not included Lithuania, but at a second meeting with von Ribbentrop this was reluctantly conceded to him. Stalin informed the governments of the three Baltic states that he required military and naval bases and intended to place military garrisons on their soil. They were in no position to do anything but submit, whereupon, in the middle of 1940, Stalin decided to absorb them altogether, extending the frontiers of the Soviet Empire beyond those of Peter the Great's Russia. Beria was charged with ridding the Baltic states of undesirable elements as the liberated countries were promised socialist governments and their own armies. The governments were staffed by puppets, and as for the armies, after a month or so compulsory conscription was declared and the armies recruited and sent on maneuvers. There they were surrounded by NKVD units, disarmed and shipped to the gulag. At the same time Beria arrested all leading figures of the bourgeoisie, intelligentsia and church, about 100,000 families in all, and deported them to Siberia.[27]

Stalin then asked Finland for bases and an adjustment in the frontier near Leningrad. He wanted to be able to bar the entrance to the Gulf of Finland against attack by England or, he added, Germany, for although relations with Hitler were good, "everything in the world may change"—a further indication that Stalin did not trust Hitler blindly. Indeed, one Finnish negotiator believed it to be Germany that Stalin really feared. When the two sides failed to agree, the Soviets began a savage anti-Finnish propaganda campaign, and, on November 3, 1939, they invaded, confident that the war would soon be over. "See you in Helsinki" was *Pravda*'s comment, while Red Army commanders were warned to respect the neutrality of Sweden at the end of their invading sweep. It was assumed that the Finnish proletariat would greet the liberating Soviet soldiers with flowers, while the Finnish Army would melt away.

It was not like that. The Soviets were initially outfought and outgeneraled. Their junior officers lacked the personal initiative required by a highly mobile war, while Mannerheim, the Finnish commander, likened the Russian handling of their forces to a powerful orchestra without a conductor. But significantly he added that they learned fast from their mistakes. It was a cold winter that year, so cold that Moscow's electric trams could not run.[28] Soviet casualties were heavy— between 80,000 and 100,000 men—and every hospital in Leningrad was full. The Finns took some 30,000 prisoners, and the summary of their interrogations makes fascinating reading:

They appeared apathetic, without any vestige of patriotic feeling, simply wanting the war to end as quickly as possible. They displayed a remarkable ignorance, believing their country had fought a defensive war against both Poland and Finland. They professed a dislike of the Soviet régime but thought that any replacement would be worse. They were fatalistic, apathetic yet capable of incredible hardship. They had the narrowest of horizons. In the army they had been browbeaten, bullied, starved, frozen, half-killed and mutilated. Some had been shot and left for dead by their own commanders, or seen friends shot, others had liquidated their own officers. Now they fully expected to be tortured and then executed. In talking to these men their interrogators constantly bore in mind how they would behave to the Finnish population in the event of their emerging the victors, and it was not a pretty thought. [29]

The Hitler-Stalin pact had come as a total surprise to the Soviet troops, since Germany had seemed the natural enemy for many years. "The masses shook their heads and said that the pact could lead to no good and that in the end Hitler would cheat Stalin." [30]

That December Hitler sent Stalin birthday greetings, and *Pravda* published a congratulatory telegram from von Ribbentrop together with Stalin's reply: "I thank you, Minister, for your congratulations. The friendship between the peoples of Germany and the Soviet Union, sealed with blood, has every reason to be enduring and steadfast." [31] The blood was presumably Polish.

The Finnish War did not delight Hitler since it threatened the supplies of nickel and timber that Finland provided. It also came close to involving Great Britain. A diplomatic report writes of the volunteers and matériel that both Britain and Italy supplied and states that preparations were in hand for the dispatch of more aid still when a peace treaty was signed. The British had even contemplated sending troops, but the Swedes declined to let them through. British behavior increased Soviet suspicion of His Majesty's government. [32]

It may have been the threat of foreign intervention that persuaded Stalin, whose troops finally broke the Finns in the spring of 1940, to sign an armistice which granted surprisingly benign terms. The cease-fire was set for noon on March 14, and hostilities died down that morning—until eleven forty-five, when the Soviets laid down a savage artillery barrage all along the front. Since Finnish units were already pulling out, casualties among soldiers and civilians alike were heavy.

The Winter War offered one further glimpse of the shape of things to come. When the Finns repatriated some 30,000 prisoners of war, they were greeted at the frontier with bands and flowers, only to disappear immediately into the maw of the gulag—because they had seen too much and some of them could be traitors. Returning officers were for the most part shot. Although this anticipates Stalin's treatment of returning POWs in 1945, it is not the first time that being an ex-prisoner of war was sufficient grounds for arrest. In 1937 Stalin had already arranged for the arrest of all prisoners from the Great War since they might have been recruited by the Germans.

CHAPTER THIRTY-EIGHT

Barbarossa

Facts are obstinate things.
—STALIN

It would be wrong to think that the Soviet Union sent supplies of raw materials flooding into Germany throughout 1940 and early 1941. The stream was only unremitting in the last months of peace before Hitler invaded. Earlier it had varied in intensity, reflecting the Soviet assessment of how well its ally was doing. Stalin cut supplies back sharply early in 1940, when he thought that the British might hold Norway and, together with Denmark, control the entrance to the Baltic. When both countries fell, supplies were renewed with an apology for temporary stoppages caused by the oversight of a "subordinate," who was none other than Mikoyan, the commissar for foreign trade. By and large the Germans were pleased with the arrangement; the Russians did not fare as well. For example, they had asked for three battleships and were beaten down to one which they never got. Admittedly Hitler ensured that the Czech arms company of Skoda delivered them 88 mm anti-aircraft guns and 205 mm cannon. The 88 in particular, subsequently manufactured in the Soviet Union, proved invaluable both as an anti-aircraft and an antitank weapon.[1]

Stalin had rejected Tukhachevsky's view that the next war would be highly mobile and involve armor acting independently of motorized infantry. He believed that it would be another positional war, and unfortunately his views had been confirmed in Spain where tanks had served as infantry support. As an old Cavalry Army man Stalin also believed in that arm and expanded it accordingly. At the outbreak of hostilities in the West he had expected the Allies and the Germans to fight a rerun of the Great War and was dismayed by the success of the *Blitzkrieg* and the fall of France. It is largely forgotten, incidentally, that when German troops entered working-class districts of Paris, they were hailed by French Communists, who welcomed them with fists raised in greeting and cries of "Comrade!" There was collaboration between the French Communist party and the Gestapo, while plans to republish the Communist paper *L'humanité* were only interrupted by the invasion of Russia.

Stalin began to understand that time was running out and that his plan for exploiting a protracted war was unlikely to succeed. As Molotov congratulated the German ambassador on victories in the West, he informed him that the Soviet Union was annexing the Baltic states. A little later Red Army troops marched into northern Rumania, occupying Bessarabia and encroaching on the German sphere in northern Bukovina, as, in Molotov's words, they "solved" the Bessarabian question. The Soviets also ran a propaganda campaign against the British. Stalin's articles in *Pravda* condemned Britain for starting the war, and British Communists, in emulation of their French comrades, did what they could to sabotage their country's war effort. On August 23, 1940, when the Battle of Britain was in full swing, *Pravda* celebrated the anniversary of the Ribbentrop pact: "We are neutral, and this pact . . . has been of great advantage to Germany, since she can be confident of peace on her eastern borders."

On June 17, Michael Foot, a future leader of Britain's Labour party, published a curious article in the *Evening Standard* which stated that "America is far away. . . . Her army is small, much of her airforce is obsolete. America could not speedily change the aspect of war in this continent." He suggested that Britain should look for salvation to Stalin, who had acted so shrewdly in his pact with Hitler. Shortly afterward the new ambassador in Moscow, Sir Stafford Cripps, tried to persuade Stalin not to send material comfort to Britain's enemy. Stalin declined, but nevertheless as a good socialist Cripps expressed the groundless view that Stalin was really Hitler's enemy and that the stream of raw materials was his way of buying time. There was a plan in Foreign Office circles to bring Stalin into the war by disseminating rumors of a separate peace with Hitler, who would then turn his attentions to the east. It was abandoned as likely to alienate American support and precipitate a Soviet-German military alliance, but rumors may well have reached Stalin.[2]

By the autumn of 1940 the trade agreement showed signs of breaking down as Germany fell behind in its deliveries and the Soviet Union replied in kind. In an effort to improve relations, von Ribbentrop wrote a letter to Stalin describing current foreign policy and reminding its recipient that the three-power pact with Italy and Japan did not violate agreements with the Soviet Union. The letter ended with an invitation to Molotov to come to Berlin for further talks. Stalin miscalculated once again, badly overplaying his hand. Acting to orders, Molotov laid down a series of conditions under which the Soviet Union would consent to join the Axis. These included a German withdrawal from Finland, control of the Black Sea straits, a pact with Bulgaria and the acceptance of Soviet domination of the Persian Gulf. The conditions were obviously unacceptable, but Stalin had looked on them as an opening bid in what was to be a protracted process of bargaining.[3]

Hitler had already concluded that he would have to "tackle the Russian problem" since hope of a Soviet alliance appeared to be preventing Britain from suing for peace. In early August he warned his generals that they should expect to attack Russia soon, and by early December he was talking of the need to "eradicate the Soviet Union from the face of the earth. Then England will rapidly lose her remaining influence in the world."[4] He did not take kindly to reminders that the Soviet Union was a large place and its army of unknown capabilities and "replied sharply that it was Germany's destiny to launch this great crusade against Bolshevism."[5] On December 18, 1940, Hitler signed Directive 21, Operation Barbarossa, which stipulated that the Wehrmacht must destroy the Soviet Union in a lightning attack before completing the war with England.[6]

Two events in early January 1941 point up the contradictions in Stalin's attitude to Hitler. On January 1 the Soviet Union increased its deliveries of oil and wheat to Germany. At about the same time Stalin, at a postmortem of the December maneuvers, told a group of senior staff officers that he considered eventual war with Germany inevitable. Thus six months before Germany's surprise attack Stalin had ceased to trust Hitler blindly—if that is what he had ever done. He would later complain to Harry Hopkins, Roosevelt's special assistant, that he had trusted Hitler and that the fiend had let him down, but better confess to blind trust than admit to miscalculating as few statesmen have ever miscalculated.

Granted the premise of poor judgment, two complementary reasons appear to account for Stalin's actions in 1941, and both of them were bad. On the strategic level Stalin overestimated his strength. He did not believe that Hitler could attack in the near future, supposing his military position to be such that he could continue bargaining with him for some time. His long-term planning arrangements suggest that he expected to enter the war late in 1942. In the meantime, with no inkling of how precarious his position was, he believed he could continue to negotiate, vary the flow of supplies and seek diplomatic advantages. He was like an inexperienced poker player who thinks two pairs look good because they are almost a full house. His mistaken strategic assessment was made worse by the absence of a fallback position. This meant that Stalin had no tactical options. His greatest fear was a premature attack by Germany which might be triggered by mistake. Hence he felt unable to prepare for war. It would be all too easy to provoke Hitler into invading before Stalin was ready for him. Inappropriate moves along the frontier by his own army or a treacherous initiative by the British were the dangers he feared most. Stalin's grasp of Hitler's motives was minimal; Hitler was driven by many and various forces, but unjustifiable suspicion in the sense that Stalin imputed to him here was not one of them.

Stalin was cornered by his own ineptitudes. Trust Hitler or not, his only choice was to appease and play for time. He was convinced that it would be impossible for him to resist Hitler; an invasion would be fatal both to him and to his regime since it was inconceivable that the people he had been persecuting for so long would fight for him. Besides, any attempt to ready his country for war might provoke the very attack that would destroy him. Stalin did nothing to prepare for Barbarossa throughout 1941 because he was afraid to. As he received signal after signal of Hitler's hostile intentions, all he could do was hope they were untrue. In March the U.S. government informed Umansky, the Soviet ambassador, that Hitler would invade in the spring, and in April Churchill ordered Sir Stafford Cripps to convey a similar warning. At about the same time Stalin's own master spy in Japan, Richard Sorge, suggested an invasion was imminent, but there was nothing Stalin could do about it.

He elected to interpret the warnings as a British plot. Perhaps his contacts within the Foreign Office had told him that something of the sort had been proposed. Yet he now did something so provocative that it is inexplicable. Late in March the Yugoslav regent had joined the tripartite pact, only to be overthrown by a coup the following day. On April 5 the Soviet Union signed a nonaggression pact with the new government, which had rescinded the German treaty signed by its predecessor. However, the Soviets offered no kind of military convention, and the German armies went into Yugoslavia and Greece that same day. Stalin's gesture of support was both provocative and futile. He derived no advantage from the arrangement, while Hitler was infuriated by his behavior. Nothing that the Russians did between 1939 and 1941 made him angrier.[7] Stalin may well have underestimated the German army and exaggerated the Yugoslavs' capacity to resist. Even so, it is hard to see why Stalin should have provoked Hitler in this way—unless he thought he still had the bargaining power to fence-sit. In view of his record in foreign affairs, it does him no injustice to credit him with yet another colossal misapprehension.

Ironically it was the Yugoslavs who gained Stalin that precious time which has been used to justify his deal with Hitler. Their repudiation of the treaty with Germany prompted Hitler to invade, a decision that made him postpone Barbarossa by five weeks. Had it not been for the delay, the German Army would have had the time to cruise into Moscow before its advance was slowed by winter weather.

Observing yet another successful *Blitzkrieg* fought over unsuitable terrain, Stalin reverted to policies of appeasement. In a remarkable *volte-face* he suddenly accepted the German interpretation of a Lithuanian boundary dispute, sped up deliveries of raw material and ceased to apply pressure on Finland to secure the transfer of a nickel concession. Tangible actions were accompanied by a symbolic one which observers considered extraordinary. On April 13 Stalin signed a neutrality pact with Japan (this incidentally, coupled with the reports of Richard Sorge which told him Japan had no intention of attacking, enabled him to commit his Siberian reserves to the Battle of Moscow later in the year). After the pact was signed, Stalin accompanied the Japanese Foreign Minister, Yosuke Matsuoka, to the station. This in itself was an unusual departure from Stalin's customary behavior. But this became stranger still; acting like an inept Western politician on his first walkabout, he approached the German ambassador, threw an arm round his shoulder and emphasized how important it was that the Russians and the Germans should be friends. He then did as much to the German acting military attaché, von Krebs, having first ascertained that he was indeed a German, observing that their friendship must be a lasting one. Stalin's actions are so out of keeping with his normal habits that one cannot help sensing a hysterical, and perfectly justifiable, urgency behind his insistence upon the need for good relations.

The flight of the Nazi leader Rudolf Hess to Scotland on May 10, 1941, in what appeared a personal initiative to establish an Anglo-German alliance against the Soviet Union, was just the kind of event to fuel Stalin's capacity for suspicion. He concluded that Hess was doing what he would have done in similar circumstances; persuade the British to conclude a separate peace with Germany. Moreover, he could not imagine the British failing to agree, thereby diverting Hitler's attentions to the Soviet Union. It took him years to accept that the British had done nothing of the sort. For the moment, though, he was convinced.

Writing of Stalin in these last months before the war, the Soviet historian A. M. Nekrich considered the Hess affair vital:

> Those of Stalin's actions which are hardest to explain were the product of a schematic understanding of the outside world which he judged on the basis of such information as he received, or rather wished to receive. . . . It is obvious from his statements, speeches and addresses that he considered Great Britain as the chief enemy of the Soviet state. . . . Hess's flight made a big impression on Stalin; he was certain that Britain was inciting Germany to attack the USSR, that secret negotiations were taking place in London. . . . If these circumstances are not taken into account it is very difficult to understand Stalin's bitter hostility toward any new reports in the course of the last month before the war, about Germany's preparations for an attack upon the Soviet Union. He considered such reports a British provocation.[8]

Fears of provocation were also a way of rationalizing the need to bury the head deep in sand. For by now that scenario was Stalin's only hope. So passionately did he attach himself to it that even after the German invasion he lingered in the belief that the hand of perfidious Albion was driving them over his frontiers.[9] In the meantime, a steady stream of intelligence suggested that Hitler was about to attack. However, this view was so emotionally unacceptable that people were shot for advancing it. Soviet military intelligence had been observing the German buildup on the Polish frontier and had concluded that this was the first stage of an invasion. However, NKVD intelligence, as presented by Beria, took a different view. It maintained that Hitler had moved the bulk of his forces to the west as a preliminary to a mass invasion of Britain by parachute and that the Polish troop concentrations were there for rest and recreation. Although spring was very late that year and the last snow left Moscow only on June 6, no one seems to have pointed out that it made no sense to send troops to eastern Europe for their R and R.

Disagreement between military intelligence and Beria's NKVD came to a head at a special meeting of the Politburo. After Beria had put forward the NKVD case, this was calmly and decisively demolished by the head of army intelligence, Lieutenant General Proskurin. Despite being interrupted by frequent ironic interjections from Beria and from Stalin, too, Proskurin left the meeting believing he had won the day. Within twenty-four hours he was arrested and shot; military intelligence was informed that henceforward it would adhere to Beria's interpretation of the facts since this was what Stalin wanted.[10] The incident illustrates the shortcomings of a command structure which stifled any views that did not comply with those held at its apex. For by now many people in the armed services and industry believed a German attack to be imminent, but the system left no room for initiative at any level. Stalin's obstinacy meant that no one could prepare for the military equivalent of a rainy day. For example, since the official view was that the USSR would fight an offensive war, no defensive strategies were prepared; to have done so would have invited charges of treasonable defeatism.

Hilger and his ambassador, von der Schulenberg, were convinced that war with Russia would be a disaster. Acting with characteristic personal courage, the ambassador committed high treason in an attempt to prevent it. Together with Hilger, he arranged to meet Dekanozov, his opposite number in Berlin, and the two Germans did all they could to warn him of the threatening danger. Dekanozov responded like a true Soviet bureaucrat: He stonewalled and kept asking on what authority they were addressing him, making it clear that the unofficial *démarche* had failed. Indeed, he ignored it. Throughout the early weeks of June fresh embassy staff and their families continued to arrive in Berlin, doubtless sharing trains with the large numbers of German Embassy staff and families that von der Schulenberg was sending home. On June 14, the day that the evacuation began, *Izvestiya* published an article denying the possibility of war. In the meantime, there was no reduction in pro-German propaganda as the press continued to vilify the British.

In the final days before the invasion a stream of intelligence reports came in. For example, a Czech Communist deserted from his German Army unit at 10:00 P.M. on the twenty-first and crossed the lines with the news that the attack would begin at 3:30 A.M. on Sunday, June 22. The report reached Stalin with remarkable speed, and his reaction was in character: He ordered that the bringer of bad news be shot at once.[11]

Some military districts at last began to prepare for an invasion, but lack of time, the nature of the command structure and lack of experience rendered their preparations totally inadequate. It should be remembered that although Barbarossa saw the greatest invasion army in history, numbers were still against the Germans—a fact that Soviet historians do not dwell upon. At the moment of the invasion the Germans were outnumbered by some thirty divisions, while the Soviets enjoyed a seven to one superiority in tanks and a four and a half to one superiority in aircraft.[12] As German units advanced to the start line, they were amazed to see freight trains speeding west, full of the raw materials which the Russians continued to supply up to the very moment of invasion.

At a meeting of the Politburo on the afternoon of Saturday, June 21, the possibility of an invasion was conceded, and Stalin invited suggestions. Budenny thought it a good idea to order the removal of the guy ropes holding down the planes of the Soviet Air Force, so that they might be moved from their neat parade positions next to the runway, but nothing came of this. One frontier air force unit held a dance that night and was still dancing when the Luftwaffe hit the next morning, while the garrison of Brest-Litovsk held a ceremonial parade that same Saturday afternoon.[13] It has been estimated that the military, some of them anyway, had a whole three hours to prepare for invasion. German agents had been operating successfully behind Russian lines for some time—despite relentless Soviet vigilance—and many frontline units had had their lines to headquarters severed. Since they had no radios, they were obliged to rely on their own initiative when the Germans attacked. Molotov had called on the German ambassador at 9:30 on Saturday night to clarify the situation. Up to and even after the invasion Stalin was still trying to make a deal with Hitler; it was his only option. Then at 3:00 A.M. on the twenty-second von der Schulenberg received a telegram from Berlin informing him that war was declared; an hour later he communicated the news to Molotov, whose reply has gone down in history: "Is this supposed to be a declaration of war? Surely we have not deserved that?"[14]

June 22 was not a good day to invade Russia. Superstition aside, the fact that it was within a day of the start of Napoleon's invasion meant that it was probably too late in the year. Curiously both Hitler and Napoleon were led by the mildness of the Russian autumn to suppose that reports of the Russian winter had been grossly exaggerated. Anyone accustomed to a continental climate knows that it can easily be seventy degrees in November and twenty below zero the following month. June 22 was a bad day for the Russians, too. According to a legend, the day that anyone disturbed the tomb of Tamerlaine in Samarkand would herald a disaster greater than any of his causing; a professor of anthropology named Gerasimov opened it on June 22, 1941.

The German success was total. Three-quarters of the Soviet Air Force was destroyed on the ground, while those planes that got into the air were shot down in a process the Luftwaffe commander termed infanticide. Successes on the ground were no less spectacular. All along the line Soviet units were overrun or surrendered en masse as lack of a command structure and the poor quality of their officers turned them into a rabble. However, when properly led, they showed stiff resistance from the start. It would be wrong to suppose that the Red Army welcomed the invader with its hands up. The truth is more complicated.

If Stalin's refusal to face the fact of imminent invasion had been a flight from reality, then that reality now broke him. As someone long protected by his power from the harsher facts of life, the uncontrollable situation now confronting him was more than he could face, and he seems to have gone into shock. Thus it was Molotov, not Stalin, who broadcast to the nation at noon on Sunday, to inform them that they were at war. This was not just a case of Stalin's using a scapegoat. To judge by a remark attributed to him by Khrushchev, he really thought the end had come. "Now all Lenin's work has been undone forever," he allegedly said. It seemed inconceivable to Stalin, taking into account the events of the last twenty-four years, that the Soviet people would actually fight for their masters—rather than turn on them wholesale. Invasion must needs mean the end of the regime since no people could be stupid enough to lay down their lives for leaders like them. Once again Stalin put himself in the place of others, crediting them with his own perspicacity and clarity of purpose. Obviously it must all be over, and history would remember him not as Lenin's great heir but as the bungler who destroyed his work.

To judge by the mood of Moscow, he may well have been right. The first British Embassy report expresses surprise at the atmosphere of sullen calm in the city. There was no sign of any kind of patriotic demonstration, spontaneous or organized, "which one might expect in the capital of a country engaged in the biggest war of its history. A point which has attracted some attention is the absence of any pronouncement under the name of Stalin. It is intelligible that he should not have broadcast personally, owing to his pronounced accent which Russians find somewhat comic, but that he should not have issued any personal call to the people is very difficult to understand."[15]

Although accounts differ in their details, Stalin certainly broke down and withdrew from public life for the better part of a fortnight, remaining in his residence in Kuntsevo in a condition of despairing and allegedly intoxicated withdrawal. Yet it says much for the system he had created that no one ventured the faintest move against him. In the meantime, government ceased to function. The Soviet ambassador in Great Britain, Russia's only ally, received no communication from the Kremlin for many days.[16]

Stalin was not heard from until he broadcast to the nation on July 3, at the peculiar hour of 6:00 A.M. Allegedly the script had been prepared by Molotov, who had had great difficulty in persuading his master to emerge. Whatever the truth of that claim, this address was very different from his usual speeches. He referred to his audience as "brothers and sisters" and urged them to fight to the death for Russia, immediately making that appeal to patriotic values which would become a rallying point for courage and decency for the next four years and for narrow-minded chauvinism thereafter. The speech also contained a warning against the enemy within, who would be accorded even shorter shrift than usual. It was not a good broadcast; Stalin sounded terribly nervous, and every now and then there was a pause while he sipped a glass of water that clattered against his teeth.[17] It was the hitherto-unheard-of form of address that really frightened people; the situation must be far worse than they had supposed if Stalin was addressing them as "brothers and sisters."[18]

CHAPTER THIRTY-NINE

Total Enough for Anyone

The war brought great sorrow and made life very hard. But it had been even harder before the war because then everyone was alone in their sorrow.

—SHOSTAKOVICH

The British had been expecting the German attack, and Churchill had his speech of welcome to Britain's ally virtually written in advance. He did not disguise his view of the USSR, observing "The Nazi regime is indistinguishable from the worst features of Communism," but, as he observed to his private secretary, his sole purpose was the destruction of Hitler and "if Hitler invaded hell I would at least make a favourable reference [to the devil] in the House of Commons."[1] This was a sensible attitude. For all its shortcomings the Soviet Union was Britain's only ally—Pearl Harbor was still some six months away—and it must have seemed evident to many realists that only Hitler's invasion of Russia could save Britain from an otherwise-inevitable defeat. Yet Churchill's view of his new ally seems to have been forgotten no sooner than advanced. Instead of being seen as a mass murderer who had never made a secret of his hostility to Britain, Stalin was almost immediately cast in the role of an insecure barbarian whose trust was to be won by convincing him that the Western powers were well disposed and could teach him to use the political equivalent of a knife and fork. Before long the gentleman that Churchill had associated with "the devil himself" was to become "Uncle Joe" and be described by the prime minister to his people as "that great and good man."

From the moment that Hitler invaded Russia, the British and the Americans began to develop an increasingly benign view of the USSR, based on inexcusable ignorance and a sentimental sense that because the Soviets were fighting Nazi Germany, they, too, must be crusaders against evil, sharing that same sense of noble purpose that Churchill and Roosevelt loved to invoke. Although Churchill professed to find Soviet politics incomprehensible, describing the Kremlin as "a riddle wrapped in an enigma," it should have been nothing of the sort. A clear, accurate and surprisingly complete account of Stalin and his regime was to be found in the files of the Foreign Office, there to be read. Yet it did not even require a reading of the files to arrive at certain obvious truths. From the outset it should have been clear that the invasion of Russia, which had saved Britain, should be used to prevent a German victory, equally clear that a German defeat would create a power vacuum that Stalin would not hesitate to fill. It should also have been obvious that there was little to choose between Hitler and Stalin. Had such views defined the basis of the Western Allies' wartime relationship with the USSR, today's map of Europe would look rather different. In the event the Allies misread Stalin quite as badly as he misread Hitler and had less excuse for their mistake.

From the start Churchill, as he put it, "tried to win Stalin over" with warm personal telegrams of the kind that had worked so well with Roosevelt. Stalin, who was not accustomed to receiving warm personal telegrams, which could only have fired his suspicion, countered with outraged demands for a second front. This soon became a deliberate policy based on the shrewd advice of Ambassador Maisky, who quickly sensed that the British were embarrassed by the knowledge that on the ground at least, the Russians were doing all the fighting. Maisky recognized that the situation made the British leadership feel guilty. Where Stalin would have been delighted to have others do his fighting for him, Churchill felt apologetic and inadequate. Maisky advised Stalin to exploit that attitude by clamoring for a second front and making the most extravagant demands for aid at the same time. He was confident that the British inability to provide the former would send them to improbable lengths to supply the latter. The disastrously costly northern convoys would show that Maisky was right.

• • •

Stalin had expected Soviet rule to collapse in the face of invasion, and to some extent his fears were justified. It is true that in many places the invaders were greeted by peasants bearing icons and the bread and salt of hospitality.[2] The welcome was warmest in the Baltic states and the Ukraine, where anti-Russian sentiment came into play. However even in Russia itself the invaders often got a friendly reception. In Smolensk there was a "Russian Liberation Committee" prepared to raise an anti-Stalin army. It presented an illuminated address and one of Napoleon's cannon to Field Marshal von Bock, to express its gratitude for the liberation of the city.[3] At first the invaders were particularly popular in the villages, where collective farming ceased as the peasants divided the livestock and hid their share in the forests.[4] Some villagers even handed crashed Soviet aircrew over to the Germans, gagged and bound.[5] The population was happy to receive the invaders as liberators because they knew no better. "After three decades of living in their hermetically sealed fastness, what could people possibly know about Hitler and Nazism?"[6]

For a moment early in the war order and government threatened to melt away as a sense of chaos mounted; or so at least it seemed to members of hastily formed Polish units on their way from Soviet POW camps to the front. The local people seemed sullen, hostile to Soviet rule and lacking in any desire to fight Germans.[7] For the moment at least there were no hurrahs, no patriotic surge to arms. Alexander Pyatigorsky, then working in a factory in the Urals, had firsthand experience of the Soviet workforce. They had nothing but poor food, work, vodka and drunken brawls; a life of empty brutishness. They professed no loyalty to Stalin nor to his regime and many looked forward to the impending arrival of the Germans who would restore order and get rid of the Jews. If Stalin had died the next day it would have disturbed them not at all.

The dominant mood was one of demoralized indifference; a general lack of motivation to fight. This was compounded by shocked amazement at the ease of the German victories. For years people had been told that they must make great sacrifices to render their armed forces invincible; now they had collapsed at first contact with a serious enemy. According to General Grigorenko, it was this that demoralized many Red Army men and encouraged them to surrender,[8] or at least disinclined them to obey Stalin's order to keep the last bullet for themselves.[9] Yet sullen indifference and apathy were as far as Soviet man went against his masters; contrary to the worst expectations of the Politburo, which had anticipated widespread organized mutiny led by senior officers.[10] Even in the camps the political prisoners were mostly anti-German; only the criminals wanted Hitler to destroy the "Black Thief."

As for the men of the Red Army, many of them were reluctant to attack German armor with petrol bombs (Molotov cocktails), while the number of troops that surrendered suggests an unwillingness to fight on the part of men badly led at every level of command. But they were ready enough to fight and fight well under good officers, and these in turn fought well under good senior commanders. The picture sometimes painted of an army and civilian population universally hostile, demoralized and potentially inclined toward treason is dangerously simplistic. Elements may be partly true, but on the whole the nation's mood was no worse than a kind of punch-drunk indifference. Certainly Stalin had feared worse.

Nevertheless, such attitudes were no foundation upon which to fight a Great Patriotic War, which introduces one of the great "ifs" of modern history. What would have happened if the Germans had operated an enlightened policy in the occupied territories, installing puppet regimes manned by nationals and treating the local population with a measure of decency? We get an answer of a kind from local reaction to the Rumanian armies of occupation in Odessa, the capital of their new-won province of Transistria, formerly southwestern Russia. The Rumanians restored private enterprise, taxed moderately and permitted the use of railroads for private goods shipments. They opened schools and re-opened the university. Even the opera house functioned, and the markets had an abundance of food not seen since the days of the NEP. Despite the fact that the government was corrupt, it was extremely popular.[11] Elsewhere even the German occupation had its supporters:

> Another factor in [postwar] discontent in Kharkov is the relations that existed between the Germans and the population during the occupation. Apart from massacring all the Jews, for which the people of Kharkov express gratitude and approval, the Germans are said to have behaved very well, and I have heard from more than one person that the population had been dismayed to see the Red Army arrive. . . . some of the women of Kharkov referred to the occupation as the best two years of their lives. The Germans loved the town dearly and referred to it as "Kleine Paris."[12]

When the Germans had to pull out of the Caucasian town of Kislovodsk, "The Russian population lived for two weeks under the threat of massacre by mountain tribes that had no reason to love them."[13] In many regions the potential was there for the creation of puppet governments, and an end to Soviet rule would have been welcome on those terms. It is easy to imagine the Germans' gaining and keeping control of all the western and southern parts of the Soviet Union, including Georgia and Armenia, which would in turn have allowed them to dominate Persia and Britain's oil supplies. Stalin would have been driven back behind the Urals, and Britain obliged to sue for peace. Certainly almost everything that Lenin had achieved would have perished.

However, it was not like that. Hitler appointed a Russian-born Balt and fanatical anti-Christian, Alfred Rosenberg, minister in charge of eastern territories, and under his stewardship the Germans failed to exploit their greatest trump card, the promotion of a religious revival in the countryside; it was left to Stalin to do so in their stead. Hitler made other mistakes: The decree that all commissars be shot, that 100 Communists be killed for every German soldier to die in the occupied territories, his recruitment of slave labor and the refusal to recognize that Slavs were members of the human race all helped destroy the goodwill created by his invasion. It has been alleged by a German source that Stalin gave orders to provoke the occupying forces into savage reprisals against the civilian population. Although the allegation is unconfirmed, it would certainly have made sense for Stalin to have done so, yet nothing we know of German behavior in World War II suggests that such provocation was needed. The greatest of all Hitler's mistakes was his treatment of Soviet POWs. Since the USSR had not signed the Geneva Convention, he felt under no obligation to treat them according to the rules of war, nor did he, allowing them to starve to death in appalling conditions. Once news of this reached the front, surrender ceased to be an attractive option. The last word on the whole sorry subject has been attributed to General Guderian, who is said to have observed sadly: "We started to mistreat them too soon."[14]

Stalin treated German POWs no better. In the winter of 1941 a Polish officer saw some captured Germans, stripped of uniform tunics and boots, being shipped east in open freight cars with no effort made to prevent them from freezing to death.[15] Not that this constituted cruel and unusual punishment by the standards of the gulag. An acquaintance who is still a Soviet citizen was traveling east in a cattle truck around this time when he noticed that he was developing frostbite in his foot. He drew the guard's attention to it, and the guard inquired: "What of it?"

"I could develop gangrene and lose my foot."

"Don't worry, we have plenty of feet in the gulag."

The flow of arrestees actually increased during the early months of the war. Stalin expected widespread betrayal and moved to counter this before it occurred. He deported thousands of Volga Germans, who had been living in that region for some 200 years and whose loyalty to the Soviet Union could not be in serious doubt. Elsewhere the NKVD often liquidated inmates of prisons that lay in the line of the German advance rather than go to the trouble of evacuating them, while it was a time when it was remarkably easy to be shot on suspicion of espionage or treason. In Moscow alone thousands were executed in the first months of the war.[16] As a matter of course any Red Army man who had been captured and escaped, or who had made his way back through enemy lines, was arrested as a potential spy. Stalin also sought to protect his people from enemy propaganda by confiscating all the radio sets in the land; henceforward broadcasting was to be done by the loudspeakers to be found on most street corners.

CHAPTER FORTY

Typhoon

Stalin returned to work in late June, when a decree was published announcing the creation of a Committee for State Defense consisting of Stalin, Molotov, Voroshilov, Beria and Malenkov. From this moment Stalin seems to have recovered and taken charge, making the administrative machine more personal than ever. For he now involved himself in military as well as civilian affairs. Already the party's general secretary and chairman of the Council of People's Commissars, he now became people's commissar for defense, head of the Stavka or (supreme headquarters), and supreme commander in chief of the armed forces. Yet almost from the start, unlike Hitler, Stalin made good use of advice. Like the excellent chief executive that he became, he never accepted the views of his experts without questioning and probing. More important, while taking those views into account, he never let experts make decisions for him. They provided information and analysis, but the decisions were his.[1] In the early stages of the war Stalin covered himself, issuing orders in the name of the general staff and never signing them in person. But appearances notwithstanding, no important decision could be made without his approval, and he was ultimately responsible for the conduct of the war.

At first Stalin seemed to have had no sense of the scale or nature of the invasion. His response was to send orders to stand and fight, while calling for countless and expensive counterattacks, which invariably consisted of a three-minute artillery barrage followed by a mass frontal assault.[2] His early decisions were costly. For example, he insisted on defending Kiev long after the situation was hopeless, with the result that he lost the commander in chief of the southwestern front together with 665,000 men. The performance of the Red Army in the early months of the war was dismal. Its first commanders, Budenny, Kulik, Voroshilov and Tulyenev, were manifestly incompetent and soon dismissed, but at least they were not shot. In fact, Stalin stopped shooting senior commanders quite early, although junior officers remained at risk for the duration. The first months of the war showed up inadequacies throughout the system, from military strategy to industrial supply. These problems were compounded by compulsive face-saving and cover-up at every level. One of the problems facing military planners was their lack of information about the pace of the Soviet retreat and the location of the front line. They would be issued communiqués stating that the line had fallen back to an obscure village scarcely to be found on any map. It would then transpire that the village was adjacent to a major city too humiliating to name. Then there were the phantom armies that seemingly retreated sixty miles overnight; in other words, they had been annihilated and their place and designation taken by reserves. So poor was military intelligence that staff officers found themselves telephoning managers of collective farms near the front to ask if the Germans had arrived.[3]

Granted such widespread incompetence, one is tempted to wonder why the Germans did not win. In the first place, it was only thanks to such incompetence, to the purges and the destruction of the military high command, to the overcentralization of government and industry that they got as far as they did. By rights the Soviet Union should have been invincible, and victory should *never* have required three years of bitter fighting and more than 20 million dead. Secondly, even as matters stood, it is doubtful whether Germany could ever have won, considering the massive reserves of Soviet manpower. Finally, Stalin proved Hitler's superior in his conduct of the war; the failure to take Moscow in 1941 was entirely Hitler's fault. Moreover, in the course of the war Hitler deteriorated steadily as a warlord, relying increasingly on his own intuition at the expense of expert advice and eventually, of reality itself, making one bad decision after another. In contrast Stalin grew enormously, and he learned fast; Guderian points out that after the Kiev disaster Stalin never made the same mistake.

Hitherto, except in the field of foreign affairs, Stalin had been able to impose his policies whether they worked or not. Now he had to get it right or perish. Over the war years he grew from a dictator operating in a void to become a skilled manager of men, who was able to listen to advice, knowing how to make use of it and when to ignore it, who could extract the last ounce of work from his executives and who withstood the extraordinary strain which his system imposed upon him. Although Soviet Russia in the autumn of 1941 was a disgrace, the situation improved on every level as the war went on. It was the Soviet nation, not Stalin, which won that war, but most certainly he could have lost it.

Hitler made his first mistake in July 1941, when he interrupted the advance on Moscow for two months. Despite the objections of Guderian, who was convinced he could capture the capital within weeks, he transferred his panzer group to Army Group South to be aimed at the southwest.[4] The Germans' failure to take Moscow marks the beginning of their defeat.

Stalin was anything but confident of victory. His learning process began in the recognition that his situation was desperate—a complete contrast to his ostrichlike behavior before the invasion. One of his sisters-in-law came to him in August in search of comfort. Novgorod, her native city, had fallen, and she hoped that Stalin might assure her that there were no grounds for panic. Instead, she discovered that he was as disturbed as she was. He already foresaw the fall of Moscow and urged her to leave while she could and move east of the Urals.[5] His daughter believes that one reason why he later sent his sister-in-law to prison for ten years was to prevent her from recalling this embarrassing exchange.

One of the factors contributing to the strain that Stalin felt at this time—those who saw him during these months were struck by the way he had aged—was the fate of his son, Yasha, captured in the first weeks of the war. It was not paternal love, but shame, that was the source of his distress. Feeling his firstborn had disgraced him before the entire world and convinced that he had surrendered on purpose, Stalin reacted with a classic variant on the theme of "I have no son." He observed to a foreign correspondent that there was no such thing as a Russian prisoner of war, only Russian traitors, with whom he would deal when the war was over. In the meantime, he contented himself with arresting Yasha's Jewish wife. The Germans sensibly tried to make capital out of the young Djugashvili. After the Battle of Stalingrad they proposed to exchange him for the captured Field Marshal Friedrich von Paulus, only to elicit the retort that Stalin did not swap field marshals for common soldiers.[6] Yasha remained in a camp for special prisoners, where he gave Russian lessons to Elie de Rothschild.[7] At the end of 1942 he was transferred to Sachsenhausen, a POW camp with a fifty percent survival rate, where he shared a hut with Molotov's nephew and some English prisoners. They did not get on, and Yasha became increasingly depressed. Tension had long been high when a fight broke out one afternoon after the British contingent had accused Yasha of shitting on the lavatory floor. The young man apparently broke down, refused to reenter the hut at curfew and charged the wire, yelling "Shoot me, shoot me," which one of the guards obligingly did. It was the British who first learned of his death after the war, from captured German archives. Stalin had long been anxious to discover details of his son's fate and had spoken eloquently to Churchill of the agony of not knowing. He had posted a million-rouble reward for news of the boy—doubtless for fear that he might be used against him. However, with a display of that low-grade *Realpolitik* which sometimes characterizes the actions of the British Foreign Office, it was decided, despite the fact that Stalin was still an ally and a "great and good man," not to tell him how his firstborn had died. As Michael Vyvyan, a senior Foreign Office official, put it, "Our own inclination here is to recommend the idea of communication to Marshal Stalin should be dropped. . . . It would naturally be distasteful to draw attention to the Anglo-Russian quarrels which preceded the death of his son."[8]

Shortly afterward Stalin experienced a further disappointment in his family life. His daughter only learned of her mother's suicide late in 1941. Hitherto she had believed that she died of appendicitis, and the discovery estranged her from her father. It was probably the need to find a substitute father figure that made her fall in love with Aleksey Kepler, a Jewish filmmaker some twenty years her senior. They saw each other for a few months, going to galleries, cinemas and the theater together, before Stalin had Kepler arrested on suspicion of being a British spy (he remained in prison until Stalin's death). Stalin summoned his daughter and flew into a rage at her betrayal, struck her and accused her in the coarsest language of sleeping with her lover. He understood that she too had betrayed him; henceforth she had no place in his affections. Indeed, so little did he now care that two years later he gave her permission to marry a Jewish student, even though he felt certain that the marriage had been arranged by Zionists. "It's spring, I suppose. To hell with you, do what you like," was how he gave his blessing.

• • •

The people of the Soviet Union are well disposed toward the
Poles, but officials can make mistakes.
                    —STALIN TO THE POLISH AMBASSADOR

That Stalin experienced a sense of urgency close to panic in the early
months of the war is reflected in his attitude to potential allies. He told
Harry Hopkins that he would not object to the presence of an American
army on Soviet soil. This was a remarkable concession; by the time that
the situation had improved, the only U.S. presence he countenanced
was a single air force base in the south, which was used as a terminal for
shuttle bombing, was unwelcome and did not last long. He also opened
diplomatic relations with General Sikorski's Polish government-in-exile
and favored a plan to turn the thousands of Polish prisoners of war on
Soviet soil into a Soviet-equipped army that would fight on his western
front. To this end a select group of Polish officers was taken from prison
and transferred to a villa outside Moscow to plan the raising of a new
army. When reviewing the officers available to lead it, the Poles wondered why those sent to certain camps did not appear on the NKVD list
of available personnel. V. N. Merkulov, Beria's second-in-command,
dealt obliquely with the question with a muttered retort that has gone
down in history: "In their case we made a fatal mistake." A mistake
indeed; the embarrassment of thousands of dead Polish officers lying in
Katyn Forest loomed over Stalin.

As the military picture improved, Stalin began to backpedal on his
plans for a Polish army, sharply reducing food and military supplies for
the luckless Poles assembling at bleak staging posts in central Asia. As a
visiting American diplomat put it, "The new Polish divisions fell into
two categories; those with shovels and those without. The former could
dig themselves underground shelters, the latter had to freeze on the
surface of Central Asia."[9] Stalin became increasingly uncooperative and
even played a game of cat and mouse with Kot, the Polish ambassador,
when Kot raised the matter of 10,000 missing officers. Stalin went
through the charade of telephoning Beria, pretending he knew nothing
of the matter and asking him what had happened to the missing men.
He listened for a while, nodded, grunted and returned to Kot, smiling
to himself. "Beria says they are a long way away and will take a very
long time to get here." Another specimen of Stalin's sense of humor.

• • •

The war was by now total enough for anyone.
—GUDERIAN

The German advance on Moscow was resumed on September 3, when Operation Typhoon began. Early losses had been made up, and the army consisted of battle-hardened troops. However, their preparation was deficient in one respect: Army units had no winter equipment; no warm clothing, no antifreeze, no calks to make tank treads grip in the snow. It was the army's mistake, *not* Hitler's. Both the Luftwaffe and the Waffen SS had all the winter equipment they needed.

Typhoon took the Russians by surprise. They had not expected an attack so late in the season. However, Guderian discovered that they had learned from early mistakes. They no longer counterattacked with combinations of men and armor and had learned to deploy their tanks separately, moving them in from the flanks. The Germans also came up against well-prepared defensive positions and were exposed to intense artillery bombardments. The going was easy no longer.

However, Stalin was fighting the greatest military machine ever assembled, and the machine was advancing at the rate of 10 miles a day over a 400-mile front. Guderian moved into Orel, 200 miles southwest of Moscow, so fast that the trams were still running as his tanks went in. But then the advance began to slow. On October 6 the rains came, and everything turned to mud, reducing the rate of advance to 4 miles a day. Still the Germans could not be held. The fall of Moscow seemed imminent, and with it the end of Soviet rule in Europe. The Politburo had been discussing the issue of whether the city should be defended. Beria insisted that it must be held, while Malenkov was anxious to depart. Evacuation had begun in August, with the dismantling of factories and the laying off of thousands of workers, adding chronic unemployment to the city's problems.

Unlike London, Moscow was not dangerous to live in. Soviets who went from Moscow to London in 1942 were appalled at the bomb damage that they saw, while one was astounded to see swans swimming in the Serpentine; in Moscow they would not have lasted five minutes before being killed for food or fun.[10] In contrast American citizens touring Moscow in 1941 tended to attribute the normal condition of the city to enemy action: "It was hard to tell where Soviet construction left off and German bombing began."[11] The civilian population was lucky not to be bombed, for the authorities countered the threat from the skies by constructing "ten thousand mud huts equipped with beds and stoves that are to be built to serve as air raid shelters."[12]

As the Germans came closer, the pace of evacuation increased. The railways were jammed, and senior officials fled the city in cars crammed with valuables, a spectacle reminiscent of the great exodus from Paris in 1940 and which infuriated those obliged to stay. There were numerous instances of cars' being stopped and stripped by angry workers, who sometimes beat their occupants to death. A British Embassy report describes peasants with pitchforks robbing fugitives and looting the country abodes of the privileged.[13] The flight also brought out that anti-Semitism which is never far beneath the surface of Soviet Russia, its being widely believed that many wealthy Jews were among those making their escape.[14] Arrangements had been made to move the government to Kuibyshev, 400 miles southeast of Moscow, where a house had been prepared for Stalin. Early in October foreign embassies were directed to move there, together with the foreign press, although correspondents were told to continue to dateline their copy "Moscow."

Stalin had not entirely regained his lost confidence, refusing, for example, to appear before a plenum of the Central Committee in early October, pleading he was too busy.[15] As the situation deteriorated, he kept a lightplane on permanent standby in Red Square and at one point seems to have abandoned the capital. For in the middle of October Moscow was given up for lost. On October 15 special NKVD units and engineers mined the city with a view to its total demolition (the mines remained in place till the end of 1942.)[16] On that day and the next Moscow was an open city. The rule of law evaporated. Hospitals ceased to function, stores were looted, warehouses opened, and remarkable scenes of sexual and alcoholic frenzy were to be witnessed. The city seemed to be coming apart, as deserters from the front streamed into the capital. Curiously, although there was chaos, looting and normal Russian disorder, there was no political protest, not a single antigovernment graffito, no anti-Stalin demonstrations. However, those who lived through those days agree that on the afternoon of the sixteenth a handful of paratroopers or even a squad of traffic police could have taken the city. At this point Stalin rallied and decided that Moscow would be defended. By the afternoon of the following day, when Stalin probably returned to the Kremlin, order had been restored with remarkable and creditable ease. The great panic was over; but it had its curious, if characteristic, aftermath. Those courageous senior officials who elected to stay at their posts were suspected of "waiting to welcome the enemy"; many of them were arrested and shot.[17]

In the meantime, German tanks reached the suburb of Khimki, half-way between the city center and its main airport and no one could understand why they checked when there was nothing to stop them. It was a battle in which, as the German commander put it, "The last battalion will decide the issue," and a final effort, apparently just beyond the strength of the invader, would have given him the city. But suddenly the balance began to swing. Soviet resistance stiffened as fresh Mongolian units, often unable to speak Russian, were committed to battle. At the same time the Germans first encountered the finest ground weapon of the war, the magnificent T34 tank, with tracks that could take it through any mud and with armor that made it difficult to knock out. They also met the *katyusha*, or multiple rocket launcher, the Stalin Organ, as they called it. (Its inventor, A. G. Kostikov, had spent years in prison, where his talk of multiple rockets had been viewed as the ravings of a saboteur.[18]) Along with the new weapons came the cold. The shift from mud to deep frost was dramatic—a matter of days—and the results were disastrous to the Germans. Synthetic fuel froze in the tanks, and the men in their denim uniforms suffered more than the machines. "We were cold too," observed a Red Army man, "but only a little colder than usual."[19] For the Germans it was very different, as soldiers made overshoes of straw and even put on women's clothes to try to stay warm. "Only he who saw the endless expanses of Russian snow during this winter of our misery and felt the icy wind that blew across it, who drove for hour after hour . . . only to find too thin shelter, with insufficiently clothed men, and who also saw by contrast the well-fed, warmly clad and fresh Siberians, fully equipped for winter fighting . . . can judge the events that now occurred."[20]

The Red Army counterattacked successfully in early December, obliging the Germans to withdraw. Guderian wrote in his diary: "The offensive for Moscow has ended. All the sacrifices and efforts of our brilliant troops have failed. We have suffered a serious defeat."[21] More important still, the Red Army had turned a *Blitzkrieg*, which they could never have won, into a war of attrition, which they could not lose. Victory would prove costly enough in human lives, but human life had long ceased to be a significant factor in the Soviet account books.

All decisions and dispositions for the Battle of Moscow had had to be ratified by Stalin, and in that sense it was he who had won, or at least not lost this, the most important land battle of the war. Army men did not always find it easy to work with him. There are instances of clashes between army intelligence and Beria, who rejected reports of alarming German rates of advance as "treason and sabotage" until discovering that they were true. [22] There were also serious clashes between Beria and Zhukov as each tried to win Stalin to his own view. According to Zhukov, Stalin still ordered occasional bloody and useless counterattacks but on the whole had learned fast from his mistakes. He could also take a personal interest in matters of detail that bordered on the eccentric. There is a famous story about his telephoning Zhukov with the news that the Germans had taken a town named Dedovsk. Stalin ordered its immediate recapture. Zhukov discovered that Dedovsk was still in Russian hands but that a small village, Dedovo, had fallen. He tried to point out that Stalin was mistaken but the chief executive simply repeated his order. Zhukov was obliged to take personal charge of the hamlet's recapture and arranged for a rifle company and two tanks to dislodge a platoon of Germans. [23]

Yet Stalin was usually better than that. He was no strategist and, unlike Hitler, soon gave up pretending to be one, but he coordinated his strategists' work, allocated resources, determined the interrelation of ground and air forces; in short, he ran the war as a manager, not a general. Of his role in the Battle of Moscow Zhukov writes: "Stalin was in Moscow organising forces and equipment. . . . He did a great job of organising the strategic reserves and the material and technical means needed for armed combat. In the period of the battle around Moscow he was always attentive to advice, but unfortunately sometimes made decisions that the situation did not call for, such as launching an offensive on all fronts." [24]

As the war developed, Stalin took advice increasingly well and began to listen to his field commanders. A Soviet admiral recalls seeing army men express disagreement with Stalin's views. He would respond by suggesting they all reconsider and would often come around to their opinions. He seemed to respect people who stood up to him, although his civilian advisers would urge the military men never to oppose him. Whereas he stopped shooting generals after some twenty or so had suffered that fate, they remained liable to demotion, dismissal or relegation to a penal battalion for failures both major and, sometimes, trivial.

As the war develops, we can see the emergence of a distinct and unpleasant "house style" of management: Always be abusive and impute the worst motives to your juniors; always use threats; always increase the target by fifty percent; do not distinguish between explanations and excuses, and make extravagant promises to your superiors for your inferiors to deliver. Failure is never excusable, while the reward for success is to keep your job and be told to do better. It is a style of management not unknown in corporate life and is particularly effective in organizations from which it is difficult to resign. It was tailor-made for the Red Army under Stalin.

This vicious style of management did not deaden Stalin's sense of public relations and the need to appear before the nation as a leader. It was his decision to hold the November 7 parade in Red Square as usual, reviewing units on their way to the front. The action had great impact, acting as a rallying point for a nation that was beginning to have something to be proud of for the first time in years. For many people it was on November 7, 1941, that their faith in Stalin attained its summit.[25]

Stalin and the Allies

We represent . . . a society in which the manifestations of
evil have been carefully buried and sublimated. For this
reason . . . the mainsprings of political behavior in Russia
tend to remain concealed from our vision.
—GEORGE KENNAN

The failure of Allied policy makers to appreciate the kind of man and
regime they were dealing with has no single and simple cause. Undoubtedly the courage, tenacity and success of the Red Army were factors. As a British diplomat in Washington later observed, "There are
people who think the defence of Stalingrad proves there is no GPU."[1]
Those who had maintained their faith in the Soviet Union throughout
the terror now found that faith vindicated as the *Daily Worker's* head-
lines changed from STOP THIS IMPERIALIST WAR to SECOND FRONT
NOW, an opinion shared by the newspaper magnate Max Beaverbrook,
whom Churchill had brought into his government, after a visit to Moscow in 1941. He came back convinced that he had won Stalin's trust,
where Stalin had won his. Henceforth his newspapers and personal
voice would be pro-Soviet and anti-Polish.

Other factors were in play. Within the U.S. State Department there
had been a struggle, for some years, between those who thought that the
Soviets were opportunistic thugs, and those with a more favorable opinion. The latter view prevailed, with the result that the department's
Eastern division was subordinated to the European division, and there

was even an attempt to destroy its priceless collection of files and documents.[2] It was not prudent for career diplomats to profess anti-Soviet views at the time; early in 1942 Harry Hopkins asked a State Department man whether he was a member of the "anti-Soviet clique" and held forth on how marvelous the Russians were.[3]

Curiously, and doubtless coincidentally, a remarkable change of attitude is to be seen in the British Foreign Office. Up to the middle of 1941 the sum of papers and views to emerge from the embassy and the Foreign Office gives an accurate and unflattering picture of Stalin, the regime and the hardships of everyday life. From the autumn of 1941 the documents have a different feel; an increasing emphasis on the need to win, or rather to buy Stalin's trust and allay Soviet suspicions. There also develops a tendency to deny any unpleasant allegations and prevent their further publication even when it is reluctantly conceded they might be true. Certain Foreign Office officials pursue this line with remarkable zeal.

However the pro-Soviet bias emerging in the Foreign Office and the embassy did little more than complement the no less strong and puzzling views of the British foreign secretary, Anthony Eden. The papers show that he was urgent to the point of hysteria in his support of the Soviet Union, and was impatient and intransigent in his dealings with the Polish government in exile. He took his bias and hostility to curious lengths, for example making the preposterous claim that: "The Polish forces fighting on our side had been recruited chiefly from the eastern provinces which the Soviets were claiming,"[4] implying that they were fighting for Russia while other Poles were pro-German. There is a considerable discrepancy between the foreign secretary's memoirs, where the bias is scarcely apparent, and the surprisingly strident views he expressed in government papers. One often comes across minutes written by Eden that deliver a sharp slap to the wrist of any Foreign Office official who appears critical of the Soviet Union. It is scarcely surprising that those holding such opinions began to keep them to themselves.

When Stalin met Eden in Moscow in December 1941, he asked for British recognition of his absorption of the Baltic states and the readjusted frontiers with Finland and Rumania. He insisted that this was "the main question for us in the war." He was content to let the issue of the Polish frontier remain open but indicated that he wanted it moved west. At the same time he harped on the British inability to help the Soviet Union in any substantial way, playing upon their sense of inadequacy to secure concessions elsewhere.[5] As it turned out, Stalin was preaching to the converted. While Eden told him that he had no authority to grant recognition, he prepared a minute which stated that Stalin was highly dissatisfied with the negative reply he had received and that "The Soviet Government regarded this question as a test of our real intention to cooperate as allies. There can be no doubt that we shall not succeed in removing M. Stalin's suspicions of ourselves and the US Government unless we agree to these claims. It is true that the claims seem difficult to reconcile with the first three clauses of the Atlantic Charter. . . ."

Eden used this paper to prepare a memorandum for Churchill in which he made three essential points. First, it was necessary to meet Stalin's claims to allay his suspicions. Secondly, "The case for recognition is based on the essential need at the present time for really close cooperation and consultation with the USSR, which, if we do not meet them on this, will I feel sure be limited to matters on which they require our help and that of the USA. This may make all the difference after the war as we all know." His third and only realistic point was that the Allies could do nothing about it. The paper bears a note in an unknown hand: "As far as their claims on Finland and the Baltic States are concerned it is in our own interest that they should be in a strong position in the Baltic."[6]

It is hard to see why Eden attached such importance to winning Stalin's trust or to cooperation on a wide range of issues after the war. He treats the issue as long decided, although as far as the papers show, it was never discussed at all. Churchill's initial response was one of indignant surprise. He pointed out that the territorial gains his government was being asked to recognize had been achieved by acts of aggression in shameful collusion with Hitler. The transfer of peoples of the Baltic states to Soviet Russia against their will would be contrary to all the principles for which his country was fighting and would dishonor their cause. Besides, the Russians had been no help to Britain in its hour of need but had added to its burdens "in our worst danger." Churchill added: "They are fighting for self-preservation and have never had a thought for us. We on the contrary are helping them to the utmost of our ability because we admire their defence of their own country and because they are ranged against Hitler."[7]

Despite Churchill's protests, it is Eden who prevailed. Early in 1942 one can see the emergence of the official view that Stalin's demands were made to "test our sincerity." In a paper to Lord Halifax Eden wrote: "We must therefore recognise that our refusal to satisfy Stalin's demand may be the end of any prospect of fruitful co-operation and may cause Soviet policy to revert to the pursuit of purely selfish aims."[8]

Eden's assumption that the Soviets had undergone a change of heart and opted for "unselfish aims" is inexplicable since the only evidence of such a change was the fact that they were fighting Germans. A further paper recognizes that the Soviet Union would emerge from the war as a major power and suggests that it must be courted by kindness; Eden wrote to Churchill suggesting that he reconsider his ban on the *Internationale*: "I think now that the *Internationale* like the *Marseillaise* has lost its revolutionary character in the public mind and become a national anthem."[9]

Eden's was not the only view to be found in Foreign Office papers at this time. Thomas Preston, who had long been British consul in Leningrad and who understood the Soviet Union as well as anybody, wrote: "I know literally scores of cases in which Soviet Russians in all walks of life have proclaimed it as their firm conviction that when 'the Imperialist Powers' become war tired, the Soviets will spread their sway westwards throughout Germany and then to England. This was certainly the belief of the Red Army of Occupation amongst soldiers and officers alike in the Baltic States."[10]

A more elaborate warning came from Gavrilovic, the Yugoslav ambassador in London at the end of 1941. In his view Stalin would not allow cooperation with the British to modify his postwar foreign policy aims, which would remain the extraction of "maximum benefit from the weakening and exhaustion of the contending powers." After the war Russia would expand as far as it could to the west. Britain and the United States should "consider how to bridle Russia when she has served the purpose of contributing to the defeat of the Germans." Stalin had tried to stay out of a war, which he wanted neither side to win, but now badly needed Britain and the United States and would listen to any proposal. He would honor any agreement in the first instance, but "It will be necessary to bring such agreements up to date at frequent intervals." Gavrilovic concluded by stating that:

> Stalin has a fanatical belief in Marxist doctrine as resting on scientific laws which it is necessary to discover, elucidate and follow carefully in order to succeed. He believes himself to be presiding over the vastest experiment in human history; he sees it as the birth of a child and dismisses the terrible birth throes as inevitable and certain to be forgotten after the child is born. . . . Stalinism . . . may be regarded

as the pure and concentrated essence of a virtually infallible
doctrine.[11]

The report is remarkable for the clear way it picks out Soviet intentions. It also reminds us of the continuing role of ideology which
served to legitimize Stalin's actions in his own eyes. Insofar as the teachings of Marxism would triumph because they were true, and insofar as
he was their instrument, it was clear that all he had done had been
necessary and no cause for sleepless nights.

Such realistic assessments of Stalin had no appeal to Eden. When a
number of Members of Parliament, including Harold Nicolson and
Duff Cooper, objected to the government's proposed recognition of Soviet claims in the Baltic, Eden observed to Churchill: "Opposition
comes so far mainly from the most ardent supporters of Munich.
Munich was a collapse before a foe and the betrayal by France of an
ally. It has of course no resemblance to the present project."[12] Eden's
views were supported by Beaverbrook, who observed: "The Baltic States
are the Ireland of Russia. Their strategic control is essential to the Russians as the possession of the Irish bases would be valuable to us. . . . It
should be clearly established that the principle of self-determination laid
down in the Atlantic Charter can only be applied when it does not
conflict with the needs of strategic security."[13]

In the event, the British readiness to disregard the Atlantic Charter
proved unacceptable to Roosevelt, which is not to say that he was hostile to the USSR. Indeed, his views on Stalin and Russia sometimes
suggest that he was out of touch with political realities beyond the borders of the United States. He was ill equipped by circumstance to make
an accurate assessment of Stalin and frequently professed the view that
he could be won over by "appeals to high morality."[14] Listening to
William C. Bullitt, first U.S. ambassador to the Soviet Union, who
eventually concluded that Stalin was a "Caucasian bandit whose only
thought when he got something for nothing was, the other fellow was
an ass," Roosevelt remonstrated: "Bill, I don't doubt your facts, and I
don't dispute the logic of your reasoning. I just have a hunch that Stalin
is not that kind of man. Harry [Hopkins] says he's not . . . and I think
that if I give him everything I possibly can and ask for nothing from him
in return, *noblesse oblige*, he won't try to annex anything and will work
with me for a world of democracy and peace."[15]

Roosevelt's emphasis upon decency, the winning of trust and the expectation of moral behavior in others derives in part from the role of

positive moral attitudes in U.S. domestic politics in the twenties and thirties, notably since the introduction of Prohibition, a crucial piece of legislation based entirely upon moral considerations. Maturing in such a political climate gave Roosevelt an "ideological" bias. He came to foreign affairs with a set of a priori assumptions acquired at home, as indeed had Stalin. Unfortunately Stalin's assumptions meshed more comfortably with international *Realpolitik*. It was this that informed Roosevelt's belief that Stalin could be cajoled into a moral view of the world, as a wild mustang can be broken. His misreading was in part the product of cultural circumstance, the consequence of a clash between two political value systems and of certain benign assumptions about the essential decency of human nature.

On this occasion Roosevelt's moral stance prevented the British from selling out the Baltic states, obliging them to settle for a friendship treaty with the Soviet Union that made no mention of frontiers. This set the tone for Allied views of Stalin's territorial aspirations. It was tacitly acknowledged that these were potentially embarrassing and should not be discussed in the hope that under the moderating influence of his allies Stalin could be persuaded to moderate his desiderata. In the meantime, Ambassador Maisky was accorded the extraordinary accolade of being elected an honorary member of the Athenaeum, a London club so conservative and respectable that members have been known to refer to it as the Dead Man's Club.

Not all the mighty Russian people had responded to the Battle of Moscow by regaining their national pride and an eagerness to repel the invader, as the following story told by a Polish soldier makes all too clear. He was standing in a bread queue, which was approached by a soldier on crutches who had lost his leg in the historic struggle.

> He asked politely if he might enter the queue without having to wait,
> for he had only been out of hospital a few days and found it difficult to
> stand for any length of time. . . . He was answered by a hostile
> murmur and maliciously told that he need be in no hurry, for with
> only one leg he would not be taken back to the front anyway. . . .
> Thus the contempt for a damaged machine . . . has permeated all the
> strata of the Russian people. . . . Besides the war itself was not
> particularly popular in Vologda in January 1942. The queues were full
> of complaints about food shortages and the chaotic conscription which
> had left many families without a single bread winner, and twice I even

overheard the whispered question: "When are the Germans coming?"[16]

Stalin's counterattacks in the spring of 1942 had borne mixed results. In the center they had succeeded in pushing the enemy back some 200 miles in places, but they had incurred heavy casualties in the northern sector, and an attempt to recapture Kharkov in the south had resulted in the loss of three armies, four generals and over a quarter of a million men. Moreover, the Germans had continued to advance, capturing the Crimea and thrusting toward the Caucasus. Stalin continued to press his Allies for a second front. Not only would this relieve pressure, but he also saw it as a way to weaken Allied land forces, which were bound to take heavy casualties. In the meantime, despite a stream of exhortative and congratulatory telegrams from Churchill, his suspicion of the British remained unabated. Putting himself in the prime minister's place, he could not conceive that his intention could be other than to keep to the sidelines and allow Russia to defeat Germany on Britain's behalf.

It is hard to exaggerate the sense of inadequacy that the British felt when their contribution to the war on the ground consisted in the not very successful engagement of two to three German divisions in the Western Desert. Nevertheless, Churchill was determined to avoid a second Dunkirk and adamantly opposed an invasion of Europe, which he considered premature. Alas, Molotov had returned from a trip to Washington in the spring of 1942 with a White House communiqué, drawn up without consulting the British, referring to "the urgent need of opening a second front in Europe in 1942." Stalin chose to interpret it as a commitment to invade that year and had everything to gain by so doing. As a negotiator it was his custom to open the bidding as high as possible, putting the most preposterously favorable interpretation upon any document.

Whatever possibilities there might have been for a second front were scotched by Rommel's spectacular success in the desert campaign and the threat he posed to Cairo and the Suez Canal. Churchill decided to break the news to Stalin in person, hoping that he might establish some kind of working relationship with him. He got off to a poor start in his role as the bringer of bad tidings by hailing Soviet crowds with his "V for Victory," a two-finger greeting immediately interpreted as the promise of a second front. Regardless of the fact that the Russian for *victory* begins with a *P*, it is clear that the prime minister had been badly briefed. He assumed that Soviet newsreel material and photographs had portrayed him in his favorite pose often enough for it to be recognized. They had done nothing of the sort, and this one fact shows how little Churchill had been told, or chose to find out, about Soviet Russia.

The actual talks must have been a curious experience for Stalin. Churchill, whom the Soviets held responsible for the Allied intervention during the civil war, was an old enemy. Moreover, this was the first occasion for years that Stalin faced an equal. The British ambassador, Sir Archibald Clark Kerr, even suggested that Stalin enjoyed Churchill's company because the prime minister was not a terrified underling, and this is doubtless true. But enjoyment did not prevent Stalin from running rings around him.

He was well placed to do so. Any disappointment at the news that there would be no invasion did not prevent Stalin from trying to make Churchill feel as bad as possible, stepping up demands for convoys and matériel or teasing him about the seeming lack of belligerence of the British fighting man. (Stalin never believed that an invasion could succeed; he regarded it as a bargaining tool and a way of increasing Allied involvement in the war to their disadvantage.) Churchill did not allow himself to be provoked, but he made the mistake of letting Stalin see what he expected of him. During a particularly tough bargaining session he complained that Stalin's attitude had "no ring of comradeship." A little earlier U.S. Ambassador Averell Harriman had cabled home the view that Stalin, though disappointed, clearly felt he had "binding ties" with Great Britain and the United States. In other words, both the British and the Americans made it clear they had come seeking "friendship." They thereby gave Stalin, who never had the slightest wish to be friends with anybody, a wonderful opportunity to manipulate his allies and make them dance to his tune. He even exploited their unaccountable ignorance of Soviet political realities to the point of pretending that on some issues his hands were tied, in part by the Politburo, in part by public opinion (there had been no opinion of any kind in the Soviet Union, public or private, for more than twenty years).

One cannot hold Churchill or Harriman alone responsible for failure to grasp the nature of their associate. Once again it was a case of bad briefing and the failure to use information readily available. However, others who had dealings with the Soviets viewed them in a different light. Before taking up his post, Sir Gifford Martel, the British military attaché, had sought advice on how to treat them. "Officials holding senior posts in the Foreign Office were unanimous in saying the best way was to be very forthcoming and friendly to the Russians and give in to them whenever one could reasonably do so. The advice was definitely one of appeasement. I gathered I would receive the same advice . . . from the Ambassador."[17]

However, when he consulted more junior people, he was told that "the only way to get on with the Russians was to be very forthright and outspoken from the moment one set foot on Rusian soil."[18] Sir Gifford followed this excellent advice, despite subsequent pressure from, among others, the foreign secretary, who maintained that the goodwill gained by giving in to, or avoiding, controversial issues, would lead to the eventual solution of every difficulty.[19] Sometime later the Foreign Office tried to prevent Sir Gifford from addressing Conservative MPs on "The True Position in Russia" and the failure of the policy known in Foreign Office circles as casting one's bread upon the waters.[20]

Lord Alanbrooke, who had accompanied the prime minister to Moscow, found the Foreign Office attitude distasteful: "We have bowed and scraped to them, done all we could for them and never asked them for a single fact or figure in return. As a result they despise us and have no use for us except what they can get out of us."[21] The reference to facts and figures is apposite since it appears that Stalin and Molotov deliberately misrepresented the military situation, concealing the truly colossal Soviet reserves, in order to extort the maximum contribution from the Allies by exaggerating the seriousness of their plight.[22] No poker player reveals that he holds a full house when he can take the pot with two pairs.

Churchill and Alanbrooke were much impressed by Stalin the man and his grasp of the subjects under discussion. For example, he immediately "understood" the significance of Churchill's proposed invasion of North Africa or at least convinced Churchill that he saw in it a strategic value that Churchill was delighted to have him discover. This convinced the prime minister that he possessed "a military brain of the very highest calibre. Never once in any of his statements did he make any strategic error, nor did he fail to appreciate all the implications of a situation with a quick and unerring eye. In this respect he stood out compared with his two colleagues."[23]

These wartime close-ups of Stalin are the first we have that are free of prejudice or sycophancy. It is clear that he had come a long way from the opportunistic bungler of the civil war, clear, too, that he was anything but the intellectual mediocrity that enemies such as Trotsky had made him out to be. Above all, the war, by confronting him with the need to make decisions that were correct not just objectively but actually as well, had sharpened him and encouraged him to learn. It would be a great mistake to accept the view of Stalin the bungling warlord proposed by Khrushchev, who mocks him for planning strategic operations on a globe. Stalin the warlord was anything but negligible, and as for the globe, which was seven feet in diameter, it was an excellent planning tool.

Stalin pitilessly exploited Churchill's wish to make friends. After three days of being, as the official papers put it, "cold and difficult," he suddenly rang the changes and invited Churchill to dinner:

> It was clear that M. Stalin had thought better of his attitude of the day before and was anxious to make amends. He was at pains to make himself agreeable. . . . When saying goodnight he told the PM that he was a rough man and begged that his roughness should not be misunderstood and that the difference between him and the PM was nothing more than one of method[!]. He accompanied the PM through the vast gallery which separated the dining room from the door by which we had come into the Kremlin. This long walk, or rather trot, for he had to be brisk in order to keep pace with Mr Churchill, is I understand without precedent in the history of the Soviet Kremlin.[24]

The prime minister returned with a communiqué affirming the alliance between the USSR, Great Britain and the United States and with nothing else, except perhaps for the delusion that he had gone some way toward winning Stalin's personal friendship. The Soviet Union quickly resumed its pressure upon Britain, using as a pretext the decision not to put Rudolf Hess on trial until after the war. It was pointed out that Britain still had everything to gain from a separate peace with Germany. There was also an assertion that the bombing of Britain had mysteriously ceased after Hess's flight. A newspaper article described Britain as "a sanctuary for gangsters."

Once again the trick worked. Eden instructed his ambassador to say that the Soviet attack was an unfriendly act, an unjustifiable slur upon the honor of an ally. So far so good. He further ordered him to endeavor to ascertain the true nature of the Soviet grievance. It was thus assumed that in some mysterious sense Britain must be in the wrong. Although Eden rounded off his communication with the order to use strong language with Stalin, it was the latter, as usual, who held the cards. On the one hand, he only had to "blow hot" for the slight to be forgiven at no cost to the Soviets; alternatively the faintest hint that there was a genuine grievance would have secured immediate concessions. In the meantime, the British felt hurt and indignant but also inexplicably guilty. They both protested and declared themselves ready to make amends, whatever they might be; the playing fields of Eton were no place to learn to deal with Stalin. Shortly afterward Maisky told Eden in confidence that the Hess affair had indeed been a pretext. The fact of the matter was that feeling inside Russia was very bad because of the absence of a second front.[25]

A Slowly Turning Tide

Despite Stalin's increasing confidence, his war was far from won. In the middle of 1942 Germans still occupied the greater part of European Russia. As the journalist Alexander Werth put it, "What melancholy names the Moscow railway stations have to-day. Leningrad Station, Kursk Station, Kiev Station, Rzhev Station, Belorussia Station, stations to nowhere."[1] The Red Army was still no match for the Germans in summer campaigns. Man for man the Wehrmacht was much too much for them, and the Soviets were regularly outfought and outled. However, the odds were seldom man for man those days; the Soviets had vast superiority in numbers and were winning the war of attrition. The German invasion was breaking down. Hitler had failed to take Leningrad—which city he had planned to raze from the face of the earth—and although the Crimea had fallen, Voronezh, on the Don, had held, and there was no breakthrough in the center. Hitler now decided on a two-pronged advance in the south, on the Transcaucasian oilfields and on Stalingrad. The Germans made a successful incursion into the northern Caucasus until their advance ran out of fuel and a stiffening resistance prevented them from reaching the oilfields. Now the entire German war effort concentrated on Stalingrad. Hitler hoped to break through, cutting Stalin off from the south and from Siberia, and mount a two-pronged attack on Moscow from the west and the southeast. The objective had great symbolic significance for Stalin, and hence for Hitler, who badly needed a victory to compensate for the failure to take either Leningrad or Moscow.

The attack began in July 1942, and by September 19 many Soviet leaders professed the view that the city could not be held.[2] What ensued fills one of the greatest pages in Russian military history, one in which the names of buildings, the Red October Plant, the Barricades Plant, or a mound, the Mamayev Kurgan, have all the resonance of Russia's historic battlefields such as Kulikovo, Borodino or Kursk. If the Battle of Moscow ensured that the Soviet Union would not lose the war, then the Battle of Stalingrad ensured that it would win it. It was the moment that the Red Army, its commander in chief, its commanders, its fighting men all found themselves, the greatest triumph of Russian arms since Peter the Great defeated Charles XII of Sweden at Poltava. It was a battle fought and won not by divisions, regiments or battalions but by companies, platoons and squads. In fact, units functioned with such independence that supply problems were regularly solved by stealing from one another.[3]

> The extreme example of a unit's self-sufficiency was offered by Senior-Lieutenant Bezditko. His crack mortar company became so widely publicized . . . that he was given special supplies of food, clothing and liquor to keep morale high for visiting photographers. One day Lieutenant Bezditko's vodka supply ran out, despite repeated and unavailing telephone calls . . . asking for more. . . . When nothing more was promised Bezditko threatened to blow up his battalion supply dump and did so with two well-placed rounds. . . . No one was killed and Bezditko was not punished. The regimental commander . . . merely ordered the supply-office to make good the vodka deficiency.[4]

Khrushchev gives an example of Stalin's management style at this time. In the middle of the battle he received an angry telephone call from Stalin about proposals he had made to evacuate what was left of the city. Khrushchev indignantly denied that such proposals existed, and the matter ended there. It was only later that he realized that Stalin was probing.[5]

By the end of October the Russians had no more than a toehold in the city but were able to operate freely in the hinterland. Then, on November 19, Zhukov launched a counteroffensive with three armies which managed to surround von Paulus's Sixth Army. After bitter fighting he then checked a relief column led by von Manstein that was trying to break through the Russian ring, and, on February 2, 1943, shortly after the capture of von Paulus and twenty-three German generals, the remainder of his army surrendered. Henceforth the German position in the south would be untenable, while in the north the siege of Leningrad was shortly to be broken. The tide of war had started to turn.

As he issued an order of the day congratulating his troops on their victories all along the front, Stalin signed himself supreme commander in chief for the first time. It was indeed he who, in the first instance, commanded both the armed forces and the civilian war effort. As his confidence grew, he became more flexible, involving field commanders in the planning of operations, retaining the advantages of a centralized structure while giving more scope to local expertise. He had also proved that when obliged to, he could pick the right commanders, in contrast with his earlier support of mediocrities such as Voroshilov and Budenny. Stalingrad was a proving ground for his young generals, and six of those who fought there—Zhukov, Vasilievsky, Rokossovsky, Chuikov, Tolbukhin and Malinovsky—would become marshals within two years.

General Grigorenko has provided two glimpses of Stalin working with his generals in which he appears in an uncharacteristic light: as a first-class handler of subordinates, effortlessly winning their loyalty as only a true leader can. The first concerns a senior commander of Far Eastern forces, Opranasenko, who was suddenly relieved of his command and recalled to Moscow. He returned expecting the worst and was summoned by Stalin, who gave him a remarkable reception. Referring to himself throughout as Stalin, he chided Opranasenko, attributing to him a string of imaginary grievances occasioned by his apparent and undeserved dismissal, and then he explained. It was not for lack of trust that he had removed him. On the contrary, now the Far East was safe from a Japanese threat, lesser men could command there. In the interests of his career Stalin was giving him a combat assignment on the western front, but since he had no experience of active service, he was going to start him as Rokossovsky's second-in-command. The episode, which Grigorenko vouches for, projects the image of a considerate commander in chief, prone to slightly sadistic teasing but obviously concerned for the welfare of officers whose loyalty he sought and won.

The second story concerns a lieutenant general who was close to Stalin throughout the war years and who found in him that peculiar simplicity and humanity, possessed by some great men, that are born of total self-confidence. He always felt he could talk freely with him and in due course had reason to feel grateful when Stalin exonerated him personally after his name had appeared on the list of those responsible for losing the Kerch Peninsula in the Crimea.[6] The stories have an authentic ring to them (Grigorenko, publishing in the West, had no reason to love Stalin). They suggest that Stalin could win the loyalty of fighting men and that he did not operate through fear alone.

He now rewarded the entire officer corps for their successes by restoring the tsarist symbols of their rank, epaulets and other insignia, the start of an epidemic of gold braid. Shortly afterward nonmilitary personnel, railwaymen, judges and diplomats, too, were put into uniform, as they had been in tsarist days. Stalin's family nanny, who had been in service before the Revolution, felt she had seen it all. "First they abolish epaulets; then they bring epaulets back."[7] So it goes.

The Red Army now observed military etiquette more strictly even than the British. Their officers were much more of a separate cast than their allied counterparts. For example, a junior officer in the U.S. Army was paid about 3 times as much as a private; in the British Army 4 times; in the Red Army, 100.[8] The lot of Soviet enlisted men, or junior officers for that matter, was far from happy. They were considered expendable, especially by Zhukov, who even among Soviet commanders had the reputation of being profligate with his men. The army attitude toward manpower was an important aspect of life in wartime Russia and is best summed up by Frederick the Great's observation to his troops when wilting under enemy fire: "Dogs, do you want to live forever!" A key part in Red Army attacks was played by NKVD units armed with automatic weapons, who went in behind the first wave, with the result that, as Stalin observed, "In the Red Army it takes more courage to retreat than to advance."[9] There was also a standing order that any soldier should shoot his neighbor if he appeared to be holding back during an assault—the Soviet version of the honor system.

It is curious to see a British Foreign Office official attempt to refute a Red Army man's allegation that NKVD units were thus employed. Dismissing his claim, Thomas Brimelow minuted: "The Red Army may well use screens of reliable men to see that less reliable elements do not turn tail in battle, but the whole description has an exaggerated air."[10] He added that since two-thirds of the Red Army were not members of the party they could not be used as cannon fodder, in which respect he was wrong. Zhukov later observed to Eisenhower that he used penal battalions to clear minefields with their feet, while it was customary not to clear mined roads but simply to accept the losses.[11] Mines were, however, cleared sometimes, as an American journalist noted:

> Elsewhere in the world mine detection is divided into two phases; first the problem of detecting the mine and second that of rendering it harmless. Here they are combined in the following manner. They send a lot of Russians poking into the weeds with a lot of poles. Presently you hear a loud bang and see a Russian rising out of the air on a column of smoke. This indicates not only the detection of the mine, but the fact that it is simultaneously rendered harmless. [12]

They adopted a similar attitude toward river crossings. As one Red Army officer put it, "Parachute troops were dropped [and] seized certain points on the German side of the river. These troops were doomed and their task consisted in pinning down the German defences for two or three days until the main body of the Soviet army completed its preparations for crossing . . . no steps were taken to ensure their withdrawal, they were bound to fight to the bitter end." [13]

At least they had parachutes. Not all units were so lucky, as the wife of a German officer recalled. "He had told me he had watched Russian soldiers leaping out into the snow behind German lines from low-flying aircraft without parachutes. Some died, some were wounded, the survivors joined the partisans." [14]

As Sir Gifford Martel observed, "The Russians can not understand why we set such great store on human life." [15] Yet this breathtaking callousness was not the most dismal aspect of the Red Army. Still worse, it was the only army of modern times not to grant home leave. A Red Army man would remain on active service until victory, assuming that he was fit to do so. This imparts real poignancy to the most popular poem of the war, a sentimental piece by the writer Konstantin Simonov in which a soldier tells his woman: "Wait for me and I'll be back. . . ."

CHAPTER FORTY-THREE

Teheran

After Stalingrad perceptible changes occurred in civilian as well as military life. The concentration camp loudspeakers, silent since the outbreak of war, came to life again. Everywhere there was a renewed emphasis upon the cult of Stalin, a cult which he had allowed to abate with the invasion. Political controls were tightened, and journalists, who had hitherto enjoyed considerable freedom, were reined in once more. At the same time Stalin continued to appeal to patriotic and nationalistic feelings. The churches were reopened in 1943, and increasing emphasis was placed upon Russian military heroes. The Soviet Information Bureau established a Jewish Antifascist Committee that included Molotov's wife, Zhemchuzhina, and Mikhoels, the greatest Yiddish actor of the age.

Military success notwithstanding, life was very hard for ordinary people. The British Embassy reported that workers in Moscow were dying of malnutrition at the rate of some 300 a month,[1] and for the first time since the civil war apartments went unheated.[2] Shortages of manpower were made up by the conscription of teenage labor at the rate, in 1942, of 2 million a year.[3]

The summer of 1943 saw the third of the great Soviet victories, the Battle of Kursk, which marked the moment that Stalin completed his education as a strategist.[4] Intelligence reports had established that the Germans would attack both flanks of a large Soviet salient around Kursk. The question was whether to attack first or to try to absorb the German onslaught and counterattack. Stalin chose the second course. The Red Army had never beaten the Germans in a summer campaign, and it took nerve to wait for them to attack. Russian defenses held in the south, and the Germans, who, for all the Russian preparations, still managed an astounding twenty-mile advance in the north, were obliged to withdraw. The Russians counterattacked with an armored thrust but were outfought by some understrength panzer divisions and had to resort to tactics of attrition, massed frontal attacks with heavy losses on both sides, which they alone could afford. As Sir Gifford Martel noted, their armor acting independently was never a match for the panzers. Still, for the first time they were beating the Germans in a summer campaign and beginning to push them back.

Soviet relations with the Allies had undergone a hiccup in April, when the Germans revealed the mass graves of thousands of Polish officers in the forest of Katyn. After trying to pass it off as a medieval burial site, the Soviet Union published a cover story stating that the Poles had been shot by Nazis in 1941, and the Western press enthusiastically followed suit, the American military paper *Stars and Stripes* publishing a cartoon of a Polish officer falsely supposed to have been killed by the Soviets.[5]

The Polish prime minister, General Sikorski, initially asked the International Red Cross to investigate the affair but was reluctantly compelled to accept that this was bringing comfort to the enemy. The British felt that no matter who had killed the Poles, their main concern was to preserve good relations with the Soviet Union. Despite the remarkable contribution of Poles in exile to the British war effort, notably to the Battle of Britain, it was felt that their feelings and interests must be disregarded. Besides leaning on Sikorski, Churchill censored the Polish press in Britain, forbidding it to express hostility toward the Soviet Union.[6] Stalin, all injured innocence, severed diplomatic relations with a "hostile" Polish government. Eden's comment on the affair was "least said, soonest mended," and the *Daily Worker* mounted an anti-Polish campaign.

At first the State Department stated that insufficient evidence was available to justify a stand, although it had known about Katyn for some eighteen months and subsequently obtained corroborative reports. However, long afterward it preferred to rely on the testimony of the twenty-five-year-old daughter of the ambassador to the Soviet Union, Kathleen Harriman, who later visited the graves under Soviet supervision and accepted the Soviet interpretation of the facts. Official pressure prevented discussion of Katyn in U.S. government circles as late as 1950; a Polish historian of the massacre concluded: "When the handling of the

Katyn affair by the agencies of the US Government is reviewed it appears that on the highest policy making level there were definite attempts to suppress information concerning it, particularly when such information contradicted the Soviet version . . . the men who voiced their opinion about the possibility of Soviet guilt seem to have been punished."[7]

We find further evidence of a pro-Soviet bias in senior Allied circles that summer, when representatives of the British Special Operations Executive in Russia produced a report recommending that top-level negotiators should stand firm on issues such as Russia's postwar frontiers, and that the practice of lavishing flowery praise on Russian military valor should cease forthwith. They concluded with the warning that after the war the Soviet Union alone would possess a large standing army to back the demands it would bring to the peace conference. The paper, with its realistic assessment, enraged the foreign secretary, who rejected it in its entirety with a scrawled minute to the effect that "I am not impressed with this stuff," without giving any consideration to the views expressed.[8]

Eden went to Moscow in the autumn of 1943 for a foreign ministers' conference to pave the way for a meeting of the "Big Three" later in the year. He was determined to avoid any issue of a controversial nature; when the Foreign Office proposed that the question of the Soviet-Polish frontier be placed on the agenda, he declined. Personally he was prepared to accept Soviet proposals but anticipated that the Americans would object. "We cannot do this, we should have to tell the Americans in advance who would not agree," he minuted.[9] The Polish issue was accordingly sidestepped. "An exchange of views took place," in the words of the protocol, while U.S. Secretary of State Cordell Hull suggested that the Polish Home Army might help its cause by rising behind German lines as the Red Army approached and making "a material contribution to shortening the war,"[10] a respect in which it obliged, man, woman and child, in the Battle of Warsaw. His allies' decision to ignore Katyn must have shown Stalin the true strength of his hand.

Stalin paced the conference with his usual care. For five days Molotov appeared intractable, in order to get as much as possible out of the Allies, before suddenly relenting on a number of issues, declining to clamor for an invasion of France and committing his country to war with Japan. The conference ended with a banquet at which Stalin bullied Eden mercilessly, as the journalist Edward Crankshaw recalled. The banquet was attended by so many senior Red Army officers that it was hard to say who was fighting the war, especially since they all got drunk. Stalin turned to Eden in mock despair and asked him if British generals got drunk in public, too, a question to which Eden evidently found it impossible to reply. Stalin then drank a series of toasts standing beside him. Each time he drank he flexed his knees, rather, Crankshaw told me, like a music hall caricature of a British policeman, and each time he placed a hand upon Eden's shoulder and made him flex, too, until the foreign secretary was to be seen bobbing helplessly up and down, smiling a toothy and self-conscious smile. Stalin then toasted other guests, further exercising his sense of humor by chucking Beria under the chin and referring to him as "my Himmler" (he did indeed bear a passing resemblance to his German opposite number). He also called upon Molotov to explain that curious pact he had concluded with von Ribbentrop. The British left Moscow with the feeling that their relationship with the Soviet Union had improved enormously. Eden's telegram to the prime minister had more than a hint of self-congratulation. Of Stalin he wrote in his diary: "Joe was friendly enough to me personally, even jovial. But he still has that disconcerting habit of not looking at one when he speaks or shakes hands. A meeting with him could in all respects be a creepy, even a sinister experience if it were not for his readiness to laugh when his whole face creases and his little eyes open."[11]

• • •

On his way to the Teheran Conference in late November 1943 Roosevelt made it clear that one of his motives for going was to get himself liked by Stalin.[12] He may or may not have succeeded, but he came away with a powerful impression: "Do you suppose that [training for the priesthood] made some kind of difference in Stalin? Doesn't that explain part of the sympathetic quality in his nature which we all feel?"[13] One wonders what he would have made of Talleyrand.

Stalin played Roosevelt beautifully, using his habitual technique of early aloofness. For three days he remained cold and unbending until Roosevelt tried to break the ice by teasing Churchill for being British and smoking cigars. This amused Stalin greatly, and the president felt that enough ice had been broken for him to call him Uncle Joe. "From that time our relations were personal."[14] It is understandable that the president should have sought a personal relationship with Stalin, incomprehensible that he should have been so ill prepared for his encounter with him. There was no shortage of first-class State Department men like Kennan and Bohlen in an excellent position to brief the president on the lack of effect that training for the priesthood had had upon Stalin.

When considering the Teheran Conference, one cannot help feeling that Stalin controlled affairs from the start. He even ensured that the president stay in the Soviet Embassy grounds, not in his own legation, upon the pretext that his agents had discovered an assassination plot and he would be safer there. Apart from the symbolic impact of Stalin's power play there is no reason to suppose that Roosevelt's residence had not been wired for sound.

The Big Three discussed military strategy, notably the date of the invasion of France, with Voroshilov making a splendid contribution to the planning of Operation Overlord. He observed that the Red Army had discovered that crossing rivers was easy so that the English Channel should not be a serious obstacle! In retrospect it appeared to Western military observers that Stalin was anxious to discourage an Allied advance through Italy and welcomed a proposal to divert forces from that theater to the south of France, despite the fact that the plan was strategically unsound. It was in his interests to keep his allies as far from the Balkans as possible.[15]

Roosevelt threw away his bargaining position on Poland by telling Stalin that he could not involve himself since he intended to run for reelection and could not alienate his Polish vote. He also observed, and a nod in such cases is quite as good as a wink, that he did not anticipate declaring war on the Soviet Union in the event of its absorbing the Baltic states. So much then for the Atlantic Charter. This was not a sudden concession. Already in July Roosevelt had told the British that he would not object to such reincorporation. "But the matter must be arranged in a manner that would give least offense to American public opinion." The British were committed to the proposal anyway but added: "We and the Americans have suggested that some provision might be made for allowing those who wish to do so to leave, but the Russians have showed no enthusiasm."[16] So much the worse for millions of Balts.

Churchill and Stalin determined the Polish frontier together. They agreed on the so-called Curzon Line, with some disagreement on what it was. Stalin insisted that Lwow be included, thereby winning at the conference table the city he had failed to take by force in 1920. Churchill agreed to Stalin's proposals and cheerfully proposed to compensate the Poles by giving them a part of Germany. This was a bad decision, making for an unstable Poland that would have to depend upon its stronger neighbor in the east, ensuring that it became a Russian protectorate.[17]

Churchill and Roosevelt then invited Stalin to participate in a joint postwar peacekeeping operation as one of the "four policemen," the fourth to be China. Stalin was skeptical at first, wondering aloud what would happen if one of the policemen turned out to be a bandit, but subsequently agreed to the proposal; once more he had nothing to lose. Apart from the beginnings of a deal on Poland and the Baltic states, Stalin also came away with a firm commitment from his allies to proceed with the invasion of France in May. As Lord Ismay put it, looking back, "The Russians had got exactly what they wanted. We for our part were in the position of a man who has signed a formal agreement to purchase a property at some future date without knowing how much it is going to cost, or whether he will have the money to pay for it when the time comes or whether a more desirable property will not be on the market before the purchase is completed."[18]

On the last night of the conference there was a dinner at the British Legation to celebrate Churchill's birthday at which Birse, the prime minister's interpreter, noticed that Stalin was feeling uncomfortable. He sat on the edge of his chair looking at the various knives and forks before him, turned to Birse and said: "This is a fine collection of cutlery! It is a problem which to use. . . . You will have to tell me, and also when I begin to eat. I am unused to your customs."[19] Stalin, whose experience of formal banquets was extensive, undoubtedly knew more about the protocol of dining than did Birse, although he may have recognized that conventions could vary from nation to nation. (He had been demonstrably upset when Churchill attended a Kremlin banquet in his "siren suit"—a one-piece garment with a zip designed to go over pajamas in the event of an air raid, which Churchill was very fond of.) However, here he made use of his "ignorance" in order to win the interpreter over: "To me, a small cog in the machinery, he was amiable, friendly and considerate. . . . There was something in his personality which revealed pre-eminence, a grasp of the essentials, the alert mind. He relied to a minimum on his assistants . . . he carried the details in his head. Nor did he miss any weaknesses in the arguments of his opponents, on whom he would pounce like a bird of prey."[20]

Birse contrasted Stalin with Roosevelt: "He knew little of Soviet mentality or had been badly advised. It was not enough, as he evidently thought, to clap Russians on the back and say they were good fellows, in order to reach a mutually advantageous agreement with them. Something more subtle was required."[21]

However, at least one real advantage accrued to the Allies. Up to Teheran Stalin had not discounted the possibility of a separate peace with Germany and had maintained the beginnings of a skeleton government, consisting of a Free German Committee staffed by captured senior officers opposed to Hitler. Unlike the Allies, he understood that there was such a thing as a German resistance movement. After the guarantees he was given by the Allies, the committee was allowed to fade into the background.[22]

At the conference Churchill presented Stalin with the famous sword that commemorated the victory of Stalingrad. All witnesses agree that both men appeared very moved by the military accolade and Churchill's rousing rhetoric. Accounts differ on whether it was Stalin or Voroshilov who rounded the ceremony off by dropping the sword. There is no reason to suppose that Stalin was anything but moved by the sight of a British prime minister giving him a symbol of knighthood, valor and honor to commemorate the magnificent defense of his city. The presentation could have been the proudest moment in Stalin's life.

Although Ambassador Harriman was delighted by the Teheran talks, professional U.S. diplomats such as Bohlen were less impressed. In its aftermath they foresaw a fragmented Europe dominated by the Soviet Union, "the only important military and political force on the continent of Europe." A power vacuum was being created and it was obvious who would fill it. On the way home Roosevelt observed to an aide: "I wish someone could tell me about the Russians. I don't know a good Russian from a bad Russian."[23] But by then it was much too late.

CHAPTER FORTY-FOUR

The Alliance

Well, Harry, all I can say is nice friends we have now.
—ADMIRAL LEAHY TO HARRY HOPKINS
AFTER TEHERAN

Stalin's daughter noted that her father returned from Teheran in high spirits. Indeed, he had every reason to be pleased. He was convinced of the good faith and naivety of his allies and began to make confident plans for expansion into Europe. He had little confidence in the fighting ability of Allied ground forces, had been unimpressed by the Battle of El Alamein, which, by the standards of the Russian front, was a skirmish, and expected them to remain locked in a long and bloody struggle on the French beaches or even be driven back into the sea. However, he was confident that they meant what they said, would never conclude a separate peace with Germany and were committed to an unconditional surrender.

The Allied view was that Teheran had set a high watermark in the process of civilizing the Soviet Union and that its agreements boded well for the future. The Polish government was tiresomely reluctant to accept its new frontier, notably the loss of Lwow, which one Pole compared to the loss of Canterbury. However, Eden made it clear that the Poles had no choice. This view was not held universally. O'Mally, British ambassador to the Polish government, wrote a letter to Eden in the aftermath of Teheran which is a model of foresight and common sense, evidence that not everyone was deceived by Stalin. It says of the Polish agreement:

The Prime Minister sees this crisis mainly as a chapter in the business of winning the war but his perspective and proportions seem to me to be faulty. There is clearly a very strong probability that we shall win the war. Surely it is high time to lend increasing weight to things which bear primarily on international relations after the conclusion of the war! The Prime Minister attaches great importance to those ties supposedly created between Russia and ourselves at Teheran; but these are feebler than he thinks. There is small warrant for the belief that the Soviets' actions will be determined by anything but pure *raison d'état*.

The Prime Minister thinks he has made Poland a fair offer which Poland might reasonably accept. This hardly seems to me to be so. The Poles would be most unwise to accept the Curzon Line. The prospect held out to them as wardens of a defeated Germany's eastern marches is a mixture of the picturesque and the unreal. The offer to press the Soviet Government to recognise the [Polish] Government is illusory unless we greatly strengthen the language we have conditionally undertaken to use to them. The real choice . . . seems . . . to lie between on the one hand selling the corpse of Poland to Russia and finding an alibi . . . and on the other putting the point of principle to Stalin in the clearest possible way, and warning him that our position might have to be explained publicly. [1]

Eden's reply was unhelpful: "The real choice lies between doing our best to see that a free and independent Poland emerges after the war or seeing the Russians overrun the country in the tide of war." This was an unrealistic assessment that failed to address O'Mally's arguments.

Stalin was refusing to have any dealings with the Polish government-in-exile, while as Secretary of State Cordell Hull put it, with the invasion of France about to take place, the Allies could "not afford to become partisan (*sic!*) in the Polish question to the extent of alienating Russia at the crucial moment."[2] It does not seem to have occurred to anyone that Stalin should have been required to earn his second front by making concessions in other spheres. In the meantime, it was conveniently forgotten, until a junior Foreign Office official reminded his masters, that the British had undertaken not to conclude any agreement compromising Poland's territorial status—a memorandum which Eden minuted: "Where did we say this?"[3] With his electoral problems now over, Roosevelt was inclined to be sympathetic to the Soviet view and even sent two American Poles of known Soviet sympathies to Moscow to open unofficial talks. Churchill, meanwhile, requested Stalin to recognize the Polish government, "If only because of the deep association between the three Allies," a representation which Stalin, in the words of the British ambassador, "dismissed with a snigger."[4]

As the Red Army moved into Poland, it was told that many Poles were pro-German and turned captured Soviet partisans over to the enemy. This did not help Russo-Polish relations.[5] True, there were times when Soviet forces and the Polish Home Army fought side by side against Germans, but these battles were not always happy affairs. On one occasion the Polish 27th Infantry, after fighting a successful joint action with the Soviets, saw their "allies" suddenly withdraw from a crucial sector, allowing the Germans to surround and virtually annihilate them. Elsewhere the Soviets shot Polish officers, disarming and deporting other ranks. On April 27, 1944, the Polish commander in chief summed the situation up in a message to London: "The attitude of the Soviet authorities towards us has to be assessed realistically. No good can be expected of them. We have no illusions about the insincerity of their propositions of loyalty and comradeship with the Polish Independent Movement."[6]

In the light of an overwhelming body of evidence and such sober evaluations, the subsequent decision to attack the Germans in Warsaw as the Russians drew near to that city was unforgivably foolish, and the outcome of that tragic act of bravery should not have come as a surprise.

Reports of Stalin's attitude to Poland and of the behavior of his troops exasperated Churchill, who proposed a cooling off in personal relations. Eden advised against this, suggesting "we let matters drift for a while." When Churchill replied that he wished only to save as many Poles as possible from being murdered, Eden answered: "The Polish affair stands in a category by itself, and I am afraid that the Soviet Government are determined to maintain their point of view."[7]

One can now detect a serious division in British circles between the military planners, who took a realistic view of the future role of the Soviet Union, and an element in the Foreign Office, led by the foreign secretary, that acted as a fierce advocate of Soviet interests. Two names stand out in the documents, those of G. M. Wilson and Thomas Brimelow. Wilson, who had been chairman of the Oxford University Labour Club in 1930, was once described by the late Edward Crankshaw as "a quaker of the cold-blooded kind, (the chillest kind of person on earth to my understanding). He had been Cripps' Private Secretary in Moscow, and had stayed on when he went home. He was not so much pro-Russian as anti everybody else; that is to say the slightest criticism of anything to do with Russia turned you into a Fascist at once." Crankshaw described Brimelow as "a tight, vain little man, bursting with cherubic self-satisfaction and a kind of brilliant, blank and patronising contempt for everyone else. . . . [He changed from being] creepily pro-Russian in the early days of the war to rather ferociously pro-Russian towards the end of his career." As Crankshaw recalled, the tension between military opinion and the Foreign Office view started in the Soviet Union.

> Eden was at the heart of the matter. . . . In no time at all I discovered that the Embassy and the Military Mission were barely on speaking terms. The soldiers had a proper view of the difficulties they were in for, and the diplomats refused to recognise that such difficulties existed. I remember once the Head of the Mission signalling and saying that he really must be allowed to protest to Stalin about such and such happening and by return came a telegram saying "Spare the Russians in their agony" with a great rigmarole to follow about how we must do everything to make it easy for them. When we pointed out that it was not easy to make things easy when they were trampling all over our faces this did not go down well. . . . When Eden came out he was assailed by outraged servicemen begging for support from the Foreign Office in the face of Russian behaviour. . . . Eden, buck teeth at the ready, smiled and soothed . . . assuring the Heads of Mission that he had fixed everything with Stalin and we should have no more trouble. If generals and admirals had been allowed by protocol to boo that is what would have happened.[8]

By 1944 the divergence of opinion had reached far beyond Moscow. The Joint Chiefs of Staff, already aware of Russia's probable role as the future enemy, prepared a paper suggesting the formation of a Western European group, the beginnings of NATO in effect, which would include at least part of Germany as an ally. They felt that "the dangerous possibility of a hostile Russia making use of the resources of Germany must not be lost sight of and that any measures which we now take should be tested by whether or not they help to keep that contingency from arising." Ironically enough the paper was circulated a day or so after the July 20 Plot, when German army officers attempted to assassinate Hitler.

The Foreign Office reacted with outrage. Eden's minute reads: "This is very bad. I must speak to Ismay about it," while a memorandum written by Wilson observes: "This sounds suspiciously like a policy of trying to win the Germans to our side against the Soviet Union, our twenty years' ally." Wilson conceded the possibility of a Soviet threat but felt this should be countered by the staging of "regular military talks and conversations on the subject of common, or even individual interest." He continued: "As a corollary we should have to recognise Russian vital interests in Eastern Europe or even take a leaf out of their book and make this suggestion first."[9] Russia's vital interests may reasonably be assumed to include its territorial ambitions.

A minute in an unknown hand welcomes the proposal since hitherto Foreign Office representatives had had some difficulty in stifling anti-Soviet attitudes among the military because they had had no concrete alternative to put forward. The papers reveal pro-Soviet attitudes' being advanced with remarkable urgency. Sometimes these occurred in the strangest places. The Foreign Office file for 1943 includes a memorandum from the British consul in Kashigar, India, who suggested that His Majesty's government should bring out an Anglo-Soviet songbook with a view to improving Anglo-Soviet relations.[10] In a further report Wilson expressed alarm at the steadily increasing popularity of anti-Soviet views. He had received complaints from D. N. Pritt (of Moscow trial fame) and from Rothstein, the Tass correspondent.[11] On the strength of his paper Eden composed a long memorandum to Churchill.

Stalin's view of his allies emerges in conversations he held with the Yugoslav leader Milovan Djilas. Stalin emphasized that just because the British were fighting Germans, this did not make them friends. At one session Stalin and Molotov briefly discussed the possibility of tricking the British into recognizing Tito and his Communist partisans as the legitimate government of Yugoslavia—just as the British wanted Stalin to recognize the Polish government-in-exile—but the suggestion was dismissed as absurd; in any event, it would take a whole year before such recognition was forthcoming. Stalin also warned Djilas that the British loved to deceive their allies and that Churchill, unlike Roosevelt, was not to be trusted. To illustrate his point, it was, he said, British intelligence that had killed General Sikorski and covered his murder by arranging for his plane to crash.[12] The charge is farfetched, although we should remember that thanks to Stalin's infiltration of British intelligence, he was in a position to know a thing or two that others might not.

Stalin went on to drop an unconscious hint to Djilas of his plans for

Europe. Djilas had observed that the southern Slavs had desired liberation, whereas the tsars had aimed at imperialist expansion. Stalin replied that the Russian tsars had "lacked horizons" and went straight on
to ask about the power struggle in Yugoslavia, with an evident view to
exploiting it. [13]

He was already making plans for expansion into Europe and was encouraging hostility toward the Allies, an encouragement reflected in
party instructions and secret circulars which stressed that the British and
Americans had hated the Soviet Union before the war and that nothing
had changed. [14] As for the second front and the military situation in the
west, a senior officer of Soviet military intelligence makes it clear that
Stalin was not eager for Allied success:

> As the months passed the second front was required increasingly in
> order to engage the British-American forces in what was considered an
> impossibly difficult and costly adventure. When the armies of
> Eisenhower and Montgomery moved swiftly forward, Army General
> Antonov, the Chief of General Staff, was seen issuing from Stalin's
> presence as scarlet as a boiled beetroot, so roundly had the Boss cursed
> him for his inaccurate information . . . while news of the German V1
> and V2 rocket attacks on Britain caused considerable delight in
> military circles. [15]

The same source states that elaborate plans had been made for the
occupation of Western Europe in anticipation that Overlord would
fail:

> The Kremlin was not concerned merely to occupy Germany. Stalin's
> predecessor Alexander I had seen his armies in Paris. . . . This time,
> once there, the Russian armies would not be moved back so quickly.
> Detailed plans had been prepared. Card indices had been combed
> through and key men were already marked for key posts in occupied
> Europe. My own instructions issued well in advance were to study and
> master every detail of the Göttingen and Aachen districts, for here
> were to be found German aerodynamical institutes. Nikolchenko, a
> personal friend, had specialised in Belgium. For him Brussels was the
> subject of study. Another friend was preparing for work at Meudon
> near Paris, and so on. The Air Force command was busy drawing up
> plans for basing our squadrons not on Eastern Germany but down the
> Rhine. [16]

Had it not been for the remarkable success of Overlord, the iron curtain would have traced its way down the coastline of France. The most significant achievement of British and American arms in World War II was not the defeat of Germany but the containment of the Soviet Union. In this respect at least hindsight must surely find that the British military planners were a great deal more realistic than the Foreign Office.

CHAPTER FORTY-FIVE

Warsaw

The first task facing the would-be conqueror of Europe was to complete the job begun in the forests of Katyn and dispose of potential Polish opposition in the form of its Home Army. This numbered between 100,000 and 500,000 men, loyal to their government-in-exile but capable of acting independently, especially now that it was known that the eastern territories of Poland had been negotiated away. Its offensive planning was dominated by the so-called Big Scheme, whereby Poland would liberate itself without the help of its Russian enemy. The rapid Soviet advance was making it clear that the Poles would have to move fast if they were to liberate Warsaw themselves. The sense of urgency increased when, on July 23, 1944, the Soviets established a Polish National Committee of Liberation in Lublin, evidently the nucleus of a future puppet government. In the meantime, there were signs of an imminent German retreat as banks, offices and army supply stores were evacuated. These factors combined to fan that special kind of Polish flame that has always been a focus for the despairing admiration of the rest of the world. As the Red Army commander Rokossovsky, himself of Polish descent, approached the city, a Soviet broadcast called the people of Warsaw to arms: "Poles, the time for freedom approaches! Poles take to arms! There is not a second to lose! Warsaw is shaken by the sounds of guns. Soviet units are engaged in an assault and are approaching Praga. People of Warsaw to arms! Throw out the German invader and take your freedom!"[1]

It seems harsh to judge the Polish commanders on the eve of one of their disastrous finest hours, yet they should have taken account of two newly arrived German armored divisions and of the recent fate of their officers. However, the call to honor and freedom proved irresistible, and on August 1 Warsaw rose in armed revolt. The rising occurred as the Polish prime minister and two colleagues were traveling to Moscow to discuss their country's future with Stalin. It would be surprising if that were a coincidence since one good reason for what now took place, or rather did not take place, would have been Stalin's wish to discredit the Polish leaders.

The Polish Home Army, lightly armed and scarcely trained, hit the Germans hard, causing up to eighty percent casualties in some units and pinning several divisions down for two months. The action would have been a spectacular success had Rokossovsky continued his advance, but by August 4 his guns were silent. The Red Army stopped fighting and settled down to watch. Churchill quickly expressed his apprehension to Eden, who tried to reassure him, observing that the War Office had explained that the Russian delay was caused by a German attack that had "surrounded and annihilated a Russian armoured division that was advancing on the city."[2] No other record of such an engagement, or indeed such a unit, has come to light. In the meantime, pro-Soviet sources, including the *Daily Worker*, were playing down the scale of the Polish action, reducing it to a series of desperate and ill-considered skirmishes. However, eyewitness accounts of the fighting came out by radio, and these described men, women and children fighting and destroying German tanks with Molotov cocktails and bare hands, while German units advanced behind screens of Polish children. As the Germans gradually regained control, the Poles took the fight to the sewers, the only channels of communication left between units cut off from one another on the ground.

Churchill made despairing appeals to Stalin to advance or at least to allow Allied aircraft to land behind his lines after dropping supplies. But Stalin declined to involve himself in the Poles' "reckless adventure" and greatly exaggerated the extent of Soviet attempts to make contact with the insurgents. Churchill wrote to Eden, expressing surprise at how little coverage the Polish struggle was being given in the British press and even wondered whether the Ministry of Information had put a stop on the story. Part of the answer lay with Beaverbrook, who took the view that: "Whatever the outcome of the tragedy, the friendship of Russia is far more important to us than the future of Anglo-Polish relations."[3]

Churchill also tried to secure the support of Roosevelt, who proved surprisingly lukewarm, while both State and War departments expressed concern at the pressure that Churchill was trying to put on Stalin. The State Department even urged Ambassador Harriman to content himself with establishing that the Soviets would not hinder Allied relief operations, even though these were impossible without their active cooperation.[4] Although it is hard to understand that stance, the president's paramount concern was to win the war at a minimum cost in American lives; this meant ensuring that the Soviet Union would eventually declare war on Japan—a concern that made the fate of Warsaw a lesser consideration.

Soviet attitudes changed somewhat in September; after six weeks of silence they started to shell German positions and even dropped some supplies, few of which got through. In the meantime, the house-to-house fighting continued until October 2, when the remnants of the army surrendered. Of the 1 million inhabitants of the city 200,000, including 15,000 combatants, had died. The Germans lost 17,000 killed, 9,000 wounded, while the city of Warsaw disappeared.

Of the various accounts of the rising, two will stand forever. The first is a telegram sent by the women of Warsaw to the pope:

> Most Holy Father, we Polish women in Warsaw are inspired by sentiments of profound patriotism and devotion to our country. For three weeks . . . we have lacked food and medicine. Warsaw is in ruins. The Germans are killing the wounded in hospitals. They are making women and children march in front of them in order to protect their tanks. There is no exaggeration in reports of children fighting and destroying tanks with bottles of petrol. . . . Holy Father, no one is helping us. The Russian armies, which have been for three weeks at the gates of Warsaw, have not advanced a step. The aid from Great Britain is insufficient. The world is ignorant of our fight. God alone is with us. Holy Father, Vicar of Christ, if you hear us, bless us Polish women, who are fighting for the church and for freedom.

The second is one of the last broadcasts to come out of the city:

> This is the stark truth. We were treated worse than Hitler's satellites, worse than Italy, Rumania, Finland. May God who is just pass judgment on the terrible injustice suffered by the Polish nation. . . .
>
> Your heroes are the soldiers whose only weapons against tanks, planes and guns were their revolvers and bottles filled with petrol. Your heroes are the women who tended the wounded and carried

messages under fire, who cooked in bombed and ruined cellars to feed children and adults and who soothed and comforted the dying. Your heroes are the children who went on quietly playing on the smoldering ruins. These are the people of Warsaw.

Immortal is the nation that can muster such universal heroism. For those who have died have conquered, and those who live on will fight on, will conquer and again bear witness that Poland lives where Poles live.

There may have been reasons for Rokossovsky's guns to have fallen silent for three weeks, but if so, they have not been produced. Stalin had everything to gain from acting as he did; little to lose. The very ferocity of the Polish onslaught suggests that he would have been wise to dispose of such potential enemies. Churchill's memoirs make no attempt to conceal the situation. His account suggests that he understood from the beginning and was powerless to do much more than appeal to Stalin's better feelings, especially since Roosevelt had made it clear that he would not countenance more drastic measures. Besides, there was little that Britain or the United States could have done. However, it should have become evident that Stalin had acted with a callous cynicism that was every bit as evil as any act of Hitler's. His actions should have made the scales fall from all eyes and brought about a sharp modification of Allied attitudes toward him and his country.

It did nothing of the sort. Once again Stalin had gambled on his assessment of his allies, and once again he had won. As with the case of the Moscow trials he recognized that "They'll swallow it." Considered from a distance of some forty years, the destruction of Warsaw seems to have been forgotten within the month, when Churchill traveled to Moscow for a third meeting with Stalin. Once again, as with Katyn, "Least said, soonest mended" appeared the order of the day. The failure of the Allies to respond to Stalin's astounding behavior and modify its attitudes remains one of the great puzzles of the war. To be fair, there was unofficial criticism of Stalin in Great Britain. A Conservative MP made a speech in which he described him as "a cold blooded realist who abandoned Warsaw in its hour of need, believing truth, honour and straight dealing to be bourgeois prejudices." G. M. Wilson observed of that speech: "The most objectionable point is the accusation against Marshal Stalin. That does seem to call for a rebuke. It would be safer to ignore . . . the denunciation of the betrayal of Warsaw."[5]

• • •

When Churchill and Eden visited Moscow in October, Stalin seems to have run rings around them once again. He sought to win Churchill over by appealing to his love of spectacle, inviting him to stand up alone in his box in the Bolshoi Theater to receive the ovation of the crowd. It was not like Stalin to encourage the acclaim of others, and one may presume that he did so in the hope that it would have a softening effect upon the prime minister. Apparently he succeeded, for the talks were conducted in a cordial atmosphere; Churchill felt the ties between himself and Stalin to be closer than ever. Although they were joined by the Polish premier, two members of his government and three representatives of the Lublin committee, no agreement was reached on Poland's future, and there was no discussion of its immediate past. At least it became clear to Churchill that the Lublin Poles were Moscow's stooges. However, Stalin deceived him once again by suggesting that both he and Molotov favored a soft line on Poland but that their hands were tied by other figures both military and political.[6] Once again the prime minister had been inadequately briefed on Stalin's situation.

Churchill reached agreement with Stalin on the extent of British and Soviet spheres of influence in the Balkans, enjoying himself as a latter-day Palmerston, apportioning percentages of each country's influence: equal in Yugoslavia and Hungary, ninety percent British in Greece, ninety percent Russian in Rumania and seventy-five percent Russian in Bulgaria. Stalin also agreed to permit the liberated countries to determine their own forms of government—a simple task after liberation at the hands of the Red Army and the NKVD. Churchill felt he had secured significant guarantees. Stalin knew that he had conceded nothing.

Churchill was gratified to discover that Stalin insisted major war criminals should only be executed after a trial, failing to observe that Stalin's turn of phrase made the outcome of such trials a foregone conclusion. He took this as an indication of a moral "ultrarespectability" in Stalin, having forgotten the forms that Soviet justice took. The meetings ended in a welter of goodwill, and the embassy cabled home: "One reason is an increase in friendship and cordiality on the part of the Russian leaders. The moral of this is that even if no perfect solution of the problems is achieved, reaction on Anglo-Soviet relations of failure to do so will not be so severe as it would have been. . . . The Russians are certainly concerned to maintain good relations with us."[7]

Churchill wrote to Stalin saying that he had come away "Refreshed and fortified by the discussions. . . . This memorable meeting . . . has

shown that there are no matters that cannot be adjusted . . . when we
meet together in frank and intimate discussion. . . . May we soon meet
again."[8]

In fact, the prime minister had come away with little except a guarantee for Greece. The Polish question remained unsettled, and a plan for
the trial of Nazi war criminals was scarcely a major issue. Stalin, on the
other hand, had learned that even in the aftermath of Warsaw, his allies
still wanted to be liked. As long as he continued to give the appearance
of doing so, he could proceed as he pleased in Eastern and Central
Europe.

• • •

Allied confidence, which had been high in October 1944, had been
jolted by the German offensive in the Ardennes. Soviet sources have
subsequently maintained that Stalin, with all the impulsive generosity of
a Jan Sobieski, or for that matter a Nicholas II, mounted a winter offensive ahead of schedule to rescue the Allies. Military historians in a position to be impartial do not agree. They point out that the German
offensive had already petered out before the Russians moved and that it
was the perfect time to attack since German forces in the east had been
depleted to mount the Ardennes offensive. Nevertheless, Stalin was able
to point to his action as tangible evidence of goodwill when he met
Churchill and Roosevelt again in Yalta in February 1945. (As late as the
preceding October there had been serious doubts in Allied circles about
Stalin's readiness to cross the German frontier, some planners fearing
that he would call a halt once he had driven the enemy from Polish
soil.[9])

The Allies were not in a strong position at Yalta. Their forces had not
yet crossed the Rhine, their scientists had not yet perfected the atomic
bomb, the German offensive had made them revise their estimates of
the duration of the war in Europe and the American military believed it
would still be fighting Japanese in 1947. The need to cajole Stalin into
declaring war on Japan as soon as Germany should be defeated was
considered paramount. Unfortunately this view was no secret, and even
had it been one, it is reasonable to assume that Communists in the
State Department would have brought it to Stalin's notice soon enough.
Alger Hiss, who attended the Yalta Conference, was deputy director of
the Office of Special Political Affairs at the time. (He went on to play a
leading role in the San Francisco Conference, at which the United
Nations was established. So popular was he with the Soviets that in

September 1945 they tried to secure his appointment as the first secretary-general of that organization.[10]) Thus, on the eve of Yalta, Stalin held all the cards. Not only were Churchill and Roosevelt in the position of indebted supplicants, but it was already clear that Soviet forces would soon be in command of Poland, Czechoslovakia, the Baltic states and a considerable slice of Germany, while the Allies had yet to cross the Rhine.

There were further complications. Both President Roosevelt and Harry Hopkins were sick men. Moreover, Roosevelt, who had been inaugurated for his fourth term some days before the conference and had had a number of official engagements, was virtually unprepared for it and had traveled with a State Department briefing file which remained unopened.[11] Churchill and Eden had hoped to have preliminary talks with him before meeting Stalin, but this proved impossible.[12] In the event, the Yalta Conference was not the sellout that it has sometimes been termed. It is true that the chief issue was Poland and that Churchill and Roosevelt were prepared to countenance a shift of Polish frontiers toward the west. However, after talks that produced nearly 20,000 words of written record, an agreement of sorts was reached on the constitution of the Polish government. Although the dominant role of the Lublin Poles was temporarily acknowledged, it was agreed that free elections would be held soon and that members of parties other than the Communist party would participate in the government of Poland and other liberated countries. The Big Three all agreed that democratic institutions would be installed in the liberated territories.

It might be argued that any agreement implying power sharing with Communists was unrealistic. As Charles Bohlen put it, "A non-Communist premier with Communist ministers would be like a woman trying to stay half pregnant."[13] The Allied advisers had forgotten their Bolshevik history and the speed with which Lenin's party disposed of its political associates in 1918. Moreover, no attempt seems to have been made to explore the substantive differences in what Soviets and Westerners meant by the term democracy. Roosevelt and, to a lesser degree perhaps, Churchill breathed a sigh of relief when they were promised free elections and did not press for controls to ensure that they really would be free. In that sense the Yalta Agreement was a sellout. Certainly that is how it appeared to some senior American naval officers, erstwhile members of the Russian nobility, who had once played as children in the imperial and grand ducal palaces in which they were now staying. One of them "described Roosevelt as being 'mesmerised' by Stalin. He thought he could win him over by agreeing to everything. Europe was written off as easily as slivers of cake. They moved matches round on the map. It made you shiver *[Zhutko bylo]*. The Russians were amazed at what they had achieved, for they had been prepared for arduous bargaining and they got it all for nothing."[14]

But as far as Eastern Europe was concerned, the Allies had nothing to bargain with. All they could, and did, do was ask Stalin to be kind, to relent and, for example, let the Poles keep Lwow; an approach which did not work. Stalin had no intention of giving an inch on the issue of Poland. The 150,000 Poles under arms might have been fighting for many things, but a free Poland fit for heroes to live in was no longer one of them. Stalin assured his allies that Polish hostility to Russians evaporated once they were liberated by the Red Army.[15]

Yet Stalin did make concessions at Yalta, notably on the design of a future UN. He no longer insisted that all Soviet republics be individually represented. He agreed to the French's being granted a zone of occupation in Germany and a place on the Allied Control Commission. He accepted an American position on postwar reparations. However, he also won important concessions in the Far East as the price of declaring war upon Japan, namely, the Japanese half of the island of Sakhalin, the port of Dairen, a naval base at Port Arthur and the Kuril Islands. He also secured the repatriation of all Soviet nationals in Allied hands.

The sorry story of the "victims of Yalta" has been told with sufficient eloquence not to require repeating here. However, Stalin's motives call for comment. He knew Russian history well enough to understand that the army returning from Alexander I's invasion of Europe in 1815 brought back with it political unrest and serious destabilizing influences. He had no intention of permitting history to repeat itself, which is why he treated anyone of suspect loyalty who had had experience of Europe with particular severity. This was a "prophylactic measure" designed to render potential enemies and infiltrators harmless. Thus ex-POWs would discover, on their release from German camps, as had their predecessors after the Winter War, that they had simply exchanged one prison for another; survivors of the most vicious death camps, such as Auschwitz, were dealt with especially harshly, their survival being suspect in itself. It was also in Stalin's interests to secure the return of the thousands of actual traitors, who had collaborated with the enemy, some out of conviction, most in order to stay alive. It has been calculated that by the end of the war there were more than 1 million *Hilfswillige (Hiwis)*, or Soviet volunteers serving in German Army and

SS units.[16] It was inconceivable that Stalin would permit treason on such a scale to go unpunished or allow proven traitors to remain at liberty beyond his frontiers. As the Soviet ambassador in Paris put it, "No nation consists exclusively of heroes, but the motherland would not be a mother if she did not love all her family, even the black sheep. Therefore all our citizens abroad will be received home."[17]

The agreement called for the return of all military personnel, all Soviet citizens in liberated countries and all citizens captured in German uniform. Whereas the Americans were prepared to treat these as Germans should they resist repatriation, the British were not.

Thanks to Lord Bethell and Count Nikolai Tolstoy, we know that the British implemented the policy of repatriation with a zeal beyond the call of duty, even though the Foreign Office soon realized that batches of returnees were being shot at their disembarkation points. Once again the names of Wilson and Brimelow feature among the more zealous executors of the policy. For example, we find Wilson anxious to muzzle the press in the case of three Soviet citizens who had committed suicide to avoid repatriation. He suggests the press be told that they had collaborated with the enemy and that "This is in fact probably true."[18] The worst case of all concerns the Andronov family. The couple had married in Germany during the war, had a child, were in love and due to be repatriated, separately. Mrs. Andronov sent the Foreign Office letters beseeching it not to send her husband back, letters that even made an official suggest they be allowed to escape, a suggestion quashed by Wilson. Finally the wife and child were allowed to remain while the husband was returned. The file, with the pleas of the wife and the cold decisions of civil servants, constitutes a pocket of pain tucked away in the Public Record Office, as awful to read today as it was when first put together forty years ago. The last word was with Wilson, who minuted: "We shall only get into the most hopeless muddle if we decide cases of this nature on humanitarian grounds and not on the facts as we know them."

Yalta now appears a one-sided affair in which Stalin got what he wanted. He was eager to enter the war with Japan anyway, needing no inducement to expand to the east as he was expanding to the west. He had no intention of observing even the letter, let alone the spirit, of his undertakings on occupied Europe. The French zone of occupation was to be carved from the Allied sectors and would not diminish his own gains. In return for his sending back a modest number of Allied POWs, whom he would probably have returned anyway, he was to receive more than 1 million traitors and potential enemies. It is true that he had outnegotiated the others, but this was scarcely surprising since he was negotiating from strength.

Yet the speeches he made at banquets, the impression he conveyed were not that of a leader about to stab his allies in the back. It is true that there is nothing remarkable about his responding to Churchill's flowery rhetoric with the compliment that a man like the prime minister was to be found only once in a hundred years. He lost nothing by thanking President Roosevelt for the invaluable help lend-lease had given the Soviet war effort. Yet across the years such speeches do more than strike a note of conventional goodwill to match those of Churchill and Roosevelt. It was as if, for a moment, Stalin really did look upon the other two as allies, fellow members of the Big Three, as if that inferiority complex which is the source of Russian chauvinism and insecurity had lifted for a moment and he realized that his country truly was a superpower, with a rightful place at the top table, and as if, briefly, that new realization mellowed him and made him adopt something close to the language of a statesman, as he said:

> I am talking as an old man, that is why I am talking so much, but I want to drink to our alliance, that it should not lose its character of intimacy, its free expression of views. In the history of diplomacy I know of no such close alliance of three Great Powers as this, when allies had the opportunity of so frankly expressing their views. . . . I propose a toast to the firmness of our Three Power Alliance. May it be strong and stable, may we be as frank as possible. [19]

While it should by now be obvious that no one was a more successful deceiver than Stalin, instinct, which is sometimes all a biographer can go on, senses that here Stalin briefly struck a different sort of note. There is an emphasis on friendship among equals, something which he never knew before and which suggests that he attached real value to the new intimacy he had found with his opposite numbers, so much in contrast with his habitual isolation. He sustained the note when continuing with a sensible warning. Shortly after Churchill had toasted him as a mighty leader of a mighty nation "whose people had driven tyrants from her soil," he replied: "It is not so difficult to keep unity in time of war, since the joint aim is to defeat the common enemy. The difficult time will come after the war when diverse interests tend to divide allies. It is our duty to see that our relations in peace time are as strong as they have been in war."[20] Stalin seems to have believed, if only for a moment, that some kind of cooperation with the Allies would be possible. If he had wanted to deceive them, there was no need for the warning note; better to let them bask in their illusory friendship. Although Stalin would never consider sacrificing a material advantage in the interests of cooperation, it would appear, at least in the flush of the banquet and its accompanying oratory, that some kind of cooperation in the future did not seem impossible. The prospect was more than enough to cause the conference to break up in a glow of euphoria. As Harry Hopkins put it, "We really believed in our hearts that this was the dawn of the new day we had all been praying for . . . that we had won the first great victory of the peace. . . . The Russians had proved that they could be reasonable and far seeing, and there wasn't any doubt in the minds of the President or any of us that we could live with them and get along with them peacefully for as far into the future as any of us could imagine."[21]

Among the private papers of Secretary of State Edward Stettinius, now with the University of Virginia, is a short letter congratulating him on the magnificent job he did at the Yalta Conference. The letter is from Alger Hiss.

CHAPTER FORTY-SIX

Not a Few Blunders

The honeymoon, such as it was, was short-lived. In the following months it became obvious that Stalin was pursuing his own foreign policy. One component entailed continuing cooperation with his allies, but this would be ruthlessly sacrificed to the creation of a security ring of satellite states and to the penetration of other countries through the abuse of democratic processes by local Communist parties—for example, the cynical take-over of Rumania. This made it obvious that certain aspects of the Yalta Agreement were already a dead letter.

The Allies should also have been alarmed by the behavior of the Red Army liberators. From Yugoslavia to Poland their motto seems to have been "When in Rome, do as the Vandals do." Their treatment of friend and foe was acknowledged by the citizens of liberated Budapest, who rechristened a Red Army monument to the Unknown Soldier "To the Unknown Rapist."[1] Milovan Djilas complained to Stalin about his army's looting and raping, only to be told that the soldiers were entitled to some fun.[2] In Czechoslovakia there were numerous instances of looting and gunpoint conscription into labor battalions, while women of all ages, nuns included, ran daily risk of rape at the hands of Red Army men, drunk and sober.[3] When the army reached Germany, it was told to treat the population as it pleased. The Red Army was master—judge, executioner and avenger rolled into one. The men behaved accordingly, killing, raping and looting on a majestic scale. One airman recalls flying over German villages: "We saw houses, whole villages even, hidden from view beneath a feathery mist from ripped pillows and eiderdowns. And all along the highways the fields were sown with multi-coloured rags of discarded loot."[4]

The airman maintained that the initiative for atrocities, which included tossing young children into burning buildings, came from the top, a view confirmed by Stalin's daughter, who states that her father encouraged his armies to lay Europe waste and took great pleasure in so doing.[5] His motives were more complex and more calculated than mere revenge. True, he was rewarding his fighting men, but he was also developing hatred. By encouraging them to misbehave in conquered and liberated territories, he ensured that they would be hated by their inhabitants, that there would be no fraternization and consequent corruption of his armies. Moreover, the looting of Europe ensured the destruction of a world offering the image of a better life. In *August 1914* Solzhenitsyn uses his experience as a soldier invading East Prussia in 1945, astounded by the standard of living enjoyed by Prussian peasants, who had brick houses with running water and curtains and whose farm buildings were finer than any equivalent Russian home. By encouraging the destruction of that world, Stalin appealed to that timeless Russian sense of cultural inferiority and spiritual superiority which always colored his country's views of the West, appealed to Russian chauvinism and delight in drunken excess, the imposition of warm Russian chaos upon cold Prussian order.

The Soviet failure to abide by the spirit of the Yalta Agreement was already beginning to make Churchill despair and had even caused the dying Roosevelt to have doubts. He was disturbed by some vituperative telegrams sent by Stalin, accusing the Americans and British of doing a deal with Marshal Kesselring, who would open the western front to them and let them move east. However, the matter was cleared up, and Roosevelt's last telegram to Churchill expressed the view that "I would minimize the general Soviet problem as much as possible because these problems, in one form or another, seem to arise every day, and most of them straighten out, as in the case of the Berne meeting. We must be firm, however, and our course thus far is correct."[6]

Almost within an hour of dictating this the president was dead.

The Red Army had started its 1945 winter offensive with an overwhelming superiority in numbers, fifteen to one on the ground, twenty to one in the air according to Guderian.[7] They began their onslaught with suicide squads of lightly armed penal battalions.[8] Not even Guderian's men could hold their positions for long against such opposition, and the Soviets advanced quickly on a broad front, led by their three most famous marshals, Rokossovsky, Konev and Zhukov. Within three weeks they had advanced between 200 and 300 miles, but on February 2 they came to a halt within thirty miles of Berlin. It has been claimed that Stalin delayed the final battle for the capital until he could be sure of victory, and Zhukov himself subsequently defended the decision not to press an attack home, irrelevantly recalling Tukhachevsky's defeat at the gates of Warsaw. In the meantime, Stalin's armies were advancing in Hungary, Austria and Czechoslovakia, while in Germany he seems to have engaged in a game of bluff with the Allied supreme commander, General Eisenhower. Eisenhower proposed a main line of Anglo-American advance along an axis to the south of Berlin, while sending Montgomery north to the Elbe (he hoped to prevent the Russians from liberating Denmark). Only then would he go on to capture Berlin. Unwisely Eisenhower communicated his intentions to Stalin, who agreed with his view that Berlin no longer had any strategic significance. Thereupon he ordered Zhukov and Konev to make all haste to capture it. Churchill's urgent representation of the importance of an Anglo-American capture of Berlin was ignored, and the Red Army had the glory of taking both Berlin and Vienna. On May 2 the German Army surrendered. Ever cautious, Stalin delayed announcing the victory for several hours. In Murmansk Allied ships were already dressed in their flags and sounding their sirens in triumph. When a Soviet tanker followed suit, it was reprimanded by a Soviet destroyer captain with the classic observation: "The Party will inform you when the war is over."[9]

Although they had failed to take Berlin, British and American forces had advanced far beyond the line of demarcation between their own and the Soviet zones, and many of the troops wanted to remain there. Churchill was eager to gain what advantages he could from the territory they had won, to apply pressure on Stalin in matters such as free elections for Poland. For once the Allies had a respectable hand to play. However, on the advice of the State and War departments President Truman, understandably committed to continuing Roosevelt's policies, suggested the troops be withdrawn without seeking a quid pro quo. On May 12, 1945, Churchill, greatly alarmed, wrote to him to say: "An iron curtain is drawn upon [the Russian] front. There seems little doubt that the whole of the region east of the line Lübeck-Corfu will soon be completely in their hands. . . . To this must be added the further enormous area conquered by the American armies, which will, I suppose, in a few weeks be occupied by the Russian power."

Harry Hopkins took the view that the Yalta Agreement would have to be honored and good faith demonstrated, while no one wanted to involve U.S. forces in further European adventures; they should be either brought home or used against Japan. Accordingly Truman replied that he was "unable to delay the withdrawal of U.S. troops from the Soviet Zone in order to use pressure in the settlement of other problems." Those sympathizing with Truman's decision have argued that the British and Americans might never have reached agreement with the Soviets on Berlin and Vienna had the withdrawal not taken place, and this may be true. However, it is undeniable that Stalin, in the same position, would never have dreamed of withdrawing without a quid pro quo, and the surprising failure of the Allies to seek one must have reinforced him in the opinion that dealing with them was like taking pennies from the blind. It was even obvious to ordinary Russians that Stalin was robbing the Allies. A popular saying had it that "the Allies were like a woman—the more you beat her the more she loves you."[10]

Stalin made no secret of his intention to impose Soviet rule upon the territories he had won. He made this clear to Djilas, although, since the latter was a believing Communist, Stalin stressed that it was ideology that he was exporting by force of arms: "Stalin repeatedly told us that Communism was to be spread by Soviet power. . . . There was no other reliable or desirable means. He had a missionary feeling about this but at heart he was motivated by Russian nationalism." Stalin understood the unique nature of conquest in World War II. It would not end like other wars with erstwhile enemies and allies trading territory at a peace conference: "This war is not as in the past; whoever occupies a territory also imposes on it his own social system. Everyone imposes his system as far as his army has the power to do so."[11] He made his attitude to adjacent countries dramatically clear in a further conversation in which he informed the Yugoslavs that he had no objection to their "Swallowing Albania. . . . At this he gathered together the fingers of his right hand and bringing them to his mouth made as if to swallow them." Djilas, an honorable man, was horrified by the naked cynicism of Stalin's gesture and observed that his country desired unification, not swallowing, to which Molotov gave the significant rejoinder "That *is* swallowing."[12]

•   •   •

On the day the surrender was signed Stalin broadcast to the nation once again:

He spoke briefly with assurance; his voice betrayed no emotions and he addressed us not as Brothers and Sisters but as Men, Women, Compatriots. . . . I thought about Stalin's speech. His lack of warmth grieved but didn't surprise me. He was the Generalissimo, the victor. What use had he for emotion? People listening to the speech shouted in reverent admiration, "Hurrah for Stalin!" This had long since ceased to astonish me. I had grown accustomed to the fact that there were people with their joys and sorrows, and that somewhere above there was Stalin.[13]

On May 24, 1945, at a reception in honor of Red Army commanders, Stalin made his most famous speech of all:

Our government made not a few blunders; there were moments of desperation in 1941 and 1942 when our army retreated, abandoned our native villages and cities . . . because it had no choice. Another nation might have said to the government, 'You have not justified our expectations, get out; we will set up a new government which will sign a peace with Germany and give us repose.' But the Russian people did not take that road because it had faith in the policy of its government. Thank you, great Russian people for your trust.[14]

This is a revealing passage. Reading its "subtext," we find confirmed the conviction that made Stalin push his head into the sand in 1941: that a foreign invasion would bring his regime down overnight. He could not believe that anyone would be stupid enough to lay down his life in its support. Knowing what we do of Stalin, we can imagine that he was secretly smiling as he proposed the toast to his people; gratitude, it will be recalled, was a dog's disease. But less important than what he may have felt is the way he phrased his thanks. "Russian" and "Soviet" are not synonyms, and here Stalin was proposing his thanks not to the citizens of the USSR but to Russians, and the phrase *great Russian people (velikomu russkomu narodu)* is uncomfortably close to *Great Russian people (veliko-russkomu narodu).*

Stalin's wish to be more Russian than the Russians, his colonial inferiority complex come to a peak here, with an insult to the millions of non-Russians under arms, for Stalin made no secret of his lack of faith in their fighting abilities. The speech initiated the persecution and deportation of entire nations which Stalin considered to have behaved disloyally during the war and was aimed in particular at the Ukrainians, whom Stalin, with good reason, suspected of separatist aspirations. As

Beria observed, the only reason that they, too, were not deported was because they were too many. The speech also sets the tone for the strident Great Russian chauvinism, anti-Semitism and persecution of minorities that marked the Soviet Union's postwar years.

Recognizing that the army offered a potential threat, Stalin increased control over it at every level of command in the latter stages of the war. He arranged for the cult to stress his role as its commander in chief, thereby gratifying long-thwarted military ambitions. These were further rewarded in June, when he promoted himself to the hitherto-unknown rank of generalissimo. A growing prominence was now given to his role as the architect of victory, while the "mistakes" he had once alluded to, not to mention the millions of victims of those mistakes, were allowed to fade into the background. Gradually the war was presented as having been "necessary," as opposed to a nation's giving its lifeblood to redeem the blindness and incompetence of its leaders. Commanders such as Zhukov had their importance diminished, although the Soviet government's refusal to allow the latter to accept an honorary degree from Cambridge University was not part of that process.

For all its horrors, to many Soviet citizens the war seemed the only honorable thing to have happened since the Revolution; they saw it as grounds for true pride, the triumph of courage and human decency. It also altered attitudes to Stalin. The writer Viktor Nekrasov, who was about to win a Stalin Prize for his novel *In the Trenches of Stalingrad* and who had until recently been a frontline soldier, told me that for him, and many like him, Stalin seemed to have redeemed himself by his victory and that whatever his past misdeeds, bygones should now be bygones. He was, Nekrasov observed, admired for having hoodwinked the Allies and secured such a good deal for his country by "swallowing" large portions of Europe. Victory also brought the widespread hope that things would now be different. People expected the future to be brighter; terror and oppression would diminish and real changes come about. Some thought that Zhukov might take over, or at the least persuade Stalin to decollectivize, since agriculture was in such a catastrophic condition. There was also the hope among the intelligentsia that there would be an improvement in foreign relations, and a modus vivendi established with the West. The best rendering of the victory mood is to be found in the last paragraphs of *Doctor Zhivago*, where characters feel that they have come through terrible ordeals, but that now it was all going to get better. Mistakes had been made, but everyone had the chance of a fresh start. The mood did not last long.

CHAPTER FORTY-SEVEN

Peacemaking

It was at the Potsdam Conference of July 1945 that the remaining scales fell from most Allied eyes, as Stalin, feeling further pretense to be unnecessary, abandoned the role of benign Uncle Joe. Some scales were still in place on the conference eve as senior diplomats discussed Russia's intentions: whether it wanted to "join the Western club but was suspicious" or was out to dominate the world.[1] That the question should have been raised at all, let alone raised in that form, is an indication of the ignorance that persisted at the highest levels. Stalin now did much to dispel it. Newsreel footage of his first meeting with Churchill and Truman is revealing. Stalin strides into the conference room carrying a briefcase, which he tosses onto the table with an unmistakably dominant air, making it clear that he is the strong man of the trio. His self-confidence emerged in other ways. For the first time in front of his allies Stalin indulged his cold sense of humor. Discussing the fate of the German fleet with Truman and Churchill, Stalin proposed they split it three ways, a suggestion which elicited an impassioned speech from the prime minister, who proposed that these were engines of destruction that should be sent to the bottom of the sea. After the peroration Stalin observed laconically, "Let us divide them anyway, and if Mr. Churchill wishes he can sink his share."[2]

At a plenary session on July 22 at which the fate of Poland was discussed again, Churchill attempted a defense of the rights of Polish Catholics. According to Admiral Leahy, Stalin reflected for a moment, stroking his mustache, and then asked the prime minister in a hard, even tone: "How many divisions has the Pope?"[3] Stalin enjoyed teasing

Churchill, which did not prevent the prime minister, even now, from observing to Eden that "I like that man."[4] The finest example of Stalin's sense of humor is the practical joke he played upon President Truman. Truman had invited Stalin to dinner. Wishing to provide appropriate entertainment, he inquired who Stalin's favorite composer was. Stalin let it be known that it was Chopin. Truman arranged to have a pianist play mazurkas and polonaises to Stalin as he dined. Stalin, who had never displayed the slightest interest in Chopin, must have enjoyed listening to him during the conference which finally extinguished any flicker of hope for a free Poland. Yet he kept the joke to himself; his sense of humor was never flamboyant.

In the perceptive eyes of George Kennan, the conference was a disaster since so many of its conclusions were unrealistic. The plan for joint administration of Germany was unworkable, and the agreement that "democratic" principles would be observed failed to explore the various meanings of that term. He was also appalled by the decision to try Nazi war criminals with the participation of Soviet judges; when it came to "crimes against humanity," the USSR could easily hold its own with Nazi Germany. Mr. Kennan was no less scathing about the cession of Königsberg to the USSR because of its "need for an ice-free port." The USSR did not want for ice-free ports in the Baltic, while Königsberg was far from ice-free.[5]

Churchill, who attended the first part of the conference before losing the general election and yielding his place to the Labour leader Clement Attlee, still seems to have considered Soviet claims in terms of "natural justice." He could see why Stalin should want to control the straits of the Bosporus and have a warm-water port in the Mediterranean. He also accepted that he was entitled to an interest in Lebanon.[6] Even now Churchill seemed prepared to negotiate on the basis of right rather than might. Nevertheless, for all the reservations we may have about Potsdam, the Allies did not give way on every issue. Admittedly they were obliged to accept unilateral decisions on Eastern Europe, but they refused to recognize Soviet-backed puppet regimes in the Balkans, rejected Stalin's claims to the Dardanelles and his call for a share in the industry of the Ruhr and declined to sever diplomatic relations with Spain. Looking back on Potsdam, Admiral Leahy found it marked a dispiriting new beginning. It had brought "into sharp world focus the struggle of two great ideas—the Anglo-Saxon democratic principles of government and the aggressive and expansionist police state tactics of Stalinist Russia. It was the beginning of the 'cold war.'"[7]

For President Truman it was the moment when he first understood what he was up against:

> Anxious as we were to have Russia in the war against Japan the experience at Potsdam now made me determined that I would not allow the Russians any part in the control of Japan. Our experience with them in Germany, Bulgaria, Rumania, Hungary and Poland was such that I intended to take no chances. . . . Force is the only thing the Russians understand. And while I was hopeful that Russia might some day be persuaded to work for peace, I knew that the Russians should not be allowed to get into . . . control of Japan.[8]

Yet it is wrong to date the start of the cold war from Potsdam; this was merely the moment when it was recognized that such a war was going on. Stalin had not suddenly changed the direction of his foreign policy; this had been consistent from the moment the Soviet Union invaded Georgia in 1921. Whenever it found itself in a position to absorb or dominate a weaker neighbor it did so, thereby thickening the security belt around the Russian heartland. Moreover, Admiral Leahy was wrong to envisage the cold war as a confrontation between conflicting ideologies, although this is how it is usually portrayed in the West. Such a view fails to recognize the peculiar role played by ideology in the Soviet mind: Ideology as such is unimportant. A country on another planet that successfully built communism according to Marx, and that had no contact with the Soviet Union, would be considered an irrelevance even though its existence might vindicate Marx's theories. The value of ideology lies in its role as a legitimizing framework for Soviet policies. Since the teachings of Marx will triumph because they are true, any Soviet action must be correct because it is carried out in the light of those teachings. Thus the cold war never was, nor could be, the counterpart of, say, a clash between Christendom and Islam. It was merely the attempt by one superpower to contain another, one that functioned according to the principle found in the well-known Russian proverb "Take when they give; when they beat you, run."

During the conference Truman and Churchill learned that the atom bomb was finally considered viable. They did not know how to explain it to Stalin, for fear of a possible demand that they share its secret with him. In the event, they concerned themselves needlessly. As President Truman put it, "On July 24th I casually mentioned to Stalin that we had a new weapon of special destructive force. The Russian Premier showed no unusual interest. All he said was that he was glad to hear it and hoped we would make "good use of it against the Japanese."9 Although his reaction has been interpreted as a failure to grasp the importance of Truman's communication, it is more likely that Stalin was playing his cards close to the chest. Many of the team working on the Manhattan Project were German physicists with left-wing sympathies, who had emigrated in the wake of Hitler's assumption of power. It is quite possible that one of their number provided Soviet agents with an inkling of the nature of their work, especially since, as Secretary of State Stettinius put it, "During the weeks just before the Big Three Conference at Yalta considerable Soviet intelligence activity was reported to be taking place on our West Coast. From these reports it was my definite impression that the Russians certainly had an indication of what was taking place [i.e., at Alamogordo]. At no time however did the Russians ever raise with the State Department the question of our atomic research."10

Stalin's lack of curiosity suggests that he knew about the bomb already and was not about to give that knowledge away.

Among the millions of corpses to be laid at Stalin's door, one might include the inhabitants of Hiroshima and Nagasaki. For Stalin might have prevented the dropping of the two atomic bombs. He failed to pass on two Japanese offers of surrender that had been made to him for transmission to the Americans. He also attempted to delay Allied warnings to the Japanese to capitulate, for the excellent reason that he wished to make territorial gains in Asia. Had Stalin relayed the Japanese peace overtures, it is just conceivable that the atom bombs would never have been used, for all the British and American eagerness to see what their new weapon would do. The first bomb was dropped on August 6; the second, two days later. The following day, August 9, the Russians declared war, and hostilities ceased on August 14. By December of that year the Russians were showing a film of their victory in the East which featured the Japanese signing terms of surrender with no victors other than Russians in sight.

George Kennan has argued that Stalin was the only statesman of the age to understand the value and limitations of the new weapon. Just because it had ended the Japanese war, it was not the devastating strategic threat that others assumed it to be. Stalin observed in an interview:

> I do not consider the atom bomb such an important force as some politicians are inclined to think. The bomb is destined to intimidate

people with weak nerves, but it cannot decide the outcome of a war; atom bombs are far from efficient for that. Of course exclusive possession of the bomb's secret creates a threat but against it at least two remedies exist. a) The secret cannot remain one for long. b) The use of the bomb will be ruled out.[11]

Stalin's grasp of the scope of the new weapon and its consequent strategies was astonishingly realistic, anticipating some forty years of nuclear standoff (the bomb would not even be used in Korea). Admittedly he arrived at it as someone who had never allowed the "fear of cockroaches" or, for that matter, of megadeaths to stand in his way.

•   •   •

If Moscow represents Bolshevism we must certainly look for something better.

—Lord Alanbrooke

Conditions in postwar Russia were terrible. Once again much of the population was living in holes in the ground. The entire nation seemed to be on the move, in search of work and food, which was desperately short and only to be had through unofficial markets.[12] In the cities the rule of law ceased at nightfall. Prostitution and hooliganism were everywhere. For example, in Odessa organized gangs, often disguised as militiamen, would ransack apartments or hold up cars at gunpoint.[13] A British Embassy official explained such behavior by the lack of any form of welfare system to assist demobilized soldiers and others whose lives had been dislocated by the war. Since those at the "base of the pyramid" had no vote, and no one accountable to them, they were left to survive as best they could.

The best was not good, as embassy reports bear witness. A factory director in the Urals complained in his cups that the Soviet Union was a slave state with grinding poverty and total lack of culture. Before the Revolution a worker would look at his pay and say, "Not enough for boots, too much for bread, just right for vodka," and nothing had changed.[14] There are reports of peasants in western Russia living on potatoes, salt and hot water, while in Siberia army men were deserting in droves and slipping away to join seminomadic tribes rather than obey their orders to put down the widespread peasant mutinies.[15] An American vice-consul traveling from Moscow to Vladivostok gained a dreadful impression of the "universal, grinding hopeless poverty of the

Russian people. Russian poverty has often been described as Asiatic. . . . But it seems to me that it can also be compared to the Negro. If a chair-leg breaks the chair is repaired, but only enough so it will stand again. . . . The same with a leaky roof, carelessly mended with paper or cloth, not permanently repaired. This is a poverty not only of shortages but also of tradition, ignorance, improvidence, laziness and hopelessness."[16]

The situation in the Ukraine was worse. It will be recalled that the occupation had not been universally unpopular, especially as it had brought a temporary end to collectivization. Now agriculture broke down under attempts to restore the collective system, producing terrible famine and the third outbreak of cannibalism in twenty-five years. A friend of mine was then teaching in an elementary school; noting after the summer vacation that one of his pupils was missing, he asked her sister about her, to be placidly informed that in the course of the summer she had died and been eaten. Famine was compounded by fierce resistance to the restoration of Soviet rule, resistance that Stalin countered by dismissing a number of officials for malpractice and incompetence and sending in the army.[17] So violent was the fighting that the troops considered themselves on active service.

Thomas Brimelow's comments on a Ukrainian defector's report of postwar conditions are curious. Brimelow denied the existence of the famine or even the fact that Ukrainian children bore signs of undernourishment, while dismissing the claim that party members received better rations than ordinary mortals. His defense went further still: Playing down the number of political prisoners and the injustice of Soviet police procedures, he stated, "I know of at least a dozen people who have emerged from the Lubyanka after questioning." A factual and accurate account of conditions in Moscow and the Ukraine was discredited with comments such as "How does he know?"; "Can this be checked?"; "Poppycock!"[18] His Majesty's government and its minister of food, John Strachey, also felt it appropriate to suppress news of the Soviet shortages, notably the Ukrainian famine, which is an even less well-known chapter in Soviet history than the famine of 1933.[19]

Despite the devastation of the war and all the lost housing and industry, we find Stalin launching one of the more curious features of mature Stalinism: grandiose architectural enterprises. It is now that the series of skyscrapers, or "many-story buildings," such as Moscow State University, begin to go up—another manifestation of Stalin's pharaonic side. He shared Hitler's love of ambitious building without taking it to the extreme of the Führer's wilder dreams. However, he took personal interest in the new enterprises, one reflected on the façade of the Moskva Hotel. Its architect submitted to Stalin a design showing two treatments of the front elevation, leaving him to choose the one he preferred. To his dismay he discovered that Stalin had signed across the line dividing the two designs, making it impossible to tell which one he had chosen. The architect was far too frightened to ask him; Stalin was notorious for the frenzies which any questioning of his architectural decisions provoked.[20] The fear he could inspire was so great that his office staff allegedly kept materials handy to clean up anyone who lost control of his bladder or sphincter in the Presence. Rather than risk choosing the wrong design, the enterprising architect employed both, which is why to this day the hotel sports a divided façade, reflecting the impact of terror upon the arts.

The postwar years saw a return of that blind Russian chauvinism already known to visitors in the sixteenth century, a sense of moral, spiritual and now also technical superiority. It manifested itself through the conviction that every wonder of the modern world, beginning with the metro, had been invented by Russians. It was impossible to persuade the citizens of Moscow that other cities also had underground transportation systems.[21] Admittedly it was true that there was only one metro in the Soviet Union, and in that sense it was unique (although at the height of the purges when prison cells were bursting, accommodation beneath the plank beds that lined cell walls was also known as the metro). These years saw a remarkable flowering of *pokazukha*, as the Soviet Union laid claim to the discovery of atomic energy, the jet engine, radio, radar, the South Pole and baseball; other inventions included the telephone, telegraph and penicillin.

One is reminded of the adoring, simpleminded mother of the writer Nikolai Gogol, who ascribed to him numerous masterpieces written by others and was not averse to suggesting that he was also responsible for the invention of the steam engine. Yet there was more here than simplemindedness. Stalin understood that too many of his citizens had seen too many Western achievements, such as the cans of American corned beef that had fed them during the war and the Studebaker trucks that had made the invasion of Europe possible, not to mention the jeep, the mud-penetrating qualities of which won the admiration of the entire Red Army. It was in Stalin's interest to persuade his nation of its superiority, fostering the image of Russia as the cradle of invention. The preposterous claims he encouraged were accepted, partly because it would be madness not to, mostly because people wanted to believe them, just as they wanted to believe that theirs was the only metro in the world.

This was a promotion of Russian, not Soviet, chauvinism, in the spirit of conservative, xenophobic and introspective old Muscovy. Indeed, the celebration of Muscovy became a prominent feature of domestic policy. To commemorate the eight hundredth anniversary of the city's foundation on September 7, 1947, Stalin published a remarkable "Salute to Moscow" which described it as having thrice liberated Russia from the foreign yoke and saw it as the symbol of a certain kind of government: "Moscow is great because it initiated the creation of a centralised Russian state."[22] It was "by the will of the great Lenin" that it became Russia's capital once again. He went on to celebrate its rebuilding and the elimination of its slums to be replaced by "many-story buildings." Stalin's salute to the capital associates Moscow, centralization and the massive new architecture, brought together with the "great Lenin" in a passage vital to his conception of the state.

The emphasis on Muscovite chauvinism was accompanied by political tightening. Not only did Stalin imprison the stream of ex-POWs and refugees returned by the Allies, but he also made energetic and successful attempts to lure back émigrés from the time of the civil war, who had settled in America and the Far East. They were told that all was forgiven, that they were free to return and bring their personal wealth with them. Those accepting his invitation were separated from that wealth as soon as they set foot on native soil; they would not be needing it in the gulag.

The British Foreign Office knew all about the gulag by now. It had been sent a wide-ranging account of it by the U.S. Embassy, which had debriefed an American ex-Communist who had escaped from Siberia to Alaska in 1946.[23] The absence of skeptical comment shows that the report was believed, yet no attempt was made to publicize it at a time when Soviet sympathizers were hotly denying that labor camps existed.[24] We find the same attitude adopted toward Stalin's mass deportation of "suspect" nations: Crimean Tartars, Chechen, Ingush. A junior Foreign Office official suggested that Stalin's behavior and his war with the Ukrainian nationalists be used as a basis for anti-Soviet propaganda; at a time when the Soviet press was praising gallant Indonesian freedom fighters, it would do no harm to point out that the Soviet Union had freedom fighters of its own. Brimelow dismissed the suggestion: "We cannot praise the people who supported the enemy against their own country, our ally." As for the notion that Stalin's deportation of nations and his annexation of East Prussia and the western Ukraine could be used as propaganda, Brimelow wrote: "I doubt it. The absorption of E. Prussia and the Transcarpathian Ukraine has taken place by agreement. . . . The disappearance of the Crimean, Chechen, Ingush, Kalmyk and Volga German Republics was due to disaffection in the face of the enemy."[25]

In July 1946 Harold Laski, a recent chairman of the British Labour party, visited Moscow and had a secret interview with Stalin, in the course of which Laski was told that the British should build their own socialism in their country and leave Europe to the Russians. Laski observed that in the event of war between Russia and America his country would side with Russia.[26] Since Labour was in power at the time, it would have been understandable if Stalin, in his ignorance of British politics, had taken Laski's words as an off-the-record statement of policy.

Resuming official attitudes toward the USSR, we can see that up to 1941 British diplomatic traffic had been unbiased. This changed, in one sense understandably, when it became Britain's only ally. Up to the end of the forties there is a powerful bias indeed, originating with Eden and furthered by a number of Foreign Office officials. The consistency of pro-Soviet attitudes in officials of a certain generation is obvious and unprofessional, yet understandable enough, if we derive it from the same sincere convictions that drove Burgess, Maclean, Philby and Blunt to commit treason or inspired their alma mater to offer Zhukov an honorary degree. The anti-Polish and pro-Soviet bias of Anthony Eden is stranger since his was a different generation.

At all events the Soviets were well aware of these prejudices and consciously exploited them. Nikolai Krasnov was a White Russian whom the British "repatriated." He was the son of General Krasnov, a tsarist commander who later fought the Soviets and who was also repatriated and subsequently shot. Krasnov junior was interviewed by V. N. Merkulov, Beria's deputy, in 1945, before being sent to the gulag, from which he was miraculously released in 1955. Merkulov, who did not expect him to survive, had nothing to lose by mocking him for having trusted the British. Merkulov suggested that the Soviets had successfully manipulated their ally all along. He observed that: "Their Foreign Office is a brothel in which sits its head, a great diplomatic madam. They trade in foreigners' lives and their own conscience."[27] He implied that the Soviets had planned the process of repatriation, which they had persuaded the British to put into effect. "And now they are forced to dance to our tune, like the last pawn on the board."[28]

Merkulov invites one to wonder who the "great madam" might have been, forcing one to conclude that the person best fitted by that expression was the foreign secretary himself. But his words do not imply that Eden was a traitor. Rather, Merkulov suggests a lack of moral principle, which, in his terms, would have meant unswerving commitment to Britain. He was probably taunting the susceptible and idealistic young Russian with hints of a British betrayal of their own interests and of their supporters, too, engineered by the manipulation of naive pro-Soviet goodwill. Thanks to Soviet penetration of the Foreign Office, there can be no doubt that the Russians knew of the pro-Soviet bias of some of its officials, which they very sensibly exploited as best they could, with consequences that were damaging to Allied interests. That is as far as one may legitimately go before lapsing into irresponsible speculation about moles in high places and fourth, fifth and sixth men. It is most unlikely that the full story, if indeed there is one, will ever be revealed.

•   •   •

Stalin's attacks on Ukrainians and other minority races were accompanied by an increase in anti-Semitism. It was widely held that the "victory over the German invader has been won primarily by the Russians, Russian troops everywhere bore the brunt of the fighting. A product of this fierce Russian nationalism is the re-emergence on the surface of an age-old anti-semitism."[29] Stalin's anti-Semitism was popular and in keeping with the new xenophobia. It was a hatred which he had nursed for many years, but only now permitted to emerge as it came to dominate the last six years of his life. He suggested to his daughter that the entire older generation was "infected by Zionism."[30] *Infected* was a sinister expression that suggested it was time for a rerun of those purges which had eliminated a generation in which Jews featured prominently.

One of the earliest manifestations of the new anti-Semitism was a murder. The actor Mikhoels, president of the Jewish Antifascist Committee, obtained an interview with Molotov in the autumn of 1947 to complain of government discrimination against Jews, who were banned from all posts which brought them into contact with foreigners, from the army, the navy and atomic research.[31] Soon afterward the press announced his death; allegedly he had been murdered by anti-Semites.[32] It is virtually certain that the murder was arranged by Stalin; his daughter believes that she overheard him ordering "an automobile accident" for him.[33] Stalin also had S. A. Lozovsky, Mikhoels's colleague on the committee, shot and had Molotov's Jewish wife arrested. All three were said to be agents of American Zionism.[34] Stalin completed his assault upon "alien elements" with a new call for nationalism and ideological orthodoxy. In a meeting with the leading Soviet writers Simonov and Fadeev, he ordered them to stress patriotism and combat Russian feelings of inferiority. As a British Embassy report put it, "There has been a stepping up of ideological conditioning, a most powerful and all-embracing drive for orthodoxy and Soviet self-sufficiency in the cultural sphere . . . in its recent development it has attained a quite new degree of intensity and its gradual expansion along the whole intellectual front has been methodical, inexorable and overwhelming."[35]

One of its first manifestations was an attack upon Zoshchenko, a writer of comic short stories, and on Russia's greatest living poet, Anna Akhmatova, both citizens of Leningrad. One of the side effects of Stalin's neo-Muscovite attitude was a resurgence of hostility to that city. However, he had not always been hostile to its writers. His respect for artists of real talent reemerged during the siege of Leningrad, when the only persons to have been evacuated from that city by special aircraft and at the express orders of Stalin himself, first across German lines and then to Tashkent, were none other than Zoshchenko and Akhmatova.[36] However, this did not prevent a subsequent vicious attack upon them— if only in print. The attack was probably triggered by a poetry reading that a group of Leningrad poets gave in Moscow shortly after the war. When Akhmatova appeared, the audience rose to their feet and cheered as only Russians can cheer a poet of genius, in an extraordinary manifestation of spontaneous enthusiasm. Akhmatova rightly foresaw that no good could come of this. As soon as a report of the audience's behavior reached Stalin, he asked, with characteristic suspicion: "Who organized the standing up?"[37]

CHAPTER FORTY-EIGHT

Stalin and the Muses

The war had exhausted Stalin, who had coordinated his country's efforts without interruption throughout its duration. In 1946 he took his first holiday in five years. His physique showed the strain he had been under: He appeared to have shrunk, his cheeks were sunken, his mustache was thinner and his color had become dangerously high. His contact with reality was also diminishing. A dictator, or any chief, surrounded by frightened or blindly loyal subordinates has to exert great energy to break through the soothing blanket in which they cocoon him. During the war Stalin had found that energy, seemingly without effort, but now it was gone, and increasingly he sank into preoccupation with trivia and morbidly suspicious musings.

Incipient loss of grip was quickly picked up by the British Embassy. The ambassador found Stalin alarmingly ill informed on foreign affairs, gaining the impression that he no longer read digests of the foreign press and only had contact with foreigners such as Harold Laski whose views were sympathetic, while his own diplomats sent only favorable reports. [1] The situation was made worse by the fact that those close to him had no experience of foreign affairs. The domestic situation was not much better. Stalin had no political contact with anyone beyond a small entourage. The official machinery of government no longer turned. The Central Committee no longer met, nor, as far as we know, did the Politburo, while the first party congress for twelve years was held in October 1952. Apparently Stalin governed through his secretariat, headed by Poskrebyshev, whose increasing importance is attested by the rank of lieutenant general, which he attained during the war, and by Stalin's nickname for him, *Glavnyi* ("Chief").

Stalin's one window on the world had become the cinema, of which he was passionately fond. He enjoyed seeing films after dinner, when he would lead a slowly winding crocodile of dignitaries across the darkened squares of the Kremlin to the viewing theater, where they would settle and watch one, two and sometimes three full-length features. Many of the films were American. He liked cowboy films and also Charlie Chaplin but had, according to Viktor Nekrasov, a veritable passion for Tarzan movies and owned a complete set of them. The films had no subtitles and the minister of cinematography, I. I. Bolshakov, was supposed to translate the dialogue. However, all he needed to do was describe the action in his own words. "Now he's leaving the room, now he's going down the street; look he's fallen over." In the meantime, Stalin would keep up a running commentary of his own.

The other important feature of his private life was the interminable sessions at table at which everyone ate and drank too much and, apparently, ran the country. The love of long banquets, formal toasting and large quantities of roast meat were among the few traces Stalin had retained of his Georgian past. The dinners were drunken, rambling affairs at which Stalin would repeat the same jokes and stories time after time. They were also the occasion of cruel, crude and childish practical jokes. Rotten tomatoes were placed on people's chairs; guests were obliged to swallow glasses of wine laced with vodka or filled with salt, while it was usual for them to get so drunk that each one had an NKVD man assigned to clean them up and get them home. The impression is one of sterility, the mechanical parody of celebration and feasting, presided over by a flushed and senile little man of immense power slowly lapsing into atrophy.

Yet Stalin still radiated energy of a kind. One of the most valuable aspects of Svetlana's portrait of her father, and one which evades translation, is her ear for the way he spoke. She conveys a mode of speech that is vivid, direct and often shatteringly crude—one can well believe that he called his mother an old whore—but that is also remarkably salty and alive, the liveliest thing about him, in fact, and a far cry from the colorless repetitions of his formal oratory.

Although his system appeared to be slowing down, the old man remained as dangerous as ever. In that respect his dinners did not lack spice. Bulganin once remarked that when you left Stalin's table, you could never be sure whether you would end up at home or in the Lubyanka. He was capable of looking at a man and deciding with self-indulgent intuition that he seemed shifty that night, so "Off with his head." His capacity for suspicion was increasing daily, partly because he had little else to absorb his energies and partly because it was inconceivable that no one should be trying to kill him. Stalin's terror of assassination had many manifestations: No one knew in advance which of his various, identically furnished bedrooms he would occupy each night. The route he would take to the Kremlin would be decided only at the last minute, while plans were in hand for a private metro line to run from the Kremlin to Kuntsevo. This still exists; from the city center to Kiev Station two metro lines run in parallel. The upper line was to be taken on to Kuntsevo, but work on it was abandoned on Stalin's death, and it was reopened only with the building of the Fili-Kuntsevskaya extension.[2]

His congenital anti-Semitism led him to conclude that there was a world Zionist plot, involving Wall Street, Russian Jews and Molotov's wife—a fairly ordinary sort of conspiracy theory. However, one aspect of those suspicions is revealing, for Stalin's sense of conspiracy had a further, almost comical extension. In his last years he became convinced that his government had been penetrated by foreign spies, notably British ones, and that Voroshilov was a British agent. Stalin liked to invest enemies with his own shortcomings, and now we see a variant upon that theme. So successful had he been at penetrating the governments and security services of the West (not to mention Japan and Nazi Germany) that Stalin was unable to accept that his enemies had not done as much to him. The thought drove him to frenzy since he could never find any evidence to support it, yet it surely must be true. For it was impossible to establish that the British, whom he had penetrated so successfully, had not penetrated the Kremlin in return. Stalin remained tormented by the certainty that he was surrounded by spies, as the blindest loyalty sufficed to render a henchman suspect.

For all his power and eccentricity, Stalin looked disturbingly ordinary. Shostakovich had occasion to observe him at close quarters at this time: "He was an ordinary shabby little man, short, fat, with reddish hair. His face was covered with pock-marks and his right hand was noticeably thinner than his left. He kept hiding his right hand. He didn't look anything like his numerous portraits."[3] Shostakovich was convinced that Stalin was at least half-mad, observing in his laconic manner that "there's nothing odd about that, there are lots of crazy rulers, we've had our share in Russia."[4] Khrushchev also believed that Stalin's suspicions had unhinged him, to the point of making his guests always sample the food at his table before trying it himself, although he could never persuade Beria to do so since he was a vegetarian. However, in

Stalin's situation it seems reasonable to fear an assassination attempt. The only evidence of serious mental derangement is the alleged mode of his medical examinations. The British Embassy reports that Stalin's doctor was required to examine a series of men all looking like the general secretary, so that he would not know which of them was Stalin.[5] In view of the attitude that Stalin would shortly adopt toward the leading medical practitioners in the land, the story is not as improbable as it sounds.

*   *   *

One of the strangest sides of Stalin's personality was his respect for the arts. This revealed itself in a somewhat macabre manner. Although the purges were a time when anyone of distinction was an automatic candidate for arrest, a great many practitioners of the arts survived. While it is true that quantities of hacks were purged, a remarkable percentage of major authors, artists and performers, including anyone associated with the Bolshoi theater, escaped arrest, a survival rate far higher than any other category. There were exceptions, but in every case there was a reason. Russia's greatest poet, Mandelstam, had, as we have seen, actually been released for a time after uttering the only known criticism of Stalin beyond graffiti scrawled on the walls of prison cells in the blood of condemned men. Gorky was probably poisoned when he began to try to moderate Stalin's enthusiastic prosecution of the purges. Isaac Babel, another victim, not only was Jewish but had written unflatteringly realistic accounts of the doings of the First Cavalry Army, Stalin's favorite military unit. Boris Pilnyak not only had resisted Ezhov's attempts to write a novel for him but in a short story, "The Tale of the Unextinguished Moon," had accused Stalin of murdering Frunze. By the standards of the day these all were capital offenses. However, numbers of distinguished writers survived, though not in any great comfort or security. Three major poets—Yesenin, Mayakovsky and Marina Tsvetayeva—all committed suicide, but at a time when people could be arrested for disseminating the poetry of Yesenin, Pasternak or Akhmatova, both the latter poets escaped arrest. When Stalin saw the name of Mayakovsky's widow on one of the death lists he signed daily, he struck it out, observing that she should not be touched. The science-fiction writer Yevgeny Zamyatin, who once observed to Stalin that life in his country was becoming intolerable, was even permitted to go abroad. Ilya Ehrenburg, another Jewish writer, was personally protected by Stalin. The country's top composers—Shostakovich, Prokoviev,

Khatchaturian—all escaped arrest, while Soviet painters went entirely untouched.

We also have direct evidence of his interest in the arts. He was very fond of grand opera, never missing a performance of *Boris Godunov*, one of the greatest musical explorations of the problems of absolutism and personal guilt. He was also fond of *Aïda*, yet another manifestation of his pharaonic side. However, the most remarkable of all his theatrical interests was his concern with a play written by the Christian novelist and playwright Mikhail Bulgakov, one of the greatest prose writers of the era and another author whom Stalin allowed to die a natural death. Bulgakov's play *The White Guard*, which describes the vicissitudes of a family of well-to-do Russians in Kiev during the civil war, is unique in the annals of Soviet art. Unlike other treatments which divide the cast into heroes and villains, both sides equally stylized, we have a balanced characterization, portraying the family, whose menfolk are officers fighting the Reds, as normal people trying to conduct their lives in the midst of civil war, in their cozy middle-class apartment. Entirely without propaganda, the play portrays the way they lived then. It was useless to the socialist state in which it was written, especially since it recalled a time of relative plenty in an age when millions were starving. In the circumstances it is understandable that the censor should have rejected the play. Yet it was put on at Stalin's express instruction, and he went to see it no fewer than seventeen times.

Seventeen times are a lot for anyone to see a play, but for a head of state like Stalin it must have been close to impossibility. It is hard to say why the play drew him so. Perhaps it gave him a window upon a way of life that he had never known. This seems to be what he looked for in the arts, if we are to judge by a strange incident reported by his daughter. Returning with her father from a Black Sea vacation, she was leafing through an art magazine which contained reproductions of drawings in the Tredyakovsky Gallery. Stalin picked it up, looked at it intently and said with a sigh that he wished he could quietly go and see the originals for himself, without all the rigmarole that such a visit would have involved. It was then that she understood how isolated and ultimately lonely he was. It may be that great art, with its capacity, unique within the Soviet Union, to tell the undistorted truth, provided him access to an honest world that he could otherwise never reach and that this induced him to treat artists with the nearest he ever came to something resembling respect.

Stalin read a lot of history, military history especially, and saved the historian Tarle, the biographer of both Talleyrand and Napoleon, from prison. He studied Russian history, if only to learn from the mistakes of earlier rulers, and based his conception of the state upon models of old Muscovy. He also enjoyed Russian literature and read Chekhov and Gogol with great pleasure. He was particularly fond of the satirist Salt-ykov-Shchedrin. One of his favorite stories, "Contemporary Idyll," concerns a governor who decides to benefit his province by doing it the greatest harm possible, in the certain knowledge that only good can come of this. Among his more ambitious projects was a plan to "abolish America," but after he had issued the order, it struck him that this did not fall within his competence—a phrase that Stalin quoted with relish in the speech that introduced his constitution. Though the story was written late in the nineteenth century, it was discovered and published in the early 1930s, when it was considered to have a direct relevance to Stalin himself.[6]

In later years Stalin found increasing time to take a personal interest in the arts. We find him telling a publisher what the respective print runs should be for works by Akhmatova and Sholokhov.[7] He would also intervene in other ways. Viktor Nekrasov had been told that his Sta-lingrad novel had been short-listed for the Stalin Prize but that he would not get it since the book had underestimated the role of the high command, overemphasizing the courage and endurance of junior of-ficers and enlisted men. He won the prize nevertheless; he was told that Stalin, who had seen his name crossed off the list, had restored it per-sonally. Something similar happened to Ehrenburg. In 1948 Stalin had asked Fadeev, chairman of the Stalin Prize Committee, why Ehren-burg's novel *The Fall of Paris* was entered only for a second prize. Fadeev replied that it was incorrect since it portrayed a Frenchwoman falling in love with a Soviet citizen. "But I like this Frenchwoman," said Stalin, "she's a nice girl. And, besides, such things happen in real life. As regards heroes I think that few people are born heroes, it is ordinary people who become them."[8] Ehrenburg got his first prize.

Stalin's interest in the arts extended to his appointing himself arbiter of the taste of the nation. He would view every product of the Soviet film industry, and no film could be released without his approval. He was especially fond of civil war films that portrayed him in a heroic light and would comment aloud on his remarkable appearance, always refer-ring to himself in the third person. He also listened to every new record, classifying it according to whether it was "good," "bad" or "rubbish." He did not have sophisticated musical taste, although in earlier years he had enjoyed sitting down at a player-piano. His favorite melody was the Georgian folk tune "Suliko," although Djilas paints a ghastly portrait of a drunken Stalin repeatedly playing an ingenious record made by a group of singing dogs, a mockery of human achievement that would undoubtedly have appealed to him. He also enjoyed the White Russian crooner Alexander Wertinsky, who used to sing with a permanent wrench in his throat, and, more significantly, in a bland *ancien régime* accent as far from Soviet speech as an Oxford accent is from Cockney.

It was on Stalin's initiative that modernist trends in Soviet music were condemned after the war, when Prokoviev and Shostakovich were called upon to produce music that could be hummed. It was also thanks to Stalin that Shostakovich's opera *Lady Macbeth of Mtensk* was taken off after a successful run, since he felt its music to be rubbish. However, his strangest involvement with the arts is also recounted by Shostakovich. One night in his villa Stalin heard a broadcast of the pianist Yudina playing Mozart's Twentieth Piano Concerto. He enjoyed it so much that he telephoned the studio and asked for the record. No one dared tell him that the performance had been live. Instead, the musicians were called back for an agonizing all-night recording session, and Stalin was duly presented with his record the next morning. Curiously, according to Shostakovich, it was found upon his gramophone after his death.

That Stalin took pleasure in art was not to say that others should be permitted to do so in the land where, in the words of Solzhenitsyn, "ninety-nine men cry and one is laughing." Yet his interest is one of the few sides of his temperament that cannot be related to his all-encompassing determination to win and keep power at any cost. It is not easy to find anything positive to say about Stalin's character, hard to get beyond Shostakovich's observation that "I was remembering my friends and all I saw was corpses, mountains of corpses."[9] Nor can one say that artists were permitted to do more than survive in Stalin's Russia or that the production of fourth-rate genteel rubbish was discouraged. But had Stalin treated artists as he had treated politicians, soldiers and everybody else of distinction, there would have been no Soviet art at all.

•   •   •

The savage verbal attack upon Zoshchenko and Akhmatova marked the start of a period of extreme regulation of all aspects of intellectual and aesthetic endeavor, from film and music to biology, culminating in a preposterous excursion into the field of linguistics. The movement was designed to check undue admiration for the West and in this respect ran parallel to the sudden spate of Russian inventions and historical claims, which finally extended to maintaining that Achilles was a Slav. It was a period when one could be arrested for "excessive praise of Western achievement." There was also an attack on "rootless cosmopolitans," or Jews, who were considered "un-Russian," a feeling which endures in many circles to this day. The attack was also intended to break up academic cliques considered capable of forming some kind of community independent of the central establishment.

The initiative for this process almost certainly came from Stalin. The U.S. Embassy recorded a conversation with a senior Soviet journalist who said that "he knew for a fact that the recent tightening up was on Stalin's personal instructions. He had decided that strong measures were needed to effect a return to pre-war conceptions. Otherwise dangerous foreign ideas which had taken root among the fourteen million Russian soldiers who had seen other countries and among the seventy million Soviet citizens who had lived under foreign occupation might spread throughout the country . . . what was happening now was exactly similar to the beginning of the purges."[10] Stalin was determined not to "lose the peace" after winning the war, ensuring that the energies the war had released be properly channeled and contained. If his purpose was to avoid destabilization, he was spectacularly successful, although the price his people paid for stability was high. It was a time of the most stifling atrophy and terror,[11] when people kept pillows over their telephones in case they could be used as listening devices.[12]

The attack upon the two writers initiated the so-called Leningrad affair, a final manifestation of Stalin's hostility toward that city. Viewing its magnificent war record and the pride of its survivors as the possible basis for an opposition, he turned on it yet again. The assault upon Akhmatova and Zoshchenko had been conducted by Andrei Zhdanov, who had been the city's party secretary during the siege and had come to be thought of as "the savior of Leningrad."[13] Djilas described him as short, with a high forehead, a pointed nose and bad color. Narrow and dogmatic, he had a smattering of general knowledge acquired through Marxist literature.[14] At the time of the attack upon the writers he took some relish in telling Djilas that his criticism of Zoshchenko had caused the latter to be deprived of his ration card. His zealous witch-hunt was partly intended to counter a dangerous rival, Malenkov, currently intriguing against him. Malenkov had attacked Zhdanov's stewardship of Leningrad, hinting that he had played no part in the defense of the city and had been removed from all his posts by a local committee which put A. A. Kuznetsov in his place.[15] Zhdanov now assaulted the writers with a savagery designed to demonstrate his loyalty and dissociate himself from any local faction.

The rivalry between Malenkov and Zhdanov was compounded by signs that Stalin was preparing further purges. He began with the armed forces, as Zhukov, the commanders of Soviet artillery and armor and the heads of both the navy and the air force were all replaced. In the meantime, Zhdanov appeared to be winning his power struggle, as Malenkov ceased to be secretary of the Central Committee and an associate, G. F. Aleksandrov, lost his place as head of propaganda, to be replaced by Mikhail Suslov. This was considered to be the result of Zhdanov's attacks upon the arts. However, Stalin was playing one man against the other. For Zhdanov's star suddenly went into serious decline, probably because of his association with Leningrad. He failed to appear on Lenin's tomb on May 1, 1947, and Stalin's daughter recalls her father abusing him at a dinner; Zhdanov, who was in poor health, did not eat or drink much, in itself a potential irritant, prompting Stalin to round on him for "sitting there like Jesus Christ."[16] The final phase of the rivalry ended with Malenkov's return to the Secretariat on July 20, 1948, followed a month later by the death of Zhdanov at the age of fifty-two. Although he had been in poor health for some time, the possibility of a murder cannot be excluded in the case of someone dying so apropos.[17]

Malenkov's triumph was made obvious by the *Izvestiya* photograph which shows Zhdanov's bier flanked on one side by Stalin and Malenkov, on the other by Molotov and Beria, who had grown fatter over the years and whose tiny, round metal-framed spectacles made him look more like Heinrich Himmler than ever. The obituary praised Zhdanov as the defender of ideological orthodoxy but said nothing of his role in the defense of Leningrad.[18] His death, and the subsequent rise of Malenkov, marked a further stage in the dominance of Stalin's secretariat and its cadres. It also heralded another assault upon prominent Leningraders. The purge was conducted by Abakumov, whom Stalin had appointed minister of state security. During the war he had been in charge of Smersh, the counterespionage organization, and the frequency of his recourse to the firing squad had amazed even Stalin.[19] Now he moved on Zhdanov's Leningrad associates, including Voznesenksy, a Politburo member; Kuznetsov, a Central Committee secretary; and Rodionov, chairman of the Council of Ministers of the

Russian Federal Republic, together with the secretaries of the Leningrad and district party organizations. They were all arrested and shot while some 2,000 lesser officials were also purged.

Kuznetsov was informed of his disgrace in a characteristic way. Stalin had him invited to dinner, but when he appeared and approached to shake his host's hand, Stalin kept his at his side and said, "I did not summon you," obliging him to leave.[20] There was also an attack upon the city itself. The Museum of the Defense of Leningrad was closed, and its massive collection of records and documents pertaining to the great siege removed. A final insult was delivered to its inhabitants. The city had maintained the famous wartime signs along Nevsky Prospekt and Sadovaya Street which read: "Citizens in the event of shelling this side of the street is the more dangerous." These mementos were now painted out.

• • •

> Asked whether he would like his people to be loyal out of fear
> or conviction, Stalin replied, "Fear. Convictions can change
> but fear remains."
> —WEISSBERG

December 21, 1949, was Stalin's seventieth birthday, an occasion which created problems for the British Foreign Office. It had already devoted much energy, ink and paper during the preceding year to deciding whether the secretary of state for foreign affairs should continue sending greetings to the Soviet Union on November 7. The prime minister had eventually decided to discontinue the practice.[21] Now there was the problem of the birthday. The ambassador observed: "He will doubtless receive messages of congratulation from all over the world. If our relations with the Soviet Union were in accord with the spirit of the Anglo-Soviet Treaty it would be natural for the Prime Minister to send a congratulatory message. Even in the present circumstances I cannot believe that an anodyne message of congratulation could be turned to our disadvantage."[22]

Further awkwardness was created by the Luxembourg minister's suggestion that the diplomatic corps give Stalin a present, a proposal that elicited the following bureaucratic gem: "The Treaty department tells us that although they cannot give us a positive assurance of there not being a diplomatic precedent for such a presentation they cannot call one to mind. In their experience it is not unknown for diplomatic representatives to make presentations to heads of state on appropriate occasions, but they would regard such a presentation to a Prime Minister as being unusual."[23]

The absence of a present from Britain is unlikely to have made Stalin feel deprived. He received hundreds of thousands of them from all over the world, enough to fill the Museum of Revolution and subsequently constitute a museum of its own in Gori. Fortunately the birthday celebrations themselves went according to plan, by no means always the case (during that year's May Day parade three army transport planes had lost their way and entered secured airspace over the capital, requiring them to be shot down).[24] They culminated in Stalin's apotheosis, as batteries of searchlights illuminated the night sky, picking out a gigantic portrait of him suspended over Moscow from a balloon. A special celebration was held at the Bolshoi Theater with Stalin, his Politburo and heads of visiting delegations onstage.

> Thirty-four speakers vied with each other in the fullness of their adulation. . . . The prize for oratory went to Togliatti [the leader of the Italian Communist party], but the Polish spokesman Juzwiak deserved at least an honourable mention for his solemn assertion that twice in twenty-five years the Polish people had gained their freedom and independence thanks to the Soviet Union. Stalin himself was silent throughout the proceeding apart from a muttered aside sufficiently audible to be picked up by the loud speaker system in which he inquired why the Polish speaker did not use his own language rather than Russian.
>
> *Pravda* was twelve pages rather than the usual four and apart from two column inches reporting the womens' world chess championship, consisted entirely of articles in honour of Stalin.[25]

The Stalin cult, which had begun on his fiftieth birthday, had now reached its apogee, as his image hung in the sky like that of a hero of antiquity become a constellation. I asked one ex-Soviet citizen whether in those days as a young academic he had really "loved Stalin." His reaction, though kind, made it clear that only an idiot could have asked such a question. Everybody loved Stalin, he replied, because the notion that you might not love him with all your heart was so terrifying that you could not dare concede the possibility.

Truly Stalin had won universal love through fear. My informant recalled the May Day parade he attended that year. In the company of his colleagues he had seen Stalin standing on the far side of Red Square. As he watched and cheered, he had been appalled at the thought that he physically might not be able to cheer with the required pitch of enthusiasm and that this might be noticed—in which case his colleagues would have lynched him on the spot, out of self-defense, since failure to have done so would have brought them down with him. It was not possible to have anything less than blind faith in Stalin. The expression of the faintest doubt or qualification would automatically be rewarded by a bullet to the back of the neck.

CHAPTER FORTY-NINE

Endgame

I am finished. I trust no one, not even myself.

—Stalin

Stalin was in decline. Increasingly he complained to his daughter of loneliness and took to paying regular visits to the grave of his dead wife. He had an old man's tiredness and had even lost the desire to take his annual trips to the south; he never left Moscow after 1951. His interest in things of the mind expressed itself in a preposterous excursion into the field of linguistics when he mounted an attack upon the theories of a linguistician named N. Ya. Marr, who had died in 1934. The attack had no obvious political or ideological motivation, and its basis may actually have been intellectual. Marr proved no match for Stalin in the ensuing debate.

Marr was a Georgian scholar, archaeologist, ethnographer and founder of Japhetology, the study of the so-called Japhetic languages, which included Georgian, Basque and Etruscan. He derived all language from four primordial linguistic elements, *sal*, *ber*, *yon* and *rosh*. As a Marxist he ascribed language to the cultural superstructure which derives from the economic base. Language was a class phenomenon, and with the coming of communism a universal language would eventually prevail: "If the revolution is not a dream there can be no talk of any palliative reform of language. . . . It is not reform that is needed but fundamental reconstruction and the transfer of the whole of the super-structural world on to new rails, a new rung in the development by stages of human speech and onto the path of the revolutionary creation of a new language."[1]

A British Embassy official, H. T. Willetts, whose dispatches were invariably intelligent and often funny, observed: "There are many stimulating hypotheses to be extracted from Marr's work. Unfortunately his exuberant and untidy mind expressed itself in a style which is always difficult and often painfully obscure and he had a sublime disregard for the ordinary rules of scientific evidence and logical argument."[2]

In the spring of 1950 Marr's views provoked a discussion in the pages of *Pravda* in which Stalin took a hand. It is hard to say what aroused him; perhaps he was reaching back to his youthful interest in Esperanto and his analysis of the relationship between nationality and language. At all events his essay had the naivety of an autodidact trying to untie complicated philosophical knots by an appeal to barroom common sense. He refutes the contention that language is part of the superstructure by asserting that the base has changed since tsarist days while the language has not—in itself a questionable contention, which makes no allowance for the "leads and lags" of linguistic change. He concedes that semantics play a part in linguistics but "One must be careful not to over-estimate that importance or abuse it," which is like saying that one must not exaggerate the importance of chemistry as a branch of natural science. "I have in mind certain linguisticians who get too preoccupied by semantics, neglect language as the immediate realization of thought, separating thought from language, maintaining that language has had its day and we can dispense with language, thereby heralding a new era in linguistics."

He then tells us that thought and language are inseparable, that for every thought there must be language and that semantics, which he seems to regard as distinct from language, must "know its place." His comments on class and language are equally pitiful. The influence of class is limited; since everyone employs the language of the "existing national language," there can be no "class grammar."[3] The fact that Stalin's idiotic ramblings were acclaimed by no fewer than eight professors of linguistics who published panegyrics in the same edition of *Pravda* is a miserable indication of his regime's reduction of every field of human endeavor to the crudest thuggery. The Soviet Union was no place in which to profess anything but boundless admiration for the emperor's new clothes.

The British ambassador, who was puzzled by the importance suddenly assumed by linguistic theory, found a magnificently fatuous explanation: "The simplest answer to this question is in my view the most satisfactory; the intervention of the most powerful authority was deemed desirable because the decisions involved were held to be of very great importance."[4] As a Russian saying goes, he appeared to have discovered the whereabouts of the sky.

Further evidence to suggest that Stalin was losing his grip is supplied by his handling of Far Eastern affairs. He failed to anticipate a Communist China and even signed a pact with Chiang Kai-shek in August 1945, undertaking not to aid any Chinese faction in return for recognition of Mongolia's status as a Soviet dependency. He did subsequently supply limited aid to Mao, and in 1949 a Sino-Soviet pact was signed after two months of negotiation. However, George Kennan has argued convincingly that Stalin encouraged the North Koreans—who were pro-Soviet, as North Vietnam would later be—to invade the South in 1950, hoping to establish a threat to China on the Korean Peninsula. He did not anticipate U.S. intervention in what he presumed would remain a local war between North and South Koreans. When Secretary of State Acheson left Korea outside his tracing of the American defense line in the Pacific, Stalin had assumed he was being sent a signal and encouraged the North Koreans to attack. The U.S. intervention surprised and embarrassed him greatly. He then allowed himself to be outmaneuvered in the United Nations. When the Americans brought the Korean issue to the Security Council, the Soviet member could have blocked them by exercising his veto. Instead, acting to instructions from Moscow, he walked out of the meeting, thereby permitting the United States and its allies to pass a vote obliging all members of the United Nations to send troops to Korea. Stalin's local war had become three years of international conflagration which threatened to turn into a global conflict. However, on this occasion at least, he managed to prevent his own country from becoming directly involved. Nevertheless, he was obliged to maintain the Soviet economy on something very close to a war footing. The greatest advantage that Stalin derived from the conflict was the wedge it drove between the United States and China. The Chinese subsequently professed the view that the Russians launched the Korean War and then used it to exacerbate Sino-American relations for years.[5]

His foreign policy had suffered a further setback when Tito broke with Moscow in 1948. The Soviet Union had frustrated Yugoslav attempts to annex Trieste and further exasperated them by an unsuccessful attempt to infiltrate their army and police. Despite Stalin's promise that "I shall shake my little finger and there will be no more Tito," Yugoslavia removed itself from the Soviet sphere of influence to pursue its own national road to socialism, setting a dangerous example to other countries in the Eastern bloc, one which Stalin countered with purges and executions in Czechoslovakia, Bulgaria, Hungary and, to a lesser degree, Poland.

Stalin seems to have looked beyond purges and executions to military conquest to extend and consolidate Soviet power. According to Karl Kaplan, a Czech who defected in 1976 and who had had access to party archives, in January 1951 Stalin had called a three-day meeting attended by the party secretaries and defense ministers of East Germany, Poland, Hungary, Bulgaria, Rumania and Czechoslovakia, at which he announced that the Americans must be swept out of Europe before their increasing military and political power could be consolidated. This, observed Stalin, would have to take place before 1955, by which time the U.S. nuclear strike capacity would make a war unacceptable to the USSR. He had earlier expected he would reach the Atlantic by peaceful means by 1957, at which time the United States would have withdrawn from Europe. Now the lamentable performance of U.S. forces in Korea had made him favor the use of force. The ministers agreed to place their armed forces under Russian command in the event of a war which, as it transpired, the plight of the Eastern bloc's economy prevented him from fighting.[6]

At the same time the Soviet Union was busy wooing and winning new friends among the ordinary people of Western Europe by means of a peace campaign which represented Western governments as warmongers. It was particularly successful in France and Italy. The British ambassador reported from Moscow in September 1951:

> All this really means of course is that Western Governments are having to conduct a nerve war on two fronts, of which the home front, their own public opinion, is the greater danger. It was an appreciation of this that led the Kremlin to implement that stroke of genius the Peace Campaign, which has . . . achieved a great deal of its purpose. There is every reason to believe that the Soviet leaders have been quite sincere in the sharp line they have drawn between the people and their Government. Their policy would be quite senseless if the idea had not been continually present in their minds of appealing to the people over the heads of their Governments.[7]

As Alexis de Tocqueville once observed: "In history there are many copies and few originals."

Stalin's daughter has made much of Beria's growing influence over her father. Certainly he acquired considerable power and moral authority. Khrushchev wrote of Beria's infiltration of Stalin's personal staff—Stalin's housekeepers always reported to him, and he had placed his own Georgians in a number of domestic positions—and of his growing influence during the war, after he had "held Stalin's hand" during his days of collapse. This may be true, but Khrushchev was party to Beria's arrest and execution soon after Stalin died, a circumstance likely to affect the way he wrote about him. Thus, although he alleges that Beria was fond of raping young girls, an allegation that has been questioned in recent years, he has nothing to say about his remarkable intellect. In the postwar years Beria seems to have allied himself with Malenkov, and it was he who had restored Malenkov to favor after his fall from grace. The Malenkov-Beria combination was dangerous since it brought together the police and the Secretariat, the two most effective branches of government. Stalin tried to counterbalance it by bringing Khrushchev in from the Ukraine, where he had been languishing in temporary disgrace. In a further move against Beria he had placed Abakumov in charge of the security services. Unfortunately Abakumov remained loyal to Beria, whom he always consulted before reporting to Stalin, which is no doubt why the latter dismissed him in July 1951. It was stated that the Central Committee was dissatisfied with the work of the security services, and since it was evident that Abakumov was Beria's man, it was clear that the latter was the real target.

Immediately after the fall of Abakumov his replacement, S. D. Ignatiev, made a "knight's move" against Beria. The latter had supported Gomulka in Poland and Slansky in Czechoslovakia. Both men were Jews. It is a little known fact that both Beria and Malenkov were philo-Semitic, often forcefully so and to Stalin's face. Beria had done much to improve the economic circumstances of Georgian Jews and even established a Jewish ethnographical museum in Tiflis, probably the first of its kind in the Soviet Union. It is very likely that he had Jewish blood on his mother's side. Stalin now moved on his protégés, notably in Czechoslovakia, where Beria had filled all the key posts with his own people after the Communist take-over in 1948. Stalin took a special interest in the Czech purges, right up to the trial and execution of Slansky. He was beginning to close in on Beria himself.

Stalin's next move was the so-called Mingrelian affair of November 1951. Mingrels were a race found in the Caucasus to which Beria belonged. Stalin sent Ignatiev to Georgia with instructions to make a clean sweep of Beria's men, who were to be accused of separatism, nationalism and conspiring with Turkey. The charges were intended as a signal to Beria to remind him that he had once been a Mussavat, or Azerbaijani separatist, agent. Turkey was mentioned because the Mussavat who had recruited him was now in that country, together with the ex-leader of the party, who had allegedly escaped from the Soviet Union with Beria's connivance.[8] Stalin thoroughly enjoyed elaborating the detail of his scenario. However, Beria sidestepped Stalin's onslaught with some elegance, as Khrushchev remembered:

> Because Stalin was old and sick he wasn't consistent in following through his scheme. Beria turned the whole thing round in his favour and shrewdly insinuated himself as Stalin's henchman. None of the rest of us would have dared interfere in a matter relating to the Georgian Republic. Beria assigned himself to go to Georgia and administer the punishment of the Mingrels, the imaginary enemies. Those poor fellows were led like sheep to the slaughter.[9]

The purge disposed of 427 local party secretaries, almost the entire Central Committee and half the local Politburo. According to Khrushchev, success made Beria insufferable. "Beria was arrogant about everything. Nothing could be decided without him. You couldn't even read a report to Stalin without getting Beria's support in advance. If you made a report and you hadn't cleared it with him beforehand he would be sure to tear your report down in Stalin's eyes with all sorts of questions and contradictions."[10]

Yet Khrushchev is surely wrong to conclude that the move failed because Stalin's powers were waning. Rather, it was because he did not feel strong enough to bring Beria down and was reluctant to move before he was certain he could annihilate him. Ignatiev was a bureaucrat, not a man of blood, and could not be certain of the loyalty of those in the security services, who remembered Beria fondly. Once again, perhaps once too often, Stalin would rather be patient than move too soon.

The Nineteenth Party Congress, the first since 1939, gathered in October 1952. Khrushchev, Malenkov and Beria all made major speeches, and there was much antagonism between Khrushchev and the other two, as they attacked one another's policies.[11] Significantly Khrush-

chev's speech complained of "lack of vigilance."[12] The expression implied criticism of the security services and of Beria. It had last been
heard in 1937 on the eve of the disgrace of Ezhov and the purge of the
NKVD. There is good reason to suppose that Stalin had a repeat performance in mind. That an attack was being leveled at Beria is borne out
by the report of the meeting held on the morning of October 5, which
demoted him from third to fifth place in the order of rank. He occupied
the same position in the record of the afternoon's proceedings. Beria
countered with an incisive speech that was remarkable for its covert
criticism of Stalin. He described the "Communist Party under the leadership of Stalin" as the architect of victory, whereas it was customary to
ascribe victory to Stalin alone.[13] More important, he defined the three
priorities of the party's nationalities policy as (1) fighting great power
chauvinism, which sounds like an echo of Lenin's criticism of Stalin;
(2) the dangers of bourgeois nationalism; (3) the dangers of cos-
mopolitanism.[14] Between the lines, Beria was saying that Stalinist chauvinism was a greater danger than either the bourgeois nationalism on
which the Mingrelian affair had been based or the Zionist threat which
was the basis of Stalin's anti-Semitic campaign. Nevertheless, Beria was
restored to third place in the hierarchy within ten days, although he
failed to get two protégés, Merkulov and Dekanozov, elected to the
Central Committee, while the Georgian party failed to mention his
name at its own congress.

It is impossible to draw any conclusion from these meager facts. Avtorkhanov, who believed that Beria and others murdered Stalin, ad-
vances the view that the latter was already hamstrung by Beria and
Malenkov by the time of the October congress. Roy Medvedev, the
dissident historian with remarkable access to official archives, dismissed
Avtorkhanov's contentions as preposterous. It would not be in the interests of recent Soviet leaders to have it supposed that Stalin was first
contained by Beria and then murdered.

One feature of Medvedev's argument concerns an incident that took
place during the congress. Apparently Stalin offered to resign his post as
general secretary. Almost certainly this would have been a ruse to test
his colleagues; anyone expressing anything but horror at the idea would
have been placing his head upon the block. If Stalin were indeed planning a fresh purge, this would have served as a useful preliminary reconnaissance, and indeed, he had already done something of the sort at
the Seventeenth Congress in 1934, taking a back seat on the eve of the
purge. Medvedev claims that no one accepted the suggestion; rather, the

entire Central Committee very prudently fell to its knees begging Stalin not to forsake it—rather like the people of Muscovy in Eisenstein's *Ivan the Terrible*.[15] Avtorkhanov, on the other hand, claims that the proposal was in part accepted, a contention Medvedev dismisses without bothering to consider the evidence. *The Encyclopaedic Dictionary* (Moscow: 1955), states under the entry "Stalin" that he was general secretary of the party up to the congress of October 1952, at which he became secretary of the Central Committee and a member of the Praesidium, as the Politburo was renamed. The same facts reappear in the index of a *Complete Works* of Lenin, published during the Brezhnev era (vol. xliv, p. 651). It is hard to say what these changes mean, but it remains most unlikely that Stalin was deprived of his offices against his will.

The change may have been related to a reorganization of the party that was now taking place. The Orgburo was abolished, and its functions were assigned to the Secretariat; the Politburo, rechristened the Praesidium, was enlarged to comprise twenty-five full members and eleven candidates, while the Central Committee was doubled in size. This looks like another stage in the buildup to a purge. Once again Stalin was bringing in a younger generation to fill dead men's shoes. Twenty-eight percent of the new Praesidium had joined the party in or after 1924, while the old guard, the erstwhile Politburo, was in a minority. The significance of Stalin's move escaped nobody. It was obvious to Khrushchev that he and his colleagues were destined to be purged, just as obvious to intelligent outsiders that something bad was going to happen. Alexander Pyatigorsky was terrified by the promotion of a batch of unknowns to the most senior posts in the party. He and his friends saw this as a certain sign of an imminent purge, which would have Malenkov and Beria as its main targets.

Apart from a few closing words Stalin did not speak at the congress. Almost certainly he was husbanding his strength. Years of sedentary existence and too many dinners were taking their toll. He had been obliged to give up smoking, and his face looked unhealthily flushed. According to Medvedev, the advocate of his natural death, he had been sick for some time, the illness dating from before his seventieth birthday.[16] Avtorkhanov maintains, on the other hand, that he was in excellent health, while Stalin's daughter, who has no ax to grind, suggests that her father was beginning to look unhealthy, but she makes no mention of an illness.

Shortly after the congress some remarkable changes took place in Stalin's personal entourage. The first concerns Poskrebyshev, whom Churchill's interpreter once described as "About five feet tall, with broad shoulders, a bent back, large head, heavy jowl, long hooked nose and eyes like those of a bird of prey."[17] Poskrebyshev knew more about Stalin than anyone living or dead. He was the frequent butt of his master's cruel teasing, while Stalin had gained an additional hold over him with a favorite device: the arrest of his wife.[18] Now, in December 1952, Stalin decided that his *homme de confiance* of twenty-five years was leaking classified documents. By January 1953 he was no longer head of the Secretariat, and shortly afterward he disappeared. Stalin replaced him with V. I. Malin, apparently a protégé of Malenkov's.[19] Poskrebyshev actually survived Stalin to die a natural death. He was last glimpsed in the Kremlin hospital in 1962 and probably died there after years of illness in the autumn of 1966.[20] One can only assume that during his years with Stalin he managed to take out some powerful life insurance cover, for his survival is otherwise inexplicable.

No less important were the changes that took place in Stalin's personal bodyguard, the Guard Directorate. It was purged, reduced in numbers and subordinated to the MGB, as the security services were now known. Surviving members braced themselves for a rerun of the security service purges of 1937.[21] More important, the head of the directorate, and Stalin's longest serving associate, Vlasik, disappeared around the time that Poskrebyshev was dismissed and was replaced by V. Khrustalov, a Beria man. About the same time S. M. Shtemenko, chief of the general staff, was dismissed, and the Guard Directorate lost its seat on that body. Then, on February 15, the deputy head of the Kremlin command, Major General Peter Koryakin, died "unexpectedly." That month saw another untimely death, that of Lev Mekhlis. During the war he had been head of the Political Directorate of the Red Army, and he had just been elected a full member of the Central Committee. It has been claimed that he was arrested in early February and died in a prison hospital later that month. Although his ashes were buried in Red Square, Stalin did not attend his funeral.[22] Before blame for his murder is laid at the door of anybody other than Stalin, it should be recalled that Mekhlis was Jewish, which would admittedly have helped anyone trying to render him suspect in Stalin's eyes.

It cannot be said what lay behind these moves. Avtorkhanov suggests that they were the doing of Beria, who had walled Stalin in and deprived him of any political initiative. It is claimed that Beria had engineered the leak that caused Poskrebyshev's disgrace and had also arranged the dismissal of Vlasik and the demotion of the Guard Directorate. He certainly knew how to manipulate Stalin's capacity for suspicion and was in a better position than anyone to secure the removal of Stalin's closest associates and replace them with his own men. The possibility that he would play a leading role in the coming purge cannot have escaped him. Stalin had always believed in winning popular support by tossing police chiefs to the wolves. On the other hand, it may be argued that Stalin's capacity for increasingly irrational suspicion was more than enough in itself to persuade him to make the changes. It had certainly not been Beria who had made him conclude that Voroshilov was a British agent and Molotov a closet Zionist. In the present state of knowledge we can only talk in terms of probabilities.

· · ·

> Comrade Stalin warned many times that our achievements
> also have a darker side.
> —*Pravda*, January 13, 1953

In the aftermath of the party congress *Pravda* published articles about the need to bring new blood into the Party, and on December 10 it echoed an expression used by Stalin at the Eighteenth Congress in 1939, when he reminded survivors of the purges that these had made possible the promotion of half a million newcomers. The article stated that the leading positions in industry, agriculture and government should be occupied by persons of undisputed loyalty, "Capable of introducing new currents, and advocating everything advanced and progressive." There was no shortage of such persons; it was simply a matter of seeking them out.

This was fighting talk. The article implied that the present leaders were grown too old and inefficient and that their loyalty was open to question. It also promised rich rewards to those with the courage and the ability to replace them.

Thus far Stalin's plans may be considered rational if one accepts the need to dispose of prominent members of senior management at regular, in this case twenty-year, intervals. Besides, if Stalin had come to fear Beria, for one, it made excellent sense to remove him, as it would have made sense to a succession of U.S. presidents to have disposed of J. Edgar Hoover. However, the form that Stalin imparted to his purge, the so-called doctors' plot, assumed the coloring of, to say the least, personal eccentricity.

Stalin had come to fear not just assassination but death itself and even its symbols. He had uprooted the cypresses that surrounded his Black Sea villa because they reminded him too much of death. Although he had never cared much for the medical profession or, for that matter, for dentists, he now came to abhor doctors as the bringers of bad news and had been especially incensed by one who had been foolish enough to observe to him that the medical capacity to sustain human life had its limits.[23] In recent months Stalin had turned his back on his own doctor, Vinogradov, and taken to treating himself. Suddenly, in late December 1952, Vinogradov and most of the Kremlin medical staff were arrested on charges of espionage and medical murder. Most of the doctors were Jews.

CHAPTER FIFTY

Checkmate

This was the sole instance in the history of the Soviet state
when the interests of the government coincided with those of
the people.
— AVTORKHANOV ON STALIN'S ALLEGED MURDER

It is fitting that Stalin should have begun his last purge with a trumped-
up charge of medical murder. We have seen before how he gave himself
away by imputing his crimes to others. The chief "victim" of the plot,
Zhdanov, may or may not have been killed by Stalin. However, the
theme of medical murder runs through Stalin's life like a red thread,
taking one back to the death of Frunze in 1925 and farther still to the
possibility that Stalin hastened the end of Lenin. The "doctors' plot"
closes the circle. Peter Deriabin, a onetime member of the Guard Directorate, maintained that the scenario had taken almost a year to prepare. Work on it had started shortly after the Mingrelian affair had
failed to bring Beria down. Among the planners we can probably count
Ignatiev, even though he was the only senior policeman to survive Stalin's death by any significant span, while its chief architect was Ignatiev's deputy, M. D. Ryumin. Significantly the *Pravda* article calling
for new blood was published immediately after the doctors' arrest. The
timing suggests careful orchestration, introducing the themes of victims
and beneficiaries in the same movement.

The instrument of the doctors' arrest was a junior Kremlin physician,
Lydia Timashuk. She had first come to Stalin's notice in 1939, when,

as an ambitious young medical student, she had proposed a competition
for the maximum prolongation of the life of Comrade Stalin, "So precious to the USSR and all progressive humanity."[1] Now she wrote a
letter to Stalin accusing her seniors of trying to curtail the lives of Soviet
leaders by sabotaging their medical treatment. The campaign against the
doctors was launched in a *Pravda* article published on January 13,
1953, denouncing physician-saboteurs who killed their patients by pre-
scribing the wrong kind of treatment: "Hiding behind the honored and
noble calling of physicians, men of learning, those monsters and murderers trampled the sacred banner of science. . . ."

The piece went on to accuse them of murdering Zhdanov and weakening the health of certain members of the armed forces. Like
Voroshilov, they were agents of British and American intelligence, operating through a "corrupt Jewish bourgeois nationalist organization."
One of its leaders had been the deceased actor Mikhoels, who conveniently happened to be a relation of one of the arrested doctors. The
article ended by castigating the security services for "lack of vigilance."
The conclusion alone would have pointed to Beria as the main target,
even without the Jewish and bourgeois nationalist additions to the subtext. In that respect it was a rerun of the Mingrelian affair. There were
other targets, too. For example, although Marshal Konev was named as
one of the plot's military victims, nothing was said about Zhukov, and
this marked him as a possible target.

The first article was followed by others hinting at widespread conspiracy and a rapid vengeance that would visit those responsible. On January 31 *Pravda* established links between the conspiring doctors and
plotters such as Slansky and Gomulka recently unmasked in satellite
countries—yet another dig at Beria. The plot had a further component.
It was the cue for a surge of open anti-Semitism. This was a time when
persons of Jewish appearance found it prudent to avoid walking past beer
halls, regular danger spots where they ran the risk of being beaten to
death by patriotic drunks as the militia looked on in amused detachment. There were numerous cases of Jewish children, often of eminent
parents, being beaten up at school. When one parent complained, he
was arrested for disseminating anti-Soviet propaganda, since all races
were equal in the Soviet Union anti-Semitism could not exist. The
Russians' natural love of Jew baiting was given fuller rein in the last
months of Stalin's life than at any time since the heady days of Nicholas
II, when Jewish blood flowed freely in the gutters of small towns in
southern Russia and the Ukraine.

Something close to a wave of hysteria swept the nation. The notion that throughout the country Jewish doctors were secretly trying to murder their patients struck a deep-rooted phobia—the fear of the expert in the white coat whose knowledge gives him power of life and death. The phobia was linked to more traditional anti-Semitic sentiments and joined just as easily to that genuine delight that Soviet citizens had long been encouraged to take in the unmasking of enemies of the people. After Dr. Timashuk was given the Order of Lenin to reward her vigilance, a veritable spate of doctors' plots burst upon the land. Everywhere Jewish doctors were being unmasked. Mme. Mandelstam writes of a medical student in Tashkent, who secured the dismissal of a doctor by claiming she had tried to murder the student's baby, resurrecting that age-old anti-Semitic myth of the ritual murder of Christian babies by the evil Jew. "Similar scenes were played out all over the place; everyone raved about saboteurs and killer doctors."[2]

Stalin, who understood the dark side of his nation so well, had tapped a rich mine of hidden fear and hatred. No Nazi attack on money lenders, capitalist bloodsuckers or profiteers ever stirred passion at so deep a level as did Stalin's assault on Jewish doctors. It was backed up by newspapers which published pieces about Jewish black marketeers, speculators and Zionist agents, while the housemaids and taxidrivers of Moscow spread rumors to the effect that a group of Jewish saboteurs at the Stalin Automobile Factory were preparing to blow up the city.[3] Yet even now there were still jokes, such as the one about the brilliant young physicist defending his doctoral thesis, who kept referring to the outstanding theoretical work of the hitherto-unknown scientist named Odnokamen'. After he was awarded his doctorate, his examiners took him to one side to ask him who Odnokamen' was. It transpired that he was none other than a Russified form of *Einstein*. *Odno* = *Ein*; *kamen'* = *Stein*.[4]

By spring 1953 restrictions on Jews included quotas for places of higher learning and for residence in big cities. Loss of jobs and organized pogroms were prevalent, notably in the Ukraine, where old habits died even harder than elsewhere. The final touch came with Stalin's plan, which enjoyed the enthusiastic and vocal support of leading Jewish intellectuals, to deport all Jews to Siberia in order to help them to make a fresh start.[5] Stalin was putting the clock back once again, as he had when he restored serfdom. Now he re-created the conditions of Jews under the tsars, when most of them were obliged to reside within the Pale of Settlement, when they had quotas for admission to universities and for residence in Moscow and St. Petersburg and there were regular pogroms in the Ukraine. One of the principal features of the Revolution had been the emancipation of the Jews, who at last took their rightful place in Russian society, a process to which Stalin now intended to call a halt. Yet suddenly something happened. On March 2 *Pravda*, which had been busy denouncing Jewish crimes as diligently as any Nazi publication, suddenly suspended its campaign. Something extraordinary must have taken place.

•   •   •

That day Malenkov telephoned Stalin's daughter, telling her that her father was seriously ill and that she should come to Kuntsevo at once. She found the normally silent villa noisy and disordered as a team of doctors, whom, with one exception, she had never seen before, jostled with members of the Politburo. She was informed that Beria, Malenkov, Bulganin and Khrushchev had dined with Stalin on the night of February 28 and that dinner, as usual, had ended between five and six in the morning. Nothing had been heard from Stalin on Sunday, a day of rest; he had been found lying by a sofa on the floor of his room early on the morning of the second.

Svetlana had not been to Kuntsevo for some time and found her father had made strange alterations to his room. He had decorated it with reproductions of sketches of Soviet writers—his respect for the arts emerging once more—including one of Gorky, and with photographs of children and animals which he had cut out of illustrated magazines, as if seeking images of honesty, innocence and tenderness. One portrayed a little girl leading a goat by its horns. The room was still dominated, as it had been for years, by a huge Chinese tapestry of a ferociously snarling tiger, the kind of detail that no biographer dare hope for, especially when his subject is a man who liked to doodle wolves in red ink as he talked.

Stalin had been incapacitated by a cerebral hemorrhage. He was surrounded by terrified doctors who even resorted to traditional forms of treatment by applying leeches. According to his daughter, all his colleagues succeeded in expressing grave sorrow except for Beria, who had difficulty in concealing his delight. Khrushchev recalls that Beria alternated between bouts of glee and, at the rare moments that Stalin regained consciousness, acts of groveling devotion as he fell to his knees and bathed the dying man's hand with his tears, spitting as he faded away again.[6] On March 4 *Pravda* published a bulletin stating that Stalin had been taken ill in the Kremlin and that Beria, Malenkov, Bulganin and Khrushchev had assumed the burdens of office. In response to the announcement the pope ordered prayers for Stalin's health, as did the chief rabbi of the USSR.

Stalin finally died at 9:50 P.M. on March 5, but not before a last terrible moment when he appeared to regain consciousness to raise his right hand at his colleagues in a gesture of threatening admonition worthy of the last moments of Boris Godunov or Ivan the Terrible, only to sink back and die.

These are the bare bones of Stalin's last days, as his daughter tells them and as recounted by Khrushchev. They do not necessarily tell us what happened, especially since Khrushchev had an interest in blackening Beria and turning him into a scapegoat. There can be no doubt that Khrushchev already had assumed a leading role. Contemporary publications, such as the illustrated journal *Ogonyek*, show him to be the chief signatory of official announcements relating to Stalin's death, eclipsing both Beria and Malenkov. If his power struggle was indeed already won, his account of Stalin's death is all the more suspect.

There are numerous versions of Stalin's death, variously assessing the timing of the stroke and whether or not it was naturally induced. Many begin with a confrontation between Stalin and his dinner guests on the twenty-eighth, at which his plan to deport all Jews was resisted and his resignation asked for. This does not ring true. It is unlikely that anyone would take such a risk on the eve of a purge. It was not a time when a Politburo member could rely on the support of his colleagues, while one may seriously wonder whether anyone was brave enough to oppose Stalin to his face.

We have one hard fact to help us date the stroke. *Pravda* dropped its anti-Semitic campaign in its March 2 issue, which was printed late on the afternoon of March 1. No one would have dared order such a change if Stalin had not already been a dying man. It therefore seems probable that he was stricken some time between the night of February 28 and the following afternoon. It would seem that the leadership gave itself twenty-four hours before letting his daughter know that something was wrong, presumably in order to have the time to arrange a smooth transmission of power. This would explain why his daughter, who tried to telephone Stalin on March 1, was unable to get through. Khrushchev's early version of Stalin's death makes no mention of a medical presence at first, suggesting that the doctors were only summoned later. It also mentions an episode in which Stalin appears to come to. Khrushchev describes him being fed tea with a spoon and pointing jokingly at the picture of the girl with the goat as an image of his own impotence. He is also said to have shaken hands with his colleagues. All this must have happened before Svetlana arrived, or else she would have mentioned it. By the time she got there her father was no longer capable of such actions.

Avtorkhanov has confidently proposed that Stalin was murdered. Others, notably Medvedev, disagree. Avtorkhanov produces a version derived from recent émigré sources, which he cannot reveal, according to which Beria, Malenkov, Khrushchev and Bulganin, recognizing that they were in imminent danger of being shot and after reviewing alternatives such as forcing Stalin to resign, concluded that the solution was to have Beria arrange a murder. They code-named the operation Mozart, after Pushkin's *Mozart and Salieri* in which Salieri poisons Mozart. Beria, it is alleged, did as much for Stalin and was then arrested and shot by his colleagues. This scenario is as good a basis as any for examining the likelihood of Stalin's having been murdered.

It is obvious that Beria, Malenkov, Khrushchev and Bulganin all had a motive to murder Stalin. It was a case of kill or be killed, "your turn today and mine tomorrow." No one with a recollection of the thirties could be in any doubt as to the boss's intentions. That the "doctors' plot" was his doing alone is revealed by the fact that all the surviving doctors were released immediately after Stalin's death. Although he did all he could to protect himself from assassination and feared poison most particularly, the changes that Beria had brought about in Stalin's personal staff could have created new opportunities for a poisoner, while there was no shortage of expertise when it came to medical murder. Stalin died with singular apropos, for the doctors were due to go on trial within ten days. It may have been a coincidence, but for more than thirty years it had been prudent to ascribe timely deaths of leading figures in Soviet life to something other than the unaided hand of God. Finally there are some curious facts or echoes of facts that favor the view that Stalin was murdered.

Shostakovich claims that Yudina's record of the Mozart piano concerto was on Stalin's gramophone when he died. The conspirators allegedly invited one another to "come and listen to Mozart" when they met. It may be that Shostakovich picked up a distant echo of the plot and unwittingly changed a code word into a record, which is how legends are created. Alternatively, one of the assassins may have put the record on as a macabre private joke. Less speculative and tenuous is the way that Beria acted after Stalin's death. Stalin's daughter suggests that he mounted a rapid tidying-up operation. He had the villa stripped of all furniture and contents, while the staff, who worked for the MGB, was at once dispersed, and two officers of Stalin's immediate guard shot themselves. Although she sees this as evidence of their grief, one may find it curious that hard-boiled policemen should have found the prospect of life without Stalin unbearable. At one time Khrushchev certainly wanted it believed that Stalin had been assassinated. In a speech he made on July 19, 1964, he said of Stalin's crimes that they could not be whitewashed and that "the history of mankind has seen its share of cruel tyrants but they all died by the axe, as they governed by the axe."[7] These words were omitted from the printed version of the speech, but their burden, broadcast to millions of listeners, was inescapable: Stalin had died as he had lived.

• • •

Andrey Sinyavsky was in his parents' apartment when he heard the news. Everyone broke down and started to howl, except for Sinyavsky and a friend whose eye he caught. They moved unobtrusively to another room, locked the door and danced in silent celebration. The poet Joseph Brodsky, a Leningrader, had the news broken to him in school; he was almost thirteen at the time. His schoolmistress, a devout Stalinist, greeted the class with tears streaming down her face and ordered them to go down on their knees to receive the news that the entire nation had been orphaned. Somewhat bewildered by the universal spectacle of conspicuous grief, Brodsky went home to the communal apartment he and his family lived in. There too, to his amazement, he found everyone racked with sobs, everyone, that is, except his father, who caught his eye and slyly winked at him, while pretending to match the rest with expressions of irreparable loss. When he heard the news, Viktor Nekrasov opened a bottle of vodka and toasted the defunct leader in the foulest old soldier's language. Other members of the intelligentsia were in less of a hurry to celebrate, regardless of their hostility to Stalin. "It gets worse maybe" (*kak by khuzhe ne stalo*) was the reaction in Jewish circles, where it was widely feared that Stalin might be succeeded by someone who would hold the entire Jewish population responsible for his death and liquidate them all. Ilya Ehrenburg: "Tried to think out what would happen to us all now but was quite unable to do so. Like so many of my compatriots at that moment I was in a state of shock."[8]

In the gulag news of the Black Thief's death was by and large greeted with delight, especially by the criminals. However, many of the faithful despaired, supposing that with his demise they had lost their last chance of justice.[9] Others used the occasion to subject their fellow inmates to a loyalty test, angrily challenging anyone who appeared suspiciously dry-eyed.[10] However, by and large, celebration or skepticism was the exception. A surprising diversity of people met the news with genuine howls of grief. Vladil Krilenko, a senior merchant seaman before he left the USSR, heard the news on his way south to investigate the alleged sabotage of a tanker. Although still a young man, he had an unusually clear idea of the darker sides of the regime and was not in the least disturbed by Stalin's death. But as he traveled south, he was amazed by the spontaneous and unaffected grief that continued to greet him. A Polish ex-prisoner on a collective farm recalled the tearful dismay of its laborers: Stalin had abandoned them, left them weak and defenseless in a hostile world of capitalist encirclement. How could they survive without his leadership and wisdom?[11] Everywhere there were scenes of grief that verged on collective hysteria among the faithful, who allowed themselves to be overwhelmed with a sense of conspiracy and paranoia. One woman in Mme. Mandelstam's institute was driven by news of the death to claim that Jews had poisoned all the water jugs in the building.[12]

Public reaction to Stalin's death was complex. Even if we regard the hysterical behavior of Mme. Mandelstam's colleague as exceptional, there is no doubt that there was a genuine sense of loss. There was also the fear that his death might bring forth the anarchy and bloody chaos that ever dwell just below the surface of Russian life. Moreover, Stalin was mourned because he was popular. He had won the war, turned his nation into a great power and provided his people with a constant outlet for their fear, their hatred and their longing to tell others how to conduct their lives.

His death also inspired a reaction of a different kind, a strange sense of surprise that a leader who had so long been thought of as remote and godlike could do anything as ordinary and human as to die. Besides, no one could tell what was going to happen, so that the safest course was to grieve as conspicuously as possible. By the time of Stalin's death any Soviet citizen with the skills of a survivor had long been as expert as any specimen of corporate man in the public profession of ardent zeal and loyalty. Not to have howled with grief at the news of Stalin's death would have been as inconceivable to such persons as failing to have a good time at the company picnic. As the novelist Alexander Zinoviev puts it:

And the Soviet people, conditioned by decades of lies and pretense, effortlessly, freely and gladly made themselves feel sincere grief—just as they would very shortly, and with all the ease of well-trained creatures of Communism, put themselves into a state of sincere rage at the thought of the evil actions of their idol and his vile henchmen, actions about which they had seemingly known nothing, although it was they who had helped Stalin's henchmen carry them out.[13]

By 10:00 A.M. on March 6 a crowd had gathered in Red Square. Supposing that Stalin had died in the Kremlin, they expected to see his coffin brought forth through the Spassky Gate. It was that unusual Soviet phenomenon, a spontaneous crowd, even though it was controlled and herded by large numbers of MVD units. By noon the security forces had taken over the city. Extra troops had been brought in from Leningrad, and the trucks and tanks posted at every major crossroad had brought traffic to a halt, while no more trains or cars were allowed into Moscow. The city had been sealed off against the possibility of a mass popular disturbance or even a military coup.

Stalin's body was to lie in state in the Hall of Columns, where he had once had his own colleagues tried and sentenced. A huge crowd gathered outside, less to pay him their last respects than to get to see the man whose face had long been reduced to the iconic lines of official art, who only appeared as a remote figure on the far side of a great square or loomed over them in the night sky. Russian authorities have a poor record in crowd control, a form of policing which Russian crowds seem to require more than most. The rush to see Stalin's corpse was a case in point. Igor Golomstok looked down on the scene from one of the tallest towers in Moscow. It was obvious that the control was not working. The enormous crowd, which seemed to stretch for miles up Gorky Street and far beyond, was being forced to keep to the pavements, creating dreadful compression.

It was a strangely quiet crowd with remarkably few drunks. But the press was terrible, and people soon began to go down. The lucky ones were squeezed along the sides of buildings till they escaped into doorways and side entrances; others were crushed to death against the masonry or simply trampled. The police greeted the spectacle with an indifference which turned to violence as they tried to arrest and beat up the "troublemakers."[14] There has never been any official record of how many hundreds of victims marked Stalin's lying at rest, but they left him a peculiarly appropriate monument. On his way to work the next morning Golomstok saw huge piles of empty overshoes that had come off in the press of the day before. Some were hanging from the trees, but most had been stacked in pyramid piles along the wayside like so many rubber skulls arranged to commemorate the passing of the Muscovite pharaoh.

Epilogue

We think of terror as the reign of those who inspire terror; on
the contrary it is the reign of people who are themselves
terrified. Terror consists of useless cruelties perpetrated by
frightened people in order to reassure themselves.
—MARX TO ENGELS DURING THE PARIS COMMUNE

Stalin is very much inside each one of us.
—JOSEPH BRODSKY

Dr. Arnold A. Hutschnecker, who once had Richard Nixon as a patient, has tried to analyze what he refers to as the "drive for power."[1] He
derives it from a painful sense of one's own insignificance, a fear of
death and the wish to have others die. It is associated with a low sexual
drive and an inability to love. "It moves on the wings of aggression to
overcome inferiority. . . . Those whose power to love and consequently
create has been broken will choose war in order to experience an intoxicating sense of power or excitement."[2] A sense of failure, inferiority
and the inability to love frequently derive from a child's lack of respect
for his father and from an overaffectionate mother whose love is taken
for granted and never has to be won.

Certainly Stalin despised and hated his father, certainly he was unable to love and there is every indication that he had a developed sense
of inferiority. The young would-be revolutionary was rejected by Zhordania because he did not know his Marx properly. Later he was the

silent, sullen man of the people, surrounded by brilliant talkers, who considered him a semiliterate colonial who never lost the accent that marked him as coming from the empire's outer rim. In later years he was bitterly envious and wished to destroy anyone who outshone him; it was never considered prudent to beat him at chess, skittles or billiards.

Stalin was single-minded in his drive for power, well suited to a one-party system which allowed for its maximum concentration without any checks, balances or accountability. The personality cult and his apotheosis were logical developments for a man who had attained such heights and who could never bear to be wrong. Stalin, the shoemaker's son, was spectacularly successful in his reaching out after power, in the way he outflanked and destroyed his apparently brilliant rivals. He displayed remarkable, seemingly passionless patience, was always ready to wait for his time to come and never allowed a surge of adrenaline to precipitate a premature move. He showed an instinctive grasp of the principles of machine politics and was always working to create an organization within the organization. It is impossible to exaggerate the importance of his practice of placing "his men" at every level of the party hierarchy or, for that matter, the importance of the Secretariat itself. It was a stroke of genius to allow this to evolve into the machinery of government, a staff operation monitoring the official administrative line. He understood the effect upon ambitious young men of proximity to a power which they transmitted as personal assistants, knowing that he could count on their loyalty and certain that they would be efficient executors of his will.

It has grown easier, over the years, to see the Soviet Union as it developed under Stalin in its historical perspective. Peter the Great had brought the power of the autocracy to a new peak, developing a conception of the state whereby everyone, whatever his estate, was obliged to serve. His new Table of Ranks, the civil and military hierarchy, was supposed to supersede traditional forms of nobility as the ladder to power and prestige. However, the nobility soon freed itself from Peter's obligation to serve and developed a significant degree of independence, as did the military. Russian history, from Peter to the October Revolution, traces the development of a series of increasingly independent social groups, bodies of opinion, and power bases, all of which hampered the prerogative of the tsars. By the time of Nicholas II these groups included the imperial grand dukes, the army, the intelligentsia, the press, elected politicians, financial and industrial circles, writers and groups of "concerned persons." None of these had the constitutional power to hamstring the tsar, but they had the capacity to hinder him and ultimately to bring about his downfall.

By the time that Stalin completed his purges all trace of these or equivalent restraining forces had been swept away. Public opinion as Nicholas II had known it at the time, say, of the Rasputin scandal was gone forever. There were no independent groups left to act as a check upon the reemergent absolutism, nor were there any persons of authority or prestige with experience of a pre-Stalinist past. The purges were aimed not at individuals but at a generation. Through them Stalin avoided that transmission of *ancien régime* values and political attitudes, unwittingly passed on by an older generation, that undermined the French Revolution. Stalin dealt with that problem by ensuring that the generation ceased to exist. This enabled him to make a genuine new beginning, one unaffected by the habits and attitudes of the immediate past, and made for the emergence of the most powerful and efficient central authority that Russia has ever known, one without a trace of checks and balances and a logical culmination of the Russian political tradition.

Stalin used his power to create a certain kind of state, one with its roots deep in Russia's past, combining elements of the Russia of Nicholas I, Peter the Great and Ivan the Terrible. Stalin's state was based on the pyramid, making use of the widest conceivable differentiation of privilege and material reward to secure the cooperation of the best and the brightest, offering them seats aboard the greatest gravy train their country had ever known. He created a new version of the service state, one far more extensive than Peter's, from which there was no escape, which rewarded loyal and intelligent effort in every field of human endeavor, from the arts to industrial management, with spectacular lavishness. Those who climbed the pyramid successfully developed an increasing interest, as they ascended, in ensuring the survival of the system and the hand that fed them. This contributed greatly to the system's stability. Able conformists grew rich, powerful and privileged, while dissidents remained ineffectual, poor and lacking in prestige.

It would be a great mistake to assume that the regime born of this system would collapse overnight if everyone were able to listen to Voice of America or that it could be destabilized by the prospect of universal prosperity as it is known in the West; jeans and stereos for all. To suppose this is to fail to understand Stalin's deployment of privilege, exemplified by the story Mme. Mandelstam tells of a young party man who had risen high in the hierarchy just after the war and who observed that he especially enjoyed the taste of his steaks when recalling that others didn't have any. Successful Soviet citizens who get their fair share of the good things of the West, and who might be in a position to bring about economic and political changes, are opposed to any notion of prosperity for all since it would erode their privileged situation; the key to the executive washroom would lose its value. Those in a position to bring about change are those most committed to the status quo. This does much to explain the remarkable political stability of the Stalinist state which has scarcely altered in the course of fifty years.

A further stabilizing factor is the subtle role assumed by ideology, again a process initiated by Stalin. By 1941 no one except the fanatics believed that Marx's prophecies were going to come true. The ideology had lost the predictive power once ascribed to it. However, it continued to function as a framework of belief that legitimized the past—all those millions must not be thought of as having died in vain—and as a guiding principle for the future. It justified all forms of expansionist action since Soviet nationalism was furthering the cause of world revolution. No longer a guideline for action, it served, and still serves, to invest action in the cloak of legitimacy. Soviet man can have his cake and eat it, safe in the conviction that, ideologically speaking, he is correct and that generations of Poles, Czechs and Afghans as yet unborn will live to thank him.

Of course, it is not the case that the Stalinist or post-Stalinist state is remorselessly monolithic—any more than a pyramid is. The system accommodates all kinds of special-interest groups, universities, the arts, the military, industrial management, the security services, while the party acts as a clearinghouse where these interests meet and are reconciled. Moreover, the Soviet Union enjoys a mixed, not a socialist, economic system: on one side the state-owned enterprises; on the other the no less important and flourishing black economy. It is possible to anticipate increasing flexibility in this and other areas of Soviet life. The Stalin generation was rigidly conformist, consisting of literal-minded first-generation university graduates with excessive faith in what their elders told them and in what they read in books. But after three generations of higher education one may expect the emergence of a new type of Soviet graduate, sophisticated enough to be more flexible and less inclined to go by the book.

Stalin appears to have modeled both his behavior and his political designs on historical precedent. In certain respects he echoes the style and the obsessions of Peter the Great. Like him, he had a passion for monumental works carried out by slave labor, such as canal building. Like him, he had an obsession with the navy; heavy cruisers were a passion of Stalin's. In his personal life, his long, drunken dinners with their aggressive hospitality are remarkably close to Peter's own All Drunken Assemblies. Like Peter, Stalin enjoyed investing his inferiors with humorously extravagant titles, and like him, he enjoyed adopting the pose of a supplicant inferior in letters to his daughter. But above all, Stalin saw himself, like Peter, as the architect of a new society. He was overcoming backwardness and ignorance to create a service state, a concentrated and rationalized form of government dependent not on hereditary rank or wealth but on ability. He further refined Peter's system with the addition of the creative use of terror. This prevented the formation of any permanent power base in the army, police or administration, creating a society of privileged officeholders; a ruling class without tenure, denied the prospect of alternative and more secure employment elsewhere. *

It was as if Stalin had turned the Soviet Union into a company town in which the company was ruthless in its treatment of personnel, but in which the rewards could be colossal. Stalin's style of management reached right down the pyramid, for no one had any means of redress against his superior, and every boss became a petty Stalin to his underlings. Everyone treated those below him badly, kept a wary eye on his equals and flattered those above—while measuring himself for their jobs.

Stalin's admiration for Peter did not extend to the latter's love of the West. Stalin feared Europe, which made him feel inferior. This helps account for his hostility toward Leningrad and the increasing emphasis on the values of conservative, xenophobic, inward-looking and ideologically orthodox Muscovy. He professed an admiration for Ivan the Terrible, and once observed to the actor playing Ivan in the Eisenstein movies that the tsar's only error had been his failure to kill all boyars opposed to his policies, a mistake that Stalin managed to avoid. There is much in Ivan's regime that is echoed by Stalin—for example, Ivan's use of the *oprichnina*, an organization that combined characteristics of the Secretariat and the security services, with which he attacked the boyars.

* It must be conceded however that in recent years the Soviet elite, like elites everywhere, has become increasingly adept at passing its benefits on to its children. Besides, the process of seeking a position in the so-called *nomenklatura*, appointments requiring the approval of a higher authority—in other words, membership of the party elite—is uncannily reminiscent of the way in which North American academics seek tenure, whereas the benefits of the two kinds of appointment are not dissimilar.

Ivan was also capable of putting the population of an entire city to the sword for reasons best known to himself.

More important than such superficial analogies is the fact that in Ivan's day Muscovy still retained a vital feature of the ideal service state: conditional land tenure. Grants of land were made in recognition of and dependent on service and could be and frequently were revoked. This represents the essence of the Stalinist conception of privilege. The development of societies favoring Western democratic institutions and individual rights is inextricably bound up with the emergence of unconditional property tenure; each informs the other. The essence of Stalin's system and its attitude to the rights of individuals derive from a totally opposing conception of the way in which property should be held.

The creation of the modern Soviet state was Stalin's main achievement. Historians of a Marxist bent often wonder whether he was "necessary" or indeed "inevitable," questions that have no meaning beyond the Marxist framework. Had it not been for Stalin, one could anticipate the emergence of some kind of collective leadership which would have been quite ready to continue spilling blood for the good of the cause— especially if Trotsky had been a part of it. Collectivization was so much a part of the ideology, distrust of peasants rooted so deeply in the intelligentsia, that it would have been imposed without Stalin, but probably not accompanied by a man-made famine. One must hold Stalin responsible for initiating the purges, for a wasteful form of industrialization and for involving his country in World War II. Undoubtedly the Soviet Union would have fought better had it not been for the manpower losses of the thirties, not to mention the million-odd able-bodied men guarding the inmates of the gulag. That being said, Stalin's manipulation of the Allies was masterly, and his management of both war and peace impressive. Finally, without Stalin the Soviet Union might have boasted fewer untimely deaths, but it is unlikely that it would have been less brutal. Diderot once observed that it was foolish to expect men to be grateful if you gave them the chance to get away with ingratitude; true enough of mankind in general, the observation is truer still of those set in authority over us. The one-party system reduced managerial accountability to a minimum. A corporation has unions and shareholders to deal with, not to mention competition. The Soviet leadership had no such threats, apart from foreign invasion, and it treated its citizens accordingly.

Yet in one respect it could be argued that such coercive treatment was indeed "necessary." Critics of the regime have suggested that had Russia not had a revolution, it would have evolved along the lines, say, of Japan, since by the beginning of this century it was poised for industrial takeoff. Yet Russia could never have become a superpower without a coercive regime. It was a Grain Belt culture, its manpower unsuited to industrial discipline, entirely lacking that mysterious quality which makes the Japanese seemingly enjoy the drudgery of production line labor. When it comes to industrial discipline, Russians are free spirits, incapable of creating their own work ethic. Stalin's labor regulations were essential if his country was to become an industrial superpower.

Stalin was not alone. It was not a question of one evil man dominating a country of the oppressed. He enjoyed nationwide support at every level because he and his style of government were popular; he was truly a dictator of the people. The party followed him because it saw him as a winner, a practical politician who could be relied upon to lead them at a time when it was a case, for that tiny body of men and women, of sink or swim. He also appealed to the populace, satisfying elements deeply rooted in the culture: a hatred of Jews, foreigners and intellectuals. He proved able to tap that particular form of messianic nationalism that had made Moscow the "third Rome," making the Russian people feel they had a peculiar historic role. He converted this uniquely Russian feeling into Soviet man's acute sense that he is special.

Stalin also appealed to the Russian passion for telling others how to conduct their lives and for correcting them vociferously if they strayed from the proper path, invoking a longing for order and for the authority to impose order upon others. He gave them their first victory over the Germans since the days of Alexander Nevsky, and half Europe into the bargain. He restored the puritanical values of Old Muscovy, where everyone served tsar and state as best he could because such service was morally right and there was no room for doubt, dissent or troublemakers.

The assent enjoyed by Stalin is reflected in the fact that no one has ever been put on trial for his crimes; to do so would require the indictment en masse of several generations. As Nadezhda Mandelstam has pointed out, there was not just one "leader"; they were legion: "anyone with a scrap of power, every investigator, every janitor. . . . Petty dictators sprung up everywhere; our country swarmed with them, and still does. . . ."[3] Far from being put on trial, the ex-KGB officers, murderers, torturers are now honorable and decent old pensioners enjoying a well-earned rest, happily playing dominoes in the open spaces of Moscow and Leningrad. Any Soviet citizen over the age of seventy has certainly bayed for blood in his day and probably been a police informer into the bargain.

Stalin created a system that worked because people worked it, willingly, for privilege, out of idealism, out of hatred of their neighbors, and sometimes also out of love. Moreover, Stalin's popularity is deep-rooted enough to have survived some thirty years of official semidisgrace. Even today his image retains an extraordinary mythic presence, radiating a blend of terror, love and authority which makes it infinitely more ambiguous and more seductive than that of Hitler, who, after all, was a loser. The sheer power of the Stalin icon is such that it is inconceivable that it will not be restored to official favor. It represents so much that is of the very essence of the Soviet conception of the state. It is fashionable these days for Soviet truck and taxi drivers to display large pictures of Stalin in their cabs. Usually accounted for by "experts" as protests against the inadequacies of today's leadership, the explanation is simpler than that: Such iconic displays express the mighty Russian people's enduring love of the last "great man" in their history and perhaps even their nostalgic longing for a return to the "good old days."

Notes

Chapter One   Georgia

1. Lang, *Modern History of Georgia*, p. 18.
2. Farson, *The Way of a Transgressor*, p. 575.
3. FO 371 N 9429 18 38.
4. Lang, *op. cit.*, p. 108.
5. *Ibid.*, p. 17.
6. Koestler, *The Invisible Writing*, p. 78.
7. Kaminsky, ond Vereshchagin, "Detstvo i yunost' Vozhdya," *Molodaya Gvardiya*, p. 32.
8. Kuusinen, *Before and After Stalin*, p. 30.
9. Souvarine, *Staline*, p. 12.
10. Joffé, M. *One Long Night*, p. 67.
11. Iremashvili, *Stalin und die Tragödie Georgiens*, p. 6.
12. *Ibid.*, p. 18.
13. Serge, *Portrait de Staline*, p. 19.
14. Fischer, *The Life and Death of Stalin*, p. 14.
15. Joffé, *op.cit.* p. 67.
16. *Ibid.*
17. Alliluyeva, S. *Tol'ko odin god*, p. 314.
18. Avtorkhanov, *Tekhnologiya vlasti*, pp. 114–5.
19. Gusarov, *Moi papa ubil Mikhoelsa*, pp. 182–4.
20. *Russkaya mysl'*.
21. Kopelev, *I sotvoril sebe kumira*, p. 283.
22. Alliluyeva, *op. cit.*, pp. 313–4.
23. Medvedev, *On Stalin and Stalinism*, p. 2.
24. Arsenidze, *Novyi Zhurnal*, 224.

Chapter Two   The Young Marxist

1. *Ibid.*

493

2. *Cult of the Individual*, p. 6.
3. Lang, *op. cit*, p. 15.
4. Kolakowski, *Main Currents of Marxism*, vol. 1., pp. 323–4.
5. *Ibid.*, p. 373.
6. *Ibid.*, vol. 2, pp. 94–5.
7. Valentinov, *Encounters with Lenin*, pp. 22-3
8. *Ibid.*
9. Deutscher, *Heretics and Renegades*, p. 70.
10. Lang, *op. cit.*, p. 124.
11. Vakar, *Posledniye Novosti*

Chapter Three   In the Underground

1. *The Alliluyev Memoirs*, pp. 29–30.
2. *Istoricheskie mesta Tbilisi*, p. 68.
3. Lang, *op. cit.*, p. 138.
4. Iremashvili, *op. cit.*, p. 22.
5. Vakar, *op. cit.*
6. Uratadze, *Reminiscences*, p. 67.
7. Antonov-Ovseenko, *The Time of Stalin*, p. 235.
8. Souvarine, *op. cit.*, p. 46.
9. Solzhenitsyn, *Arkhipelag gulag*, vol. 1, p. 79.
10. Medvedev, *op. cit.*, pp. 17–18.

Chapter Four   Bolsheviks and Mensheviks

1. Arsenidze, *op. cit.*, 218–9.
2. Antonov-Ovseyenko, *op. cit.*, pp. 236–7.
3. Arsenidze, *op. cit.*, pp. 220–1.
4. Ulam, *Lenin and the Bolsheviks*, pp. 210–1.
5. Trotsky, *Nashi politiicheskiye zadachi*, p. 54.
6. Arsenidze, *op. cit.*, p. 221.
7. Kolakowski, *op. cit.*, vol 2, p. 149.
8. Antonov-Ovseenko, *op. cit.*, pp. 237–8.
9. Arsenidze, *op. cit.*, p. 224.
10. Uratadze, *op. cit.*, p. 67.
11. Arsenidze, *op. cit.*, pp. 234–5.
12. *ibid.*

Chapter Five   1905

1. Lang, *op. cit.*, pp. 162–4.
2. Arsenidze, *op. cit.*, pp. 230–1.
3. Souvarine, *op. cit.*, p. 92.
4. *Ibid.*, pp. 98–89.
5. Glenny, "Leonid Krassin," *Soviet Studies*, October 1970. No 22.
6. Arsenidze, *op. cit.*, pp. 232–3.
7. *Ibid.*, p. 225.
8. Uratadze, *op. cit.*, pp. 196–7.
9. Arsenidze, *loc. cit.*

10. Stalin, *Collected Works*, vol. 6, p. 56.
11. Shub, *Lenin*, p. 30.
12. Stalin, *op. cit.*, vol. 2, p. 188
13. Vereshchak, *Dni*.

Chapter Six   Exile

1. Iremashvili, *op. cit.*, pp. 30 and 39.
2. Antonov-Ovseenko, *op. cit.*, p. 247.
3. Iremashvili, *op. cit.*, p. 40.
4. Khrushchev, *Khrushchev Remembers*, p. 301.
5. Alliluyev, *op. cit.*, p. 137.
6. Hyde, *Stalin: The History of a Dictator*, pp. 96–7.
7. *ibid.*, p. 225.
8. McNeal, *Survey*, p. 140.
9. Smith, E. E. *The Okhrana*, pp. 235–6.
10. Valentinov, *op cit.*, p. 245.
11. *Ibid.*, p. 246.
12. *Ibid.*, p. 248.
13. *Zarya Vostoka*, December 23, 1925.
14. Dubinsky-Makhadze, *Ordzhonikidze*, pp. 92–4.
15. Alliluyev, *op. cit.*, p. 132.
16. *Ibid.*

Chapter Seven   Promotion

1. Shub, *op. cit.*, p. 130.
2. Alliluyev, *op. cit.*, pp. 138–9.
3. Medvedev, *Let History Judge*, p. 337.
4. Souvarine, *op. cit.*, p. 127.
5. Alliluyev, *op. cit.*, p. 141
6. *Ibid.*, p. 144.
7. Pipes, *The Formation of the Soviet Union*, p. 37.
8. *Ibid*, p. 36.
9. Stalin, *Collected Works*, vol. 11, pp. 147–8.
10. Deutscher, *The Prophet Armed*, p. 209.

Chapter Eight   Siberia

1. Antonov-Ovseenko, *op. cit.*, p. 240.
2. Medvedev, *On Stalin and Stalinism*, p. 6.
3. Sverdlova, K. T. *Ya. M. Sverdlov*, M. 1960. p. 199.
4. Sverdlov, Ya. M. *Izbrannye proizvedeniya*, M. 1957 vol. 1, pp. 276–7.
5. Bazhanov, *Vospominaniya*, pp. 94–5.
6. Ciliga, *The Russian Enigma*, p. 556.
7. Antonov-Ovseenko, *op. cit.*, p. 242.
8. *Life Magazine*, October 2, 1939.
9. S. Alliluyeva, *Tol'ko odin god*, p. 323.
10. Alliluyev, *op. cit.*, pp. 216–7.
11. Khrushchev, *op. cit.*, p. 320.

12. Alliluyev, *op. cit.*, p. 243.
13. Lenin, *Works*, 48, pp. 101 and 106.
14. *Kratkaya biografiya*, p. 56.
15. Sverdlova-Novgorodtseva, *Oktyabr'*, 1956, No 7, p. 150.
16. Medvedev, *op. cit.*, pp. 6–7.
17. Alliluyev, *op. cit.*, p. 189.
18. *Kratkaya biografiya*, p. 189.
19. Baikaloff, *I Knew Stalin*, pp. 27–9.

Chapter Nine   Revolution

1. Alliluyev, *op. cit.*, p. 187.
2. *Ibid.*, p. 188.
3. Schapiro, *The Communist Party of the Soviet Union*, p. 324.
4. Medvedev, *op. cit.*, p. 7.
5. Ulam, *op. cit.*, p. 324.
6. *Survey*, p. 160.
7. Sukhanov, *The Russian Revolution*, p. 230.
8. Sukhanov, *Zapiski o revolyutsii*, vol. 3, pp. 6–8.
9. Bazhanov, *op. cit.*, pp. 114–5.
10. Schapiro, *op. cit.*, p. 165.
11. *Pravda*, April 21, 1917.
12. Stalin, *Collected Works*, vol. 1, pp. xii–iii.
13. Shub, *op. cit.*, p. 225.
14. Sukhanov, *op. cit.*, vol. 3, p. 52.
15. *Ibid.*, pp. 56–7.
16. E. E. Smith, *The Young Stalin*, p. 333.
17. *Shestoi s'ezd RSDRP bol'shevikov. Avgust 1917. Protokoly.* M. 1958, p. 250.

Chapter Ten   October

1. Valentinov, *op. cit.*, p. 239.
2. *Kratkii kurs.*, M. 1953, p. 197.
3. Lenin, *Collected Works*, vol. 21, p. 444.
4. *Ibid.*, p. 507.
5. Ulam, *op. cit.*, pp. 361–7.
6. Joffé M., *Vremya i my*, no. 19 (1977), p. 178.
7. *Ibid.*, p. 367.
8. Medvedev, *op. cit.*, p. 10.
9. Monkhouse, *Moscow 1911–33*, pp. 66–7.
10. *Ibid.*

Chapter Eleven   Communism

1. Trotsky, *My Life*, pp. 233–4.
2. Trotsky, *Stalin*, pp. 246–7.
3. Duranty, *I Write as I Please*, p. 170.
4. Poretsky, *Proletarskaya Revolyutsiya*, no. 10 (1922), pp. 93–103.
5. Stalin, *op. cit.*, vol. 4, pp. 87–9.
6. Poretskty, *op. cit.*

7. Ulam, *op. cit.*, p. 404.
8. *Protokoly tsentral'novo komiteta RSDRP (b)*, pp. 211–3.
9. Souvarine, *op. cit.*, p. 439.
10. Ulam, *op. cit.*, p. 404.
11. *Ibid.*, p. 407.
12. Daniels, *The Conscience of Revolution*, 1960, p. 39.
13. *Ibid.*
14. von Laue, *Why Lenin? Why Stalin?*, p. 138.
15. Cohen, *Bukharin*, p. 87.
16. *Ibid.*
17. Ameel, *Red Hell*, pp. 4–5.
18. Berkman, *The Bolshevik Myth*, p. 264.
19. *Ibid.*, p. 248.
20. *Ibid.*, p. 255.
21. Fainsod, *Smolensk Under Russian Rule*, p. 38.
22. Shostakovich, *Memoirs*, p. 48.
23. Schapiro, *op. cit.*, p. 194.
24. Joffé, *Vremya i my*, no. 20 (1977), p. 179.

Chapter Twelve   Civil War

1. Pipes, *op. cit.*, p. 108.
2. Souvarine, *op. cit.*, p. 212.
3. Stalin, *op. cit.*, vol. 4, pp. 118–21.
4. *Ibid.*
5. Avtorkhanov, *Tekhnologiya vlasti*, p. 285.
6. Erickson, *The Soviet High Command*, p. 70.
7. Voroshilov, *Stalin and the Armed Forces*, M. 1951, p. 19.
8. Medvedev, *Let History Judge*, p. 13.
9. Antonov-Ovseenko, *op. cit.*, p. 11.
10. Medvedev, *op. cit.*, p. 14.
11. P. A. Zhilin, ed. *Ocherki po istoriografii sovetskovo obshchestva*, M. 1965, p. 18.
12. Trotsky, *My Life*, pt. 2, pp. 171–5.
13. Bazhanov, *op. cit.*, pp. 82–3.
14. Trotsky, *Kak vooruzhilas' revolyutsiya*, vol. 1, pp. 350–1.
15. Erickson, *op. cit.*, p. 58.
16. *Ibid.*, p. 45.
17. *Ibid.*, p. 43.
18. *Ibid.*, p. 46.
19. Stalin,*op. cit.*, vol. 4, p. 261.
20. Trotsky, *My Life*, pp. 432–3.
21. Souvarine, *op. cit.*, p. 229.
22. Trotsky, *Stalin*, p. 329.
23. Erickson, *op. cit.*, p. 99.

Chapter Thirteen   The Bolshevik Character

1. Cohen, *op. cit.*, p. 201.
2. Pethybridge, *Social Prelude to Stalinism*, p. 113.

3. Grigorenko, V *podpolye*, pp. 64–5.
4. Deutscher, *The Prophet Armed*, p. 495.
5. *Red Sword*, August 18, 1919.
6. *Red Terror*, November 1, 1918.
7. Doumbadze, *Na sluzhbe cheka i kominterna*, p. 22.
8. Poretsky, *Our Own People*, p. 42.
9. Bazhanov, *op. cit.*, p. 208.
10. Possony, *Lenin: The Compulsive Revolutionary*, p. 368.
11. Solzhenitsyn, *op. cit.*, vol. 1, p. 306.
12. Kolakowski, *op. cit.*, vol. 1, p. 508.
13. Solzhenitsyn, *op. cit.*, vol. 1, p. 46.
14. Abramovich, *The Soviet Revolution*, p. 415.
15. Deutscher, *The Prophet Unarmed*, pp. 438–40.
16. Rubin, *Moscow Mirage*, p. 211.
17. Balabanoff, *My Life as a Rebel*, p. 206.
18. Mandelstam, *Vospominaniya*, p. 141.

Chapter Fourteen   Promotion and a Marriage

1. Lockhart, *Memoirs of a British Agent*, p. 257.
2. Serge, *Portrait de Staline*, p. 52.
3. *Odinnadsatyi s'ezd RKP(b). Mart-Aprel' 1922. Stenograficheskii otchet* M. pp. 84–5, 143.
4. Schapiro, *op. cit.*
5. Tokaev, *Betrayal of an Ideal*, p. 160.
6. Medvedev, *Stalin and Stalinism*, pp. 80–1.

Chapter Fifteen   Cannibalism and Reform

1. Duranty, *I Write as I Please*, pp. 105–6.
2. Berkman, *op. cit.*, p. 292.
3. Strong, *I Change Worlds*, p. 123.
4. Abramovich, *op. cit.*, p. 206.
5. Solzhenitsyn, *op. cit.*, vol. 1, p. 147.
6. Besseches, *Stalin*, 1951 p. 150.
7. Ransome, *Six Weeks in Russia*, p. 55.
8. *Voina i revolyutsia*, 1926.
9. Berkman, *op. cit.*, p. 292.
10. Deutscher, *The Prophet Armed*, p. 514.
11. *Ibid.*, p. 494.
12. *Ibid.*
13. Bazhanov, *op. cit.*, pp. 116–7.
14. FO 318 N3592 4783 38.
15. Lewin, *Lenin's Last Struggle*, p. 24.
16. Schapiro, *op. cit.*, p. 218.
17. Agabekov, *GPU zametki chekista*, p. 43.
18. Grigorenko, *op. cit.*, p. 90.
19. Parvilhati, *Beria's Gardens*, p. 150.

Chapter Sixteen   The Stalin Machine

1. Daniels, *op. cit.*, p. 152.

2. *Ibid.*, p. 169.
3. Duranty, *Stalin & Co.*, p. 39.
4. Ulam, *op. cit.*, p. 547.
5. Stalin, *Voprosy Leninisma*, p. 477.
6. Barmine, *Memoirs of a Soviet Diplomat*, p. 257.
7. Zinoviev, *Ziyaushchie vysoty*, p. 298.
8. Bazhanov, *op. cit.*, p. 32.
9. Brzezinski, *The Permanent Purge*, p. 51.
10. Bazhanov, *op. cit.*, p. 24.
11. *Ibid.*
12. Scheffer, *Seven Years in Soviet Russia*, p. 340.
13. Rusanov, *Sotsialisticheskii Vestnik*, (1953) nos. 7–8.
14. Bazhanov, *op. cit.*, p. 53.
15. *Ibid.*
16. *Ibid.*, p. 82.
17. Schapiro, *Survey*, vol. 21, no. 3 (1975), p. 96.

Chapter Seventeen   Immeasurable Power

1. Kennan, *Russia and the West*, p. 184.
2. Kolarz, *Russia and Her Colonies*, p. 226.
3. Souvarine, *op. cit.*, p. 282.
4. *Ibid.*
5. Lang, *op. cit.*, p. 235.
6. Cole, *Stalin*, p. 59.
7. Lenin, *op. cit.*, vol. 42, p. 356.
8. Lang, *op. cit.*, pp. 238–9.
9. *Ibid.*
10. Trotsky, *Stalin*, p. 357.
11. Possony, *op. cit.*, p. 367. Bazhanov, *op. cit.*, p. 40.
12. Ulam, *op. cit.*, p. 559.
13. Kharmandarian, *Lenin i stanovlenie zakavkazsko federatsii 1921–23*. Erevan 1969, pp. 214–5.
14. Schapiro, *op. cit.*, p. 233.
15. Ulam, *op. cit.*, p. 559.
16. Randall, *Stalin's Russia*, p. 147.
17. Lewin, *op. cit.*, p. 40.
18. Carr, *The Triumvirate in Power*, p. 263.

Chapter Eighteen   God Votes Again

1. Joffé, M., *Vremya i my*, no. 19 (1977), p. 195.
2. Scheffer, *op. cit.*, p. 166.
3. Alexandrov, *Joseph Stalin*, p. 2598.
4. Carr, *Socialism in One Country*, p. 158.
5. Sukhanov, *Zapiski*, vol. 3, p. 218.
6. Bazhanov, *op. cit.*, p. 63.
7. Duranty, *Stalin & Co.*, p. 37.
8. Lenin, *op. cit.*, vol. 54, pp. 327–8.
9. Fotieva, *Iz vospominanii*, pp. 64–5.

10. Lenin, *op. cit.*, vol. 45, pp. 606–7.
11. *Ibid.*, vol. 54, p. 329.
12. *Ibid.*
13. Trotsky, *My Life*, p. 485.
14. Khrushchev, *op. cit.*, p. 44.

Chapter Nineteen   The Triumvirate

1. Ulam, *op. cit.*, p. 576.
2. Antonov-Ouseenko, *op. cit.*, p. 22.
3. *Ibid.*
4. Joffé, M., *Vremya i my*, no. 20 (1977), p. 183.
5. *Pravda*, May 16, 1923.
6. Stalin, *Works*, vol. 5, pp. 266 and 268.
7. Schapiro, *op. cit.*, p. 274.
8. Trotsky, *Moya Zhizn'*, vol. 2, p. 207.
9. Brzezinski, *op. cit.*, p. 51.
10. XIV *c'ezd VKP(b) Stenograficheskii otchet*. M. 1926. p. 506.
11. Carr, *The Triumvirate in Power*, p. 287.
12. Bazhanov, *op. cit.*, p. 74.
13. FO 371 N 5805 250 38.
14. Carr, *op. cit.*, part 3, p. 305.
15. Trotsky, *On the Suppressed Testament of Lenin*, New York: 1946, p. 38.
16. Bazhanov, *op. cit.*, p. 79.
17. Agabekov, *op. cit.*, p. 43.
18. Bazhanov, *op. cit.*, p. 80.
19. Trotsky, *Moya Zhizn'*, vol. 2, p. 240.

Chapter Twenty   We Vow to Thee, Comrade Lenin

1. Medvedev, *op. cit.*, p. 203.
2. Parvilhati, *op. cit.*, p. 140.
3. Werth, *The Year of Stalingrad*, p. 315.
4. Mandelstam, *Vtoraya kniga*, p. 233.
5. Bazhanov, *op. cit.*, p. 88.
6. Duranty, *I Write as I Please*, p. 210.
7. Bazhanov, *op. cit.*, p. 113.
8. Urban, *Stalinism*, p. 26.
9. Medvedev, *Let History Judge*, p. 224.
10. Beylis was a Russian Jew who was charged with the ritual murder of a Christian baby just before the First World War. Somewhat surprisingly he was acquitted, although Nicholas II remained convinced of his guilt.
11. Besseches, *op. cit.*, p. 117.
12. Bazhanov, *op. cit.*, p. 113.
13. Stalin, *Voprosy Leninsma*, p. 514.
14. Urban, *op. cit.*, p. 211.

Chapter Twenty-one   The Triumvirate Destroyed

1. XIII *C'ezd RKP(b) Stenograficheskii otchet*, M. 19245, p. 515.

2. Urban, *op. cit.*, p. 17.
3. Antonov-Ovseenko, *op. cit.*, p. 23.
4. Urban, *op. cit.*, p. 18.
5. Carr, *op. cit.*, p. 360.
6. Urban, *op. cit.*, pp. 18–20.
7. Erickson, *op. cit.*, p. 171.
8. Scheffer, *op. cit.*, p. 130.
9. *Ibid.*
10. Bazhanov, *op. cit.*, p. 140.
11. S. Sirotinskii, Poslednie Dni, *Krasnaya Zvezda*, October 31, 1930.
12. *Ibid.*
13. Antonov-Ovseenko, *op. cit.*, p. 42.
14. *Ibid.*
15. Carr, *The Struggle in the Party*, part 3, p. 67.
16. Antonov-Ovseenko, *op. cit.*, p. 30.
17. Cohen, *op. cit.*, p. 241.
18. Trotsky, *Stalin*, p. 417.
19. Bazhanov, *op. cit.*, p. 196.
20. *XIV S'ezd VKP(b) stenograficheskii otchet.* M. 1926, p. 875.
21. Khrushchev, *op. cit.*, pp. 26–7.

Chapter Twenty-two   The Beginnings of Stalinism

1. For a detailed discussion see Fainsod and Hough, *How the Soviet Union Is Governed*, pp. 138–40.
2. Tucker, *Stalin as Revolutionary*, p. 369.
3. *Ibid.*, p. 370.
4. Souvarine, *op. cit.*, p. 406.
5. Grigorenko, *op. cit.*, p. 88
6. Erickson, *op. cit.*, p. 210.
7. Medvedev, *Let History Judge*, p. 325.
8. Kuusinen, *op. cit.*, p. 30.
9. Antonov-Ovseenko, *op. cit.*, p. 233.
10. FO 371 N3410 309 38.
11. *Rabochaya Moskva*, May 26, 1924.
12. Solonevich, *Escape from Russia in Chains*, p. 248.
13. Serge, *Memoirs*, pp. 205–6.
14. FO 371 N 3504 245 38.
15. Carr, *The Triumvirate in Power*, p. 283.
16. *XIV S'ezd VKP(b) stenograficheskii otchet* M. 1926, pp. 504–5.
17. Carr, *The Economic Revival*, p. 200.
18. Stalin, *Works*, vol. 7, pp. 25–8.

Chapter Twenty-three   Trotsky Leaves the Stage

1. Fainsod, *Smolensk*, p. 48.
2. *Ibid.*, p. 52.
3. Tucker, *op. cit.*, p. 399.
4. Khrushchev, *op. cit.*, pp. 27–8.

5. FO 371 N 5455 31 38.
6. Berger, *Shipwreck of a Generation*, p. 76.
7. Rosenfeldt, *Knowledge and Power*, pp. 175–6.
8. Doumbadze, *op. cit.*, pp. 123–4.
9. Medvedev, *op. cit.*, pp. 28–9.
10. Scheffer, *op. cit.*, p. 168.
11. Fischer, I., *Men and Politics*, p. 30.
12. Medvedev, *On Stalin and Stalinism*, p. 58.
13. Khrushchev, *op. cit.*, p. 30.
14. *Ibid.*
15. Schapiro, *op. cit.*, p. 343.

Chapter Twenty-four   A Visit to Siberia

1. Ludwig, *Leaders of Europe*, p. 373.
2. Grigorenko, *op. cit.*, pp. 98–9.
3. Kopelev, *I sotvoril sebe kumira*, p. 232.
4. Petrov, *Empire of Fear*, p. 33.
5. Strong, *I Change Worlds*, p. 283.
6. Petrov, *op. cit.*, p. 38.
7. Fainsod, *Smolensk*, p. 129.
8. Besseches, *op. cit.*, p. 165.
9. Davies, *The Industrialisation of Russia*, p. 213.
10. Strong, *op. cit.*, p. 293.
11. FO 371 N 1771 75 38.
12. Lyons, *Assignement in Utopia*, p. 287.
13. Mandelstam, *Vospominaniya*, p. 82.
14. Lyons, *op. cit.*, p. 346.
15. *Ibid.*, pp. 114–5.
16. FO 371. N 1612 55 38.
17. FO 371. N 1874 18 38.
18. Cohen, *op. cit.*, p. 289.
19. Dmitrievsky, *Sovetskie Portrety*, p. 65.
20. Serge, *From Lenin to Stalin*, p. 169.

Chapter Twenty-five   Collectivization

1. Kopelev, *op. cit.*, pp. 203–3.
2. Conquest, *The Great Terror*, p. 41.
3. Poretsky, *op. cit.*, p. 186.
4. Czapski, *The Inhuman Land*, p. 194.
5. Glovatski, *The Pharaoh and the Priest*, p. 84.
6. *Ibid.*, p. 135.
7. FO 371 N 1612 55 38.
8. Poretsky, *op. cit.*, p. 102.
9. FO 371 N 6118 55 38.
10. FO 371 N 2207 55 38.
11. Lyons, *op. cit.*, p. 227.
12. Scheffer, *op. cit.*, p. 107.

13. Poretsky, *op. cit.*, p. 91.
14. Abramovich, *op. cit.*, p. 339.
15. Avtorkhanov, *Tekhnologiya vlasti*, p. 291.
16. Fainsod, *op. cit.*, p. 150.
17. Serge, *Memoirs*, pp. 246–7
18. Solonevich, *Escape from Russia in Chains*, p. 270.
19. FO 371 N 8574 88 38.
20. Grigorenko, *op. cit.*, p. 115.
21. Khravchenko, *op. cit.*, p. 90.
22. *Ibid.*
23. Solonevich, *op. cit.*, p. 269.
24. FO 371 N 5454 55 38.
25. Lyons, *op. cit.*, p. 283.
26. *Ibid.*, p. 284.
27. FO 371 N 1777 75 38 and 611 55 38.
28. Wickstead, *My Russian Neighbours*, p. 119.
29. Duranty, *I Write as I Please*, p. 264.
30. Wickstead, *op. cit.*, p. 119.
31. Cole, *op. cit.*, p. 85.
32. Medvedev, *Let History Judge*, p. 87.
33. Dmitrievsky, *op. cit.*, and FO 371 N 1951 75 38.
34. Tucker, *Stalinism*, p. 209.
35. Stalin, *Works*, vol. 12, pp. 191–9.
36. R. W. Davies, *op. cit.*, p. 271.
37. Scheffer, *op. cit.*, p. 276.
38. Stalin, *op. cit.*, vol. 12, p. 213.
39. Grigorenko, *op. cit.*, p. 114.
40. Szamuely, *Soviet Studies*, 16 (1966), p. 320.
41. Petrov, *op. cit.*, p. 31.
42. Cohen, *op. cit.*, p. 339.
43. Beck and Godin, *Russian Purge*, p. 17.
44. Solzhenitsyn, *op. cit.*, vol. 2, p. 34.

Chapter Twenty-six The Plan

1. Souvarine, *op. cit.*, p. 493.
2. Cohen, *op. cit.*, p. 295.
3. Knickerbocker, *The Soviet Five-Year Plan*, p. 155.
4. McNeal, *The Bolshevik Tradition*, p. 111.
5. Randall, *op. cit.*, p. 176.
6. Monkhouse, *op. cit.*, p. 207.
7. Low, *Low's Russian Sketchbook*, p. 73.
8. Strong, *op. cit.*, p. 318.
9. Knickerbocker, *op. cit.*, p. 87.
10. *Ibid.*, p. 13.
11. Lyons, *Moscow Carrousel*, pp. 336–7.
12. Labin, *Stalin's Russia*, p. 206.
13. Serge, *Memoirs*, p. 312.

14. Kolakowski, *op. cit.*, vol. 3, p. 39.
15. Parvilhati, *op. cit.*, p. 190.
16. *Ibid.*
17. Monkhouse, *op. cit.*, p. 266.
18. Solonevich, *Russia in Chains*, p. 175.
19. Knickerbocker, *op. cit.*, p. 221.
20. *Pravda*, April 21, 1937.
21. Solzhenitsyn, *op. cit.*, vol. 2, pp. 75–7.
22. Swianiewicz, *Forced Labour*, p. 161.
23. Deutscher, *La Russie après staline*, p. 56.
24. Dallin and Nicolaevsky, *Forced Labour in the Soviet Union*, p. 100.
25. Solonevich, *Escape from Russia in Chains*, pp. 226–7.
26. Khravchenko, *op. cit.*, p. 336.
27. Herling, *A World Apart*, p. 16.
28. Conquest, *The Great Terror*, p. 679.

Chapter Twenty-seven   A State of Terror

1. FO 371 N 2566 75 38.
2. FO 371 N 7744 7743 38.
3. Rosenfeldt, *op. cit.*, p. 176.
4. Schapiro, *op. cit.*, p. 393.
5. *Ibid.*
6. Urban, *op. cit.*, p. 103.
7. Lyons, *Assignment in Utopia*, p. 342.
8. Mandelstam, *Vospominaniya*, p. 277.
9. Agabekov, *op. cit.*, p. 246.
10. In a letter smuggled out of Russia in 1930.
11. Conquest, *The Great Terror*, p. 382.
12. Khravchenko, *op. cit.*, p. 75.
13. Solzhenitsyn, *op. cit.*, vol. 2, p. 291.
14. Lyons, *op. cit.*, p. 361.
15. Avtorkhanov, *op. cit.*, p. 408.
16. Zinoviev, *op. cit.*, p. 342.

Chapter Twenty-eight   New Society

1. Knickerbocker, *op. cit.*, p. 11.
2. Solonevich, *Escape from Russia in Chains*, pp. 326–7.
3. FO 371. N 854 75 38.
4. FO 371 N 8574 75 38.
5. Lyons, *Assignment in Utopia*, p. 359.
6. Solonevich, *Russia in Chains*, p. 119.
7. Lyons, *op. cit.*, p. 486.
8. *Ibid.*
9. Solonevich, *op. cit.*, pp. 137–8.
10. Ameel, *op. cit.*, p. 160.
11. Grigorenko, *op. cit.*, p. 414.
12. Granovsky, *All Pity Fled*, p. 26.

13. Weissberg, *op. cit.*, p. 186.
14. Koestler, *op. cit.*, p. 59.
15. Gusarov, *op. cit.*, p. 415.
16. Mandelstam, *Vtoraya kniga*, p. 255.
17. Weissberg, *op. cit.*, p. 279.
18. Lyons, *op. cit.*, p. 430.
19. Dutt, *George Bernard Shaw*, p. 1.
20. Redlich, *O Staline*, p. 216.
21. Grigorenko, *op. cit.*, p. 115.
22. Kopelev, *op. cit.*, p. 286.
23. Beal, *Word from Nowhere*, p. 258.
24. Kopelev, *op. cit.*, p. 289.
25. Redlich, *op. cit.*, p. 217.
26. Beal, *op. cit.*, p. 252.
27. *Ibid.*, p. 253.
28. FO 371 N 5514 113 38.
29. FO 371 N 6565 113 38.
30. Abramovich, *op. cit.*, p. 345.
31. Khravchenko, *op. cit.*, p. 129.
32. *Ibid.*, pp. 122–3.
33. FO 371.N 6514 6514 38.
34. FO 371.N 1914 113 38.
35. Lyons, *op. cit.*, p. 568.
36. A. Smith, *I Was a Soviet Worker*, p. 196.
37. Kopelev, *op. cit.*, p. 291.
38. FO 371 N 4964 119 38.

Chapter Twenty-nine   Terror Begins at Home

1. Orlov, *The Secret History of Stalin's Crimes*, p. 318.
2. *Ibid.*
3. Barmine, *op. cit.*, p. 263.
4. Medvedev, *Stalin and Stalinism*, p. 83.
5. Lermolo, *Face of a Victim*, p. 226.
6. S. Alliluyeva, *Dvadtstat' pisem k drugu*, p. 180.
7. Orlov, *op. cit.*, p. 319.
8. FO 371 N 6848 6426 38.
9. Deriabin, *The Secret World*, p. 231.
10. FO 371 N 6859 6426 3.
11. Koestler, *op. cit.*, p. 155.
12. Serge, *Memoirs*, p. 259.
13. FO 371. N 1433 113 38.
14. Ivanov-Razumnik, *T'yurmy i ssylki*, p. 200.
15. Mandelstam, *Vtoraya kniga*, p. 543.
16. Monkhouse, *op. cit.*, p. 274.
17. FO 371 N 3177 461 38.
18. Ivanov-Razumnik, *op. cit.*, p. 201.
19. Fainsod and Hough, *op. cit.*, p. 165.

20. FO 371 N 480 113 38.
21. Lermolo, *op. cit.*, p. 181.
22. Nicolaevsky, *Power and the Soviet Elite*, pp. 45–6.

Chapter Thirty   The Cult

1. Ludwig, *Leaders of Europe*, p. 350.
2. N. Gold, *The Twentieth Congress and After*, pp. 5–6.
3. Biagi, *Svetlana*, p. 51.
4. Barmine, *op. cit.*, p. 299.
5. Labin, *op. cit.*, p. 71.
6. Bortoli, *op. cit.*, p. 17.
7. Ehrenburg, *Men Years Life*, vol. 6, p. 303.
8. Antonov-Ovseenko, *op. cit.*, p. 175.
9. Avtorkhanov, *Zagadka smerti Stalina*, p. 309.
10. Shostakovich, *op. cit.*, p. 210.
11. Solzhenitsyn, *op. cit.*, vol. 1, pp. 81–2.
12. Deriabin, *op. cit.*, p. 171.
13. Agabekov, *op. cit.*, pp. 169–70.
14. Weissberg, *op. cit.*, pp. 402–3.
15. Vyshinsky, *Teoriya sudebnykh dokazatel'stv*, p. 23.
16. *Ibid.* p. 265.

Chapter Thirty-one   Reconciliation

1. V. and E. Petrov, *Empire of Fear*, pp. 88–9.
2. *Pravda*, February 7, 1964.
3. Poretsky, *op. cit.*, p. 144.
4. Hilger, *The Incompatible Allies*, p. 268.
5. *Pravda*, February 7, 1964.
6. Antonov-Ovseenko, *op. cit.*, pp. 79–80.
7. FO 371 N 1420 18 38.
8. Nicolaevsky, *op. cit.*, pp. 46–7.
9. Mandelstam, *Vospominaniya*, p. 154.

Chapter Thirty-two   The Kirov Affair

1. Antonov-Ovseyenko, *op. cit.*, p. 89.
2. *Ibid.*
3. S. Alliluyeva, *Dvadtsat' pisem k drugu*, p. 131.
4. Orlov, *op. cit.*, p. 34.
5. Lermolo, *op. cit.*, p. 124.
6. Antonov-Ovseyenko, *op. cit.*, p. 91.
7. Medvedev, *Let History Judge*, p. 161.
8. *Ibid.*, p. 159.
9. Antonov-Ovseyenko, *op. cit.*, p. 94.
10. *Ibid.*, p. 95.
11. V. and E. Petrov, *Empire of Fear*, p. 256.
12. A. Smith, *op. cit.*, p. 254.
13. Granovsky, *op. cit.*, p. 27.

14. Kopelev, *op. cit.*, pp. 319–20.
15. Mandelstam, *Vospominaniya*, p. 202.
16. Berger, *Shipwreck of a Generation*, p. 167.
17. Wolfe, *Khrushchev and Stalin's Ghost*, p. 181.
18. Orlov, *op. cit.*, pp. 253–4.
19. FO 371 N 1868 6 38.
20. Solzhenitsyn, *op. cit.*, vol. 1, p. 70.
21. Fischer, *Men and Politics*, p. 495.
22. Serge, *Memoirs*, p. 315.

Chapter Thirty-three   Terror by Day, and by Night

1. Bohlen, *Witness to History*, p. 144.
2. FO 371 N 1017 6 38.
3. FO 371 N 3422 250 38.
4. Berger, *op. cit.*, p. 73.
5. *Ibid.*
6. Brzezinski, *op. cit.*, p. 62.
7. V. Petrov, *It Happens in Russia*, pp. 17–18.
8. FO 371 N 103 23 38.
9. Erickson, *op. cit.*, p. 401. Soloviev, *Nine Lives in the Red Army*, p. 107.
10. Grigorenko, *op. cit.*, p. 282.
11. Tokaev, *Betrayal of an Ideal*, pp. 285–6.
12. Katkov, *The Trial of Bukharin*, p. 93.
13. FO 371 N 569 559 38.

Chapter Thirty-four   Four Years Late

1. Alliluyeva, *Dvadtsat' pisem k drugu*, p. 34.
2. Dan, *Novyi Zhurnal*, p. 181.
3. *Ibid.*
4. Weissberg, *op. cit.*, p. 427.
5. Vogeler, *I Was Stalin's Prisoner*, p. 33.
6. Saltykov Shchedrin, *Sochineniya*, M. 1954, p. 68.
7. Orlov, *op. cit.*, p. 70.
8. FO 371 N 4329 565 38.
9. Medvedev, *Stalin and Stalinism*, p. 99.
10. *Ibid.*
11. Orlov, *op. cit.*, p. 350.
12. FO 371 N 4331 565 38.
13. Nicolaevsky, *op. cit.*, p. 66.
14. Bohlen, *op. cit.*, p. 51.
15. Strang, *The Stalin Era*, p. 63.
16. Adler, *The Witchcraft Trial in Moscow*, p. 19.
17. Pritt, *The Zinoviev Trial*, p. 4.
18. Barmine, *op. cit.*, p. 295.
19. Orlov, *op. cit.*, p. 162.
20. Avtorkhanov, *Reign of Terror*, pp. 44–7.
21. Barmine, *op. cit.*, p. 254.

22. Mandelstam, *Vospominaniya*, p. 55.
23. Kennan, *op. cit.*, p. 306.
24. Soloviev, *op. cit.*, pp. 277–8.
25. FO 371 N4329 565 38.

Chapter Thirty-five   Up to Our Elbows in Blood

1. Orlov, *op. cit.*, p. 193.
2. FO 371 N 4872 24 38.
3. FO 371 N 111 11 37.
4. Avtorkhanov, *Tekhnologiya vlasti*, p. 422.
5. Conquest, *op. cit.*, p. 263.
6. Kolarz, *op. cit.*, p. 230.
7. Orlov, *op. cit.*, pp. 248–9.
8. Medvedev, *Let History Judge*, p. 174.
9. *K istorii plenuma TsK VkP(b)*. M. 1937.
10. Orlov, *op. cit.*, pp. 248–9.
11. *Ibid.*, p. 222.
12. Conquest, *op. cit.*, pp. 408–9.
13. *Ibid.*
14. Chaney, *Zhukov*, p. 30.
15. Grigorenko, *op. cit.*, pp. 210–1.
16. FO 371 N 4776 250 38.
17. FO 371 N 5024 250 38.
18. Ginzburg, *Into the Whirlwind*, pp. 20–1.
19. Ivanov-Razumnik, *op. cit.*, p. 342.
20. Begin, *White Nights*, p. 154.
21. Granovsky, *op. cit.*, p. 69.
22. Kolakowski, *op. cit.*, vol. 3, p. 87.
23. Orlov, *op. cit.*, p. 154.
24. Ginzburg, *op. cit.*, p. 105.
25. Carmichael, *Stalin's Masterpiece*, p. 150.
26. Ivanov-Razumnik, *op. cit.*, pp. 182–3.
27. Deriabin, *op. cit.*, p. 141.
28. Ginzburg, *op. cit.*, p. 136.

Chapter Thirty-six   The Final Phases of the Terror

1. FO 371 N 26 26 38.
2. *Cult of the Individual*, p. 35.
3. *Ibid.*, p. 34.
4. Orlov, *op. cit.*, p. 214.
5. Conquest, *op. cit.*, pp. 354–5.
6. Medvedev, *Let History Judge*, p. 296.
7. Mandelstam, *Vospominaniya*, p. 371.
8. Poretsky, *op. cit.*, p. 181.
9. Fischer, *Men and Politics*, p. 435.
10. FO 371 N 6180 26 38.
11. Beck and Godin, *op. cit.*, p. 156.

12. Mandelstam, *op. cit.*, p. 375.
13. FO 371 N 6234 250 38.
14. FO 371 N 5732 250 38.
15. FO 371 ·N 6432 250 38.
16. *Pravda*, January 27, 1938.
17. Orlov, *op. cit.*, p. 251.
18. Poretsky, *op. cit.*, p. 179.
19. Alexandrov, *op. cit.*, p. 216.
20. Poretsky, *op. cit.*, p. 200.
21. Orlov, *op. cit.*, p. 292.
22. Duranty, *The Kremlin and the People*, pp. 84–5.
23. FO 371 N 1506 26 38.
24. V. and E. Petrov, *op. cit.*, p. 46.
25. Katkov, *op. cit.*, p. 185.
26. FO 371 N 1291 26 38.
27. Medvedev, *Let History Judge*, p. 333.
28. *Ibid.*, p. 311.
29. Khrushchev, *op. cit.*, p. 108.
30. FO 371 N 5720 250 38.
31. Khravchenko, *op. cit.*, p. 304.
32. Berger, *op. cit.*, pp. 122–3.
33. Medvedev, *On Stalin and Stalinism*, p. 110.
34. *Ibid.*
35. Yakovlev, *Tsel' zhizni*. M. 1966, p. 179.
36. Stalin, *Voprosy Leninizma*, p. 594.
37. *Ibid.*, p. 596.
38. *Ibid.*

Chapter Thirty-seven   Foreign Policy

1. Cohen, *op. cit.*, p. 293.
2. Kuusinen, *op. cit.*, p. 90.
3. O'Neill, *Men of Destiny*, p. 76.
4. Buber, M., *Under Two Dictators*, p. 9.
5. Schapiro, *op. cit.*, p. 490.
6. Tokaev, *Comrade X*, p. 169.
7. FO 371 N 1599 132 38.
8. *Ibid.* p. 82.
9. von Ribbentrop, *Memoirs*, p. 111.
10. *Ibid.*, p. 113.
11. Hilger, *op. cit.*, p. 314.
12. *Ibid.*, p. 316.
13. S. Alliluyeva, *Dvadsat' pisem k drugu*, p. 340.
14. Nord, *Iz bloknota sovetskoi zhurnalistki*, p. 85.
15. Urban, *op. cit.*, p. 199.
16. J. E. Davies, *Mission to Moscow*, p. 293.
17. Grigorenko, *op. cit.*, p. 238.
18. Maisky, *Memoirs of a Soviet Ambassador*, p. 31.

19. Liddell Hart, *The Soviet Army*, p. 74.
20. *Ibid.*, p. 75.
21. Urban, *op. cit.*, pp. 201–2.
22. FO 371 N 8304 1551 38.
23. Liddell Hart, *op. cit.*, p. 76.
24. Herling, *op. cit.*, p. 3.
25. Granovsky, *op. cit.*, p. 229.
26. Wittlin, *Commissar*, pp. 270–1.
27. Liddell Hart, *op. cit.*, p. 82.
28. Eeman, *Inside Stalin's Russia*, p. 159.
29. FO 371 N 3288 32 38.
30. *Ibid.*
31. *Pravda*, December 25, 1939.
32. FO 371 N 1570 1570 38.

Chapter Thirty-eight   Barbarossa

1. Khrushchev, *op. cit.*, p. 136.
2. FO 371 N 5969 30 38.
3. Lissan, *Survey*, p. 56.
4. Turney, *Disaster at Moscow*, p. 25.
5. *Ibid.*
6. *Ibid.*
7. Hilger, *op. cit.*, p. 326.
8. *Survey*, p. 172.
9. FO 371 N 10521 1 38.
10. Grigorenko, *op. cit.*, p. 253.
11. Chaney, *op. cit.*, p.86.
12. Erickson, *op. cit.*, p. 584.
13. Tokaev, *Comrade X*, p. 170.
14. Hilger, *op. cit.*, p. 336.
15. FO 371 N 3147 114 38.
16. Maisky, *op. cit.*, p. 160.
17. Werth, *Russia: The Post-War Years*, p. 2.
18. Khravchenko, *op. cit.*, p. 359.

Chapter Thirty-nine   Total Enough for Anyone

1. Churchill, *Second World War*, vol. 3, p. 331.
2. E.g., Guderian, *Panzer Leader*, p. 156, Soloviev, *op. cit.*, p. 205; Schapiro, *op. cit.*, p. 502.
3. Strik-Strikfeldt, *Against Stalin and Hitler*, p. 46.
4. Soloviev, *op. cit.*, p. 235.
5. Pirogov, *Why I Escaped*, p. 100.
6. Soloviev, *op. cit.*, p. 205.
7. Czapski, *op. cit.*, pp. 16–17.
8. Grigorenko, *op. cit.*, p. 582.
9. Soloviev, *op. cit.*, p. 248.
10. Kalinov, *Le Figaro littéraire*, no. 185 (November 5, 1949).

11. FO 371 N 1111 624 38.
12. FO 371 N 79 1631 38.
13. Schellenburg, *op. cit.*, p. 311.
14. Randall, *op. cit.*, p. 275.
15. Wittlin, *op. cit.*, p. 293.
16. Khravchenko, *op. cit.*, pp. 355–7.

Chapter Forty   Typhoon

1. Bialer, *Stalin and His Generals*, pp. 340–1.
2. Erickson, *op. cit.*, p. 613.
3. Grigorenko, *op. cit.*, p. 274.
4. Guderian, *op. cit.*, pp. 158–60.
5. S. Alliluyeva, *Tol'ko odin god*, p. 324.
6. Biagi, *op. cit.*, p. 47.
7. *Sunday Times*, February 24, 1980.
8. Thayer, *Bears in the Caviar*, p. 224.
9. V. and E. Petrov, *op. cit.*, p. 96.
10. Thayer, *op. cit.*, p. 211.
11. *Pravda*, September 4, 1941.
12. FO 371 N 4108 521 38.
13. FO 371 N 4307 551 38.
14. Avtorkhanov, *Tekhnologiya vlasti*, p. 467.
15. Khravchenko, *op. cit.*, p. 375.
16. Solzhenitsyn, *op. cit.*, vol. 1, p. 91.
17. Tokaev, *Comrade X*, p. 205.
18. *Ibid.*, p. 229.
19. Guderian, *op. cit.*, p. 194.
20. *Ibid.*, p. 128.
21. Bialer, *op. cit.*, pp. 275–6.
22. *Ibid.*, pp. 328–9.
23. Chaney, *op. cit.*, p. 184.
24. Bialer, *op. cit.*, p. 349.
25. Kopelev, *op. cit.*, pp. 207–8.

Chapter Forty-one   Stalin and the Allies

1. Bohlen, *op. cit.*, p. 126.
2. *Ibid.*, pp. 40–1.
3. *Ibid.*, p. 122.
4. Eden, *The Reckoning*, p. 437.
5. FO 371 N 841 114 38.
6. FO 371 N 108 5 38.
7. *Ibid.*
8. FO 371 N 1093 5 38.
9. FO 371 N 428 428 38.
10. FO 371 N 841 114 38
11. FO 371 N 7316 114 38 and FO 312 N 3147 114 38.
12. FO 954 SU 42 80.

13. FO 954 SU 42 2 V.
14. Hull, *Memoirs*, p. 1266.
15. Farnsworth, *William Bullitt and the Soviet Union*, p. 3.
16. Herling, *op. cit.*, pp. 230–1.
17. Martel, *The Russian Outlook*, p. 46.
18. *Ibid.*
19. *Ibid*, p. 112.
20. *Ibid.*, p. 144.
21. Bryant, *Turn of the Tide*, p. 380.
22. Kerr, *The Secret of Stalingrad*, pp. 32–5.
23. Bryant, *Triumph in the West*, p. 90.
24. FO 954 SU 42 23.
25. FO 371 N 527 252 38.

Chapter Forty-two   A Slowly Turning Tide

1. Werth, *The Year of Stalingrad*, p. 315.
2. FO 954 SU 42 253. Litvinov in a conversation with HM ambassador in Washington, September 3, 1982.
3. Deriabin, *op. cit.*, p. 47.
4. *Ibid.*
5. Khrushchev, *op. cit.*, p. 191.
6. Grigorenko, *op. cit.*, pp. 284–6.
7. S. Alliluyeva, *Dvadsat' pisem*, p. 210.
8. C. A. Smith, *Escape from Paradise*, p. 110.
9. Urban, *op. cit.*, p. 74.
10. FO 371 N 607 24 38.
11. FO 371 N 4307 55 38.
12. White, *Report on the Russians*, p. 159.
13. FO 371 N 4307 55 38.
14. Metternich, *Tatiana*, p. 187.
15. Martel, *op. cit.*, p. 6.

Chapter Forty-three   Teheran

1. FO 371 N 2172 52 38.
2. FO 371 N 583 52 38.
3. Khravchenko, *op. cit.*, p. 406.
4. Tucker, *Stalinism*, p. 264.
5. Conquest, *op. cit.*, p. 643.
6. Zawodny, *Death in the Forest*, p. 36.
7. *Ibid.*, p. 181.
8. FO 371 N 2354 52 38.
9. FO 371 N 5121 66 38.
10. Hull, *op. cit.*, p. 1317.
11. Eden, *op. cit.*, p. 413.
12. Perkins, *op. cit.*, p. 83.
13. *Ibid.*, p. 142.
14. *Ibid.*, p. 84–5.

15. Ismay, *Memoirs*, p. 339.
16. Bryant, *Triumph in the West*, p. 91.
17. FO 371 N 4099 4069 38.
18. Kennan, *Russia and the West*, p. 361.
19. Ismay, *op. cit.*, p. 340.
20. Birse, *Memoirs of an Interpreter*, p. 160.
21. *Ibid.*, p. 212.
22. White, *op. cit.*, p. 131.
23. Perkins, *op. cit.*, p. 86.

Chapter Forty-four   The Alliance

1. FO 954 Pol 44 10.
2. Hull, *op. cit.*, p. 1237.
3. FO 317 N 4099 4069 38.
4. Feis, *Churchill, Roosevelt, Stalin*, p. 297.
5. Pirogov, *op. cit.*, p. 185.
6. Kusnierz, *Stalin and the Poles*, pp. 214–6.
7. FO 371 N 2128 36 38.
8. In a private letter.
9. FO 371 N 5126 36 38.
10. FO 371 N 2544 36 38.
11. FO 371 N 6214 36 38.
12. Djilas, *Conversations with Stalin*, p. 61.
13. *Ibid.*, p. 65.
14. Tokaev, *Betrayal of an Ideal*, p. 278.
15. *Ibid.*, pp. 279–80.
16. *Ibid.*, pp. 280–1.

Chapter Forty-five   Warsaw

1. Stypulkowski, *Invitation to Moscow*, pp. 123–4.
2. FO 954. SU 44 167.
3. FO 954 Pol 44 180.
4. Feis, *op. cit.*, pp. 386–7.
5. FO 371 N 1441 18 38.
6. Churchill, *Second World War*, vol. 6, p. 207.
7. FO 371 N 6523 36 38.
8. Churchill, *op. cit.*, *vol. cit.*, pp. 211–2.
9. Strang, *Home and Abroad*, p. 213.
10. Weinstein, *Perjury. The Hiss-Chambers Case*. New York: 1976, p. 361.
11. Byrnes, *Frankly Speaking*, p. 23.
12. Eden, *op. cit.*, p. 512.
13. Bohlen, *op. cit.*, p. 164.
14. Metternich, *op. cit.*, p. 280.
15. Stettinius, *Roosevelt and the Russians*, p. 193.
16. Hart, *op. cit.*, p. 96.
17. FO 371 N 2059 19 38.
18. FO 371 N 3589 409 38.

19. Churchill, *op. cit.*, *vol. cit.*, p. 316.
20. Byrnes, *op. cit.*, p. 44.
21. Clemens, *Yalta*, p. 268.

Chapter Forty-six   Not a Few Blunders

1. Vogeler, *op. cit.*, p. 33.
2. Djilas, *op. cit.*, p. 76.
3. C. A. Smith, *op. cit.*, pp. 28–30.
4. Pirogov, *op. cit.*, p. 197.
5. S. Alliluyeva, *Tol'ko odin god*, p. 339.
6. Churchill, *op. cit.*, *vol. cit.*, p. 398.
7. Guderian, *op. cit.*, p. 309.
8. *Ibid.*, p. 316.
9. FO 371 N 6914 18 38.
10. Suvorov, *op. cit.*, p. 17.
11. Djilas, *op. cit.*, p. 90.
12. *Ibid.*, p. 111.
13. Ehrenburg, *op. cit.*, vol. 5, p. 189.
14. Fischer, *The Life and Death of Stalin*, p. 172.

Chapter Forty-seven   Peacemaking

1. Dixon, *Double Diploma*, p. 165.
2. Truman, *Year of Decisions*, p. 275.
3. Leahy, *I Was There*, p. 476.
4. Eden, *op. cit.*, p. 545.
5. Kennan, *Memoirs*. p. 264.
6. Eden, *op. cit.*, p. 546.
7. Leahy, *op. cit.*, p. 500.
8. Truman, *op. cit.*, p. 342.
9. *Ibid.*, p. 346.
10. Stettinius, *op. cit.*, p. 40.
11. Urban, *op. cit.*, pp. 394–5.
12. Mandelstam, *Vtoraya kniga*, p. 103.
13. FO 371 N 1111 624 38.
14. FO 371 N 677 389 38.
15. FO 371 N 15177 24 38.
16. FO 371 N 12414 24 38.
17. FO 371 N 607 24 38.
18. Thomas, *John Strachey*, p. 86.
19. FO 371 N 10905 24 38.
20. Nicolaevsky, *op. cit.*, p. 136.
21. White, *op. cit.*, p. 246.
22. Werth, *Russia: The Post-war Years*, p. 292.
23. FO 371 N 4872 24 38.
24. Conquest, *op. cit.*, pp. 450–1.
25. FO 371. N 14905 627 38.
26. The *Times* of London, May 6, 1977.

27. Tolstoy, *Stalin's secret War*, p. 324.
28. *Ibid., loc. cit.*
29. FO 371 N 3353 42 38.
30. S. Alliluyeva, *Dvadsat' pisem k drugu*, p. 182.
31. FO 371 N 14870 389 38.
32. FO 371 N 653 68 38.
33. S. Alliluyeva, *Tol'ko odin god*, p. 134.
34. Khrushchev, *op. cit.*, p. 260.
35. FO 371 N 12261 389 38.
36. FO 371 N 375 24 38.
37. Shostakovich, *op. cit.*, p. 272.

Chapter Forty-eight   Stalin and the Muses

1. FO 371. N 15903. 24 38.
2. Tucker, *Stalin and Stalinism*, p. 233.
3. Shostakovich, *op. cit.*, p. 254.
4. *Ibid.*, p. 192.
5. FO 371 N 1925 18 38.
6. Ivanov-Razumnik, *op. cit.*, 206–8.
7. Nord, *op. cit.*, pp. 57–8.
8. Ehrenburg, *op. cit.*, vol. 6, p. 48.
9. Shostakovich, *op. cit.*, p. 276.
10. FO 371 N 2375 24 38.
11. Mandelstam, *Vtoraya kniga k drugu*, pp. 102–3
12. S. Alliluyeva, *Dvadsat' pisem k drugu*, p. 183.
13. Werth, *Russia: The Post-war Years*, p. 201.
14. Djilas, *op. cit.*, p. 116.
15. FO 371 N 2796 24 38.
16. S. Alliluyeva, *Tol'ko odin god*, p. 333.
17. Medvedev, *Stalin and Stalinism*, p. 150.
18. *Izvestiya*, August 2, 1948.
19. Avtorkhanov, *Tekhnologiya vlasti*, p. 487.
20. Alliluyeva, *op. cit.*, p. 333.
21. FO 371 N 11809 18 38.
22. FO 371 N 1055 33 19612 38.
23. FO 371 N 8702 19612 38.
24. Randall, *op. cit.*, p. 123.
25. FO 371 N 1055 33 19616 38.

Chapter Forty-nine   Endgame

1. *Pravda*, May 30, 1950.
2. FO 371 N 1012 31 5.
3. *Pravda*, July 4, 1950.
4. FO 371 NS 1012/5.
5. Kennan, *Russia and the West*, p. 431.
6. *Times* of London, May 6, 1977.
7. FO 371 NS 1015/68.

8. Avtorkhanov, *Zagadka smerti stalina*, pp. 121–2.
9. Khrushchev, *op. cit.*, p. 312.
10. *Ibid.*, p. 313.
11. *Ibid.*, p. 276.
12. Wittlin, *op. cit.*, p. 370.
13. *Pravda*, October 9, 1952.
14. *Ibid.*, October 15, 1952.
15. Medvedev, *Stalin and Stalinism*, p. 157.
16. *Ibid.*, pp. 154–5.
17. Birse, *op. cit.*, p. 99.
18. Berger, *op. cit.*, p. 235.
19. Avtorkhanov, *op. cit.*, pp. 178–9.
20. *Times* of London, October 3, 1967.
21. Deriabin, *op. cit.*, p. 167.
22. Avtorkhanov, *op. cit.*, p. 197.
23. Berger, *op. cit.*, p. 235.

Chapter Fifty   Checkmate

1. Alexandrov, *The Kremlin*, p. 311.
2. Mandelstam, *Vtoraya kniga*, p. 432.
3. Bortoli, *op. cit.*, p. 179.
4. *Ibid.*, p. 177.
5. Medvedev, *Stalin and Stalinism*, pp. 158–60.
6. Khrushchev, *op. cit.*, p. 318.
7. Avtorkhanov, *op. cit.*, p. 244.
8. Ehrenburg, *op. cit.*, *vol. cit.*, p. 301.
9. Solzhenitsyn, *op. cit.*, vol. 2, p. 337.
10. Kuusinen, *op. cit.*, p. 206.
11. Berger, *op. cit.*, pp. 236–7.
12. Mandelstam, *op. cit.*, pp. 431–3.
13. Zinoviev, *Svetloe budushchee*, p. 45.
14. *Ibid.*, p. 46.

Epilogue

1. New York, 1974.
2. *op. cit.*, pp. 83–4.
3. Mandelstam, *Vospominaniya*, p. 284.

Selected Bibliography

Unless otherwise stated, all English-language titles are published in London.

M = Moscow, L = Leningrad.

Books

Abramovich, R. *The Soviet Revolution 1917–1939*. 1962.
Abbe, E. *I Photograph Russia*. 1935.
Agabekov, G. *GPU, Zametki chekista*. Berlin: 1930.
Alexandrov, V. *The Kremlin*. 1962.
———. *The Tukachevsky Affair*. 1962.
The Alliluyev Memoirs, ed. D. Tutaev. 1968.
Alliluyev, S. *Proidenniy put'*. M. 1946.
Alliluyeva, A. *Vospominaniya*. M. 1946.
Alliluyeva, S. *Dvadsat' pisem k drugu*. 1967.
———. *Tol'ko odin god*. 1969.
Amba, A. *I Was Stalin's Bodyguard*. 1952
Ameel, J. *Red Hell*. 1941.
Antonov-Ovseenko, A. *The Time of Stalin*. New York: 1982.
Armstrong, J. A. *The Politics of Totalitarianism*. New York: 1961.
Auty, P. *Tito: A Biography*. 190.
Avtorkhanov, A. (A. Uralov). *Proizkhozhdeniya partokratii*. 2 vols. Frankfurt: 1973.
———. *Tekhnologiya vlasti*.
———. *The Reign of Stalin*. 1953
———. *Zagadki smerti Stalina*. Frankfurt: 1976.

Baikaloff, A. V. *I Knew Stalin*. 1949.
Bailey, G. (pseud). *The Conspirators*. 1966.

Bajanov, B. *Avec Staline dans le Kremline*. Paris: 1929.
———. *Stalin: Der Rote Diktator*. Berlin: 1931.
———. *Vospominaniya*.
Balabanoff, A. *Impressions of Lenin*. Ann Arbor, Mich.: 1964.
———. *My Life as a Rebel*. 1938.
Barmine, A. *Memoirs of a Soviet Diplomat*. 1938.
Beal, F. *Word from Nowhere*. 1937.
Beck, F. and W. Godin. *Russian Purge and the Extraction of Confessions*. 1951.
Begin, M. *White Nights: The Story of a Prisoner in Russia*. 1977.
Berger, J. *Shipwreck of a Generation*. 1971.
Berkman, A. *The Bolshevik Myth*. 1976.
Besseches, N. *Stalin*. 1951.
Bessedovsky, G. *Revelations of a Soviet Diplomat*. 1931.
———. *Staline: 'L'homme d'acier.'* Paris: 1933.
Biagi, E. *Svetlana: The Inside Story*. 1967.
Bialer, S. ed. *Stalin and His Generals*. 1970.
Birse, A. H. *Memoirs of an Interpreter*. 1967.
Bohlen, C. E. *Witness to History*. 1973.
Bor-Komorowski, T. *The Secret Army*. 1950.
Brook-Shepherd, G. *The Stormy Petrels*. 1977.
Brouée, P. *Le procès de Moscou*. Paris: 1964.
Bryant, A. *The Turn of the Tide*. 1965.
———. *Triumph in the West*. 1959.
Brzezinski, Z. *The Permanent Purge*. 1956.
Buber (Neumann), M. *Under Two Dictators*. 1949.
Byrnes, J. F. *Frankly Speaking*. 1947.

Carmichael, J. *Stalin's Masterpiece*. 1976.
Cassidy, H. C. *Moscow Dateline*. Boston: 1943.
Carr, E. H. *Foundations of a Planned Economy, 1926–9*. 3 vols. 1969–78 (with R. A. Davies).
———. *Socialism in One Country, 1924–6*. 2 vols. 1958–9.
———. *The Bolshevik Revolution, 1917–23*. 3 vols. 1950–3.
———. *The Interregnum, 1924–6*. 1954.
Chamberlin, W. H. *Russia's Iron Age*. 1935.
———. *The Russian Revolution, 1917–21*. 2 vols. 1935.
Chambers, W. *Witness*. 1953.
Chaney, O. P. *Zhukov*. Newton Abbott. 1972.
Churchill, W. S. *The Second World War*. 6 vols.
Ciliga, A. *The Russian Enigma*. 1940.
Ciszek, W. S. *He Leadeth Me*. 1974.
Clemens, D. S. *Yalta*. 1965.

Cohen, S. *Bukharin and the Bolshevik Revolution.* 1980.
Cole, D. M. *Josef Stalin: Man of Steel.* 1942.
Conquest, R. *Power and Politics in the USSR.* 1961.
————. *The Great Terror.* 1968.
————. *The Human Cost of Communism.* Washington, D.C.: 1970.
————. *The Soviet Deportation of Nationalities.* 1962.
Crankshaw, E. *Khrushchev.* 1966.
————. *Russia Without Stalin.* 1956.
Cult of the Individual. Belfast: 1975.
Czapski, E. *The Inhuman Land.* 1958.

Dallin, D. J., and B. I. Nicolaevsky. *Forced Labour in Soviet Russia.* 1947.
Daniels, R. V. *The Conscience of Revolution.* 1960.
Darel, S. A *Sparrow in the Snow.* 1974.
D'Astier, J. *Sur Staline.* Paris: 1963.
Davies, J. E. *Mission to Moscow.* 1942.
Deane, J. R. *The Strange Alliance.* 1947.
Dedijer, V. *Tito Speaks.* 1953.
Delbars, Y. *The Real Stalin.* 1952.
Deriabin, P., and F. Gibney. *The Secret World.* 1960.
Deutscher, I. *Stalin: A Political Biography.* 1967.
————. *The Prophet Armed: Trotsky, 1879–1921.* 1959.
————. *The Prophet Unarmed: Trotsky, 1921–1929.* 1959.
————. *The Prophet Outcast: Trotsky, 1929–1940.* 1963.
Dixon, P. *Double Diploma.* 1968.
Djilas, M. *Conversations with Stalin.* 1962.
Dmitrievskii, S. *Sovetskie portrety.* Berlin: 1932.
————. *Stalin.* Stockholm: 1930.
————. *Za kulisami kremlya.* Paris: 1933.
Douglas, W. O. *Russian Journey.* New York: 1956.
Doumbadze, E. V. *Na sluzhbe cheka i kominterna.* Paris: 1930.
Duranty, W. *I Write as I Please.* 1935.
————. *Stalin & Co.* 1949.
————. *The Kremlin and the People.* 1942.

Eden, A. *Memoirs: The Reckoning.* 1965.
————. *The Avon Papers.* FO954 nos. 19–21, 24–26.
Eeman, H. *Inside Stalin's Russia.* 1977.
Ehrenburg, I. *Men, Years, Life.* 6 vols. 1963–6.
Eisenhower, D. D. *Crusade in Europe.* 1948.
Elleinstein, J. *The Stalin Phenomenon.* 1976.
Erickson, J. *The Soviet High Command.* 1962.
Estorick, E. *Stafford Cripps.* 1949.

Fainsod, M. *How Russia Is Ruled*. Cambridge, Mass.: 1953.

———. *Smolensk Under Russian Rule*. 1959.

———. and J. F. Hough. *How the Soviet Union Is Governed*. Cambridge, Mass.: 1983 ed.

Farnsworth, B. *William Bullitt and the Soviet Union*. Bloomington, Ind.: 1967.

Farson, N. *The Way of a Transgressor*. 1935.

———. *Seeing Red*. 1930.

Feis, H. *Churchill, Roosevelt, Stalin*. Princeton, N.J.: 1966.

———. *Between War and Peace: The Potsdam Conference*. Princeton, N.J.: 1960.

Fischer, G. *Soviet Opposition to Stalin*. Cambridge, Mass.: 1952.

Fischer, L. *Men and Politics*. 1941.

———. *The Life and Death of Stalin*. 1953.

Fishman, J. *The Private Life of Josif Stalin*. 1962.

Fotieva, L. A. *Iz zhizni Lenina*. M. 1959.

Getty, J. A. *Origins of the Great Purges*. 1985.

Ginzburg, E. S. *Into the Whirlwind*. 1967.

Glovatski, A. (pseud. B. Prus.). *The Pharaoh and the Priest*. 1910.

Gold, N. *The Twentieth Congress and After: A Vindication of J. V. Stalin and His Policy*. Dublin: 1953.

Gorbatov, A. V. *Years Off My Life*. 1964.

Granovsky, A. *All Pity Choked: The Memoirs of a Soviet Secret Agent*. 1955.

Grigorenko, P. *V podpol'e mozhno vstretit' tol'ko krys*. New York: 1981.

Guderian, H. *Panzer Leader*. New York: 1980.

Gusarov, V. *Moi papa ubil Mikhoelsa*. Frankfurt: 1978.

Harriman, W. A. *Peace with Russia?* 1960.

Herling, A. K. *The Soviet Slave Empire*. New York: 1951.

Herling, I. *A World Apart*. New York: 1951.

Hilger, G. *The Incompatible Allies*. 1956.

Hingley, R. *Joseph Stalin: Man and Legend*. 1974.

———. *The Russian Secret Police*. 1970.

H.M.S.O. *The History of the Second World War*.

Hull, C. *Memoirs*. 2 vols. 1948.

Hutton, J. B. *Stalin, the Miraculous Georgian*. 1961.

Iremashvili, J. *Stalin und die Tragödie Georgiens*. Berlin: 1932.

Ismay, H. L. *The Memoirs of General the Lord Ismay*. 1960.

Ivanov-Razumnik, R. V. *T'yurmy i ssylki*. New York: 1953.

Joffé, M. *One Long Night*. 1978.

Karski, J. *Story of a Secret State*. Boston: 1945.

Katkov, G. *The Trial of Bukharin*. 1960.

Kennan, G. F. *Memoirs 1925–50*. Boston: 1967.

——. *Russia and the West Under Lenin and Stalin*. 1961.

Kerr, W. *The Secret of Stalingrad*. 1979.

Khravchenko, I. *I Chose Freedom*. 1947.

Khrushchev, N. S. *Khrushchev Remembers*. 1971.

——. *The Crimes of the Stalin Era: Special Report to The Twentieth Congress of the Communist Party of the Soviet Union*. New York: 1956.

Knickerbocker, H. R. *The Soviet Five-Year Plan and Its Effect on World Trade*. 1931.

Koestler, A. *Darkness at Noon*. 1940.

——. *The Invisible Writing*. 1954.

Kolakowski, L. *The Main Currents of Marxism*. 3 vols. Oxford: 1978.

Kolarz, W. *Russia and Her Colonies*. New York: 1952.

Kopelev, L. *I sotvoril sebye kumira*. Ann Arbor, Mich.: 1978.

Kot, S. *Conversations with the Kremlin and Dispatches from Russia*. 1962.

Krivitsky, W. *In Stalin's Secret Service*. New York: 1939.

——. *I Was Stalin's Agent*. 1939.

Kusnierz, B. *Stalin and the Poles: An Indictment of the Soviet Leaders*. 1949.

Kuusinen, A. *Before and After Stalin*. 1974.

Labin, S. *Stalin's Russia*. 1949.

Lakoba, N. *Stalin i Kashim 1901–2*.Sukhum: 1934.

Lang, D. M. *A Modern History of Georgia*. 1962.

Latey, M. *Tyranny: A Study in the Abuse of Power*. 1969.

Laue, T. von. *Why Lenin? Why Stalin?* 1966.

Leahy, W. D. *I Was There*. 1950.

Lenin, V. I. *Collected Works*. 14 vols. M. 1960–70.

Lermolo, E. *Face of a Victim*. 1955.

Levine, I. D. *Stalin's Great Secret*. New York: 1956.

——. *The Mind of an Assassin*. 1950.

Levytsky, B. *The Uses of Terror*. 1971.

Lewin, M. *Lenin's Last Struggle*. 1969.

Liddell Hart, B. H. *The Soviet Army*. 1956.

Lockhart, R. Bruce. *Memoirs of a British Agent*. 1974 ed.

Low, D. *Low's Russian Sketchbook*. 1932.

Ludwig, E. *Leaders of Europe*. 1934.

——. *Stalin*. 1933.

Lyons, E. *Assignment in Utopia*. 1938.

——. *Moscow Carrousel*. 1935.

——. *Stalin: Czar of All the Russias*. Philadelphia: 1941.

——. *Workers' Paradise Lost*. New York: 1967.

Maclean, F. *Eastern Approaches*. 1949.

McCauley, M. *The Stalin File*. 1979.

McNeal, R. H. *Lenin, Stalin, Khrushchev: Voices of Bolshevism*. Englewood Cliffs, N.J.: 1957.

———. *Stalin's Works (Bibliography)*. Stanford, Calif.: 1967.

———. *The Bolshevik Tradition*. New York: 1975.

Maisky, I. *Journey into the Past*. 1962.

———. *Memoirs of a Soviet Ambassador*. 1967.

Mandelstam, N. *Vospominaniya*. New York: 1970.

———. *Vtoraya kniga*. Paris: 1972.

Martel, G. *The Russian Outlook*. 1947.

Mead, M. *Soviet Attitudes to Authority*. New York: 1951.

Medvedev, R. *Let History Judge*. 1971.

———. *On Stalin and Stalinism*. 1979.

Menon, K. *The Flying Troika*. 1963.

Metternich, T. *Tatiana: Five Passports in a Shifting Europe*. 1976.

Molotov, V. *Stalin and Stalin's Leadership*. M. 1950.

———. *Speech at the Funeral of Joseph Vissarionovich Stalin*. M. 1953.

"Monitor." *The Death of Stalin Investigated by Monitor*. 1958.

Monkhouse, A. *Moscow 1911–1933*. 1933.

Montagu, I. *Joseph Stalin. 70 Years*. 1949.

Muggeridge, M. *Winter in Moscow*. 1934.

Murphy, J. T. *Stalin 1879–1944*. 1945.

Nazi-Soviet Relations 1939–1941. Documents from the Archives of the German Foreign Office. Washington, D.C.: 1948.

Nicolaevsky, B. I. *Power and the Soviet Elite*. 1965.

Nord, L. *Inzhenery dushi*. Buenos Aires: 1954.

———. *Iz bloknota sovetskoi zhurnalistki*. Buenos Aires: 1958.

Nove, A. *Was Stalin Really Necessary?* 1964.

O'Neill, H. C. *Men of Destiny*. 1953.

Orlov, A. *The Secret History of Stalin's Crimes*. 1954.

Paloczi-Horvath, G. *Khrushchev: The Road to Power*. 1960.

Panin, D. *The Notebooks of Sologdin*. 1976.

Parvilhati, U. *Beria's Gardens*. 1960.

Pavlov, V. *Leningrad and the Blockade*. Chicago: 1965.

Payne, R. *The Rise and Fall of Stalin*. 1966.

Perkins, F. *The Roosevelt I Knew*. 1947.

Pethybridge, R. *The Social Prelude to Stalinism*. 1972.

Petrov, V. *It Happens in Russia.* 1951.
Petrov, V. and E. *Empire of Fear.* 1956.
Pipes, R. *The Formation of the Soviet Union.* Cambridge, Mass.: 1964.
Pirogov, P. *Why I Escaped.* 1950.
Poretsky, E. *Our Own People.* 1969.
Possony, S. T. *Lenin: The Compulsive Revolutionary.* Chicago: 1964.
Pritt, D. N. *The Truth About the Soviet Union.* 1951.
———. *The Zinoviev Trial.* 1936.

Randall, F. B. *Stalin's Russia: An Historical Reconsideration.* New York: 1965.
Ransome, A. *Six Weeks in Russia in 1919.* 1919.
———. *The Crisis in Russia.* 1921.
Rauch, G. von. *A History of Soviet Russia.* New York: 1958.
Redlich, R. *O Staline i Stalinizme.* Frankfurt: 1971.
Reed, J. *Ten Days That Shook the World.* 1919.
Ribbentrop, J. von. *The Ribbentrop Memoirs.* 1954.
Rigby, T. *The Stalin Dictatorship: Khrushchev's Secret Speech and Other Documents.* Sydney, Australia: 1968.
———. *Stalin.* Englewood Cliffs, N.J.: 1966.
Rosenfeldt, N. E. *Knowledge and Power.* 1978.
Rubin, J. H. *Moscow Mirage.* 1935.

Salisbury, H. E. *Moscow Journal.* Chicago: 1961.
———. *Stalin's Russia and After.* 1955.
———. *The 900 Days: The Siege of Leningrad.* 1970.
Schapiro, L. *The Communist Party of the Soviet Union.* 1970.
Scheffer, P. *Seven Years in Soviet Russia.* 1931.
Schueller, G. K. *The Politburo.* Stanford, Calif.: 1951.
Seaton, A. *The Russo-German War, 1941–45.* 1971.
Serge, V. *From Lenin to Stalin.* 1937.
———. *Memoirs of a Revolutionary, 1901–41.* 1963.
———. *Portrait de Staline.* Paris: 1940.
Sharkat Usmani. *I Met Stalin Twice.* Bombay: 1953.
Shostakovich, D. D. *Memoirs.* 1979.
Shub, D. *Lenin.* New York: 1948.
Shukman, H. *Lenin and the Russian Revolution.* 1968.
Sinel'nikov, S. *S. M. Kirov.* M. 1964.
Smith, A. *I Was a Soviet Worker.* 1937.
Smith, C. A., ed. *Escape from Paradise.* 1954.
Smith, E. E. *The Okhrana: A Bibliography.* Stanford, Calif.: 1967.
———. *The Young Stalin.* 1968.
Smith, W. B. *Moscow Mission, 1946–9.* 1950.
Snow, E. *The Pattern of Soviet Power.* New York: 1945.

Solonevich, I. *Escape from Russia in Chains*. 1939.
———. *Russia in Chains*. 1938.
Soloviev, M. *My Nine Lives in the Red Army*. 1955.
Solzhenitsyn, A. I. *Arkhipelag gulag*. 3 vols. New York: 1970–74.
Souvarine, B. *Staline: Aperçu historique du bolshévisme*. Paris: 1935.
Stalin, J. V. *For Peaceful Co-existence. Post War Interviews*. New York: 1951.
———. *Sochineniya*. 13 vols. M. 1946–51.
———. *Sochineniya*. 3 vols. ed. R. H. McNeal. Stanford, Calif.: 1967.
———. *Voprosy Leninizma*. M. 1945.
Stettinius, E. R. *Roosevelt and the Russians*. 1950.
Strang, Lord. *Home and Abroad*. 1956.
Strik-Strikfeldt, W. *Against Stalin and Hitler*. 1970.
Strong, A. L. *I Change Worlds*. 1935.
———. *The Stalin Era*. 1957.
Stypulkowski, Z. *Invitation to Moscow*. 1951.
Sukhanov, N. N. *The Russian Revolution, 1917*. 1955.
———. *Zapiski o Revoliutsii*. M. 1922.
Suslov, I. *Rasskazy o Tovarishche Staline*. Ann Arbor, Mich.: 1981.
Suvorov, V. *The Liberators*. 1983.
Svanidze, B. *My Uncle Joseph Stalin*. New York: 1953.
Sverdlova, K. T. *Jacob M. Sverdlov*. M. 1945.
Swianiewicz, S. *Forced Labour and Economic Development*. Oxford: 1968.

Tchernavin, T. *Escape from the Soviets*. 1937.
Thayer, C. W. *Bears in the Caviar*. 1952.
———. *Hands Across the Caviar*. 1953.
Tokaev, S. A. *Betrayal of an Ideal*. 1954.
———. *Comrade X*. 1953.
Tolstoy, Count N. *Stalin's Secret War*. 1982.
Trotsky, L. *My Life*. 1930.
———. *Kak vooruzhilas' revolutsiya*. M. 1924.
———. *Military Writings*. New York: 1969.
———. *Stalin*. 1946.
———. *The History of the Russian Revolution*. 3 vols. 1932–3.
———. *The Stalin School of Falsification*. New York: 1962.
———. *The Trotsky Papers*. The Hague: 1964.
———. *Trotsky's Diary in Exile*. 1959.
Truman, H. S. *Year of Decisions, 1945*. 1955.
———. *Years of Trial and Hope, 1946–1953*. 1956.
Tucker, R., ed. *Stalinism*. New York: 1977.
———. *Stalin as Revolutionary, 1879–1929*. 1974.
Turney, A. *Disaster at Moscow*. 1971.

Ulam, A. *Lenin and the Bolsheviks*. 1966.

————. *Stalin: The Man and His Era.* 1974.
Uratadze, G. *Reminiscences of a Georgian Social Democrat.* Stanford, Calif.: 1968.
Urban, G. R., ed. *Stalinism.* 1982.

Valentinov, N. N. *Encounters with Lenin.* 1968. .
Vogeler, R. A. *I Was Stalin's Prisoner.* 1952.
Vishinsky, A. Y. *Teoriya sudebnykh dokazatelstv v sovetskoi prave.* M. 1950.

Weissberg, A. *Conspiracy of Silence.* 1952.
Werth, A. *Moscow 1941.* 1942.
————. *Russia: The Post-war Years.* 1971.
————. *The Year of Stalingrad.* 1946.
White, D. *The Growth of the Red Army.* Princeton, N.J.: 1944.
White, W. L. *Report on the Russians.* 1945.
Wickstead, A. *My Russian Neighbours.* 1934.
Wittlin, T. *Commissar.* 1973.
Wolfe, B. D. *Khrushchev and Stalin's Ghost.* 1957.
————. *Three Who Made a Revolution.* 1956.
————. *Strange Communists I Have Known.* 1966.
Woodward, Sir L. *British Foreign Policy in the Second World War.* 1962.

Zawodny, J. K. *Death in the Forest.* Notre Dame: Mich.: 1962.
Zhukov, G. K. *Marshal Zhukov's Greatest Battles.* 1969.
————. *Vospominaniya i razmyshleniya.* 1969.
Zinoviev, A. *Svetloe Budushchuye.* 1983.
————. *Ziyayushchiue Vysoty.* 1981.

Articles

Arsenidze, R. "Iz Vospominaniii o Staline," *Novy Zhurnal,* no. 72 (June 1963).
Avtorkhanov, A. "Zakulisnaya istoriya pakta Ribbentrop-Molotov." *Kontinent,* vol. 4 (1978).

Bazhanov, B. "Pobeg iz nochi." *Kontinent,* nos. 8–10 (1976).

Dan, L. "Vospominaniya." *Noviy Zhurnal,* 1064. no. 75 (1964).

Floyd, D. "Generalissimo Stalin." *Daily Telegraph* (July 8, 1965).

Joffé, M. "Vospominaniya." *Vremya i my* nos. 19–20 (1977).

Kennan, G. (pseud. "X") "The Sources of Soviet Conduct." *Foreign Affairs.* July 1974.
Kessel, G. "La Nuit où Staline est mort." *Paris Match* (March 30, 1963).

Lasky, M. J. "From Sartre to Solzhenitsyn." *Encounter,* no. 45 (July 1975).

Lissan, M. "Stalin the Appeaser." *Survey,* no. 76 (1970).

Lunghi, H. "Stalin Face to Face." *The Observer* (February 24, 1963).

Kaminsky, V. and I. Vereshchagin. "Detstvo i iunost' Vozhdya." *Molodaya Gvardiya,* no. 12 (December 1939).

McNeal, R. H. "Caveat Lector: A Preface to Stalin's *Sochineniya. Survey,*" (October 1963).

————. "Soviet Historiography on the October Revolution." *American Slavic and East European Review,* vol. 17, no. 2 (October 1958).

Rusanov, P. "Voskhozhdeniya Malenkova." *Sotsialisticheskii Vestnik,* nos. 7–8 (July-August 1953).

Salisbury, H. E. "Stalin Survivors Tell Their Story." *Times* of London (October 3, 1967).

Schapiro, L. "The General Department of the CC of the CPSU." *Survey,* vol. 21 (1975).

Shaumyan, L. "Na Rubezhe pervykh pyatiletok." *Pravda* (February 7, 1964).

Szamuely, T. "The Elimination of the Opposition Between the Sixteenth and Seventeenth Congresses of the CPSU." *Soviet Studies,* vol. 17 (January 1966)

Vakar, N. "Stalin po vospominaniyam N. N. Zhordania." *Posledniye Novosti* (December 16, 1936).

Vereshchak, S. "Stalin v tyurme," *Dni,* 23 (January 4, 1928).

Index

527